6.00

THE ACQUISITION OF SCRAMBLING AND CLITICIZATION

STUDIES IN THEORETICAL PSYCHOLINGUISTICS

VOLUME 26

Managing Editors

Lyn Frazier, *Dept. of Linguistics, University of Massachusetts at Amherst*
Thomas Roeper, *Dept. of Linguistics, University of Massachusetts at Amherst*
Kenneth Wexler, *Dept. of Brain and Cognitive Science, MIT, Cambridge, Mass.*

Editorial Board

Robert Berwick, *Artificial Intelligence Laboratory, MIT, Cambridge, Mass.*
Manfred Bierwisch, *Zentralinstitut für Sprachwissenschaft, Akademie der Wissenschaften, Berlin*
Merrill Garrett, *University of Arizona, Tucson*
Lila Gleitman, *School of Education, University of Pennsylvania*
Mary-Louise Kean, *University of California, Irvine*
Howard Lasnik, *University of Connecticut at Storrs*
John Marshall, *Neuropsychology Unit, Radcliffe Infirmary, Oxford*
Daniel Osherson, *M.I.T., Cambridge, Mass.*
Yukio Otsu, *Keio University, Tokyo*
Edwin Williams, *Princeton University*

The titles published in this series are listed at the end of this volume.

THE ACQUISITION OF SCRAMBLING AND CLITICIZATION

edited by

SUSAN M. POWERS
*University of Potsdam,
Germany*

and

CORNELIA HAMANN
*University of Geneva, Switzerland,
University of Tübingen, Germany*

KLUWER ACADEMIC PUBLISHERS
DORDRECHT / BOSTON / LONDON

A C.I.P. Catalogue record for this book is available from the Library of Congress.

ISBN 0-7923-6249-7

Published by Kluwer Academic Publishers,
P.O. Box 17, 3300 AA Dordrecht, The Netherlands.

Sold and distributed in North, Central and South America
by Kluwer Academic Publishers,
101 Philip Drive, Norwell, MA 02061, U.S.A.

In all other countries, sold and distributed
by Kluwer Academic Publishers,
P.O. Box 322, 3300 AH Dordrecht, The Netherlands.

Printed on acid-free paper

All Rights Reserved
© 2000 Kluwer Academic Publishers
No part of the material protected by this copyright notice may be reproduced or
utilized in any form or by any means, electronic or mechanical,
including photocopying, recording or by any information storage and
retrieval system, without written permission from the copyright owner.

Printed in the Netherlands.

TABLE OF CONTENTS

SUSAN M. POWERS & CORNELIA HAMANN 1
Introduction: The Acquisition of Clause-internal Rules

Part I: Scrambling

HUBERT HAIDER 19
Scrambling: What's the State of the Art?

ISABELLA BARBIER 41
An Experimental Study of Scrambling and
Object Shift in the Acquisition of Dutch

JEANNETTE SCHAEFFER
Object Scrambling and Specificity in Dutch Child Language 71

SUSAN M. POWERS 95
Scrambling in the Acquisition of English?

ZVI PENNER, ROSEMARIE TRACY, & JÜRGEN WEISSENBORN 127
Where Scrambling Begins: Triggering Object Scrambling at the
Early Stage in German and Bernese Swiss German

Part II: Cliticization

ANNA CARDINALETTI & MICHAL STARKE 165
Overview: The Grammar (and Acquisition) of Clitics

MARCO HAVERKORT & JÜRGEN WEISSENBORN 187
Parameters and Cliticization in Early Child German

BERTHOLD CRYSMANN & NATASCHA MÜLLER 207
On the Non-parallelism in the Acquisition of Reflexive
and Non-reflexive Object Clitics

PIERO BOTTARI, PAOLA CIPRIANI, & ANNA MARIA CHILOSI 237
Dissociations in the Acquisition of Clitic Pronouns by Dysphasic
Children: A Case Study from Italian

VICENÇ TORRENS & KENNETH WEXLER 279
The Acquisition of Clitic Doubling in Spanish

SHYAM KAPUR & ROBIN CLARK 299
The Automatic Identification and Classification of Clitic Pronouns

MARTHA YOUNG-SCHOLTEN 319
The L2 Acquisition of Cliticization in Standard German

Part III: Related Issues

THOMAS ROEPER & BERNHARD ROHRBACHER 345
Null Subjects in Early Child English and the Theory of
Economy of Projection

GUNLØG JOSEFSSON & GISELA HÅKANSSON 397
The PP-CP Parallelism Hypothesis and Language Acquisition:
Evidence from Swedish

CORNELIA HAMANN 423
Negation, Infinitives and Heads

JACQUELINE VAN KAMPEN 479
Left-branch Extraction as Operator Movement: Evidence from Child Dutch

INDEX 505

SUSAN M. POWERS   CORNELIA HAMANN

THE ACQUISITION OF CLAUSE-INTERNAL RULES

1. INTRODUCTION

Rather than focusing on different approaches to language acquisition, this collection of papers investigates two specific linguistic phenomena from an acquisition point of view. Observations on the acquisition of scrambling or pronominal clitics can be found in the literature, but up until the recent past they were sparse and often buried in other issues. This volume fills a long existing gap in providing a collection of articles that target acquisition while giving a more complete view of the overarching syntactic issues involved. It also provides an overview of L1 and L2 acquisition data from a number of different languages as well as from different theoretical points of view with these two clause-internal processes at the center.

The study of language acquisition bears on three basic research questions within the field of linguistics in general. First, acquisition data can potentially establish - though not disprove - the early availability of principles of UG. That is, the patterns observed in the acquisition data immediately raise the question of how much information is input-given as opposed to UG-given. Second, acquisition data can validate analyses of specific linguistic phenomena. It is this aspect of acquisition research which has received more attention in the recent literature as the data from a given developmental stage, have been compared to the data linguists collect from a newly discovered language or dialect as was common in earlier approaches (see Brown & Fraser, 1963). Wexler (1996) even encourages acquisitionists to "be bold" and stop desperately fitting and bending their results into the frame of the latest theory, but rather, point out the theoretical consequences of their findings, changing the theory if need be. Hopefully, it is this interpretation of acquisition data that will become more commonplace in the future permitting linguistic theory and acquisition research to enter into a relationship of mutual give and take, equals in theoretical relevance. The third question raised by acquisition research is how the attested acquisition data fit together not only with our ideas of how language development proceeds but also, and perhaps more importantly, how development can be best described by linguistic theory.

While there are many ways in which the child grammar could differ from the adult, holding UG constant shifts the locus of the dissociation between child and adult grammars to other aspects or modules of the grammar. For example, perhaps the child grammar differs from the adult grammar only in one sub-area of syntax. For example, perhaps the best account of the variation across and within child language is tied to the emergence of functional projections (cf. Meisel, 1992). This provides a number of possibilities for language acquisition (see Thráinsson, 1996 for a review). Since the parametric variation observed in scrambling and cliticization is considerable, acquisition data may be able to clarify some issues on parameters and parameter setting.

When "The Workshop on the L1 and L2 Acquisition of Clause-internal Rules" was held in January of 1994, many of the above issues were passionately discussed but only a little was actually known about the acquisition of scrambling and cliticization. The meeting in Berne highlighted the importance of accurately describing these two sub-areas of syntactic acquisition. As a consequence, intensive work on these subjects began. This volume is the culmination of these investigations, including the earliest thoughts on these topics and should be thought of as a starting point for further research in the acquisition of scrambling and cliticization.

2. SCRAMBLING

2.1 Defining the Phenomenon

Very loosely construed, the term 'scrambling' refers to word order in simple clauses. For example, languages like English and French which display a fairly rigid order of constituents contrast starkly with languages like German, Japanese, and Turkish in which nearly all variations of constituents are permitted. For example, consider the Japanese example in (1) below from Otsu (1994).

(1) a. Taroo-ga   Hanako-ni   hon-o   ageta.
        Taroo-NOM   Hanako-DAT   book-ACC   give+PAST
        'Taro gave a book to Hanako.'
     b. Taroo-ga   hon-o   Hanako-ni ageta.
     c. Hanako-ni   Taroo-ga   hon-o   ageta.
     d. Hanako-ni   hon-o   Taroo-ga   ageta.
     e. hon-o   Taroo-ga   Hanako-ni ageta.
     f. hon-o   Hanako-ni   Taroo-ga   ageta.

Almost all of the logically possible re-orderings of the syntactic constituents (i.e., DPs) of (1a) are grammatical.

There is still no consensus on how to best characterize scrambling even in the adult grammar (see Haider, this volume). The implicit assumption is that scrambling is a syntactic phenomenon because as Roeper (1996) notes, most non-syntactic acquisition theories of word-order variation prove inadequate:

Broad claims about parsing or pragmatic differences are totally incapable of explaining differences between children's two-word utterances, for instance why [English-speaking] children say *you big* and never *big you*...

Scrambling can be distinguished from other syntactic processes such as heavy NP shift, object-shift, or functionally motivated movement (e.g., passive). Further refining the definition of the phenomenon in this way as Barbier (this volume) suggests leads to the problem of how to accurately describe the acquisition of scrambling which, unlike object shift, is an optional syntactic process. This optionality only adds to the already daunting task of accurately characterizing the emergence of obligatory syntactic processes.

The phenomenon called 'scrambling' (irrespective of the right definition) is attested in languages like Dutch, German, and Swedish. Most reports of word order errors in the acquisition literature come primarily from languages with relatively fixed word order (e.g., child English, child French). This is because children acquiring scrambling languages like German, typically produce the adult word order patterns from the outset (Park, 1971; Roeper, 1973).

2.2. Analyzing the Phenomenon

There are two main syntactic analyses that have been offered to explain scrambling. In the first, the different word orders observed are base-generated as such. In the second, these different orders are derived via syntactic movement. Each of these theories, inasmuch as they are models of the adult grammar, should be licit language acquisition theories. Theories of language acquisition however, are based on empirical acquisition data. The acquisition fact, which any theory of the acquisition of scrambling must accurately capture, is that different child languages manifest different orders already at the two-word stage. In addition, fundamental assumptions about phrase structure have an effect on which of these two syntactic accounts is to be preferred.

For example, the hypothesis that the observed orders are freely base-generated has been widely adopted for the different orders attested during development. Interestingly, this explanation is the most popular for child languages that have fairly rigid word order. For example, Gruber (1967), Radford (1990), and Felix (1991) claim that word order errors found in child English are base-generated as such. Similarly, Pierce (1992) and Tsimpli (1991) both argue that post-verbal subjects in child French are base-generated. These accounts all adopt the hypothesis that the child grammar initially lacks projections of functional categories like inflection, determiner, and complementizer (Radford, 1986, 1990; Lebeaux, 1988; Guilfoyle & Noonan, 1988, 1992 and others). The alternative word orders are freely base-generated and will be fixed later in a target-consistent fashion when functional projections emerge (Felix, 1991). This approach predicts an early stage of word order variability across all child languages. As noted above, the fact is that across languages, children manifest target-consistent word order as early as the two-word stage. For example, OV is not found in the initial stages of child English (Bowerman, 1973; Brown, 1973; Powers, this volume) while this is the prevalent order in child German (Roeper, 1973).

How does the hypothesis that the scrambled orders are derived by movement fare? If the order of constituents in all languages is underlyingly the same (Kayne, 1994; Zwart, 1993) and the different surface orders are derived by movement, then perhaps the fact that word order is target-like from the outset is best accounted for by assuming that the child's grammar does not initially lack functional structure. The problem for the movement account comes from the acquisition evidence which suggests that crucial syntactic operations like the ability to form A-chains (Borer & Wexler, 1987) or the ability to move constituents at all are initially lacking (deVilliers, Roeper & Vainikka, 1990; Powers, 1996). Adopting the Universal Base Hypothesis, the No Functional Projections Hypothesis, and the movement account makes the same false prediction as the base-generation account namely that different child languages will be similar at the initial state.

The movement account could be modified by adopting the hypothesis that the child's grammar initially lacks functional projections altogether but that in those languages that have scrambling, functional structure is projected sooner than in those that do not. This means that all child languages initially have the same "non-functional" grammar but in languages with verb-movement (e.g., German) children project functional categories almost immediately (see Radford, 1996). This would account for the target-consistent patterns of word order found at the period of first word combinations while allowing child languages to vary exactly as adult languages do. This analysis is consistent with the fact that word orders that depend on functional projections in languages like Turkish are initially infrequent. According to Kornfilt (1994), the only order not dependent on functional projections, SOV, is the most frequent three-constituent word order in child Turkish (see Otsu, 1994 for similar results on child Japanese). These data are also compatible with the hypothesis that phrase structure varies from language to language and that children somehow set the language-specific parameters (e.g., the head-direction parameter) before their two-word combinations emerge (Roeper, 1992). Even though, Japanese and Turkish permit all logical combinations of constituents; initially, only the adult-base order SOV is attested. Similarly Bowerman (1990) finds that only orders which are consistent with adult English base order SVO (i.e. SV, VO) are found in the initial stages (see Powers, this volume). Only this latter hypothesis accurately predicts the prevalence of licit base-generated word orders at the first stage of word combinations.

Because there are different kinds of syntactic movement (functionally motivated and not), (at least) five different theories of scrambling have been advanced for the adult grammar (see Haider's summary). Similarly, all of these possibilities have found advocates in the acquisition literature:

(2)   a. Base-generation: Felix, 1991; Tsimpli, 1991
                b. A-chain (substitution): Kornfilt, 1994
                c. A-chain (adjunction): Powers, this volume
                d. A'-chain (substitution): Otsu, 1994
                e. A'-chain (adjunction): Barbier, this volume; Kornfilt, 1994; Otsu, 1994; Lakshmanan & Ozeki, 1996

The correct theoretical characterization of scrambling both across and within languages is an area of much debate which as Haider notes in his contribution, could be settled by a correct empirical generalization:

The empirically correct characterization of the phenomenon should lead to the adequate choice of the theoretical position. What is the problem? As a matter of fact, the discussion has not reached the level of descriptive adequacy yet.

It is the goal of the papers in the first part of this collection to provide the requisite descriptive adequacy as each focuses on the emergence of scrambling in the acquisition of the adult languages in which it is attested (Dutch, German, Bernese Swiss German) and in which it is not (English). The correct empirical classification of word order variation across a range of child languages is crucial to establish not only if the child data mirror the adult, but also to be able to make the "adequate choice of the theoretical position". In this way, the acquisition data could lead to the adequate choice of theoretical position and allow us to decide between the competing analyses of scrambling in adult grammars.

2.3. Studies on the Acquisition of Scrambling

The fact that word order is (for the most part) target-like from the beginning of acquisition is the primary reason that there have been so few systematic studies on the acquisition of word order. The large acquisition studies that do exist contain sweeping statements like "the violations of normal order are triflingly few...." (Brown, 1973:156). Is the lack of word order errors due to the nature of spontaneous speech? Perhaps this is just a problem of inadequate sampling. Inasmuch as spontaneous samples can be divided into stages by some meaningful developmental criterion (e.g., MLU), these data can provide important information about the frequency or lack of particular word orders. Previous literature on the acquisition of Turkish (Kornfilt, 1994) have revealed that even though SOV is the most frequent word order found in spontaneous speech, Turkish children understand the other licit word order variations in comprehension experiments and manifested preferences for particular orders in elicited imitation tasks. Otsu (1994) reports similar results for Japanese.

Schaeffer's paper in this volume investigates spontaneous child Dutch data. She claims that the phenomenon of scrambling pronouns is obligatory in adult Dutch, but optional in child Dutch. Schaeffer relates the lack of scrambling to the lack of fully specified DPs in child Dutch. Similar accounts are given by Lakshmanan & Ozeki (1996) for the lack of object scrambling in child Japanese, and by Schönenberger, Penner, & Weissenborn (1997) for child German. As Barbier points out in her contribution, spontaneous data from child Dutch and child German has not led to consensus among child researchers. She chooses to help settle the debate by experimentally inducing the environment in which scrambled structures are most felicitous. She uses stimuli containing negation in an elicited imitation task, in order to determine if children have the competence for object shift and scrambling. Barbier maintains that object shift reflects an "unmarked" option in the grammar as it is triggered by licensing principles of UG.

Diary studies of child language are particularly useful for determining if a certain pattern does not occur or just happens to be very infrequent. That is, the micro-stages of acquisition which Roeper (1992) claims are often "neglected" are rather "undetected" in spontaneous and experimental studies. Several papers in this volume search for the "missing links" in the acquisition sequence by investigating diary data. Schaeffer investigates child Dutch in order to confirm the patterns she finds in spontaneous data. Penner, Tracy, & Weissenborn seek the earliest evidence of target-like behavior in German and Bernese Swiss German; while Powers charts the emergence of both grammatical and ungrammatical orders in Bowerman's child English diary data. The paper of van Kampen, continues along this theme finding reordering violations in Dutch as late as eight years of age.

In addition to the possibilities discussed above that the child's grammar either lacks functional phrase structure or lacks specific syntactic operations, yet another possibility is that there is a lack of the required lexical items. That is, if only DPs scramble and child grammars initially contain no DPs (Radford, 1990; Guilfoyle & Noonan, 1988; Powers, 1996) then we would predict that scrambling proper would be lacking at the earliest state. Similar ideas are presented in the papers of Penner *et al.* and Schaeffer. These contributions focus on determining the categorial or X-bar status of the earliest lexical items. If these are identical to the adult, then target-like behavior is predicted. If particular lexical items are not amenable to the adult analysis, then the way in which these lexical items come to bear adult properties is the issue. The Håkansson & Josefsson paper in the Related Issues Section claims that the same lexical item is two different syntactic heads while Penner *et al.* claim that two lexical items, a focus particle and negator, are initially classified as having the same function. Hamann maintains that German negation is correctly classified as a specifier from the outset of acquisition.

As can be most clearly seen in the contribution of Haverkort & Weissenborn it is the syntactic behavior of DPs that unites scrambling and cliticization thus providing an important bridge between the two halves of this volume. With respect to scrambling, the phrase structural status of nominals and especially pronouns crucially determines whether an item has to scramble or not, if a functional projection exists, or whether there are potential blockades to movement. Other aspects of the pronominal system are examined in greater depth in the second half of the book to which we now turn.

3. THE ACQUISITION OF THE PRONOMINAL SYSTEM

3.1. The properties of clitics and earlier results

The acquisition of the pronominal system of a language bears on all the aspects discussed above by providing unique evidence of the relevance of acquisition research both within linguistics in general as well as being potentially decisive for acquisition questions. Since they occupy designated positions in the clause, pronominal clitics provide evidence *par excellence* of what categories and operations are present from the outset of acquisition and can help answer the questions of what is acquired later, and why and how. The pronominal clitic acquisition data relate directly to the early existence of functional categories, movement processes, licensing, and locality constraints. The attachment of the clitic to the inflected verb indicates the existence of the agreement system and the existence of head movement. Romance pronominal clitics illustrate the case in paradigmatic fashion appearing pre- or post-verbally and obeying constraints not observed with strong pronouns or lexical DPs. These clitics (subjects and objects) differ from lexical nominals in that they cannot be used in isolation (as in 3), cannot be conjoined (as in 4), cannot be modified (as in 5), cannot receive focal stress (as in 6), and cannot be separated from the verb as in (7) below.

(3) a. Qui est venu?   * Il
        who is come   *he
        'Who came?'
     b. Qui as-tu vu?   * Le
        who has-you seen   *him
        'Who did you see?'

(4) a. *Il et elle viendront
        he and she will come
        'He and she will come.'
     b. *Je le et la connais.
        I him and her know
        'I know him and her.'

(5) a. *Seuls ils viendront.
        only they will come
        'Only they will come.'
     b. *Je seul le connais.
        I only him know
        'I only know him.'

(6) a. *IL viendra (pas Marie).
        HE will come (not Mary)
        'HE will come (not Mary).'
     b. *Je LE connais (pas Marie).
        I HIM know (not Mary)
        'I know HIM (not Mary).'

(7) a. *Il probablement viendra.
        he probably will come
        'He will probably come.'
     b. *Pierre le probablement connaît.
        Pierre him probably knows
        'Pierre probably knows him.'

Similar to the acquisition of word order, the surprising observation across Romance languages is that clitics are used early and once they appear, they are always used correctly (cf. Haverkort & Weissenborn, 1991 for errors with object clitics in imperatives in child French). The child French results from Pierce (1989, 1992) Friedemann (1992), and Hamann *et al.* (1996) as well as Guasti's findings (1992) for child Italian are corroborated in this volume by Cardinaletti & Starke (for child Italian) and Torrens & Wexler (for child Spanish).

In French, a rare Romance language because it is not *pro*-drop, subjects clitics only occur with finite verbs and never with infinitives. This fact, first observed for the L1 acquisition of French by Weissenborn *et al.* (1989), Pierce (1989), Meisel (1990), was later confirmed by Friedemann (1992), Kaiser (1994), Hamann *et al.* (1996) and White (1996) for L2-acquisition. Clark (1985) was the first to discover that object clitics appear later than subject clitics in child French. This finding has also been corroborated by Friedemann (1992), Kaiser (1994), and Hamann *et al.* (1996). Although these studies found a significant delay, the overall appearance of object clitics was rare and as the latter authors show, 'accelerates' only about six months after the first appearance of subject clitics. The significant delay of object clitics with respect to subject clitics in child French was also found in elicited production studies (Jakubowicz *et al.*, 1996). In Italian and Spanish, which have only object clitics, object clitics appear much earlier in development than in child French. In the acquisition of these languages, object clitics appear at about the time as subject clitics appear in French, but are initially rare (see Guasti, 1992 for child Italian; Torrens & Wexler, this volume, for child Spanish).

The acquisition of clitics in non-romance languages does not as yet show such definitive patterns of emergence. Penner's (1991) Bernese Swiss German data are suggestive and Haegeman (1996) essentially confirms the Romance findings: subject clitics do not occur with finite verbs in child Dutch, and object clitics are similarly delayed. This brief overview shows that a clear picture is beginning to emerge, but these observations were unique or based on unconfirmed data at the time of the Berne conference.

3.2. Clitics and Linguistic Theory

Many questions about the analysis of Romance and Germanic pronominal clitics are still unresolved. One of these unresolved questions is: should Germanic and Romance clitics be treated on a par? In other words, are Germanic clitics functional heads like their Romance counterparts? It is this question which Haverkort & Weissenborn pursue in their contribution and they bring to bear acquisition evidence quite crucially on their decision to assign the pronominal clitics in the two language families different status in terms of X-bar theory. Young-Scholten also provides an overview of the problems and possible analyses of Germanic clitics.

The other current debate about the X-bar status of clitics is whether Romance subject clitics (which occur in French and in some Northern Italian dialects) are agreement markers and thus, heads or if they have a different syntactic status. In effect, the two competing analyses are (8a) and (8b), where (8a) represents a *pro*-drop language.

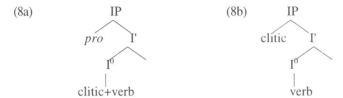

The structure in (8a) is a viable analysis for the Northern Italian dialects in which there is free inversion of the subject and which allows quantifiers in clitic-doubling structures. Especially subject inversion is a property which normally co-occurs with *pro*-drop. The claim is that languages with subject clitics are *pro*-drop (for a different view see Friedemann, 1995). The close connection of *pro*-drop and cliticization can also be seen in Roeper & Rohrbacher's investigation in this volume.

The structural representation of clauses (in 9) suggests, however, that subject clitics are not heads and are, in fact, rather different from object clitics.

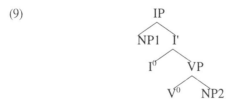

If the clitic position is associated with I° (the surface position of the inflected verb in French), a clitic can legitimately bind a trace in object position, but not in subject position, for the simple reason that I° does not c-command NP1. Analysis (8a) runs into a similar problem because *pro* must be licensed by the clitic.

This problem can be solved by assuming that subject clitics are full NPs in the syntax, i.e., occupy position NP1 at S-Structure, so that on this level (and at LF), trace binding is not a concern. They undergo a cliticization process only in the phonology, where the proper binding requirement is irrelevant (Kayne, 1975; Rizzi, 1986). As phonological cliticization is limited to linearly adjacent positions, this option is not open to object clitics, which must undergo movement. The common properties of subject and object clitics follow, in this approach, from the fact that all are clitics in the phonology, even though their syntactic status is very different. Only Young-Scholten deals with the phonological side of cliticization in her L2 acquisition study. All the other contributions consider the syntactic side of cliticization.

Another possible account of the differences in the two types of clitics, comes from Cardinaletti & Starke who propose a three valued system for the pronominal system of languages: strong pronouns > weak pronouns > clitics. In their system, French subject and object clitics represent two different kinds of structurally impoverished elements: the former are 'weak pronouns', constrained to occur in a strict specifier-head configuration with the licensing head; while the latter are genuine clitics, undergoing head movement to be associated to their licensing head. The common properties of subject and object clitics follow, under this approach, by their both being 'impoverished elements', even though to a different extent.

The approaches discussed thus far assume that the position of clitics high in the clause, indicates movement in the case of complement clitics. This is a natural assumption needed to account for the fact that the designated clitic position is typically different from the canonical complement position (Belletti, to appear). The classical movement approach for this property of clitics goes back to Kayne (1975). Adopting this approach to complement clitics, raises several theoretical questions:

- Why do clitics move?
- Why is clitic movement obligatory?
- Where exactly do clitics move to in the clause structure?

If clitic movement is fundamentally triggered by the case-checking mechanism and its interaction with requirements of checking verbal morphology (Belletti, 1993; to appear), then results on the acquisition of clitics will provide evidence of the early availability of feature-checking, of the knowledge of case features, of head-movement triggered by these requirements, and of the existence of landing sites outside of VP.

The phenomenon of clitic doubling seems to preclude a simple movement analysis, however, because under this analysis two elements carry the same case and theta-role. This is not a real problem for the movement account, if a slightly more articulated structure for clitics is assumed for independent reasons (as suggested by Cardinaletti & Starke). On the other hand, there are approaches like Borer (1984) and Sportiche (1992) which avoid the problem by assuming that the clitic is base-generated in a special clitic projection, called 'clitic voice'. Both Torrens & Wexler and Crysmann & Müller provide good overviews of the problems with both of these approaches. The latter authors question in particular the creation of projections for accommodating morphological material (Siloni, 1994; Belletti, to appear). Nevertheless, the issue remains open. On the face of it, the predictions of the two approaches to acquisition and the existence of positions outside VP are remarkably alike. Crysmann & Müller provide very subtle evidence on the acquisition of reflexive object clitics compared to referential object clitics in French in an analysis which treats object clitics as morphologically derived affixes and reflexive clitics as involving argument absorption. Torrens & Wexler, on the other hand, present data that the correct use of clitic-doubling in child Spanish and the concomitant occurrence of other crucial phenomena, argue directly for Sportiche's (1992) analysis of object clitics. Bottari *et al.* rather interpret their results on clitic use in the speech of children with a specific language impairment in the framework of a movement analysis. They show that though a moderate performance with simple clitic constructions is reached by Italian dysphasic children, the real problem lies in the occurrence of clitic clusters or the occurrence of clitics in complex structures, i.e., in structures with an auxiliary or a modal. They attribute the difficulty to an incomplete mastery of chain-formation, i.e., to a basic difficulty with conditions on movement.

3.3. Clitics and Functional Projections

The results on the early emergence of clitics and their correct placement are important. In a full continuity approach, every phase of language acquisition is assumed to be a possible UG-consistent grammar. However, there is no consensus on how to explain the obvious difference from adult grammars. On the one hand, is the hypothesis that children start with only lexical and thematic positions, so that the early structure is in effect a small clause (Radford, 1986, 1990). Projections are consecutively built up one on top of the other with the acquisition of functional items and paradigms. On the other hand, there are arguments for the early availability of the full array of functional projections (Hyams, 1986; Pierce, 1989, 1992; Weissenborn, 1990; Poeppel & Wexler, 1993). The obvious lack of similarity between adult and child speech, is explained by assuming that certain parameters are open in the beginning or set to a default value or even that certain UG principles mature.

The small clause approach is, at first glance, very convincing as it explains the observed absence of determiners, inflectional endings pronouns and complementizers by assuming the absence of the D, the I and the C system. Arguments against this account show that the child is aware of the syntactic consequences of morphological processes in form-position correlations. As discussed in 3.1 above, the fact that subject clitics co-occur exclusively with finite verbs, suggests that the clitic is placed higher than VP and the verb has presumably moved. Guasti (1992) claimed that clitic placement indicates that Italian children distinguish finite and non-finite structures early on. She found that whenever object clitics were used (which was not often), they were used correctly:

(10)   clitic + Vfin   *Vfin + clitic
         Vinf + clitic   *clitic + Vinf

Apart from the existence of the clitic position outside the VP, another relevant issue is the categorization of object clitics. If these are D-heads, at least in their surface position, then their occurrence and correct placement is direct evidence for the presence of the D-system. The findings on the delay of object clitics in French could argue for an initial absence of this projection (see also Crysmann & Müller who claim that this delay is due to the early absence of the C-system), but the results on Italian and Spanish argue for an early availability of DP.

In addition, the observation that subject clitics occur only with finite verbs (Weissenborn *et al.*, 1989; Pierce, 1989) is relevant for the debate on the presence of functional categories. The non-occurrence of subject clitics in infinitives indicates that certain constructions, namely root infinitives, do not involve the full structural tree. This is so because the simple assumption that the infinitive must stay in a projection below ArgSP is not enough to explain the absence of subject clitics - the tacit assumption being that the subject clitic necessarily attaches to open verbal material. However, as Haegeman (1996) shows, this is not the case as clitics can attach to phonologically empty positions. The availability of the position should make it possible for the clitic to appear unless there are special assumptions about the morphological spell-out of agreement or tense features as Wexler (1997) has suggested.

Another question, which has led to notorious debate, is whether adult learners of a second language have direct access to both the principles and parameters of UG. As the evidence in favor of an affirmative answer accumulates, some areas remain unexplained. These are taken up by Young-Scholten who asks: Why do adult language learners often fail to acquire various functional categories and a native-like phonology? She investigates the acquisition of pronominal clitics of Standard German and finds that some of the syntactic aspects of German clitics are not mastered even by advanced L2 learners. She speculates that this is not due to inaccessibility of UG, but rather that the learner's phonological competence is incomplete and cannot represent the input required to set the parameters correctly.

3.4. Pronominal clitics and parametric variation

The considerable cross-linguistic variation of subject clitics, indicates the following possibilities for languages:

- non *pro*-drop with subject pronouns (English)
- non-*pro* drop with subject clitics (Standard and Colloquial French)
- *pro*-drop with subject clitics (Fiorentino)
- *pro*-drop (Standard Italian, Spanish)

Hyams' early work explored these parametric possibilities by attempting to explain the occurrence of null subjects in child English. In this volume, Roeper & Rohrbacher investigate the use of null subjects in comparison to the use of pronouns in English and discuss the possibility that the projection of the agreement system is parameterized across languages following the Principle of Economy of Projection (Speas, 1994). They analyze the use of null subjects and infinitives in wh-questions and argue that dropped subjects are indeed *pro*. The parametric variation regarding the use of *pro*, is well-documented in target and child languages.

Another not as well investigated area of considerable parametric variation is the placement of object clitics. Some languages do not raise the clitic out of the lower clause in modal embedding contexts, others either allow or require enclisis. A closely related fact is that some languages allow enclisis with infinitives (e.g., Italian) while others always have proclisis with infinitives (e.g., French). How far a clitic can raise even varies within a language, depending on the embedding verb. Another difference, probably due to a parametric difference is that some languages, notably Spanish, allow (object) clitic-doubling, while other languages do not.

Yet, despite this complexity, the Romance child, *grosso modo*, places clitics correctly. This raises again the notoriously recalcitrant question for acquisition theory: How are parameters set by the child in the course of development? Assuming default settings, what are the triggering data and situations that can trigger a reset? Assuming that parameters are initially not set, then what are the learning algorithms and triggering mechanisms? Kapur & Clark investigate these questions from a computational perspective and show that a symbolic algorithm combined with a statistical entropy measure applied to the input can presort available data so that trigger detection is guided. Parameter setting on the basis of this presorting is already biased in the right direction and thus precludes the problems of random setting and testing. By monitoring positional properties, especially closeness to the verb, their algorithm can successfully and quickly distinguish clitic pronouns from free pronouns. As Romance clitics are correctly placed by the child very early in development, a lot depends on the speed which such a technique allows for trigger detection.

This volume unites articles on clitics from very different points of view. Cardinaletti & Starke provide a cross-linguistic, theoretical view on pronominal clitics, introducing a new analysis and classification system for pronouns. Bottari *et al.* look at clitics from the point of view of language impairment and Kapur & Clark from that of computational linguistics. Crysmann & Müller as well as Roeper & Rohrbacher analyze their data in a structure-building framework, while Haverkort & Weissenborn use a full competence approach and use acquisition data to settle a theoretical question about the syntax of Germanic clitics. Torrens & Wexler take the same approach for a specific problem of the syntax of Romance clitics. Young - Scholten approaches German clitics from the point of view of L2 acquisition and focuses on the phonological side of clitics. We can also look at the collection of articles from another perspective: Haverkort & Weissenborn and Young-Scholten treat Germanic clitics, Kapur & Clark and Crysmann & Müller treat French, Bottari *et al.* and Cardinaletti & Starke present data on the acquisition of Italian clitics, and Torrens & Wexler deal with Spanish.

4. CONCLUSION

As the foregoing discussion has shown, both scrambling and cliticization intersect with a number of syntactic issues and acquisition issues. Many similarities in the analyses exist. For example, both movement and base-generation accounts have been offered for each of these processes. Determining of the categorial and X-bar status of the constituents involved is crucial in determining what kind of movement is involved. The goal of this volume is to enrich our understanding of the adult phenomena by studying the patterns of emergence found cross-linguistically. The most amazing fact uniting scrambling and cliticization is that the syntax of these clause-internal processes is indeed very complex, but children converge on the target very quickly. While linguists and acqusitionists are still debating about the analysis of the target, children seem to have figured it out. With this in mind, we now turn to the individual contributions.

ACKNOWLEDGEMENTS

We would like to acknowledge Hans Bennis, Liliane Haegeman, Paola Merlo, and William Snyder for providing additional reviews. Cornelia Hamann was supported by the SFN Grant No. 1213-042212.94 and by the Geneva University Interfaculty Project on "Language and Communication". Susan Powers was supported by the Linguistics Department at the University of Potsdam.

REFERENCES

Belletti, A.: 1993, 'Case Checking and Clitic Placement: Three Issues on (Italian/Romance) Clitics', *GenGenP* **1 (2)**, 101-118.
Belletti, A.: to appear, '(Italian/Romance) Clitics: Structure and Derivation', In H. van Riemsdijk (ed.) Clitics in the Languages of Europe. *EUROTYP* **8**, Mouton de Gruyter, Berlin.
Borer, H.: 1984, *Parametric Syntax*, Foris, Dordrecht.
Borer, H. and K. Wexler: 1987, 'The maturation of syntax', in T. Roeper & E. Williams (eds.), *Parameter setting*, Reidel, Dordrecht, 123-172.
Bowerman, M. F.: 1973. *Early Syntactic Development: A Crosslinguistic Study with Special Reference to Finnish*. Cambridge University Press, London
Bowerman, M. F.: 1990, 'Mapping Thematic Roles onto Syntactic Functions. Are Children Helped by Innate Linking Rules?' *Linguistics* **28(6)**, 1253-1289.
Brown, R. W., and C. Fraser: 1963, 'The acquisition of syntax', In C. N. Cofer & B. S. Musgrave (eds.) *Verbal Behavior and Learning: Problems and Processes*, McGraw-Hill, New York.
Brown, R. W.: 1973. *A First Language: The Early Stages*. Harvard University Press, Cambridge.
Cardinaletti, A. and M. Starke: 1995, 'The Tripartition of Pronouns and Its Acquisition: Principle B Puzzles are Ambiguity Problems', in J. Beckman (ed.) *NELS* **25**, 1-12.
Clark, E.: 1985, 'The Acquisition of Romance with Special Reference to French', in D. Slobin (ed.) *The Cross-linguistic Study of Language Acquisition,* Lawrence Erlbaum, Hillsdale, 687-782.
de Villiers, J., T. Roeper and A. Vainikka: 1990, The Acquisition of Long-distance Rules. In L. Frazier & J. deVilliers (eds.) *Language Processing and Language Acquisition*, Kluwer Academic Publishers, Dordrecht, 257-297.
Felix, S.W.: 1991, Language Acquisition as a Maturational Process, In Weissenborn, J., Goodluck, H, and Roeper, T. (eds.) *Theoretical Issues in Language Acquisition: Continuity and Change in Development*, Lawrence Erlbaum, Hillsdale, 25-52.
Friedemann, M.-A.: 1992, 'The Underlying Position of External Arguments in French', *GenGenP* **0(1-2)**, 123-144.
Friedemann, M.-A.: 1995, 'Sujets syntaxiques; positions, inversions et pro'. Doctoral dissertation, University of Geneva.
Gruber, J.S.: 1967, 'Topicalization in child language', *Foundations of Language* **3**, 37-65.
Guasti, M.T.: 1992, 'Verb Syntax in Italian Child Grammar', *GenGenP* **0 (1-2)**, 145-162.
Guilfoyle, E. and M. Noonan: 1988, 'Functional Categories and Language Acquisition'. Paper presented at *The Boston University Conference on Language Development*.
Guilfoyle, E. and M. Noonan: 1992, 'Functional Categories and Language Acquisition', *Canadian Journal of Linguistics* **37**, 241-272.
Haegeman, L.: 1996, 'Root Infinitives, Clitics and Truncated Structures', in H. Clahsen (ed.) *Generative Perspectives on Language Acquisition*. John Benjamins, Amsterdam, 271-308.
Hamann, C., L. Rizzi, and U. Frauenfelder: 1996, 'The Acquisition of Subject and Object Clitics in French', in H. Clahsen (ed.) *Generative Perspectives on Language Acquisition*. John Benjamins, Amsterdam, 309-334.

Haverkort, M. and J. Weissenborn: 1991, 'Clitic and Affix Interaction in Early Romance', paper presented at the *16th Boston University Conference on Language Development*, October.
Hyams, N.: 1996, 'The Underspecification of Functional Categories in Early Grammar', In H. Clahsen (ed.) *Generative Perspectives on Language Acquisition*. John Benjamins, Amsterdam, 91-128.
Jakubowicz, C., N. Müller, O.-K. Kang, B. Riemer, and C. Rigaut: 1996, 'On the Acquisition of the Pronominal System in French and German', in A. Stringfellow *et al.* (eds.) *Proceedings of the Boston University Conference on Language Development* **20**, Cascadilla Press, Somerville, 374-385.
Kaiser, G.: 1994, 'More about INFL-ection and Agreement: The Acquisition of Clitic Pronouns in French', in J. Meisel (ed.) *Bilingual First Language Acquisition. French and German Grammatical Development*. John Benjamins, Amsterdam. 131-160.
Kayne, R.: 1975, *French Syntax*, MIT Press, Cambridge.
Kayne, R.: 1994, *The Antisymmetry of Syntax*. MIT Press, Cambridge.
Kornfilt, J.: 1994, 'Some remarks on the interaction of Case and Word Order in Turkish: Implications for Acquisition', In B. Lust *et al.* (eds.) *Syntactic Theory and First Language Acquisition: Crosslinguistic Perspectives*, Lawrence Erlbaum, Hillsdale, 171-199.
Lakshmanan, U. and M. Ozeki: 1996, 'The case of the Missing particle: Object Case Assignment and Scrambling in the early Grammar of Japanese', In Stringfellow *et al.* (eds.) *Proceedings of the Boston University Conference on Language Development* **20**, Cascadilla Press, Somerville, 431-442.
Lebeaux, D.: 1988, Language Acquisition and the Form of the Grammar. Ph.D. Dissertation, University of Massachusetts Amherst.
Meisel, J.: 1990, 'INFL-ection: Subjects and Subject-Verb Agreement in Early Child Language', in J. Meisel (ed.) *Two First Languages. Early Grammatical Development in Bilingual Children*, Foris, Dordrecht. 237-298.
Meisel, J. (ed.) 1992: *The Acquisition of Verb Placement: Functional Categories and V2 Phenomena in Language Acquisition*, Kluwer, Dordrecht.
Meisel, J. and N. Müller: 1992, 'Finiteness and Verb Placement in Early Child Grammars: Evidence from Simultaneous Acquisition of French and German Bilinguals', in J. Meisel (ed.) *The Acquisition of Verb Placement. Functional Categories and V2 Phenomena in Language Acquisition*. Kluwer, Dordrecht, 109-138.
Müller, N.: 1994, 'Parameters Cannot be Reset, Evidence from the Development of Comp', in J. Meisel (ed.) *Bilingual First Language Acquisition. French and German Grammatical Development*. John Benjamins, Amsterdam, 235-269.
Otsu, Y.: 1994, Early acquisition of Scrambling in Japanese, In Hoekstra, T. & B. Schwartz (eds.) *Language Acquisition Studies in Generative Grammar*, John Benjamins, Amsterdam, 253-264.
Park, T.-Z.: 1971, 'A Study of German Language Development', Ph.D. Dissertation, University of Berne.
Penner, Z.: 1991, 'Pronominal Clitics in Bernese Swiss and their Structural Position. Evidence from the acquisition process', in H. van Riemsdijk and L. Rizzi (eds.) Clitics and their Hosts. *EUROTYP Working Papers*, 253-268.
Pierce, A.: 1989, 'On the Emergence of Syntax: A Cross-linguistic Study', Ph.D. Dissertation, MIT.
Pierce, A.: 1992, *Language Acquisition and Syntactic Theory*, Kluwer, Dordrecht.
Poeppel, D. and K. Wexler: 1993, 'The Full Competence Hypothesis of Clause Structure in Early German', *Language* **69**, 1-33.
Powers, S. M.: 1996, 'The Growth of the Phrase Marker: Evidence from Subjects'. Ph.D. Dissertation , University of Maryland.
Radford, A.: 1986, 'Small Children's Small Clauses'. *Transactions of the Philological Society* **86**, 1-46.

Radford, A.: 1990, *Syntactic Theory and the Acquisition of English Syntax*, Blackwell, Oxford.
Radford, A.: 1996, Towards a Structure-building Model of Acquisition. In H. Clahsen (ed.) *Generative Perspectives on Language Acquisition*, John Benjamins, Amsterdam, 43-90.
Rizzi, L.: 1986, 'On the Status of Subject Clitics in Romance', in O. Jaeggli & C. Silva-Corvalan (eds.) *Studies in Romance Linguistics*, Foris, Dordrect. 391-419.
Roeper, T.: 1973, 'Connecting children's language and linguistic theory'. In T. E. Moore, (ed.) *Cognitive development and the acquisition of language*. Academic Press, New York, 187-196.
Roeper, T.: 1992, 'From the Initial State to V2: Acquisition Principles in Action', In J. Meisel (ed.) *The Acquisition of Verb Placement. Functional Categories and V2 Phenomena in Language Acquisition*. Kluwer, Dordrecht, 333-370.
Roeper, T.: 1996, 'Merger Theory and Formal Features in Acquisition', In H. Clahsen (ed.) *Generative Perspectives on Language Acquisition*, John Benjamins, Amsterdam, 415-450.
Schönenberger, M., Z. Penner and J. Weissenborn: 1997, 'Object Placement and Early German Grammar', In *Proceedings of the Annual Boston University Conference on Language Development* 21, Cascadilla Press, Somerville, 539-549.
Siloni, T.: 1994, 'Noun Phrases and Nominalizations'. Ph.D. Dissertation, University of Geneva.
Speas, M: 1994, Null Arguments in a Theory of Economy of Projection. *University of Massachusetts Occasional Papers in Linguistics* 17, 179-208.
Sportiche, D.: 1992, 'Clitic constructions', ms., UCLA.
Thráinsson, H.:1996, 'On the (Non-)Universality of Functional Categories', In W. Abraham *et al.* (eds.) *Minimal Ideas:Syntactic Studies in the Minimalist Framework*, John Benjamins, Amsterdam, 253-281.
Tsimpli, I-M.: 1991, 'On the Maturation of functional Categories: Early Child Speech'. *UCL Working Papers in Linguistics* 3, 123-148.
Weissenborn, J., M. Verripps and R. Berman: 1989, 'Negation as a Window to the Structure of Early Child Language', ms. Max-Planck Institute.
Weissenborn, J.: 1990, 'Functional Categories and Verb Movement: The Acquisition of German Syntax Reconsidered', in M. Rothweiler (ed.) Spracherwerb und Grammatik. Linguistische Untersuchungen zum Erwerb von Syntax und Morphologie. *Linguistische Berichte, Special Issue* 3, 190-223.
Wexler, K.: 1996, 'What Children *Don't* Know Really Tells Us a Lot about Linguistic Theory', paper presented at WCHTSALT, OTS, Utrecht. June.
Wexler, K.: 1997, 'Explanatory Models of Language Acquisition', plenary talk presented at *GALA*, Edinburgh. April.
White, L.: 1996, 'Clitics in L2-French', in H. Clahsen (ed.) *Generative Perspectives on Language Acquisition*, Benjamins, Amsterdam, 335-368.
Zwart, C. J-W.: 1993, 'Dutch Syntax', Ph.D. Dissertation, University of Groningen.

SUSAN M. POWERS
University of Potsdam

CORNELIA HAMANN
University of Geneva &
University of Tuebingen

HUBERT HAIDER

SCRAMBLING - WHAT'S THE STATE OF THE ART?

1. INTRODUCTION

Anything goes still appears to be the adequate motto summarizing the present stage of the theoretical debate on scrambling. All options available in the theory of grammar have been exploited for the reconstruction of this phenomenon, that is the variable constituent order within a clause in languages like German, Hindi, or Japanese, to name just a few. Consensus about what the correct overarching theory of scrambling is has not been reached however. Even for one and the same language, various analyses are still in competition. Given this situation, why is this so? There are two possible answers: Either the phenomenon is still not sufficiently understood or the present theories are not fully adequate for capturing it.[1]

What is the range of anything goes? First, the various alternative orderings may be viewed as alternative base orders. Secondly, scrambling might be treated as a stylistic rule that operates on the PF-representation and does not belong to syntax proper. Thirdly, scrambling may be, and in fact, most often is, taken to be a genuine syntactic phenomenon: The scrambling order is analyzed as a derived order. It is derived from a base order by means of syntactic operations. Since there are two basic types of movement (adjunction or substitution) and two different types of dependencies (A-chains or A'-chains), the logical space for theorizing contains four possible options.

It should be easy, one might think, to narrow down the set of explanatory options. Since they embody different predictions which can be checked empirically, the empirically correct characterization of the phenomenon should lead to the adequate choice of the theoretical position. What is the problem? As a matter of fact, the discussion has not reached the level of descriptive adequacy yet: There is still an ongoing debate as to what the theoretically significant generalizations are. This will be highlighted in the discussion of the role of the parasitic gap phenomenon in Section 2.

Section 2 briefly reviews word order phenomena of Germanic languages that constitute the empirical basis of the scrambling phenomenon. Section 3 introduces the background for the analytic decision between a movement and a non-movement analysis and arguments for the choice of the movement type. Section 4 provides additional empirical support: The structure dependent properties of focus spreading in scrambling constructions are evidence for verb-class specific base orders. Section 5 deals with semantic effects that correlate with scrambling. Section 6 examines, and argues against, the claim that there are German infinitival constructions that allow for long scrambling. The last section is a short descriptive appendix. It draws a distinction between scrambling proper and the distribution of pronouns.

2. THE RANGE OF SCRAMBLING IN GERMANIC LANGUAGES[2]

In the non-technical usage, scrambling is used as a synonym for free word order in languages like German in contrast to the more rigidly fixed word order in languages like English. Scrambling refers to word order variation within the simple clause (local scrambling) or out of an embedded clause (long-distance scrambling) that is not triggered by an overt morphological marker. Functionally triggered word order variation is understood either as wh-movement (as in the case of question formation, relative clause formation) or as NP-movement (as in the case of passive or subject-to-subject raising in English).

The non-technical usage covers a wider range of word order variation than the technical usage. In the technical usage (see Haider, Olsen & Vikner, 1995:14-21), scrambling proper (as in example 1b) is distinguished from heavy NP-shift (as in (2); see Postal, 1974) and object shift (as in (3)) in Scandinavian languages (see Vikner, 1995; Holmberg & Platzack, 1995):

(1)   a. daß keiner den Mann kennt
          that nobody the man knows
      b. daß den Mann$_i$ keiner e$_i$ kennt
          that the man nobody knows

(2)   a. *I would like to introduce to you [linguists]
      b. I would like to introduce to you [linguists who have never worked on scrambling]

Heavy NP-shift reorganizes the VP-internal word order in such a way that a sufficiently complex NP ends up in the final position. VP-external subjects are not shifted. That English subjects cannot be post-posed by means of heavy NP-shift has been pointed out by Postal (1974).

Object shift (as in 3b) refers to a switch in the relative order of DP-objects and adverbials that derives the order in (3b) from the order in (3a). Object shift does not change the relative order of objects in multiple object constructions, however. PP-Objects do not participate in object shifting. In addition, object shift is contingent on V-fronting: No verb is allowed in the domain of object shifting. If the VP contains an overt verb in surface structure, object shift is ungrammatical (see 3c). In the continental Scandinavian languages, object shift is restricted to pronouns. This restriction does not hold for Icelandic.

(3)   a. ì gær las Pètur eflaust ekki bòkkina   [Icelandic]
         yesterday read Peter undoubtedly not book-the
     b. ì gær las Pètur [bòkkinai eflaust ekki ei]
     c. *ì gær hefur Pètur [bòkkinai eflaust ekki lesi_ ei]

The order relations among DP-objects must be distinguished from the order relations of PPs, not only in the case of object shift. PPs, both arguments and adjuncts, occur in alternative orders even in a language with a highly fixed order like English:

(4)   a. He does not talk to everyone about scrambling.
     b. He does not talk about scrambling to everyone.

To sum up, heavy NP-shift is observed in all Germanic languages, Object-shift is a phenomenon of Germanic VO-languages, and scrambling proper is found only in Germanic OV-languages. The latter facts need to be correlated (see below).

The Germanic OV-languages, notably Dutch and German, differ significantly with respect to their scrambling options, though. In German, scrambling in a clause like (5a) produces all possible permutations of the DP-constituents. So, there are five variants of (5a) that differ in the order of the DP-arguments. In Dutch, the relative order of subject, indirect objects and direct objects must not be changed. Scrambling in (5b) would produce ungrammatical results (see Geerts *et al.*, 1984:988). What changes is the order relative to adverbials. PPs, however, may change their positions, irrespective of object (as in 6a,b) or adverbial status.[3]

(5)   a. daß der Mann dem Bürgermeister die Malerei angeboten hat
         that the men (to) the mayor the painting has offered
     b. dat de man de burgemeester de schilderij heeft aangeboden

(6)   a. dat de man [aan de burgemeester] de schilderij heeft aangeboden
that the men to the mayor the painting has offered
b. dat de man de schilderij [aan de burgemeester] heeft aangeboden

Scrambling of a PP-object to the left of a transitive subject in Dutch, however, is ungrammatical in general. This is possible only under clause internal topicalization, that is, with an intonational pitch on the fronted element and strong focusing intonation on the clause final phrase. Under these restricted conditions, DPs may appear in an inverted order (see Neeleman, 1994:396):

(7)   a. dat [zulke boeken]$_i$ zelfs Jan niet e_i koopt
that such books even Jan not buys
b. dat Jan [zulke boeken]$_i$ zelfs Marie e_i niet geeft
that Jan such books even Mary not gives

This double pitch contour is a clear signal for reconstruction: The element with the first pitch (rising) is reconstructed into its base position. This can be checked with scope interaction: The relative scope of the elements identified with the pitch accents is computed according to their base positions (see Krifka, 1998).

(8)   a. /Alle Bilder$_i$ hat er den Besuchern \nicht e_i gezeigt
[wide scope negation]
all pictures has he (to) the visitors not shown
b. Alle Bilder$_i$ hat er den Besuchern nicht e_i gezeigt
[narrow scope negation]

Under the pitch contour indicated in (8a), the fronted constituent is reconstructed into its gap position. So, wide scope is assigned to the negation. In (8b), the scope is assigned according to the c-command relations in S-structure.[4]

What is referred to as scrambling in Dutch in the literature is the order of adverbials relative to the argument expressions. The relative order of the nominal arguments remains constant. Hence, what is called scrambling in Dutch is subject to the same restriction as object shift in Scandinavian languages. In (9), a time adverbial like *gisteren* 'yesterday' may occur in any of the slots indicated by the sign # (see Neeleman, 1994:419; Geerts *et al.*, 1984:992f.):

(9)   dat # Jan # de mannen # de foto # toonde
        that Jan the men the photograph showed

It should be kept in mind that in current theorizing it is not the adverbial that is suspected to scramble, but the arguments. This implies, of course, that the leftmost position in (9) is the base position. If arguments are moved to the left of the adverbial, it apparently shifts to the right. Consequently, all the arguments must have been moved across the adverbial if it appears in the rightmost position in (9). The premise, however, is not self-evident. Its empirical support is of indirect nature only (see Diesing, 1992; de Hoop, 1992; Haider & Rosengren, 1998).

What are the significant descriptive generalizations? The two most important parameters are the headedness-parameter and the case-parameter. Scrambling of the German type is restricted to OV-languages. In addition, the language must have a non-structural linking system for arguments. If arguments are positionally linked, they do not scramble. This property is the division line between German and Dutch. German has a morphological system of linking. Dutch has a positional system: Objects are not differentiated by morphological means, that is, by case or an equivalent linking device (see Haider, 1988).

(10)   a. Generalization 1:
           No scrambling across heads of phrases
        b. Generalization 2:
           No scrambling of positionally linked arguments

Generalization 1 rules out scrambling to the left in VO-languages. In fact, it rules out scrambling out of head-initial constituents altogether (see Haider, 1995). Scrambling to the right in OV-languages would be forbidden by (10a). But there is a more general constraint against targeting positions to the right (see Haider, 1992; Kayne, 1994). This rules out scrambling to the right in VO- languages as well.

3. SCRAMBLING: MOVEMENT OR BASE GENERATION?

The main bifurcation in the search tree for an adequate account of scrambling is that between a movement approach and a base generation approach. According to the former, scrambling yields an antecedent gap configuration. Hence, one expects to see properties associated with this configuration. To establish the fact and prove that the properties are fulfilled by scrambling is a non-trivial enterprise, however.

It is not sufficient to realize (as Webelhuth, 1989:341-47) that scrambling parallels wh-movement by virtue of the fact that it does not violate island constraints, in order to jump to the conclusion that movement is involved:

(11) a. *weil ihre Freiheit$_i$ die Leute [für e$_i$] kämpften
  [PP-island]
  since their freedom$_i$ the people [for e$_i$] fought
 b. *weil sich Faßbinders$_i$ jemand [e$_i$ Film] ansah
  [left branch]
  since refl. Faßbinder's someone [e$_i$ movie] watched
 c. *weil ihn$_i$ jemand [e$_i$ und Maria] anmeldete
  [coordinate structure island]
  since him$_i$ someone registered [e$_i$ and Mary]

Sentences like these are ruled out in a base generation approach as well. If scrambling shares with movement constructions the lack of certain properties, this does by no means prove that movement is involved: If movement is not involved at all, movement violations trivially cannot arise.[5]

There is a phenomenon that is known to be directly related to the existence of a specific movement configuration, namely the parasitic gap construction. Parasitic gaps are licensed by A'-traces, but not by A-movement traces (see Chomsky, 1982; Postal, 1993). So, if scrambling licenses parasitic gaps, scrambling must be an instance of A'-movement. Webelhuth (1989:410f.), however, admits that the impact of this area of grammar is puzzling: Scrambling seems to license parasitic gaps on the one hand, and on the other hand scrambled DPs can serve as the antecedents of anaphors. The latter feature is a property of A-positions, not of A'-positions. The licensing of parasitic gaps is indicative of an A'-position. Moreover, A'-movement triggers cross-over effects.

(12) a. ?Er hat jeden$_i$ Gast [ohne *pg$_i$* anzuschauen] seinem$_i$ Nachbarn e$_i$ vorgestellt
  he has every guest [without to-look-at *pg*] (to) his neighbor introduced
 b. ?Er hat die Gäste$_i$ [ohne *pg$_i$* anzuschauen] einander$_i$ e$_i$ vorgestellt
  he has the guests [without to-look-at *pg*] (to) each$_i$ other introduced

According to Webelhuth's analysis, the scrambled phrase is the antecedent for the gap in the infinitival adverbial clause. This gap is claimed to be a parasitic gap. In addition, the scrambled quantified NP in (12a) binds a pronoun without a weak crossover effect, and in (12b), the scrambled object binds an anaphor. These properties are associated with A-positions, however. Since in the current theory a position cannot simultaneously be treated as A and A', there are either two movement steps involved (see Mahajan, 1994), or the dichotomy must be relaxed (see Deprez, 1994), or the data must be reevaluated for their validity. There are good reasons to take the latter path and discard the idea that (12) involves parasitic gaps.

First of all, the gaps in adverbial infinitival clauses do not have the properties of parasitic gaps in English, as the comparison between (13a-c) and (14a-c) illustrates. Second, the typical cases of English (as in 13d) are strongly deviant in German (see 14d).

(13)   a. *Where did Elaine work e_i without ever living pg_i? (Postal, 1993:737)
                  b. *What he became e_i without wanting to become pg_i was a linguist (Postal, 1993:746)
                  c. *This is a topic about which$_i$ you should think e_i before talking pg_i (Postal, 1993:736)
                  d. ?Which disease$_i$ did everyone who caught pg_i want Dr. Jones to study e_i (Postal, 1993:738)

(14)   a. ?Wo hat Elaine, anstatt mit dir zu wohnen, ihr Büro eingerichtet?
                  b. ?Was er wurde, ohne eigentlich werden zu wollen, war ein Linguist
                  c. ?Das ist ein Thema, über das wir, anstatt zu schwätzen, nachdenken sollten
                  d. *Welches Haus wollte jeder, dem er pg_i zeigte, e_i sofort kaufen?
                     which house$_i$ did everyone, who he showed pg_i (to), want to buy immediately?

Finally, the gaps in infinitival adverbial constructions are not restricted to a single occurrence, as (15a) illustrates. This immediately rules out a parasitic gap analysis. Fanselow (1993:33-38) notes parallels between this construction and conjunction reduction and concludes that *ohne* 'without' and *anstatt* 'instead' function syntactically like coordinating heads. The alleged parasitic gaps are the result of ellipsis rather and not the result of variable binding mechanisms. Viewed from this perspective, it is not surprising that the alleged parasitic gap construction may contain more than one gap.

(15) a. daß er eine Frau$_i$ einem Mann$_j$ [anstatt e$_i$ e$_j$ vorzuziehen] unterordnen will
that he a woman a man [instead to prefer] subordinate wanted
'that he wants to subordinate a woman to a man instead of preferring [her to him]'
b. daß er eine Frau einem Mann zuerst unterordnete und dann --- vorzog
'that he first subordinated a woman to a man and then preferred ---'

Fanselow's reanalysis of the alleged parasitic gap construction in German on the one hand removes the puzzling conflict between A- and A'-properties illustrated in (18), and on the other hand it does away with the main support for an A'-movement analysis of scrambling in German.

We may nevertheless continue to ask whether there is direct evidence for the status of movement involved in scrambling. If scrambling is A'-movement, it is expected that the class of elements that admit wh-movement also admit scrambling. In addition, it is predicted that the relations a wh-moved element may or may not enter are available or unavailable for scrambled elements. Topicalization is an uncontroversial instance of wh-movement in German. Hence, a comparison between topicalization and scrambling should reveal common properties if there are any. Table (16) presents but an illustrative sample. The example sentences corresponding to (16a) to (16d) are listed in (17) - (20). The brackets signify that the respective property cannot be checked by simple inspection in German, because other factors may interfere (see Frey, 1993; Haider, 1993).

(16)

categories	SCR.	wh-chain type	A-chain-type
a. result predicate	*	+	*
b. VP	*	+	*
c. particles	*	+	*
d. idiom chunks	*	+	(+)
relations			
e. binding	+	–	+
f. weak crossover	–	(+)	–
g. scope sensitive	+	(–)	+

(* = ungrammatical; + = grammatical; – = does not apply)

(17) a. *wenn er hart$_i$ sein Ei e$_i$ gekocht hat
'if he has boiled his egg hard'
b. Hart$_i$ hat er sein Ei e$_i$ gekocht

(18) a. *daß er [sein Problem erklärt]i niemandem e$_i$ hat
that he [his problem explained] (to) no one has
b. [sein Problem erklärt]$_i$ hat er e$_i$ niemandem

(19) a. *wenn sein Entschluß fest in dieser Sache schon steht,...
if firm his decision in this matter stands
b. Fest steht sein Entschluß in dieser Sache schon lange
firm stands his decision in this matter already for a long time
'Already for a long time he is determined on his decision in this matter'

(20) a. *daß sich Fragen$_i$ keiner e$_i$ stellen muß
that refl. questions$_i$ no one e$_i$ puts must
'that no one needs to ask himself (put questions =ask)'
b. Fragen$_i$ muß sich keiner e$_i$ stellen

What this sample shows is that there are elements that can be displaced under wh-movement but not under scrambling. The following examples show that scrambling differs from wh-movement also with respect to reconstruction effects: On the one hand, scrambling creates new binding possibilities (illustrated in 21b), if a potential binder is scrambled into a position c-commanding the bindee. On the other hand, (21c) shows the converse, namely that scrambling the bindee destroys the binding relation. Wh-movement does not incur this effect.

(21) a. *Ich habe einander$_i$ die Gäste$_i$ vorgestellt
I have (to) each other the guests introduced
b. Ich habe die Gäste$_i$ einander$_i$ e$_i$ vorgestellt
c. *Sie haben [auf einander$_i$]$_j$ die Hunde$_i$ e$_j$ gehetzt
They baited against each other$_i$ the dogs$_1$
d. [Auf einander]$_j$ haben sie die Hunde$_i$ e$_j$ gehetzt

Scrambling does not exhibit weak crossover effects and it enlarges the scope domain of a quantifier if the quantifier is scrambled (see Frey, 1993; Haider, 1988, 1993). This is a characteristic property of A-chains, but not of A'-chains.

These facts cast doubt on the viability of a wh-movement approach but - what should not be overlooked - they do not discriminate between A-movement and base generation. So, what we need is clear evidence for the existence of a gap in scrambling constructions. Again, there have been adduced constructions which seem to provide the desired evidence but the evidence is not always reliable. For instance, Giusti (1990), who follows Sportiche (1988), has claimed that Q-stranding identifies the base position of a scrambled NP.

(22)   a. Er hat [die Bücher darüber]$_i$ schon fast alle e$_i$ gelesen
            He has the books about it already almost all read
     b. [Fast alle die Bücher darüber] hat er schon gelesen
     c. *[Die Bücher darüber fast alle] hat er schon gelesen

(23)   [Die Männer$_i$ angerufen] hat sie damals alle e$_1$
     The men phoned up has she then all   (Fanselow, 1993)

If Q-stranding is the effect of scrambling, the scrambled element must bind a trace in the base position. But, since Q-stranding occurs with VP-topicalization (23), Q-stranding cannot be the exclusive result of dissociating the NP and Q by movement, as Fanselow (1993) argues: The VP-internal NP could not bind the trace.[6]

3.1. Evidence for gaps?

There is an area of grammar which provides a crucial testing ground for the presence of a structural gap-position in scrambling constructions. This area is the interaction between base order, sentence accent and focus projection. Höhle (1982) expounded the relevance of word order and sentence stress for the focus potential of a sentence. He correlates normal word order and normal intonation with maximal focus potential:

(24)   Was ist passiert? (What has happened? or What's new?)
     [X$_F$ = focus exponent]
     a. [Es [hat [jemand [einer Frau [*eine Nachricht$_F$* hinterlassen]]]]]
         there has someone (to) a woman a message left
     b. %[Es [hat [jemand [*einer Frau$_F$* [eine Nachricht hinterlassen]]]]]
     c. %[Es [hat [jemand [eine Nachricht$_i$ [*einer Frau$_F$* [e$_i$ hinterlassen]]]]]]

Examples (24b,c) are felicitous answers only for questions which focus on the dative object. They are infelicitous answers, however, to a question which focuses on the whole event. Why is this so? It is so because the focus on a higher position does not project to the whole clause. Why does it project in (24a) then?

Focus projects if the pitch accent of the clause rests on the most deeply embedded position. This is the default position of sentence stress (see Cinque, 1993). Stress on a position higher in the structure (cf. 24b) amounts to narrow focus. The focus does not project (for details see Haider, 1993:212f). Let us now compare (24b) and (24c). If scrambling structures contain a gap in the base position, as indicated in (24c), the stressed NP in (24c) occupies the very same position as in (24b). Hence, the effect on focus projection is the same. If, however, scrambling would be the result of the generation of alternative base orders, the prediction would be that focus in (24c) unlike in (24b) projects.

Of course, one might try to defend a base generation approach by relating the focus potential to a distinguished order without invoking a gap. But the point of the discussion must not be overlooked: In Cinque's conception of stress assignment, it is the syntactic structure that determines the prosodic structure. There is no extra stress rule that could relate to a distinction like standard and non-standard word order, or canonical versus non-canonical projection of A-structure. In combination with the assumption that scrambling involves gaps, the result follows without stipulation. Moreover, as expected, scrambling interferes with focus projection only in case the most deeply embedded argument is scrambled.

(25) es hat einer Frau$_i$ jemand e$_i$ eine *Nachricht$_F$* hinterlassen
there has a woman (DAT) someone a message left
'Someone has left a message for a woman'

In (25), scrambling does not affect the focus potential because scrambling does not involve the direct object, that is the most deeply embedded phrase in (25). The criterion of focus projection provides additional evidence which bears directly on scrambling: The base order of arguments in the VP is a function of the argument structure of the verb and not a function of structurally fixed case positions.

(26)   Possible primary serializations (for transitive and intransitive verbs):
   a. NOM-AKK {*betreten* 'enter', *verlassen* 'leave', ...}
   b. AKK-NOM {*interessieren* 'interest', *stören* 'bother',...}
   c. NOM-DAT {*helfen* 'help, *gratulieren* 'congratulate',...}
   d. DAT-NOM {*gefallen* 'please', *fehlen* 'lack', ...}
   e. NOM-DAT-AKK {*anvertrauen* 'entrust', *verbieten* 'forbid',...}
   f. NOM-AKK-DAT {*aussetzen* 'expose', *unterordnen* 'subordinate', ...}

All the verbs in (26) are unergative ones. Whether a given NP-NP-V sequence is a primary serialization (= base sequence) or a scrambled one, cannot be decided without recourse to the A-structure of the verbal head. A given order of arguments can be either a base order for one class of verbs (cf. 27a,c) or a scrambled order for another class of verbs (see 27b,d). The base order reflects the ranking of the arguments in the argument structure of the head (see Haider, 1992, 1993 based on the theory of M. Bierwisch), which is a function of the lexical-conceptual structure.

(27)   a. [NOM [AKK V]]   b. [AKK$_i$ [NOM [e$_i$ V]]]
       c. [AKK [NOM V]]   d. [NOM$_i$ [AKK [e$_i$ V]]]

The focus projection property is a diagnostic for establishing the base order: If in the following sentences the NP immediately preceding the verb is the exponent of sentence stress, the focus projection potential is as indicated. The difference in the focus potential is a direct reflex of the difference in base order. In the scrambled order, the focus exponent is not the most deeply embedded NP.

(28)   a. daß Linguisten$_{NOM}$ Balladen$_{ACC}$ interpretieren
          [maximal focus]
          that linguists interpret ballads
       b. daß Linguisten$_{ACC}$ Balladen$_{NOM}$ interessieren
          [maximal focus]
       c. daß Balladen$_i$ Linguisten$_{NOM}$ e$_i$ interpretieren
          [minimal focus]
       d. daß Balladen$_i$ Linguisten$_{ACC}$ e$_i$ interessieren
          [minimal focus]
          that ballads interest linguists[7]

The same contrast applies to the relative order of dative and accusative:

(29)   a. Man wird einem Psychologen$_{DAT}$ ein Experiment$_F$ verbieten [maximal focus]
'they will forbid a psychologist an experiment'
b. Man wird ein Experiment$_i$ einem Psychologen$_F$ e$_i$ verbieten [minimal focus]
c. Man wird einem Psychologen$_i$ ein Experiment$_F$ e$_i$ unterstellen [minimal focus]
d. Man wird ein Experiment einem Psychologen$_F$ unterstellen [maximal focus]
they will subordinate an experiment (to) a psychologist
'they will put a psychologist in charge of an experiment'

It is worth pointing out that the order restriction is independent of definiteness. If in (28) and (29) the indefinite NPs are replaced by definite ones, the focus effects remain unaffected. This is unexpected if definiteness were the trigger for moving a DP to higher specifier positions. The relative order of specifier positions should not be contingent on the argument structure of the verb: The fact that the base order is a function of the argument structure for definite as well as indefinite argument DPs is incompatible with the idea that the order of definite DPs reflects the order of specifier positions that host these DPs and thereby determine the serialization.

4. CHAIN FORMATION

This section briefly reviews the range of theoretical approaches to scrambling from a theoretical point of view. The theory of grammar provides two basic types of movement (substitution, adjunction) and two types of positions (A- or A'-positions). Hence, there are four logically possible derivational analyses for capturing the word order variation plus a fifth possibility, namely base-generation with canonical and non-canonical projection of A-structure.

(30)   a. Scrambling = substitution into A-positions
b. Scrambling = substitution into A'-positions
c. Scrambling = adjunction as an A'-position
d. Scrambling = adjunction as an A-position
e. Scrambling = base-generation of alternative base orders

All of these options have found advocates with the exception of (30b). This analysis is only partially used in Deprez (1994). A choice of the pertinent literature is listed under (31). Webelhuth (1989) calls for a mixed type of position, that is compatible with the mixed behavior of scrambled DPs in parasitic gap constructions (but recall the negative evaluation of the parasitic gap evidence above).

(31) a. A-chain (substitution): Deprez, 1989; Fanselow, 1990; Moltmann, 1990; Van den Wyngaerden, 1989;
  b. A'-chain (substitution): Deprez, 1994; as a partial option.
  c. A'-chain (adjunction): Hoekstra, 1984; Müller & Sternefeld, 1993; Saito, 1989;
  d. A-chain (adjunction): Haider, 1993; Rosengren, 1993; Haider & Rosengren, 1998;
  e. Base generation: Fanselow, 1993; Haider, 1984; Neeleman, 1994

The substitution accounts assume that scrambling is the effect of movement to the specifier position of a functional projection. Case driven movement would yield A-chains. In this view, it would be unclear, however, why scrambling is optional. Deprez (1994) relates scrambling to a case assignment alternative: In scrambling languages, Case is either assigned as a governed case or a functional case. The specifier position that hosts an NP may count as an A-position, if the head assigns case to the NP (functional case), or as an A'-position if case is assigned in the base position (governed case). Scrambling as A'-chain formation by means of adjunction to VP or IP is a straightforward theoretical option but it has to face the empirical obstacles discussed above: The class of elements that can be scrambled is not the class of elements that enter A'-chains.

In order to motivate the fourth type, a brief comment on the status of A-positions is necessary. A-positions are positions in which a lexical NP is licensed. Since the licensing of an NP involves two types of relations, there are two types of A-positions, that is linking positions and A-structure projection positions. The position in which S-structure linking (= Case checking) takes place is an A-position, and the projection positions (= θ-positions) licensed by the argument structure of the head are A-positions as well. If the two licensing requirements are not checked in a single structural position, we find an NP-chain that relates the linking position with the projection position. The A-chain found with scrambling is the result of dissociating the linking license and the projection license. Since linking is only possible once per head of a chain, the foot of the chain counts as an unlinked projection position. Thus, the A-chain of scrambling shares the characteristic property of A-chains with the familiar NP-movement chains.

This account relates two properties of scrambling: A-type scrambling is clause bound and it is found only in OV-languages. The reason is as follows: The checking domain of the verb in an OV-VP exceeds its minimal projection domain: Compare a structure like (32a) and (32b) with (32c).

(32)   a. [NP2$_i$ [NP1 [e$_i$ V[A1, A2]]]] (illustrated by 27b,d)
     b. NP1 [NP2 V [A1, A2]]] (illustrated by 27a,c)
     c. [NPa [NPb [NPc V]]]

Example (32c) is a possible VP-structure in an OV language. It could occur with a verb that projects three argument positions, for instance. But it is also a possible structure for a two-argument verb, if it involves an A-chain, as indicated in (32a). In this case, one of the NP-positions must be the foot of an A-chain. The foot is the projection position and the head of the chain is the position in which linking is checked. Since linking is possible in either position, scrambling is optional. The projection of the A-structure determines the base order. If the actual order of the argument NPs does not correspond to the base order, the arguments are heading A-chains that terminate in the base position. This constellation cannot arise in VO-languages. In these languages the verb licenses and checks A-positions on the right side. Expanding the VP would create positions on the left. These positions are not in the checking domain of the verb.[8]

Thus, base generated adjunction to VP within the checking domain of a head creates A-positions. Actually, adjunction is a potentially misleading term. What looks like base generated adjunction is the licit extension of the V-projection in terms of a checking domain above the minimal projection domain. In this view it is predicted that long-distance scrambling (see Müller & Sternefeld, 1993) must differ from clause bound scrambling. The former type must involve A'-chains because it cannot fulfill the locality requirement on A-chains.

There are various empirically testable differences between an adjunction and a substitution approach. First, (30a) predicts a fixed order for scrambled elements, given that the functional projections that host the scrambled elements are non-arbitrarily ordered. The German examples under (33) illustrate, that the scrambling positions are not ordered with respect to case.

(33)   a. daß [meinem Onkel$_{DAT}$]$_i$ [die Möbel$_{ACC}$]$_j$ eine hiesige Firma e$_i$ e$_j$ zugestellt hat
that (to) my uncle the furniture a local company delivered has
b. daß [die Möbel]$_j$ [meinem Onkel]$_i$ eine hiesige Firma e$_i$ e$_j$ zugestellt hat
that the furniture (to) my uncle a local company delivered has

Second, non-nominal elements can be scrambled as well. As exemplified in (34) and (35), sentential and prepositional constituents may scramble as well. This is problematic, if the scrambling position is characterized as an Agr-O position, if the element in the spec of an AGR-position needs features which are checked by the head. The fact that sentential constituents and PPs, but not NPs, may be extraposed in German, shows that the licensing properties are different.

(34)   a. daß bis jetzt jeder [die Tür zu öffnen] vergeblich versucht hat
that until now everyone [the door to open] in-vain tried has
b. daß bis jetzt [die Tür zu öffnen]$_i$ jeder e$_i$ vergeblich versucht hat
that until now [the door to open] everyone in vain tried has

(35)   a. daß jetzt keiner mehr [auf die Farbe] achtet
that now no one anymore [to the color] attention-pays
b. daß jetzt [auf die Farbe]$_i$ keiner mehr e$_i$ achtet
that now [to the color] no one anymore pays-attention

In the adjunction approach to scrambling it is predicted that a phrase which can be linked within the VP has more than one potential linking position. Case checking is but one linking device. Whatever linking device links a PP or a clause VP-internally, the structure will display the same variation as case linking displays. A substitution approach would predict that only those elements scramble that can occur in the specifier of a higher functional head.

Third, scrambling is possible within topicalized VPs. If scrambling involved functional heads, the topicalized constituent would have to be larger than a VP. It would have to be a functional projection. In this case, the functional head of the projection is part of the topicalized projection as well. This functional head, however, would be a head position in the head chain of the finite verb. But the fronted VP must not contain the trace of the finite verb, as (36) demonstrates.

(36)   a. [Dein Gepäck$_i$ einem Fremden e$_i$ anvertrauen] solltest du nicht
[Your luggage (to) a stranger entrust] should you not
b. *[Dein Gepäck$_i$ einem Fremden e$_i$ an-e$_j$] vertraute$_j$ sie
c. Dein Gepäck vertraute$_j$ sie einem Fremden an-e$_j$

In sum, the main line of demarcation between the accounts listed under (30) that involve antecedent-gap relations is the question whether the S-structure positions of scrambled arguments are A-positions or not.

A final consideration that bears on the choice between A- chains and A'-chains is a comparative issue: In an A'-chain approach, it is unexplained why scrambling is confined to the Germanic OV-languages. If scrambling were A'-adjunction to VP, it should not be barred from VO-languages. If, however, the scrambling positions must be potential checking positions and the checking domain of the verb is subject to a directionality requirement, adjunction to VP creates positions outside the checking domain in VO-languages, but not in OV-languages.

5. SCRAMBLING AND THE SYNTAX-SEMANTICS INTERFACE

It has been claimed that there is a direct correspondence between syntactic phrasing and semantic interpretation. Diesing (1992:15) suggests that the VP be mapped on the nuclear scope part of the semantic representation while the rest of IP maps on the restrictor part. Particles like *ja, doch, denn,* are taken to mark the left boundary of the VP (Diesing, 1992:37). The nuclear scope part is the domain of existential closure. Therefore, indefinites receive an existential interpretation only in the nuclear scope.

Sentences like in (37) provide evidence against the equation of the VP with the nuclear scope domain. According to Diesing's argumentation, the scrambled object NP in (37a) remains within VP because it follows the particles. Nevertheless, the interpretation changes. The interpretation of (37a) is paraphrased in (38a). (38b) is the interpretation of (37b), the clause without scrambling.

(37) a. Damals hat (ja doch) Dollars$_i$ jeder e$_i$ gegen Yen eingetauscht
then has (particles) Dollars everyone into Yen exchanged
'At that time everyone changed dollars for Yen'
b. Damals hat (ja doch) jeder Dollars gegen Yen eingetauscht

(38) a. If someone changed dollars at that time, he changed them for Yen
b. If someone changed (money) at that time, he changed dollars for Yen

It seems more adequate to equate the minimal projection domain of V with the nuclear scope domain of arguments.[9] The minimal projection domain is the minimal V-projection that contains the base position of all the arguments. In this view, the scrambling of objects (see 39) does not preclude existential closure unless the scrambling position is outside the minimal V-projection.

(39) Damals hat ja doch einer Geheimdokumente$_i$ Journalisten e$_i$ übergeben
then has prtcls. someone secret documents (to) journalists handed-over

If this is the correct way to look at it, the mapping relation identifies the minimal V-projection only. Since in non-scrambling languages the minimal V-projection is identical with the maximal V-projection with respect to A-positions, Diesing's hypothesis is correct in this case but it is not correct for the V-projection in scrambling languages.

Researchers who adopt Chomsky's Minimalist Program (see deHoop, 1992; Meinunger, 1995) suggest that scrambling is triggered by a syntactic prerequisite for semantic interpretation: They surmise that indefinite DPs that are not interpreted under existential closure need to be moved to specifier positions of functional heads (object agreement positions) in order to be licensed for a strong (e.g., specific, generic, distributive) interpretation.

(40) a. daß ja hier immer Linguisten herumlungern [existential]
that PRT here always linguists loiter around
'There are always linguists that loiter around here'

b. daß ja Linguisten hier immer herumlungern   [generic]
that PRT linguists here always loiter around
'It is typical for linguists that they always loiter around here'

In order to capture this difference it is sufficient to realize that the c-command relation between the scope sensitive elements is different. A more simple assumption suffices to capture these phenomena: An indefinite DP outside the scope of an element that modifies the minimal domain of existential closure cannot be interpreted under existential closure. If adverbials may be generated in more than one position - an unavoidable assumption for English - and if the OV-languages offer more adverbial positions than the VO-languages, the difference in (40) and related phenomena is captured without scrambling.

6. THE DISTRIBUTION OF PRONOUNS

Pronouns tend to be fronted in Germanic languages. It is only the domain of fronting that differs. In German, object pronouns are fronted to a position following the topmost functional head, that is the complementizer or the finite verb.[10] In Dutch, an object pronoun must not be fronted across an unergative subject (41b). In English, pronouns are fronted within the VP. In the continental Scandinavian languages pronouns must be fronted in the so-called object-shift configuration (see Vikner, 1995: 97-100).

(41)   a. daß es$_i$ jemand e$_i$ zurück-stellte
        b. *dat het$_i$ iemand e$_i$ terug-zette
        c. *that someone put back it

In German, there are distributional restrictions that seem to differentiate between pronoun fronting and scrambling. Fronted negation in *if*-clauses and the particles discussed in Section 5 may precede scrambled NPs, unless they are pronominal. In this case, they follow the pronouns.

(42)   a. wenn/weil damals nicht/ja den {Mann$_i$, *ihn$_i$} jemand e$_i$ gewarnt hätte
        if/since then not/prtc. the man {someone,*him} warned had
        'if/since someone would have warned {the man, him} then'
        b. wenn/weil damals {den Mann$_i$, ihn$_i$} nicht/ja jemand e$_i$ gewarnt hätte

The following example shows, however, that there is a general restriction against pronouns in the c-command domain of the particles including negation:

(43) a. daß der Mann ja doch *sie/die Frau gesehen hat
      that the man particles she/the woman seen has
      'that the man has seen the woman after all'
   b. daß der Mann sie/die Frau ja doch gesehen hat

The contrast between (43a) and (43b) parallels the contrast in (42). Hence, it is independent of scrambling. The only difference between scrambling and pronoun fronting is an order restriction. The preferred order for fronted pronouns is Nom-Acc-Dat. There is no such restriction for scrambled non-pronominal DPs (see Lenerz, 1993).

7. SUMMARY

The theoretical modeling of scrambling is still a controversial issue. In this overview, the emphasis has been put on the controversial theoretical aspects and on empirical evidence that bears on the choice of the theoretically adequate analysis of scrambling. The crucial parameter for the existence of clause bound scrambling is claimed to be the size of the checking domain of the verb. Scrambling is analyzed as an A-type-dependency, that is a dependency that relates a position with linking license and a position with a projection license. A-type scrambling is contingent on the OV-order of the projection.

NOTES

[1] There is of course also the third possibility, namely human insufficiency: Some of the competing accounts are based on different sets of data, each of which does not fully cover the whole range of relevant data.

[2] In terms of data presentation, this contribution concentrates on Scrambling in Germanic languages. Scrambling, however, is found in all OV-languages. There is, for instance, an extensive literature already on scrambling in OV-languages like Japanese (cf. MIT Working Papers #24: Formal Approaches to Japanese Linguistics). Japanese is prototypical for OV-languages with both clause internal and long distance scrambling. Scrambling in Germanic languages is clause internal, not regarding controversies on the nature of the "third construction".

[3] Variable order of P-objects and NP-objects is found in OV-languages as well, for instance in Italian:
   i. Mario ha messo sulla tavola due monete
       Mario has put on the table two coins
   ii. Mario ha messo due monete sulla tavola

[4] If there is no extraction site lower than the phrase with the falling pitch, the double pitch contour does not lead to the inversion of the scope relations:

    i. /Alle Leute$_i$ haben e$_i$ kein Bild\ betrachtet [narrow scope negation]
       'all people have no picture watched'

Reconstruction does not change the c-command relations in this case because the extraction site is higher than the position of the object.

[5] "Proof": If X is derived by movement, it has property Y. X has property Y. Therefore, X is derived by movement. This reasoning is not valid, of course.

[6] The particle *alle* does not move to the left and cannot be topicalized:

    i. *Er hat alle$_i$ der Frau e$_i$ die Bücher gezeigt.
    ii. *Alle$_i$ hat er der Frau e$_i$ die Bücher gezeigt.

[7] In English the obligatory raising of the would-be-nominative to Spec, IP I masks its VP-internal base position: NP$_i$ [V e$_i$]. It is revealed by its binding properties, however:

    a. [Pictures of herself$_j$]$_i$ do not [interest her$_j$ e$_i$ at all]
    b. *[Pictures of herself$_j$]$_i$ do not [e$_i$ describe her$_j$ accurately]

[8] Of course one may ask why these languages do not allow scrambling to the right. The answer proposed in (Haider, 1992) is simple: Projection lines are constrained universally: The branching node must not be on the left side. Scrambling to the right would created left branching nodes. Apparent instances of scrambling to the right in OV-languages (Hindi, Turkish) are base-generated structures with the verb moved to the left.

[9] Operator-elements like negated indefinites or frequency adverbials may narrow down the nuclear scope domain even within the minimal VP.

[10] They need not be adjacent, however. Adverbials may intervene, as in (i.):

    i. daß in diesem Fall man/er sich nicht wundern muß
       'that in this case one/he refl. not marvel needs'

REFERENCES

Chomsky, N.: 1982, *Some Concepts and Consequences of the Theory of Government and Binding*, MIT Press, Cambridge.

Cinque, G.: 1993, 'A Null Theory of Phrase and Compound Stress', *Linguistic Inquiry* 24, 239-297.

de Hoop, H.: 1992, 'Case Configuration and Noun Phrase Interpretation', Ph.D. Dissertation University of Groningen.

Deprez, V.: 1989. 'On the Typology of Syntactic Positions and the Nature of Chains', Ph.D. Dissertation, MIT.

Deprez, V.: 1994. 'Parameters of Object Movement', In N. Corver & H. van Riemsdijk (eds.) *Studies on Scrambling*, Mouton de Gruyter, Berlin, 101-152.

Diesing, M.: 1992, *Indefinites*, MIT Press, Cambridge.

Fanselow, G.: 1990, 'Scrambling as NP-Movement'. In G. Grewendorf & W. Sternefeld (eds.) *Scrambling and Barriers*, Benjamins, Amsterdam, 113-140.

Fanselow, G.: 1993, 'The Return of the Base Generators', *GAGL* 36, 1-74.

Frey, W.: 1993, Syntaktische Bedingungen für die semantische Interpretation. Studia Grammatika XXXV. Akademie Verlag, Berlin.

Geerts, G. & W. Haeseryn, J. de Rooij, and M.C. van den Toorn.: 1984, A*lgemene Nederlandse Spraakkunst*, Wolters-Noordhoff, Groningen.

Geilfuß, J.: 1991, 'Verb- und Verbphrasensyntax', Arbeitspapiere des SFB 340, #11. University of Tübingen.

Giusti, G.: 1990, Floating Quantifiers, Scrambling and Configurationality. *Linguistic Inquiry* 21, 633-41.

Haider, H.: 1984, 'The Case of German', In J. Toman (ed.) 'Studies in German Grammar', Foris, Dordrecht, 65-101.
Haider, H.: 1988, 'Theta-tracking Systems - evidence from German', In L. Marácz & P. Muysken (eds.) *Configurationality*, Foris, Dordrecht, 185-206.
Haider, H.: 1992, 'Branching and Discharge', Working Paper #23 of the SFB 340. University of Stuttgart.
Haider, H.: 1993, *'Deutsche Syntax, generativ'*, Narr, Tübingen.
Haider, H. 1995, 'The Basic Branching Conjecture', In *Studies on Phrase Structure and Economy* SFB 340 Working Papers #70, Universität Stuttgart. 1-30.
Haider, H., S. Olsen & S. Vikner (eds.): 1995, Introduction to: *Studies in Comparative Germanic Syntax*, Reidel, Dordrecht, 1-45.
Haider, H. & I. Rosengren: 1998, 'Scrambling. Sprache und Pragmatik' #49; Germanic Institute, University Lund. 1-104.
Höhle, T.: 1982, 'Explikation für "normale Betonung" und "normale Wortstellung"', In W. Abraham (ed.) *Satzglieder im Deutschen*, Narr, Tübingen, 75- 153.
Hoekstra, T.: 1984. *Transitivity - Grammatical Relations in Government-Binding Theory*, Foris, Dordrecht.
Holmberg, A. & C Platzack.: 1995, *The Role of Inflection in Scandinavian Syntax*, Oxford University Press, Oxford.
Krifka, M.: 1998, 'Scope Inversion and the Rise-Fall Contour in German', *Linguistic Inquiry* 29, 75-112.
Lenerz, J.: 1993, 'Zur Syntax und Semantik deutscher Personalpronomina. In Marga Reis (ed.)*Wortstellung und Informationsstruktur*, Niemeyer, Tübingen, 203-249.
Mahajan, Anoop. 1994. Towards a Unified Theory of Scrambling. In N. Corver & H. van Riemsdijk (eds.) *Studies on Scrambling*, Mouton de Gruyter, Berlin, 301-330.
Meinunger, A.: 1995, 'Discourse Dependent DP Deplacement', Ph.D. Dissertation. Universität Potsdam.
Moltmann, F.: 1990, 'Scrambling in German and the Specificity effect', ms., MIT.
Müller, G. & Sternefeld, W.: 1993, 'Improper Movement and Unambiguous Binding', *Linguistic Inquiry* 24, 461-507.
Neeleman, A.: 1994, ' Scrambling as a D-structure Phenomenon", In N. Corver & H. van Riemsdijk eds. Studies on Scrambling, Mouton de Gruyter, Berlin, 387-429.
Postal, P.: 1993, Parasitic Gaps and the Across-the-board Phenomenon. *Linguistic Inquiry* 24, 735-54.
Postal, P.: 1974, *On Raising*, MIT-Press: Cambridge, Mass.
Rosengren, I.: 1993, 'Wahlfreiheit mit Konsequenzen-Scrambling, Topikalisierung und FHG im Dienste der Informationsstrukturierung', In M. Reis (ed.) *Wortstellung und Informationsstruktur*, Niemeyer, Tübingen, 251-312.
Saito, M.: 1989, 'Scrambling as Semantically Vacuous A'-movement', In M. Baltin & A. Kroch (eds.) *Alternative Conceptions of Phrase Structure*, Chicago University Press, Chicago 182-200.
Sportiche, D.: 1988, 'A Theory of Floating Quantifiers and its Corollaries for Constituent Structure', *Linguistic Inquiry* 19, 425-449.
Vikner, S.: 1995, 'Verb movement and Expletive Subjects in the Germanic Languages', Oxford University Press, Oxford.
Van den Wyngaerd, G.: 1989, 'Object Shift as an A-movement Rule', *MIT Working Papers in Linguistics* 11, 256-71.
Webelhuth, G.: 1989, 'Principles and Parameters of Syntactic Saturation', Ph.D. Dissertation. University of Massachusetts.

HUBERT HAIDER
University of Salzburg

ISABELLA BARBIER

AN EXPERIMENTAL STUDY OF SCRAMBLING AND OBJECT SHIFT IN THE ACQUISITION OF DUTCH

1. INTRODUCTION

Currently, there is an ongoing debate in the literature about whether or not young children have the competence for leftward movement of constituents out of the VP. This paper focuses on whether children acquiring Dutch as their first language demonstrate early competence for this type of movement.[1] Two constructions in which the non-finite verb and its DP complement are no longer adjacent will be examined. The first of these constructions is illustrated in (1).

(1) Ik wil dat boek niet lezen.
     I want that book not read
     'I don't want to read that book.'

If, as is generally assumed, the direct object is generated as a sister to the verb, it is expected that in the underived order, direct object and verb would be adjacent. Therefore, the order in (1) must be a derived order. Zwart (1993) accounts for this order by assuming, in the spirit of the minimalist approach, that the DP complement must be licensed in the specifier position of a functional projection AgrOP (see also Vanden Wyngaerd, 1989 for Dutch and Santelmann, 1989 for German). The fact that the DP complement and the verb are no longer adjacent is the result of overt movement of the object to this specifier position. The overt movement is presumably triggered by the presence of strong N-features in AgrO which need to be eliminated in overt syntax.[2] I will refer to this A-movement of the DP complement into a licensing position Spec, AgrOP as 'object shift'.[3] In the case of negation in example (1) above, the DP must precede the negation *niet* in order to obtain a wide scope, sentential negation reading. If the DP follows the negation, a constituent (*viz.*, of the DP) negation reading is obtained as shown in (2). Such narrow scope, constituent readings are obtained only under a rising terminal intonation and it is expected that the sentence be continued with a contrastive statement.

(2) I will niet dat boek lezen (maar de krant).
I want not that book read (but the paper)
'I don't want to read that book (but the paper).'

The other construction in Dutch and German where the direct object and the non-finite verb are not adjacent is illustrated in (3a).

(3) a. Jan heeft zijn paraplu vaak vergeten.
Jan has his umbrella often forgotten
'Jan has often forgotten his umbrella.'
b. Jan heeft vaak zijn paraplu vergeten.
Jan has often his umbrella forgotten
'Jan has often forgotten his umbrella.'

In this construction, which involves adverbs, direct object and verb can be adjacent, as in (3b) or separated by the adverb without any (substantial) difference in meaning, as in (3a). It is a common assumption that adverbs such as *vaak* are VP adjuncts. Presumably, the movement of the object across the adverb would involve adjunction to the VP as well. In the literature, placement of the object preceding the negation and placement of the object preceding the adverb have often been treated as the same phenomenon, under the label 'scrambling'. The fact that a difference of order results in a significant difference in meaning for the negation sentences, but not for the adverb sentences suggests, however, that these phenomena are distinct. I will refer to this A'-movement of the object into an adjoined position preceding the adverb as 'scrambling'.[4] What will be important from the perspective of acquisition is that object shift and scrambling differ in the following two ways. First, there is a configurational difference between object shift and scrambling. Object shift is A-movement into the specifier of a functional projection, Spec, AgrOP while scrambling is A'-movement to an adjoined position. Second, there is a difference in the motivation for object shift and scrambling. Object shift is triggered by the need for DPs to have their (strong) N-features (e.g., [+case]) checked in a licensing position in the functional domain. Since all DPs carry the [+case] feature, object shift will apply to all DPs. For this reason, object shift is obligatory. It is, however, only in the case that some element, *viz.*, negation intervenes between the base-position of the DP and the Spec, AgrOP position, that this movement can be directly observed for Dutch. As far as scrambling is concerned, not all DPs carry the special feature, presumably a [+scope] or [+focus] feature which triggers scrambling. For this reason, scrambling will be defined as 'optional'.

With regard to object shift, since all DPs carry the [+case] feature, both direct and indirect objects obligatorily undergo object shift in Dutch. As shown in (4), this results in the order indirect object+direct object+negation., i.e., the indirect object must precede the direct object.

(4) a. Jan will Lisa dat boek niet geven.
     Jan wants Lisa that book not give
     'Jan doesn't want to give Lisa that book.'
  b. *Jan will dat boek Lisa niet geven
     *Jan wants that book Lisa not give

This restriction on the order of indirect object and direct object is reminiscent of the superiority effects found in multiple *wh*-preposing. It is generally assumed that, in multiple *wh*-preposing constructions, one *wh*-element moves into Spec, CP, while the other *wh*-elements have to adjoin to CP. Such adjunction allows these elements to satisfy the *wh*-criterion, but they do not enter into the same basic specifier-head agreement relation as the *wh*-element in the specifier position. Similarly, for double object constructions, there is only one Spec, AgrOP position in which more than one element needs to be licensed. Only one element, *viz.*, the direct object can occupy Spec, AgrOP and enter the special specifier-head agreement relation. The indirect object adjoins to AgrOP and while it can have its features licensed in that position, it cannot enter the special specifier-head relation the direct object does.

As far as the [+scope] or [+focus] feature is concerned, it is awkward in Dutch to have both the direct object and the indirect object carry this feature and be scrambled to a position preceding the adverb, as shown in (5). Presumably, this reflects the fact that multiple focus in Dutch is not felicitous.

(5) ? Jan zal Lisa dat boek straks niet geven.
     ? Jan shall Lisa that book presently not give

2. PREVIOUS RESEARCH ON THE ACQUISITION OF OBJECT SHIFT IN DUTCH AND GERMAN

Currently, there is an ongoing debate in the acquisition literature about whether or not early child Dutch and early child German evidences competence for object shift. As mentioned above, object shift can be observed directly only when negation intervenes between the base-position of the DP and the Spec, AgrOP position. Hence, the debate focuses on whether or not the placement of the DP complement *vis-à-vis* the negation is correct in early Dutch and German acquisition.

Clahsen (1990) and Hoekstra & Jordens (1994) describe for the acquisition of German and Dutch respectively an early stage in which the placement of DP complements *vis-à-vis* the negation *nicht, niet* 'not' appears to be deviant, as shown in (6a) (from Clahsen, 1990) and (6b-d) (from Hoekstra & Jordens, 1994).

(6)   a. kann nicht das zumachen.   J. 2;4
             can not that close
             'I can't close that.'
        b. Ik mag niet modewijzer.   J. 2;1
             I may not fashion designer
             'I may not have the/a fashion designer.' (name of a toy)
        c. Ik kann niet Maria zoeken.   J. 2;1
             I can not Mary seek
             'I can't seek Mary.'
        d. Ik will niet dit.   J. 2;1
             I want not this
             'I don't want this.'

In these utterances, the DP complement follows the negation. As mentioned earlier, this order is different from the adult order, shown in (7).

(7)   a. Ich kann das nicht zumachen.
             I can that not close
             'I can't close that.'
        b. Ik will dit niet.
             I want this not
             'I don't want this.'

Recall that, in order to obtain a sentential negation reading, the DP needs to move out of the VP and into a position preceding the negation (With indefinites, a different negation, *viz.*, the fused negator *kein, geen* is used). The order found in (6) is not impossible in the adult language, but results in the narrow scope, constituent negation reading.

If there were indeed such a 'stage' of post-negation DPs in early German and Dutch, then it would presumably not be expected that deviant structures would be found after the appearance of adult-like structures nor that such deviant structures would persist till a relatively late age.

As far as the first objection is concerned, there seems to be evidence that Clahsen's child J. does produce adult-like structures with negation, a month before the sample Clahsen uses as evidence of a 'stage'. In Hamann (1993) the following utterance by Julia at the age of 2;3 years is mentioned (see also Penner *et al.*, this volume).

(8)   Ich schaff das nich.   Julia 2;3
         I manage that not
         'I can't manage that.'

With regard to the second objection, Hamann (1993, 1996, this volume) also gives some examples from older children, as shown in (9).

(9)   a. kanne nich Haus machen.   Math. 3;0
            can not house make
            'I can't make the house.'
         b. Krisjan mag nich gouter.   Elena 3;1
            Christian like not biscuits
            'Christian doesn't like the biscuits.'

Similar examples for Dutch from Schaeffer (1995) are given in (10).

(10)   a. Ik wil niet Sinterklaas kijken.   Niek 3;9
            I want not Santa Claus watch
            'I don't want to see Santa Claus.'
         b. dan kan je niet mij speen hier afpakken. Niek 3;9
            then can you not my pacifier here away-take
            'Then you can't take away my pacifier.'

While the evidence for a 'stage' of post-negation direct objects appears to be scant, there does appear to be evidence that deviant utterances occur and that they may persist till a relatively late age.

Cases of DPs in post-negation position have also been observed by Weissenborn (1990) in his natural speech data. Weissenborn mentions that these cases are apparently rather rare since he found only the following two in the natural speech data of child S.

(11)   a. brauche nicht lala.   S. 2;0
            need not pacifier
            'I don't need the pacifier'
         b. häschen braucht nicht windel   S. 2;1
            bunny need not diaper
            'Bunny doesn't need diaper'

Besides this small number of utterances with direct objects in post-negation position, Weissenborn (1990) also observed a systematic absence of objects in the post-verbal/ pre-negation position in his early German natural speech data, i.e., the adult order is not observed at all.

The results reported in Penner *et al.* (this volume) do not seem to indicate such a stage in the acquisition of two children acquiring Bernese Swiss German either. Their data show that in Michael's corpus, definite objects are correctly shifted to the left of *nicht*, as in (12a), while indefinites remain *in situ* from the beginning, as in (12b) (also see Penner *et al.* (this volume)).

(12)   a. das nid uspakche.
                 this not unpack
                 'don't unpack this.'
        b. nei, nid e blaus dra (mache)
                 no, not a blue one (put) on it
                 'no, don't put a blue one on it'

These results lead Penner *et al.* (1993; this volume) to the conclusion that these children make the distinction between definite and indefinite DPs and that object shift, i.e., A-movement into a specifier position is available from the beginning. This conclusion is the opposite of what Clahsen (1990) proposes. Clahsen (1990) suggests that the 'stage' of deviant post-negation DPs he observed, evidences a lack of competence for what he refers to as 'scrambling' (object shift in my terminology). He offers as a possible solution that the competence for 'scrambling' may mature as the result of a maturational schedule, as proposed by Borer & Wexler (1987). In this maturational schedule, the competence for A' chains is available before the competence for A-chains, which matures. It could then be said that the alleged initial absence of object shift is due to the fact that object shift is an instance of A-movement, hence needs to mature. If however, as Penner *et al.* (this volume) conclude, object shift is available from the beginning, the deviant structures require a different explanation. Two main types of explanations are found.

Weissenborn (1990) and Hamann (1996; this volume) conclude that the most likely analysis for deviant structures is an analysis in terms of constituent negation. Recall that the post-negation position of DPs results in a constituent negation reading in the adult language. The problem with this proposal, however, is that such constituent negation interpretations are always contrastive. These interpretations are only obtained under a rising terminal intonation and it is expected that the sentence be continued with a contrastive statement. In none of the child utterances in question however, is there any indication that the sentence is continued with such a contrastive statement. Therefore, it seems rather unlikely these utterances were intended as constituent negations.

Hoekstra & Jordens (1994) note for Dutch that, as soon as determiners are acquired, the DPs they are part of seem to behave as expected. Therefore, they argue that the delay in the acquisition of object shift is due to some delay in the acquisition of the determiner system. If object shift is movement to Spec, AgrOP for licensing of case, then, if there are no determiners yet, the nominal element would not be a DP but rather a NP, hence not subject to this type of movement. This explanation might also explain why object shift is particularly frequent with demonstratives, which may be the first elements to be recognized as DPs. Schaeffer (1995, this volume) proposes a similar account, based on an initial underspecification of the functional head D with regard to specificity.[5]

Hoekstra & Jordens (1994) also note the late acquisition of the fused negator *geen* used with indefinite DPs, which does not seem to appear before the age of 2;9 years in their Dutch corpus. This late appearance of *geen* can be explained as the result of the fact that the child has to learn that there is a specific lexical item to be used with indefinite DPs. Hence, it could be argued that cases of *niet* followed by an indefinite DP are not due to an absence of object shift, but due to the wrong choice of negation.

Weissenborn *et al.* (1989) also analyze German cases as the result of the fact that these children have not yet acquired the knowledge that with nonspecific indefinite direct objects a negation different from *nicht*, namely the fused negation *kein* must be used. Penner *et al.* (1993) observed for one of the children studied that indefinite objects were negated with *nicht* until the age of 2;8 when the *kein* paradigm appeared. Constructions of the type shown in (13a) are successively replaced by *kein* structures shown in (13b).

(13) a. Mami bruucht nid es Chüssi.
Mummy needs not a pillow
'Mummy doesn't need a pillow'
b. da het's keni meh.
Here there is no more
'There isn't any left here'

It certainly seems that this proposal can take care of the examples in (9) which appear to be nonspecific indefinites since they lack a determiner. This solution cannot work for (6a, c and d) however, where the object is clearly definite and substituting *kein* for *nicht* would still result in an ungrammatical utterance. Hamann (1993) gives some other examples of clear definite DPs, where such substitution would not work, as in (14).

(14) mag die Maus nicht das Gruene   Andrea 2;0
like the mouse not the green
'The mouse doesn't like the green one'

3. PREVIOUS RESEARCH ON THE ACQUISITION OF SCRAMBLING IN DUTCH AND GERMAN

Dokter (1995) (reported in Wijnen & Verrips, 1996) investigated the relative placement of direct objects and adverbs in the natural speech corpora of several children acquiring Dutch and found that both scrambled and non-scrambled word-orders started to appear at about the same time in the children's natural speech, roughly between 2;3 and 2;5 months of age. Definite NPs were found both scrambled and non-scrambled with a preference for the non-scrambled order. Scrambling was not found to be lexically bound, i.e., with each adverb investigated, both scrambled and non-scrambled NPs were found.

Schaeffer's results (1995; this volume) also seem to indicate that both scrambled and unscrambled orders are found, as shown in the examples (15) from Schaeffer, 1995) .

(15)   a. wil je mijn portomonnee even zoeken   L. 3;6
               want you my wallet just search
               'Could you look for my wallet'
        b. jij gaat ook altijd jij oren wassen.   L. 3;7
               you go also always your ears wash
               'You are also always going to wash your ears'

4. THE EXPERIMENTAL STUDY

4.1. Rationale

It is the purpose of this experimental study to determine whether there is evidence for early competence for object shift in Dutch. As we have seen, it is only when some element, *viz.*, negation intervenes between the base-position of the DP complement and the licensing position, Spec, AgrOP to which it moves, that the movement of the DP can be directly observed for Dutch. Hence, studying the acquisition of structures with negation offers a way to investigate early competence for object shift in Dutch. Such a study is particularly warranted in view of the fact that, as discussed above, there is a debate in the literature about whether or not the placement of the DP complement *vis-à-vis* the negation is correct in early child Dutch and German. It was shown that the analysis of natural speech data has lead different researchers to different conclusions. Therefore, an experimental task, *viz.*, the elicited imitation task was chosen. As will be discussed below, the logical structure of the elicited imitation task involves looking for critical contrasts in the variance of imitation data (both quantitatively and qualitatively) in accord with the variables in the design of the stimulus sentences. Thus, the negation structures should be compared to some other structures and the results of this comparison should tell us something about children's competence for object shift. The obvious choice for these other structures were structures which, in fact, have often been lumped together with the negation structures, but which were shown to be critically different from the latter, as discussed in the introduction. These structures involve the position of DPs *vis-à-vis* adverbs. We have noted that object shift and scrambling differ in the following two ways. There is a configurational difference between object shift and scrambling. Object shift is A-movement into the specifier of a functional projection, Spec, AgrOP while scrambling is A'-movement to some adjoined position. In addition, there is a difference in the motivation for object shift and scrambling. Object shift is triggered by the need for DPs to have their (strong) N-features (e.g., [+case]) checked in a licensing position in the functional domain. Since all DPs carry the [+case] feature, object shift will apply to all DPs. For this reason, object shift is obligatory. As far as scrambling is concerned, not all DPs carry the special feature, presumably a [+scope] or [+focus] feature which triggers scrambling. For this reason, scrambling can be viewed as 'optional'. Another way of looking at this, is to say that the scrambled order is 'marked' compared to the unscrambled order since it involves a special feature. As far as object shift is concerned, we can say that object shift is 'unmarked'. Note that 'unmarked' order does not necessarily mean 'underived' order. Object shift is 'unmarked' in the sense that it is triggered by UG licensing principles, applies to all DPs and results in the 'unmarked' sentential negation interpretation. Absence of object shift is 'marked' in the sense that it results in a constituent negation reading (of the DP) and requires a special intonational pattern as well as a contrastive statement.[6]

It is the purpose of this study to test experimentally whether, at the earliest testable age, children are sensitive to these differences between object shift and scrambling. The hypothesis is the following: If children have the competence for object shift, then this should be evidenced in a critical difference in their imitation data between object shift structures and scrambling structures (structures which on the surface look very similar. In fact, so similar that in the literature they have often been lumped together). The imitation data are expected to differ in a manner to be made more precise in the hypotheses below. The general idea, however, is that the difference between the 'obligatory' or 'unmarked' nature of object shift and the 'optional' or 'marked' nature of scrambling will be reflected in the success rate of imitation of these structures as well as in the 'errors' in imitation.

Since the elicited imitation task is extremely sensitive to constituent order, it can be hypothesized that a significant proportion of errors of imitation would consist of attempts to move constituents back to their unmarked position. That is, for the scrambling stimulus sentences, we can hypothesize that there will be attempts to move the DP back to the 'unmarked' position following the adverb, as shown in (16).

(16)   Ik lees vaak dat boek.
       I read often that book
       'I often read that book.'

For the object shift stimulus sentences, corresponding attempts to move the DP back to the position following the negation, as shown in (17), would result in a 'marked', i.e., constituent negation structure.

(17)   Ik lees niet dat boek (maar de krant).
       I read not that book (but the paper)

The comparison of the success rate of imitation between object shift and scrambling structures as well as the rate of attempts to move constituents back to their 'unmarked' position should evidence what the unmarked order for each of the structures is for the children. If children have competence for object shift, then it is expected that the object shift order will be the unmarked order. As far as scrambling is concerned, it is expected that the scrambled order will be the marked order.

With regard to object shift, we have seen that since all DPs carry the [+case] feature, both direct and indirect objects obligatorily undergo object shift in Dutch. There is, however, a restriction on the relative order of indirect object and direct object: the indirect object must precede the direct object. In the introduction, it was assumed that for double object constructions of this type, there is only one Spec, AgrOP position in which more than one element needs to be licensed. Only one element, *viz.*, the direct object, can occupy Spec, AgrOP and enter the special specifier-head agreement relation. The indirect object adjoins to AgrOP and while it can have its features licensed in that position, it cannot enter the special specifier-head relation the way the direct object does. It is the purpose of this study to test experimentally whether, at the earliest testable age, children are sensitive to this difference between object shift of the direct object and the indirect object. The hypothesis is the following: If children have competence for object shift, this competence can be expected to be evidenced in a critical difference in their imitation data between object shift stimulus sentences with a direct object and object shift stimulus sentences with an indirect object.

4.2. Experimental Task

The decision to pursue these questions experimentally, rather than by an analysis of natural speech corpora was based on the fact that the analysis of natural speech data has lead different researchers to different conclusions with regard to early competence for object shift. The investigation of object shift through an experimental task can provide converging evidence for one of these conclusions.

In the elicited imitation task, the experimenter orally presents one by one a series of 'model' stimulus sentences to the subject, taking care to regulate intonation by giving even, natural emphasis to all parts of the sentence. The subject is asked to repeat the 'story' the experimenter has told. The elicited imitation task is preceded by a set of pre-training sentences, which do not involve the experimental factors being tested. The purpose of the pre-training sentences is to give the child practice with the task. A full description of the elicited imitation task is given in Lust *et al.* (1996).

The elicited imitation task allows a principled and quantitative evaluation of variance in the child's production *vis-à-vis* the adult model, i.e., a quantitative assessment of imitation success. Regarding constituent order, it has been shown that variance in imitation success varied significantly with variation in constituent order of stimulus sentences (Lust & Wakayama 1981). In addition, analysis of 'errors' in imitation confirms the non-random nature of elicited imitation, e.g., a significant proportion of errors of imitation consists of attempts to move constituents back to their unmarked position. Thus, the elicited imitation task evidences children's competence to link surface structures related by movement, to each other. The design of the stimulus sentences involves experimentally manipulated variables. Controlled design, administration, and analyses of the elicited imitation task provide a set of reliable, non-random results where the variance in the imitation data is significantly constrained (both quantitatively and qualitatively) in accord with the variables in the design of the stimulus sentences. All data were scored independently in accordance with established, standardized written criteria available to the author. Lexical errors such as substituting a different name were ignored. Any structural change (i.e., word order changes such as movement of DPs, omissions and reductions, elaborations etc.) were scored as incorrect.

4.3. Design

The stimulus sentences in this study consisted of simple sentences which were varied by two factors. The first factor involved the type of movement tested, *viz.*, object shift versus scrambling. In the stimulus sentences, object shift is signaled by the presence of the negation *niet* 'not'. Scrambling is signaled by the presence of the adverbs *nu* 'now' and *straks* 'soon'. I will refer to this factor as the MOVEMENT TYPE factor. The second factor concerns the syntactic function of the DP(s) which have undergone movement and precede the negation (object shift) or the adverb (scrambling). I will refer to this factor as the DP TYPE factor. Two types of DPs are tested, *viz.*, direct objects and indirect objects. Actually, rather than simple indirect objects, it is double object constructions (*viz.*, indirect object and direct object) which are tested. I will, however, refer to these sentences as 'indirect object' constructions. In the object shift stimulus sentences, both indirect and direct object are shifted across the negation. For the scrambling stimulus sentences, however, only the indirect object is scrambled across the adverb in order to avoid presenting the children with unnatural sentences (Recall that multiple focus in Dutch is not felicitous). In sum, the design involved four sentence types: (i) scrambling/direct object, (ii) scrambling/indirect object, (iii) object shift/direct object, and (iv) object shift/indirect object. Two sentence tokens were presented for each one of the four sentence types, for a total of eight sentences. All sentences were 7-9 words in length and 11-12 syllables long. The stimulus sentences are shown in (18).

(18)   **Scrambling**
Direct Object
a. Caroline mag de pop nu in het bad stoppen.
Caroline may the doll now in the bath put
'Caroline may now put the doll in bath.'
b. Peter zal het hondje straks op zijn schoot houden.
Peter shall the doggie soon on his lap keep
'Peter shall soon keep the doggie on his lap.'

Indirect Object
c. Lisa zal mama straks een cadeautje geven.
Lisa shall mummy soon a present give
'Lisa shall soon give mummy a present.'
d. Anna mag de baby nu een flesje geven.
Anna may the baby now a bottle give
'Anna may now give the baby a bottle.'

Object Shift
Direct Object
e. Eva mag haar vinger niet in haar neus steken.
   Eva may her finger not in her nose put
   'Eva can't put her finger in her nose.'
f. Mama zal het speelgoed niet uit de kast halen.
   Mummy shall the toys not out the closet get
   'Mummy won't take the toys out off the closet.'

Indirect Object
g. Steven zal Rita het poesje niet geven.
   Steven shall Rita the pussycat not give
   'Steven won't give Rita the pussycat.'
h. Papa mag Tom het verhaaltje niet vertellen.
   Daddy may Tom the story not tell
   'Daddy can't tell Tom the story.'

4.4. Subjects

The subjects for this experimental study were sixty-one children attending nursery schools in Gent, Belgium, who were acquiring Dutch as their first language. The subjects were divided in four developmental groups by age ranging from 2;8 to 6;3 with a mean age of 4;9. Thus, development has been systematically varied as an independent factor. Mean age range and number of subjects for each group and total for all the groups are shown in Table 1.

Table 1.
Subject Information

Age group	# of Subjects	Age Range	Mean Age
Group I	7	2.8-3.3	2.11
Group II	18	3.6-4.5	4
Group III	18	4.7-5.4	5
Group IV	18	5.7-6.3	5.11
Group V	61	2.8-6.3	4.9

4.5 Hypotheses

The design allowed an assessment of the following hypotheses:

1. If children have the competence for both object shift and scrambling, then it is expected that there will be a critical difference in the imitation data between object shift structures and scrambling structures. If children have the competence for object shift, their imitation data is expected to evidence the 'obligatory' or 'unmarked' nature of object shift. If children have the competence for scrambling, their imitation data is expected to evidence the 'optional' or 'marked' nature of scrambling. It is expected that the difference between the 'obligatory' or 'unmarked' nature of object shift and the 'optional' or 'marked' nature of scrambling will be reflected in the success rate of imitation for these structures as well as in the imitation 'errors', *viz.*, in children's hypothesized attempts to move the DPs back to their 'unmarked' position.

a. In particular, if children know the difference between 'obligatory' or 'unmarked' object shift and 'optional' or 'marked' scrambling, then this competence should be reflected in a significant difference in the success rate of imitation between object shift stimulus sentences and scrambling stimulus sentences. It is expected that the success rate of imitation will be significantly higher for object shift stimulus sentences than for scrambling stimulus sentences. In particular, it is expected that the success rate of imitation will be significantly higher for object shift stimulus sentences with direct objects than for scrambling stimulus sentences with direct objects. Similarly, it is expected that the success rate of imitation will be significantly higher for object shift stimulus sentences with direct objects than for scrambling stimulus sentences with indirect objects (But see Hypothesis 2).

b. In addition, if children know the difference between 'optional' or 'marked' scrambling and 'obligatory' or 'unmarked' object shift, then this competence is expected to be reflected in a significant difference in the occurrence and nature of children's errors, in particular with regard to children's hypothesized attempts to move the DPs back to their 'unmarked' position. I will refer to hypothesized 'errors' of this kind as reconstitution responses. It is predicted that the rate for spontaneous structural conversion into a reconstitution response will be significantly higher for scrambling stimulus sentences (where this results in the 'unmarked' order) than for object shift stimulus sentences (where this results in the 'marked' order, *viz.*, the constituent negation reading).

In particular, it is expected that the conversion rate into a reconstitution response will be significantly higher for scrambling stimulus sentences with direct objects than for object shift stimulus sentences with direct objects. Similarly, it is expected that the conversion rate into a reconstitution response will be significantly higher for scrambling stimulus sentences with indirect objects than for object shift stimulus sentences with indirect object. (But see Hypothesis 2).

If, on the contrary, children lack competence for object shift and/or scrambling, then no critical difference is expected in children's imitation data between object shift structures and scrambling structures. The success rate of imitation as well the occurrence and nature of the children's errors is expected to be random.

2. If children have the full competence for object shift, no critical difference is expected between the object shift stimulus sentences with direct object and the object shift stimulus sentences with indirect object. If, on the other hand, children have early competence for object shift of the direct object, which is movement into Spec, AgrOP but experience a delay in the competence for object shift of the indirect object, which is movement into an adjoined position, then a critical difference is expected in the imitation data between object shift stimulus sentences with direct object and object shift stimulus sentences with indirect object. It is expected that such a developmental delay would be reflected in a significant amount of imitation 'errors' for object shift stimulus sentences with indirect objects. Some hypothesized imitation 'errors' are responses where the indirect object is dropped as well as responses where the indirect object is changed into a prepositional phrase. If children experience a delay in the licensing of indirect objects, then it is expected that this delay will also be evidenced in the imitation data for the scrambling stimulus sentences with indirect object since indirect objects must first be licensed by object shift before they can be scrambled.

3. Developmentally, if children have competence for object shift and scrambling, then this is predicted to be evidenced at the earliest testable age. At the same time, it is expected that there will be developmental changes with regard to the full competence for object shift, i.e., licensing of the DP in an adjoined position (indirect object) will take time to develop. With regard to scrambling, which is in a sense the 'marked' option, it is also expected that there will be some developmental changes with regard to the full competence for scrambling over time.

5. RESULTS

5.1. Results with regard to Hypothesis 1

5.1.1. Result 1a: Success rate of imitation

Table 2 represents the mean number of correct responses by movement type, XP type, and Age. The possible score range was 0-2, i.e., two tokens per sentence type. Overall mean correct in this study was 0.92.

Table 2.
Mean Number of Correct Responses (by Movement Type, XP and Age)

Age group	SCRAMBLING		OBJECT SHIFT		
	DO	IO	DO	IO	Group Mean
Group I	0.00	0.15	0.15	0.15	0.11
Group II	0.72	0.61	1.11	0.66	0.77
Group III	0.72	0.77	1.60	0.77	0.96
Group IV	0.94	1.44	1.66	1.25	1.32
Overall	0.71	0.85	1.31	0.81	0.92

The results show that, as hypothesized, there was a difference in the success rate of imitation between object stimulus sentences and scrambling stimulus sentences.

In particular, object shift sentences with direct objects were imitated correctly more often (mean 1.31) than scrambling sentences with direct objects (mean 0.71) (t-statistic = 5.889, df = 60, $p < 0.0001$). This result suggests that children know the difference between 'obligatory' or 'unmarked' object shift and 'optional' or 'marked' scrambling of direct objects.

Statistically, the higher success rate of imitation for object shift stimulus sentences with direct object than for scrambling stimulus sentences with direct object is significant for the third group (t-statistic = 4.499, df = 17, p = 0.0003) and the fourth group (t-statistic = 4.075, df = 17, p = 0.0008) but not for the first (t-statistic = 1.00, df = 6, p = 0.3559) or the second group (t-statistic = 1.941, df = 17, p = 0.0690).

With regard to development, even though the difference is not statistically significant for these two groups, the result is clearly in the same direction with the mean rate of correct imitation for object shift stimulus sentences with direct object (mean 0.15 for the first group and mean 1.11 for the second group) higher than the mean rate of correct imitation for scrambling stimulus sentences with direct object (mean 0.00 for the first group and mean 0.72 for the second group).

With regard to stimulus sentences with indirect objects, the results showed that there was no significant difference in amount of correct responses between object shift stimulus sentences with indirect object (mean 0.81) and scrambling sentences with indirect object (mean 0.85) (t-statistic = 0.402, df = 60, p = 0.6893). The fact that a difference is found between the direct object stimulus sentences and the indirect object stimulus sentences with regard to object shift suggests that object shift of the direct object is different from object shift of the indirect objects. Other results, discussed in Result 2 below will confirm this hypothesis. Note that with regard to age, the statistical analysis of the correct responses for indirect object stimulus sentences shows that age is very significant ($F(3,57) = 8.8651$, $p < 0.0001$).

5.1.2. Result 1b: Spontaneous structural conversion rate

Table 3 represents the mean number of reconstitution responses by movement type, XP type, and Age. Overall mean of reconstitution responses for this study was 0.48. On the average, 45.1% of all errors in imitation are due to reconstitution.

Table 3.
Mean Number of Reconstruction Responses (By Movement Type, XP Type and Age)

Age group	SCRAMBLING		OBJECT SHIFT		Group Mea
	DO	IO·	DO	IO	
Group I	0.76	0.61	0.15	0.15	0.42
Group II	0.88	0.77	0.44	0.16	0.56
Group III	1.00	0.66	0.28	0.05	0.49
Group IV	1.00	0.27	0.22	0.11	0.39

The results show that, as hypothesized, there was a difference in the rate for spontaneous reconstitution responses.

In particular, children gave significantly more reconstitution responses to scrambling stimulus sentences with direct objects (mean 0.94) than to object shift sentences with direct objects (mean 0.30) (t-statistics = 5.579, df = 60, p = 0.0001). Statistically, this difference is significant for the third group (t-statistic = 3.424, df = 17, p = 0.0032) and the fourth group (t-statistic = 4.082 , df = 17, p = 0.0008), but not for the first (t-statistic = 1.922, df = 7, p = 0.1030) or the second group (t-statistic = 1.810, df = 17, p = 0.0880). Again, even though the difference is not statistically significant for these two groups, the result is clearly in the same direction with the reconstitution rate for scrambling stimulus sentences with direct objects higher (mean 0.76 for the first group and mean 0.88 for the second group) than for object shift stimulus sentences with direct objects (mean 0.15 for the first group and mean 0.44 for the second group). These reconstitution results thus also confirm that children know the difference between 'obligatory' or 'unmarked' object shift and 'optional' or 'marked' scrambling.

Although the reconstitution rate was significantly higher for scrambling stimulus sentences with direct object than for object shift stimulus sentences with direct object, as hypothesized, some reconstitution responses for stimulus sentences with direct object and negation were found. There were 18 such reconstitution responses, more or less evenly distributed over the two tokens, *viz.*, 10 and 8 of each token respectively. They were also distributed over the four age groups. There was one such response in Group 1, eight such responses in Group 2 (for 6 children), five such responses in Group 3 (for four children) and four such responses in Group 4 (for four children).

There are at least two possible ways to explain these few occurrences. Under either explanation, the source of the reconstitution is situated with negation, not with object shift *per se*. The fact that these occurrences are found in all age groups, up to the eldest age group suggests that perhaps these residual cases ought to be interpreted as cases of constituent negations (cf. Weissenborn *et al.*, 1989; Hamann, this volume -- see the discussion above) in which case they are perfectly grammatical. Such a constituent negation interpretation requires, however, a particular intonation pattern. The analysis of the intonation pattern of these responses did not prove to be conclusive. While these responses occur in all age groups, it is also true that many of these cases occur in the youngest age groups. From the qualitative analysis of the responses of the children in the youngest group, it appears that some children are having trouble with the placement of the negation *'niet'*, as evidenced by cases of negation doubling. In fact, all five occurrences of negation doubling were found in the first two age groups. In addition, there is one occurrence of the incorrect use of *niet* with the indefinite article instead of the correct *geen* negation in the response of one child aged 3;6 years. Hamann (1993) suggests that cases of doubling of the negation could be interpreted as evidence that children initially incorrectly categorize *niet* as both a head and a specifier. The problem with this proposal is that the cases of negation doubling found involve utterances where the negation immediately precedes and follows the object, as shown in (19). This response is from a child aged 3;6 years.

(19)   Eva mag niet haar vinger niet in haar neus steken.
         Eva may not her finger not in her nose put

If the negation doubling is the result of a miscategorization of the negation as both head and specifier, the question arises as to what position the direct object occupies since there is no position between the head and the specifier for the direct object to occupy (but see Hamann, this volume). The standard assumption in the acquisition literature regarding copies of this sort is that they are the lexical spell-out of the trace of a moved element (Roeper, 1991). This suggests that the negation doubling responses show that in these responses the negation has moved. Such movement of the negation is perhaps not surprising considering the fact that negation is associated with scope and that many movements are triggered by scope. The syntax and semantics of negation is very intricate. The child acquiring Dutch has to learn how in its target language, constituent negation, and sentential negation are expressed differently. There are issues dealing with intonation. There are lexical issues dealing with a different lexical form, *viz.*, a fused negation *geen* instead of *niet,* and the indefinite article. In conclusion, there is evidence that problems dealing with the relative order of direct object and negation might be due to some problem with negation rather than with object shift *per se*. There is an alternative explanation for the negation doubling, *viz.*, that *nicht* and *niet* are classified as a simple adverb in the beginning (see Hamann, this volume) and that adverbs can be attached in different positions. Notice though, that in that case, one would not predict any significant difference in the treatment of stimulus sentences with adverbs and stimulus sentences with negation.

Children also gave significantly more reconstruction responses to scrambling stimulus sentences with indirect objects (mean 0.57) than to object shift sentences with indirect objects (mean 0.11) (t-statistic = 4.823, df = 60, p < 0.0001). Statistically, this difference is significant for the second group (t-statistic = 3.335, df = 17, p = 0.0039) and the third group (t-statistic = 3.335, df = 17, p = 0.0039), but not for the first (t-statistic = 1.441, df = 6, p = 0.1996) or the fourth group (t-statistic = 1.144, df = 17, p

= 0.2687). Again, although the difference is not statistically significant, the result is in the same direction with the reconstitution rate for scrambling stimulus sentences with indirect objects higher (mean 0.61 for the first group and mean 0.27 for the fourth group) than for object shift stimulus sentences with indirect objects (mean 0.15 for the first group and mean 0.11 for the fourth group).

Recall that for scrambling stimulus sentences with indirect object, only the indirect object preceded the adverb in the stimulus sentences because scrambling of both the indirect object and the direct object is awkward. Therefore, a reconstitution response for this type of stimulus sentence involves reconstitution of the indirect object only. This is in contrast with the object shift stimulus sentences with indirect object, where both the indirect object and the direct object precede the negation. As a result, a reconstitution response can involve reconstitution of the direct object, as in (20a) or both the indirect object and the direct object, as shown in (20b).

(20)   Stimulus: Steven zal Rita het poesje niet geven.
                   Steven shall Rita the cat not give
                   'Steven shall not give Rita the pussycat'

        Response: a. Steven zal Rita niet het poesje geven
                     Steven shall Rita not the cat give

        Response: b. Steven zal niet Rita het poesje geven
                     Steven shall not Rita the cat give

Since almost all the reconstitution responses for object shift stimulus sentences with indirect object involved reconstitution of the type shown in (20a), only this type of conversion is included in the means given in table 3 above. There are 7 reconstitution responses for object shift stimulus sentences with indirect objects. These responses are more or less evenly distributed over the two tokens, *viz.*, 3 and 4 respectively. They are also distributed over the four age groups. There is one such response in Group 1, three such responses in Group 2 (for three children), one such response for Group 3 and two such responses in Group 4 (for two children). As mentioned above, the means in Table 3 only include those reconstitution responses for indirect object stimulus sentences which involve reconstitution of the direct object. There are also three responses, *viz.*, one for Group 1, and two (for two children) in Group 2, which involve reconstitution of both the indirect and the direct object. Such a response is given in (21).

(21)   Stimulus: Papa mag Tom dat verhaaltje niet vertellen.
                    Daddy may Tom that story not tell

         Response: Papa mag niet Tom dat verhaaltje vertellen
                    Daddy may not Tom that story tell

5.2 Results with Regard to Hypothesis 2

With regard to indirect objects, the results show that the hypothesized difference in the responses between object shift stimulus sentence with indirect object and scrambling stimulus sentences with indirect object is not always statistically significant. We had also hypothesized, however, that there might be developmental changes with regard to the full competence for object shift because the direct object and the indirect object are licensed in different positions. They both need to be licensed in Spec, AgrOP. Only one element, however, *viz.*, the direct object can move into the Spec, AgrOP proper, while the indirect object has to be licensed in an adjoined position. Presumably, full competence for this type of last resort adjunction takes time to develop.

Wijnen & Verrips (1996) summed up the available information on Dutch children's acquisition of dative verbs as follows:

The available evidence suggests that dative verbs (with both internal arguments overtly realised) appear first between 2;6 and 3;0...Niek and Thomas produce their first prepositional datives after their first double object datives. Hein produces the first of each in the same file... Before 3;0, both realisations are very infrequent in Dutch child speech...

They conclude:

The low frequency of dative constructions in child speech makes the study of spontaneous speech a questionable method for investigating children's knowledge: the less frequent a construction is used, the smaller the chance that it will appear in a recording session. Experimental research should be carried out to extend the picture.

Penner *et al.* (1993) found in their analysis of natural speech data that there initially seems to be a problem with double object constructions, where both direct and indirect object need to shift to the pre-negation position. At this point, double object shift seems to be blocked, as shown in the example in (22). In this utterance, a prepositional phrase is used instead of a double object construction.

(22)   I cha das pyjama nid am Bäri aalege.
       I can the pajama not to bear put on
       'I can't put the pajama on the bear.'

We find a similar response in the imitation data, *viz.*, 7% of all responses for indirect object stimulus sentences involve a conversion of indirect objects into prepositional phrases. In these responses, the relative order of direct object, prepositional phrase, and adverbial varies in different ways, as shown in (23).

(23)   Stimulus: Papa mag Tom dat verhaaltje niet vertellen
                   Daddy may Tom that story not tell
                   'Daddy can't tell Tom that story'

       Child 3;6: Papa mag het verhaaltje niet aan Tom vertellen
                   Daddy may the story   niet to Tom tell
                         DO   NEG PP

       Child 3;0: Papa wil niet aan Tom dat verhaaltje vertellen
                   Daddy wants not   to Tom that story tell
                              NEG PP   DO

       Child 5;0: Papa mag niet het verhaaltje aan Tom vertellen
                   Daddy may not   the story   to Tom tell
                         NEG DO   PP

In addition, we find a significant amount of indirect object drop responses. The mean number of argument drop responses are presented in Table 4 as differentiated by design factors.[7]

Table 4.
Mean Number of Argument Drop Responses (By Movement Type, XP Type and Age)

Age group	SCRAMBLING		OBJECT SHIFT		Group Mean
	DO	IO	DO	IO	
Group I	0.15	0.61	0.3	0.46	0.38
Group II	0.11	0.33	0.05	0.55	0.26
Group III	0.11	0.33	0	0.5	0.23
Group IV	0	0.11	0.05	0.4	0.13
Overall	0.07	0.27	0.06	0.48	0.23

Overall mean of argument drop responses for this study was 0.23. Children gave significantly more argument drop responses for indirect object stimulus sentences than for direct object stimulus sentences. In particular, children gave significantly more argument drop responses to object shift stimulus sentences with indirect objects (mean 0.48) than to object shift stimulus sentences with direct objects (0.06) (t-statistic = 5.443, df = 60, p < 0.0001). They also gave significantly more argument drop responses to scrambling stimulus sentences with indirect objects (mean 0.27) than to scrambling stimulus sentences with direct objects (mean 0.07) (t-statistic = 2.867, df = 60, p = 0.0057).

This very strong tendency for omission of indirect objects contrasts starkly with the virtually complete absence of omission of direct objects. Within object shift, the difference between omission of direct objects and omission of indirect objects is particularly high. Only four responses for stimulus sentences with negation and direct object involved direct object drop. If there were a systematic absence of objects in the post-verbal/pre-negation position, as observed by Weissenborn (1990), it is conceivable that children, when confronted with stimulus sentences for which they don't have the grammatical competence, would omit the direct object. Thus, the small amount of object drop responses in object shift stimulus sentences disconfirms the alleged systematic absence of objects in post-verbal/pre-negation position.

5.3. Results with regard to Hypothesis 3

Both in the case of the success rate of imitation and in the case of the reconstitution rate, the statistical analysis does not reveal much for the two youngest age groups. As mentioned in the description of the experimental task above, the scoring criteria for correct responses were very strict: the children's responses were scored as 'correct' only if the response involved absolutely no change to the stimulus sentence except for lexical changes such as name changes. However, the responses of the youngest children often involved changes other than name changes to the stimulus sentences. For example, in a typical response, part of the stimulus sentence would simply be omitted. Partial responses of this kind were not included in the means given in Tables 2 and 3. Nevertheless, partial responses can often provide evidence for the grammatical competence of the youngest children. For this reason, the responses of the seven children in the youngest age group will be looked at individually, in particular with regard to the question whether there is evidence that even the youngest children tested produce sentences with object shift as required for a sentential negation interpretation.

As regards the question whether there is evidence for early competence for object shift in the youngest age group, there is one response (out of four tokens) from the youngest child tested in this experiment, child 2601 (2;8 years) which evidences object shift. In her response, the child has dropped the indirect object, but the direct object is correctly shifted to the pre-negation position, i.e., is imitated correctly, as shown in (24).

(24)　　　　Stimulus:　Papa zal Tom het verhaaltje niet vertellen
　　　　　　　　　　　　Daddy shall Tom the story not tell

　　　　　　Child 2;8:　Papa zal verhaaltje niet vertellen
　　　　　　　　　　　　Daddy shall story not tell

The fact that the direct object is correctly shifted to the pre-negation position, as in the stimulus sentence, even though part of the sentence is omitted, becomes even more significant when one considers that this same child's response to a scrambling stimulus sentence with indirect object involves reconstitution so that the indirect object follows the adverb, as shown in (25).

(25)　　　　Stimulus:　Mama mag de baby nu een flesje geven
　　　　　　　　　　　　Mummy may the baby now a bottle give

　　　　　　Child 2;8:　Mama gaat nu baby een flesje geven
　　　　　　　　　　　　Mummy goes now baby a bottle give

This difference in response suggests that this child knows the difference between the 'obligatory' nature of object shift and the 'optional' nature of scrambling. There is another response from this child which provides interesting information about the child's grammatical competence. This response involves a double negation, as shown in (26).

(26)　　　　Stimulus:　Steven zal Rita het poesje niet geven
　　　　　　　　　　　　Steven shall Rita the pussycat not give

　　　　　　Child 2;8:　niet poesje niet geven
　　　　　　　　　　　　not pussycat not give

This child's responses to the two other object shift tokens involve one argument drop response and one response with just a few words, which contain neither the negation nor the direct object.

The responses of the second youngest child 2602 (2;9 years) involve four words at the most. Yet, even in these very limited utterances there is evidence for object shift as shown in (27), where the direct object is correctly shifted to the pre-negation position, i.e., is imitated correctly.

(27) Stimulus: Steven zal Rita het poesje niet geven
                 Steven shall Rita the pussycat not give

      Child 2;9: poeske niet geven
                 pussycat not give

For child 2603 (2;9 years), there are several responses which provide evidence for object shift with negation, as shown in (28).

(28) Stimulus: Eva mag haar vinger niet in haar neus steken
                 Eva may her finger not in her nose put

      Child 2;9: Mama mag haar niet in haar neus steken
                 Mummy may her not in her nose put

      Stimulus: Steven zal Rita het poesje niet geven
                 Steven shall Rita the pussycat not give

      Child 2;9: dat poesje niet geven
                 that pussycat not give

      Stimulus: Papa mag Tom het verhaaltje niet vertellen
                 Daddy may Tom the story not tell

      Child 2;9: Dat kindje mag dat niet vertellen
                 That child may that not tell

Child 2604 (2;11 years) was the only child, who did not produce any responses which explicitly showed object shift. Two of her responses involved reconstitution.

For child 3001 (3;1 years) it is impossible to tell whether his responses involved object shift with negation or not because the relevant responses all involved double negation, as shown in (29).

(29) Stimulus: Mama zal het speelgoed niet uit de kast halen
                 Mummy shall the toys not out the closet get

      Child 3;1: Mama zal nie speelgoed nie uit de kast halen
                 Mummy shall not toys not out the closet get

Stimulus: Mama zal Rita het poesje niet geven
Mummy shall Rita the pussycat not give

Child 3;1: Mama wil niet dat poesje niet geven
Mummy wants not that pussycat not give

For child 3002 (3;2 years), (30) shows object shift and negation responses.

(30) Stimulus: Steven zal Rita het poesje niet geven.
Steven shall Rita the pussycat not give

Child 3;2: Steven gaat het poesje niet geven
Steven goes the pussycat not give

Stimulus: Lisa mag haar vinger niet in haar neus steken.
Lisa may her finger not in her nose put

Child 3;2: Lisa mag haar vinger niet in haar neus steken
Lisa may her finger not in her nose put

And there is one example for child 3003 (3;3 years), as shown in (31).

(31) Stimulus: Lisa mag haar vinger niet in haar neus steken
Lisa may her finger not in her nose put

Child 3;3: Ik mag dat niet in mijn neus steken, die vinger
I may that not in my nose put, that finger

In conclusion, even though the quantitative analysis of success of imitation discussed in Result 1 does not provide evidence for early competence for object shift, a qualitative analysis of the often only partial responses of the children in the youngest age group reveals that there is evidence for competence for object shift, particularly of the direct object, from the beginning because the youngest children tested seemed to treat object shift stimulus sentences differently from scrambling stimulus sentences with regard to reconstitution.

With regard to the early competence for scrambling, there is evidence that the children in the youngest age group give more reconstitution responses to scrambling stimulus sentences than correct responses. In the youngest age group, there were nine reconstitution responses (for five children) for scrambling stimulus sentences and only one correct response. In addition, there were four adverb drop responses (for two children). This suggests that the full competence for scrambling might take time to develop. This is not unexpected in view of the fact that scrambling is in a sense the 'marked' option since it only applies to DPs carrying the special [+scope] or [+focus] feature.

6. CONCLUSIONS

In sum, the results provide evidence for early competence for object shift, in particular of the direct object. The few cases of responses where the object was apparently not shifted to the pre-negation position can be explained in terms of evidencing problems the children have with regard to the syntax and semantics of negation rather than a lack of competence for object shift *per se*. There appears to be some developmental delay in the full competence for object shift with indirect objects. This is presumably due to the fact that direct objects are licensed in Spec, AgrOP proper while indirect objects have to be licensed in an adjoined position. The results also show that, from the earliest testable age, children know the difference between object shift and scrambling. Evidence suggests that full competence for scrambling might take time to develop. This is presumably due to the fact that scrambling only occurs with DPs carrying a special [+focus]feature.

ACKNOWLEDGEMENTS

I would like to thank two anonymous reviewers as well as the audience at GALA in Durham in September 1993, where an earlier version of this paper was presented, for their comments.

NOTES

[1] This paper focuses on the acquisition of Dutch. There will, however, be references to the acquisition of German because adult Dutch and German behave very similarly with regard to the syntactic phenomena discussed. In addition, most of the previous acquisition research has focused on the acquisition of these phenomena in German.

[2] Object shift can be observed directly only when negation intervenes between the base-position of the DP and the Spec, AgrOP. Presumably, however, the trigger for this movement of the DP complement into a licensing position Spec, AgrOP is also active when the direct object movement can not be directly observed, as in (i).

(i)   Ik wil   dat   boek   lezen
            I want   that   book   read
            'I want to read that book'

Zwart (1993) argues that the O(bject)-V(erb) order, which is traditionally assumed to be the underived order of Dutch and German VPs (Koster, 1975) is itself a derived order. He further argues that this OV word order is derived from a basic VO order, i.e., that Dutch VPs are head-initial. For some acquisition evidence supporting Zwart's proposal, see Barbier (1995; 1996).

[3] Depending upon the literature, this movement has also been called 'pseudo-scrambling', 'scrambling by substitution', 'triggered scrambling' or 'local scrambling'.

[4] Zwart refers to the movement of the direct object to a position preceding the negation as scrambling and reserves the term object shift for the pronoun movement in Mainland Scandinavian languages. As far as the adverb order is concerned, he assumes that this results from the property of adverbs that they can be base-generated in different positions

[5] It is difficult to interpret Schaeffer's results because object shift and scrambling are considered one and the same phenomenon, labeled 'scrambling' in her work (But see Schaeffer's Tables 1-4 in this volume). A similar observation can be made about the discussion of the acquisition of leftward movement in Haegeman (1996).

[6] Strictly speaking, even in constituent negation readings, object shift has taken place, i.e., the whole DP constituent, including the DP internal negation moves to Spec, AgrOP. For ease of description in this paper, however, I refer to constituent negation readings as evidencing absence of object shift.

[7] One reviewer suggested it would be useful to comment on the kinds of utterances that were to be found in the 'none of the above category', i.e., those that did not made it into Tables 2, 3, or 4. As discussed in the section on the results regarding Hypothesis 1, some responses involved negation doubling. As discussed in the section on the results regarding Hypothesis 2, some responses involved dropping the indirect object or the direct object, as well as conversion of the indirect object to a prepositional phrase. As discussed in the section on the results regarding Hypothesis 3, a number of responses, particularly those of the younger children, involved omission of large parts of the sentence. Some other responses not mentioned in the discussion of the results involved mainly a few instances of omission of the adverb, the negation, or the modal verb.

REFERENCES

Barbier, I.: 1995, 'The acquisition of embedded clauses with finite verbs in nonfinal position in Dutch', In E. Clark (ed.) *Proceedings of the twenty-sixth annual child language research forum*, 147-158.Cambridge University Press, Cambridge.

Barbier, I.: 1996, 'The head-direction of Dutch VPs: evidence from L1 acquisition', In C. Koster & F. Wijnen (eds.) *Proceedings of the Groningen Assembly on Language Acquisition*, 97-106.

Borer, H. & K. Wexler: 1987, 'The maturation of syntax'. In T. Roeper & E. Williams (eds.) *Parameter Setting*, Reidel, Dordrecht, 123-172.

Clahsen, H.: 1990, 'Constraints on parameter setting. A grammatical analysis of some acquisition stages in German child language', *Language Acquisition* **1**, 361-391.

Dokter, N.: 1995, '"Mag ik zo klein kipje hebben?" De Basisgeratietheorie van Scrambling Getoetst aan Kindertaaluitingen, M.A. Thesis, Utrecht University.

Haegeman, L.: 1996, 'Root infinitives, clitics and truncated structures', In H. Clahsen (ed.) *Generative Perspectives on Language Acquisition*, Benjamins, Amsterdam, 271-307.

Hamann, C. : 1993, 'On the acquisition of Negation in German', ms., Université de Genève.

Hamann, C.: 1996, 'Negation and truncated structures', in M. Aldridge (ed.) *Child Language*, Multilingual Matters, Clevedon.

Hoekstra, T. and P. Jordens: 1994, 'From adjunct to head', In T. Hoekstra & B. Schwartz (eds.) *Language Acquisition Studies in Generative Grammar*, John Benjamins. Amsterdam, 119-150.

Koster, J.: 1975, 'Dutch as an SOV language', *Linguistic Analysis* **1**, 111-136.

Lust, B. and T. Wakayama: 1981, 'Word order in first language acquisition of Japanese', In P. Dale and D. Ingram (eds.) *Child Language - An International Perspective*, University Park, Baltimore, 72-90.

Lust, B., Flynn, S. and C. Foley: 1996, 'What children know about what they say: Elicited Imitation as a research method for assessing children's syntax', In D. McDaniel, C. McKee and H. Smith Cairns (eds.) *Methods for assessing children's syntax*, MIT Press, Cambridge, 55-76.

Penner, Z., Tracy, R. and J. Weissenborn: 1993, 'Scrambling', ms., University of Berne, University of Tübingen, and University of Potsdam.

Roeper, T. 1991, 'How a marked Parameter is chosen: Adverbs and do-insertion in the IP of child grammar', In T. Maxfield & B. Plunkett (eds.) *Papers in the Acquisition of WH - Special Edition of University of Massachusetts Ocaassional Papers in Linguistics*, GLSA Publications, Amherst. 175-202

Santelmann, L.: 1989, 'Object Movement in German: Evidence from Negation', ms., Cornell University, Ithaca, NY.
Schaeffer, J.: 1995, 'On the Acquisition of Scrambling in Dutch', In D. MacLaughlin & S. McEwen (eds.) *Proceedings of the 19th Annual Boston University Conference on Language Development*, Volume 2, Cascadilla Press, Somerville, 521-533.
Vanden Wyngaerd, G.: 1989, 'Object Shift as an A-movement Rule', *MIT Working Papers in Linguistics* **11**, 256-271.
Weissenborn, J.:1990, 'Functional categories and verb movement: The acquisition of German syntax reconsidered', In M. Rothweiler (ed.) *Spracherwerb und Grammatik: linguistische Untersuchungen zum Erwerb von Syntax und Morphologie*, Westdeutsche Verlag, Opladen, 190-224.
Weissenborn, J., Verrips, M. & R. Berman: 1989, 'Negation as a window to the structure of early child language', MS., Max Planck-Institut, Nijmegen.
Wijnen, J. & M. Verrips: 1996, 'The acquisition of Dutch syntax', *OTS Working Papers* TL 96-102.
Zwart, J. W. (1993). *Dutch Syntax. A Minimalist Approach.* Unpublished doctoral dissertation, University of Groningen.

ISABELLA BARBIER
University of Queensland

JEANNETTE SCHAEFFER

OBJECT SCRAMBLING AND SPECIFICITY IN DUTCH CHILD LANGUAGE

1. INTRODUCTION

During the past decade, many investigators of child language have reported that in early grammar verbs often surface without finite morphology in root clauses (for example, Jordens (1990), Weverink (1989) for Dutch). Wexler (1994) refers to this phenomenon as the *optional infinitive stage* because such examples occur alongside finite sentences. Examples of optional infinitives are given in (1) for Dutch, French, and German:

(1)   a. pappa schoenen wassen   *Dutch* (from Weverink, 1989)
              'daddy shoes wash'
          b. ik ook lezen
              'I also read'
          c. pas manger la poupée   *French* (from Pierce, 1989)
              'not eat the doll'
          d. Michel dormir
              'Michael sleep'
          e. Zähne putzen   *German* (from Wexler, 1994)
              'teeth brush'
          f. Thorstn das haben
              'Thorsten that have'

A natural way to account for sentences as in (1) is to assume that the verb has failed to raise to the inflectional head I, where finite morphology is checked. This suggests that verb raising, an obligatory process (either overt or covert) in adult language is optional in the child's. Hyams (1996) accounts for the phenomenon of optional infinitives by claiming that the temporal specificity of children's root clauses can be underspecified with respect to finiteness.

Given this optionality in the child's verbal system, and given the parallels which are often drawn between the verbal and the nominal system, we might expect a similar type of optionality within the nominal system. In this paper, I will argue that this is the case for Dutch child language. I will show that just as the sentences in (1) are underspecified for temporal specificity or finiteness, children's nominal expressions can be underspecified with respect to nominal specificity. This is stated in (2):

(2) Hypothesis
Children's nominal expressions can be underspecified with respect to specificity.

We define the notion 'underspecification' in this hypothesis as follows: a nominal expression is underspecified with respect to specificity if the syntactic feature 'specificity' is absent. The hypothesis that nominal expressions can be underspecified with respect to specificity makes two predictions for Dutch child language, which are stated in (3):

(3) (i) scrambling of object nominals will not always take place in obligatory contexts;
(ii) determiners will often be omitted in obligatory contexts.

To explain the first prediction, many object nominals undergo obligatory movement in languages such as Dutch and German. This process is known as scrambling, on which I will elaborate in a moment. Assuming that it is the notion of specificity that is responsible for scrambling, as Diesing (1992) argues, we expect that in the cases in which specificity is underspecified, children will not scramble objects.

Regarding the second prediction, determiners are traditionally thought to specify the definiteness of a Noun Phrase. Furthermore, determiners (or definiteness) are largely responsible for the specificity of a nominal expression. For example, if a nominal is definite, it is specific. If a nominal is indefinite, it can be either non-specific or specific. Thus, if specificity is not specified, we predict that the determiner is absent, because specificity cannot be established without the presence of a determiner. We propose that specificity is a feature located in D. Furthermore, we assume that nominals with a definite determiner or a specific indefinite determiner have a structure as in (4a) and non-specific nominals with an indefinite determiner as in (4b):

(4)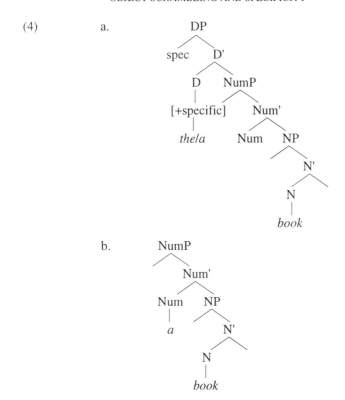

Before turning to the child language data, we will first elaborate on the phenomenon of scrambling in adult Dutch.

2. SCRAMBLING IN ADULT DUTCH

The position of the Dutch (and German) object is rather controversial. The domain between C and the finite V in Dutch contains at least three fields, or zones, in which an object can appear, as is exemplified in (5). A plus-sign indicates that the relevant nominal can appear in that position; the star-sign indicates that it is ungrammatical for the relevant nominal to appear in that position.

(5)   *Possible positions for objects in Dutch*

	1	adverb	2	negation	3	Vfin
pronoun	+		*		*	
definite DP	+		+		+	
proper name	+		+		+	
specific indefinite	+		+		+	
non-specific indefinite	*		*		+	

As (5) shows, the clearest cases of scrambling in adult Dutch are pronouns, which *obligatorily* scramble. Illustrations of the position of object pronouns are given in (6); the position of definite object DPs is exemplified in (7), and examples of proper name objects are given in (8). In each example, the object is bold-faced. The number in parentheses after each example indicates the zone that contains the object.

(6)   *object pronoun*
      a. *dat Saskia waarschijnlijk niet **het** gelezen heeft   (3)
         that Saskia probably not it read has
      b. *dat Saskia waarschijnlijk **het** niet gelezen heeft   (2)
         that Saskia probably it not read has
      c. dat Saskia **het** waarschijnlijk niet gelezen heeft   (1)
         that Saskia it probably not read has

(7)   *definite object DP*
      a. dat Saskia waarschijnlijk niet **het boek** gelezen heeft
         (maar naar de bioscoop is gegaan)   (3)
         that Saskia probably not the book read has
         (but to the cinema is gone)
      b. dat Saskia waarschijnlijk **het boek** niet gelezen heeft
         that Saskia probably the book not read has   (2)
      c. dat Saskia **het boek** waarschijnlijk niet gelezen heeft
         that Saskia the book probably not read has   (1)

(8) *proper name*
    a. dat Saskia waarschijnlijk niet **Jan** gebeld heeft
       (maar Marieke een briefje heeft geschreven)   (3)
       that Saskia probably not Jan telephoned has
       (but Marieke a letter has written)
    b. dat Saskia waarschijnlijk **Jan** niet gebeld heeft   (2)
       that Saskia probably Jan not telephoned has
    c. dat Saskia **Jan** waarschijnlijk niet gebeld heeft   (1)
       that Saskia Jan probably not telephoned has

The position of *in*definites is a little trickier. If the indefinite stays in Zone 3, it receives a non-specific interpretation, as is illustrated in (9a). If the indefinite occurs in Zone 2, it cannot have a non-specific reading, but must be specific, or perhaps generic, as exemplified in (9b). Finally, an indefinite in Zone 1 cannot be interpreted as non-specific either, but must be specific or perhaps generic, as illustrated in (9c).

(9) *indefinite object*
    a. dat Saskia waarschijnlijk **geen** (niet + een) **science-fiction boek** gelezen heef   (3)
       that Saskia probably no (not + a) science-fiction book read has
       [OK if non-specific - * if specific]
       'that Saskia probably hasn't read any science-fiction book'
    b. dat Saskia waarschijnlijk **een science-fiction boek** niet gelezen heeft   (2)
       that Saskia probably a science-fiction book not read has
       [OK if specific - * if non-specific]
       'it is probable that there is a particular science-fiction book such that Saskia has not read it' or
       'there is a particular science-fiction book such that Saskia
       has probably not read it'
    c. dat Saskia **een science-fiction boek** waarschijnlijk niet gelezen heeft   (1)
       that Saskia a science-fiction book probably not read has
       [OK if specific - * if non-specific]
       'there is a particular science-fiction book such that Saskia has probably not read it'

3. WHAT FORCES SCRAMBLING?

The Dutch facts suggest that there is some principle forcing or allowing certain objects to move leftwards out of the VP. In the literature, there are many theories that try to account for this type of movement. Some people claim it is a Case-driven movement (for example Mahajan, 1990), some people propose that intonation is the driving force behind scrambling, such as Zwart (1994), others propose that scrambling is forced by scope requirements (for example Diesing, 1992). I assume that scrambling is a scope-driven movement: certain specific nominals must be in the scope of an element such as an adverb or negation.

Diesing (1992) proposes a Mapping Hypothesis which maps semantic domains to the syntactic structure of a sentence. The Mapping Hypothesis is illustrated in (10):

(10)   Mapping Hypothesis

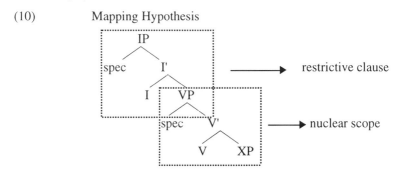

Object nominals can either stay in the "nuclear scope", a semantic domain which corresponds to the syntactic VP, or it can move to the "restrictive clause", which maps on the syntactic IP.

If a nominal is non-specific, it introduces a novel variable, which must be bound in the nuclear scope. In this case, the nominal stays within the VP. If a nominal is specific, it introduces a familiar variable, which must be bound in the restrictive clause, as Heim (1982) proposes. Therefore, the object moves out of the VP/nuclear scope to a higher position within the IP/restrictive clause. Although this is a very sketchy representation of Diesing's and Heim's ideas regarding scrambling, it suffices for our purposes.

4. SCRAMBLING IN DUTCH CHILD LANGUAGE

Let us turn now to our developmental findings. We searched through all the available files of Niek (collected by Frank Wijnen, in CHILDES, MacWhinney and Snow, 1985).The entire corpus includes transcripts of 46 recordings of 60 minutes each between the ages of 2;7 and 3;11. A second child, Laura (data collected by Jacqueline van Kampen), was also included, whose utterances were not computerized, but consisted of diary notes of Laura's speech corresponding to 205 dates between the ages of 1;10 and 6;4.[1] We used the notes corresponding to 195 dates between the ages of 1;10 and 5;4. For Niek, we pulled (using the KWAL command) from the database all sentences with a verb, an object and negation and all utterances with a verb, an object and one of the following adverbs: *ook* 'also', *zo* 'this way' or 'in a minute', *weer* 'again', *even* 'for a minute', *maar* (?), *altijd* 'always', *morgen* 'tomorrow'. For Laura we (manually) counted all utterances containing a verb, an object, and negation *niet* 'not', or an adverb. Non-intelligible utterances and repetitions (of parent's/experimenter's and of own utterances) were excluded in the counts. The sentences were grouped into the categories as described in (11):

(11)   (i) Pronouns: - scrambled
                                                    - unscrambled
                   (ii) Proper names: - scrambled
                                                    - unscrambled
                   (iii) Definite NPs: - scrambled
                                                    - unscrambled
                   (iv) Indefinite NPs: - scrambled
                                                    - unscrambled
                   (v) Determinerless NPs: - scrambled
                                                   - unscrambled

Furthermore, in order to show development, both corpora were divided up into two stages, as is shown in (12):[2]

(12)   Niek: Stage I: 2;7 - 3;5
                            Stage II: 3;6 - 3;11

                Laura: Stage I: 1;10 - 3;4
                            Stage II: 3;5 - 5;4

The proportions of scrambled and non-scrambled objects in Niek are given in Tables 1 and 2 for Stage I and II, respectively. All cases which would be ungrammatical in adult Dutch are marked with an asterisk.[3]

Table 1.
Proportions of scrambled (scr) and non-scrambled (non-scr) objects in Niek Stage I

	pronoun		proper name		definite DP		indefinite		determiner-less	
	scr	non scr	scr	non scr	scr	non scr	scr	non scr	scr	non scr
total	15 71%	*6 29%	0	1 100%	2 67%	1 33%	0	1 100%	*11 18%	*50 82%
neg	4 67%	*2 33%	0	0	1 100%	0	0	0	*2 10%	*19 90%
adv	11 69%	*4 31%	0	1 100%	1 50%	1 50%	0	1 100%	*9 23%	*31 77%

Table 2.
Proportions of scrambled (scr) and non-scrambled (non-scr) objects in Niek Stage II

	pronoun		proper name		definite DP		indefinite		determiner-less	
	scr	non scr	scr	non scr	scr	non scr	scr	non scr	scr	non scr
total	50 78%	*14 22%	0	1 100%	11 55%	9 45%	1 7%	13 93%	*10 23%	*33 77%
neg	14 88%	*2 12%	0	1 100%	4 80%	1 20%	0	6 100%	*5 38%	*8 62%
adv	36 75%	*12 25%	0	0	7 47%	8 53%	1 12%	7 88%	*5 17%	*25 83%

The proportions of scrambled and non-scrambled objects in Laura are given in Tables 3 and 4 for Stage I and II, respectively:

Table 3.
Proportions of scrambled (scr) and non-scrambled (non-scr) objects in Laura Stage I

	pronoun		proper name		definite DP		indefinite		determiner-less	
	scr	non scr	scr	non scr	scr	non scr	scr	non scr	scr	non-scr
total	3 30%	*7 70%	0	2 100%	1 50%	2 80%	1 20%	4 80%	0	*18 100%
neg	3 50%	*3 50%	0	1 100%	1 50%	1 50%	1 25%	3 75%	0	*13 100%
adv	0	*4 10%	0	1 100%	0	1 100%	0	1 100%	0	5 100%

Table 4.
Proportions of scrambled (scr) and non-scrambled (non-scr) objects-Laura Stage II

	pronoun		proper name		definite DP		indefinite		determiner-less	
	scr	non scr	scr	non scr	scr	non scr	scr	non scr	scr	non scr
total	7 88%	*1 12%	0	1 100%	2 67%	1 33%	0	3 100%	0	*1 100%
neg	5 83%	*1 17%	0	1 100%	1 50%	1 50%	0	1 100%	0	*1 100%
adv	2 100%	0	0	0	1 50%	1 50%	0	2 100%	0	0

The following generalizations emerge from Tables 1, 2, 3, and 4:

(13) A. There are a large number of unscrambled determinerless object nouns in Dutch child language, which are prohibited in adult Dutch;
B. Scrambling of pronouns is *not obligatory* for Dutch children as it is for adults;
C. Scrambling of definite objects (nouns with definite determiners and proper names) are adult-like in that it is *not obligatory*;
D. Scrambling of indefinite objects is *rare* in Dutch child language.

The sentences in (14) illustrate result A, that there are a large number of unscrambled determinerless nouns.

(14) a. Niekje ook [ ] boot maken   Niek 2;8
         Niekje also boat make-INF
      b. even [ ] huis maken   Niek 2;10
         for-a-minute house make-INF
      c. niet [ ] neus snuiten   Niek 3;0
         not nose blow-INF
      d. papa heeft ook [ ] trein   Niek 3;0
         daddy had also train
      e. hier zit niet [ ] licht in   Niek 3;1
         here sits not light in
      f. ik kan niet [ ] brandweerauto maken hee   Niek 3;1
         I can not fire-engine make-INF
      g. mag die ook [ ] gordijn dicht doen?   Niek 3;2
         may that also curtain closed make
      h. ik maak even [ ] brug   Niek 3;2
         I make for-a-minute bridge
      i. jij even [ ] autootje bouwen   Niek 3;2
         you for-a-minute car build-INF
      j. hij heb ook [ ] grote bak hee   Niek 3;4
         he has also big tray/car huh
      k. hier lig niet [ ] stenen op   Niek 3;4
         her lies not rocks on
      l. nou laat heel even [ ] verf staan Niek 3;5
         now let for-a-minute paint stand
      m. mag ik weer van blokjes [ ] toren bouwen? Niek 3;5
         may I again of blocks tower build
      n. vind jij ook [ ] huis mooi?   Niek 3;6
         find you also house beautiful

o. doe jij even [ ] deur dicht?   Niek 3;6
    do you for-a-minute door closed
p. heef jij ook [ ] beetje moestuin?   Niek 3;7
    has you also bit vegetable garden
q. moet even [ ] kachel open toch?   Niek 3;7
    must for a minute heater open
r. hij heef niet [ ] auto en [ ] fiets wel bij je   Niek 3;8
    he has not car and bicycle with you
s. ik ga ook [ ] boef pakken   Niek 3;8
    I go also bad guy grab
t. dan heef ik weer [ ] speen in mond   Niek 3;9
    then has I again pacifier in mouth
u. hij heef ook nog [ ] papegaai en muizen   Niek 3;10
    he has also yet parrot and mice
v. wegenbouwers kan ook [ ] huis bouwen   Niek 3;11
    roadbuilders can also house build
w. ikke ook [ ] kietje aai   Laura 2;1
    I also knee stroke
x. ik vind niet [ ] bietje lekker   Laura 2;10
    I find not beet-root nice
y. ik is even [ ] kussen wegzetten   Laura 2;10
    I is for a minute cushion away put
z. ik ga niet [ ] slabje omdoen   Laura 3;1
    I go not bibby on do
z'. heb jij nog niet [ ] thee opedaan?   Laura 3;8
    have you yet not tea up done

Hoekstra & Jordens (1994) find similar results for the Dutch children they studied, as is illustrated in (15):

(15)   a. ik mag niet [ ] modewijzer   Jasmijn 2;1
               I may not fashion designer
            b. dat jij niet [ ] lolly heb   Jasmijn 2;8
               that you not lollypop have

Furthermore, Weissenborn (1990) (as in 16a-b) and Hamann (1993, 1996; this volume) in 16c, report that German children produce many unscrambled, determinerless NPs as well. See also Clahsen (1988) and Penner *et al.* (this volume).

(16) a. brauche nicht [ ] Lala   Simone 2;0
         need not pacifier
      b. haschen braucht nicht [ ] Windel   Simone 2;1
         bunny need not diaper
      c. kanne nich [ ] Haus machen   Mathias 3;0
         can not house make

The examples in (17) illustrate result B, that scrambling of pronouns is not obligatory.[4]

(17) a. mama **dat** ook proberen (scrambled)   Niek 3;0
         mommy that also try-INF
      b. ik zie **'t** niet (scrambled)   Niek 3;4
         I see it not
      c. heb jij **dit** ook nog nodig? (scrambled)   Niek 3;6
         have you this also yet needed
      d. ik ga **het** even vertellen (scrambled)   Niek 3;10
         I go it for a minute tell-INF
      e. ik ook **dat** hebben (unscrambled)   Niek 2;11
         I also that have-INF
      f. Niekje heb ook **die** (unscrambled)   Niek 3;2
         Niekje has also that
      g. mag even **dit** dicht? (unscrambled)   Niek 3;6
         may for a minute this closed
      h. nu doe ik niet meer **die** (unscrambled)   Niek 3;9
         now do I not anymore that
      i. ik hoef **het** niet hemmen (scrambled)   Laura 2;9
         I must it not have-INF
      j. ik salt **dat** wel doen (scrambled)   Laura 4;1
         I will that AFF do-INF
      k. ik hoefe niet **die** opeten (unscrambled)   Laura 2;5
         I must not that eat-up
      l. waarom dan mag ik niet **dit** hebben?   Laura 3;6
         (unscrambled)
         why then may I not this have-INF

Again, these results are confirmed by Hoekstra & Jorden's (1994) findings for Dutch, as is illustrated in (18), and by Clahsen's (1991) findings for German child language, as is illustrated in (19):

(18) ik wil niet **dit** (unscrambled)   Jasmijn 2;1
      I want not this

(19) kann nicht **das** zumachen (unscrambled)   Julia 2;4
      can not that close

OBJECT SCRAMBLING AND SPECIFICITY

The sentences in (20) and (21) illustrate result C, that scrambling of definite objects is not obligatory. Sentences with adverbs are in (20), (21) contains sentences with negation.

(20)   a. doe ik **dit** kussens zo hier op schuiven   Niek 3;5
(scrambled)
do I this cushions this way here on push
b. moet **dit** blok even in (scrambled)   Niek 3;7
must this block for a minute in
c. hij doet **het** mes altijd (scrambled)   Niek 3;10
he does the knife always
d. ik ga zo oma opbellen (unscrambled)   Niek 3;5
I go in a minute grandmother upcall
e. moet even **die** kiepauto hier (unscrambled) Niek 3;7
must for a minute that truck here
f. even weer **die** huis opbouwen   Niek 3;10
(unscrambled)
for a minute again that house upbuild
g. hallo Ben, wil je **mijn** portemonnee   Laura 3;6
even zoeken? (scrambled)
hello Ben, want you my wallet for a minute search
h. wil je soms pappa bellen? (unscrambled)   Laura 2;10
want you ADV daddy call-INF
i. jij gaat ook altijd **jij** oorden wassen?   Laura 3;7
(unscrambled)
you go also always your ears wash

(21)   a. **mijn** speentje niet ophalen (scrambled)   Niek 3;1
my pacifier not uppick
b. anders krijg hij **die** briefje niet (scrambled) Niek 3;10
otherwise gets he that letter-DIM not
c. dan kan jij niet **mij** speen hier
afpakken (unscrambled)   Niek 3;9
then can you not my pacifier away-take
e. ik wil niet Sinterklaas kijken (unscrambled) Niek 3;10
I want not Santa Claus watch
f. ik kan **mijn** eigen niet dragen (scrambled) Laura 3;4
I can my own not carry
g. ik vind niet Manon leuk (unscrambled)   Laura 2;10
I find not Manon nice
h. ik heb niet Sinterklaas zien (unscrambled) Laura 3;7
I have not Santa Claus seen

Interestingly, the only unscrambled definite NPs that are non-adult-like are the proper names in (21g and h). Hoekstra & Jordens (1994) report the same phenomenon and give the following example which would be ungrammatical or at least marginal in adult Dutch:

(22)   ik kan niet Maria zoeken (unscrambled)   Jasmijn 2;1
       I can not Maria look for

The examples in (23) show that indefinite objects occur mostly unscrambled.

(23) a. mama mag ook **een** pap (unscrambled)   Niek 3;1
         mommy may also a porridge
      b. neem nou niet **een** appel (unscrambled)   Niek 3;9
         take now not an apple
      c. hebben ze weer **een** nieuw   Niek 3;10
         bootje maak (unscrambled)
         have they again a new boat made
      d. dit is ook nog **een** boortje (unscrambled)   Niek 3;11
         this is also yet a gimlet
      e. ik heb niet **een** boterham pindakaas   Laura 2;3
         (unscrambled)
         I have not a slice of bread peanut butter
      f. ik ga ook **een** heleboel schrijven   Laura 3;6
         (unscrambled)
         I go also a lot write

5. DISCUSSION AND ANALYSIS

How do we analyze these data? In the discussion and analysis of the observed facts, we will focus on Eesults A and B, since these differ most clearly from adult Dutch. Results A and B are repeated in (24):

(24)   Result A:
       There are a large number of unscrambled determinerless object nouns in Dutch child language, which is prohibited in adult Dutch;
       Result B:
       Scrambling of pronouns is *not obligatory* for Dutch children as it is for adults.

Although the object might make a short move, say, to Spec, VP or to Spec, AgrOP, for Case reasons, further movement of, for example, pronouns to the IP domain does not always take place in Dutch child language. Recall that this is obligatory in adult Dutch. Thus, prediction (i) is borne out: scrambling of object NPs does not always take place in obligatory contexts. In particular, as result B shows, scrambling of *pronouns* does not always take place. As for the position of pronouns, we follow Koopman (1998) in the assumption that pronouns are base-generated in N and assume furthermore that they move from N-to-D (cf. Longobardi, 1994). This supports the hypothesis that the functional head D may be underspecified with respect to specificity, the feature which forces scrambling. If this is the case for pronouns, the object pronoun stays within the VP. The utterances with unscrambled pronouns in Dutch child language then correspond to a tree as in (25):

(25)
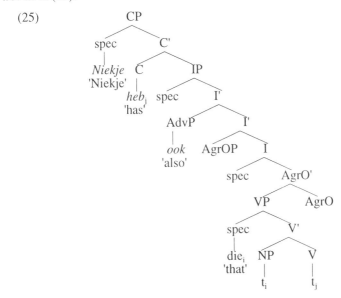

The second prediction is borne out, too: determiners are often omitted in obligatory contexts. As was illustrated in (14), a large number of object nouns occur without a determiner. During the first stage, 94% of Niek's full object nominals appears without a determiner, as we can see in Table 5:

Table 5.
Proportion of determinerless objects during Stage I and II in Niek

stage	total full objects	determinerless nouns	pronouns	
			scrambled	non-scrambled
I	65	61 (94%)	15 (71%)	6 (29%)
II	77	43 (56%)	50 (78%)	14 (22%)

Laura produces 70% full objects without a determiner during the first stage, as is shown in Table 6:

Table 6.
Proportion of determinerless objects during Stage I and II in Laura

stage	total full objects	determinerless nouns	pronouns	
			scrambled	non-scrambled
I	26	18 (69%)	3 (30%)	7 (70%)
II	7	1 (14%)	7 (88%)	1 (12%)

The second stage shows a considerable drop in determinerless nouns, but the proportion is still quite high for Niek (56%). In Laura's corpus, the proportion of determinerless nouns during Stage II is only 14%.

Developmentally, we observe an interesting pattern. While the percentage of determinerless NPs decreases (from 94% to 56% for Niek - Table 5; from 69% to 14% for Laura, Table 6), the percentage of scrambled pronouns increases (from 71% - 78% for Niek - Table 5; from 30% to 88% for Laura - Table 6). This pattern suggests that the acquisition of scrambling and nominal specificity are related.

Interestingly, the majority of the determinerless nouns occur unscrambled, as we can see in the Tables 1 - 4 (82% and 77% for Niek's Stages I and II; 100% and 100% for Laura's Stages I and II, respectively). A chi-square test performed on both scrambled and non-scrambled determinerless nouns and nouns preceded by a definite determiner indicates that this result is significant, at least for Niek Stage I and II and for Laura Stage I, as is illustrated in the Tables 7 - 10:

Table 7.
Connection between lack of object scrambling and determiner drop in Niek Stage I

	w/ definite determiner	w/o determiner	$x^2(1)$	p
scrambled	2	11	4.18	.04
non-scrambled	1	50		

Table 8.
Connection between lack of object scrambling and determiner drop in Niek in Stage II

	w/ definite determiner	w/o determiner	$x^2(1)$	p
scrambled	11	10	6.19	.01
non-scrambled	9	33		

Table 9.
Connection between lack of object scrambling and determiner drop in Laura - Stage I

	w/ definite determiner	w/o determiner	$x^2(1)$	p
scrambled	1	0	6.30	.01
non-scrambled	2	18		

Table 10.
Connection between lack of object scrambling and determiner drop in Laura - Stage II

	w/ definite determiner	w/o determiner	$x^2(1)$	p
scrambled	2	0	1.33	.25
non-scrambled	1	1		

The Tables 7-9 show that the proposed connection between the absence of determiners and the absence of scrambling is real. Unfortunately, the relevant data in Laura's Stage II are too scarce, which explains the high p-value and the low chi-square value. However, the absolute numbers point into the right direction: the one determinerless noun has not scrambled, and two out of the three nouns preceded by a definite determiner have scrambled.

The result that the majority of determinerless object nouns do not scramble is not surprising, since if there is no determiner, specificity cannot be established, which means that no variable is introduced and thus there is nothing to force scrambling. Again, this result supports the hypothesis that the acquisition of scrambling and specificity are related. Notice, however, that both Niek and Laura leave definite DPs unscrambled, too (cf. Tables 3 and 4). We assume that in these cases, D is also underspecified with respect to specificity, and that the overt definite determiner is expletive (cf. Longobardi, 1994). We propose that the relationship between the acquisition of scrambling and specificity is mono-directional: the absence of a determiner implies absence of specificity, and therefore of scrambling. On the other hand, the presence of a determiner does not necessarily imply the presence of specificity (since it can still be underspecified), and therefore scrambling of definites does not always take place.

Concluding, both predictions formulated in (3) are borne out supporting the hypothesis that at this stage of development the functional head D can be underspecified with respect to specificity.

To sum up, an underspecified D gives rise to two effects: first, no variable is introduced and hence there is no necessity for objects to scramble. Since there is no necessity to scramble, considerations of Economy (Chomsky, 1991) or Procrastinate (Chomsky, 1993) dictate that it will not. Second, we find an absence of determiners.

Of course, the question arises as to how DPs with an underspecified D are semantically interpreted in the early grammar. If D is not specified for specificity then it is unclear how the DP is hooked up to the discourse. Underspecified DPs must be interpreted somehow, since they clearly have a meaning in the child's language. Let us first consider the determinerless nouns.

On the basis of the context, we established that some of the determinerless nouns must be interpreted as familiar, others as novel. Unfortunately, there is also a residual group of nouns without a determiner for which it is very difficult to establish (on the basis of the context) whether they are interpreted as familiar or as novel objects by the child. The numbers are given in the Tables 11 and 12:

Table 11.
Numbers and Percentages of interpretation of determinerless nouns in Niek

stage	familiar	novel	?
I	22 (44%)	13 (26%)	15 (30%)
II	13 (39%)	8 (24%)	12 (36%)

Table 12.
Numbers and Percentages of interpretation of determinerless nouns in Laura

stage	familiar	novel	?
I	8 (44%)	6 (33%)	9 (22%)
II	1 (100%)	0 (0%)	0 (0%)

We propose that the determinerless nouns with a novel interpretation have a NumP structure, similar to non-specific indefinite nominals, mass nouns and bare plurals in adult language, and that determinerless nouns with a familiar interpretation have a DP structure, as definite nominals in adult language.[5] Thus, novel determinerless nouns arrive at this novel interpretation in the same way as adults do with non-specific indefinites, mass nouns or bare plurals. There is no D position, as was shown in (4b), so no specificity feature, and therefore the nominal is non-specific, or novel. However, it is not immediately clear how determinerless nouns with a DP structure arrive at their familiar interpretation. Recall that D is underspecified with respect to specificity in these cases, which is never the case in adult language. Thus, the child cannot arrive at a familiar interpretation in the same way as the adult does.

I would like to propose an analysis of semantic interpretation partly based on Hyams (1996), who mainly deals with the interpretation of Optional (or 'Root') Infinitives, another instance of underspecification. Suppose DPs have a D(et) Operator, located in Spec, DP, as shown in (26):

(26)
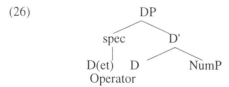

The function of the D(et) Operator is to hook up D to the discourse. In other words, the D(et) Operator provides D with an interpretation. Analogous to Guéron & Hoekstra's (1994) Binding ideas regarding a Tense Operator (which links the clause to the *here and now* by default, creating a 'T-chain'), Hyams proposes that the default value of the D(et) Operator consists of the contextually salient and presupposed (or familiar) NPs, that is, the discourse domain. Furthermore, again along the lines of Guéron & Hoekstra's theory regarding Tense, we could say that if the head of DP, D, bears the same index as the D(et) Operator, the DP is interpreted as specific. In other words, if D and the D(et) Operator are co-indexed, they pick out a familiar NP. This is illustrated in (27):

(27) $(D(et)Op_i) [D_i]$ the book ->   familiar

Returning now to the question how determinerless nouns with an underspecified D arrive at a familiar interpretation in child language, Hyams proposes that when D is underspecified, it is without an index. In this case, it receives a *familiar* interpretation by co-reference, rather than by syntactic binding. This implies that D and the D(et) Operator can accidentally refer to the same entity in the world, without being co-indexed. In this sense, children's bare nouns are the nominal analogue of root infinitives. As Hyams (1996) argues, children's root infinitives (as described in (1)) have an unindexed T, and therefore no T-chain is formed. The interpretation of root infinitives can be established by co-reference of T and the T(ense) Operator, rather than by syntactic binding of T by the T(ense) Operator.

Notice that bare nouns whose interpretation is familiar in child language, arrive at this interpretation through co-reference, and not through the adult syntactic binding. Like all other bare nouns, these familiar bare nouns do not have a D, and therefore no specificity feature. Consequently, even though they receive a familiar interpretation, they do not scramble. This is analogous to children's root infinitives in the sense that root infinitives are often interpreted as finite, present tense constructions (again, through co-reference), but, despite that interpretation, do not undergo V2.

The question now is why the co-reference option is blocked in the adult grammar. Hyams suggests that there is a parallel with binding phenomena of NPs. In the adult language, co-reference between two NPs is ruled out just in case the resulting interpretation would be indistinguishable from bound anaphora. This is the essence of a pragmatic principle first formulated by Reinhart (1983), called Rule I. Translating this to the interpretation of DPs, this pragmatic principle excludes co-reference between D and the D(et) Operator in adult language, since it would yield an interpretation which is indistinguishable from the bound variable interpretation. (The bound variable interpretation being syntactic binding of the specificity feature in D by the D(et) Operator).

Grodzinsky & Reinhart (1993) have claimed, and Chien & Wexler (1991) under a slightly different formulation, that children have not yet acquired this pragmatic principle. Therefore, children have two ways to arrive at a familiar interpretation of a DP: first, they can co-index D and the D(et) Operator (if D contains a specificity feature, as in adult language); second, they can let D and the D(et) Operator co-refer to the same entity in the discourse, which is a familiar object, since the value of the D(et) Operator picks out familiar entities by default. The former is an instance of syntactic binding, the latter a case of co-reference. In the case of determinerless DPs with a D, that is, DPs underspecified for specificity, there is no specificity feature, and thus co-indexation is not possible. Thus, in these cases children rely on the co-reference mechanism to interpret the determinerless DPs as familiar.

In summary: there are two possible interpretations of determinerless nouns in Dutch child language: either they are NumPs, and receive a novel interpretation in an adult-like way, or they are DPs, in which case they are interpreted as *familiar* by virtue of co-reference between D and the D(et) Operator. This is stated in (28):

(28)   *Determinerless nouns* in Dutch child language are:
         (i)   NumPs -> novel interpretation in adult-like way
         (ii)   DPs -> familiar interpretation by virtue of co-reference (not available in adult language)

What about pronouns? We have assumed that pronouns which do not scramble are underspecified for specificity, i.e., they have no specificity feature in D. However, it is clear from the contexts in which the children's pronouns occur, that they should all be interpreted as *familiar*, whether they have scrambled or not. This is not surprising given the idea that they move from N to D (cf. Longobardi, 1994). In other words, pronouns are DPs. As we have just seen, DPs which are underspecified for specificity can receive a *familiar* interpretation through co-reference in child language. It follows that the scrambled pronouns, whose D is specific, receive a familiar interpretation in the adult way, that is, by syntactic co-indexation between D and the D(et) Operator. On the other hand, unscrambled pronouns, whose D is underspecified with respect to specificity, are interpreted as familiar by virtue of *co-reference*. This is stated in (29):

(29)   *scrambled pronouns*
D is specific -> familiar interpretation by virtue of co-indexation (adult-like)
non-scrambled pronouns
D is underspecified w.r.t. specificity -> familiar interpretation by virtue of co-reference (not available in adult language)

6. CONCLUSION

In this paper we have shown that the underspecification of the functional head D with respect to specificity can account for a) the fact that object nominals do not always scramble in obligatory contexts and b) for the fact that many nouns occur without a determiner in Dutch child language.

As for the interpretation of underspecified DPs, we elaborated on Hyams' (1996) idea that the child has access to a co-reference mechanism which allows the child to interpret underspecified determinerless DPs and pronouns as familiar. The novel interpretation of the other determinerless nouns was accounted for by the assumption that they are NumPs, rather than DPs.

The analysis just sketched supports the parallelism between the verbal and the nominal system in the sense that optional infinitives, determinerless nominals, and optionality of scrambling can be handled in a unified way, namely as the effects of underspecified functional heads.

NOTES

[1] We are grateful to Jacqueline van Kampen for making Laura's data available to us.

[2] The stages were divided up on the basis of the child's behavior with respect to the position of the pronoun: as long as the majority (70%) of the pronouns remained unscrambled, the data were classified as 'Stage I'; 'Stage II' started at the point in development at which the majority of the pronouns were no longer unscrambled.

[3] We only counted determinerless nouns which would be ungrammatical in adult language. In other words, we excluded mass nouns without a determiner, bare plurals, etc.

[4] Notice that the examples in (17) only involve the neuter third person singular pronoun *het* 'it' and demonstrative pronouns. This might suggest that the failure of scrambling is restricted to these types of pronouns, and that other pronouns (such as first and second person personal pronouns) behave differently. Although this would be interesting to investigate further, Niek and Laura's utterances with an adverb/negation do not include enough first and second person pronominal objects to draw definitive conclusions from.

[5] Thanks to Teun Hoekstra who suggested this idea to us.

REFERENCES

Chomsky, N.: 1991, 'Some Notes on Economy of Derivation and Representation', In R. Freidin (ed.) *Principles and Parameters in Comparative Grammar*, MIT Press, Cambridge, 417-454.
Chomsky, N.: 1993, 'A Minimalist Program for Linguistic Theory' In K. Hale and S. J. Keyser (eds.) *The View from Building 20*, MIT Press, Cambridge, 1-52.
Chien Y-C. and K. Wexler: 1991, 'Children's Knowledge of Locality Conditions on Landing as Evidence for the Modularity of Syntax and Pragmatics', *Language Acquisition* 1, 225-295.
Clahsen, H.: 1988, 'Kritische Phasen der Grammatikentwicklung', *Zeitschrift für Sprachwissenschaft* 7, 3-31.
Clahsen, H.: 1991, 'Constraints on parameter setting. A grammatical analysis of some acquisition stages in German child language', *Language Acquisition* 1, 361-391.
Diesing, M.: 1992, *Indefinites*. MIT Press, Cambridge.
Grodzinsky, Y. and T. Reinhart: 1993, 'The Innateness of Binding and Reference', *Linguistic Inquiry* 24, 69-102.
Guéron, Jacqueline and T. Hoekstra: 1995, 'The temporal interpretation of predication." In A. Cardinaletti and M. T. Guasti (eds.) *Syntax and Semantics 28:Small Clauses*, Academic Press, New York.
Hamann, C. : 1993, 'On the acquisition of Negation in German', ms., Université de Genève.
Hamann, C.: 1996, 'Negation and truncated structures', in M. Aldridge (ed.) *Child Language*,
Heim, I.:1982, 'The Semantics of Definite and Indefinite Noun Phrases', Ph.D. Dissertation, University of Massachusetts, Amherst.
Hoekstra, T., and P. Jordens: 1994, 'From Adjunct to Head', In T. Hoekstra and B. D. Schwartz (eds.) 'Language acquisition studies in generative grammar, John Benjamins, Amsterdam, 119-149.
Hyams, N.: 1996, 'The Underspecification of Functional Categories in Early Grammar", In H. Clahsen (ed.) *Generative Perspectives on Language Acquisition*. John Benjamins, Amsterdam, 91-128.
Jordens, P.: 1990, 'The Acquisition of Verb Placement in Dutch and German', *Linguistics* 28, 1407-1448.
Koopman, H.: 1998, The internal and external distribution of pronominal DPs', in K. Johnson and I. Roberts (eds.) *Papers in Memory of Osvaldo Jaeggli*, Reidel, Dordrecht, 91-132.
Longobardi, G.: 1994, 'Reference and Proper Names: A Theory of N-Movement in Syntax and Logical Form', *Linguistic Inquiry* 25, 609-665.
MacWhinney, B. and C. Snow: 1985, 'The Child Language Data Exchange System', *Journal of Child Language* 12, 271-196.
Mahajan, A.: 1990, 'The A A' Distinction and Movement Theory', Ph.D. Dissertation, MIT.
Pierce, A.: 1989, 'On the emergence of syntax: A cross-linguistic study', Ph.D. Dissertation, MIT.
Reinhart, T.: 1983, *Anaphora and Semantic Interpretation*. Croom Helm, London 1983.
Weissenborn, J.: 1990, 'Functional Categories and Verb Movement: The Acquisition of German Syntax Reconsidered', in M. Rothweiler (ed.)., Spracherwerb und Grammatik. Linguistische Untersuchungen zum Erwerb von Syntax und Morphologie. *Linguistische Berichte, Special Issue* 3, 190-223.
Weverink, M.: 1989, ' The Subject in Relation to Inflection in Child Language', Master's thesis, University of Utrecht.
Wexler, K.: 1994, 'Optional Infinitives, Head Movement and the Economy of Derivation in Child Grammar', In D. Lightfoot and N. Hornstein (eds.) *Verb Movement*, Cambridge University Press, Cambridge.
Zwart, J-W.: 1994, 'Word Order, Intonation and Noun Phrase Interpretation in Dutch', Paper presented at WECOL XXIV, UCLA, Los Angeles.

JEANETTE SCHAEFFER
Ben Gurion University of the Negev

SUSAN M. POWERS

SCRAMBLING IN THE ACQUISITION OF ENGLISH?

1. INTRODUCTION

Word order errors in child English have two things in common with the phenomenon of scrambling. First, the same explanations which have been offered for scrambling namely, clause–internal movement and base-generation, have been offered for word order errors. Second, just as little else in the scrambling literature besides the rough definition of scrambling as the permutation of two elements which are clause-mates is conceded (see Haider, this volume), the only recognized fact is that children acquiring English sometimes produce word order errors. It is not certain when these errors emerge, what their overall frequency is or if one type of word order error is more frequent than another. Consider the representative samples in Table 1.

Table 1.
Sources of child English early word order data

Child	Age (months)	Source
Gia	19	Bloom 1970
Kendall	22	Bowerman 1973
Susan	22	Miller & Ervin 1964
Adam	27	Brown 1973

Of all these samples, the only word order errors are those listed in Table 2.

Table 2.
Some Word Order Errors in Child English

Order	Utterance	Child	Age (months)
OV	balloon throw	Gia	19
OV	doggie sew	Kendall	22
OV	Kimmy kick	Kendall	22
OV	Kendall pick-up	Kendall	22
OV	book read	Susan	22
OV	paper write	Adam	27
OV	paper find	Adam	27
VS	hug Mommy	Kendall	22
VS	see Kendall	Kendall	22
OVS	Mommy hit Kendall	Kendall	22

It is virtually impossible to compare across these samples because the Character of Data (to borrow a term from Brown, 1973) varies from sample to sample. For example, the data of Kendall (Bowerman, 1973) constitute two full days of the child's productions which were transcribed at the scene, while the data from Adam (Brown, 1973) was taped over a period of several months. The varying character of these samples makes quantitative analysis impossible. Both types of data however provide important information about the development of word order. Only diary data can tell us about the emergence of each type of word-order error, while data which constitutes a day's worth of productions can tell us the frequency of a certain production on any given day. These data are especially useful when data from more than one point in time have been collected.

This paper focuses on the earliest word order errors produced by children acquiring English. First, diary data are examined in order to chart the emergence of both correct and incorrect word orders. Then data that constitute a day's worth of productions (hereafter, Day-Data) are used for a frequency analysis of early word order errors. After establishing the emergence and frequency of word order errors, an analysis in terms of both base-generation and movement is given. This is followed by an examination of supporting data. In the final part of the paper, this analysis is extended to word order errors in spontaneous child English.

2. EARLY WORD ORDER

2.1. Emergence of Word Orders - Diary Data

All of the child utterances considered here contain a verb and at least one other thematic argument (e.g., an object, or a subject). Utterances without verbs have not been analyzed. The motivation behind this exclusion comes from the lack of word order errors in other word combinations in child English. For example, word order errors in nominals as in (1) below are not attested (Bloom, 1990; Brown, 1973; Miller & Ervin, 1964).

(1)   *book my   (cf. my book)
           *a that cup   (cf. that a cup)

In order to ascertain the significance of word order errors for syntactic development in general, it is crucial to determine the overall acquisition sequence for both target-consistent word orders as well. Such fine-grained detail can only be found in diary data in which the parent carefully charts the emergence of specific types of utterances. Table 3 gives the word order patterns for two children acquiring American English (as recorded by Bowerman, 1990).

Table 3.
Emergence of Word Orders (Bowerman Diary Notes)

	Eva	Christy
SV	16;4	17;1
VO	16;4	17;2
VS	18;3	17;3
OV	19;2	18;4
SVO	19;1	21;1

For both children, the orders SV and VO emerge before the order VS. Moreover, all three of these orders emerge before OV. The probability of exactly this emergence for two children is extremely low (p = .0002767).[1] An important observation, first made by Bowerman (1990), is that all two-constituent orders emerge before any three-constituent orders. We will return to the relevance of this observation in Section 4.1.2 below.

2.2 Frequency of Word Orders - Day Data

According to Brown (1973:156), out of thousands and thousands of well-ordered utterances "the violations of normal order are triflingly few". His claim is based on spontaneous data samples from seventeen children learning American English but since the numbers of both correct and incorrect orders which the children produced are not provided, the exact rate of word order errors cannot be reliably determined.[2] Diary data are inappropriate for frequency counts as these data chart the emergence of tokens, not the frequency of particular types of utterances. In an experimental study of seven American children's earliest productions, Ramer (1976) found that the highest rate of word order error among her subjects was 3.8% out of the total syntactic output.[3] In Table 2 above, OV appears to be the most common word order error as all children produce at least one instance of OV. In order to determine if this is a fact or just an artifact, the Day-Data from Kendall (Bowerman, 1973) have been analyzed. These Day-Data are particularly good because there are data from two different points in development. Her MLU is 1.10 at Time I, and 1.10 at Time II, her MLU = 1.48. Table 4a lists all of Kendall's word combinations that contain a verb and a subject or an object at Time I. All these combinations are only two constituents long. That is, there are no subject, verb, and object combinations.

Table 4a
All Kendall's Utterances with a Verb at Time I

Order: S V   V O
        Kendall sit   find Mommy (n=3)
        Kendall read   close... door
        Kendall walk   close ... bathroom
        Kendall bounce   taste cereal (n=2)
        Daddy sit
        Daddy hide
        Daddy walk
        Daddy write (n=2)
        Mommy read
        Mommy tie-it
        Kimmy read
        Kimmy bite
        horse walk
        horse run
        spider move (n= 6)
        Melissa walk
        Bill talk

Order: V S   O V
                               hand clean (n=3)

2.2.1. Excluded Utterances

Similar to the above analysis of Bowerman's diary data, only Kendall's utterances containing a verb and another thematic constituent (e.g., a subject or an object) were considered. That is, utterances containing null verbs (2a) or other null constituents like prepositions (2b) were excluded.

(2)   a. Kendall shower   (= Kendall takes a shower)
        b. sit lap   (= sit on lap)

While the interpretation of these utterances is clear from the context notes, these utterances were not included in the analysis.

Table 4b below lists all of Kendall's word combinations containing a verb and subject or object (or both) at Time II.

Table 4b.
All Kendall's Utterances with a Verb at Time II

Order:	S V	V O	S V O
	Kendall bark	read ... book	Mommy pick up... Kendall
	Kendall swim	writing book	Mommy sew doggy
	Kendall bite	bite...finger	Kimmy ride bike
	Kendall break	break Fur-Book	Kimmy eat hand
	Kendall turn	open...lotion	Kendall turn page
	Kendall fix-it (n=2)		
	Kimmy spit		
	Kimmy come		
	Kimmy swim		
	Kimmy blow (n=2)		
	Kimmy bite		
	Kimmy running		
	Kimmy eat (n=2)		
	Mommy bounce		
	Mommy sleep		
	Mommy read		
	Mommy break it		
	Daddy pick up		
	Daddy break it		
	Melissa bounce		
	Melissa read		
	Phil running (n=2)		
	Pam running		
	Scott scream		
	cow moo (n=4)		
	doggie bark		
	pillow fell		
	thread break		
Order:	VS	OV	OVS
	hug Mommy	doggie sew (n=5)	Mommy hit Kendall
	see Kendall	Kimmy kick	
		Kendall pickup	

2.2.2. Distribution of Word Orders

The number of Kendall's utterances with a verb and a subject or an object (or both) is in Table 5 below.

Table 5.
Kendall's Correct and Incorrect Word-Orders

	SV	VO	SVO	VS	OV	OVS	Totals
Time I	24	7	0	0	3	0	34
Time II	31	5	5	2	7	1	51
Totals	55	12	5	2	10	1	85

Out of 85 utterances with verbs, 13 (15%) were incorrect word orders. The errors are distributed unevenly however. Out of 63 utterances which contain a subject and a verb, there were 5% (n=3) errors while out of 22 utterances with object and verb 50% (n=11) were errors. This confirms the pattern reflected by Table 2 namely, OV is a more frequent error than VS. In addition, similar to the diary data of Bowerman, Kendall produces more word order errors at Time II. The difference in the number of errors at Time I and Time II is significant.

2.3. Summary of Early Word Orders

The discussion above revealed the following facts about early word order:

1. two-constituent orders emerge before three-constituent orders
2. SV and VO emerge before VS and OV
3. VS emerges after SV and VO
4. OV emerges after SV and VO and VS
5. OV is more frequent than VS
6. There are significantly more errors later in development
7. OV and the first instance three-constituent order SVO emerge roughly at the same time

Any account of early word order must be able to provide an account of these facts of emergence and frequency. Before presenting such a theory, some of the previous syntactic accounts of word order errors in child English are considered. Interestingly, all of the accounts claim that deviant word order is base-generated as such. After pointing out the weaknesses in each of these accounts, I present a theory in which both base-generation and movement play a role in accounting for the word order facts listed above.

3. PREVIOUS ACCOUNTS OF DEVIANT WORD ORDERS

The main problem with the previous analyses of deviant word orders in child English is that none adequately accounts for the emergence of correct word orders as well. Moreover, almost all of the accounts focus on just one type of deviant order (OV or VS).

3.1. Base Generated Accounts

3.1.1. Base-generated Post-verbal Subjects

A base-generation account of VS is advocated by Tsimpli (1991). She claims that VS order is due to the possibility of the subject to adjoin to either side of the VP as in (3a-b) below.

According to Tsimpli, the attested variation in the position of the subject only occurs at the early stages because the child's phrase marker has no functional projections. When functional projections emerge, the phrase marker position of subjects will be fixed (see also Pierce, 1992).

3.1.2. Base-generated Post-verbal Topics

According to Gruber (1967), nouns appearing on either side of the verb in child English are topics co-generated with the rest of the clause as in (4).

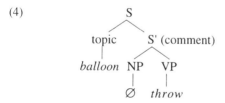

In his analysis of the OV utterance *balloon throw*, the noun *balloon* is co-generated as a topic, which proceeds the comment, and the subject position (marked by ∅) is empty.

3.1.3. Base-generated Pre-verbal Objects

Radford (1990) claims that dislocated NPs are base-generated as adjuncts to verbal small clauses. Following Hyams (1986), he hypothesizes that there is a null *pro* subject (denoted by the italicized *pro*).

(5) [$_{VP}$ [$_{NP}$ balloon][$_{VP}$ *pro* [$_V$ throw] **pro**]]

According to Radford, the second *pro* (in boldface) "designates an understood null resumptive pronominal complement of the verb *throw*, interpreted as co-referential with the dislocated NP *balloon*" (1990:80). That is, the object *balloon* appears to the left of the verb but it is co-indexed with **pro** on the right.

3.1.4. Base-generated Freely Ordered VP

According to Felix (1991), neither subjects nor objects are base-generated in a fixed order with respect to the verb. This means that there are four possible freely ordered VPs (in 6a-d).

(6)

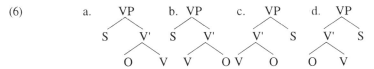

Allowing the VP to be freely ordered provides these four possible orders.[4] The only grammatical order in English is SVO (6b).

3.2. Problems with Base-generation Accounts

3.2.1. Lack of Generality

All of the above accounts have the problem that they are too specific in focus. For example, Tsimpli can account for VS but does not give an account of OV. Similarly, Radford focuses on OV and leaves VS errors aside. While these may be viable accounts of each type of error, they are inadequate accounts of word order in general. In addition, none of the accounts address the fact that OV emerges after VS or the fact that OV is a more frequent error than VS.

3.2.2. Prediction of Unattested Error: OSV

Both Radford and Gruber maintain that there is an unfilled structural subject position. If there is a subject position, then we predict the occasional use of both topic and overt subject as in (7) and the structures they propose (in 8).

(7)   *balloon, I throw

Especially since English-speaking children do not omit subjects 100% of the time at this stage (Valian, 1991), the complete lack overt subjects with topicalized objects is unexpected.

(8)

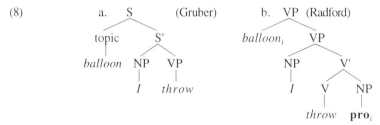

Utterances with overt subjects like (7) are unattested at this stage. Only the order OV is found, not OSV (Radford, 1990).

3.2.3. Prediction of Unattested Error: VOS

In Tsimpli's account, the subject can either left- or right-adjoin to the VP (like in 3a & 3b). This falsely predicts that the unattested order VOS will emerge at the same time as SVO. According to Bowerman's diary data, VOS emerges only after SVO and SOV.

3.2.4. Prediction of Unattested Error: SOV

Felix posits a freely ordered VP because he claims that "It thus appears that at this early developmental stage the position of subjects and objects relative to the verb is not fixed, but variable" (1991:35). If the position of subjects and objects were in fact variable (with respect to the verb), more variation than is attested should occur. That is, Felix predicts the order OSV (like Gruber and Radford), VOS (like Tsimpli) and the order SOV as well. Not one of these orders is attested at the earliest stage.

3.2.5. False Prediction: No Cross-linguistic Variation

According to Tsimpli and Felix, word order is variable until a later point in development when functional projections emerge. This means that perhaps all child languages will reflect the same variability at the initial state. That is, the earliest productions of children learning languages in which the order is VO (e.g., English) should be similar to the earliest data from children learning languages in which the target order is OV (e.g., German). This similarity across child languages is not attested. In his study of three German children at the two to three word stage, Park (1971) found that the object occurs before the verb in 80% of their utterances (see Roeper, 1973 for similar findings).[5]

3.2.6. Frequency

As noted above, neither Tsimpli's nor Felix's account is compatible with the acquisition sequence. Tsimpli falsely predicts the simultaneous emergence of SVO and VOS while Felix predicts that SVO, SOV, VOS, and OVS will all appear at the earliest stage. An additional problem for Felix comes from the frequency facts. If the word order variation attested in child English is due to an intrinsically unordered VP, then all word orders are equally likely to occur. That is, there is no reason for VO to be more frequent than OV or for OV to be more frequent than VS. Recall that out of all of Kendall's two-word utterances with verbs, the error types OV and VS, occur significantly less often than the orders SV and VO.

4. EARLY WORD ORDER - A MIXED ACCOUNT

None of the accounts above claim that word order errors are due to movement though each of these accounts is compatible with the hypothesis that children's grammars initially lack A-movement altogether (Felix, 1991; deVilliers, Roeper, & Vainikka, 1990). In contrast to the above accounts, I analyze the word order OV as an instance of A-movement. Assuming that OV is a result of A-movement, but adopting the hypothesis that child grammars initially lack A-movement, predicts that OV will not be one of the earliest word orders. The data further support this analysis. Recall that OV emerges **after** SV, VO, and VS. My claim is that the initial lack of the word order OV is due to the initial lack of A-movement.

4.1. Early Word Orders - Stage 1

4.1.1. The No Functional Projections Hypothesis

Before providing an explanation of the word order patterns described above, it is necessary to sketch out in detail my theoretical assumptions of child syntax. I assume that as soon as the child uses two-word combinations, there is a syntactic representation (or phrase marker). Moreover, I adopt the hypothesis that child clauses differ from adult clauses in that the child's phrase marker lacks functional projections altogether (Guilfoyle & Noonan, 1988; Lebeaux, 1988; Radford, 1986, 1990; and many others). Under the No Functional Projections Hypothesis (hereafter, the NFP Hypothesis), the children's earliest word combinations with verbs are VPs.

4.1.2. Two-constituent Orders

One of the most interesting facts is that the earliest word orders are only two constituents long. Recall my claim that the lack of certain word orders (e.g., OSV) argues against the base-generation accounts of word order errors. Since the earliest word combinations (both grammatical and ungrammatical) are only two constituents in length (Bowerman, 1990), the initial lack of word order errors comprised of subject, object and verb is most likely due to the lack of three-argument combinations in general. The lack of three constituent combinations is not predicted by any of the above analyses under which the child's phrase marker is at least a VP (or in Gruber's analysis, an entire sentence). If the child's phrase marker were a VP, then both subject and object position could be overtly occupied. The fact that three-constituent utterances emerge later suggests that a VP is not an accurate syntactic description of the earliest word combinations.

4.1.3. The Base-generation of Simple Binary Trees

According to LaPorte-Grimes & Lebeaux (1993), the child's initial phrase marker is a simple binary branching structure. While they do not discuss how such a structure is generated (but see Powers, in press), the initial VO and SV orders could be accommodated by a simple binary tree as in (9).

(9)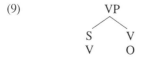

Recall that no three-word combinations are initially attested. If the phrase marker were a regular adult VP, the (at least sporadic) appearance of three-constituent utterances is expected. The phrase marker in (9) can accurately capture the lack of such structures. As there are only two phrase structure positions provided by the syntax, only two-word combinations should be attested.

The next word order to emerge after SV and VO is VS as in (10) below.

(10)   a. break pumpkin   Mackie (Gruber, 1967)
         b. go truck   Mackie (Gruber, 1967)

According to Pierce (1992), 90% of post-verbal subjects in child English occur with unaccusatives.[6] In a traditional analysis of unaccusatives (Burzio, 1986; Perlmutter, 1978) the subject of the unaccusative predicate is base-generated post-verbally. The appearance of VS orders with unaccusatives is not surprising if this is the base-structure.[7] Consider also the data in (11).

(11)   a. bye-bye Calico   Andrew (Braine, 1976)
         b. Calico bye-bye   Andrew (Braine, 1976)

According to Lebeaux (1988), *bye-bye* functions as an unaccusative predicate for the child roughly equivalent in meaning to *disappear*.[8] The orders in (11) show that the subject occupies either its post-verbal base-generated position (11a) or its pre-verbal surface position (11b). In child English, VS with unaccusatives is attested before SV with unaccusatives (Powers, 1998).

This analysis can account for the following three facts about early word order:

1. two constituent orders emerge before three constituent orders
2. the target-consistent orders SV and VO emerge before any target-inconsistent orders
3. the target inconsistent order VS emerges after the target consistent orders SV and VO but before SV with unaccusative verbs

Fact 1 is explained by the limit on the early representation to a singular binary branching tree. The accounts that postulate that the child's phrase marker is a VP or bigger have to claim that there are phonetically null syntactic constituents like *pro* at this time. Those accounts also predict the sporadic overt appearance of these constituents, which are not attested at Stage 1. The hypothesis that the child's phrase marker is a singularly binary tree better accounts for the attested orders. Fact 2 is explained as SV and VO are the canonical word orders for English. The later emergence of VS (Fact 3) could be due to the fact that this is a non-canonical (but licit) base-order in English. The emergence of these combinations in this particular order is statistically significant. My hypothesis is that at Stage 1, there are only base-generated binary trees. There is no A-movement and in fact, no position in the phrase marker which could serve as a landing site. This is why the order SV with unaccusative verbs, which (by hypothesis) involves movement, is not attested at this stage.

4.2. Early Word Order - Stage 2

4.2.1. Emergence of OV and SVO

There is a conflicting pattern of emergence of the orders SVO and OV. In Christy's data (see Table 3 above), OV emerges three months before SVO, while in Eva's data, SVO emerges one week before the first OV is attested. Nonetheless, I claim that the same phrase marker, a doubly binary VP, is responsible for both OV and SVO. My hypothesis is that the order SVO is base-generated, while OV is a result of movement of the object from the post-verbal base-generated position to the pre-verbal position. The orders OV and SVO emerge later because each reflects a new development in the child's grammar. The most important fact about these two orders is that they both follow all the grammatical two-word combinations and precede any ungrammatical three-word combinations.

4.2.2. A Mixed Analysis of Stage 2

At Stage 2, the phrase marker of verbal utterances changes from the binary VP structure in (9) above to VP as in (12) below. Evidence for this phrase marker comes from the emergence of the first three-constituent order: SVO.

(12)

The reason why no three-constituent orders are observed at Stage 1 is due to the lack of a phrase marker position for three arguments. There is only the singularly binary branching structure in (9) above.

The order OV is the only order which is not base-generated. The VP in (12) accommodates this order also: OV results from movement of the object to the VP adjunct position as in (13) below.[9]

(13)

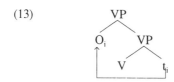

This analysis is consistent with proposals that there is a universal base-order of VO and that the order OV is derived through movement (Kayne, 1994; Zwart, 1993). My analysis is slightly different however, as the object adjoins to VP. This is also the base-generated position of the subject (Kayne, 1994; Manzini, 1989; Powers, 1994, 1996; Tsimpli, 1991). That is, either a subject is base-generated as a VP adjunct as in (12) or the object moves and adjoins to the VP as in (13).[10]

4.2.3. Three Predictions

Above I claimed that emergence of the VP-adjunct position is heralded by the order SVO. I also hypothesized that the contemporaneous availability of this position and A-movement is responsible for the ungrammatical order OV as well. If the VP-adjunct position hosts either a moved object or a base-generated subject then orders where both subject and object precede the verb (e.g., SOV) should not be attested at this time. This analysis also predicts that other instances of A-movement from the post-verbal position to the pre-verbal position will be attested and perhaps other instances of base-generated VP-adjuncts.

4.2.4. A-movement to VP Adjunct

The possibility of A-movement and the existence of a pre-verbal position to serve as a landing site predicts that the first pre-verbal subjects of unaccusative predicates will emerge at about the same time as OV. Even though Christy's first SVO does not appear until 21;1, her first pre-verbal unaccusative subject, in the utterance *bear come*, emerges at the same time as her first OV (at 18;4).

Table 6.
Christy's Unaccusative Subjects (data from Bowerman diary notes)

Order	Utterance	Age	Context
OV	horsie...ride	18;4	
OV	kiddie car ride	18;4	(not riding now)
VS	come bear	18;4	(taking beary with her)
SV	bear come	18;4	
SV	blanket come	18;4	(picking up blanket to leave house)

Recall that in the traditional analysis of unaccusatives the subject is base-generated post-verbally and moves to the pre-verbal position. Thus, the order SV with unaccusative predicates requires movement of the subject to the VP-adjunct position. At Stage 2, this movement (shown in (14) below) becomes possible and the first SV orders are attested.

(14)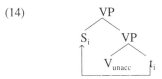

The emergence of the first unaccusatives at 18;4 supports the hypothesis that Christy's OVs result from a bigger phrase marker even though her first SVO is somewhat delayed.

4.2.5. Base-Generation of VP-adjuncts

More support for the hypothesis that Christy's phrase marker is a VP before her first SVO at 21;1 comes from Bowerman's diary data in (15) below.

(15) a. awa see-gum   Christy 19;2
      b. awa see car   Christy 19;2
      c. awa see.man   Christy 19;2
      d. awa write.leg   Christy 19;2

According to Bowerman, the child invented form *awa* is equivalent to 'I want'. These data are amenable to the analysis of Powers (1996), according to which *want* and lexical subjects are in complimentary distribution in child English because they occupy the same phrase structure position, the VP-adjunct position (see 16).

(16)

Similarly, *awa*, an amalgam of *want* and subject, could occupy the VP-adjunct position as in (17) below.

(17)

Thus even though Christy produces her first SVO much later than her first OV, her pre-verbal subjects of unaccusatives and utterances with *awa* support the hypothesis that there is at least a VP at this stage.[11]

4.2.6. Uniqueness of VP adjunct

Following Kayne (1994), I assume that multiple adjunction to a non-head is prohibited and that all specifiers are an instance of adjunction. In my analysis thus, there is only one VP-adjunct (or specifier) position. Either an object or unaccusative subject moves to this position, or the subject (of a transitive verb) is base-generated there. This means that the two orders where both subject and object precede the verb namely, SOV, and OSV, should not be attested. This prediction is borne out. The only three-constituent order attested at Stage 2 is SVO.

4.3. Summary of Early Word Order Errors

The first three early word order errors facts were accounted for in 4.1 above.

1. two constituent orders emerge before three constituent orders
2. SV and VO emerge before VS and OV
3. VS emerges after SV and VO
4. OV emerges after SV and VO and VS
5. OV and the first three constituent order SVO emerge about the same time
6. OV is more frequent than VS
7. There are significantly more errors later in development

Facts 4-7 are accounted for by the analysis just presented in which the joint development of the VP-adjunct position and A-movement is responsible for the two grammatical orders: SV (with unaccusatives) and SVO as well as the

ungrammatical order OV. That is, the Stage 2 word orders are explained by assuming that two syntactic developments occur:
1. The representation becomes a doubly binary branching VP
2. The operation of A-Movement enters the child's grammar

More specifically, Fact 4 is related to the change in the phrase marker. The order OV is due to A-movement and requires a bigger phrase marker than the other two constituent orders. The change in the phrase marker from single binary branching to doubly binary branching is also supported by Fact 5 namely, the concurrent emergence of SVO. Why should OV be more frequent than VS (Fact 6)? It may be because VS is only a licit as a base-order. The child first determines the base-order of the target language (see note 7).[12] Once movement is part of the child's grammar, it applies to base-structures so all VS base-structures will surface as SV. The order OV reflects A-movement from a post-verbal position to the VP-adjunct position. In this way, the word order errors which appear later in development reflect developments in the phrase marker.[13] This analysis accounts for the pattern of emergence of these word orders listed in Table 3 above.

5. SUPPORTING DATA

5.1. The No Functional Projections Hypothesis

According to the NFP Hypothesis, words which correspond to functional categories (e.g., inflections, determiners) are initially lacking from the child's output because the phrasal projections of these categories are missing in the child's syntax. While none of the earliest word combinations have case-marked pronominal subjects or objects (e.g., *me*, *I*), the pronouns *it*, *that*, and *this* do appear. If these pronouns are members of the category determiner (Abney, 1987), then the No Functional Projections Hypothesis and the analysis above must be abandoned. An alternative analysis of these pronouns as verbal clitics (which I argue for below) not only permits us to pursue the analysis developed above but in fact, further supports it.

5.2. The Distribution of Caseless Pronouns

Table 7 lists all utterances with a verb and the pronouns *it*, *that* and *this*.

Table 7.
Caseless Pronouns in Early Child English

Order	Utterance	Child/Age	Source
V*it*	tie-it (n=2)	Kendall I	Bowerman, 1973
	carry-it	Kendall I	Bowerman, 1973
V*it*+S	tie-it self	Kendall I	Bowerman, 1973
	carry it, Mommy	Kendall I	Bowerman, 1973
S+V*it*	Mommy tie-it	Kendall I	Bowerman, 1973
	Kendall fix-it (n=2)	Kendall II	Bowerman, 1973
	Daddy break-it	Kendall II	Bowerman, 1973
	Mommy break-it	Kendall II	Bowerman, 1973
V*it*+O	gimme...this...toy	Eric 21 months	Braine, 1976
	want this ...egg	David 21 months	Braine, 1976
	want this ...soap.	David 21 months	Braine, 1976
	want this ... music.	David 22 months	Braine, 1976
	want this ... light.	David 22 months	Braine, 1976
	gimme that ... blow	David 22 months	Braine, 1976
	fix it that.	David 22 months	Braine, 1976
	have it egg.	Johnathan 24 months	Braine, 1976
	have it milk.	Johnathan 24 months	Braine, 1976
	have it fork.	Johnathan 24 months	Braine, 1976
	leave-it heel	Kendall II	Bowerman, 1973
O+V*it*	horse... see it	Kendall 1	Bowerman, 1973
S+V*it*+O	Mommy fix-it ear	Kendall II	Bowerman, 1973

In the majority of these examples, the pronoun *it* occurs after the verb. The pronouns *that* and *this* also appear but to a lesser extent. Importantly there are no other pronouns at all (i.e., *I, me, you, he*). In the words of Radford "it would seem that it is not pronouns as such that children avoid, but rather pronouns overtly inflected for case" (1990:102). We could assume that these pronouns are uninflected caseless pronominal NPs, not DPs (Bloom, 1970; Guilfoyle & Noonan, 1988; Radford, 1990), however while *it* is similar to *this* and *that* (being a case-less pronominal), *it* differs from *this* and *that* in a number of important ways which favor an alternative analysis.

5.3. The Determiner Analysis

Some of the data in Table 7 are compatible with analyzing *it* as a determiner on a par with *this* and *that*, even though this use of *it* (i.e., *it book*) is ungrammatical in adult English (cf. *this/that book*).[14] The square brackets in (18-20) indicate the determiner analysis. The data from David, Eric, and Johnathan are from Braine (1976) and Kendall's data is from Bowerman (1973).

(18)	gimme [that ... blow]	David 22 months
(19)	a. gimme...[this...toy]	Eric 21 months
	b. want [this ...egg]	David 21 months
	c. want [this ...soap.]	David 21 months
	d. want [this ... music]	David 22 months
	e. want [this ... light]	David 22 months
(20)	a. fix [it that]	David 22 months
	b. have [it egg]	Johnathan 24 months
	c. have [it milk]	Johnathan 24 months
	d. have [it fork]	Johnathan 24 months
	e. leave [it heel]	Kendall II
	f. Mommy fix [it ear]	Kendall II

The first argument against this analysis comes from the pause denoted by ... in the examples with *this* and *that*. If these elements were determiners, no pause is expected to occur between the determiner and noun. No pause between *it* and the following NP is attested.

Radford (1990) similarly rejects the analysis of *it*, *this* and *that* as determiners in early child English because he claims it is only possible to classify an item as a determiner if we can demonstrate that it productively combines with nominal complements. While the data in (20) above are compatible with the hypothesis that *it* is a determiner, the rest of the combinations with *it* from Table 7 (listed below) argue against this analysis.

(21)	horse... see it	Kendall I (Bowerman, 1973)
	tie-it (n=2)	Kendall I (Bowerman, 1973)
	carry-it	Kendall I (Bowerman, 1973)
	tie-it self	Kendall I (Bowerman, 1973)
	carry it, Mommy	Kendall I (Bowerman, 1973)
	Mommy tie-it	Kendall I (Bowerman, 1973)
	Kendall fix-it (n=2)	Kendall II (Bowerman, 1973)
	Daddy break-it	Kendall II (Bowerman, 1973)
	Mommy break-it	Kendall II (Bowerman, 1973)
	Mommy fix-it ear	Kendall II (Bowerman, 1973)

According to the notes of Bowerman and Braine, *it* is clitic-like (as denoted by the - between the verb and *it*).

Another argument against analyzing *it* as a determiner comes from its distribution. The pronoun *it* appears in the following six syntactic environments:

1. verb it
2. subject verb it
3. verb it subject
4. verb it object
5. object verb it
6. subject verb it object

while the pronouns *this* and *that* uniformly appear in the single syntactic environment in (22).[15]

(22)   verb *this/that* object

This distributional difference is not expected if the child treats *it*, *this*, and *that* on a par.

5.4. The Clitic Analysis

According to the notes of Bowerman and Braine, *it* is a clitic, which always occurs with a verb. That is, *it* does not appear in isolation and does not seem to vary with other NP objects. Under the analysis of Keyser & Roeper (1992), the pronoun *it* is a base-generated verbal clitic which is co-indexed with the object NP as in (23) below.

(23)
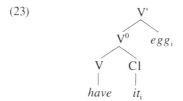

The advantage of this approach is that there is no need to postulate that the NP *egg* is right-adjoined. Recall that one of the problems with the base-generated account of VS was that the subject occurs pre-verbally significantly more often than post-verbally. The opposite pattern is attested with the pronoun *it* which always appears to the right of the verb. If *it* is a base-generated verbal clitic, then V*it* is the only possible order.

5.5. Simple Binary Trees

Another important feature of these V*it* constructions is that only one out of 24 occurs with both a subject and an object i.e., S+V*it*+O. Above I argued that the lack of any three-constituent structures at Stage 1 is due to the presence of a simplex binary tree. Similarly, if *it* is a verbal clitic rather than a syntactic constituent, then the earliest V*it* constructions can be accounted for with the simple binary structure in (24) below.

(24)
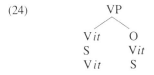
```
         VP
        /  \
      Vit   O
      S    Vit
      Vit   S
```

This phrase marker can account for the most frequent orders V*it*+O, V*it*+S, and S+V*it* combinations (almost all of which appear at Stage 2). These three orders occur much more often than O+V*it* and S+V*it*+O which each only occur a single time. Moreover, the single instance of O+V*it* attested at Stage 1 is dubious because there was a significant pause after the object (denoted by ...).

(25)   horse... see it   Kendall 1 (Bowerman 1976)

Consider also the single instance of both subject and object occurring with V*it*, namely, Kendall's *Mommy fix-it ear*. According to the *it*-as-clitic analysis presented above, this utterance is three constituents long and is thus predicted to occur only at Stage 2. This prediction is borne out as this single instance of S+V*it*+O appears at Kendall II.

5.6. Summary

The analysis above explains the following five facts about the V*it* constructions:

1. *it* always follows V
2. *it* occurs more often than other caseless pronominal (e.g., *that*, *this*)
3. mostly O or S plus V*it*
4. S+V*it* +O occur later
5. O+V*it* not attested

The first two facts are accounted for by the analysis of *it* as a base-generated verbal clitic. Facts 3-4 are accounted for by postulating that the initial syntactic representation is a binary branching tree. Moreover, there is no movement at this time. If we treat the O+V*it* constructions on a par with OV above, then the O+V*it* combinations require a bigger phrase marker and movement.

6. LATER WORD ORDER ERRORS

The later word order errors found at Stage 3, namely OSV, SOV, VSO, VOS, and OVS, seem to be related to the Stage 2 utterances with the pronoun *it*. In this section, these utterances are shown to play an important syntactic role initially occupying positions which will later serve as landing sites for moved arguments.

6.1. The Emergence of IP

Under the NFP hypothesis, the child's phrase marker is initially devoid of functional projections. Functional projections become part of the phrase marker later in development. Inasmuch as the NFP hypothesis explains the lack of words corresponding to functional categories by the lack of functional projections, it predicts an observable change in the child's productive repertoire when functional projections enter the child's phrase marker system. Following Guilfoyle & Noonan (1992), Radford (1990), Powers (1996), and Vainikka (1994), the child's use of nominative pronominal subjects, indicates one such change in the phrase marker namely that from VP to IP as in (26) below.

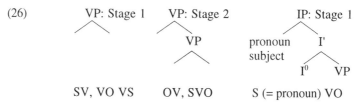

(26)   VP: Stage 1   VP: Stage 2   IP: Stage 1

SV, VO VS   OV, SVO   S (= pronoun) VO

Pronominal subjects appear only later when IP becomes part of the phrase marker.[16] The pronominal subject is assigned nominative Case by I^0. The VP Internal Subject Hypothesis of Koopman and Sportiche (1991) is compatible with the account presented here (as the subject is sister to VP not to an intermediate projection of V). The initially VP-internal subject moves to Spec, IP.

In the account presented above, in the absence of a base-generated VP subject, the object can move to the VP-adjunct position. Additionally, I will assume (following Powers, 1996) that when pronominal subjects emerge, they are base-generated directly in the specifier of IP as in (27) below.

(27)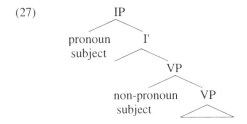

Non-pronominal subjects are base-generated in the VP-adjunct position. Only nominative pronominal subjects are initially base-generated in Spec, IP.[17]

6.2. Later Word Order Errors

In Bowerman's diary, later word order errors emerge in the order shown in Table 8 below.

Table 8.
Later Word Orders (from Bowerman Diary Notes)

	Eva	Christy
SOV	20;3-4	21;4
OSV	21;1-2	22;2
VSO	21;1-2	22;2
OVS	21;1-2	------
VOS	21;1-2	22;4

The order SOV emerges after SVO. All the other three-constituent orders OSV, VSO, OVS and VOS emerge at (or about) the same time. Both Christy and Eva produce SOV before the other ungrammatical three-constituent orders: OSV, VSO, and VOS.

Considering the emergence information we have from the diary data, we can now turn to spontaneous data to confirm these patterns. Powers (1996) defines three stages of pronominal subject use in Adam's and Eve's data (from Brown, 1973) as in Table 9.

Table 9.
Three Stages in IP Development (from Powers, 1996)

	Eve	Adam
IP: Stage 1	1;6-1;9	n/a
IP: Stage 2	1;10	2;3.4 -3;5
IP: Stage 3	2;2	3;5 and up

The word order error SOV emerges in both Adam and Eve between Stages 1 and 2 in the development of pronoun subjects.

6.3. SOV as Scrambling

As noted above, both Adam and Eve (Brown, 1973) produce SOV but only with pronominal subjects.

(28)   a. I sock put on   Eve 1;7
            b. I doughnut get you   Adam 2;6

As the subject of both utterances in (28) is the nominative pronoun *I*, which is by hypothesis, base-generated in Spec, IP (see (27) above) the object can occupy the VP-adjunct as in (29) below.

(29)
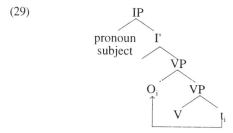

Since the subject is neither base-generated in, nor moved out of the VP-adjunct position, the object occupy this position yielding the order SOV. This analysis of SOV is identical to the analysis of the early word order error OV: the object occupies the VP-adjunct position.

According to Grewendorf and Sternefeld (1990), the following are properties of the phenomenon commonly referred to as scrambling:[18]

1. scrambling is clause bound
2. scrambling is adjunction to VP, IP or AP
3. scrambling is not allowed to cross over a pronominal subject

These are exactly the properties of the SOV constructions, as the object adjoins to VP not crossing the pronominal subject. Moreover, the object does not move out of the clause containing it. Because the subject is not base-generated in the VP-adjunct position but rather directly in Spec, IP at this stage, the object can occupy the VP-adjunct position.

Another possibility is that a caseless subject is base-generated in the VP-adjunct position. This predicts what Powers (1996) calls "double" subjects in (30). Adam's data come from Brown, 1973, Douglas' data from Huxley, (1970) and the example in (30e) from Thornton (personal communication).

(30) a. I Adam ride dat. (n=2)   Adam 2;3.18
      b. I Adam driving.   Adam 2;3.18
      c. I Adam don't <sit Adam foot> [?]   Adam 2;4.3
      d. I, Douglas picks up big cards on floor. Douglas 2;8
      e. I want Aurora swing   Aurora 1;6.26

These caseless proper name subjects which are base-generated in the VP-adjunct position are co-referent with the nominative subject in Spec, IP. A verb can also overtly occupy I^0 as example (30e) from Aurora demonstrates. These data support the hypothesis that there are two subject positions at this stage as the lower VP-adjunct position is filled with co-referential lexical material as in (31) below.

(31)

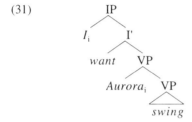

According to Powers (1996), the base-generated position of the subject is initially linked to its surface position via co-indexing, rather than by A-movement.[19] Similar to the double-subject cases, there are double objects in which the pronoun *it* co-refers to objects as in the examples from Brown, 1973 in (32) below.

(32) a. Papa, you fix it my fingernail?   Eve 2;2
      b. Mommy get it my ladder   Adam 2;3.4
      c. cowboy miss it my hat   Adam 2;7
      d. I miss it, truck   Adam 2;6.3
      e. I miss it cowboy boot   Adam 2;6.3
      f. I drop it cowboy boot (n=2)   Adam 2;6.17
      g. I drink it milk   Adam 2;7
      h. I found it another one   Adam 2;7
      i. I found it soakie   Adam 2;7
      j. I break it airplane   Adam 3.6

These data are also similar to the SOV constructions as most of the subjects are nominative pronouns. These data differ from the clitic use of *it* described above as co-referential DPs as well as NPs appear after *it*. Similar to the analysis in (31) above, these data can be analyzed as in (33).

(33)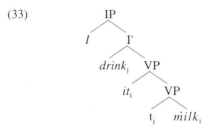

The pronoun *it* base-generated in the VP-adjunct position co-refers to the object *milk*, not to the subject *I*. The base-generation of nominative subjects in Spec, IP is crucial because if subjects moved from the VP-adjunct position to Spec, IP, a trace would occupy the VP-adjunct position. This would preclude movement of the object to this position as well as the base-generation of caseless DPs like *it* in this position.[20]

6.4. THE EMERGENCE OF CP

6.4.1. Pseudo Topics and it

Before real topics appear, both Adam and Eve produce utterances in which fronted topic DPs co-refer with the pronoun *it*. I will call these "pseudo-topics" as the pronoun *it* still appears in the base position.

(34)   a. Horse see it.   Adam 2;3.4 (Brown, 1973)
          b. Daddy's suitcase go get it.   Adam 2;3.4 (Brown, 1973)

In example 34b, the pronoun *it* refers to the topicalized object 'Daddy's suitcase' which is base-generated in Spec, IP and the VP-adjunct position is occupied by a null subject (denoted by *pro*) as shown in (35) below.

(35)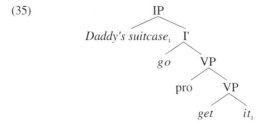

Similar to the initial linking of the two subject positions before real topics appear, the topicalized object is linked via co-indexing to the pronoun *it* which appears in the base-generated object position.

Later, even nominative pronominal subjects appear with pseudo-topics as shown in Eve's data (from Brown, 1973) in (36) below.

(36) a. oh # my sponge I can't find it.   Eve 1;10
      b. that a green one # I buy it.   Eve 2;1

Since a nominative subject occupies Spec, IP these topicalized NPs must be outside IP as in (37) below.

(37)

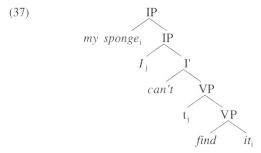

The pronoun *it* can no longer be base-generated in the VP-adjunct position because the two subject positions are now linked by movement (as in 37) therefore the trace of the moved subject occupies this position.

6.4.2. Real Topics

Once the topic position and the object position are linked by movement, the pronoun *it* disappears and the adult topics in (38) are attested.

(38) a. two I have.   Eve 2;3
      b. cotton balls I had (in) my hand.   Adam 2;11
      c. three times I missed.   Adam 3;3

As in (37) above, the nominative subject has moved out of the VP to occupy the specifier of IP. Now the object DP which was previously generated directly in the topic position (cf. (35) and (37) above) moves from the object position to the topic position adjoined to IP as in (39) below. The co-referential pronoun *it* is no longer attested.

(39)
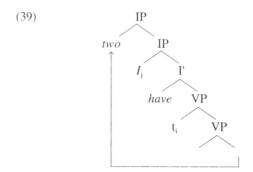

Following May (1985), Fanselow (1990) claims that quantified NPs may adjoin to both IP and VP. Notably, all the topics in (38) are quantified NPs.

7. ARE WORD ORDER ERRORS SCRAMBLING?

In this analysis of early word order, the object moves from its base-generated post-verbal position and adjoins to VP (and later to IP). This movement of the object is a pre-cursor to true topicalization which is similarly analyzed as adjunction to IP. The initial lack of IP altogether, in conjunction with the hypothesis of Powers (1996) that nominative subjects are base-generated in Spec, IP when IP emerges, elegantly accounts for the first three-constituent word order error SOV as well as a number of constructions in child English. Moreover, the pronoun *it* was shown to play an important role as a syntactic place holder.

When scrambling is simply defined as the clause internal reordering of constituents, child English has scrambling. Moreover, the attested child English word order errors obey restrictions on scrambling, e.g., never crossing pronominal subjects. I have extensively argued that all word order errors (except VS) are best analyzed as instances of NP-movement. According to Bayer & Kornfilt (1994) however, the problem with the NP-movement analysis of scrambling comes from the definition of scrambling of NP-movement to an adjoined position. If scrambling is a simple case of adjunction (to VP, IP, or AP), then the adjunct position created is an A-bar position and by definition, cannot host an argument as the landing site for an NP must be an A-position. One solution would be to claim that adjunction sites are both A and A-bar positions at the same time (see similar suggestions by Müller, Crysmann & Kaiser, 1994 for child German; and Vainikka, 1994 for child English). Another possibility would be to follow

Barbier (this volume) who suggests that object-shift is A-movement while scrambling is A-bar movement of the object into an adjoined position.

I avoided this problem by claiming that the VP-adjunct position is the base-generated position of the subject. The subject is not a typical adjunct but rather one that is theta-marked when present at D-structure.[21] This differs from other adjuncts e.g., the IP-adjunct/topic position which is a true A-bar position. This is a somewhat radical approach, however, I have supported the notion that the VP-adjunct position is an A-position by showing that NPs may move to this position and that other NPs (the caseless pronoun *it*) are base-generated there. Whether this treatment of the VP-adjunct position is viable for adult theories of scrambling is a question for future research.

ACKNOWLEDGEMENTS

I am grateful to Melissa Bowerman for giving me access to her diary data. Thanks also to the participants of the Workshop on L1 and L2 Acquisition of Clause Internal Rules, Theodore Marinis, and an anonymous reviewer, for useful comments. Special thanks to Chris Hoffmeister for assistance with the statistical analysis.

NOTES

[1] Significant at $p < .05$.
[2] The samples in Table 1 are only a subset of the samples Brown (1973) considered.
[3] Two other subjects had even lower rates of word order errors and one never produced any word order errors at all.
[4] As Ouhalla points out, "The remaining two logically possible orders, VSO and OSV, are excluded by the constraints imposed by X-bar on the structural representation of categories, e.g. the constraint on crossing branches (1990:18)."
[5] Schönenberger, Penner, & Weissenborn (1997) report that there are hardly any violations of object verb order in early Swiss German and High German.
[6] Although it is not clear where this number comes from as there is no mention of how many utterances with unaccusatives verbs there are in total or even how many utterances with post-verbal subjects were found in the samples she considered.
[7] The interesting and as yet unanswered question is how the child determines the base structure as the order VS will not be found in the input. This is especially interesting for the acquisition of English which lacks other unaccusativity diagnostics (e.g., auxiliary selection). See Powers (1998).
[8] This interpretation of *hi* and *bye-bye* come from the original context notes of Braine (1976) and Bloom (1970). See also Tomasello (1992) and Powers (1998).
[9] Weissenborn (personal communication) suggests that like the adult grammar, the object moves to AgrOP however unlike in the adult grammar, in the child grammar this movement happens at S-structure not at LF. According to his (1993) Syntactic Precedence Principle, when faced with a choice between covert (LF) movement and overt (S-Structure) syntactic movement, the child prefers the over (or S-Structure) movement. Under this hypothesis, we predict OSV and OVS neither of which are attested at this stage.

[10] If the subject were base-generated in [Spec, VP], then the object could not move into this position (cf. Johnson, 1991) such a restriction does not hold when the pre-verbal slot is an adjunct.

[11] In fact, the following two utterances with *awa*: would require the phrase marker to be even bigger than VP:

    i.   awa man... watch   Christy 19;2
    ii. awa Christy ...see   Christy 19;2

[12] This predicts that the word order of utterances from children learning OV languages like German or Dutch will also be target-consistent. Such target-consistent word order is attested from the outset of word combinations. Under the Universal Base Hypothesis, we would have to claim children learning these languages have a bigger phrase marker and syntactic movement at the initial state. An alternative to this is proposed by Schönenberger et al. (1997) who claim that the initial OV orders are lexical rather than syntactic.

[13] See Powers (1996) for a more explicit explanation of syntactic development along these lines.

[14] The analysis of *it* as a determiner in these combinations was suggested to me in three different personal communications with Hans Bennis, Luigi Burzio and Stephen Crain.

[15] Except for the single example

    i.   fix it that   David 22 months (Braine, 1976)

[16] Powers (1996) claims that DP emerges as well.

[17] Note that only nominative pronominal subjects appear at Stage 1. Non-nominative pronominal subjects appear at IP Stage 2. See Powers (1996) for a review.

[18] This term originally comes from Ross (1967).

[19] This was suggested by Lebeaux (1987) for apparent Condition C violations in acquisition.

[20] This account also explains the single instance of a subject co-referential with *it*:

    i.   tape recorder it go round round   Eve 1;9 (Brown, 1973)

[21] See Lebeaux (1987), Speas (1990), and Powers (1996) for more on theta-marked adjuncts present at d-structure.

REFERENCES

Abney, S.: 1987, 'The Noun Phrase in its Sentential Aspect', Ph.D. Dissertation, MIT.
Bayer, J and J. Kornfilt: 1994, 'Against Scrambling as an Instance of Move-alpha', In N. Corver & H. van Riemsdijk (eds.) *Studies on Scrambling. Movement and Non-Movement Approaches to Free Word-Order Phenomena.* Mouton de Gruyter, Berlin, 17-60.
Bloom, L.: 1970, *Language Development: Form and function in emerging grammars*, MIT Press, Cambridge.
Bloom, P. :1990, 'Syntactic distinctions in child language', *Journal of Child Language* 17, 343-355.
Bowerman, M.: 1973, *Early Syntactic Development: A Crosslinguistic Study with Special Reference to Finnish.* London: Cambridge University Press.
Bowerman, M.: 1990, 'Mapping Thematic Roles Onto Syntactic Functions: Are Children Helped By Innate Linking Rules?' *Linguistics* 28(6), 1253-1289.
Braine, M.: 1976, 'Children's first word combinations'. *Monographs of the Society for Research in Child Development* 41, 1-97.
Brown, R.: 1973, *A First Language: The Early Stages*, Harvard University Press, Cambridge.
Burzio, L.: 1986, *Italian Syntax*, Reidel, Dordrecht.
de Villiers, J., T. Roeper and A. Vainikka: 1990, 'The Acquisition of Long-distance Rules', In L. Frazier & J. deVilliers (eds.) *Language Processing and Language Acquisition*, Kluwer Academic Publishers, Dordrecht, 257-297.
Fanselow, G.: 1990, 'Scrambling as NP-Movement'. In G. Grewendorf & W. Sternefeld (eds.) *Scrambling and Barriers*, John Benjamins, Amsterdam, 113-140.

Grewendorf, G. and W. Sternefeld: 1990, 'Scrambling Theories', In G. Grewendorf & W. Sternefeld (eds.) *Scrambling and Barriers*, John Benjamins, Amsterdam, 3-37.
Gruber, J. S.: 1967, 'Topicalization in child language'. *Foundations of Language* **3**: 37-65.
Guilfoyle, E. and M. Noonan: 1988, 'Functional Categories and Language Acquisition'. Paper presented at *The Boston University Conference on Language Development*, Boston, Mass.
Guilfoyle, E., and M. Noonan: 1992, 'Functional Categories and Language Acquisition'. *Canadian Journal of Linguistics* **37**, 241-272.
Huxley, R.: 1970, 'The development of the correct use of subject personal pronouns in two children', In G. Flores d'Arcais, & W. Levelt (eds.) *Advances in psycholinguistics*. Elsevier - N. Holland, Amsterdam.
Hyams, N. : 1986, *Language acquisition and the theory of parameters*, Reidel, Dordrecht.
Johnson, K.: 1991, 'Object Positions', *Natural Language and Linguistic Theory* **9**, 577-636.
Kayne, R.: 1994, *The Antisymmetry of Syntax*. Cambridge, Mass: MIT Press.
Keyser, S. J. and T. Roeper: 1992, 'Re: The Abstract Clitic Hypothesis', *Linguistic Inquiry* **23**, 89-125.
Koopman, H. and D. Sportiche: 1991, 'The Position of Subjects', *Lingua* **85**, 211-258.
Kornfilt, J.: 1994, 'Some Remarks on the Interaction of Case and Word Order in Turkish: Implications for Acquisition', In B. Lust, M. Suñer & J. Whitman (eds.) *Syntactic Theory and First Language Acquisition: Crosslinguistic Perspectives*. Volume 1: Heads Projection and Learnability, Lawrence Erlbaum, Hillsdale. 171-199.
LaPorte-Grimes, L., and Lebeaux D.: 1993, 'Complexity as a Tool in Child Language'. Paper presented at *Signal to Syntax*, Brown University, March.
Lebeaux, D.: 1987, 'Comments on Hyams', In T. Roeper & E. Williams (eds.) *Parameter Setting*. Reidel, Dordrecht.
Lebeaux, D.: 1988, 'Language Acquisition and the Form of the Grammar'. Ph.D. Dissertation, University of Massachusetts Amherst.
Manzini, M. R.: 1989, 'Categories and Acquisition in the Parameters Perspective', *UCL Working Papers in Linguistics* **1**, 181-191.
MacWhinney, B. and C. Snow: 1990, 'The Child Language Data Exchange System: An Update', *Journal of Child Language* **17**, 457-472.
May, R.: 1985, *Logical Form*, MIT Press, Cambridge.
Miller, W. and Ervin-Tripp, S.: 1964, 'The Development of Grammar in Child Language'. *The acquisition of language* **29** (1).
Müller, N., Crysmann, B. and G. Kaiser: 1994, 'Interactions between the Acquisition of French Object Drop and the Development of the C-System', Paper presented at the *Workshop on the L1 and L2 acquisition of Clause Internal Rules: Scrambling and Cliticization*, Berne, Switzerland. January.
Ouhalla, J.: 1990, 'Functional Categories, Agrammatism and Language Acquisition', *Linguistiche Berichte* **5**: 1-35.
Otsu, Y.: 1994, 'Early Acquisition of Scrambling in Japanese', In T. Hoekstra & B. Schwartz (eds.) Language Acquisition Studies in Generative Grammar, John Benjamins, 253-264.
Perlmutter, D.: 1978, 'Impersonal Passives and the Unaccusative Hypothesis', *Berkeley Linguistics Society* **IV**, 157-189.
Pierce, A. E.: 1992, *Language Acquisition and Syntactic Theory : A Comparative Analysis of French and English Child Grammars*, Kluwer Academic Publishers, Dordrecht.
Powers, S.M.: 1994, 'The Acquisition of Pronoun Subjects: Implications for the Phrase Marker'. Master's Thesis, University of Maryland.
Powers, S.M.: 1996, 'The Growth of the Phrase Marker: Evidence from Subjects', Ph.D. Dissertation, University of Maryland.
Powers, S.M.: 1998, 'Early Unaccusatives', Invited paper presented at *The Workshop on Unaccusativity*, Zentrum für Allgemeine Sprachwissenschaft Berlin, Germany. May.
Powers, S.M.: in press, 'A Minimalist Account of Phrase Structure Acquisition', In G. Alexandrovia & O. Arnaudova (eds.) *The Minimalist Parameter, Current Issues in Linguistic Theory*, John Benjamins, Amsterdam.

Radford, A.: 1986, 'Small Children's Small Clauses', *Transactions of the Philological Society* **86**, 1-46.
Radford, A.: 1990, *Syntactic theory and the acquisition of English syntax: The nature of early child grammars of English*. Basil Blackwell, Oxford.
Ramer, A.: 1976, 'Syntactic styles in emerging language', *Journal of Child Language* **3**, 49-62.
Roeper, T.: 1973, 'Connecting children's language and linguistic theory', In T. Moore (ed.) *Cognitive development and the acquisition of language*, Academic Press, New York.
Ross, J. R.: 1967, 'Constraints on Variables in Syntax', Ph.D. Dissertation, MIT.
Schönenberger, M., Z. Penner and J. Weissenborn: 1997, 'Object Placement and Early German Grammar', In *Proceedings of the Annual Boston University Conference on Language Development* **21**, Cascadilla Press, Somerville, 539-549.
Speas, M.: 1994, 'Null Arguments in a Theory of Economy of Projection', *University of Massachusetts Occasional Papers in Linguistics* **17**, 179-208.
Tomasello, M.: 1992, *First verbs : a case study of early grammatical development*. Cambridge University Press, New York.
Tsimpli, I-M.: 1991, 'On the Maturation of Functional Categories: Early Child Speech', *UCL Working Papers in Linguistics* **3**, 123-148.
Vainikka, A.: 1994, 'Case in the Development of English Syntax', *Language Acquisition* **3**, 257-325.
Valian, V.: 1991, 'Syntactic subjects in the early speech of American and Italian children'. *Cognition* **40**, 21-81.
Weissenborn, J.: 1993, 'Mommy's sock almost fits: Constraints on children's grammars', Paper presented at *Sixth International Congress for the Study of Child Language*, Trieste, Italy: July.
Zwart, C. J-W.: 1993, 'Dutch Syntax', Ph.D. Dissertation, University of Groningen.

SUSAN M. POWERS
University of Potsdam

ZVI PENNER   ROSEMARIE TRACY   JÜRGEN WEISSENBORN

WHERE SCRAMBLING BEGINS: TRIGGERING OBJECT SCRAMBLING AT THE EARLY STAGE IN GERMAN AND BERNESE SWISS GERMAN

1. PRELIMINARIES

At a very young age, children are capable of producing utterances, which we could hardly improve upon. The following sentences were spoken by a small German boy named Valle who was about 26 months old at the time:[1]

(1) a. das sind alle legos die ich ausgeschüttet hab\
     that are all lego blocks which I out-dumped have
     'Those are all the lego blocks which I dumped out'
  b. das is die tür wo man immer raus und rein kann\
     that is the door where one always out and in can
     'That is the door through which one can leave and enter'
  c. macht da der bauer die tür zu daß es nicht in den bulldog regnet\
     makes there the farmer the door shut that it not in the bulldozer rains
     'The farmer closes the door there so that it doesn't rain into the bulldozer'

In this paper, we will take a step back from the time at which complex sentences like those in (1) are used productively. That is, we will focus on an earlier developmental period during which recursive structures manifest themselves for the very first time.

We will claim that already at the time of two-word utterances there are special lexical elements which fulfill a pioneering function for syntactic structure building, namely the so-called focus particles like German *auch* 'also/too' and the negation particle *nicht* 'not'. It will be argued that these particles provide the basis for the first 'Affect Configurations' (Haegeman, 1992 and related work) above the VP, i.e., phrases in which operators are formally licensed by means of specifier-head configurations. Once these configurations emerge, a specifier position becomes available as a landing site outside the VP, giving rise to a type of movement which we will consider as 'local scrambling'.

Our theoretical position falls within the spectrum of current Continuity perspectives on language acquisition (see Roeper, 1992; Weissenborn, 1992, 1994; Penner, 1994b; Tracy, 1995; Hyams, 1996; Penner & Weissenborn, 1996). The core assumption is that, while the knowledge concerning both language-specific and universal phrase-structure rules as well as formal licensing conditions are available to the child from early on, the feature matrix of certain functional nodes may be 'underspecified'. This kind of underspecification affects features such as X-bar status of constituents (e.g., specifier versus head in an operator configuration), agreement spell-out, etc. The state of underspecification leads to stage-specific interim solutions (default choices, placeholder insertion, etc.), the common denominator being that they do not violate the requirements of the parametric system of the target grammar. This differentiated continuity approach enables us to deal with the tension between continuity on the one hand and developmental change on the other. Rather than place the burden for differences between the child's intermediate grammars or between the child's and the adult's systems on the immaturity of his or her processing system (Valian, 1992) or on maturational accounts (Felix, 1992), we will explore grammar-internal reasons, such as accessibility of crucial triggers in the input, for the developmental sequence which we observe.

The structure of the paper is as follows. Section 2 is mainly descriptive. It starts with some general observations on the emergence of focus particles (including negation) in German as well as their syntactic and discourse functions in early care-giver/child interactions. In Section 3, we introduce the theoretical framework that underlies our analysis of both the adult's and the child's systems, taking into account the grammars of both High German and Swiss German. We will characterize the target system in terms of parameter setting and discuss the accessibility of relevant triggers. In particular, we predict that the focus particle *auch* will be acquired prior to the negative marker *nicht,* which involves a complex pattern of cross-modal learning procedure. In Section 4, we present a detailed model of the step-by-step acquisition of the focus particle *auch* and the negative marker *nicht* on the basis of a Swiss German case study. Section 5 is a quantitative presentation of the data and a refinement of our account. It will be shown that while the scrambling mechanism itself is available to the child from early on, the application of object scrambling can be initially restricted. This is due to the fact that, initially, the child prefers to treat certain object nouns as 'light nouns', i.e., as part of complex predicates, rather than projecting them onto fully-fledged phrases. We will conclude with some explanatory hypotheses concerning the acquisition order observed, highlighting the pioneering function of *auch* as a trigger for early scrambling and for structure building in general.

1. THE PHENOMENA IN FOCUS: SOME INITIAL OBSERVATIONS ON FOCUS PARTICLES

When we look at the earliest word combinations of monolingual German-speaking children, we find that they invariably include the focus particle *auch* (cf. Miller, 1976; Tracy, 1991; Penner, 1994b).[2] Quite often, these utterances have no verb at all or only a verbal particle. Example (2), for instance, was recorded at a time when the child, Julia, produced hardly any lexical verbs (i.e., verb stems not prefixes) in combination with other words.

(2)   Julia 1;7

J. puts blocks in box	daREIN\ there-in
picking up another block	AUCH darein\ also there-in

For Julia, corpora of 400-500 utterances each between the ages of 1;7 and 1;8 would mainly consist of single-word utterances and of 20-30 two-word constructions. Most of the latter are combinations of a deictic particle and a noun (*da ball* 'there ball'), of two nouns (*mama kette*, mama chain, 'Mummy has a chain'), or nouns and verbal particles (*brille ab,* glasses off, 'take off your glasses'). While main verbs appear in isolation, there are just about two to four utterances per corpus which exhibit a lexical main verb in construction with other lexical elements as in *vogel aufziehn*, bird up-wind, 'wind up the (mechanical) bird'.[3]

The example in (3) is attested several months later, after Julia has begun to produce three-word utterances and the first inflected verbs:

(3)   Julia 1;11

J. puts toys in a box	EINräum\
	in-put
A.	Einräumen willst du sie wieder?
	'You want to put them away again?'
J. placing goat in box	ziege AUCH/ ... tracy AUCH einräum/
	goat also ... tracy also in-put/
	'T. should also start putting things away'
A.	Ich soll auch?
	I shall also?
	'Me too?'

Although Julia produces the first inflected verbs at this time, *auch* occurs consistently with non-finite main verbs. As a matter of fact, of 20 three- and four-word utterances with a non-finite verb in final position, 13 have *auch*. In addition, there are still plenty of constructions with *auch* without any verb at all (*mami auch kette*, Mummy also chain, 'Mummy has a chain, too' *da auch räder*, there also wheels, 'There are wheels, too'), etc.

The table below gives an impression of the frequency of occurrence of *auch* in two early corpora from other children, each based on a single hour of recording. The percentages refer two- and multi-word utterances, disregarding single-word occurrences of *auch*. The percentages in the last columns were calculated with respect to the respective sums of two- and multiword utterances:

Child	age	utterances total	2-word utterances	3-4 word utterances	utterances with *auch*
Stephanie	1;8	143	37	1	8 (= 21%)
Benny	2;2	292	67	17	19 (= 23%)

As was the case for Julia, Stephanie's and Benny's utterances with *auch* may lack a verb altogether, have a non-finite verb or just a particle in final position. Benny's corpus has a couple of (arguably) finite verbs in final position and even two instances of *ich auch will fee* 'I also want coffee', a deviant order for both main and subordinate clauses in German.

The early *auch* constructions are probably the first utterances which contain a focus-like discourse representation with two-member sets. We will return to this observation below. In addition to set formation, two kinds of interpretation of utterances with *auch* can be assigned on the basis of verbal and nonverbal contexts with adult interlocutors:

(a) boulemaic reading, where the particle can be said to fulfill some modal function, as in (2)-(3);
(b) an existential reading, cf. (4)-(6), or a possessive interpretation as in (8) below.

Consider the following examples:

(4)   Florian 2;8

| F. pointing at bird house outside his window. | da AUCH'n futter drin\ there also-a food inside 'there's also some food in there' |

(5)   Florian 2;8

| F. is watching several trucks. | lastwagen AUCH so groß\ truck also so big 'the truck is also so big' |

(6)   Florian 2;8

| F. pointing at windmill in a picture (Mirko = his friend, Floa = Florian) | Mirko AUCH eine windmühle klein ... M. also a windmill small ... 'M. also has a small windmill..' FLOA eine GROße\ F. a big 'F. has a big one' |

These examples already indicate that the use of *auch* entails quite complex discourse representations for both children and adults. In (3) above the adult relies on the child's remembering enough of the previous context to interpret an elliptical question *Ich soll auch* 'I should too?' Me too? (meaning 'You want me to tidy things up as well?'). In the episode in (7), for instance, one of two adult interlocutors, the one who did not participate in the event (collecting acorns and chestnuts), has problems understanding what the child is trying to say, while the other one, who had been on the scene, interprets the child's statement without difficulty:

(7)   Stephanie 1;10

Adult1 picking up pine cones	Was ist das denn? 'What's that?!'
S.	das sin EIcheln\ that are acorns
Adult1	Eicheln? Habt ihr die heute gefunden? 'Acorns? Did you find them today?'
S.	kastanien AUCH/ chestnuts also
Adult1 (failing to understand)	Was meinst du? 'What did you say?'
S.	kaSTAnie auch\ chestnut too
Adult2 (confirming)	Kastanie auch, ja.

It should be emphasized that in our data *auch* is acquired before *nicht* (the negation particle *not*) is attested. In the following episode, for example, we find a typical *auch* construction, while the child resorts to anaphoric *nein* 'no' in combination with a head-shaking gesture in order to express negation. The child does not appear to have problems with the semantics or pragmatics of negation; what appears to be lacking, however, is the adult syntactic form:[4]

(8)   Stephanie 1;8 (= S., R.= adult, F: Father)

R. is looking at a toy monkey called Bobo w/ a necklace around its neck	....der Bobo mit seiner schönen Kette, ne? B. with his pretty chain, right?
S. looking at R's necklace	ROsi auch\ R. also
R.	Ja, ich hab auch eine Kette, das stimmt. 'Yes, I also have a chain, that's right.'
S. touching her own neck, shakes head	Stefanie NEIN nein\ S. no no 'S. (doesn't) have a necklace'
R.	Nein? 'No?'
S. looking again at R's necklace	ROsi kette\ R. chain 'R. has a chain'
S. turns around to father, shaking her head	Papa AUCH/...NEIN nein\ Papa also no no 'Daddy doesn't have a chain either'

Auch emerges long before the V2 rule is established. Crucially, at the time when these *auch* structures first manifest themselves, none of the children provide us with compelling evidence for productive V2 beyond precursor structures. That is, there may be formulaic V2-like patterns (such as [ge:tiç] for *geht nicht* 'doesn't work', or [da:z ball], *da ist der Ball* 'there's the ball') but no object topicalization and no wh-questions with verbs other than the copula.[5]

Indeed, what looks like an impeccable root clause without *auch* takes on a different quality once *auch* appears. Thus, we find within one and the same corpus *Stefan weint* 'Stefan cries' alongside the deviant verb-final *Stefan auch weint* 'Stefan also cries' instead of the appropriate V2 pattern *Stefan weint auch*. There is, by the way, no question that both *Stefan weint* and the verb-final *Stefan auch weint* are to be interpreted as independent root clauses. Similarly, we encounter the well-formed *Papi geht arbeiten* 'Daddy goes (to) work' next to *Nina auch geht arbeiten* 'Nina also goes (to) work' instead of *Nina geht auch arbeiten* (cf. Tracy, 1991:201f.) Thus, clauses involving *auch* seem to be more conservative in terms of verb placement.

Note further that, even after V2 is established, patterns with *auch* continue to occur without verbs or tend to be non-finite. This holds not only for expressions with an imperative or future-oriented (modal) reading but also for descriptions of past and current affairs. The next two examples, both from one child, Florian (cf. Tracy, 1991), illustrate these points. The episode in (9) shows the complementary distribution of *auch* and the finite possessive *haben*,[6] and in (10) *auch* occurs in an infinitival declarative:

(9)   Florian 2;8

F. looking at Christmas photos	Mirko AUCH weihnachten\ M. also Christmas
A.:	Wer hat Weihnachten? 'Who is celebrating Christmas?'
F. pointing at children in picture	kindern hat weihnachten\ children has Christmas ... mirko AUCH weihnachten\ ...m. also Christmas 'the children are having Christmas ... M. is also having Christmas'

(10)   Florian 2;8

F. points at picture of a train conductor	der AUCH einsammeln\ ... AUCH sammel\ he also in-collect .... also collect 'He also collects (tickets)'

Indeed, the *sammel* of the follow-up in (10) could possibly be interpreted as an attempted self-correction, rendering the verb finite, albeit with a deviant zero-inflection instead of the required 3rd person singular -*t*. However, even if this interpretation were correct, the position of the verb would still have to be considered inappropriate for a German main clause. The same holds for (11) where we have two clearly finite clauses with *auch*, and yet the verb does not raise to where it should be, given a root interpretation.

(11)   Florian (2;8)

| F. lies down and places a small toy man next to himself. Pulling blanket over toy man | mann AUCH schlaft\ ...mann\ ... mann AUCH schlaf möchte\

man also sleep\... man\ ...man also sleep want\ |

The example in (12), from Stephanie, is therefore quite unique and progressive in exhibiting both *auch* and a finite verb in V2 position; and yet, the very same episode also contains the more frequent pattern, i.e., the verbless *auch* construction *Sabine AUCH augen*, Sabine also eyes, 'Sabine has eyes, too'.

(12)   Stephanie 1;10

Adult inquires about S.'s monkey "Bobo"	Wo sind die Augen vom Bobo? 'where are the eyes of Bobo?'
S. pointing	da ... hat AUCH augen\ there ... has also eyes
A.	Ja, der hat auch Augen. 'Yes, he has also got eyes'
S. looking at adults present looking at Sabine	ALle hamen augen .. all have eyes Sabine AUCH augen\ Sabine also eyes

As compared to Stephanie and the other children, Florian's first attested V2-plus-*auch* construction occurs much later, see (13). Actually, the whole episode around this example provides striking evidence for the child's attempt to assemble various independently existing options. Recall that Florian also refers to himself as "Lo", "Flo" or " Floa".

(13)   Florian 2;8

| F. and T. are looking at pictures. T. asks F. | Was macht der Polizist da? 'What's the policeman doing there?'

STEIne holt\ ... LO auch⁾ steine\...lo hat AUCH steine\. stones got ... F. also stones ...F. has also stones\

... LO auch--... hat auch-- ...FLOrian ... AUCH steine holt\ ...F. also--.. has also-- ...F.   ... also   stones got 'F. also went and got some stones' |

These various observations lead us to conclude that even after V2 effects are productive in principle, structures with *auch* still behave conservatively. This goes for utterances with an existential reading as in (12) as well as for cases like (14) below from Julia, with a boulemaic (modal) interpretation. At this time, the overall corpus in which (14) occurs contains about 150 V2 clauses, including utterances with the modal verbs *können* 'can', *wollen* 'want', *müssen* 'must'. Nevertheless, Julia resorts to a non-finite pattern with *auch*.

(14) Julia 2;4

J. telling T. about bee sting.	de hat ein ein BIEne reinstich\... there/it has a a bee in-stung 'A bee stung me (there)' [...]
(Florian = the friend she was going to visit)	Julia Florian AUCH in nase stechen\ J. F. also in nose sting 'J. wants to sting Florian too'

It is remarkable that utterances containing *nicht* are equally conservative. In Florian's first and last utterance in (15), for instance, the finite verb does not raise across the negative particle. Note also the non-finite verb in the context of *auch* in the declarative statement *Schiff auch passen* 'ship also fit' within the same episode.

(15) Florian 2;8

F. pushing ship under bridge	NICHT runterpasst\ not under-fits 'The ship doesn't fit underneath' die brücke runtermachen\ the bridge down-make 'Let's lower the bridge'
pushing a ship which fits	schiff AUCH passen\ ship also fit 'This ship fits also'
pushing others	dies AUCH passt\ this-one also fits ... dies NICHT passt\ ... this-one not fits

At the same time, target constraints on clause-internal movement (see below) are observed from the beginning. We found that subjects reliably raise across the particle, as in the examples given so far. At 2;4 inherently definite objects (e.g., demonstrative pronouns) raise to the left side of the negation particle as in (16):

(16)   Julia 2;4

| J. looking at picture of a spoon | ein löffel kann das nicht machen\ a spoon can that not do 'A spoon can't do that' |

In contrast, at the same age the definite noun phrase *die schubkarre* 'the pushcart' in (17) remains inside the infinitival complement on the right side of the negation particle (i.e., scrambling does not occur). Note that this is a licit target option in German provided that the negation particle preceding the infinitive phrase is focus-stressed:

(17)   Julia 2;4

| J. leading little doll, pretending that it is trying to push a pushcart | da kann nicht die schubkarre schiebe\ there/he can not the pushcart push 'He can't push the pushcart' |

In contrast to (16)-(17), indefinite objects do not raise at all in accordance with the target. See for example (18) and (19) with the generic object (note that in the latter article insertion is ruled out in German):

(18)   Stephanie 1;11

| S. refusing pillow offered by interlocutor | will nis kissen\... will nis ein kissen\ want not pillow...want not a pillow |

(19)   Julia (1;11)

| J. after kicking ball to T. | tracy AUCH fussball spielen\ |

These observations on the development of *auch* clauses and negation can be summarized as follows:

- In the acquisition of German, the focus particle *auch* appears early, i.e., already in two-word utterances. These utterances are often verbless; occurring verbs tend to be non-finite.
- In addition to set formation, *auch* expresses either existentiality or boulemaic modality.
- *auch* appears developmentally earlier than negation with *nicht*. In the data investigated here, it appears to be the very first operator-type element acquired by German-speaking children; a few others, like *noch(mal)/wieder* 'again', etc. appear to occur around the same time.
- Extensive use of *auch* precedes the emergence of V2 effects.
- Even after V2 has become productive, utterances with *auch* are often verbless, the verb is non-finite, or it does not raise.
- From the beginning, constraints on scrambling are observed, i.e., (a) subjects raise, (b) definite objects may or may not raise, and (c) indefinite objects do not raise.

After this initial review of the data we now introduce the theoretical background for our analyses. Subsequently, in Section 3, we will turn to a more fine-grained case study.

2. ON THE SYNTAX OF NICHT AND AUCH IN GERMAN AND SWISS GERMAN

2.1. Focus Particles and Word Order in the Middle Field: The Notion of Local Scrambling

In recent literature the status of scrambling in Continental West Germanic languages has received considerable attention. It has been emphasized in various works that scrambling is a cover term for A- and A'-movement within the middle field.[7] The former, A-movement, appears to be the more local type which we find in the familiar case of the obligatory raising of definite objects to the left side of focus particles such as *auch* and negative markers like *nicht*. Consider, for instance, examples (20a-c), keeping in mind that local scrambling applies regardless of whether the main verb is finite or not:

(20) a. ich habe diesen Film$_i$ nicht t$_i$ gesehen.
      I have this movie not seen
      'I did not see this movie.'
   b. ich habe diesen Film$_i$ auch t$_i$ gesehen.
      I have this movie *also* seen
      'I also saw this movie.'

c. ... dass ich diesen Film$_i$ nicht/auch t$_i$ sah
    ... that I this movie not/also saw
    '... that I didn't see this movie/also saw this movie'

In general, the landing site of the locally-scrambled constituent is identical with the position of the focus-stressed wh-*in-situ* element. This is shown in (21):

(21)   .... wo ich WELCHEN FILM$_i$ nicht/auch t$_i$ sah?
        ..... where I which movie not/also saw?
        .... 'What movie did you say I didn't see/saw too?'

In terms of phrase structure, the landing site of a locally scrambled constituent could be either Spec, AGRO or the specifier position of the movement-triggering particle in a focus particle phrase (FPP).

Within the Minimalist Program of Chomsky (1992) and the Antisymmetry approach of Kayne (1994), object scrambling is best captured in terms of movement to Spec, AGRO. A scrambling analysis along these lines has been developed in Zwart (1993) for Dutch. Working within this framework, Eisenbeiss (1994) has argued that movement to the left side of *nicht* in German is an instance of raising to Spec, AGRO. According to this view, (20a) should be analyzed as (22):

(22)   Ich habe[$_{AGROP}$ diesen Film$_i$ [$_{NegP}$ *nicht* [$_{VP}$ t$_i$ gesehen]]]

Alternatively, if local scrambling targets the specifier position of the focus particle (Spec, FPP), the analysis would correspond to (23):

(23)   Ich habe [$_{FPP}$ diesen Film$_i$ [$_{FP'}$ FP°[VP t$_i$ gesehen]]]

The structure in (23) constitutes a special case of the 'Affect Configuration' in the sense of Haegeman (1992) and related work. The basic assumption is that the focus particles *auch* and *nicht* in German entail contrastive sets.[8] As such, focus particles have the formal properties of quantificational operators and adhere to well-formedness conditions on operator configurations. These formal conditions were first formulated in Rizzi (1991) who argues that question formation is subject to the so-called Wh-Criterion. This well-formedness condition requires *wh*-operators to be licensed in a specifier-head agreement configuration such as (24):

(24)   Spec, CP   C^0
            [+wh]   [+wh]

Extending Rizzi's proposal, Haegeman (1992, 1995) postulates that the requirement on specifier-head agreement holds for any affective operator. This requirement is formulated in (25):

(25) The Affect Criterion
 a. An [AFFECTIVE] operator must be in a specifier-head configuration with an [AFFECTIVE] X°
 b. An [AFFECTIVE] X° must be in a specifier-head configuration with an [AFFECTIVE] operator

In Haegeman & Zanuttini (1991, 1996) and Haegeman (1992), the application of the Affect Criterion to negative operators is discussed in detail. As in the case of question formation, negative operators are claimed to be licit only if they occur in a specifier-head agreement configuration as in (26):

(26) Spec, NegP Neg⁰
 [+neg] [+neg]

The implementation of this principle can be seen best in languages with negative concord, an issue to which we will return below. Another instance of a specifier-head configuration, which can be captured in terms of the broad definition of the Affect Criterion, is the V2-focus configuration in languages like Hungarian. This idea has been worked out in Puskas (1992). Thus, parallel to Neg- and wh- configurations one would find focus agreement as in (27), a configuration that comes close to (24) above:[9]

(27) Spec, CP C⁰
 [+FOCUS] [+FOCUS]

In addition, one would hope to be able to show that the choice between the Spec, AGRO and the Spec, FPP options for local scrambling is not arbitrary but rather parametrically determined.

Starting with negation, and confining our discussion to sentential negation, we will now look more closely at the relevant facts. Our point of departure is the following division of labor among the negation markers in Standard German and Bernese Swiss German.

Negation markers in German
↙ ↓ ↘
Anaphoric negator Existential negator Negative particle
nein 'no' (Bernese: *nei*) *kein* (Bernese: *ke(s)*) *nicht* (Bernese: *nid*)
(sentence adjunct) (DP-internal)

The negative particle *nicht* is employed to negate both transitive clauses with definite objects (and complement clauses) and intransitive clauses. As mentioned above, the definite object must be raised, i.e., locally-scrambled, to the left of *nicht*. Adopting Zanuttini's (1991) terminology, we will not assume that *nicht* is part of the inflectional complex of the verb (INFL) but that it represents a phrase in its own right. Following Hamann (1996; this volume), we further assume that *nicht* is the specifier of an 'Affect Configuration' dominating the VP. That is, *nicht* behaves on a par with French *pas*, rather than *ne*. That *nicht* and *pas* display the same distribution can be seen in (28a-c). Both are excluded whenever a negative quantifier occurs:

(28) a. Jean (**ne**) viendra *(**pas**) [French]
    Hans kommt **nicht** [German]
    dr Hans chunnt **nid** [Bernese]
    'John will not come'
  b. Jean **ne** viendra *(**jamais**)/(***pas**) [French]
    Hans kommt **nie** / (***nicht**) [German]
    dr Hans chunnt **nie**/(***nid**) [Bernese]
    'John will never come'
  c. Jean **ne** parlera *(**à personne**) /(***pas**) [French]
    Hans spricht mit **niemandem**/(***nicht**) [German]
    dr Hans ret mit **niemerem**/(***nid**) [Bernese]
    'John will not talk to anybody'

Given these assumptions, local scrambling triggered by *nicht* would most likely involve Spec, AGRO as the landing site (cf. (22) above):

(29) ich habe[$_{AGROP}$ diesen Film$_I$ [$_{NegP}$ *nicht* [$_{Neg'}$ [$_{VP}$ t$_i$ gesehen]]]

In contrast with *nicht*, the existential negator *kein* negates transitive clauses with indefinite objects and intransitive clauses with indefinite nominal predicates. Superficially, the object (as well as the predicate) remains in its base position:

(30) ich habe kein Brot bekommen. [German]
    I ha kes Broot übercho. [Bernese]
    I have no bread got
    'I didn't get bread.'

To conclude this section, it must be pointed out that the so-called 'light nouns' are exceptional in this intricate system (see Schönenberger, Penner & Weissenborn, 1997). In contrast with 'heavy nouns' which are fully-fledged (quantified) noun phrases with a determiner position, object-verb clusters in light noun constructions are spelled out as complex predicates as in English *lose face, make love*, etc. or German *abschied nehmen*, leave take, 'to take leave', *bahn fahren*, railway ride, 'to ride on a train', *platz nehmen*, seat take, 'to have a seat', *schwein haben*, pig have, 'to be lucky' *gas geben*, gasoline give, 'accelerate' etc. Although generic, light nouns are negated by *nicht*, and not by *kein* (as in (30)). More importantly, light nouns resist scrambling. That is, they behave very much like verbal prefixes in complex predicates and not like object nouns.

In what follows we shall discuss how this intricate system can be acquired by the child.

2.2. Predictions for the Acquisition of Local Scrambling: *auch* versus *nicht*

The essential conclusions to be drawn by the learner can be captured in the following parametric terms referring to the X-bar-status of *nicht*:

(a) The independence of the projectional domain:
Nicht spells out an Affect Configuration in a Neg Phrase dominating the VP rather than part of the inflectional complex,
(b) The status within the projectional domain:
Nicht occupies the specifier of the Neg Phrase rather than its head position.

Both parameters are of the standard type. We can now ask how the relevant triggers are encoded in the input. As for (a), concerning the independent status of *nicht*, it seems that the child is exposed to unambiguous evidence, which comes from verb movement to C°, or simply to a higher INFL node in root clauses. That is, a standard degree-1 triggering frame should consist of a main and a subordinate clause as in (31):

(31)   Das kaufen wir **nicht** bevor wir es **nicht** sehen   [German]
         Das choufe mir **nid** bevor (dass) mir's **nid** gseh   [Bernese]
         this buy we not before (that) we it not see (1 pl.)
         'We won't buy this without having seen it.'

where the asymmetry between post-verbal and pre-verbal negation provides the child with the crucial information that verb movement does not affect *nicht*. This evidence should be sufficient to deduce that the inflected verb and *nicht* are independent constituents.

The next task for the learner, as suggested in (b), would be to assess the function of *nicht* within the Affect Configuration itself. Recall that the evidence for the function of negative markers can be unraveled in double-negation structures (see (28) above). Intuitively, one might want to say that whenever a language has overt negative markers for both specifier and head positions, the latter, not the former, may be optional. This intuition has recently been claimed to be confirmed not only, for French (see (29a) above where *ne*, but not *pas* can be dropped), but also in the so-called 'negative concord' constructions in West Flemish (Haegeman & Zanuttini, 1991).

If this is universally true, the child would indeed come equipped with a powerful data-sorting device, which should help him or her to bootstrap the relevant triggering frame. The deduction procedure could run along the lines of (32):

(32) If only a single negation marker occurs, it must be the specifier element of an Affect Configuration, provided that there is evidence that the negation marker is not part of the inflectional complex.

However, careful examination of cross-linguistic data reveals that this cannot be the right deduction. Consider, for instance, Bayer's (1990) analysis of negative concord in Bavarian (*kein* followed by *nicht*):

(33) also brauchst keine Angst nicht haben.
      thus need-you **no** fear **not** have
      'Thus you don't have to worry.'

In (33), the *kein*-negated object co-occurs with *nicht*. Bayer analyzes the latter as a head adjoined to V°. Within the framework of the Affect Configuration approach of Haegeman (1992), the *kein*-negated object is analyzed best as a specifier element. Thus, Bavarian *nicht* would be predicted **not** to occur in isolation in simply-negated clauses (on a par with French *ne*). However, this prediction is not borne out by the data.

Given these considerations, the occurrence of German *nicht* in simply-negated structures cannot count as a reliable trigger for the acquisition of the X-bar status of the negation particle. We will therefore assume that in order to set the parameter concerning the function of *nicht* in German, the child will have to extend the triggering frame. More precisely, the child will need a broader triggering frame that renders visible at least a subset of the structural relations expressed in the German examples in (28) above. That is, the minimal triggering frame, which the child needs to take into account, must include negative quantifiers displaying complementary distribution with *nicht*. In sum, we would like to propose that the acquisition of the negation particle in German *nicht* involves a cross-modal learning procedure which combines cues both from verb movement (on the basis of root-/non-root asymmetries) and the distribution of negative quantifiers.

We will now proceed to compare the parametric status of nicht with the one of the focus particle auch (Bernese o, ou, o no). As already mentioned by Jacobs (1982, 1983), German nicht and focus particles such as auch are syntactically related. The following aspects are relevant for our discussion:

- Like *nicht*, *auch* is a scope-bearing element.
- If *auch* precedes the VP, the entire proposition is within the scope domain of the particle. This is shown in (34):

(34)   Ich will auch klavier spielen.   [German]
        i wott *ou* klavier schpile.   [Bernese]
        I want also piano play
        'I also wunt to play the piano.'

- Where the VP involves a transitive verb, the sentential-scope reading is retained only if the definite object is raised to the left side of *auch*. Note that the focus intonation is assigned to the particle itself:

(35)   Ich kenne Dani AUCH.   [German]
        I kenne dr Dani OU.   [Bernese]
        I know (the) Dani also
        '(You know/someone knows Dani) and I know Dani too.'

- Indefinite objects remain VP-internal. Sentential scope is obtained by focusing (i.e., focus stressing) the particle *auch*. Constituent scope results from focusing the object:

(36)   a. Ich will AUCH ein Brot.   [German]
           I wott OU es Broot.   [Bernese]
           I want also a bread
           '(You want bread/someone wants bread and) I want some bread too.'
        b. Ich will auch ein BROT.   [German]
           I wott ou es BROT.   [Bernese]
           I want also a BREAD
           'I want (something and) some bread too.'

We will further assume that in (36a) *auch* is VP-external. In (36b), on the other hand, *auch* could be adjoined to the object inside the VP. The same effect can be observed in the case of subjects:

(37)   [Auch DANI] kommt auf die Party.   [German]
        [Ou DR DANI] chunnt a d Party.   [Bernese]
        also (the) Dani comes to the party
        '(Someone will come to the party) Dani will come too.'

Simplifying somewhat, we would like to suggest that the focus particle *auch* unifies the functional domains of both *nicht* and *kein*, i.e.,

- *auch* behaves on a par with *nicht* whenever it is focus-stressed. Sentential scope then requires raising the definite object out of the VP.
- *auch* behaves on a par with *kein* when it is adjoined to a focused constituent.

Given these observations and hypotheses, it becomes plausible to assume that the acquisition of *auch* in German involves fewer steps than the acquisition of the negation marker(s). This follows directly from the fact that the syntactic feature [Focus Particle] is spelled out by one single lexical item, namely *auch*. Negation, on the other hand, is marked by several items. In addition to the anaphoric negator *nein* 'no', negation in German is realized by *nicht* and *kein*, each linked to different syntactic functions. This discrepancy between *auch* and the negation marker(s) is summarized in the table below:

Negation markers in German			Affirmative Focus Particle
↙	↓	↘	↓
Anaphoric negator *nein* 'no' (sentence adjunct)	Existential negator *kein* (DP-internal)	Negative particle *nicht* (specifier of an independent NegP)	Uniformly spelled out as *auch*

There is yet another domain where similar accessibility considerations may become relevant for pacing individual steps in the acquisition of focus particles and negation markers. With respect to negation, we have assumed that parameter setting is likely to refer to information concerning the presence or the absence of negative concord in order to determine whether a given negation marker functions as a specifier or a head element. This decision problem is not to be expected for *auch* since, to the best of our current knowledge, there is no *auch* counterpart to negative concord. In fact, *auch* is a pure 'syncategorematic expression' which is, as suggested by Bayer (1990), in the unmarked case analyzed as a head ($X°$). We therefore postulate that the null hypothesis of the child will be that *auch* is a head. This initial hypothesis will be revised only when the child encounters evidence to the contrary.

In light of these facts, we will assume that the focus particle *auch* in German is more accessible in terms of lexical bootstrapping (spell-out of a given syntactic function) and syntactic bootstrapping (discovery of X-bar-status) than the syntactically closely related negation markers.

2.3. Three Possible Accounts of the Emergence of Scrambling

In concluding this section, we shall briefly review three competing hypotheses concerning the developmental schedule of local scrambling:

- *The Morphological Readiness Hypothesis*
  According to the view that Spec, AGRO is the target site of local scrambling (see (22)), and that the objective Case is assigned to the raised DP in this position, the Lexical Learning Approach (see Eisenbeiss, 1994) predicts that the acquisition of overt accusative marking must precede (or at least correlate with) the emergence of local scrambling.

From the perspective of the Morphological Readiness Hypotheses then, the Bernese Swiss German data, which will be reviewed in the next section, should be particularly important. In contrast with High German, Bernese German has 'nominative-accusative syncretism' (i.e., there is no distinct accusative marking). If the Morphological Readiness Hypothesis has a principled character, we would expect differences in the emergence of scrambling in children acquiring High German and Bernese Swiss German.

- *The Semantic Readiness Hypothesis*
  As shown above, local scrambling of object nouns in German is triggered by the feature [Definiteness]. On the assumption that nominals in early grammar are underspecified with regard to the feature [Definiteness], Hyams (1996), following Schaeffer *et al.* (1994) and Schaeffer (this volume), argues that local scrambling is unlikely to apply regularly as long as the feature content of the DP is not fully specified.

- *The Configurational Readiness Hypothesis*
  This is the position, which we argue for in the remainder of this paper. Negators and focus particles are intrinsically specified as [+affective], hence require formal licensing via specifier-head agreement configurations. The acquisition of negators and focus particles should therefore be a sign of the emergence of Affect Configurations. Given our assumption that local scrambling is *inter alia* a special case of local movement into the specifier position of the licensing agreement configuration (see (23) above), we would expect local scrambling to emerge as soon as the first operator-like head is licensed by means of some Affect Configuration. More precisely, we assume that the knowledge concerning the scrambling mechanism itself is likely to be represented in the learner's grammar **prior** to the

emergence of *nicht* and *auch* in the production repertoire. Once these elements are projected in the syntax, scrambling is forced to apply by the formal system of the grammar. This is the point where the latent knowledge of scrambling is rendered visible in the child's utterances.

In what follows, we will argue that the Configurational Readiness Hypothesis provides us with an adequate account of the acquisition data. The main claim is that the acquisition of local scrambling is best accounted for as a natural by-product of syntactic structures hosting Affect Configurations. Thus, at least structurally, no "special learning" of scrambling is needed. The core of the developmental process and the major burden of the learning task is to be located in another domain. On the one hand, the order of acquiring 'affective heads' is determined by the extent to which they lend themselves to lexical and syntactic bootstrapping. On the other hand, in order to apply object scrambling correctly, the child must be capable of distinguishing between 'heavy' and 'light nouns'. As shown in Schönenberger, Penner & Weissenborn (1997), children initially overgeneralize the light noun option. The projection of fully-fledged object nouns is acquired piecemeal (essentially item-by-item) and begins to be productive shortly after the second birthday. Given that light nouns resist scrambling, we expect there to be an initial subject/object-asymmetry. This asymmetry follows from the mechanism of lexical learning and is independent of the scrambling rule itself.

3. EARLY DEVELOPMENT OF NEGATION AND FOCUS PARTICLES IN BERNESE SWISS GERMAN: THE MODEL

This section concentrates on the acquisition of negation markers and the focus particle *auch* in Bernese Swiss German. The analysis presented is a slightly revised version of the model developed in Penner (1994b), which is based on the diary data of one boy, J. [10]

3.1. Acquiring the Negation Particle

Detailed treatments of the acquisition of negation can be found in Wode (1977), Clahsen (1988), Weissenborn *et al.* (1989), Hamann (1996; this volume) for German, and Hoekstra & Jordens (1994) for Dutch. By and large, the developmental schedule proposed by these authors agrees with the Bernese data, which can be best captured as a multiple stage development:

Stage 1 - until 1;8

At this early stage, the only negation marker attested is the anaphoric *nein* (Bernese: *nei*). Since this negator appears to fulfill different functions, the following sub-stages can be identified:

(i) - around 1;3

The particle *nein* functions as an alethic negator, negating the existence of objects as in:

(38) Ditsi nei
      cookies *nein*
      'I have no more cookies'

(ii) - until 1;7

At this sub-stage, the child distinguishes two ways of realizing *nein*. The particle ***nei*** (with a word-initial dental-nasal) occurs in last position, expressing alethic/epistemic negation, cf. (39):

(39) Mama nei
      audio cassettes *nein*
      'the audio cassette is not in the recorder'

The *nein* particle, spelled out as ***mei*** (with a word-initial labio-nasal), figures as a boulemaic negator; it occurs as a one-word utterance meaning 'I don't want'.

(iii) - until 1;8.7

Boulemaic *mei* gradually disappears during this stage. The alethic/epistemic particle *nei* is now uniformly pre-posed as in:

(40) nei faffe (schlaafe)
      nein sleep
      'I don't want to sleep'

Existential negation is first expressed by a gap, i.e., a "silent negator", accompanied by a negating gesture (recall Stephanie's head shaking in example (8)):

(41) a. Mami --- da
         Mammy (not) here
      b. Nomi --- da
         Naomi (not) here

and later by a consonantal pre-lexical placeholder (noted here as [CCC]):

(42)   Nomi [CCC] da
         Naomi [CCC] here
         'Naomi is not here'

Given these observations, the *nein* stage in Bernese can be captured as a superordinate term for three parametric processes:

1. Initially, the target marker for negation *nicht* is unavailable. The child starts out with *nein* as a negation marker, assuming that negation is part of the inflected verb or a negative auxiliary. The final position of the negation element agrees with the general pattern of verb placement at this stage. This assumption is in accordance with Clahsen's (1988) and Hoekstra & Jordens' (1994) analyses of early negation in German and Dutch, respectively. Employing various forms of the *nein* negator, the child construes a complex system which expresses existence and diverse modal functions.
2. At the second sub-stage, the child treats the negation marker and verbal inflections separately. The overt manifestation of this shift is the transition from an utterance-final pattern with the negative auxiliary to an utterance-initial pattern with a right-adjoined *nein* particle.
3. The third sub-stage is characterized by the emergence of pre-lexical place holders (see Bottari *et al.*, 1993/4 and literature cited therein) for the negation marker. As we will see below, these place holders herald the shift from *nein* to *nicht* negation.

We now turn to the second stage in the acquisition of negation:

Stage 2 - until 2;1
This stage is characterized by the emergence of *nicht* and *kein* negation. The negation marker *nicht* occurs in existential constructions replacing the pre-lexical place holders of Stage 1. Example (43) below is typical of Stage 2.

(43)   Nomi nid da
         Naomi not here
         'Naomi is not here'

The existential negator *kein* is still infrequent at this time (cf. Penner, 1993). In this period, four utterances with *kein* are attested all of which are structurally "incomplete". That is, they either involve a gap in the noun position, no verb, or both.

Stage 3 - until 2;3-7

The negation marker *nicht* occurs with both finite and non-finite verbs. The prevailing pattern is *(i) wott nid* 'I want not'. Indefinite objects (article-resistant 'light nouns' in this case) remain *in situ* as in (44):

(44)   a. nei, i wott nid Windeli aalege   2;03.15
              no, I want not diaper on-put
              'I don't want to put on my diaper'
      b. wott nid Musik lose   2;03.30
              want not music listen
              'I don't want to listen to music'

while (inherently) definite objects are regularly raised to the left side of *nicht*. This happens, for instance, in the case of the demonstrative pronouns in (45).

(45)   a. i ha das nid gno   2;06.15
              i have this not taken
              'I didn't take it'
      b. i wott das nid ässe   2;07.01
              I want this not eat
              'I don't want to eat this'

Note that, with the exception of PPs, which are exempted from scrambling in German, no definite noun phrases occur in the object position during this period.

3.2. Acquiring the Focus Particle auch

In order to understand the triggering mechanism of the successive shift from the *nein* to the *nicht* stage, we will now take a closer look at the parallel development of the related focus particle *auch*. Here, J.'s corpus provides us with the following developmental schedule:

Stage 1 - 1;07.13

Initially, there is a "silent *auch*" stage, i.e., the focus particle, while implicitly part of the sentence meaning (in (46), for instance, another nose had been mentioned in the preceding context), is not spelled out overtly:

(46)   Nomi --- Nase
                Naomi --- nose
                'Naomi has a nose too'

It must be stressed, however, that (46) is the only utterance in J.'s corpus which could count as evidence in support of a "silent *auch*" stage.

Stage 2 - 1;07.13-26
First overt *auch* particles occur. They are still positionally unstable:

(47) a. o no Dindun (Pingu)
      also Pingu (= a puppet)
      'I also have the Pingu book in my bed'
   b. Dindun o no   [a few hours later]
      Pingu also

In this period, 6 cases of *auch* are attested.

Stage 3 - 1;07.27-1;11.11
Subjects raise from Spec,VP to the left of *auch* as in (48)

(48) Nina [= Tina] o cho
      Tina also come
      'Tina also came'

In this period 25 cases of *auch* are attested, 16 of these are the type in (48).

Stage 4 - 1;11.11 on
There are now first constructions with object raising to the left of *auch*. It should be emphasized that in the corpus under investigation no violation of the scrambling rule is attested, i.e., there are no occurrences of unmoved definite objects: (*=ungrammatical if article is omitted)

(49) a. Schnägg o gässe   1;11.11
         *(**the**) snail also eaten
         '(It) ate the snail too'
      b. Schue o no aalege   2;01.23
         *(**the**) shoes also on-put
      c. das o no abzieh   2;01.29
         this also off-take
      d. Laschtwage o no choufe   2;04.04
         *(**the**) truck also buy

It should be pointed out that object scrambling with *auch*, although structurally stable, remains marginal until 2;4 (4 cases of object scrambling out of 49 *auch* constructions). It is however, interesting to see how these object nouns behave with regard to the feature [Definiteness]. The demonstrative pronoun in (49c) is deictic and therefore intrinsically definite. What about the object nouns in (49a, b, d)? It has become a standard assumption in recent models to distinguish between two subtypes of definiteness, depending on how a given noun is anchored in the speaker's knowledge: 'discourse linking' (explicit definiteness) as opposed to 'situation linking' ("situative unica" or implicitly definite nouns).[11] These two subtypes are also formally distinguished in German: discourse linking is overtly marked by the accented article, while the situation-linked noun is marked by an expletive, clitic article. Both discourse- and situation-linked object nouns are subject to the requirement on obligatory scrambling. A close look at the data reveals that none of the object nouns in (49a, b, d) are explicit definite in the sense of discourse linking. Although the article is systematically absent, the object nouns in (49a, d) are to be interpreted as unique in the specific situation of the utterance, hence implicitly known in the sense of situation linking. The object noun in (49b) is potentially ambiguous in early grammar. The target perspective is the one of situation linking (I want to put on my own shoes). However, early grammar does not exclude the light noun interpretation (see (59) below). The fact that the object noun in (49b) has been scrambled, however, indicates that at the age of 2;2 the child already opts for the target choice.

Note that the fact that the observed object nouns are restricted to situation linking is by no means random. As shown in detail in Penner & Weissenborn (1996), all the occurrences of definite articles in early grammar spell out situation linking (or proper names). In contrast, discourse linking is a very late phenomenon. Penner & Hamann (1998) ascribe this delay to the fact that discourse linking presupposes explicit anchoring via the complementizer system. The restriction to situation linking can be best accounted for in terms of 'default'.

Interestingly enough, the above examples reflect an unbalanced state of knowledge with regard to the target rule. On the one hand, the fact that the above examples are well-formed with regard to word order reveals that the child is aware of the target scrambling rule with regard to object nouns. On the other hand, the lack of overt articles in (49) and the restriction to situation linking clearly indicate that both the article insertion rule and the representation of the feature [Definiteness] in the child's grammar is still 'underspecified'. In more technical terms, it seems to be the case that the scrambling rule is intact, although the child systematically resorts to a default solution.

What about the role of Case marking in early scrambling in the light of the absence of the definite article in (49)? Given that Case marking in German, just like definiteness, is spelled out on the article (rather than by a nominal ending), we assume that there need not be any causal relationship between the acquisition of morphological Case marking and local scrambling. More importantly, since Bernese Swiss German, in contrast with High German, lacks accusative marking altogether, the fact that local scrambling in Bernese is operative just as early as in High German (cf. Section 1 above) shows that Case marking *per se* is not necessary as a triggering device.

Given these arguments, it seems that the scrambling rule becomes operative before the rule of definiteness exceeds the default stage and independently of overt Case marking. Thus, the strong versions of both the Morphological and Semantic Readiness Hypothesis seem to make wrong predictions with regard to the development of scrambling.

Furthermore, it is noteworthy, that *auch* occurs only exceptionally with a finite verb, a point that we already raised in Section 1. In J.'s corpus, 80 *auch* clauses are attested up to the age of 2;4 but only 9 of them (11%) involve a finite verb. Interestingly enough, all of these *auch* clauses are intransitive. These nine finite *auch* clauses are late, first attested at 2;01.21 (e.g., in the period between 1;11 and 2;0, 113 verbal utterances are attested; 53% of which are inflected, 47% are (root) infinitives; all 5 *auch* utterances are infinitives). In view of the fact that J. inflects 80-90% of all verbal constructions at 2;4, this frequency is astonishingly low. In addition, the typically "truncated" (i.e., infinitive) structure of *auch* constructions clearly contrasts with the fact that J. shifts to V2 in both declaratives and interrogatives at 2;4. A last important feature concerns the complementary distribution of subjects and objects in infinitival *auch* clauses, i.e., it is either the subject or the object nominal phrase which undergoes raising to the left side of the focus particle, but not both.

3.3. Deriving the Developmental Path of *nicht* and *auch*

The parallel development of negation and *auch* can be summarized as:

NEIN			
Stage 1 (around 1;3) An alethic particle *nei* negates existence			
Stage 2 (until 1;7) The particle *nei* figures as an alethic/epistemic negator. The particle *m ei* functions as a boulemaic negator.			
Stage 3 Boulemaic *m ei* disappears stepwise. The alethic/epistmic particle *nei* particle is now uniformly preposed	AUCH		
	Stage 1 (1;07.13) "Silent"(implicit) *auch*		
	Stage 2 (1;07.13-26) Overt *auch* emerges	NICHT	
	Stage 3 (1;7.27 -1;11.11) Subject raising	Stage 1 (until 1;8) Occurrence of "silent" *nicht,* as well as *nicht* spelled out by pre-lexical place holders	
	Stage 4 (1;11.11 on) Regular raising of (inherent/implicit) definite objects in infinitives	Stage 2 (until 2;1) Overt *nicht* in existential constructions	

Let us now turn to an analysis along the lines of the Configurational Readiness Hypothesis. Our point of departure is that what we have referred to as *Nein* Stage 3 consists of a shift from a verb-like negator to a negation marker as an adjoined, adverb-like element. At this stage, the negator and the negated expression constitute an incomplete functional complex, i.e., a 'small scope phrase' with the structure in (50):

(50)

In the case of J., the emergence of *auch* yields a complete functional complex between the ages of 1;7 and 1;8. From that time on, the focus particle, *qua* head, projects an Affect Configuration, opening a complement slot for the VP and a specifier position. The structure of this early Focus Particle Phrase is shown in (51):

(51)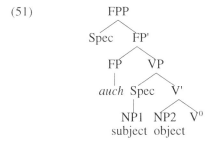

Once the Affect Configuration becomes available, either NP1 or NP2 may undergo raising to the empty Spec, FPP, i.e., they are 'locally scrambled'. As shown above, we initially find only subject raising in J.'s data; object raising is attested later (around 2;0). Recall that object scrambling remains marginal throughout the period studied here. In this sense, one might want to say that the application of local scrambling in early grammar does not reflect the acquisition of a structure-specific rule (in the traditional sense), but is rather a side-effect of the emergence of Affect Configurations.

The analysis in (51) also accounts for the observation that in the period under discussion object and subject raising are in complementary distribution: Since the Affect Configuration makes available only one single specifier position as a landing site, only one noun phrase can be raised past the focus particle.[12]

Recall that *auch* constructions are also conservative in terms of verb raising. That is, even in the period in which the inflected verb is regularly raised, *auch* constructions are preferably realized as infinitives. This pattern can be accounted for if we assume that the underlying 'minimal' Affect Configuration (with an Focus Phrase governing a VP) tends to remain unchanged during early grammar.

The emergence of the Affect Configuration in (51) has also a considerable impact on the development of other scope-bearing elements. In particular, it seems that the negation marker is assimilated to the scheme originally yielded by *auch*. In analogy with the *auch*-headed Focus-Particle

Phrase, the negation marker is initially analyzed as a head, projecting a complement slot for the VP and a specifier position. The latter then serves as the landing site for raised NPs, again either subjects or objects, but not both. The structural change of the negation marker from the utterance-initial and adverb- like adjunct of (50) to the head of an Affect Configuration is earmarked by the shift from the overextended (anaphoric) *nein* to *nicht*. The phrase marker of the negated structure at the *nicht* stage is represented in (52):

(52)
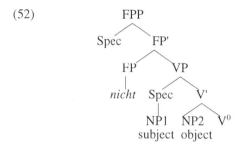

The temporal lag between *auch* and *nicht* supports our assumption that *auch* is more easily accessible to the child. Recall that we have reason to believe that the acquisition of *auch* involves *fewer* parametric and lexical decisions than those involved in the acquisition of *nicht* (cf. Section 2). In German, we find neither *auch* concord constructions nor a division of labor along the lines of *kein* and *nicht*. Hence, the focus particle, being purely syncategorematic, can be analyzed as a head in a straightforward manner. This null hypothesis gives rise to the early emergence of the Affect Configuration in (51). The task is certainly more complex in the case of negation where, if our analysis here is correct, the child has to settle the issue of negative concord before she can assess the X-bar status of *nicht*. Consequently, *nicht* is more likely to be integrated into the scheme of *auch* than vice versa.

In more technical terms, then, one could claim that in early grammar the negation particle *nicht* is underspecified with regard to the feature [X-bar Status]. The data presented above suggest an interim solution where the negative operator is a zero-level head on a par with *auch*. It may well figure as a syntactic place holder whose function it is to overtly spell out a [+Negative]-marked Affect Configuration.

In sum, the Configurational Readiness Hypothesis accounts for both the specific order of acquisition and the constraints on early *auch* and *nicht* constructions in terms of projecting Affect Configuration in early grammar. Within this approach, scrambling does not involve learning of structure-specific rule, but is rather a by-product of more formal and general properties of Affect phrases. Recall that scrambling applies target-consistently **prior** to (or independently of) the specification of the [Definiteness] and Case marking. Thus, if we take the strong versions of the Morphological Readiness Hypothesis and the Semantic Readiness Hypothesis to imply that the features [Definiteness] and [Case Marking] must be fully specified **prior** to (object) scrambling, we have to conclude that they fail to account for the specific developmental path shown here. There is, however, a tight relationship between (object) scrambling and the mode of mapping object nouns onto syntactic configuration. This is the point where the correlation between the occurrence of the article (which spells out the features [Definiteness] and [Case Marking]) and scrambling can be observed. This issue is briefly discussed in the next section.

4. REFINING THE ANALYSIS: WHICH OBJECTS UNDERGO SCRAMBLING IN EARLY GERMAN? THE SIMONE CORPUS

In the last part of the paper, we analyze the data from the German child Simone between the of ages 1;10 and 2;04 in order to focus on the issue of which objects undergo scrambling in early German.[13] As we will see, the German data clearly support the results from the analysis of the Bernese Swiss German data. In the period in question we find 144 verbal utterances containing *nicht* (n = 37) or *auch* (n =107). Of these, 68 are finite (n = 44 with *auch*; n = 24 with *nicht*), and 76 are non-finite (n = 63 with *auch*:; n = 13 with *nicht*). That is, similar to Bernese Swiss German, Simone's *auch*-utterances tend to occur more often as non-finite than her *nicht*-utterances. There are 88 utterances containing a subject and a direct object (n = 71 with *auch* (finite: n = 28 and non-finite: n = 42); n = 17 with *nicht* (finite: n = 14 and non-finite: n = 3)) (see examples in (53) below). In these cases, with the one exception shown in (54), the subject precedes the object. One utterance contained an indirect and a direct object but no subject (see (55) below):

(53)   a. mag nich kuche backe_.   Simone 1;10.20
                  want not cake bake
                  '(I) don't want to bake a cake.'
               b. brauche nich lala`.   Simone 2;00.23
                  need not pacifier
                  '(the baby) doesn't need a pacifier.'
               c. baby nich nuckel habe`.   Simone 2;00.01
                  baby not bottle have
                  'the baby doesn't have a bottle.'

  d. auch kuche backe_ auch`.   Simone 1;10.22
   also cake bake also
   '(I) also want to bake a cake.'
  e. auch creme habe`.   Simone 1;11.13
   also cream have
   '(I) also want to have cream.'
  f. mone auch laffe habe'.   Simone 1;11.13
   Simone also bottle have
   'Simone also wants to have a bottle.'

(54) des auch mone hol(en)   Simone 2;01.21
   this also Simone gets
   'Simone also gets this'

(55) baby auch labe (=Flasche) gebe   Simone 2;00.26
   to baby also bottle give
   'also give the baby a bottle'

If we look at the distribution of light versus heavy object nouns, we find that their position almost perfectly conforms to our predictions. That is, out of 114 light object nouns, 112 (98.3%) are unscrambled, appearing to the right of the negative or the focus element. Only the two light objects, shown in (56), have been scrambled (the two identical sentences were uttered just one after the other):

(56) a. mone kaukau auch trinke_.   Simone 2;02.20
   Simone cocoa also drink
   'Simone also drinks cocoa.'
  b. mone kaukau auch trinke_.
   Simone cocoa also drink
   'Simone also drinks cocoa.'

Of the 31 heavy object nominals, 26 are scrambled; that is, appear to the left of the negative or the focus element. They are, with one exception, demonstrative pronouns, which scramble obligatorily (i.e., independently of discourse and situation linking). The exception is the determinerless indirect object *baby* in (55) which, in the context, functions as a proper name and is thus inherently definite and referential. As such, it must undergo scrambling.

Of the unscrambled object nominals, only one should have been scrambled obligatorily, i.e., the object pronoun should occur to the left of the degree phrase *gar nicht* 'not at all' in (57) (note that this "error" occurs relatively late):

(57)   mag gar nicht die essen   Simone 2;04.20
         (I) do not want this to eat
         'I don't want to eat this'

All the other unscrambled objects are definite DPs which are allowed to stay *in situ* in verb-final infinitival clauses, as in (58) (cf. (17) above):

(58)   a. mone nich das eis haben   Simone 2;00.26
            Simone not the ice cream have
            'Simone doesn't have the ice cream'
         b. kann nich de knete essen   Simone 2;01.12
            (One) cannot the clay eat
            '(one) cannot eat the clay'
         c. auch de banke habe   Simone 2;00.03
            also the bench have
            '(I) also have the bench'

Again 96.2% (30 out of 31) of the heavy object nominals are placed correctly by the child.

There are two interesting cases, given in (59), of (correctly) unscrambled light object nominals which illustrate the basic assumption of the Configurational Readiness Hypothesis, namely the close relationship mentioned above between object scrambling and the mode of mapping object nouns onto syntactic configurations:

(59)   a. brauche nich lala`.   Simone 2;00.23
            need not pacifier
            '(I) do not need a pacifier'
         b. häschen braucht nich windel`. Simone 2;01.19
            bunny needs not diaper
            'the bunny does not need a diaper.'

According to our assumptions (see also Schönenberger, Penner & Weissenborn, 1997), the two object nominals *lala* and *windel* have to be analyzed as pure N°s which form a complex predicate together with the verb *brauchen* and which, exactly like the nominal *rad* 'bicycle' in *rad fahren* 'to cycle' stays behind in a V2-matrix clause, as shown in (60):

(60)   Hans fährt rad
         Hans rides bicycle
         'Hans is cycling'

In this sense, the sentences in (59) do not constitute a violation of the target language as they accord with its licensing conditions. What the child still has to find out is which subset of German nouns can appear in these complex predicates like *rad fahren* (Schönenberger, Penner & Weissenborn 1997). This is a lexical task which is independent of the scrambling rule itself.

The last example we want to discuss is shown in (61):

(61)   ande auch schuh ausziehen   Simone 2;00.01
       other also shoe take-off
       'also take the other shoe off'

We propose that this example is more evidence in favor of the analysis of pure noun+verb structures as complex predicates. Under this analysis the modifier *ande* = *andere* becomes available for the specifier position of the Affect Configuration.

To summarize, we have shown that the High German data also support our assumption that local scrambling is available from early on in both languages, independently of the degree of morphological specification of the Case and determiner system.

5. SUMMARY AND CONCLUSIONS

We have drawn attention to acquisition phenomena which have so far gone largely unnoticed, such as the remarkably early emergence of the focus particle *auch* in German, and we have underscored its crucial function in shaping the emerging phrase structure. Specifically, we have argued that the acquisition of the focus particle *auch*, a set-forming, hence quantificational element, gives rise to the first fully-fledged Affect Configuration above the VP. The specifier position, which becomes available in the process, promptly serves as a landing site for local scrambling. The next step consists in the creation of an Affect Configuration of the same type headed by the negation marker *nicht*. This temporal order, with *auch* preceding *nicht* has been attributed to the fact that *auch* is more accessible to the child in terms of syntactic bootstrapping.

Initially, local scrambling evolves around the focus particle *auch* which is the only item in the one-member class [+Affective], i.e., it is the head or a "unique" (see Roeper, 1996) or "special" projection (see Tracy, 1995). Subsequently, the [+Affective] class is extended by an additional member, namely the negative marker *nicht*. The latter figures as a 'place holder' for the feature [Negation] until the question concerning its X-bar status (specifier vs. head) has been settled. It seems, then, that local scrambling becomes operative as soon as the child has acquired at least one affective item, i.e., once the formal licensing conditions of inserting [+Affective] elements are satisfied. Since at the time both Case marking and definiteness are still 'underspecified' at the time we should not expect them to be critical in the process. For Swiss German, for instance, support from Case marking is not even an option. The asymmetry between subject and object scrambling in early grammar was ascribed to the fact that the child starts out with an overgeneralized light noun interpretation of object nouns which is later adapted to the target language in an item-by-item fashion.

While we have concentrated our discussion on *auch* and negation, one could consider taking into account other lexical items, such as *noch(mal)* and *wieder* (both meaning 'again'), which also appear very early in our data and which are sufficiently similar to *auch* to assume that they get assimilated into the same structural schema.

For the time being, we hope to have shown that there is still a lot to be gained from the investigation of children's first word combinations. More detailed reanalyses of available German data and future case studies, preferably ones involving very frequent recordings and, ideally, diary notes, should easily falsify our hypothesis concerning the bootstrapping function fulfilled by early *auch vis-à-vis nicht*.

ACKNOWLEDGEMENTS

We are indebted to the audiences of various conferences for constructive comments, in particular to B. Drubig, C. Hamann, G. Müller, T. Roeper, M. Schönenberger, S. Winkler, and to I. Gawlitzek-Maiwald for making available the early Benny corpora. The Simone data were collected by Max Miller. We want to thank him for making the data available to us. We also want to thank Susan Powers and Uli Scharnhorst for their help with the data analysis, the editors of this volume and an anonymous reviewer for helpful suggestions. The research of Rosemarie Tracy was supported by the Deutsche Forschungsgemeinschaft (DFG, Forschungsschwerpunkt "Spracherwerb"); Jürgen Weissenborn was supported by a grant of the Deutsche Forschungsgemeinschaft (DFG) in the framework of the Innovationskolleg "Formale Modelle kognitiver Komplexität".

NOTES

[1] In the presentation of examples, the following conventions will be followed: The first line shows the utterance with context, where needed. The second line contains an interlinear translation, and the third line a gloss. Accented syllables are rendered in capitals, final rising, falling and level tones are indicated by /,\ and –, respectively; "A." refers to adult interlocutors.
[2] The examples in this first section are from the four longitudinal case studies described in Tracy (1991) and one child Benny, who took part in the DFG-project (for methodological details see Fritzenschaft *et al.* (1990)).

[3] Actually, the categorial status of some of the lexical items classified as main verbs is quite dubious. For utterances such as *äffchen schauke* 'little-monkey swing', for instance, it is impossible to decide whether *schauke* represents a noun *Schaukel)*or a verb *schaukeln*; see the discussion in Tracy, 1991:162ff.

[4] Following the child's negative statement, her father, also a linguist, comments: *This form of negation is new*, referring to the combination of utterance and head shaking.

[5] Tracy (1995) refers to this stage as V2 mimicry. The syntax of wh question in early German is documented in Penner (1994a) and Tracy (1994) and the literature cited therein.

[6] Note that the deviant agreement marking (*hat* instead of the plural *haben*) may have been provoked by the input. On the other hand, Florian's agreement marking at this stage is still largely deficient.

[7] See among others, the papers in Grewendorf & Sternefeld (1990), Geilfuss (1990), and Schönenberger & Penner (1995) for Swiss German.

[8] It must be pointed out here that set formation in early grammar is probably restricted to two-member sets. The more articulated bound-variable reading is acquired much later at the age of 4;0. See Penner & Roeper (1998) for a detailed discussion of this issue.

[9] Penner (1994b) and Penner & Weissenborn (1996) propose that such an Affect Configuration is also relevant for the structure of dative possessive in (Swiss) German and their acquisition. Thus the possessor and the expletive possessive pronoun in the possessive structure in (i):

(i)　　em Vater sis Huus　　　　　(dem Vater sein Haus)
　　　to the father his house
　　　'Father's house'

creates the Affect Configuration:

Spec, DP　　　　　D^0
+POSS　　　　　　+POSS

[10] The Bernese data are taken from J.'s diary which consists of two corpora. The first corpus (age-range: 1;02-2;08; total number of utterances: 5000) contains a daily collection of all the developmentally-relevant data from the onset (first one-word utterances) until after the acquisition of V2. The second corpus focuses on the late development of subordination. What is crucial for our concern here is that this diary includes a complete representation of speech production from the onset and *all* the two- and multi-word-utterances until 2;6. This enables us to develop an articulated model for the emergence of *nicht* and *auch*.

[11] For German see Penner & Schönenberger (1995), and Penner & Weissenborn (1996) and the literature they cite.

[12] Even though in J.'s data we only find either subject or object raising, we have encountered a few exceptions in other children, though never more than a couple per child. Some of these cases, like the late (2;4) example (15) *Julia Florian auch in Nase stechen* can be explained relatively easily since at that time, the child already has further landings sites available, as shown by the prevalence of productive V2 clauses. This brings down problematic cases to very rare and early exceptions such as *Bobo Rosi auch* 'Bobo R. also' ('R. should also sit down on the monkey Bobo') by Stephanie at age 1;8 (note that the verb is dropped in this case!)

[13] The data are taken from the Simone corpus collected by Max Miller. The counting is computer-assisted (data bank).

REFERENCES

Bayer, J.: 1990, 'What Bavarian Negative Concord reveals about the syntactic structure of German', in J. Mascaro & M. Nespor (eds.) *Grammar in Progress*, Foris, Dordrecht, 13-23.

Bottari, P., Cipriani, P., and Chilosi A.M. (1993/4) 'Proto-syntactic Devices in the Acquisition of Italian Free Morphology', *GenGenP* **0(1-2)**, 83-101.

Chomsky, N.: 1992, 'A Minimalist Program for Linguistic Theory, MITOPL, 1.

Clahsen, H.: 1988, 'Critical Phases of Grammar Development: A Study in the Acquisition of Negation in Children and Adults', In P. Jordens & J. Lalleman (eds.) *Language Development*, Foris, Dordrecht, 123-148.

Eisenbeiss, S.: 1994, 'Raising to SPEC and Adjunction. Scrambling in German Child Language', Paper presented at the Workshop on the L1- and L2- Acquisition of Clause-Internal Rules: Scrambling and Cliticization, Bern, Switzerland, January.
Fritzenschaft, A, I. Gawlitzek-Maiwald and S. Winkler: 1990,'Wege zur komplexen Syntax', In *Zeitschrift für Sprachwissenschaft* **9**, 52-134.
Geilfuss, J.:1990, 'Verb und Verbphrasensyntax', *Arbeitspapiere des Sonderforschungsbereichs* 340, Bericht Nr. 11, Stuttgart.
Grewendorf, G. & W. Sternefeld (eds.) 1990, *Scrambling and Barriers*. John Benjamins, Amsterdam.
Haegeman, L. and R. Zanuttini: 1991, 'Negative Heads and the Neg Criterion', *The Linguistic Review* **8**, 233-251.
Haegeman, L.: 1992, 'Sentential Negation in Italian and the Neg Criterion', ms., University of Geneva.
Haegeman, L. and R. Zanuttini: 1996, 'Negative Concord in West Flemish', In A. Belletti & L. Rizzi (eds.) *Parameters and Functional Heads*. Oxford University Press, Oxford, 117-179.
Hamann, C.: 1996, 'Negation and truncated structures', in M. Aldridge (ed.) *Child Language*, Multilingual Matters, Clevedon. 72-83.
Hoekstra, T. and P. Jordens: 1994, 'From Adjunct to Head. In T. Hoekstra & B. Schwartz (eds.) *Language Acquisition Studies in Generative Grammar*, John Benjamins, Amsterdam, 119-150.
Hyams, N.: 1996, 'The Underspecification of Functional Categories in Early Grammar', In H. Clahsen (ed.) *Generative Perspectives on Language Acquisition: Empirical Findings, Theoretical Considerations, Crosslinguistic Comparisons*, John Benjamins, Amsterdam, 91-128.
Jacobs, J. : 1982, *Syntax und Semantik der Negation im Deutschen*, Fink, München.
Jacobs, J. : 1983, *Fokus und Skalen. Zur Syntax und Semantik der Gradpartikeln im Deutschen*, Niemeyer, Tübingen.
Kayne, R.: 1994,*The Antisymmetry of Syntax*. MIT Press, Cambridge.
Miller, M.: 1976, *Zur Logik der frühkindlichen Sprachenentwicklung*, Klett, Stuttgart.
Penner, Z.: 1993, 'The Earliest Stage in the Acquisition of the Nominal Phrase in Bernese Swiss German: Syntactic Bootstrapping and the Architecture of Language Learning', *Arbeitspapier Institut für Sprachwissenschaft der Universität Bern* **30**.
Penner, Z.: 1994a, 'Asking Questions without CPs? On the Acquisition of Wh Questions in Bernese Swiss German and Standard German', In T. Hoekstra & B. Schwartz (eds.), *Language Acquisition Studies in Generative Grammar*, John Benjamins, Amsterdam, 177-214.
Penner, Z.: 1994b, 'Ordered Parameter Setting', Habilitation Thesis, University of Berne.
Penner, Z. and C. Hamann: 1998, 'The emergence of discourse/syntax interface problems in impaired grammar', In A. Greenhill, M. Huges, H. Litttlefield & H. Walsh (eds.) *Proceedings of the 22nd Boston University Conference on Language Development*, Cascadilla Press, Somerville, 626-639.
Penner, Z. and T. Roeper: 1998, 'Trigger Theory and the Acquisition of Complement Idioms', In Z. Penner & N. Dittmar (eds.) *Issues in the Theory of Language Acquisition. Essays in Honor of Jürgen Weissenborn*, Peter Lang, Bern, 77-112.
Penner, Z. and M. Schönenberger: 1995, 'The Distribution of Nominal Agreement Features in Swiss German Dialects', In Z. Penner (ed.)*Topics in Swiss German Syntax*, Peter Lang, Bern, 331-346.
Penner, Z. and J. Weissenborn: 1996, 'Strong Continuity, Parameter Setting, and the Trigger Hierarchy', In H. Clahsen (ed.) *Generative Perspectives on Language Acquisition: Empirical Findings, Theoretical Considerations, Crosslinguistic Comparisons*, John Benjamins, Amsterdam, 161-200.
Puskas, G.: 1992, 'The Wh-Criterion in Hungarian', *Rivista di Grammatica generativa* **22**, 141-186.
Rizzi L.: 1991, 'Residual Verb Second and the Wh Criterion', *Technical Reports in Formal and Computational Linguistics* **2**, University of Geneva.

Roeper, T.: 1992, 'From the Initial State to V2. Acquisition Principles in Action', In J. Meisel (ed.) *The Acquisition of Verb Placement: Functional Categories and V2 Phenomena in Language Acquisition*, Kluwer, Dordrecht, 333-370.

Roeper, T.: 1996, 'The Role of Merger Theory and Formal Features in Acquisition', In H. Clahsen (ed.) *Generative Perspectives on Language Acquisition: Empirical Findings, Theoretical Considerations, Crosslinguistic Comparisons*, John Benjamins, Amsterdam, 415-450.

Schaeffer, J., N. Hyams, and K. Johnson: 1994, 'On the Acquisition of Scrambling in Dutch. Paper presented at the Workshop on the L1- and L2- Acquisition of Clause-Internal Rules: Scrambling and Cliticization, Bern, Switzerland, January.

Schönenberger M. and Z. Penner: 1995, 'Cross-dialectal Variation in Swiss German: Doubling Verbs, Verb Projection Raising, Barrierhood, and LF Movement', In H. Haider, S. Olsen and S. Vikner (eds.) *Studies in Comparative Germanic Syntax*, Kluwer Academic, Dordrecht, 285-306.

Schönenberger, M., Penner, Z. & Weissenborn, J.: 1997, 'Object Placement and Early German Grammar', In *Proceedings of the 21st Annual Boston University Conference on Language Development*, Cascadilla Press, Somerville, 539-549.

Tracy, R.: 1991, *Sprachliche Strukturentwicklung: Linguistische und kognitionspsychologische Aspekte einer Theorie des Erstspracherwerbs*, Narr, Tübingen.

Tracy, R.: 1994, 'Raising Questions: Formal and Functional Aspects of the Acquisition of Wh-Questions in German', In R. Tracy & E. Lattey (eds.) *How Tolerant Is Universal Grammar? Essays on Language Learnability and Language Variation*. Niemeyer, Tübingen, 1-34.

Tracy, R.: 1995, 'Child Languages in Contact: The simultaneous acquisition of two first languages (English/German) in early childhood', Habilitationsschrift, Universität Tübingen.

Valian, V.: 1992, 'Categories of First Syntax: Be, Be+ing, and Nothingness', In J. Meisel (ed.) *The Acquisition of Verb Placement: Functional Categories and V2 Phenomena in Language Acquisition*, Kluwer, Dordrecht, 401-422.

Weissenborn, J.: 1994, 'Constraining the Child's Grammar: Local Wellformedness in the Development of Verb Movement in German and French', In B. Lust, J. Whitman, & J. Kornfilt (eds.) *Syntactic Theory and Language Acquisition: Crosslinguistic Perspectives*. Lawrence Erlbaum, Hillsdale, 215-247.

Weissenborn, J., M. Verrips and R. Berman: 1989, 'Negation as a Window to the Structure of Early Child Language, ms., Max Planck Institut für Psycholinguistik, Nijmegen.

Wode, H.: 1977, 'Four Early Stages in the Development of L1 Negation', *Journal of Child Language* **4**, 87-102.

Zanuttini, R.: 1991, 'Syntactic Properties of Sentential Negation: A Comparative Study of the Romance Languages', Ph.D. Dissertation, University of Pennsylvania.

Zwart, J.W.: 1993, Dutch Syntax: A Minimalist Approach, Ph.D. Dissertation, University of Groningen.

ZVI PENNER
University of Konstanz

ROSEMARIE TRACY
University of Mannheim

JÜRGEN WEISSENBORN
University of Potsdam

ANNA CARDINALETTI   MICHAL STARKE

OVERVIEW: THE GRAMMAR (AND ACQUISITION) OF CLITICS

1. INDEXICALITY AND DEFICIENCY

Pronouns have a complex grammar. They are at the crossroad of two rather ill-understood systems: *indexicality* and *deficiency*. On the one hand, knowledge of pronouns is knowledge of an intricate "referential" system, whereby a part of a sentence can "corefer" with another, or "be a variable linked to" another, or again "point to the context" of the utterance. These intuitive descriptions of indexicality have vexed scholars in their attempt to render them precise, ever since the dawn of research on language. For instance, in the first century AC, Appolonius Dyskolus came to distinguish an anaphoric use (secondary acquaintance) from a deictic use (primary acquaintance) of pronouns. This distinction remains a lively source of bewilderment for scholars in the end of the twentieth century through discussions of "accidental coreference", "donkey-sentences", "telescoping", and other such puzzles.

On the other hand, knowledge of pronouns requires knowledge of the opposition between distinct forms of one and the same pronoun. It is a mysterious fact about pronouns that they often come in pairs, where the two elements of the pair are near-identical in meaning, but extensively different in syntax. At first sight, this opposition seems to be purely syntactic, and as such raises interesting issues about its cross-linguistic robustness, and its acquisition.

In this brief survey, we will concentrate on the problem of deficiency, providing an overview of the major facts and pointing out the most likely path of explanation. Such an analysis defines what it is that a child must learn, and in a brief appendix we look at what it is that children actually know, judging from their utterances as recorded in the CHILDES Database (MacWhinney & Snow, 1985).

2. THE GRAMMAR OF THE STRONG/DEFICIENT OPPOSITION

2.1. Strong > Weak > Clitic

In many languages, one and the same pronoun (say that which corresponds to English *you*) appears with several distinct morphological forms (say the French *te* and *toi*):

(1) a. Il a peur **de toi** maintenant.
    he fears of you now
  b. Il **te** craint maintenant.
    he you fears now
    'He is afraid of you now.'

In this example, the two forms *tu* and *de toi* seem semantically (or functionally) identical. Yet they cannot be interchanged (**il a peur (de) te* or **il (de) toi craint*). The two elements of the pair appear to have arbitrary syntactic properties. Why couldn't the *te* form occur in the usual noun-phrase positions, and why can't the *toi* form occur pre-verbally as *te* does? The existence of such arbitrary asymmetries would seem to be a quirk stemming from the arbitrary properties of the syntax itself. The facts to be learned would thus roughly be:

(2) *Deficiency #1* (non-final)
    Personal pronouns divide into two classes, defined by purely arbitrary grammatical properties (i.e., the two classes do not correlate with functional/semantic properties).
    One and the same (functionally defined) pronoun can have an instantiation in each class.

(The reason for the term "deficiency" will become transparent below.)

In fact, the puzzle is slightly deeper: grammar provides not only two but three distinct forms of one and the same pronoun, with three distinct sets of properties associated to each type of pronoun. This was first noted by Cardinaletti (1991), thanks to the transparent distribution of Romance, with the following paradigm:

(3) a. Non **gli** dirò mai *gli tutto *gli.
     b. Non *loro dirò mai **loro** tutto *loro.
     c. Non *a loro dirò mai *a loro tutto **a loro**.
        not to.him/to.them I.will.say never everything
        'I will never tell him/them everything.'

Such a tripartition is echoed in French imperatives:

(4) a. **Me** parles *me pas *me.
     b. *Moi parles **moi** pas *moi.
     c. *A moi parles *à moi pas **à moi**.
        to.me speak to.me not to.me
        'Don't speak to me.'

and in several paradigms of other language groups, such as the following Germanic examples (from Olang Tirolese), in which the *e:r* form can be a V2 initial subject both short and long distance, *es* can only be short distance, while the reduced form *s* can never occur V2 initially:

(5) a. ✓ **E:r** sagt Maria [t isch intelligent.
     a.' ✓ Maria sagt [**e:r** isch intelligent.
         Maria says he is intelligent
     b. * **Es** sagt Maria [t isch toire.
     b.' Maria sagt [**es** isch toire.
     c. * **S** sagt Maria [t isch toire.
     c'. * Maria sagt [**s** isch toire.
         Maria says it is expensive

The state of affairs to be acquired thus becomes slightly more complicated:

(6) Deficiency #2 (non-final)
     Personal pronouns divide into three classes, defined by purely arbitrary grammatical properties (i.e., the three classes do not correlate with functional/semantic properties).
     One and the same (functionally defined) pronoun can have one instantiation in each class.

In all the above cases, one of the three forms has (by and large) the properties of any noun phrase {*a lui, à moi, e:r*}. First, a noun phrase has some distributional liberty: it can be dislocated, clefted, sometimes it can appear in distinct positions within the clause as with Italian pre- and post-verbal subjects, etc. This property is shared by the "normal" pronouns, the {*a lui, à moi, e:r*} series. On the other hand, all other pronouns are distributionally "special": they can only occur in a very limited set of positions, arguably in one and only one position.

This normal/special distinction is even more transparent in coordination. The "normal" series behaves like noun phrases: it is freely coordinable (*parles à moi et à lui alors* 'speak to me and to him then'). The "special" series by opposition has a special behavior here: it cannot be coordinated:

(7) a. *Non   dirò mai **loro** e loro tutto.
     b. *Non   **gli** e le   dirò mai   tutto.
         not   to.him and to.her   I.will.say never   everything
     c. *Ne   **me et lui**   parles   pas.
     d.   *Parles **moi et lui** pas.
         not   to.me and to.him   speak   not
     e. *Es **und es**
         it and it   sain toire.
                                          are expensive

All the acceptable examples involving special pronouns become unacceptable when the special pronoun is coordinated. Again, the normal series behaves as any noun phrase of these languages, while the special series behaves specially.

Now it is a striking fact that (to our knowledge), systems of personal pronouns always divide like this: two special and one normal series. While there are languages where lexical gaps leave only one or two series, it is never the case that there are four classes, or that there are two normal and one special series, etc.

Another way to put this is that these three types of personal pronouns seem to exhaust the inventory of distinct types of personal pronouns.

Much energy has been devoted to special pronouns as those in (3a-4a) in the last twenty years. One of the few rather uncontroversial results of this investigation is that the surface occurrences of such pronouns are best treated as heads, X^0, rather than phrases, XP (this does not prejudge their underlying status), while normal pronouns are best treated as XPs, as any other noun phrase is.

This may be best illustrated by examples like the following,

(8) L'avesse Gianni organizzato con un certo anticipo, ...
it had Gianni organized with a certain advance, ...
'had Gianni organized it in advance, ...'

where the special pronoun is preposed along with the verb (an uncontroversial X^0) over the subject (an XP). Again, special pronouns are special with respect to noun phrases.

On the other hand, not much attention has been accorded to special pronouns of the type (3b-4b), with one exception: French reduced subject pronouns (such as *il*) have been the object of systematic investigation. Dealing with the latter, both Kayne (1983) and Rizzi (1986) came to the conclusion that these are surface phrases, XPs. This conclusion, which was then limited to French subject pronouns, also applies to (3b-4b), and many other cases of that type (Cardinaletti & Starke, 1994). We thus have a simple syntactic characterization of the tripartition of pronouns: there are three homogeneous classes, the normal pronouns, the special XPs, and the special X^0s.

But this is a limited and misleading way of stating the facts. Consider the following depiction of the "special" properties of "special" pronouns:

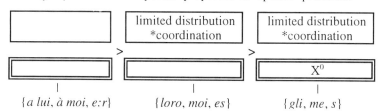

Trivially the normal pronouns have no "special properties", the *loro*-type pronouns have one set of special properties, and the *gli*-type pronouns have both this set and additional "special properties". This way of putting things brings out two more general properties of the tripartition: (i) the two "special" types share a set of properties that render them "special" (here limited distribution and non-coordination), (ii) for one of the two classes, this exhausts its "special" character, while the other has additional quirks (here X^0): it is so to speak "very special". This gives the fundamental character of the tripartition: its $x > y > z$ organization (*normal > special > very special*):

(9)   *Deficiency #3* (non-final)
Personal pronouns divide into three classes with an internal relation of *normal class* > *special class* > *very special class*.
Classes are defined by arbitrary grammatical properties (i.e., the three classes do not correlate with functional / semantic properties).
One and the same (functionally defined) pronoun can have one instantiation in each class.

From this set of observations, we now have fairly precise constraints on any theory of the pronominal system: it must be capable of expressing the systematic existence of one normal and two special classes, and must be capable of expressing the *normal* > *special* > *very special* relationship in the above sense. The obvious way of expressing that, is that human language contains two properties which render things (here personal pronouns) "special", say S1 (responsible for limited distribution and non-coordinability) and S2 (responsible for the surface X^0 status). The above observations now follow if normal pronouns are <- S1; - S2>, the special pronouns are <+S1; - S2> and the very special pronouns are <+S1; +S2>.

Some historical and terminological asides. First a warning: the above remarks may seem rather trivial or even self-evident. They are however not uncontroversial. Although no alternative has been proposed – and the facts themselves are seldom noted – this way of seeing things is both new (first proposed in Cardinaletti & Starke (in press) where it is discussed in much more detail) and sometimes contested (cf. the appended peer reviews).

More positively, it is to be noted that viewing the pronominal system as composed of three classes organized in a *normal* > *special* > *very special* fashion, enables one to look at and integrate facts which have mostly been left aside. Since traditional studies of pronominal systems focus on the opposition between "normal" and "very special" pronouns, the pronouns belonging to the intermediate "special" class were somewhat of a mystery. Attempts have been made to treat them as very special, disregarding the differences with other special pronouns, or again, more radically, some have proposed to simply ignore most of the facts and treat "special" pronouns as normal. In most cases however, these pronouns have been merely set aside. This is for instance the case of practically all continental Germanic pronouns (in their non-deictic use), and also of the English pronoun *it* (subject and object). The *normal* > *special* > *very special* distinction allows us to bring these facts back in.

Finally, a note of terminology. It is traditional to call the "normal" pronouns "strong pronouns" and the "very special" pronouns "clitic pronouns". Although some confusion may arise from the connotations of these traditional terms, we will follow this terminology. Furthermore since many of the ill-understood Germanic pronouns were referred to as "weak pronouns" (a term which has not been given any explicit signification, or worse, which sometimes is taken to mean "Germanic counterpart of Romance clitics"), we will adopt this term, but as a technical label for the intermediate class of "special" pronouns.

The tripartition thus emerges as *strong > weak > clitic* pronouns: strong pronouns behave essentially as full noun phrases, weak and clitic pronouns however differ from noun phrases. Furthermore, all properties that make weak pronouns different from noun phrases are shared by clitics, while clitics have some additional special properties on their own.

The *strong > weak > clitic* distinction established on the basis of "how special the pronoun is" is confirmed by two other properties. First the choice of pronouns: if there are three versions of each pronoun, how does one of the three get chosen in a given sentence? The choice turns out to obey the same hierarchy: *strong > weak > clitic*. That is, where both a clitic and a strong pronoun are in principle possible, only the clitic is in fact possible:

(10) a. ✓ Il **te** craint maintenant.
b. * Il craint **toi** maintenant.
he you fears you now
'He is afraid of you now.'

The strong pronoun is possible only in those constructions that exclude the clitic and weak pronouns, such as coordination, adverbial modification or some forms of contrastive stress:

(11) a. ✓ Il craint [**toi et ton frère**].
b. ✓ Il ne craint [**que toi**].
he fears you and your brother/ only you
'He is afraid of you and your brother/ only you .'
c. ✓ Il craint [**TOI, pas ton frère**].
he fears you, not your brother
'He is afraid of you, not your brother.'

This gives the typical surface paradigm of an element appearing to some leftward position, *unless* it is coordinated, modified or contrastively focussed. (In this respect, the paradigm in (4) is slightly smoothed: the strong pronoun in (4c) is only possible if the other two are independently impossible, e.g., with some form of contrastive stress. Similarly, (3) plays on distinct registers, to avoid the effects of the choice preference: (3a) is colloquial while (3b) is formal.)

The above paradigm only establishes a *clitic < strong* preference. The following two paradigms fill in the gaps:

(12) *weak < strong*
    a. ✓ **Il**   me voit.   [French]
    b. * **Lui**   me voit.
    c. ✓ **Lui** aussi me voit.
           he (also)   me sees
           'He (too) sees me.'

(13)   *clitic < weak*
    a. ✓ ... weil   **s**   toire   isch.   [Olang Tirolese]
    b. * ... weil   **es**   toire   isch.
           ... because it   expensive is
           '... because it is expensive.'
    c. ✓ **Es** isch   toire.

The French subject weak pronoun *il* is chosen over the strong form *lui* unless it is independently impossible (as with adverbial modification here), and the Olang Tirolese clitic form *s* is chosen over the weak form *es* when possible (as in the Mittelfeld, but not V2-initially), thus: *strong > weak > clitic*. (Note that if *pro* is a pronoun, it is to be classified as a weak pronoun, and it thus follows that given the choice between *pro* and a clitic, the clitic is to be chosen, contrary to what is sometimes intuitively proposed: that zero forms are always chosen over overt forms).

Similarly, the three types of pronouns often differ morphologically. When that is the case, the tendency is again systematic: strong forms are heavier than others, and weak forms are heavier than clitic forms. A transparent illustration of this is the Slovak strong/clitic pair <*jeho/ho*> where the strong from *jeho* contains the clitic form *ho*. A more complete state of affairs is given by:

(14) | | clitic | weak | | strong | |
|---|---|---|---|---|---|
| a. | ho | | < | jeho | [Slovak] |
| b. | s | < es | | | [Olang Tirolese] |
| c. | | loro | < | a loro | [Italian] |
| d. | | il | < | lui | [French] |

The *strong* > *weak* > *clitic* thus seems to be a general property of the pronominal system:

(15)   *strong* > *weak* > *clitic*
- the number of ways in which each class is distinct from noun phrases
- the choice between pronouns
- the morphological hierarchy

The characterization of the pronominal system thus becomes:

(16)   *Deficiency #4* (non-final)
Personal pronouns divide into three classes with an internal relation of *strong class* > *weak class* > *clitic class*.
This relationship reflects with hierarchies: (i) how special the pronoun is with respect to noun phrases, (ii) which class is preferably chosen *ceteris paribus,* and (iii) the "morphological weight" of the classes. The three classes are defined by arbitrary grammatical properties (i.e. they do not correlate with functional / semantic properties).

From the above paradigms, not only do we know that the general form of the pronominal system is *strong* > *weak* > *clitic*, but the properties in (15) give us one more hint as to the underlying form of the system: whatever trigger provokes the distinction between strong and weak pronouns (trigger labeled S1 above), this trigger causes both morphological reduction, and a choice-preference in favor of those pronouns that possess S1 over those that don't. On the other hand, whatever trigger provokes the distinction between weak and clitic pronouns (S2 above), it also causes both morphological reduction, and a choice-preference in favor of those pronouns that possess S2 over those that don't. This high similarity in the effects of the two triggers makes it probable that S1 and S2 are very similar, or two instantiations of an identical underlying trigger.

Finally, a word on acquisition. If one follows most of the contemporary literature on clitichood, mastery of clitics would seem to be an essentially uninteresting state: clitics are usually seen as idiosyncratic DPs, marked as [+clitic], [+specific], [+phonologically enclitic], or some similar marker, and this marker is then seen as associated with some special syntactic and/or accentual properties. In such a world, knowledge of clitics reduces to knowledge of a marker and its associated properties.

By contrast, if more paradigms are taken into account, knowledge of the pronominal system becomes a much more complex achievement, combining two instances of an underlying marker in order to produce an ordered tripartition of pronouns, with widespread surface consequences, the topic of the next section.

2.2. Across Grammar

Apart from the $x > y > z$ form of the system, a second striking (and maybe unique) fact about the tripartition is that these very same three classes differ across every part of the grammar: syntax, morphology, semantics, and phonology. This raises the delicate question of covariation between what otherwise appears to be widely distinct systems.

That weak and strong pronouns differ both in syntax (distribution, coordination, modification) and in morphology has been illustrated above. But these two classes also differ semantically: the strong pronoun can only refer to human entities while weak (and thus clitic) pronouns can refer to both human and non-human entities. The weak French *il* (17a) can refer both to a boy and a truck, while the corresponding strong *lui* can only refer to the boy, not the truck. The same holds for Italian *loro /a loro* in (18):

				+human/−human	
(17)	a.	**Il**	est beau.	✓	✓
	b.	**Lui**	est beau.	✓	*
		'He	is pretty.'		
(18)	a.	Non metterò mai **loro** il cappuccio.		✓	✓
		not I.will.put never to.them the cap			
	b.	Non metterò mai il cappuccio **a loro**.		✓	*
		not I.will.put never the cap to them			
		'I will never put the cap /pen-top on them.'			

(this has sporadically been noted at least since the Port-Royal grammar. It is systematically applied in Cardinaletti & Starke (to appear) to clarify for instance the status of some traditionally unclear German pronouns: pronouns such as *sie* 'she' are difficult to deal with until it is noted that they become weak when referring to non-human entities. The discovery that this pronoun can refer to non-human entities but cannot do so anymore as soon as it is coordinated now clearly indicates that it is ambiguous between a strong and a weak (or clitic) form.

Finally, the two classes differ not only in syntax, morphology and semantics but also in phonology. Take the French plural pronouns *ils* and *eux* 'they' in (19). The first, but not the second one undergoes *liaison*, the surfacing of a final (mute) consonant:

(19) a.   Ils   -[z]   ont   un seul bras ?
      b. Pourquoi   eux   *-[z]   ont-ils   un seul bras ?
         why   they   have (they)   one only arm
         'Why do they have only one arm?'

Before drawing conclusions from this, let us strengthen the phonological case a little bit. In (20), the contrast could be due to irrelevant reasons: *eux* might lack the underlying final /z/. To discard this, let us note first that in (20b) the subject appears twice, once between *pourquoi* and *ont*, and once between *ont* and *un seul bras*. In its first occurrence, the subject pronoun must necessarily be strong (*pourquoi **ils** ont-ils un seul bras?). In its second occurrence, it cannot be strong (*pourquoi eux ont-**eux** un seul bras?). Now in the feminine, the weak pronoun and the strong pronoun have the same morphology. Yet the asymmetry with respect to liaison still obtains even though the phonological environment is identical in the two cases: the weak *elles* in (20a) undergoes liaison, just as *ils* in (20a), and the strong *elles* in (20b) cannot undergo liaison on a par with the strong *eux* in (20b):

(20) a.   Elles -[z]   ont   un seul bras ?
      b. Pourquoi   elles *-[z]   ont-elles   un seul bras ?
         why   they   have (they)   one only arm

The remaining generalization is that weak but not strong pronouns undergo liaison (also: no perceptible prosodic boundary needs to occur between the first subject and the verb).

To put things slightly more provocatively, a simple covariation between phonology and semantics obtains in constructions of the type (20b-20b): pronouns that do not undergo liaison can only refer to human entities!

How are we to capture the fact that weak pronouns differ from strong pronouns syntactically, morphologically, semantically and phonologically? Obviously, the least desirable solution would be not to capture this at all: the worst solution would be to restipulate the weak/strong distinction once in syntax, once in semantics, once in phonology, etc. Given such a solution it would be a surprise that the class of possibly-non-human-referring entities and the class of liaison-undergoing elements is one and the same. For example, we could then have in semantics an opposition between say, *{moi, tu, il, ...}* versus *{je, toi, lui, ...}* and in phonology the usual opposition between *{je, tu, il, ...}* versus *{moi, toi, lui, ...}*. This does not seem to exist.

To capture this covariation, we need to derive all the differences from one unique underlying difference. Presupposing a T-model of grammar, where semantics and phonology do not communicate, such an underlying difference must be syntactic in nature. If weak pronouns are special in their (morpho)syntax, this marking may easily have both semantic and phonological consequences. The trigger must thus be syntactic. (This rules out many traditional approaches to the strong/non-strong distinction which attempt to reduce it either to phonology – capitalizing on the deaccentuation of weak/clitic pronouns, see below, or semantics – capitalizing on contrastive focus or theme/rheme oppositions.)

With respect to acquisition, the above makes knowledge of pronominal classes much more interesting: knowledge of pronouns presupposes an intricate and fine-grained deductive structure across grammatical modules. One property of weak pronouns in syntax must allow asymmetries with respect to such diverse linguistic aspects as coordination, the humanness of the referents and phonological liaison. In turn this presupposes knowledge of: (i) the intramodule constraints regulating these constructions (constraints on coordination, constraints on allocation of referents, constraints on liaison, etc.) and most notably (ii) the cross-module interaction which enables one property of syntax to cause asymmetries in phonology and semantics. In other words, the child who masters the pronominal system must be in possession of the relevant subparts of grammar and of their interrelations (i.e., the mapping between syntactic/phonological, syntactic/semantic representations). This last property makes acquisition of clitichood an invaluable source of insight into the nature of children's grammar.

What is true of the weak/strong distinction also obtains with the clitic/weak distinction: they differ all over syntax, morphology, semantics and phonology. The syntactic difference has already been illustrated above: one is a (surface) syntactic head while the other is a (surface) syntactic phrase. Morphological differences are illustrated in (4b-c) and (14b). Semantically, one difference is that clitic but not weak pronouns occur as "emotional" (non-referential) datives, i.e., while examples of the type (21a) with the clitic *te* occur, the corresponding (21b) with the weak *toi* does not.

(21)   a. Nous **te**   (lui)   foutrons une claque à ce mec.
          we   to.you (to.him) will.give a   smack to this guy
          'We will slap this guy.'
       b. *Foutons – **toi**   (lui)   une claque à ce mec!
          let.us.give (to.you) to.him a smack   to this guy

Finally, clitic and weak pronouns differ phonologically in that clitic pronouns never bear word-stress, while weak pronouns may do so. The situation is thus (leaving morphology out):

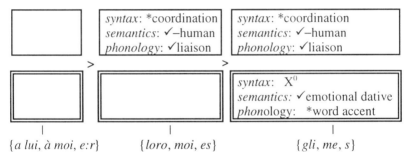

Again, the surface differences between clitic and weak elements must be due to a unique syntactic underlying trigger, for the same reasons as above. We thus have a system of *strong > weak > clitic* pronouns, where the strong/weak and weak/clitic distinctions are each due to a unique underlying syntactic trigger. The two triggers have similar effects in both cases: making the bearer of the trigger preferred over the pronoun which does not have it, triggering differences with respect to usual noun phrases, and triggering differences across all parts of grammar:

(22)   *Deficiency #5* (non-final)
Personal pronouns divide into three classes with an internal relation of *strong class > weak class > clitic class*.
This hierarchy (a) cuts across distinct components of language (syntax, semantics, phonology, morphology) with no systematic functional correlation and (b) reflects three hierarchies: how special the pronoun is with respect to noun phrases; which class is preferably chosen *ceteris paribus,* and the respective "morphological weight" of the classes.

2.3. Deficiency

In the preceding sections, clitic and weak pronouns exhibited some "special" properties with respect to noun phrases and strong pronouns. Upon closer inspection, these properties are not only special, but are special in the very same way. The clearest case is probably morphology. As noted above, each class of pronouns is not only morphological *different* with respect to the other, but is *reduced* with respect to the other. But the same is true of syntax: not only are clitic and weak pronouns different from strong forms and noun phrases, but the syntactic possibilities (i.e. distribution) of clitic/weak pronouns is *reduced* with respect to those of strong pronouns and noun phrases. The same occurs in phonology: clitic pronouns are famous for their being phonologically *deficient*, or *reduced* (sometimes they are even called atonic pronouns). Furthermore, liaison, which distinguishes clitic/weak from strong pronouns, is a phenomenon classical of reduced function words (as opposed to full lexical forms). Finally, clitic and weak pronouns are also semantically deficient: they cannot introduce a new discourse referent. They are limited to being anaphoric (old information) or expletives. It would take slightly more time to trace the asymmetry with respect to ±*human* referent to this referential limitation, but the curious reader is referred to Cardinaletti & Starke (1994) where this is discussed in more detail. (The existence of semantic differences does not contradict our initial description of deficiency. In the semantic paradigms, one class is the subset of the other, which can hardly be used to derive the syntactic asymmetries, where both classes are disjoint.)

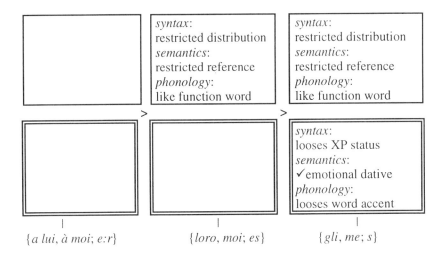

{ a lui, à moi; e:r}   {loro, moi; es}   {gli, me; s}

The systematic nature of the "special" properties is true both of the properties distinguishing weak from strong pronouns and of the properties distinguishing clitic from weak pronouns.

It would thus seem that we are not confronted to a mere *normal > special > very special* hierarchy, but to a *normal > deficient > very deficient* hierarchy:

Correspondingly, the characterization of pronominal systems becomes:

(23)   *Deficiency #6* (non-final)
Personal pronouns divide into three classes with an internal relation of *strong class > weak class > clitic class*.
This hierarchy (a) cuts across distinct components of language (syntax, semantics, phonology, morphology) with no systematic functional correlation and (b) reflects three hierarchies: how **deficient** the pronoun is with respect to noun phrases; which class is preferably chosen *ceteris paribus*, and the respective "morphological weight" of the classes.

It was already noted above that the trigger responsible for the difference between weak and strong pronouns (S1) and the trigger responsible for the difference between clitic and weak pronouns (S2) must be rather similar since they trigger similar morphological and choice-preference effects. The deficiency aspect of the system now completes this similarity: not only are S1/S2 similar with respect to morphology and choice, but also in the nature of the special properties they trigger, namely deficiencies.

2.4. Across Languages and Categories

As a final note, let us observe that the above generalization seems to have wide validity. On the one hand, we find the same pronominal system in language after language. Again, this is not to say that every language has a representative of each of the three classes of pronoun, they don't. Rather, what seems to be true is that the same three clusters of properties obtain in language after language. Every personal pronoun of every language seems to fall into one of the three classes sketched above.

To illustrate this very briefly, consider the conjunction of the coordination and the ±*human* constraint: from the above description of the three classes, it follows that if a pronoun is coordinated, it is strong, and if it is strong, it is necessarily +*human*. This entails the seemingly bizarre and arbitrary fact that a coordinated (personal) pronoun is always +*human*. Consider for instance the following set of languages:

			+*human*/- *human*	
(24)	a. German (∈ Germanic)			
	Sie und die daneben sind groß.		✓	*
	they and those besides are tall/big			
	'They and those besides are tall.'			
	b. Slovak (∈ Slavic)			
	Vidiel som **ich a tch druhch**.		✓	*
	seen I.am them and these others			
	'I have seen them and these others.'			
	c. Hungarian (∈ Finno-Ugric)			
	Láttam **öket és a mellettük levöket**.		✓	*
	I.saw them and those besides			
	'I saw them and those besides.'			
	d. Hebrew (∈ Semitic)			
	Hi ve-zot le-yad-a gvohot.		✓	*
	she and-that.one to-side-her tall/big			
	'She and the one next to her are tall.'			
	e. Gun (∈ Kwa)			
	Yélè kpo yélè kpo yon wankpè.		✓	*
	she and she and know beauty			
	'She and she are beautiful.'			

That this is indeed cross-linguistically so is a strong sign that the above arbitrary system is a general characterization of systems of personal pronouns in human language, not an idiosyncratic property of some specific languages. In fact, all the languages that we have seen in any detail seem to fit into the mold of the three arbitrary classes, with respect to the above mentioned properties.

If confirmed, such paradigms would provide a wealth of surface universals (e.g., 'coordinated personal pronouns are +*human*'), and this with respect to a large number of surface properties across syntax, morphology, semantics and phonology.

Not only does this tripartition seem to apply universally to systems of personal pronouns, but systems other than personal pronouns seem to be affected by the same arbitrary set of distinctions. Restricting ourselves to a minimal syntactic characterization of the tripartition, whereby strong pronouns have an unrestricted distribution, weak pronouns are XPs with a restricted (deficient) distribution, and clitics are X^0's with a restricted distribution, we find the same ternary distribution of possessive pronouns, interrogative pronouns, relative pronouns.

The same holds outside of the pronominal domain: Greek shows a very clear tripartition of adverbs, whereby some adverbs, the strong ones, can be coordinated, focussed, etc. while others cannot. Furthermore, among those adverbs that have a deficient distribution, one class attaches to the verb in verb-movement and thus qualifies as a head, while the other does not interact with verb-movement and thus qualifies as an XP. In fact, this tripartition seems to be a general property of any XP, or rather of any Extended Projection (in the sense of Grimshaw, 1991): any major syntactic phrase, nominal, verbal, adjectival or other, can potentially occur in any of the three formats.

The characterization of the tripartition of pronouns should thus be stated in much more general terms, stating that pronouns are submitted to a system whereby:

(25)   *Deficiency #7* (final)
        Extended Projections divide into three classes with an internal relation of *strong class > weak class > clitic class*.
        This hierarchy (a) cuts across distinct components of language (syntax, semantics, phonology, morphology) with no systematic functional correlation; across languages and across grammatical classes and (b) reflects three hierarchies: how deficient the pronoun is with respect to noun phrases; which class is preferably chosen *ceteris paribus,* and the respective "morphological weight" of the classes.

3. THEORY

It is not our goal in this overview to give a formal model capable of subsuming the above facts under one unique syntactic trigger, but we do want to illustrate that this is indeed possible. To do so we give only the bare outline of the model developed in Cardinaletti & Starke (to appear).

Two simple reasonings give the general path for the answer of the above questions:

(a) in some cases of morphological deficiency, the more deficient pronoun is a proper subset of the corresponding strong pronoun: the deficient form is literally contained in the stronger form. Here, the strong/deficient difference correlates with the presence/absence of one morpheme. Under contemporary approaches to syntax-morphology interactions, this morpheme, when present, is represented in syntax. We are then almost forced to assume that the deficient pronoun is *syntactically* deficient: the head corresponding to this morpheme is absent (or radically empty). Since we are forced to the postulation of a syntactic deficiency in deficient pronouns, let us suppose that this is what we were looking for: the unique underlying trigger of deficiency.

(b) several recent analyses of noun phrases conclude that the topmost functional projection of noun phrases is realized by "vacuous" prepositions like *of, in*, etc. But crosslinguistically the complements of these prepositions have the same properties as deficient pronouns (here we must put aside languages with "preposition stranding" such as English or Scandinavian languages, since this phenomenon intermixes with several of the relevant properties to obscure the facts). Furthermore, this part of nominal phrases which has the properties separating the strong from the deficient classes, is often morphologically present in strong pronouns, but absent in deficient pronouns (cf. *a loro* versus *loro*).

Putting these two points together we have a simple model to explain the totality of above facts: deficient pronouns seem to lack the highest functional projection of noun phrases (usually realized by dummy prepositions), and from this all their deficiency follows. The underlying trigger of deficiency is thus "lack of the highest functional projection of an extended projection", property which is easily transposed to the clitic/weak distinction. We thus arrive at the following representations of the three classes of pronouns:

(26)   a. Strong Pronouns   b. Weak Pronouns   c. Clitic Pronouns

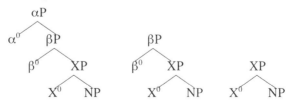

In such a representation, the presence or absence of αP and βP is the underlying cause of the properties of deficiency. It would of course take us too far afield to show how this is done in detail for each property, but let us note that the matter is *a priori* unsurprising: it is a common observation that differences in functional heads of a syntactic marker trigger all types of the needed properties: syntactic of course, but also morphological, semantic, and phonological.

APPENDIX. SOME PRELIMINARY NOTES ON ACQUISITION

As the contributions in this volume testify, the grammar of deficient pronouns has many interesting and complex ramifications in the study of language acquisition. Here, we would like to emphasize a simple but wide-ranging consequence:

(i) the grammar of deficient pronouns is intricate, in particular it presupposes a knowledge of the full functional structure of nominal projections, it presupposes a full mastery of the interaction between grammatical modules, and it presupposes knowledge of general constraints on movement, coordination, modification, expletives, and many others;

(ii) the available data seem to indicate that as soon as they start using deficient pronouns – often around 25 months, children make no errors (see below);

(iii) from (i) and (ii), it follows that by around 25 months, children know the full functional structure of nominal projections, the interaction between grammatical modules, the general constraints on movement, coordination, modification, expletives, etc.

Although the published evidence is not conclusive on these points, a preliminary examination of the CHILDES database (MacWhinney & Snow, 1985) is suggestive. Surveying 21, 222 utterances contained in the corpora of the French child Philippe (33 files; 15, 204 utterances; 2;1.19 - 3;3.12), and the Italian children Guglielmo (9 files; 2, 231 utterances; 2;2.1 - 2;11.14) and Raffaele (6 files; 3,787 utterances; 1;7.1 - 2;11.20) it is almost impossible to find an error concerning clitics (we counted all "utterances" reported in the corpora, except for repetitions by the child of the adult's previous utterance, or of the child's own previous utterances).

Let us illustrate this more precisely. Inspecting Philippe's object pronouns, we do not find a single error: all clitic pronouns are preverbal, all strong pronouns are post-verbal or post-prepositional. How relevant is this?

Philippe has 4,508 utterances that contain pronouns. Among these, 4,226 are deficient pronouns (93.7%). On the other hand, only 80 of them are post-verbal or post-prepositional objects (1.8%). If Philippe did **not** know the restriction on clitic-placement, we could expect to find that post-verbal object clitics represent 1.7% of all pronouns (0.937 x 0.018). In a corpus containing 4,226 pronouns, this means that we would expect to find that 75 out of the 80 post-verbal or post-prepositional pronouns are deficient. But we find that zero out of 80 are deficient.

This is rather suggestive evidence that Philippe indeed does master that part of grammar which leads to the constraint on deficient pronouns. We argued that the constraints underlying the grammar of pronouns are widespread and involve most of what is standardly considered as syntax. If so, these facts would lead us to conclude that by around 25-28 months Philippe knows most of syntax (movement, functional structures, representational constraints, ...).

A similar way of putting this result is to notice that within object pronouns, only two of the four possible distributions are found. A most unexpected result if Philippe did not know the grammar of deficient pronouns:

Philippe	deficient	strong
preverbal objects	746	0
post-V or post-P objects	0	80

Very much the same point can be made for Italian, where the corresponding table would be:

Italian	deficient	strong
preverbal objects	695	0
post-V or post-P objects	0	33

Obviously, more careful statistical analysis would be needed to secure the point (e.g. taking into account the total number of NP objects) but the above results are more than suggestive regarding the extent of syntactic knowledge accumulated by these children in their first 25 months.

The placement facts are not the only way to make this point. It might be noticed, for instance, that Philippe correctly restricts himself to deficient pronouns in expletive and impersonal constructions (as required by deficiency); that Guglielmo and Raffaele respect the constraint on clitic-climbing doing it optionally in optional contexts, obligatorily in obligatory contexts, and never in impossible contexts; that Guglielmo and Raffaele already follow the morphosyntactic rule which turns the clitics *mi* 'me', *ti* 'you' and *si* 'self' into *me, te, se*, when they precede another third person clitic; that these children respect the principle governing the choice of pronouns given the syntactic context, or that human referents are distributed correctly, etc.

To repeat, the most simple facts about clitic placement might well lead us to believe that Philippe, Guglielmo and Raffaele know, among others, high functional projections, cooperation between modules, the chains involved in clitic-placement, the transderivational conditions regulating choices of pronouns within a pair.

REFERENCES

Cardinaletti, A.: 1991, 'On pronoun movement: The Italian dative *loro*', *Probus* **3.2**, 127-153.
Cardinaletti, A. and M. Starke: in press, 'The Typology of Structural Deficiency. A Case Study of the Three Classes of Pronouns', in H. van Riemsdijk (ed.) *Clitics in the Languages of Europe*, Vol. 8 of *Language Typology*, Mouton de Gruyter, Berlin.
Grimshaw, J.: 1991, 'Extended Projections', ms., Brandeis University.
Kayne, R.S.: 1983, 'Chains, Categories External to S, and French Complex Inversion', *Natural Language and Linguistic Theory* **1**, 107-139.
MacWhinney, B. and Snow, C.: 1985, 'The Child Language Data Exchange System', *Journal of Child Language* **12**, 271-296.
Rizzi, L.: 1986, 'On the status of subject clitics in Romance', in O. Jaeggli & C. Silva-Corvalán (eds.) *Studies in Romance Linguistics*, Foris, Dordrecht, 391-419.

ANNA CARDINALETTI
University of Venice

MICHAL STARKE
University of Geneva

MARCO HAVERKORT   JÜRGEN WEISSENBORN

PARAMETERS AND CLITICIZATION IN EARLY CHILD
GERMAN

1. INTRODUCTION

In this paper[1], we will argue that there are a number of distinctions between the behavior of Germanic clitics and their Romance counterparts. We will argue that these distinctions are best explained if the clitics in the two language families are assigned a different status in terms of X-bar theory: Romance clitics are heads (1a), which adjoin to heads, in accordance with the principle of structure preservation, whereas Germanic clitics behave as maximal projections (1b), and can therefore only adjoin to maximal projections, following the same principle.[2] This paper will only discuss German and Swiss German clitics, but similar observations hold for clitics in a number of other Germanic languages and dialects (Haverkort, 1994).

(1)   a. $[_{IP} NP [_{I'} [_I \text{clitic I}] [_{VP} ADV [_{VP} V ...]]]]]$
      b. $[_{IP} \text{clitic}_1 [_{IP} NP [_{I'} [_{VP} \text{clitic}_2 [_{VP} ADV [_{VP} ... V]]] I]]]$

The following examples illustrate the distribution of German subject and object clitics, respectively. As the examples in (2) show, subject clitics only occur directly folowing the complementizer position, independent of whether the latter is filled with a complementizer or verb (as a result of verb second). Nothing can come between the complementizer position and subject clitic.

(2)   a. Weil'r dem Vater gefolgt hat
         because he the father followed has
         'because he has followed father'
      b. Was hat'r dem Vater gegeben?
         what has he the father given
         'What has he given father?'
      c. Hat'r dem Vater gefolgt?
         Has he the father followed
         'Has he followed father?'

The distribution of object clitics is less constrained. Object clitics can occur in a position immediately preceding the subject NP, as in (3), but they can also show up in a position following the subject NP, as in (4), though not always directly (see the discussion on scrambling below).[3]

(3)   a. Weil'm die Mutter was gegeben hat
                 because him the mother something given has
                 'because mother has given him something'
         b. Was hat'm die Mutter gegeben?
                 what has him the mother given
                 'What has mother given him?'
         c. Hat'm die Mutter was gegeben?
                 has him the mother something given
                 'Has mother given him something?'

(4)   a. Weil die Mutter'm was gegeben hat
                 because the mother him something given has
                 'because mother has given him something'
         b. Was hat die Mutter'm gegeben?
                 what has the mother him given
                 'What has mother given him?'
         c. Hat die Mutter'm was gegeben?
                 has the mother him something given
                 'Has mother given him something?'

The examples in (5) illustrate that object clitics in Bernese Swiss German have the same distribution (Penner, 1991: 252, 267).

(5)   a. I weiss wo's dr Vater verloore het
                 I know where it the father lost has
                 'I know where father has lost it.'
         b. I weiss dass dr Vater's gmacht het
                 I know that the father it made has
                 'I know that father has fixed it.'

2. GERMANIC AND ROMANCE CLITICS

In the recent literature, cliticization in Germanic has generally been analyzed in terms of head movement, on a par with the well-established analysis for Romance clitics. In his discussion of the acquisition of clitics in Bernese Swiss German, Penner (1991) adopts the structure in (6).

(6)
```
              CP
             /  \
          Spec   C'
                /  \
               C    AGR₁P
                   /    \
                AGR₁    AGR₂P
                       /    \
                    Spec    AGR₂'
                           /    \
                          TP    AGR₂
                         /  \
                      Spec   I'
                            /  \
                           VP   T
```

Following a suggestion by Cardinaletti & Roberts (1991), he assumes an AGR-projection; the head of this projection is the host for clitics. One immediate problem which arises for Penner is that there is only one landing site for clitics available under the head movement analysis, viz. AGR_1. Under the assumption that the subject occurs in the specifier of AGR_2, as in embedded clauses, the occurrence of object clitics in post-subject position remains unaccounted for. Moreover, it is precisely this order which prevails in early child German. Cardinaletti & Roberts allow AGR_1P to have a specifier, so that in languages like German and Bernese Swiss German, the subject can surface in either the specifier of AGR_1P or AGR_2P, getting Case under specifier-head agreement and government, respectively, accounting for the post- and pre-subject occurrence of clitics. This left-headed functional projection, however, is empirically not very strongly supported: because unlike other functional heads, it is not the site of the representation of morphological features.

In the remainder of this section, a number of characteristics of Germanic clitics will be discussed, which warrants treating them differently from their Romance counterparts. A more extensive discussion can be found in Haverkort (1994); see also Cardinaletti & Starke (in press, this volume) for a different perspective.

2.1. Independence of Head Movement (V-to-C)

In Romance, V-to-C will take the clitic along, as shown in (7), as expected under the assumption that the verb and the clitic end up being dominated by the same head position, some functional head in the extended projection of the verb.

(7)   a. Pourquoi m'avez-vous choisi?
                 why me have you chosen
                 'Why have you chosen me?'
         b. *Pourquoi avez-vous me choisi?
                 why have you me chosen
                 'Why have you chosen me?'

In Germanic, on the other hand, the clitic can be left stranded, while the verb moves to C, as the example in (8b) shows. As the examples in (8a) and (8c) show, a pattern which superficially looks very similar to the Romance pattern, where the clitic is adjacent to the verb in C, also occurs in Germanic. Finally, the opposite situation can obtain: where the verb remains downstairs, in the embedded clause as (8d-e), while the clitic moves up and occurs either in the pre-subject position or the post-subject position.

(8)   a. Was hat'm die Mutter gegeben?
                 what has him the mother given
                 'What has mother given him?'
         b. Was hat die Mutter'm gegeben?
                 what has the mother him given
                 'What has mother given him?'
         c. Die Mutter hat'm was gegeben
                 the mother has him something given
                 'Mother has given him something.'
         d. Weil'm die Mutter was gegeben hat
                 because him the mother something given has
                 'because mother has given him something'
         e. Weil die Mutter'm was gegeben hat
                 because the mother him something given has
                 'because mother has given him something'

2.2. Parasitic Gaps

In Romance, clitics never license parasitic gaps, as the examples in (9), from Italian and French, show respectively. Parasitic gaps are empty positions in islands (like the adjunct-PPs in the examples below), which require a gap which is the result of A'-movement at S-structure in order to be licensed; LF-movement cannot license parasitic gaps. If cliticization is an instance of head movement, we expect clitics not to be able to license parasitic gaps, because the licensing gaps left by cliticization cannot form an extended chain with the gap of the empty operator in the adjunct. Either the latter is a head too, in which case the PP would constitute a barrier for it (which cannot be voided via adjunction), or it is a maximal projection, in which case it cannot form one chain with the chain created by head movement of the clitic, due to incompatibility in terms of X-bar features (see Safir, 1984).

(9)   a. *Glie*li* dobbiamo far mettere *t* nello scaffale invece di lasciare e sul tavolo.
'We must make him put them on the shelf, instead of leaving (them) on the table'
b. *Vous *l'*avez fait signer *t* par le president en mettant e en Èvidence sur son bureau.
'You had it signed by the president by obviously putting (it) on his desk.'

In Germanic, on the other hand, cliticization can license parasitic gaps, as the German and Bernese Swiss German examples in (10) from Penner (1991: 259) indicate respectively.

(10)   a. Der Peter had'*n* [ohne *e* anzusehen] *t* zusammengeschlagen
the Peter has him without to look at beaten up
'Peter has beaten him up without looking at him.'
b. Dr Hans het'*ne* [ooni *e* aaz'luege] *t* zämegschlage
the Hans has him without to look at beaten up
'Hans has beaten him up without looking at him.'

If cliticization in Germanic is an instance of A'-movement of a maximal projection, or more specifically, an instance of adjunction to a maximal projection, this property is accounted for. This analysis also accounts for the independence of clitic movement and verb movement as A'-movement of a maximal projection is by definition freer than head movement and thus does not require verb movement in order to be licensed.

3. SCRAMBLING

Maximal projections which are base-generated in VP in German, can under certain circumstances be moved out of VP, a phenomenon that is known in the literature as scrambling. This scrambling process results in a number of alternative surface word orders, which essentially have the same underlying semantic representation. The examples from Uszkoreit (1987:18) in (11b-c) show some of the alternative orders associated with the unmarked order in (11a).

(11)   a. Dann wird der Doktor dem Patienten die Pille geben.
then will the doctor the patient the pill give
'Then the doctor will give the patient the pill.'
b. Dann wird der Doktor die Pille dem Patienten geben.
then will the doctor the pill the patient give
'Then the doctor will give the patient the pill.'
c. Dann wird die Pille der Doktor dem Patienten geben.
then will the pill the doctor the patient give
'Then the doctor will give the patient the pill.'

At first glance, clitics seem to occur in the same position that is occupied by scrambled maximal projections, as shown in (12a-b), which involve long-distance scrambling and cliticization out of an embedded clause. This suggests that cliticization in Germanic and instances of A'-movement, like scrambling are parallel. Moreover, when long-distance movement of a scrambled element is impossible, cliticization to the parallel position is also impossible, as the ungrammaticality of examples (12c-d) from Thiersch (1978:109) indicates.

(12)   a. Weil ich das Lied [eine alte Dame singen] hörte
because I the song a old lady to sing heard
'because I heard an old lady sing the song'
b. Weil ich's [eine alte Dame singen] hörte
because I it a old lady to sing heard
'because I heard an old lady sing it'
c. *Weil ich das Lied [dass eine alte Dame sang] hörte
because I the song that an old lady sang heard
'because I heard that an old lady sang the song'
d. *Weil ich's [dass eine alte Dame sang] hörte
because I it that an old lady sang heard
'because I heard that an old lady sang it'

A similar parallel between scrambling and cliticization has been observed for Bernese Swiss German by Penner (1991). In these cases as well, both processes are either allowed, as in (13), or lead to illicit results as in (14), again suggesting parallel behavior.

(13) a. I weiss dass'ne dr Dani laat la schlaafe
   I know that him the Dani lets let sleep
   'I know that Dani lets him sleep.'
  b. I weiss dass mis Buech nid auui Chind hei probiert z'läse
   I know that my book not all children have tried to read
   'I know that not all children have tried to read my book.'

(14) a.*I weiss'er dass choo isch
   I know he that come is
   'I know that he has come.'
  b.*I weiss ds Buech dass'er mibracht het
   I know the book that he brought has
   'I know that he has brought the book along.'

These instances of long-distance clitic movement are similar to instances of so-called clitic climbing in Romance, exemplified by the following examples from Italian and French, respectively, where the clitic moves out of the clause in which it is base-generated:

(15) a. Gianni li vuole vedere
   Gianni them wants to see
   'Gianni wants to see them.'
  b. Jean l'a entendu reciter les poèmes
   Jean him has heard recite the poems
   'Jean has heard him recite the poems.'

The observed parallels do not suffice to show that cliticization is an instance of scrambling. Actually, there are arguments to show that the two processes are distinct: Dutch, for instance, does have long-distance clitic climbing, but does not allow long-distance scrambling (see Zwart, 1993). Moreover, in West Flemish, clitics can occur in a number of positions where scrambled maximal projections are not allowed, even in the same clause (for relevant discussion, see Haegeman, 1992; Haverkort, 1994; Penner, 1991).

The acquisition of German and Swiss German also argues against collapsing scrambling and cliticization. As has been observed by Penner, Tracy & Weissenborn (this volume), object scrambling in the earliest stages of acquisition is blocked by VP-external subjects. That is, the order subject-verb can only obtain if the subject has left the specifier of VP. These authors explain this fact in terms of the similarity of the landing sites of both movement processes, as both are specifiers of some AGR-projection, this incurs a violation of relativized minimality.

(16)   a. Simone o ds Auto näh
Simone also the car take
'Simone also takes the car'
b. Simone o de Bitzeli Broti näh
Simone also the piece bread take
'Simone also takes the piece of bread'

Object scrambling is blocked by the presence of a VP-external subject until the age of 2;5. Crucially, however, at the same stage of development, cliticization is not constrained by VP-external subjects, indicating that, even though superficially similar, a different process must be involved.

(17)   a. Ich puste's auf   2;04.17
I blow it up
'I blow it up'
b. Ich krieg's alleine   2;04.21
I get it alone
'I get it alone'

More important however, is the observation that in adult German scrambling and cliticization can interact in a way in which cliticization and adverbials can never interact, due to the stative nature of the latter. Thus, as the following examples indicate, a clitic can never occur in VP, that is, to the right of an adverbial (d), but it can be separated from the subject by a scrambled object, as the relative acceptability of (b-c) shows.

(18)   a. Der Vater hat's gestern seinem Sohn gegeben
the father has it, yesterday his son given
'Father has given it to his son yesterday.'
b. ?Gestern hat der Vater seinem Sohn's gegeben
Yesterday has the father his son it given
'Yesterday, father has given it to his son.'
c. ?Der Vater hat seinem Sohn's gestern gegeben
the father has his son it yesterday given
'father has given it to his son yesterday.'
d. Der Vater hat gestern's seinem Sohn gegeben
the father has yesterday it his son given
'father has given it to his son yesterday.'

Under the assumption that scrambled maximal projections are moved into the specifier of some functional head in the extended projection of VP, clitics must thus be able to adjoin to such a maximal projection or the highest segment of VP (thus preventing them to follow adverbials, which are also adjoined to VP). Under the head movement alternative, we would have to assume that a number of distinct functional projections in the extended projection of the verb are left-headed, thus providing multiple landing sites for clitics (see Haegeman (1992) for such a proposal). As argued before, the left-headed AGR_1P is ill-motivated, since its sole purpose seems to be to act as host for the clitic. In German, it is also invoked in instances of embedded verb second (Cardinaletti & Roberts, 1991), but the interaction between embedded verb second and cliticization is not discussed, even though it poses some interesting empirical problems for such an approach (see Haverkort, 1994). Moreover, in many Germanic languages, Dutch being a prime example, embedded verb second cannot occur, and hence one of the motivations for AGR_1P falls away.

The interaction between cliticization and scrambling can also provide an argument in the debate about the question whether scrambled elements are base-generated in their surface position (see Neeleman, 1994) or not. If complements of the verb can be base-generated in a position that is hierarchically lower or higher (in case of scrambling) than adverbial elements, as both are within VP, the fact that clitics can occur on either side of a scrambled element, but only to the left of an adverbial element is unexplained. Since the order of these elements is due to different PS-rules, the clitic to the right of a scrambled element would be in the same hierarchical position as the clitic to the right of the adverb. Moreover, the clitic to the right of a scrambled element would still be in the VP, something that is generally excluded. Under a base-generation analysis of scrambling, the order Adverb-Clitic can only be excluded by means of an ad hoc surface filter, whereas under a movement analysis of scrambling, both clitics and scrambled elements move past the position occupied by the adverbial. That is, the surface order of clitics depends on their adjunction site with respect to the scrambled element which is either higher (clitic-NP) or lower (NP-clitic).

An additional example, taken from Bernese Swiss German, also indicates the untenable nature of a head-movement analysis of cliticization as the clitic can appear in a pre-subject position, separated from the complementizer position by a topicalized adverbial. Under a right-headed phrase structure for Germanic, examples like these are difficult to accommodate under the head-movement analysis.

(19) ?? I weiss dass morn's dr Vater bringt
      I know that tomorrow it the father brings
      'I know that tomorrow father will bring it.'

3.1. Ordering Clitics

Subject clitics occur internal to object clitics in the linear string with respect to the complementizer position. This is illustrated for German and Bernese Swiss German, respectively, in the following examples:

(20) a. hat'r's dem Kind gegeben?
         has he it the child given
         'Has he given it to the child?'
      b. Dem Kind hat'r's gegeben
         the child has he it given
         'He has given it to the child.'
      c. *hat's'r dem Kind gegeben?
         has it he the child given
         'Has he given it to the child?'
      d. *Dem Kind hat's'r gegeben
         the child has it he given
         'He has given it to the child.'

(21) a. I weiss dass'r'm's zeigt het
         I know that he him it shown has
         'I know that he has shown it to him.'
      b. I weiss dass'r's'm zeigt het
         I know that he it him shown has
         'I know that he has shown it to him.'
      c. *I weiss dass'ne'si gseh hei
         I know that him they seen have
         'I know that they have seen him.'

This can be accounted for in terms of bottom-up application of move (see the linear cycle) under the assumption that clitic movement is the movement of a maximal projection, adjoining the clitic phrase to another maximal projection, in accordance with the principle of structure preservation. If the object clitic, which is most deeply embedded, left-adjoins to IP first, followed by the subject clitic, the latter will left-adjoin to the topmost segment of IP, accounting for the grammatical order as in (22a). An alternative derivation which leads to the same result, is that the subject clitic adjoins to IP and the object clitic to VP as in (22b).

(22) a.
```
            CP
           /  \
              C'
             /  \
            C    IP
            |   /  \
            V su-cl IP
                  /  \
               obj-cl IP
```

b.
```
            CP
           /  \
              C'
             /  \
            C    IP
            |   /  \
            V su-cl VP
                  /  \
               obj-cl VP
```

At PF, both these elements cliticize phonologically to the same element, namely COMP. Thus syntactic and phonological cliticization would go in different directions, rightward and leftward, respectively (see discussion of similar cases in Klavans, 1981 and Fontana, 1993).

If clitic movement were an instance of head-movement and clitics were adjoined to the same head as the verb, this result is unexpected. We would expect precisely the opposite order, in view of the fact that the object clitic would move up prior to the subject clitic, in accordance with the restriction that head movement applies bottom-up. A separate AGR_1-projection can solve this problem, since verbs and clitics attach to different functional heads (but this would not work in cases of cliticization with embedded verb second, where both the clitic and the verb end up on AGR_1). In Romance, the order of subject and object clitics with respect to the verb is indeed the opposite, as the following example from French shows:

(23)   Il l'a vu.
        he him has seen
        'He has seen him.'

As the above discussion has indicated, there are a number of properties of German clitics, which warrant treating them as maximal projections, which adjoin to VP and IP. There are a number of other observations which point in the same direction, having to do with the behavior of clitics in Verb Projection Raising constructions, coordinate structures, and the fact that clitic clusters in Germanic can be split, unlike in Romance (a more in-depth discussion of these phenomena can be found in Haverkort, 1994). Analyzing Germanic clitics as maximal projections makes a number of predictions for their acquisition. This is taken up in the second part of the paper.

The main differences between Germanic and Romance clitics are summarized in Table 1 below.

Table 1.
Differences Between Germanic and Romance Clitics

	Germanic	Romance
Independence of verb movement	+	−
Licensing of parasitic gaps	+	−
Split clitic clusters	+	−
Interaction with scrambling	+	−
Clause-initial coordination	±	−
Clitic can move along in Verb Projection Raising	±	−

4. THE ACQUISITION OF GERMANIC CLITICS[4]

In the child's early grammar, we assume with other authors, like Boser *et al.* (1991), Hyams (1992), Poeppel & Wexler (1993), Roeper (1992), Verrips & Weissenborn (1992), Whitman (1994) and Weissenborn (1994), that the extended projection of the verb, (in the sense of Grimshaw (1991) i.e., an I- and a C-projection, or other functional projections under the split INFL hypothesis) is present in early child German. This assumption is challenged by Clahsen (1991), Meisel & Müller (1992), Penner (1991), and Tracy (1991) who argue that initially the child's finite clauses may only project to IP. We will not discuss this issue here. Instead, we present what we consider to be some evidence for the assumption that a CP projection is present. The first evidence of V-to-C movement comes from the topicalization of non-subjects (including null objects 24c-d) as in the following examples (from Verrips & Weissenborn, 1992).

(24) a. hier isse Ball   1;10.20
         here is ball
         'here is the ball'
      b. neues hat'e mitgebracht   2;02.07
         new one has he brought along
         'he has brought along a new one'
      c. baun will ich   1;10.22
         to.build want I
         'I want to build'
      d. finn ich auch   2;02.09
         find I also
         'I find (that) also'

Secondly, verbs occur to the left of adverbs and negation as shown in 25.

(25) a. das macht der maxe nicht   2;01.12
         that does the Max not
         'Max does not do that'
      b. kann ma nicht essen   2;01.12
         can one not eat
         'one cannot eat (that)'
      c. will auch ein Ball   2;01.12
         want also a ball
         '(I) want a ball, too'

Finally, verb-particle combinations are discontinuous (b-c), and auxiliaries occur in a pre-participial position (a), both indicative of verb movement:[5]

(26) a. mone hat'e puttemacht   2;02.22
         Mone has it broken
         'Mone has broken it'
      b. ah, ich puste's auf   2;04.17
         ah, I blow it up
         'Ah, I blow it up'
      c. gleich fällt's um   2;04.20
         soon falls it down
         'soon, it'll fall down'

All of these processes involve verb movement indicating the presence of CP.

4.1. Scrambling

We now turn to the question of whether and when we find evidence for scrambling in our data. We claim that forms of scrambling can be observed from early on. The availability of object scrambling from the outset of acquisition is shown by the German data in (27), and in the Swiss German data from Penner in (28). Early scrambling in Germanic is discussed in more detail in Penner, Tracy & Weissenborn (this volume) and Penner, Schönenberger & Weissenborn (1994).

(27)   a. ander auch malen   1;10.21
              other one also paint
              '(I) also paint the other one'
      b. die auch mal mitnehme   2;00.01
              that one also PRT bring
              '(I) bring along that one, too'
      c. das auch reinstecken   2;00.01
              that one also put in
              '(I) also put that one in'
      d. des auch Mone hol   2;01.21
              that also Mone get
              'Mone also gets that'

(28)   a. Mässer au i Chübu me
              knife also in pocket put
              '(I) also put the knife in the pocket'
      b. cha das au hebe
              can this also hold
              '(I) can also hold this'
      c. das nid uspakche
              that not unpack
              '(I) don't unpack that'   2;1 - 2;4

These examples show that an object can be scrambled over the particle *auch*, indicating that the object must have moved out of VP. The same holds for subjects, although initially subjects and objects cannot be moved out of VP simultaneously, an effect which can be explained in terms of Relativized Minimality (see Penner *et al.*, this volume).

4.2. Cliticization

What are the implications of what we have said so far for the issue of cliticization? The presence of generalized verb second in early finite matrix clauses implies that both VP and IP are available as adjunction sites for cliticization. The availability of scrambling predicts that object clitics should also occur, since, as we claimed above, cliticization uses the same process, namely A'-movement.

One of the first to study the acquisition of cliticization in Germanic in some detail was Penner (1991). Penner assumes that the extend projection of V emerges gradually, following essentially the pattern predicted by Weissenborn's (1994) Local Wellformedness Constraint, i.e., acquiring the relevant structure in a strictly bottom-up fashion. The following three stages are distinguished in Penner's analysis:

(29) a. the AGR_2P-system
      b. the AGR_1P-system
      c. the CP-system

(30)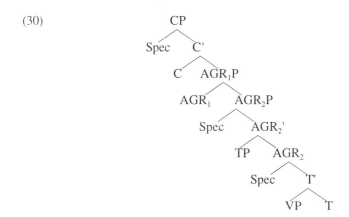

One of the crucial observations for Penner's analysis is that during the second stage, when AGR_1P has been acquired, the head of this projection is the landing site of the verb, and thus associated with *phi*-features of the verb. As a consequence, the only type of clitic that is allowed to co-occur in this head with the verb is the subject clitic: Object clitics would cause a feature clash, since they have different phi-features associated with them. The data from the acquisition of Standard German, however, do not support this observation; as both subject and object clitics can co-occur with the verb, contrary to Penner's predictions and findings for Bernese Swiss, as the following data show.[6]

(31) a. se abmache   2;00.01
     them take off
     '(I) take them off'
    b. Pudding nimmstes   2;00.03
     pudding take you it
     'the pudding, you take it'
    c. Heike kann's habe   2;02.20
     Heike can it have
     'Heike can have it'
    d. Mone hatte puttemacht   2;02.21
     Mone has it broken
     'Mone has broken it'

Thus, there is no evidence for a subject/object asymmetry in terms of the availability of cliticization, which under Penner's analysis, is the basic motivation for the assumption that the AGR_1 position is the highest functional head available during his second stage of development.

Not only do object clitics occur, they also occur in V2 structures, which is unexpected because according to Penner's analysis AGR_1P does not have a specifier position. Under his analysis, only verb first would be expected to occur, as in the following examples:

(32) a. isses das   2;00.01
     is it that
     'is that it?'
    b. is'er puttegang'   2;04.21
     is it broken
     'has it broken?'

Contrary to this prediction, as argued before (24 - 26) and as shown in the following examples, an element **can** precede the verb-clitic combination indicating that a specifier position is available.

(33) a. Mone hatte puttemacht   2;02.21
         Mone hat it broken
         'Mone has broken it'
      b. Ich puste's auf   2:04.17
         I blow it up
         'I blow it up'
      c. gleich fällt's um   2;04.20
         soon falls it down
         'soon, it'll fall down'

There is another observation which argues against the above structure; namely, up until age 3;6, there are hardly any cases of pre-subject clitics; the common order with transitive verbs is subject - verb – object clitic. Under a head movement analysis, this can only be explained in terms of unavailability of nominative case in the specifier of AGR_2P, so that subjects need to move all the way to the specifier of AGR_1P to receive case. Penner's (1991) analysis however, does not have a specifier position available there, so the attested state of affairs is completely unexpected. Under a maximal projection analysis of cliticization, children start out moving the clitic over the shortest possible distance to a licensing position, i.e., adjoin to VP (or AGR_0P), only later adjoining the clitic to IP (alternatively AGR_SP). This development is in accordance with the Subset Principle and also the Local Wellformedness Condition (Weissenborn, 1994).

Another fact that straightforwardly follows from a maximal projection analysis, is the right ordering of clitics. In (34), the subject clitic precedes the object clitic in the linear string. Under an A'-movement analysis, as mentioned before, this order can be explained by assuming that by a bottom-up application, first the lowest element, the object clitic, adjoins to VP or IP followed by the subject clitic. Whether the object clitic has adjoined to IP or VP cannot be decided on the basis of the string because no other element occurs between VP and IP. In a next step, the clitic-complex phonologically cliticizes to the verb.[7]

(34)   nimmstes   2;00.03
            take you it
            'do you take it?'

Additional evidence for the maximal projection analysis of clitic movement in early child German comes from the data in (35) below, which show the independence of verb movement and clitic movement. In this sentence, the verb must have been moved out of VP, as indicated by negation, leaving the object clitic behind.[8]

(35)   Tommy bringt nicht's   2;01.16
       Tommy brings not it
       'Tommy does not bring it'

We find the opposite pattern, namely that the clitic moves independently of the verb, only later, given that (finite) embedded clauses do not occur initially. Examples of clitics moving independently of the verb which stays behind are given in (36) below.

(36)   a. ich zeig dir mal wie Mone's immer macht   2;07.23
          I show you how Mone it always does
          'I'll show you how Mone always does it'
       b. dann kann's Tobias auch mache'   3;05.21
          then can it Tobias also do
          'Then Tobias can also do it'

5. CONCLUSION

The analysis sketched in this paper, in which Germanic cliticization is an instance of movement of a maximal projection as opposed to Romance clitics which behave as heads, can capture the facts of cliticization in adult German. Moreover, it can accommodate all instances of cliticization which are found in child German. A number of these facts were shown to be more problematic for the head movement analysis as it has been formulated for Bernese Swiss German. In addition, the A'-movement analysis of clitic placement in German presented here is compatible with the assumption that a full-fledged C-projection is available from the outset for finite clauses in the grammar of the child.

ACKNOWLEDGEMENTS

We would like to thank two anonymous reviewers for their comments on an earlier version of this paper. Special thanks go to Susan Powers, for checking the English, the logic, and doing the formatting. All remaining errors are ours.

NOTES

[1] This paper was first presented at the 17th Boston University Conference on Language Development in 1992. The majority of the research was made possible by the Max-Plank Institute for Psycholinguistics in NIjmegen.
[2] This is just a rough generalization, since there is some degree of intra-language variation, see Haverkort (to appear) and Cardinaletti & Starke (in press).
[3] In Dutch, clitics can only follow the subject; the order where they precede the subject is illicit.
[4] The data we will discuss in the following all come from the Simone Corpus which has been collected by Max Miller. Ages are given in year;month.day.
[5] Unlike Dutch, Standard German does not allow the order auxiliary-participle in the VP; moreover, the verb is finite in the (a)-example, indicative for verb movement in normally developing children.
[6] Like subject clitics in Bernese Swiss, object clitics in Child German can be doubled as shown in the (b)-example.
[7] The maximal projection analysis must assume linear cyclicity, i.e., first the deepest element moves all the way up, then the next deepest, etc., and a higher base position for the subject than for the object.
[8] This sentence is not a grammatical structure in the adult grammar: for definite elements, scrambling is obligatory and clitic elements cannot be stranded in VP. This is the only mistake we found. This attachment, error may indicate that the child has not yet learned the principle that adjunction has to be the highest IP/VP segment.

REFERENCES

Boser, K., B. Lust, L. Santleman, and J. Whitman: 1991, 'The Theoretical Significance of Auxiliaries in Early Child German, Paper presented at the *16th Boston University Conference on Language Development*, Boston.
Cardinaletti, A. and I. Roberts: 1991, 'Clause Structure and X-second', ms., University of Venice & University of Geneva.
Cardinaletti, A. and M. Starke: in press, 'The Typology of Structural Deficiency. A Case Study of the Three Classes of Pronouns', in H. van Riemsdijk (ed.) *Clitics in the Languages of Europe*, vol. 8 of *Language Typology*, Mouton de Gruyter, Berlin.
Clahsen,H.:1991, 'Constraints on Parameter Setting: A Grammatical Analysis of Some Acquisition Stages in German Child Language', *Language Acquisition* 1, 361-391.
Fontana, J.: 1993, 'Phrase Structure and the Syntax of Clitics in the History of Spanish', Ph.D. Dissertation, University of Pennsylvania.
Grimshaw, J.: 1991, 'Extended Projections', ms., Rutgers University.
Haegeman, L.: 1992, 'The Distribution of Object Pronouns in West Flemish', In L. Rizzi (ed.) Clitics in Romance and Germanic, *Eurotyp Working Papers*, 33-76.
Haverkort, M.: 1994, 'Romance and Germanic Clitics: A Comparison of their Syntactic Behavior', In T. Shannon & J. Snapper (eds.) *The Berkeley Conference on Dutch Linguistics 1993*, University Press of America, Lanham, 131-150.
Haverkort, M.: to appear, 'Prepositional Clitics as Hybrid Categories', In H. van Riemsdijk (ed.) *Clitics in the Languages of Europe*, Mouton-De Gruyter, Berlin.
Hyams, N.: 1992, 'The Genesis of Clause Structure', In J. Meisel (ed.) The Acquisition of Verb Placement, Kluwer, Dordrecht, 371-401.
Klavans, J.: 1981, 'Some Problems in a Theory of Clitics', Ph.D. Dissertation, University College London.
Neeleman, A.: 1994, 'Complex Predicates', Ph.D. Dissertation, University of Utrecht.
Meisel J. and N. Müller: 1992, 'Finiteness and Verb Placement in Early Child Grammar: Evidence from Simultaneous Acquisition of French and German in Bilinguals. In J. Meisel (ed.) *The Acquisition of Verb Placement*, Kluwer, Dordrecht, 109-139.

Penner, Z.: 1991, 'Pronominal Clitics in Bernese Swiss and their Structural Position: Jakob Wackernagel and Language Acquisition', In H. van Riemsdijk&L. Rizzi (eds.) *Clitics and their Hosts*, Eurotyp Working Papers, 253-268.

Penner, Z., R. Tracy and J. Weissenborn: 1992, 'Scrambling in Early Developmental Stages in Standard and Swiss German', ms., University of Bern & Max Planck Institute for Psycholinguistics.

Penner, Z., M. Schönenberger and J. Weissenborn: 1994, 'The Acquisition of Object Placement in Early German and Swiss German, *Linguistics in Potsdam* **1**, 93-108.

Poeppel, D. and K. Wexler: 1993, 'The Full Competence Hypothesis of Clause Structure in Early German', *Language* **69**, 1-33.

Roeper, T.: 1992, 'From the Initial Stage to V2: Acquisition Principles in Action', In J. Meisel (ed.) *The Acquisition of Verb Placement*, Kluwer, Dordrecht, 333-371.

Safir, K.: 1984, 'Multiple Variable Binding', *Linguistic Inquiry* **15**, 603-638.

Thiersch, C.: 1978, 'Topics in German Syntax', Ph.D. Dissertation, MIT.

Tracy, R.:1991, 'Raising Questions: Some Formal and Functional Aspects of the Acquisition of WH-questions in German', Paper presented at the *Max Planck Institute for Psycholinguistics*, Nijmegen.

Uszkoreit, H.:1987, 'Word Order and Constituent Structure in German', Stanford: CSLI Lecture Notes, nr. 8.

Verrips, M. and J. Weissenborn: 1992, 'Routes to Verb Placement in Early German and French: The Independence of Finiteness and Agreement. In J. Meisel (ed.) *The Acquisition of Verb Placement*, Kluwer, Dordrecht, 283-333.

Whitman, J.: 1994, 'In Defense of the Strong Continuity Account of the Acquisition of Verb Second', In B. Lust et al. (eds.) *Syntactic Theory and Language Acquisition: Crosslinguistic Perspectives, Volume 1: Heads, Projections and Learnability*. Lawrence Erlbaum, Hillsdale, 273-289.

Weissenborn, J.: 1990, 'Functional Categories and Verb Movement in Early German: The Acquisition of German Syntax Reconsidered. In M. Rothweiler (ed.) Spracherwerb und Grammatik: Linguistische Untersuchungen zum Erwerb von Syntax und Morphologie. *Linguistische Berichte, Special Issue* **3**, 190-223.

Weissenborn, J.: 1994, 'Constraining the Child's Grammar: Local Wellformedness in the Development of Verb Movement in German and French', In B. Lust et al. (eds.) *Syntactic Theory and Language Acquisition: Crosslinguistic Perspectives, Volume 1: Heads, Projections and Learnability*, Lawrence Erlbaum Hillsdale, 215-249.

Zwart, J.: 1993, 'Dutch Syntax: A Minimalist Approach', Ph.D. Dissertation, University of Groningen.

MARCO HAVERKORT
University of Groningen &
Boston University

JÜRGEN WEISSENBORN
University of Potsdam

BERTHOLD CRYSMANN   NATASCHA MÜLLER

ON THE NON-PARALLELISM IN THE ACQUISITION OF REFLEXIVE AND NON-REFLEXIVE OBJECT CLITICS

1. INTRODUCTION

In this article, we want to study the development of French reflexive clitics in relation to the acquisition of ordinary non-reflexive object clitics. In Müller *et al.* (1996), we argued that the emergence of the full object clitic paradigm and its target-consistent use is tied to the instantiation of the C-system. As for the adult system, we assumed that non-reflexive object clitics license and identify a *pro* object in syntax. Reflexive clitics, however, involve argument absorption which arguably is a presyntactic process, yielding a syntactic representation with one thematic role less (Grimshaw, 1982; Wehrli, 1986). Given this, we would expect reflexives not to interact with other syntactic constituents, like e.g., the C-system. Interestingly enough, reflexive clitics are already used sporadically during a stage where their non-reflexive counterparts are still systematically lacking. Furthermore, placement errors are attested with reflexive clitics in constructions which contain an analytic verb form, errors which are nonexistent with their non-reflexive counterparts. Moreover, these placement errors coincide with the selection of the wrong auxiliary, namely *avoir* instead of *être*. We will argue in particular that the acquisition pattern is attributed to the unavailability of complex morphological words in the child's initial grammatical representation, i.e., morphological objects which map onto more than one single syntactic atom. In contrast to the target analysis in terms of a verb cluster, the children analyze French auxiliary+participle constructions as a hierarchical VP, where the auxiliary selects a VP complement.

The paper is organized as follows: in the next section, we will discuss the processes which are operative in adult French reflexives as compared to ordinary non-reflexive clitics. Section 3 discusses the acquisition data drawn from the corpus of a French/German bilingual boy (Ivar). For reasons of comparison, we include longitudinal data from another French/German bilingual child (Caroline), as well as first results from an elicited production task carried out with ten French/German bilingual children. We will show how errors can be modeled in the light of the present approach.

2. THE ADULT SYSTEM

The status of Romance non-reflexive object clitics has been a matter of much controversial debate since the early days of the generative enterprise (Borer, 1986 for an overview; Crysmann, 1995, Chapter 2 for a critical perspective). Two main approaches dominate the overall picture: a syntactic approach (Kayne, 1975; Sportiche, 1992) and a lexical approach (Miller, 1992). Lexicalist analyses (Auger, 1993; Auger & Miller, 1995; Miller, 1992; Miller & Sag, 1995; Roberge, 1991; Simpson & Withgott, 1986; Spencer, 1991) provide us with a wide range of evidence that Romance clitics should rather be conceived of as affixes which are morphologically derived: they conform to most of the criteria suggested by Zwicky & Pullum (1983) for an element's affixal status: they are highly selective for their host (Criterion A), they exhibit arbitrary gaps in the set of combinations (B), they display morphophonological (C) and semantic idiosyncrasies (D), they cannot be manipulated by syntactic rules (E), and, finally, they can intervene between other affixes and the stem (F).

In contrast to non-reflexive clitics, the status of Romance reflexive clitics is rather uncontroversial: researchers like Grimshaw (1982, 1990), Haider & Rindler-Schjerve (1987), Jackendoff (1990), Marantz (1984), Rosen (1990), and Wehrli (1986) have proposed that reflexivization should be conceived of as a process of argument structure manipulation. As for so-called middle *se*, an analysis in terms of argument absorption is largely accepted (cf. Belletti, 1982; Manzini, 1986; Zubizarreta, 1982). Due to the projection principle, one has to assume that rules that alter the thematic structure of a lexical item apply presyntactically. Assuming some version of Lexical Integrity (Bresnan & Mchombo, 1995), one should not expect syntactic constituents to intervene between a presyntactically attached reflexive and its morphological host. As French non-reflexive object clitics are categorically positioned between the reflexive and the verb (*Il se le dit.* 'He says it to himself.'), this implies a morphological derivation of nonreflexive object clitics as well.

In this section, our main goal is to provide a unified account of both reflexive and non-reflexive object clitics in French. We will present a modified version of Wehrli's (1986) unified account of *se* and R-clitics (Crysmann, 1992).

Under a morphological approach to the treatment of French object clitics, one may assume that the clitic affixes to the verb, thus contributing its agreement features to the verbal mother node. The clitic-verb complex then defines an object agreement paradigm which is characterized by only and all derived forms and by morphological "richness" (see Table 1).

Table 1.
The French object clitic paradigm

	Singular			Plural		
	1st	2nd	3rd	1st	2nd	3rd
dir.	*me*	*te*	*le/la*	*nous*	*vous*	*les*
indir.	*me*	*te*	*lui*	*nous*	*vous*	*leur*
refl.	*me*	*te*	*se*	*nous*	*vous*	*se*

As for the theory of null objects, we adopt the kind of analysis advanced by Huang (1984) and Jaeggli & Safir (1989) which states that null arguments may either be a *pro* which has to be licensed and identified by uniform[1] and "rich" agreement morphology or a variable bound by some empty operator PRO.

In fact, as can be observed in Table 1, the conditions to license and identify *pro* are both met by the object agreement paradigm in adult French. Consequently, much in the spirit of Roberge (1991), we assume that a sentence like (1) has the underlying structure given in (2).

(1) Jean le voit
 John it sees
 'John sees it.'

(2) [Jean [$_V$ le$_i$ voit] *pro*$_i$]

One of the most striking differences between *se* and non-reflexive object clitics is that *se* functions much like a "detransitivizer" or "ergativizer", making a (two-place) transitive verb it attaches to behave exactly the same as one-place predicates with respect to constructions such as stylistic inversion, impersonals and *faire*-causatives.[2]

(3)   a. Je me demande quand partira ton ami
 I ask when will leave your friend
 'I wonder when your friend will leave.'
 b. *Je me demande quand achètera Paul la maison.
 I me ask when will buy Paul the house
 'I wonder when Paul will buy the house.'
 c. Je me demande comment s'est rasé Paul.
 I me ask how himself is shaved Paul
 'I wonder how Paul shaved himself.'
 d. ?Je me demande comment les a rasé Paul.
 I me ask how them has shaved Paul
 'I wonder how Paul has shaved them.'

(4) a. Un train passe.
     A train passes
     'A train passes by.'
  b. Il passe un train.
     It passes a train
     'A train passes by.'
  c. Quelqu'un lave une voiture.
     Someone washes a car
     'Someone washes a car.'
  d. *Il lave une voiture quelqu'un.
     It washes a car someone
     'Someone washes a car.'
  e. *Il la lave quelqu'un.
     It it washes someone.
     'Someone washes it.'
  f. Il se lave quelqu'un.
     It himself washes someone
     'Someone washes himself.'

(5) a. Jean les fait laver aux enfants
     John them makes wash to the kids
     'John makes the kids wash them'
  b. *Jean les fait laver les enfants
     John them makes wash the kids
  c. *Jean fait les laver les enfants
     John makes them wash the kids
  d. Jean fait se laver les enfants
     John makes himself wash the kids
     'John makes the kids wash themselves'
  e. *Jean fait se laver aux enfants
     John makes himself wash to the kids
  f. *Jean se fait laver les enfants /aux enfants
     John himself makes wash the kids/ to the kids

These data suggest that a verb with a *se* attached really has one θ-role less. This can be subsumed under Wehrli's (1986) generalization in (6):

(6) *se* absorbs an argument.

This means that the argument is missing entirely in the syntax (cf. Haider & Rindler-Schjerve, 1987; Rosen, 1990), not just lacking phonological content, like e.g., *pro*.

As we have already noted above, the view that affixation of *se* indeed involves some process of argument structure manipulation is quite uncontroversial in the literature. Then, due to the Projection Principle, it should follow that such a process cannot take place within syntax, but rather has to be attributed to the level of lexical morphology. This conclusion seems to be further supported by the large amount of lexicalized forms, both for reflexive (absorption of an internal argument) and middle *se* (absorption of the external argument). Wehrli (1986) has argued quite convincingly that the four different uses of *se* should be treated in a unified fashion (see Table 2). According to him, the difference in interpretation between reflexive/reciprocal and middle *se* can be modeled with reference to the distinction between internal and external arguments. Likewise, the availability of the absorbed θ-role as a controller will be attributed to a second factor, namely whether the process has been lexicalized for a particular verb (inherent pronominal and ergative) or not (reflexive and middle).

Table 2.
The different roles of French clitic se

	internal argument	external argument
- lexicalized	reflexive/reciprocal	middle
+ lexicalized	inherent "pronominal"	ergative

So far, we have argued that reflexive *se* and non-reflexive *le* are subject to quite distinct processes, namely argument absorption in one case and introduction of a restriction on referential indices in the form of object agreement in the other. In order to include the first and second person object clitics *me*, *te*, *nous*, *vous* which are neither inherently reflexive nor inherently non-reflexive, we have to ensure that argument absorption will give rise to a coindexation with the subject. Wehrli (1986) motivates his formulation of this restriction by appealing to the need for semantic recoverability. We assume the following, slightly modified version given below:

(7) If a clitic absorbs an argument of α, it agrees in person and number with the highest available θ-role of α.

Consider the examples below:

(8) a. Je_j te_i regarde [pro_i]
     b. Tu_i te_i regarde
     c. *Je_j te_i regarde
     d. *Tu_i te_i regarde pro_i

In (8a), no argument is absorbed and the clitic-verb complex licenses a *pro* in object position. (8b) is fine, too: the clitic absorbs an argument and thus triggers the agreement requirement. As the indices are nondistinct, the requirement is met. The ungrammaticality of a representation like (7c) reduces to a mere θ-criterion violation as argument absorption is blocked by the agreement requirement. The last representation (7d) captures the case where there is agreement without absorption: this can be ruled out by Principle B of Binding Theory (*pro* is not free in its BT-relevant domain).

Let us now briefly discuss how the agreement requirement works for middle *se*. Following Wehrli (1986), the middle interpretation can be attributed to the absorption of the external argument. The agreement requirement now ensures that the absorbed argument agrees with the highest remaining θ-role which is the theme role for "ordinary" transitive verbs. Assuming a lexical binding theory like the one outlined in Jackendoff (1990), the interpretation of the implicit agent should be free as there is no higher role in the thematic hierarchy that could bind it. Conversely, a nominal or pronominal realization of the theme role will always be interpreted as disjoint from the implicit agent.

The second major observation regarding the differences between *se* and its nonreflexive counterparts is that *se* is incompatible with constructions involving derived or expletive subjects.

(9)   a. *Il se semble que les candidats sont excellent
           it itself seems that the candidates are excellent
      b. Les candidats nous semblent être excellents
           the candidates to us seem to be excellent
           'To our minds, the candidates seem to be excellent.'
      c. *Les candidats se semble être excellents
           the candidates to themselves seem to be excellent

(10)   a. Jean vous est fidèle.
           John to you is faithful
           'John is faithful to you.'
      b. *Vous vous êtes fidèle
           You to yourselves are faithful

Let us first consider the raising verbs with expletive subjects: here, affixation of the reflexive absorbs the referential index of the verb's sole θ-role, the optional experiencer, effectively blocking assignment of this role in syntax. As there is no other role with an associated index in the verb's thematic structure, the agreement condition cannot be fulfilled. Hence, the derivation is ruled out.

The same seems to hold for the constructions with derived subjects (cf. (8c) and (9b)): despite the fact that there is a referential subject available in these constructions, neither the raising verb nor the copula assign a θ-role to it. This might be regarded as further evidence for a thematically based agreement requirement. To sum up, reflexive clitics need to have access to the thematic hierarchy of the verb whose argument structure they manipulate. Nonreflexive clitics, which are perfectly admissible in these constructions, do not exhibit this property: as we have claimed above, they merely contribute a restriction to the referential index.

In contrast to raising and copula constructions, *se* is realized on the auxiliary in analytic verb forms. At first glance, this is a rather unexpected observation: under the formulation of the agreement requirement given above, it follows that the main verb's thematic structure would have to be raised onto the auxiliary. One might wonder why this should be so: in general we would like to exclude such a mechanism at the level of syntax in order to maintain a principled account of the incompatibility of *se* with derived and expletive subjects.

French temporal auxiliaries, however, differ in important respects from raising verb and copula constructions. As has been demonstrated by Abeillé & Godard (1994), there does not seem to be any positive evidence that the auxiliaries *avoir* 'have' and *être* 'be' take a VP complement. As opposed to French predicative and modal constructions, the participle does not seem to form a constituent with its complements in the auxiliary+participle construction. Neither of the standard constituency tests (i.e., pronominalization, topicalization, ellipsis) may be applied in constructions with analytic verb forms.

(11) a. Jean peut venir, mais il ne le veut pas.
    John can come but he not it wants not
    'John is able to come, but he does not want it.'
  b. *Jean n'est pas arrivé à l'heure, mais Marie l'est
    John 'not is not arrived in time but Mary it is
  c. *Jean croyait avoir compris, mais il n' avait pas
    John believed have understood but he not had not

(12) a. Que veut elle? -- Partir.
    what wants she leave
    'What does she want? -- To leave.'
  b. *Qu'est elle? -- Partie
    what is she left
  c. *Qu' a-t- elle? -- Vendu ses livres
    what has she sold her books

(13)   a. Jean voudrait venir, mais il n'ose pas.
                 John would like come but he not dare not
                 'John would like to come, but he doesn't dare.'
             b. Si Jean veut venir, il peut.
                 if John wants come he can
                 'If John wants to come, he may.'
             c. *Jean n'est pas arrivé, mais Marie est
                 John not is not arrived but Mary is
             d. *Jean a fini son travail, mais Marie n'a pas
                 John has finished his work but Mary not has not

Abeillé & Godard (1994) take this as evidence that French analytic verb forms give rise to extremely flat surface structures. This view seems to be further supported by the specific behavior of temporal auxiliaries in the *tough*-construction and with *faire*-causatives. While raising of an object out of an embedded VP seems to be excluded in French, this is not the case for the object of the participle. Assuming a flat structure in this case, an explanation falls out rather naturally.

(14)   a. Cette langue est utile à apprendre.
                 this language is useful to learn
                 'This language is useful to learn.'
             b. *Cette langue est utile à savoir parler
                 this language is useful to know learn
             c. C'est le genre de gens utiles à avoir fréquenté pendant sa jeunesse.
                 this is the type of people useful to have known during one's youth
                 'This is the kind of people useful to have known during one's youth.'

Above, we mentioned that French causatives are sensitive to the transitivity of their verbal complement: while the subject of intransitives is realized as a direct object, the subject of transitives can only be expressed as the indirect object. Interestingly enough, French temporal auxiliaries are transparent for the participle's transitivity.

(15) a. Son ambition a fait avoir fréquenté les gens qu'il fallait à notre ministre.
his ambition has made have visited the right people to our minister
'His ambition has made our minister having visited the right people.'
b. *Son ambition a fait avoir fréquenté les gens qu'il fallait notre ministre
his ambition has made have visited the right people our minister
c. La frugalité fait avoir vécu jusqu'à 110 ans notre fameuse concitoyenne.
frugality makes have lived until 110 years our famous fellow citizen
'Frugality makes our famous fellow citizen to have lived until 110 years of age.'
d. *La frugalité fait avoir vécu jusqu' à 110 ans notre fameuse concitoyenne.
frugality makes have lived until 110 years our famous fellow citizen

Again, it is not clear how to account for this kind of behavior under a hierarchical analysis in a straightforward way.

We will interpret these findings in favor of an analysis where the auxiliary and the participle constitute a complex morphological object which is represented as an X^0 structure at the level of syntax (see Figure 1). Under this perspective, we are able to relate the transparency versus opacity of thematic structure to the distinction between lexical morphology and syntax, respectively. Furthermore, syntactic constituency seems to support an analysis in terms of complex morphological objects in the spirit of DiSciullo & Williams (1987) and Stiebels & Wunderlich (1992). Finally, the existence of lexicalized forms like verbs with inherent pronominal or ergative *se* may be interpreted in favor of this claim: even in these cases, the pseudo-reflexive clitic is attached to the auxiliary rather than the main verb.

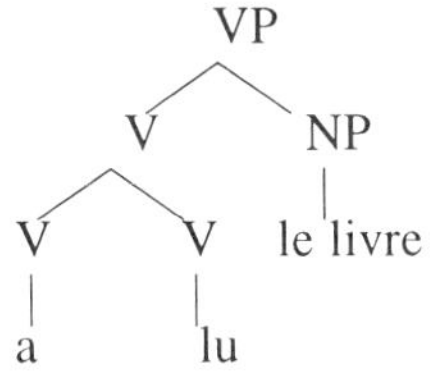

```
        VP
       /  \
      V    NP
     / \    |
    V   V  le livre
    |   |
    a   lu
```

Figure 1   The syntactic representation of temporal auxiliaries

To conclude our discussion of the adult system, we will briefly summarize the main claims. The particular process of argument absorption French clitic *se* is involved in, requires access to the complete thematic hierarchy of a predicate. We argued that such access is restricted to the level of morphology. Syntactic constituency provided us with supporting evidence that French temporal auxiliaries constitute a complex morphological object together with its participial complement. In contrast to this, such evidence could not be found for predicative constructions and modals. Consequently, we would not model them as an entity at the level of morphology. Interestingly enough, French clitic *se* may not be realized on the higher verb in these constructions. Under our approach, nonreflexives simply put a further restriction on some referential index. As this does not require access to the thematic structure of the verb, raising of the clitic does not hinge upon the creation of a verbal complex.

3. CHILD LANGUAGE

3.1. The Data

The subject of our study is a German/French bilingual boy named Ivar. The German/French bilingual girl Caroline will be included for reasons of comparison.

The data originate from the longitudinal DUFDE study (Deutsch Und Französisch-Doppelter Erstspracherwerb 'German and French-Simultaneous First Language Acquisition').[3] The analysis starts at the point in development where there is evidence for the finiteness-distinction, i.e., at about age 2;3/2;4 in Ivar and 2;0 in Caroline (Meisel, 1990a).

Furthermore, we conducted an elicited production task with ten German/French bilingual children. A detailed description of the experimental setup can be found in Section 3.1.2.

3.1.1. Longitudinal data

Recent research on child language has shown that early child utterances differ from adult speech with respect to those constructions which are related to the C-system in the grammar of the target system: this entails the absence of root wh-question formation, inversion, target-like complementizers, relative pronouns, and embedded wh-questions. In order to account for these phenomena, it has been proposed in the literature that a full-fledged C-system is not yet active (Meisel, 1992; Radford, 1987; Roeper & de Villiers, 1992; Roeper & Weissenborn, 1990; Rothweiler, 1994; Verrips & Weissenborn, 1992).[4]

This can also be attested for Ivar whose early French lacks the relevant constructions (Meisel & Müller, 1992, Müller, 1990; Müller, 1993; Müller, 1994). Inversion is absent in both yes/no questions and wh-questions. Furthermore, root constituent questions at the initial stage contain only *où*, other wh-words are not used yet. Target-like complementizers, subordinating conjunctions, and relative pronouns are lacking. Cleft constructions which are already used fairly productively always lack the obligatory relative *que/qui*. Embedded questions do neither contain wh-operators nor the wh-complementizer *si*.

As can be observed in Table 3, Ivar makes productive use of object-drop constructions in a target-deviant way up to the age of 3;0, e.g., *maman prend* 'mummy takes' (Müller *et al.*, 1996). Following Huang (1984) and Jaeggli & Safir (1989) we assumed that empty arguments may be either *pro*, which has to be licensed and identified by rich and uniform agreement morphology, or an empty R-expression *t* A'-bound by a null operator PRO. Interestingly enough, object clitics are lacking entirely from Ivar's early speech (see Table 5). Thus, Ivar's grammar lacks a device to morphologically identify the empty object. We concluded that the object drop exhibited by Ivar's early grammar of French is of the Chinese type. This view is further supported by the observation that the omitted argument corresponds to the discourse topic. Furthermore, Ivar's utterances exhibit multiple argument drop of the type *a pas trouvé* 'Ivar has not found it' which is characteristic of adult Chinese drop constructions as well.

Table 3.
Object omissions (tokens) in obligatory contexts in Ivar (2;4-3;5)

Age	MLU	+OBJ	-OBJ	-OBJ (in %)
2;4	1.33	0	1	100
2;5	2.93	20	17	46
2;6	3.58	8	7	47
2;7	3.51	8	7	47
2;8	3.96	4	4	50
2;9	4.55	11	6	35
2;10	4.90	12	4	25
2;11	4.90	15	5	25
3;0	6.79	25	0	0
3;1	5.47	23	2	8
3;2	6.01	43	4	9
3;3	6.64	23	0	0
3;4	6.81	9	0	0
3;5	5.37	5	0	0

Discussing the possibilities to license empty arguments in Ivar's early grammar of French, we concluded that they have to be conceived of as variables A'-bound by a null operator (PRO) in an IP-adjoined position, see below.

(16) $[_{IP}$ PRO$_i$ $[_{IP}$ Ivar répare t$_i$]]

Our analysis is supported by the observation that Ivar's speech exhibits productive use of lexically instantiated topicalization into a pre-S position. Due to the inactivity of the C-system at this developmental stage, we may interpret topicalization as overt evidence for the existence of an IP-adjoined position in Ivar's emerging grammar of French. Table 4 shows the exact number of topicalizations (XP Subject V$_{finite}$ (YP)) in relation to the total number of multiple constituent utterances containing a finite verb. If these assumptions are correct, it follows that Ivar has access to A'-dependencies.

(17)   a. ça on mets.   Ivar 2;05.07
        this one puts
        'This one we put [here/there].'
    b. et ça on va prendre.   Ivar 2;10.24
        and this one will take
        'And this one we'll take.'
    c. deux piqûres on va faire.   Ivar 2;11.21
        two injections one will make
        'Two injections we'll administer.'
    d. à marktstrasse on va.   Ivar 2;11.21
        to 'Marktstrasse' one goes
        'To Marktstrasse we'll go.'

Table 4.
Topicalizations in Ivar

Age	topicalizations	multiple constituent utterances
2;4.9	2	5
2;5.7	4	26
2;6.6	2	43
2;7.17	1	27
2;8.15	4	43
2;9.18	4	47
2;10.24	9	66
2;11.21	7	92

Driven by the acquisition of the C-system in its target form at the age of 3;0 (Penner & Müller, 1992; Müller & Penner, 1996), Ivar's mechanism of licensing object drop starts to converge with the target system. There is a higher position in the clause (CP) by now, and therefore an empty PRO topic in the IP-adjoined position is no longer licensed, because it is now governed from outside. As a consequence, the child resorts to the other device and starts looking for morphological material that is rich enough to license and identify a *pro* object, i.e., object clitics. The child thus switches from a topic-identified object drop system to a morphologically identified one which corresponds to adult French. One prediction which is borne out by the data is that object clitics are acquired within a very short period of time (see Table 5).

Table 5.
The emergence of object clitics in Ivar (tokens)

Age	MLU	me	te	le, la, les	lui, leur	nous, vous	se
2;4	1.33	0	0	0	0	0	0
2;5	2.93	0	0	0	0	0	0
2;6	3.58	0	0	0	0	0	0
2;7	3.51	0	0	0	0	0	0
2;8	3.96	0	0	0	0	0	1
2;9	4.55	0	0	0	0	0	13
2;10	4.90	0	0	0	0	0	0
2;11	4.90	0	0	0	0	0	3
3;0	6.79	1	2	1	0	0	3
3;1	5.47	0	4	4	0	1	3
3;2	6.01	1	2	8	0	0	6
3;3	6.64	0	0	12	0	0	0
3;4	6.81	0	1	16	0	0	4
3;5	5.37	0	0	7	0	0	1

Interestingly enough, object clitics, including *me*, *te*, *nous*, *vous*, are always placed correctly as long as they have a non-reflexive interpretation.

This is also valid for constructions with analytic verb forms (see (18c)).

(18) a. je peux le faire. Ivar 3;11.8
       I can it do
       'I can do it.'
     b. je le fais. Ivar 3;11.8
       I can it do
       'I do it.'
     c. je l' ai encore mis sur la rue. Ivar 4;0.4
       I it have also put on the road
       'I have also put it onto the road.'

Reflexives, however, do not pattern with non-reflexives in the following respects: the first difference concerns the observation that reflexives already show up occasionally during the stage where object clitics are systematically lacking, i.e., at age 2;8 (see Table 6).

(19) a. ils se battent. Ivar 2;9.18
       they each other beat
       'They beat each other.'
     b. elle se lève. Ivar 2;11.21
       she herself gets-up
       'She gets up.'
     c. ils se battent pas. Ivar 2;11.21
       they each other beat not
       'They don't beat each other.'

Compare also the following examples which are unclear utterances or imitations of the adult's speech and which were not included in Table 6.[5]

(20) a. mamam(s') (a)ppelle maman. Ivar 2;8.15
       Mummy herself calls Mummy
       'Mummy is called Mummy.'
     b. il [samo] (=ils s'amusent) Ivar 2;9.18
       they themselves amuse
       'They amuse themselves.'
     c. pas se promener (Imitation) Ivar 2;10.24
       not oneself walk
       'not walk'
     d. il (s') fait mal Ivar 2;11.21
       he himself hurts
       'he hurts himself'

Thus, the occurrence of reflexives does not seem to be dependent on the development of the C-system in its target form (around 3;0).

Table 6a.
The emergence of reflexive clitics in Ivar (tokens): 2;4 - 3;11

Age	me	te	se	nous	vous
2;4.9	0	0	0	0	0
2;4.23	0	0	0	0	0
2;5.7	0	0	0	0	0
2;5.21	0	0	0	0	0
2;6.6	0	0	0	0	0
2;6.27	0	0	0	0	0
2;7.17	0	0	0	0	0
2;8.1	0	0	0	0	0
2;8.15	0	0	1	0	0
2;9.5	0	0	0	0	0
2;9.18	0	0	13[1]	0	0
2;10.11	0	0	0	0	0
2;10.24	0	0	0	0	0
2;11.7	0	0	0	0	0
2;11.21	0	0	3	0	0
3;0.19	0	0	3	0	0
3;1.3	1	0	1	0	0
3;1.24	0	0	2	0	0
3;2.14	0	0	5	0	0
3;2,28	0	0	1	0	0
3;3,12	0	0	0	0	0
3;4,9	0	0	0	0	0
3;4,23	0	1	4	0	0
3;5,7	0	0	1	0	0
3;5,28	3	0	2	0	0
3;6,13	0	0	0	0	0
3;7,9	0	0	0	0	0
3;7,17	0	0	2	0	0
3;8,1	0	0	3	0	0
3;8,22	0	0	2	0	0
3;8,29	1	1	0	0	0
3;10,11	1	0	0	0	0
3;10,25	0	0	1	0	0
3;11,8	0	0	1	0	0
3;11,20	0	0	2	0	0

Table 6b.
The emergence of reflexive clitics in Ivar (tokens): 4;0 - 5;4

Age	me	te	se	nous	vous
4;0.4	1	1	0	0	0
4;0.18	3	0	6	0	0
4;1.2	0	0	1	0	0
4;1.14	0	0	1	0	0
4;1.28	1	0	1	0	0
4;2.4	0	1	2	0	0
4;2.11	0	0	2	0	0
4;3.16	0	0	3	0	0
4;4.14	0	0	3	0	0
4;4.21	0	0	1	0	0
4;5.0	0	0	4	0	0
4;5.14	0	0	1	0	0
4;5.28	0	0	0	0	0
4;6.13	0	0	1	0	0
4;6.20	0	0	4	0	0
4;7.24	0	0	0	0	0
4;8.4	0	0	1	0	0
4;8.17	0	0	1	0	0
4;9.1	1	0	1	0	0
4;9.15	0	1	2	0	0
4;10.15	0	0	7	0	0
4;10.29	0	0	0	0	0
4;11.14	0	0	7	0	0
5;0.25	0	1	3	0	0
5;1.8	1	0	5	0	0
5;1.22	3	0	5	0	0
5;2.6	0	1	2	0	0
5;2.28	2	1	2	0	0
5;4.6	0	0	1	0	0
5;4.30	0	0	4	0	0

Another observation concerns the placement of reflexive clitics with respect to their argument, the main verb. Reflexive clitics are always adjacent to the main verb in Ivar's speech. For non-analytic verb forms and modal constructions, this gives the correct target-like surface forms (see the examples in (20)). With analytic verb forms containing an auxiliary, he produces target deviant surface strings of the type AUX+*se*+V categorically. This is evidenced by the examples in (21).

(21)   a. on va se baigner.   Ivar 3;02.14
          one will oneself bathe
          'We will go swimming.'
       b. on peut se baigner.   Ivar 3;02.14
          one can oneself bathe
          'We can go swimming.'
       c. non moi quand je me baigne…   Ivar 3;05.28
          no me when I myself bathe…
          'No, when I go swimming… '
       d. grand-père tu te mets comme ça.   Ivar 3;04.23
          grandpa you yourself put like this
          'Grandpa, you sit down like this.'
       e. maintenant je va avec lui se battre.   Ivar 3;04.23
          now I will with him myself beat
          'Now I will fight with him.'

(22)   a. après il a se réveillé.   Ivar 3;02.14
          afterwards he has himself woken
          'Afterwards he woke up.'
       b. il a se fait mal.   Ivar 3;02.28
          he has himself made pain
          'He hurt himself.'
       c. il il faut que t'as te garée sur la rue   Ivar 4;00.04
          it is necessary that you have yourself
          parked on the street
          'It is necessary that you have parked on the street.'

Note further that Ivar has chosen the wrong auxiliary in these constructions, namely *avoir* instead of *être*. Placement errors and errors in the choice of the proper auxiliary always cooccur. Neither of these two can be attested for non-reflexive object clitics, suggesting that both the ordering of clitics and auxiliary selection are quite resistant to slips of the tongue.

Only from 4;2.4 onwards, placement errors and the erroneous selection of *avoir* disappear immediately. There is a radical shift in the child's grammatical system, not a step-by-step development.

(23) a. tu t' es trompée dans un restaurant. Ivar 4;02.04
you yourself are mistaken in the restaurant
'You have mistaken the restaurant.'
b. quand on s' est levé on mange. Ivar 4;02.04
when one oneself is woken one eats
'After we have woken up, we have something to eat.'

As the contrast between Tables 5 and 6 shows, reflexives are far less frequent in Ivar's spontaneous production data than non-reflexives. Therefore, we included data from a second bilingual child, Caroline. The same patterns that have been observed for Ivar's development can also be found in her data. They do not exhibit placement errors with non-reflexive clitics, including forms like *me* and *te* (see the examples in (24)). Furthermore, the placement of reflexive clitics is always correct with non-analytic verb forms and with modal verbs, as shown in the examples in (25) below:

(24) a. je l' a rincé. Caroline 3;01.28
I him have rinsed
'I have rinsed it.'
b. je l'ai vu là. Caroline 4;03.02
I him have seen there
'I've seen him there.'
c. je veux le sortir. Caroline 3;09.22
I want him leave
'I want him to leave.'
d. on les voit pas. Caroline 4;01.05
one them sees not
'One does not see them.'

(25) a. je me dessine. Caroline 3;10.20
I myself paint
'I paint myself.'
b. je va me chercher une biscotte. Caroline 3;09.08
I will myself look for a biscuit
'I will try to find myself a biscuit.'

On the contrary, the placement of reflexive clitics is always incorrect with analytic verb forms. As in Ivar's case, placement errors and target-deviant selection of the auxiliary -- *avoir* instead of *être* -- go hand in hand:

(26) a. la maman elle a- elle avait [sa] se   Caroline 3;08.11
fait mal et...
the mummy she has- she had has herself
made pain and...
'The mother hurt herself and . . . '
b. il a- il a se caché.   Caroline 3;09.22
he has- he has himself hidden
'He hid himself.'

3.1.2. Elicited production task

Although the types of errors found in Ivar are reflected in Caroline's data as well, the absolute number of tokens is extremely low with occurrences distributed over a large period of time. This is hardly surprising since reflexive clitics are produced far less frequently than nonreflexive clitics (see Table 6). In addition, synthetic verb forms are dominating in the spontaneous interactions investigated here. We, therefore, conducted an elicited production task with 10 bilingual French/German children (3;6 - 4;11) in a bilingual kindergarten, five girls and five boys. For the purpose of the present study, we included six children, 3 girls and 3 boys (see Table 7).

Table 7.
Subjects in Elicited Production Task

Name	Age
Pierre	3;8.12
Thierry	4;1.16
Victor	4;8.26
Diane	4;4.4
Sarah	4;10.0
Nathalie	4;11.25

For a period of approximately ten minutes, a native speaker of French presented pictures to the subjects which showed habitual (like 'to wake up') and non-habitual activities (like 'to cut oneself with a knife') in the life of a little boy (Alex) and his elder sister (Lucie). The French interviewer was instructed to prompt the children with specific contexts in order to avoid use of the imparfait, the synthetic form used for habitual actions in the past. We contrasted reflexive with corresponding non-reflexive situations (see Figure 2). In addition to true reflexive situations expressed by *se* in the target language, we also tested for lexicalized forms, i.e., inherent pronominal and ergative *se*. Furthermore, we integrated another function of *se*, namely the reciprocal use.[6]

Figure 2 *le laver* and *se laver*

The main observation is that three out of six children (Pierre, Thierry, and Victor) pattern with Ivar and Caroline: while non-reflexive clitics are always positioned correctly both with synthetic and with analytic verb forms, reflexive clitics are always attached to the lexical verb which yields the correct placement for synthetic verbs and modal constructions, but which produces target-deviant surface strings in constructions with analytic verb forms. As in the case of Ivar and Caroline, incorrect placement of the reflexive clitic and choice of the wrong auxiliary go hand in hand. In other words, Pierre, Thierry, and Victor always choose the (wrong) auxiliary *avoir* instead of *être* in reflexive constructions with an analytic verb form.

Some examples are given below:

(27) a. il l' a coupé.   Pierre 3;8.12
      he it has cut
      'He has cut it.'
   b. il l' a mis sur son pull là.   Pierre 3;8.12
      he it has put on his pullover there
      'He has put it on his pullover.'
   c. il a se peigné.   Pierre 3;8.12
      He has himself combed
      'He combed himself.'
   d. il a se coupé.   Pierre 3;8.12
      He has himself cut
      'He cut himself.'

Tables 8 and 9 contain the absolute numbers of both correct and incorrect placement of reflexive and nonreflexive object clitics, respectively. Synthetic verb forms comprise present tense as well as past tense forms (imparfait) (cf. (28)). Analytic verb forms are restricted to present perfect (passé composé) (for illustration, see (27)).

(28)   a. il se réveillait.   Pierre 3;8.12
he himself woke up
'He woke up.'
b. et là il se lave.   Pierre 3;8.12
and there he himself washes
'And there, he washes himself.'

The other three children (Diane, Sarah, and Nathalie) included here do not produce any placement errors of this kind, neither with reflexive nor with nonreflexive clitics. Furthermore, auxiliary selection corresponds to adult French. Note that these children are already at an age where also Ivar and Caroline do not produce this kind of error anymore.

Table 8.
Placement of reflexive clitics (tokens)

Child	synthetic		modals		analytic	
	correct	incorrect	correct	incorrect	correct	incorrect
Pierre	9	0	0	0	0	4
Thierry	2	0	0	0	0	6
Victor	3	0	0	0	0	3
Diane	20	0	2	0	8	0
Sarah	4	0	0	0	6	0
Natalie	10	0	0	0	3	0

Table 9.
Placement of nonreflexive object clitics (tokens)

Child	synthetic		modals		analytic	
	correct	incorrect	correct	incorrect	correct	incorrect
Pierre	4	0	0	0	3	0
Thierry	1	0	0	0	2	0
Victor	0	0	1	0	2	0
Diane	3	0	0	0	7	0
Sarah	0	0	0	0	3	0
Natalie	0	0	0	0	0	0

3.1.3. Bilingualism

One could object now that the errors concerning auxiliary selection and clitic placement are merely an effect of unsuccessful transfer from German. In German main clauses, NP objects including reflexive and nonreflexive pronouns are positioned between the auxiliary and the clause-final main verb yielding the surface order AUX+OBJ+V, the order which is used by Caroline, Ivar, Pierre, Thierry, and Victor for reflexive clitics. Furthermore, German auxiliary selection is not sensitive to the presence of the reflexive. Again, in the data of the children mentioned above auxiliary selection in French does not depend on the presence of *se*. If we conceive of transfer as a process whereby learners transfer grammatical knowledge from one language to another, rather than mere surface strings, this amounts to saying that the children who produce the aforementioned errors indeed have a representation which corresponds to their German grammar in two respects: first, they have, at least optionally, a head-final VP, and second, they analyze French reflexive clitics as strong pronouns. It follows, then, that nonreflexive clitics and full NPs should have the same distribution as *se* in the children's data, giving rise to surface strings such as (28a,b) in French. A second prediction of this claim would be that the distribution of *se* parallels the distribution of German *sich* 'oneself' in all contexts. Both predictions are not borne out by the data: first, with analytic verb forms, nonreflexive clitics and full NPs are never positioned between the auxiliary and the participle in the children's utterances. Moreover, nonreflexive clitics are always placed correctly with respect to the target grammar, and more importantly, in a position where these elements cannot be licensed in German cf. examples in (29c) and (29d) below.

(29)   a. Er hat ihn/den Hund gesehen.
He has him/the dog seen
'He has seen him/the dog.'
b. Er hat sich gesehen.
He has himself seen
'He has seen himself.'
c. *Er ihn hat gesehen
He him has seen
d. *Er ihn sieht
He him sees
e. *Er sich sieht
He himself sees

Second, *se* is always placed correctly with synthetic verb forms, preceding the finite verb. Again, this is a position not available in German main clauses (see (29e)). We believe to have shown that the specific error patterns found in the speech of the subjects cannot be simply attributed to some notion of transfer, but have to be accounted for in terms of intermediate child grammars.

With respect to auxiliary selection, we found that even monolingual French children exhibit severe problems in this area in conjunction with the acquisition of object clitics. Grégoire's data are available on the CHILDES database (Champaud, 1989; MacWhinney & Snow, 1985). With respect to the interpretation of his data, one has to be careful however because the undocumented phase before the productive use of clitics is quite long (about 2 months). Therefore, we are unable to trace back the exact developmental path he takes in the acquisition of clitics.

Grégoire seems to acquire reflexives and nonreflexives at the same stage. He experiences a complete breakdown of this part of grammar: the type of clitic present does not have any impact on the selection of the auxiliary, and, even worse, in sentences without any clitic present, he chooses correct and wrong auxiliaries at random, an observation not being made in our bilingual children of the longitudinal study. Sometimes these errors can be attested with the same verb during the same recording session (compare examples (30a,b) with (31a,b) respectively). Before he started to use object clitics productively, Grégoire did not exhibit any problems selecting the correct auxiliary. Finally, it should not remain unmentioned that Grégoire also makes a few placement errors, of the type in (30d), which are restricted to *se* and the potentially "ambiguous" forms like *me* and *te*, while placement of *le* is 100% correct. However, wrong placement of those potentially "ambiguous" forms is not systematic: Correct and wrong placements cooccur for the same verb and during the same recording.

(30) *incorrect auxiliary selection*
    a. moi j'étais, moi j'étais peur de la mer.   Grégoire 2;5.28
        me I was fear of the sea
        'Me, I was afraid of the sea.'
    b. regarde je m'ai fait mal avec la petite   Grégoire 2;5.28
        pince à linge.
        look I myself have made pain with the little clothes-pin
        'Look, I hurt myself with the little clothes-pin.'
    c. je m'ai cogné ici.   Grégoire 2;5.14
        I myself have hit here
        'I hit myself here.'

        d. et puis j'ai m'aide.   Grégoire 2;5.14
           and then I have myself help
           'And then I helped myself.'
        e. moi je m' ai couché,
           moi je m' ai caché...   Grégoire 2;5.28
           me I myself have gone-to-bed,
           me I myself have hidden ...
           'I went to bed, I hid myself... '

(31)   *correct auxiliary selection*
        a. le monsieur a pas peur de la mer.   Grégoire 2;5.28
           the man has not fear of the sea
           'The man isn't afraid of the sea.'
        b. il s' est fait mal.   Grégoire 2;5.14
           he himself is made pain
           'He has hurt himself.'
        c. et, et la jeep, elle s'est ameseé a-avec   Grégoire 2;5.28
           and the jeep she herself is amused with
           'And she amused herself with the jeep.'
        d. papa il s'est mouillé les pieds.   Grégoire 2;5.28
           daddy he himself is wetted the feet
           'Daddy has wetted his feet.'

    Other researchers, like Jakubowicz (1991) and Snyder *et al.* (1997), do not observe placement errors with reflexive clitics and auxiliary selection errors in the acquisition of reflexive clitics in the monolingual children they analyzed. There is, however, one study which also reports on placement errors, namely Nuckle (1981). Although she observes placement errors only within the clitic cluster (e.g., *ils les se lavent* 'they it themselves wash'), one of our main results is confirmed in her study, namely that the reflexive clitic is always placed adjacent to the main verb, reflecting the claim advanced here that the relation between *se* and the predicate is much closer than the relation between the predicate and non-reflexives. It would be interesting to see whether our findings, especially those related to the specific placement errors, could be confirmed in a cross-sectional or longitudinal study of monolingual French children.

    Finally we want to mention the observation that the error types discussed here for the domain of reflexive constructions are not a necessary feature of bilingual language development. There are also bilingual children who do not produce these errors.

3.1.4. Discussion

We will now turn to the discussion of the observations in the light of the analysis of the adult system outlined above.

First, the French reflexive clitics do not seem to interact with developments within the C-system: reflexives already show up occasionally at a point where ordinary non-reflexives are omitted systematically (Müller et al., 1996). Given that reflexive clitics involve the absorption of an internal argument, there should be no object present in syntax, neither overt nor covert. Since there is no null argument, there is also no need to license it by means of an A'-binding PRO. Hence, the instantiation of a syntactic constituent, like CP, should have no impact on the derivation of reflexive clitics.

A second important result is that Ivar, Caroline, Pierre, Thierry, and Victor make errors with both clitic placement and auxiliary selection in reflexive constructions which fall into the range of problem space defined by the derivation process. Recall that even with analytic verb forms the morphological derivation of non-reflexive clitics may operate on the finite part alone. Put differently, the derivation involves simple words only. Thus, in Di Sciullo & Williams' (1987) terminology, the morphological word is a single syntactic atom. Contrarily, the reflexive clitic requires access to the complete thematic hierarchy of a predicate. We have argued that the adult-like representation of reflexive clitics involves complex objects which map on more than one syntactic atom.

We assume that the systematic placement errors with reflexive clitics can be accounted for in a natural way given the child's assumption that syntactic and morphological structures be isomorphic: favoring an analysis in terms of simple words leads the child to affix the reflexive clitic to the main verb rather than the auxiliary as the process of argument absorption must have access to the main verb's thematic hierarchy. Our analysis implies that *se* does not have access to the auxiliary in some local domain, neither in morphology nor in syntax (see Figure 3). The systematic selection of the wrong auxiliary, then, is hardly surprising.

Figure 3   The children's erroneous syntactic representation of *se* with analytic verb forms

Since nonreflexive clitics do not involve access to the thematic hierarchy of the predicate, the hierarchical structure in Figure 3, where the auxiliary selects a VP complement, can also account for the correct positioning of nonreflexive clitics in the children's utterances which contain analytic verb forms.

The hierarchical structure in Figure 3 makes the prediction that the participle forms a constituent with its complements in child grammar. Thus, we would expect that the complex V[part]+object(s) be subject to syntactic processes such as topicalization, clefting, and ellipsis. We leave the empirical verification of this prediction for further research.

A further prediction would be that medial and ergative *se* pattern with ordinary ergatives as far as auxiliary selection is concerned. Unfortunately, the corpora studied do not allow us to verify nor to falsify this claim.

Finally, we have to ask what kind of data the children could use in order to revise the target-deviant structure in Figure 3 and assume a representation in terms of a verb cluster as shown in Figure 1. The trigger for the target-like analysis should be found in exactly those domains of the grammar for which a hierarchical VP structure cannot account (cf. Abeillé & Godard, 1994). These are bounded dependencies (*tough*-constructions) and causative constructions for example. Note that these constructions occur at later steps in the children's grammatical development. Therefore, we would expect that placement and auxiliary selection errors disappear at an advanced age which is the case in the children under investigation. It would be interesting to study the hypothesized interaction between correct placement of reflexive clitics and the development of bounded dependencies and causatives.

4. CONCLUSION

Comparing the acquisition of reflexive and non-reflexive clitics in French, we have found that non-isomorphic syntactic and morphological representations confront the child with a considerable learning problem. The main result of our investigation is that children favor affixation to operate on simple words rather than complex words. It is probably true that the cases in which there is one-to-one correspondence between morphological categories and syntactic categories constitutes the core or unmarked case and thus is persued by small children in the first place. That there are grammars like French which allow for mismatches between morphology and syntax is discovered only during later developmental stages. If our analysis turns out to be correct, we would expect similar problems in all domains which are characterized by diverging morphological and syntactic representations. The observation that monolingual German children cannot separate the particle from the finite verb as required for German particle verbs in main clauses could be evidence in favor of the child's erroneous analysis in terms of isomorphic structures.

ACKNOWLEDGEMENTS

The paper is the revised talk version of our contributions to the 1st Lisbon Meeting on Child Language (with Special Reference to Romance Languages) (June 1994) and to the language acquisition session at Langues et Grammaire 2 (Paris, June 1995). We would like to thank the audiences for useful comments. We are also indebted to Susanne E. Carroll, Celia Jakubowicz, Jürgen M. Meisel, Jürgen Weissenborn, and the anonymous reviewers for valuable comments.

We are particularly grateful to Gesche Seemann for drawing the pictures for us: the children loved them! Thanks also to Elizabeth Kinnaër who interacted with the children during the experiment: the children loved her too! Finally, we want to thank Eva Sobottka for proof-reading the paper before submission.

NOTES

[1] Morphological Uniformity: An inflectional paradigm P in a language L is morphologically uniform iff P has either only underived inflectional forms or only derived inflectional forms (Jaeggli & Safir, 1989:30).
[2] These and the following examples in this subsection are taken from Wehrli (1986). Of course, argument reduction yields a two-place predicate when applied to ditransitives.
[3] In the DUFDE project, bilingual German/French children are studied longitudinally. They are videotaped once a fortnight from the age of approximately 1;0,0 (Years;Months,Days) - 1;6 up to the age of 5;0 - 6;0 years. For further details see Meisel (ed.) 1990b, 1994. The project has been financed by a grant from the Deutsche Forschungsgemeinschaft (DFG) to Jürgen M. Meisel.
[4] However, for a more thorough discussion of early subordination and the successive activation of the C-system see Penner & Müller (1992) and Müller & Penner (1996).
[5] All 13 tokens correspond to one type.
[6] Although children's imitations of adult utterances surely cannot be taken as robust evidence for the availability of grammatical knowledge, it is a general observation that children tend to omit unanalyzed elements in imitation tasks.
[7] Reflexive *se*: se regarder 'to look at oneself', *se brosser les dents* 'to brush one's teeth', *se/le laver* 'to wash oneself/someone', *se/lui laver les cheveux* 'to wash one's/someone's hair', *se/le couper* 'to cut oneself/something', *se/lui couper les cheveux* 'to cut one's/someone's hair', *se salir* 'to dirty oneself', *se gratter* 'to scratch oneself', *se tirer la langue* 'to stick out the tongue to oneself', *se/le peigner* 'to comb oneself/someone'; lexicalized se: se réveiller "to wake up", *se lever* 'to get up', *se casser* 'to break', *se cogner* 'to hurt oneself'; reciprocal se: *se tirer la langue* 'to stick out the tongue to each other', *se battre* 'to beat one another'.

REFERENCES

Abeillé, A. and D. Godard: 1994, 'The Complementation of French Auxiliaries', *West Coast Conference on Formal Linguistics* **13**, Stanford University.
Auger, J.: 1993, 'More Evidence for Verbal Agreement-Marking in Colloquial French', In W. Ashby, M. Mithun, G. Perissinotto, & E. Raposo (eds.) *Linguistic Perspectives on Romance Languages*. John Benjamins, Amsterdam, 177-198.
Auger, J. and P. H. Miller: 1995, 'Les affixes pronominaux du français: à l'interface entre syntaxe, morphologie et phonologie', Manuscript, McGill University, Montrèal, Université de Lille 3.
Belletti, A.: 1982, 'Morphological Passive and Pro-Drop: The Impersonal Construction', *Journal of Linguistic Research* **2(1)**, 1-34.
Borer, H.: 1986, 'Introduction', In H. Borer (ed.) *The Syntax of Pronominal Clitics*, Vol. 19 of SYNTAX and SEMANTICS, Academic Press, New York, 1-11.
Bresnan, J. and S. A. Mchombo: 1995, "The Lexical Integrity Principle: Evidence from Bantu', *Natural Language and Linguistic Theory* **13**, 181-254.
Champaud, C. (ed.): 1989, 'Grégoire Corpus. Directions for Use', Paris: CNRS.
Crysmann, B.: 1992, 'R-Klitika im Französischen. Morphologische Derivation und ihre Implikationen für die Syntax', ms., Universität Hamburg.
Crysmann, B.: 1995, 'Klitisierung in einer HPSG des Französischen', Master's thesis, Universität Hamburg.
Di Sciullo, A.-M. and E. Williams: 1987, *On the Definition of Word*, MIT Press, Cambridge.
Grimshaw, J.: 1982, 'On the Lexical Representation of Romance Reflexive Clitics', In J. Bresnan (ed.) *The Mental Representation of Grammatical Relations*, MIT Press, Cambridge, 87-148.
Grimshaw, J.: 1990, *Argument Structure*, Linguistic Inquiry Monographs 18. MIT Press, Cambridge/
Haider, H. and R. Rindler-Schjerve: 1987, 'The Parameter of Auxiliary Selection: Italian-German Contrasts', *Linguistics* **25**, 1029-1055.
Huang, C.-T. J.: 1984, 'On the Distribution and Reference of Empty Pronouns', *Linguistic Inquiry* **15**, 531-574.
Jackendoff, R.: 1990, *Semantic Structures*, MIT Press, Cambridge.
Jaeggli, O. and K. Safir: 1989, 'The Null Subject Parameter and Parametric Theory', In O. Jaeggli & K. Safir (eds.) *The Null Subject Parameter*, Vol. 15 of Studies in Natural Language and Linguistic Theory, Kluwer, Dordrecht, 1-44.
Jakubowicz, C.: 1991, 'L'acquisition des anaphores et des pronoms lexicaux en français', In J. Guèron & J.-Y. Pollock (eds.) *Grammaire Gènèrative et Syntaxe Compareé*. Paris: Editions du CNRS, 229-252.
Kayne, R.: 1975, *French Syntax. The Transformational Cycle*, MIT Press, Cambridge.
MacWhinney, B. and C. Snow: 1985, 'The Child Language Data Exchange System', *Journal of Child Language* **12**, 271-296.
Manzini, R.: 1986, 'On Italian Si', In H. Borer (ed.) *The Syntax of Pronominal Clitics*, Vol. 19 of SYNTAX and SEMANTICS, Academic Press, New York, 241-262.
Marantz, A.: 1984, *On the Nature of Grammatical Relations*, MIT Press, Cambridge.
Meisel, J. M.: 1990a, 'INFL-ection: Subjects and Subject-Verb Agreement', In J.M. Meisel (ed.) *Two First Languages. Early Grammatical Development in Bilingual Children*, Foris, Dordrecht, 237-298.
Meisel, J. M. (ed.): 1990b, *Two First Languages. Early Grammatical Development in Bilingual Children*, Dordrecht, Foris.
Meisel, J. M. (ed.): 1992, *The Acquisition of Verb Placement: Functional Categories and V2 Phenomena in Language Development*, Kluwer, Dordrecht,
Meisel, J. M. (ed.): 1994, *Bilingual First Language Acquisition: German and French*, Vol. 7 of Language Acquisition and Language Disorders. John Benjamins, Amsterdam.

Meisel, J. M. and N. Müller: 1992, 'Finiteness and Verb Placement in Early Child Grammars. Evidence from the Simultaneous Acquisition of Two First Languages: French and German', In, J. M. Meisel (ed.) *The Acquisition of Verb Placement: Functional Categories and V2 Phenomena in Language Development*, Kluwer, Dordrecht, 109-138.
Miller, P. H.: 1992, *Clitics and Constituents in Phrase Structure Grammar*, Garland, New York.
Miller, P. H. and I. A. Sag: 1995, 'French Clitic Movement without Clitics or Movement', ms., Université de Lille 3, Stanford University.
Müller, N.: 1990, 'Erwerb der Wortstellung im Französischen und Deutschen. Zur Distribution von Finitheitsmerkmalen in der Grammatik bilingualer Kinder', In M. Rothweiler (ed.) Spracherwerb und Grammatik. Linguistische Untersuchungen zum Erwerb von Syntax und Morphologie, *Linguistische Berichte Sonderheft* **3**, 127-151.
Müller, N.: 1993, *Komplexe Sätze. Der Erwerb von COMP und von Wortstellungsmustern bei bilingualen Kindern (Französisch/Deutsch)*, Narr, Tübingen.
Müller, N.: 1994, 'Parameters Cannot Be Reset: Evidence from the Development of COMP', In J. M. Meisel (ed.) *Bilingual First Language Acquisition. French and German Grammatical Development*, Johm Benjamins, Amsterdam, 235-269.
Müller, N., B. Crysmann, and G. A. Kaiser: 1996, 'Interactions between the Acquisition of French Object Drop and the Development of the C-System'. *Language Acquisition* **5(1)**, 35-63.
Müller, N. and Z. Penner: 1996, 'Early Subordination: The Acquisition of Free Morphology in French, German, and Swiss German', *Linguistics* **34**, 133-165.
Nuckle, L.: 1981, 'Sur l'acquisition des pronoms clitiques objets chez des enfants francophones: la double-cliticisation et la simple-cliticisation', Master's thesis, Université de Montréal.
Penner, Z. and N. Müller: 1992, 'On the Early Stages in the Acquisition of Finite Subordinate Clauses in German, Swiss German, and French', *Geneva Generative Papers* **0(1/2)**, 163-183.
Radford, A.: 1987, 'The Acquisition of the Complementizer System', *Bangor Research Papers in Linguistics* **2**, 55-76.
Roberge, Y.: 1991, 'On the Recoverability of Null Objects', In D. Wanner & D. A. Kibbee (eds.) *New Analyses in Romance Linguistics. Selected Papers from the XVIIIth Linguistic Symposium on Romance Languages*, 299-312.
Roeper, T. and J. de Villiers: 1992, 'The One Feature Hypothesis'. ms., University of Massachusetts at Amherst.
Roeper, T. and J. Weissenborn: 1990, 'How to Make Parameters Work: Comments on Valian'. In L. Frazier & J. de Villiers (eds.) *Language Processing and Language Acquisition*, Kluwer, Dordrecht, 147-162.
Rosen, S. T.: 1990, *Argument Structures and Complex Predicates*, Garland, New York.
Rothweiler, M.: 1994, *Der Erwerb von Nebensätzen im Deutschen*, Niemeyer, Tübingen.
Simpson, J. and M. Withgott: 1986, 'Pronominal Clitic Clusters and Templates', In H.Borer (ed.) *The Syntax of Pronominal Clitics*, Vol. 19 of SYNTAX and SEMANTICS. New York, Academic Press, 149-174.
Snyder, W., N. Hyams, and P. Crisma: 1997, 'Romance Auxiliary Selection With Reflexive Clitics: Evidence for Early Knowledge of Unaccusativity', ms. , MIT, UCLA, University of Venice.
Spencer, A.: 1991, *Morphological Theory. An Introduction to Word Structure in Generative Grammar*, Blackwell, Oxford.
Sportiche, D.: 1992, 'Clitic Constructions', paper presented at the GLOW conference 1992, Lisbon.
Stiebels, B. and D. Wunderlich: 1992, 'A Lexical Account of Complex Verbs', *Theorie des Lexikons. Arbeiten des SFB 282* **30**, 1-43.
Verrips, M. and J. Weissenborn: 1992, Routes to Verb Placement in Early German and French: the Independence of Finiteness and Agreement'. In J. M. Meisel (ed.) *The Acquisition of Verb Placement: Functional Categories and V2 Phenomena in Language Development*, Dordrecht: Kluwer, 283-331.

Wehrli, E.: 1986, 'On Some Properties of French Clitic se', In H. Borer (ed.) *The Syntax of Pronominal Clitics*, Vol. 19 of SYNTAX and SEMANTICS. Academic Press, New York, 263-284.

Zubizarreta, M.-L.: 1982, 'On the Relationship of the Lexicon to Syntax', Ph.D. Dissertation, MIT.

Zwicky, A. and G. K. Pullum: 1983, 'Cliticization vs. Inflection: English n't', *Language* **59**, 502-513.

BERTHOLD CRYSMANN NATASCHA MÜLLER
Universität des Saarlandes *Universität Hamburg*

PIERO BOTTARI   PAOLA CIPRIANI   ANNA MARIA CHILOSI

DISSOCIATIONS IN THE ACQUISITION OF CLITIC PRONOUNS BY DYSPHASIC CHILDREN: A CASE STUDY FROM ITALIAN

1. INTRODUCTION

Developmental dysphasia (or Specific Language Impairment, according to the terminology adopted in the USA) is a pathological condition in which the linguistic disorder is not associated with deficits in other cognitive domains. Indeed, children diagnosed as dysphasic do not follow the normal course of language development but they appear to be normal in all other respects. Moreover, they do not show any neurological sign of brain damage or dysfunction. Morphosyntax and phonology are the linguistic domains most affected: speech production by dysphasic children have an 'agrammatic' shape in that function words or morphemes are significantly omitted. Moreover, the learning course is characterized by chronological dissociations; that is, sub-components of grammar that in normal development emerge together may emerge at different times or may not emerge at all.

Recently, research on dysphasia has received a new impulse not only because of clinical necessities, such as a finer definition of the syndrome against its varying manifestations and the construction of diagnostic and prognostic profiles, but also because of some exciting issues it raises at a more speculative level. In fact, the discussion has now centered on the nature of the disorder. In particular, the research on the specific aspects of the linguistic knowledge that are affected has given rise to a number of competing interpretative hypotheses. Thus, it has been proposed that dysphasics (or some subgroups) entirely lack certain deep grammatical features or competencies as a consequence of a genetic deficit (Gopnik, 1990; Gopnik & Crago, 1991). According to an alternative interpretation, the cause of the competence deficit lies in the fact that dysphasics are unable to extract from the input all the necessary information to construct a correct grammar (Leonard, Sabbadini & Volterra, 1987). Another alternative interpretation assumes that dysphasics have no problems at the competence level but that performance difficulties of various sorts emerge in their actual speech (see Fletcher, 1992).

The debate on these issues or alternative interpretations is at present very lively and calls for detailed and theory oriented analyses of the linguistic behavior of dysphasic children. Under this perspective, then, the study of dysphasia may also significantly contribute to the understanding of the general properties of grammar and to a finer definition of the strategies and the laws governing language development in normal children. On the one side, specific manifestations of the deficit hinting at dissociations among the grammatical components may provide interesting tools for evaluating theoretical interpretations of linguistic phenomena or for choosing among alternative proposals. On the other side, identifying which specific factors are involved may shed light on what specific pre-requisites are needed in the normal learning process.

The purpose of this paper is to contribute to this debate by reporting the results of a longitudinal study centered on the deviant behavior of one dysphasic child's use of clitics. The competence of clitics, because of its multi-component character, appears to be an interesting topic for investigation. Indeed, among other things, it involves the knowledge of argument structure properties, of the structural representations of functional categories, of chain formation procedures, of the assignment of control relations, and of morphological paradigms. In normal children, these pieces of knowledge seem to emerge in a rather integrated fashion (or, at least, they are rapidly integrated in the course of the development). In dysphasia, instead, the integration process does not seem to fully reach its target. This is perhaps due to the absence or the misapplication of some of the required pieces of knowledge. Indeed, we will see that the peculiar pattern of omission in the productions of this child seems to indicate a deficit in one specific component of the cliticization rule, the syntactic rule of chain formation. This result will be checked against each one of the current interpretative hypotheses with the ensuing suggestion that only some may suit the case at hand and that even these will require refinements in terms of grammatical properties.

2. SAMPLE AND METHOD

2.1. Sample

2.1.1. Case study

The dysphasic child, M. was followed from 5 years and 9 months up to 13 years and 5 months. Only data from 6 years and 2 months up to 9 years and 4 months will be reported here. Observations have been made at the Scientific Institute 'Stella Maris' - Institute of Child Neuropsychiatry of the University of Pisa. The analyses we will report concern spontaneous speech productions for a total of 13 sessions, each consists of about 250 utterances.

2.1.2 A broad outline of M.'s development 1

The dysphasic child (M.) had very limited expressive language when first seen at the age of 5 years. His cognitive development was normal as repeatedly assessed by non-verbal tests of intelligence (Leiter International Scale and WISC/R Performance Scale). Hearing was normal and no clinical signs of neurological dysfunction were present. MRIs showed no evidence of morphological brain abnormalities and chromosomal studies were normal. M. was videotaped in the clinic while interacting with a familiar adult (the mother or the therapist) at different intervals.[2]

M. shows a deficit of the so-called phonologic-syntactic subtype (see Rapin & Allen, 1983) or Grammatical SLI (Van der Lely & Stollwerk, 1997). The global linguistic profile up to 8 years and 9 months reveals deficits in various morphosyntactic domains: free morphemes (clitics, articles, prepositions, copula, auxiliaries) tend to be omitted or used incorrectly, while syntactic structures are bound to root clauses (sometimes with a missing predicate) and to coordinated clauses. Bound morphology, although restricted to a few types, is used correctly (correct agreement relations). From 9 years and 4 months on, M's productions show a visible improvement, with a rapid decrease of omissions and the emergence of new morphological types and syntactic structures. However, some important difficulties still persist with clitics, articles, relative clauses, and other constructions.

Even though we will report data from the 9 years and 4 months session, for the purpose of the present discussion we will take as relevant the period from 6 years and 2 months to 8 years and 9 months. Indeed, the focus of the present paper will be the selective pattern of occurrences and omissions of clitics that persistently characterizes this long period. The session of 9 years and 4 months simply documents the age point at which M's improvement begins (even though with some persisting difficulties with clitics to which we will return in much more detail).

2.1.3. Cross-sectional Sample and Normal Control

The analyses performed on M's productions have also been performed on a cross-sectional sample consisting of 6 dysphasic children (age range 6 years and 2 months - 11 years and 6 months) who have the same kind of deficit as M. and on the productions of a normal child, R., followed from 24months 28 days until 35 months and 9 days, for a total of 12 sessions. [3]

2.2. Method

The analysis has focused on the production of argument clitics. By argument clitic, we mean a clitic that can be replaced by a lexical NP or by a PP. So inherent clitics and 'pleonastic' clitics have been left out.

The production of clitics has been investigated by looking at 1) occurrences; 2) omissions; 3) corresponding stressed pronouns or lexical NPs (labeled here as Full NPs), in a set of possible obligatory contexts. In each session, repetitions of the same structure have been counted only once; imitations of the adult participants' utterances have not been counted.

2.2.1.Types of Contexts Investigated

The contexts for clitic insertion have been subdivided into four main types, which have been labeled as follows (the illustrative examples are not from M.).

(a) Simple INFL (present tense)

By Simple INFL, we mean contexts containing a single inflected verbal form, a present tense in most cases.

(1)   a. lo mangio
　　　　　　it I-eat
　　　　　　'I eat it.'
　　　　　b. mi chiama
　　　　　　me he-calls
　　　　　c. gli parlo
　　　　　　to-him I-speak

(b) Complex INFL ('*passato prossimo*')

By Complex (or Non-Simple) INFL, we mean compositional tenses, as for instance present perfect the *passato prossimo*.

(2)   li ha mangiati
           them he-has eaten-PLUR
           'He has eaten them.'

(c) Monoclausal infinitive constructions (modal+infinitive; semi-modal+infinitive; causative constructions)

By Monoclausal infinitive constructions, we mean constructions in which clitic climbing is allowed or obligatorily required. These include modal+infinitive; semi-modal+infinitive; causative constructions

(3)   lo vuole mangiare/vuole mangiarlo
           it he-wants to-eat/he-wants to-eat-it
           'He wants to eat it.'

(d) Obligatory contexts for post verbal clitics

Obligatory contexts for post verbal clitics include imperatives as in (4), infinitives governed by a preposition as in (5) or by a non-modal or non-causative verb.

(4)   mangialo
           eat-it
           'Eat it.'

(5)   serve per mangiarlo
           it is necessary for to-eat-it
           'It is necessary for eating it.'

(6)   dice di mangiarlo/*lo dice di mangiare (bi-clausal context)
           he-says 'di' to-eat-it/*it he-says 'di' to-eat
           'He says that he eats it.'

It must be pointed out that proper contexts for clitic insertion were considered to be only the contexts containing a word to which the clitic could attach. Thus, all the cases in which an auxiliary or a modal verb was missing have been left out of the analysis. We have counted as omissions all the cases in which one obligatory argument of a predicate is not phonetically realized (as a clitic or as an NP): it must be noted that this criterion may overestimate the omission rate since omissions may involve either a clitic or a full NP. Deciding which was the case was impossible for most situations. However, there are two facts suggesting that what is likely to be omitted is a clitic and not a full NP:

i. in almost all sessions the amount of full NPs is higher than or equal to the sum of occurrences of clitics and omissions (see Table 1 below);

ii. in his late development, when omissions significantly drop, M. still manifests a tendency to produce full NPs even in contexts where a clitic could be used (cf. Cipriani, Bottari, Chilosi, & Pfanner, 1995).

3. RESULTS

3.1. Overall Panorama

The overall panorama of M's clitic production is illustrated in Figure 1 below, which shows the percentage of presences, omissions, substitutions and erroneous uses of functors in obligatory contexts.[4]

Figure 1 Clitic pronouns in a Dysphasic Child - Relative percentages

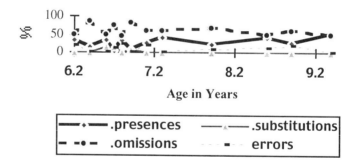

As can be seen, even though omissions prevail over occurrences throughout, clitics are significantly present from the first observation. This conforms to the general behavior M. displays with respect to other morphemes.[5] As illustrated in Figure 2, in normal development clitics show a fast evolution and are attended to very early.[6]

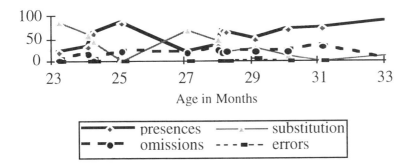

Figure 2 Clitics in Normal Development (Relative percentages)

A further fact worth considering is that in M's productions the argument slots of predicates are preferably filled with full NPs. This is also true for the other dysphasic children. Here, M's productions differ from normal children, who tend to fill the argument slots with clitic pronouns as soon as they acquire mastery of the functor. To get an idea of this difference compare Table 1 and Table 2 below, which show the evolution of clitics in Simple INFL contexts (percentages have been calculated on the total of occurrences, omissions, and full NPs).

Table 1.
Simple INFL Contexts for M (dysphasic Child)

age	Occurrences	Omissions	Full NPs
6;2	4	9	18
6;5	0	13	13
6;7	1	3	17
6;8	4	10	11
6;9	3	9	18
6;1	2	9	9
6;11	1	6	14
7;1	0	2	2
7;3	1	1	4
7;9	4	8	13
8;6	1	1	9
8;9	4	3	11
9;4	4	1	10

Table 2.
Simple INFL contexts in R. (normal child)

AGE(in months)	Occurrences	Omissions	Full NPs
24,28	4	2	5
25,15	2	1	1
27,14	1	4	2
28,28	4	3	1
29,13	13	4	13
30,13	15	1	3
31,14	16	6	22
33,06	36	5	19
34,14	17	1	6
35,09	24	1	18

M.'s tendency to avoid clitics also characterizes the period from 9 years and 4 months to 13 years 5 months, when he has mastered functors.

Of course it might well be the case that the prominence of full NPs is just an effect of the particular discourse topic (i.e., that nominal complements turn out to be novel entities in most cases). As an explanation for the prominence of full NPs is not central to the present argument, we will leave the observation at that. However, we would like to make the following remarks:

i. it is a curious fact that in so many sessions of dysphasic children's productions the discourse topic requires novel referents (prevalence of full NPs) while in most instances of the normal child's utterances referents happen to be anaphoric to discourse entities (prevalence of clitic pronouns);

ii. M. tends to avoid clitics also in narratives (see Cipriani, Bottari, Chilosi & Pfanner, 1998) where the 'frog story' experiment has been evaluated) which typically involve a high number of anaphoric referents;

iii. in principle, nothing excludes the possibility that the tendency to avoid clitics depends on a generalized difficulty dysphasics manifest in controlling the syntactic representations involved in the cliticization rule (see below for discussion).

3.2. Contexts of Realization/Omission

Let us now consider the specific contexts of clitic realization. Here an important dissociation emerges. Production of clitics is **very selective** as for what concerns contexts: occurrences are almost only attested **in contexts containing a simple verbal form** (present tense). *Passato prossimo* and monoclausal infinitives almost totally exclude the presence of clitics (we will see that the late instances of clitics with *passato prossimo* are to be considered special cases). In addition, post-verbal clitics are almost totally missing. To illustrate this point in a concise way we have devised Table 3.

Table 3.
Simple INFL contexts versus Non-simple INFL Contexts for M.

age	presences Simple INFL	presences Non-simple INFL	omissions Simple INFL	omissions Non-simple INFL
6;2	30% 4	0	9	1
6;5	0	0	13	0
6;7	25% 1	0	3	3
6;8	28% 4	0	10	1
6;9	25% 3	0	9	0
6;1	18% 2	0	9	4
6;11	14% 1	0	6	1
7;1	0	0	2	1
7;3	50% 1	0	1	0
7;9	33% 4	0	8	5
8;6	50% **1**	30% 3	1	5
8;9	57% 4	0	3	5
9;4	80% 4	35% **6**	1	11

In this table, the data concerning Simple INFL contexts are matched with a collapse of the data concerning the other types of contexts (for convenience these have been labeled Non-simple INFL contexts). The table has to be viewed according to a longitudinal perspective (indeed, if data are to be collapsed, even excluding the session at 9 years and 4 months, it will turn out that the occurrences in Simple INFL contexts amount to 25% while the occurrences in Non-simple INFL contexts amount to 10%, a non-significant difference). What this table shows, instead, is that, for a long period (more than two years) Simple INFL contexts may be filled with a clitic pronoun while non-Simple INFL contexts are not. At the end of the follow-up, at 9 years and 4 months, when M. makes visible improvements in many grammatical domains, the panorama changes somewhat (even though clitics are still preferably inserted in Simple INFL contexts). However, it is important to note that late clitics in Non-simple INFL contexts are restricted to first or second person clitics in *passato prossimo* constructions, while the majority of clitics in Simple INFL constructions consists of third person clitics. As we will argue later on, production of first or second person clitics involves some facilitating factor with respect to production of third person clitics.

This result is replicated to a certain extent by data from the cross-sectional sample, as illustrated in Table 4 in which the overall results of the analysis performed on the other dysphasic children are reported (percentages have only been calculated on total occurrences and omissions).

Table 4.
Overall production (cross-sectional sample)

	occurrences		omissions	NPs
simple INFL	52%	40	36	58
complex INFL	15%	5	28	10
Monocl. Infinitives	33%	4	8	20

Again, differences among the two context-types are not highly significant, however it appears that Simple INFL contexts are likely to be much more filled than the other contexts.

3.3. Clitic Clusters

Another crucial phenomenon M.'s productions display is the **absence of clitic clusters**, either consisting of two argument clitics or of an inherent and an argument clitic. This is a widespread phenomenon: The children in the cross-sectional sample also only very rarely produce clitic clusters.

Here, again, M. differs from normal children, who produce clitic clusters of both types very early (see the examples in (1) for an illustration). Ages are in months; days.

(7)   *Clitic clusters in normal development*
         a. te a (=la) presto.   R 31;14
            you it [FEM.] lend
            'I lend it to you.'
         b. me lo fai un sempente (=serpente)?   R 33;06
            me it_i you-do a snake_i
            'can you do a snake for me?'

There are not so many contexts for clitic clusters in both M's and the normal child's productions. However, a quantitative analysis of the obligatory contexts yields significant results: in M's transcripts 14 contexts for clitic clusters have been found, none of which happens to be occupied, while in the normal child's productions 27 contexts have been found, 24 of which are correctly occupied by a clitic cluster.

Finally, contrary to what happens in normal development, the clitics M. produces are never associated with a right-dislocated NP or PP (for an illustration, see the 7b above).

Synthesizing the results:

- notwithstanding that M. produces all the four contexts for clitic insertion, clitics mostly occur in Simple INFL contexts; moreover, this is the sole context where third person clitics have been found
- late appearance of clitics in complex INFL contexts is restricted to first or second person clitics
- clitic clusters, contrary to what happens in normal development, are totally absent
- no right-dislocation is observed in the contexts where the clitics are produced

3.4. Types of Clitics

Many forms belonging to the singular accusative, dative and locative paradigms appear at least once in the corpus. However, some forms are more frequent than others are and some are specific to particular structural contexts.

Third person clitics are especially used with simple verbal forms, with a particular preference for *lo*, notwithstanding that omission contexts call for all the forms. First and second person singular are the only clitics that occur in *passato prossimo* contexts. The partitive clitic *ne* never occurs even though M. produces NPs containing quantifiers (the appropriate contexts for *ne*-extraction).

A variety of non-clitic stressed pronouns are used both in subject and non subject position: The results of the analysis of this pronominal class are given in Table 5.

Table 5.
Stressed pronouns in Case-marked positions in M.

Pronoun	subject	non-subject
1Ps me	1	14
2Ps te	31	9
3Ps lui	21	1
3Ps lei	5	4
1Pp noi	3	2
2Pp voi	-	1
3Pp loro	4	2

It is important to note that in M.'s utterances non-subject stressed pronouns only rarely replace clitic pronouns, that is, they do not realize the direct and indirect object relations but in most occurrences they are governed by a preposition. Note, finally, that the overall panorama of stressed and clitic pronouns shows that M. is able to master pronominal reference quite well, including the agreement requirements involved.

4. QUALITATIVE EVALUATION OF THE RESULTS

From the results of the quantitative analysis, we draw the following conclusion. The selective pattern of clitic omission suggests that competence in clitics is bound to Simple INFL contexts (notwithstanding the significant values of omissions in these contexts too). Of course, these results have a weak statistical power. In particular, the somewhat limited number of occurrences raises questions concerning the existence of a real competence underlying the use of clitics, while the relatively low amount of contexts other than Simple INFL leaves open the possibility that absolute omissions in these contexts are simply due to chance factors. The fact that the children in the cross-sectional sample behave like M. supports the idea that the distribution of omissions should not be given a chance interpretation and that production of clitics in Simple INFL contexts responds to some sort of competence in cliticization. Notwithstanding that, we will now try to circumvent the statistical problems by performing a qualitative analysis in the light of certain well-known assumptions on the nature of child language and the linguistic features associated with cliticization.

4.1. Productivity of the Observed Instances of Clitics

The first question we will consider concerns the productivity of the observed instances of clitics. In particular, the question can be formulated as follows: could it be the case that the clitics M. produces are part of lexicalized chunks due to rote learning and that there is no grammar underlying their use?

For the purpose of the present discussion, this is the really crucial question. Indeed, if it turned out that no grammatical knowledge underlies the production of clitics we should conclude that the cliticization rule is entirely missing and that there is nothing more to say about the phenomenon. On the contrary, if there were arguments for assuming a rule driven interpretation for the produced clitics, no matter how few in number they are, the question why they occur only in specific contexts would gain much interest.

The following facts initially seem to support the rote-learning hypothesis:

i. the absence of clitics with Complex INFLs: clitics are inherent features of lexical predicates and not of auxiliaries or modals;
ii. cases in which there is independent evidence that the clitic cannot link an argument position (i.e., in expressions like *lo so*, where the reference of the clitic should be a proposition).

There are, however, arguments suggesting that a rote-learning account cannot suit M.'s production of clitics.

i. The lexical predicates bearing a clitic may also appear as isolated words or may be preceded by other clitics. Examples are in (8) to (12):

(8)   *portare* 'bring/take'
              a. mi botti (=porti) via ?   M 6;10
                  me you-take away?
                  'can you take me away?'
              b. a (=la) potta al mare   M 6;11
                  she he-takes to the sea
                  'he takes her to the sea'.
              c. lo potta via .   M 6;2
                  him he-takes away
                  'he takes him away.'
              d. o (=lo) potti via .   M 6;2
                  it you-take away
                  'you take it away.'

	e. c'è una stratta ti potta ciù . there is a road, you it-brings down 'there is a road, it brings you down'	M 9;4
	f. potta lolotto (=roulotte) he-brings caravan	M 6;11
	g. mio amico porta via tutte cose, porta via mia casa. 'my friend takes every thing away, he-takes away my house.'	M 6;11
(9)	*guardare* 'look at'	
	a. lo guaddo (=guardo). it I-look at 'I look at it.'	M 6;2
	b. vieni qui e guaddi (=guardi) catto (=gatto). 'you-come here and look-at cat.'	M 9;4
	c. guadda (=guarda) quetto (=questo) 'look at this.'	M 6;9
(10)	*girare* 'turn'	
	a. o siri (=giri) te . it you-turn you 'you turn it'	M 6;9
	b. te cira di qua . 'you turn this way.'	M 9;4
	c. ciri (=giri) di nuovo di qua you-turn again this way 'you turn this way again.'	M 9;4
(11)	*dare* 'give'	
	a. mi dai maggiare. to-me you-give (something) to eat 'can you give me something to eat?'	M 8;6
	b. dò ciaffone (=schiaffone) mio cane . I-give big-slap my dog 'I give a big slap to my dog.'	M 8;6
	c. mi dai kiift (=skilift) to-me you-give skilift . 'Can you give me the ski-lift?'	M 8;9

(12) *mettere* 'put'
    a. o (=lo) metto novo
       it I-put new
       'I put a new one.'
    b. metto li   M 6;5
       I-put there
       'I put (something) there.'
    c. metto cavallo .   M 6;10
       I-put horse
       'I put the horse.'
    d. mette a foco pane .   M 6;9
       he-puts in the stove bread
       'he puts bread in the stove.'

ii. If chunk memorization applied in present tense contexts, in principle, nothing should prevent it from applying in other contexts, namely, clitic clustering with frequent verbs (i.e., *dare*), *passato prossimo* (whose contexts are significantly high at a certain age), and, in particular, post verbal clitics. Moreover, within a chunk memorization hypothesis we should minimally expect that also other morphemes should be produced as an effect of rote-learning, instead, as pointed out in a preceding footnote, there are morphemes like articles that are almost completely absent for a long period in M.'s speech production.

iii. Chunk memorization would not justify the presence of certain stranded modifiers after the verb as in (13) below.

(13) *Stranded modifier*
    o metto novo   M 6;8
    it$_i$ I-put new$_i$
    'I put a new one.'

iv. If the produced clitics had no grammatical import, we would expect cases of real clitic-doubling or right-dislocation, contrary to fact. In other words, given that M. produces a consistent amount of lexical arguments, under the proviso that clitics have no meaning, it is strange that he never produces lexical arguments when a clitic is also present.

v. Both M. and the children in the cross-sectional sample never make agreement mistakes when producing a clitic. This strongly suggests that clitics have grammatical independence.

In light of the previous observations let us assume the following **first conclusion**: cliticization, even though being not so frequently employed and restricted to specific contexts, is part of M.'s competence.

4.2. Silent Clitics or no Clitics at all in Omission Contexts?

Let us now turn to a second question, which is diametrically opposed to the first one. Assuming, as we have suggested, that in Simple INFL contexts clitic production is rule driven, it is likely that in the remaining contexts, given the almost absolute absence of clitics, omissions are due to special conditions inhibiting the application of the rule. This is the most reasonable suggestion, also considering the fact that, in general, dysphasic children preferably omit clitics. However, there still remains one logical possibility, namely, that clitic omission does not correspond *in toto* to lack of cliticization. More specifically, it could be argued that, as has been proposed for normal development, in the cases of clitic omission the clitic is just phonetically dropped but syntactically present.

To illustrate the problem let us briefly consider the general problem of optional behavior in child language, that is, the fact that at given stages some specific functors are partly produced and partly omitted. As a starting point, it seems reasonable to assume that when a functor is produced at significant values in a given context it can be considered part of the child's grammar. The question then is how to account for residual omissions. In principle, there are three logical possibilities:

1. Omissions are due to performance factors. A child knows what goes there or that something goes there, but he simply does not realize it (due to articulatory overload, to difficulties in retrieving the specific form within a particularly rich morphological paradigm, etc.). A hypothesis along this line is the 'silent clitic' hypothesis advanced by McKee and Emiliani (1992), see below for details).

2. Omissions testify that nothing is there. In its stronger version, this hypothesis corresponds to the so-called 'pre-functional' stage hypothesis:[7] functional categories are really absent in the syntactic structures of children's utterances. In the case of clitics this hypothesis has very strong implications, since it predicts that syntactic realizations of predicate-argument structures are defective (incomplete).

3. Omissions are possible because syntactically licensed empty categories are replacing the missing elements. According to this hypothesis, which has recently been advocated by Weissenborn (1990), Rizzi (1992), in the early stages of language development, the relative simplicity of structural representations provides licensing conditions for empty categories otherwise disallowed. A typical case is provided by subject drop in early stages of non-pro drop languages: according to Rizzi (1992) the absence of a CP level allows for the existence of discourse governed empty variables in subject position. In the case of clitics, an explanation along this track could be implemented assuming that omissions occur in utterances whose special structural representations permit an empty category in post verbal position to be licensed. A general prediction of this hypothesis should be that occurrences and omissions (optional behavior) are to be accounted for in terms of intervening different structural or pragmatic conditions (a straightforward ensuing prediction being that optional behavior in identical contexts should present constant values)

Deciding which one among the above possibilities may in principle better account for the optional behavior lies outside the purposes of the present paper. What interests us here is to inspect whether omissions in Non-simple INFL contexts -- where no optional behavior obtains -- are to be accounted for either in terms of possibility one or in terms of possibility two or three above. In other words, whether clitics are just phonetically dropped or really absent. As for Simple INFL, where optional behavior occurs, it is difficult to take a definite stand. However, as we will see in the more general discussion, there is nothing to exclude the possibility that omissions in these contexts have the same nature as omissions in Non-simple INFL contexts.

4.2.1.The Phonological side of the problem

From a phonological point of view the Silent Clitic Hypothesis amounts to saying that because of factors such as absence of stress, monosyllabicity, and syntactic predictability, clitic pronouns, as other morphemes, are subjected to erasure in actual speech. According to this criterion phonetic drop should operate almost randomly, that is, it should not be conditioned by the particular INFL, as, instead the data we have reported testify. This argument is in itself sufficient to discard the Phonetic Drop Hypothesis for the Non-simple INFL contexts, however, a more accurate analysis of the phonetic structure of the words occurring in the *passato prossimo* contexts calls for some discussion.

The vocalic character of the *passato prossimo* auxiliaries *ho* (=[o]), *hai* (=[ai]), etc., calls (even though optionally in certain cases) for the vowelless clitic *l'* instead of the full forms *lo* and *la* (also *li* and *le* in Tuscan dialects): given that the liquid [l] is sometimes deleted in other contexts, might it be the case that with the *passato prossimo* there is just a phonologically dropped (=silent) clitic? There are some considerations suggesting that the answer to this question should be no.

i. The phone [l] is occasionally omitted when the clitic *lo* is produced in present tense contexts, however it is not systematically omitted, so we expect something analogous to happen in the case of *passato prossimo*, contrary to fact.

ii. There are (nine different) cases in which the *l'* clitic is syntactically omitted in front of the *ho* (=[o]), *hai* (=[ai]), etc. forms used as main verbs and preceded by the pleonastic *c'/ ce*. As illustrated in the first example in (14), when no clitic precedes the verb the pleonastic form is *c'*, when a clitic precedes the verb the pleonastic form is *ce*. Thus, if there were a silent clitic in these constructions we would expect *ce ho*: M. never produces such strings but only strings analogous like in (8b).

(14)   Pleonastic *ce/c'* with *avere* 'to have' as a main verb
         a. c'ho un cane - ce l'ho   M 7;9
           c' I-have a dog - *ce* it I-have
           'I have a dog, I have it.'
         b. no, c' __ ha Iccado (=Riccardo).
           no, c' (it) he-has Riccardo
           'Riccardo has (it).'

iii. If the omission of *l'* were due to phonetic factors only, say, a supposed weakness or scarce saliency of the liquids, no omission of stronger consonantal segments, such as [m] or [t] in *m'ha+past participle* or *t'ho+past participle* etc., should occur, contrary to fact.

To conclude this short overview of phonetic factors, it seems reasonable that the responsible factor for the omission of clitics in *passato prossimo* contexts (and, as a consequence, in all remaining contexts) is not to be found in certain specific phonetic features of the clitic themselves, that is, the fact that they contain a liquid.

4.2.2. The Syntactic side of the problem

The syntactic side of the problem amounts to the following : If clitics were just phonetically dropped but syntactically present, some visible syntactic effect is expected. One such effect concerns past participle agreement.

As is well known (see (15) for an illustration), in Italian *passato prossimo* the past participle obligatorily agrees in gender and number with an accusative clitic but not with a lexically realized object: in this case the past participle takes the masculine singular default form.

(15)   *Italian passato prossimo*
      a. ho preso i cavalli
         I-have taken$_{MAS-SING}$(= default form) the horses$_{MASC-PLUR}$
      b. li ho presi
         them I-have taken [MASC. PLUR]

On the basis of this alternating behavior of the past participle, it is possible to infer the presence of a silent clitic according to the following criterion: a silent clitic is likely to be present in cases where the past participle agrees with the gender and number of the contextually inferred reference of the missing argument. Of course, this criterion can only be applied to the non-default agreement cases, say feminine singular and masculine and feminine plural past participles. In the case of masculine singular past participle nothing, apart from independent argumentation, can help us to decide between assuming the presence of a silent clitic and assuming the presence of an empty post-participial object. Actually, some doubt can be cast on the past participle agreement test as a valid tool for verifying the Phonetic Drop Hypothesis. Indeed, concerning normal development, at present there are two competing hypotheses on the past participle agreement phenomena. Let us call them the 'Silent Clitic Hypothesis' and the 'Absent Clitic Hypothesis'.

(a) *The Silent Clitic Hypothesis*
According to this hypothesis, clitics are syntactically present but, due to performance factors, are not realized phonetically. The structural representation of *passato prossimo* constructions is identical to that of adult language. (cf. McKee and Emiliani (1992), Schaeffer (1992))

(b) *The Absent Clitic Hypothesis*
The clitic position is not filled at any level. The structural representation of child language *passato prossimo* differs from the corresponding one in the adult language. Borer & Wexler (1992) have elaborated a hypothesis of this kind, but some possible variants of it could be devised as well.

For the purpose of the present discussion, it is unimportant to verify which hypothesis is correct for normal child language. What interests us here is whether an (a)-like hypothesis can be maintained for the dysphasic child, say, for the specific pattern of omission he displays. Indeed, if (a) were not the case given the specificity of M.'s behavior, we could get a stronger support for the phonetic considerations and M.'s omission pattern would appear more clear-cut from a syntactic point of view. If M.'s data made it impossible to decide between (a) and (b), we would simply have a situation potentially identical to the one we find in normal development.

In order to verify which hypothesis is more consistent with M.'s productions, an analysis of the past participle agreement contexts has been performed. All the contexts requiring a feminine singular and masculine and feminine plural third person direct object, have been taken into consideration. Agreeing and non-agreeing past participles have been counted separately for contexts containing no nominal argument and for contexts containing nominal arguments. The results are reported in Table 6.

Table 6.
M.: Past participle agreement with the object

age	Missing Obj. +Agr.	Missing Obj. -Agr.	NP Obj. -Agr.	NP Obj. +Agr
6,2				
6,5				
6,7				
6,8				1
6,9				
6,1		1		
6,11			2	1
7,1	(1)		1	
7,3				1
7,9	2		3	
8,6			3	1
8,9		1		
9,4	1		2	3

In the (not so many) missing-object contexts, the past participle sometimes agrees with the referent of the missing theme and sometimes it does not, a result that, in itself, does not contrast with the silent clitic hypothesis (even though there are two cases of disagreement).

The second two columns provide more interesting results: in 7 cases the past particple incorrectly agrees with the following NP and in 11 it correctly does not. At first sight, this result seems to plead in favor of the Silent Clitic Hypothesis. The non-agreement cases are simply nominal realizations of the object argument, whereas the agreement cases could be interpreted as cases of clitic-doubling or right-dislocation. Indeed, what we would minimally expect if the silent clitic hypothesis were to be discarded is the absence of past participle agreement with the object. However, there are reasons to discard the hypothesis that the agreement cases are interpretable as cases of clitic-doubling or right-dislocation containing a silent clitic:

i. As already pointed out, full clitic-doubling or right-dislocation never occur in contexts where clitics are phonetically realized; in order to maintain the Silent Clitic Hypothesis it should be said that clitic-doubling or right-dislocation are always/obligatorily associated with phonetic drop of the clitic, a very bizarre conclusion.[8]

ii. in some of the agreement cases, the presence of a silent clitic has to be discarded for contextual and prosodic reasons; examples like those in (16) are not appropriate for clitic insertion:

(16)   *Past participle agreement with realized NP object*
    a. pecché __ messa __colla.   M 7;3
       because (I-have) put$_{\text{FEM. SING}}$ (the) glue $_{\text{FEM. SING}}$
    b. ho trovata una bimba glante   M 9;4
       I-have found $_{\text{FEM. SING}}$ a tall baby$_{\text{FEM. SING}}$
    c. poi ho chiusa __potta   M 9;4
       then I-have closed$_{\text{FEM. SING}}$ (the) door$_{\text{FEM. SING}}$
    d. mio babbo mi ha prestata __Panta.   M 9;4
       my daddy to-me he-has lent $_{\text{FEM. SING}}$ (the) Panda$_{\text{FEM. SING}}$
    e. ho trovata una bimba glante glante glante   M 9;4
       cosa te si chiama ... si chiama Sara.
       I-have found$_{\text{FEM. SING}}$ a girl$_{\text{FEM. SING}}$ grown up grown up
       like you is called...is called Sara
       'I have found a grown up girl like you whose name is Sara'

Moreover, given that in adult and (presumably) in child language what triggers the presence of agreement is the very existence of a clitic -- that is, the clitic has some saliency on its own -- it is at least surprising that clitics are **never** realized. Nothing of this kind seems to happen in normal development, where at least an optional behavior with respect to occurrences and omission is attested in *passato prossimo* contexts.

Additional support for the conclusion that no clitic is syntactically present in *passato prossimo* contexts comes from two different sources. One source is provided by M.'s productions after 9 years and 4 months: in this period he is able to realize clitics in *passato prossimo* contexts, but still has problems in checking the proper agreement relation when full NPs follow - *ha presa una rana* 12.5 'I have taken (FEMINE. SINGULAR) a frog (FEMINE. SINGULAR)'; *hanno trovata una rana*, 13.5 'they have found (FEMINE. SINGULAR) a frog (FEMINE. SINGULAR)'.

A second source of data is our joint experimental work with Emiliani on a different group of dysphasic children. The children were administered the same kind of test as employed with normal children (see McKee and Emiliani, 1992). The results show again a strong difficulty in mastering past participle agreement and plead against the hypothesis of a silent clitic in the produced utterances.

To conclude, it seems to us that the data in Table 6, together with the absolute absence of phonologically realized clitics in *passato prossimo* contexts, suggest that there is no compelling indication to assume the presence of a silent third person clitic in *passato prossimo* contexts. As for the peculiar pattern of past participle agreement, it is outside the present issue to try to account for the phenomenon. We would only like to point out that i) M.'s behavior on past participle agreement does not operate randomly, given that no error is found in contexts containing a masculine singular referent for the Theme. Instead, concerning the late occurrences of first or second person clitics in *passato prossimo* contexts let us for the moment simply observe that they differ from third person clitics in that they do not (obligatorily) trigger past participle agreement as exemplified in (17).

(17) mi ha chiamato/chiamata (female speaker)
me he-has called$_{\text{MASC. SING/FEM. SING}}$

5. DISCUSSION

5.1. Responsible Factors for the Pattern of Clitic Omission/Realization

The results of the analyses suggest that M. possesses the fundamentals of the cliticization rule but that this competence is only deployed in contexts containing a present tense verb and, very late in the period under consideration, in *passato prossimo* contexts and only in the case of first or second person clitics. For want of more statistically significant data, we have tried to provide qualitative evaluations suggesting that the conclusion hinted at by the quantitative analysis are correct. Suppose they are. The next question is what is or are the possible linguistic domains where we should search for the factors responsible for the observed pattern of clitic omission/realization. This is indeed what we will turn to in the present section. We would like to stress that in the discussion to follow we do not mean to suggest an explanation for the observed phenomena: this would require taking into account specific factors involved in actual speech production or specific modes of learning characterizing dysphasia. More simply we will look at which components of the cliticization rule may better be associated with the observed pattern, in other words we will provide a description of the deficit in terms of the grammatical properties of the cliticization rule. In the following section, we will check the obtained descriptive characterization against some of the hypotheses on the nature of dysphasia.

Let us then look at some of the properties of the clitic pronouns and try to evaluate which one or which ones may be considered in some way missing or impaired so as to account for the pattern of omission in M.'s productions. For methodological reasons, we will mainly concentrate on the Non-simple INFL contexts. Indeed, as already pointed out, data concerning Simple INFL do not allow an unequivocal explanation. However, as we will see, the conclusions we will suggest for the Non-simple INFL contexts can be coherently applied to Simple INFL as well.

5.1.1. Scarce phonologic saliency

Clitics consist of an unstressed syllable adjoined to a verb without affecting the latter's metrical pattern; learning clitics involves a capacity of paying attention to scarcely salient phonetic segments. Thus it may be hypothesized that what M. lacks is this auditory capacity and, as a consequence, that he is unable to infer the correct cliticization rule from the input. This kind of explanation, which has been proposed by Leonard, Sabbadini, and Volterra (1987) in order to account for omissions of functional categories in dysphasia, cannot be invoked for the cases at hand.[9]

In the first place, it cannot be invoked for the overall pattern of omission in M.'s productions: phonetic saliency could not explain the fact that certain free (unstressed) morphemes (i.e., articles) are omitted more than others (i.e., prepositions or copulas, or auxiliaries), and that fully stressed words like verbs are sometimes omitted. In the second place, and analogous with the case of clitic omission, we would expect a much more random pattern, with clitics also appearing in *passato prossimo* contexts, in restructuring contexts and post verbally. In the third place, we would not expect omission of clitic clusters, given their stressed or half-stressed nature and their length.

5.1.2. Argument structure

Since clitics represent arguments of various types, their mastery involves a more general knowledge of the argument structure of predicates. Since M. can realize the various types of argument entities as stressed pronouns or lexical NPs (see Table 1 and examples (3) to (6)) no deficit concerning the basics of predicate argument structure representations can be hypothesized.

5.1.3. Control

Given the nature of pronominal elements, the use of clitics is subject to the application of the general principles of Control, that is, the strategy responsible for the correct assignment of reference to all types of pronominal elements. A deficit in Control would predict that: a) clitic omissions were subject to specific contexts; b) non-clitic pronouns were subject to analogous deficits. Given M.'s rather extensive use of strong pronouns in every person, gender, and number in the various grammatical relations (see Table 5 above); his correct application of the agreement rules when producing third person tensed verbs,[10] and also considering his use of clitic pronouns in some contexts, no deficit in Control can be invoked. Moreover, the observed omission and realization patterns present no significant differences from the point of view of Control: M.'s utterances are relatively short thus preventing the activation of textual strategies of Control, which is generally performed through contextual strategies.

5.1.4. Morphological paradigms

Pronominal Control requirements and also Case requirements impose the exact choice/retrieval of a clitic form out of a quite rich paradigm, in which Case, person, gender and number are specified. Given the absence or the very scarce occurrence of some forms, a deficit in this domain cannot be excluded a priori. Indeed, for certain omissions, we could think of difficulties emerging in the retrieving *operations*, say, in the choice of the correct morphological item or even that some forms are really missing from the paradigm.[11] However, this can only be considered a partial explanation. Normal children, who omit clitics less than M., often signal the presence of a clitic by inserting a monosyllabic placeholder as shown in (18), a strategy that M. never adopts.[12]

(18)   *Monosyllabic place holders realizing clitics*
             a. [e] dai a bimba? (conjecture: mi dai la bimba?)
                [e] you-give the little girl
                'Can you give me the little girl?'
             b. [en] prende (= mi prende)
                [en] (=me) he-takes
                'He takes me.'

Moreover, and most crucially, resorting to a checking/retrieval difficulty is in itself insufficient to account for the omissions of the clitic forms M. actually uses in other contexts. More precisely, this kind of difficulty alone cannot account for the fact that the clitic *lo* is sometimes produced with present tense simple forms, but is never produced a) in *passato prossimo* contexts; b) in monoclausal infinitives; c) post verbally; d) when another clitic is present or in contexts requiring clitic clusters. Moreover, if the difficulty were solely to be attributed to retrieval, we would expect analogous deficits in the use of strong pronouns, contrary to fact. Finally, why should a retrieval difficulty affect clitic paradigms and not other paradigms? As Cipriani et al. (1996) report, this same child has no problem selecting the correct verbal forms in the case of subject agreement with not only present tense but also with complex INFL verbal structures like *passato prossimo* with the auxiliary *essere* 'be' which require past participle agreement with the subject.

Of course, it could be conjectured that the Retrieval Difficulty Hypothesis could be rescued by assuming that the retrieval difficulties are contingent on operational overload of a different kind. As an example, consider the accusative clitic *lo*. Suppose that Non-simple INFL contexts involve more operational load than Simple INFL and that this sort of overload negatively affects retrieval of the clitic form. An explanation along these lines cannot be rejected *a priori*; however, it cannot rescue the Retrieval Difficulty Hypothesis if retrieval difficulties turn out to be just a secondary effect of something else: if indeed retrieval difficulty were contingent upon string complexity, the prediction should be that string complexity is the offending factor and not retrieving *per se*. Moreover, there are some empirical facts that make the Retrieval Difficulty Hypothesis, which is based on such an assumption, not always easy to work out. First, why should this operational overload affect clitics but not the corresponding full NPs? Secondly, and most crucially, in terms of tense complexity (operational overload) contexts for post verbal clitics, which contain a simple verbal form (imperative and infinitive), should be on a par with Simple INFL contexts, contrary to fact (5 unfilled contexts for post-verbal clitics have been found to which 14 unfilled contexts for monoclausal infinitives should be added). Note that this fact suggests that even if string complexity were a relevant factor, it would be inappropriate to measure it in terms of words, morphemes, syllables, etc because present tense, imperative and infinitive forms are analogous from this point of view; thus string complexity, if taken into account, should be defined in some other way.

To conclude, we can say that a retrieval difficulty may be responsible for the absence of certain clitic forms. However, with respect to the clitic forms M. produces, this difficulty is only secondary to a different sort of difficulty, which even though it seems to be generally linked with string or structure complexity, still has to be characterized in detail.

5.1.5. *Syntactic representation*

Given the different position clitics occupy with respect to their stressed or lexical counterparts, some special syntactic procedure or device is involved in their use. As currently assumed, knowledge of clitics involves the capacity of controlling chains of some sort, which link the position occupied by the clitics to the syntactic position occupied by the lexical counterparts. This is necessary in order to interpret these different positions as if they were the same position, say, in order to interpret the grammatical relation they bear to the predicate as if it were the same grammatical relation. A simplified illustration of the clitic-chain is given in (19).

(19)   lo$_i$ prendo t$_i$
                  it$_i$ I-take t$_i$

Now, discussing the hypothesis of a retrieval difficulty we envisaged the possibility that M.'s difficulty lies in the complexity of the individual strings. We have already noted that an account in terms of complexity defined on the basis of number of words or morphemes leaves some important problems open. Therefore, if we were to discard such an account the logical conclusion -- by exclusion -- should be that M.'s difficulties with clitics reside somewhere in the chain formation procedure. Thus, following the argumentative procedure adopted so far we will take into consideration this logical possibility and try to inspect how far and in which way a difficulty in chain formation or chain representation may account for the observed pattern of omission. In discussing this possibility, we will also take into consideration the issue of string complexity raised before.

5.2. Implementing the Hypothesis of a Difficulty with Clitic-chains

In this section, we will try to specify in more detail what a special difficulty with clitic-chains could be like. Of course, at some points in the discussion, we can only make some conjectures, not only because of want of more data, but also because of the well known indeterminacy of current theories on cliticization once we look for more detail about the exact representation of the clitic-chain in the various contexts.[13] Moreover, a further complication is provided by the still unclear relationship between the details of formal representation of linguistic knowledge and the actual procedures activated in parsing or speech production. Let us circumvent this problem by assuming that chain links in some way really correspond to specific steps in the actual speech production procedures and, most importantly, that these steps are extraneous to the production of the so-called base-generated elements (i.e., full NPs or PPs).

The idea of a difficulty in clitic-chains may find indirect support in the fact that M. shows difficulties in syntactic chains other than those involved in cliticization. As reported in Cipriani et al. (1996), for instance, this child shows difficulties with the chains involved in wh-questions and relative clauses. As for clitics, the hypothesis of a difficulty with clitic-chains may be implemented in three major different ways that can be synthesized as follows:

1. *Base-generation Hypothesis*
   M.'s rule of cliticization differs from the one used by normal speakers in that no syntactic movement is involved and clitics are base-generated.

2. *Ban on long-movement*
   M. is only able to master 'short' chains, that is, chains which contain few lexical or structural material between the clitic and its trace.

3. *Ban on multi-link chains and multiple chains*
   M. is able to master structures containing chains involving just a few operations or a reduced number of chains.

We will describe and discuss each of the three hypotheses in turn

5.2.1. Hypothesis 1 – Base-generation

This hypothesis is suggested by the following conjecture: assuming that M.'s use of clitics is rule governed, it is logically plausible that the rule he is applying differs from the one operating in standard Italian. Thus, it could be hypothesized that no chain formation rule is involved in the production of clitics in present tense contexts and that clitics are base-generated, just as full NPs are, the only difference being position.

Before discussing this hypothesis, it is necessary to point out that M.'s pattern of clitic omission argues against the hypothesis that in adult language clitics are base-generated and that there is no syntactic movement. If this were the case, the production of clitics should also be expected in complex (i.e., Non-simple) INFL constructions and post-verbally. Thus, hypothesizing that clitics in M.'s productions are base-generated means one has to assume he is applying an entirely idiosyncratic rule that stems from a very special learning condition.

Let us then consider in more detail how such an idiosyncratic base-generation hypothesis could work. M.'s own cliticization rule could simply amount to the instruction 'attach an unstressed pronoun to the left hand side of the governing lexical predicate': this would be sufficient to exclude Complex INFL and Monoclausal constructions from the application of the rule, hence the regular omission of clitics in these contexts. The sense of the rule would be that M. is only able to capture the thematic relation between a clitic and a predicate under the constraint of strict locality. As stated, however, this rule makes false predictions. Indeed, ungrammatical sentences as those listed in (20) should be expected, contrary to fact.

(20) a. *ha lo mangiato
      he-has it eaten
      'He has eaten it.'
   b. *vuole lo mangiare
      he-wants it to-eat
      'He wants to eat it.'
   c. *per lo mangiare
      for it to-eat
      'Its for eating.'
   d. *lo mangia (imperative second person)
      it you-eat
      'Eat it.'

In order to prevent the structures in (20) this sort of base-generation rule should be refined taking into account the INFL component. In fact, as reported before, M. seems to be perfectly aware of the fundamental syntactic properties of the inflection morphemes he produces. So, the base-generation rule for clitics could read as follows: 'Attach a clitic to the inflected governing lexical predicate. The position of the clitic is contingent upon Inflection type'. In the spirit of this rule, attaching a clitic to an independent auxiliary or to a modal would mean retrieving the argument relation to the governing predicate through a chain of some sort. Thus, this explanation would in a sense be compatible with the conclusion that the responsible factor for selective omission of clitics is chain formation, under the special assumption that M. is able to master clitics in contexts where no chain is required.[14] Of course, this explanation would have strong implications for a global evaluation of M.'s competence: it amounts to saying that in M.'s competence chain formation rules are missing. In any case, there are arguments suggesting that this type of base-generation hypothesis also has to be excluded:

i. it is at odds with the high rate of omission in Simple INFL contexts; especially since M. has no problem in controlling pronominal reference and in producing base-generated nominal arguments, it would be somewhat curious if he had difficulties in producing base-generated clitic pronouns;

ii. it predicts the occurrence of post-verbal clitics;

iii. it predicts the occurrence of clitic clusters.

Of course, none of these predictions is borne out. It seems, then, that M.'s production of clitics in present tense contexts has to be accounted for in terms of chain formation rules.[15]

5.2.2. Hypothesis 2: Ban on long-movement

According to this hypothesis, what blocks or hampers clitic movement in the observed contexts is the amount of lexical or structural material to cross. Presumably M. possesses competence in cliticization, as the use of clitics with present tense forms testifies, but processing difficulties (i.e., memory limitations, representational overload, etc.) emerge when the head of the chain and its trace are too distant, as for instance, in *passato prossimo* or monoclausal infinitives.

This hypothesis may suit some of the cases, but it cannot account for the observed pattern in many respects. Let us put aside the fact that in some constructions clitic movement may involve more than one step and assume, for the present purpose, that each clitic involves a single-step chain. The excessive distance hypothesis turns out to be at odds with the following empirical facts:

i. it cannot explain the **absence of post-verbal clitics**, especially in monoclausal infinitives: this strategy would avoid clitic-climbing thus circumventing long-movement.

ii. it predicts that a **dative clitic** cannot co-occur with a verb followed by an accusative lexical object. The prediction is falsified, as is shown in the examples in (21):

(21)   a. mi dai maggiare   M 8;6
          to-me you-give (something) to eat
          'Can you give me something to eat?'
       b. mio babbo mi ha prestata __Panta .   M 9;4
          my daddy to-me he-has lent $_{\text{FEM.SING}}$ (the) $_{\text{PandaFEM. SING}}$
       c. mi ha pottato due giochi   M 9;4
          to-me he-has brought two toys
          'He brought me two toys'

iii. it cannot explain the existing **dissociation between first or second person clitics and third person clitics** with *passato prossimo*: why should the former escape the excessive distance condition while the latter does not?

This is a weaker counter-argument since it could be argued that, overall, structures containing third person clitics involve more computational load than structures containing first or second person clitics. This is because first or second person clitics as well as full NPs are novel in the discourse reference frame while third person clitics are anaphoric (an antecedent is to be searched for/determined), thus they require more operations. It has already been observed that, in general, M. does not seem to have special problems in controlling pronominal reference. However, even if this were the case, the computational overload raised by the special anaphoric properties of third person clitics would still be contingent on string/structure complexity, as the different pattern of omission in Simple INFL and Non-simple INFL structures shows. Moreover, *passato prossimo* structures requiring third person clitics may involve computational overload of a structural kind, given by the obligatory past participle agreement with the referents of the clitics: as we will see below, this requirement is likely to involve the control of a complex clitic-chain.

To conclude this section, even though the structural 'distance' between the two ends of the clitic-chains may play some role in preventing clitic production in some contexts (as, indeed, the protracted absence of both first or second person an third person clitics in Non-simple INFL contexts testifies), it cannot account for the whole pattern of omission.

5.2.3. Hypothesis 3: Ban on multiple chain links or on multiple chains

According to this hypothesis -- the one we are sympathetic with, notwithstanding some specific problems -- the selective pattern in M.'s production can be accounted for in terms of chain complexity: the chain in present tense contexts requires less syntactic operations than the chain in the other contexts. The chain complexity can be measured in terms of instances of movement, more specifically, either in terms of number of steps in a single complex chain (chain links, in technical terms) or in terms of number of chains in a sentence containing clitics. Thus, in principle M. knows what clitic movement is, but when the occurrences of the movement rule exceed his capabilities something goes wrong with the whole sentence: either the clitic is omitted or, when possible, a different strategy is resorted to. There are some facts supporting this intuition,

i. Hypothesis 3 is entirely consistent with the **absence of clitic clusters**. because these constructions involve two chains

ii. Hypothesis 3 can easily account for the *passato prossimo* facts. Past participle agreement, as currently assumed, requires additional movement in SPEC VP (Particple P), thus creating a complex clitic-chain. Omission of third person clitics follows.

What about the (late) presence of first or second person clitics in the same contexts? There are arguments leading us to believe that this phenomenon is perfectly coherent with Hypothesis 3. As observed, first or second person clitics do not (obligatorily) require past participle agreement, hence they do not require an intermediate step. If we assume something analogous to Sportiche's (1992) theory, we may argue that first or second person clitics in Italian behave like French clitics: only long-movement is sufficient in *passato prossimo*.

(22) a. li_i ho [t_i [letti ... t_i]]
b. mi_i ha [[chiamato ... t_i]]
me He-has called
'He has called me.'

Analogous behavior is displayed by dative clitics, as shown in the examples in (21). It is an open question why M. doesn't produce dative third person clitics in the same contexts. Note, however, that the problem is likely to reside elsewhere since third person dative clitics are not produced in present tense contexts too.

iii. Hypothesis 3 is entirely consistent with the absence of the partitive clitic *ne* in M.'s productions

Interestingly enough, in the course of a repetition test made when he was 13 years old, M. replaced the clitic *ne* with the corresponding lexical constituent or reformulated the utterance so as to insert an accusative clitic.

Hypothesis 3 presents some formal problems that cannot be solved in a straightforward way given the still high degree of indeterminacy of the theory of cliticization for some specific empirical domains. These problems, however, can be overcome by making some specific assumptions.

One problem is why M. does not produce post verbal clitics, which, in principle seem to involve a simple chain. A possible solution to this problem is to assume that these structures involve an additional instance of movement with respect to structures containing present tense, more specifically, that they involve verb movement to the C position. Thus, contexts for post-verbal clitics involve computational overload raised by the presence of two chains, the clitic-chain, and the 'complex' verb chain. The hypothesis of V-to-C movement has actually been entertained for imperatives and can be easily extended to infinitives.

Another problem is provided by a possible alternative account for the selective pattern of omission in terms of types of chain. Thus, it could be hypothesized that in M.'s grammar, at least up to 8 years of age, clitic-chains consist of bare head movement, which would account for strict locality. Of course, this hypothesis is at odds with the absence of clitic clusters, but it is not entirely implausible, especially if integrated with Hypothesis 3.[16]

5.3. Conclusions on the Offending Factors

In searching for the possible affected component in the clitic grammar of M., we have reached the following results.

Even though the clitic paradigm is incomplete (for reasons still to be identified), M. possesses some kind of competence in cliticization. We have argued that the clitics he produces are not base-generated, but are part of a clitic-chain, consistently with the adult rule. Thus, it may be concluded that none of the fundamentals of the cliticization rule is deeply compromised in M.'s grammar and that the pattern of occurrences and omissions is contingent upon the complexity of the specific string or structure requiring a clitic. However, we have also seen that measuring complexity in terms of words or general computational steps cannot account for all the observed phenomena: complexity seems to depend on the particular configuration of the clitic-chain; in particular, it seems that, rather than or in addition to the length of the chain, a significant role is played by the 'form' of the chain (the number of links in a single chain) or the amount of chains in a given structure. Finally, these results can be used to suggest an explanation for the high rate of omission in Present tense contexts -- a problem that initially we put aside for methodological reasons. It can be reasonably assumed that clitic omissions in these contexts depend on the general difficulty M. has with clitic-chains. What is special about present tense contexts is that the relative structural simplicity at times allows a clitic-chain to be formed, while in the remaining contexts the structural complexity is such that clitic-chain formation is hampered systematically.

5.4. Hypotheses on the Nature of the Linguistic Deficit

Supposing that the descriptive account of the deficit just sketched out is correct, we will now try to match it with some current hypotheses on the nature of dysphasia. As anticipated, this is essentially a tentative procedure. It is commonly recognized that dysphasics represent a heterogeneous population, so, in principle each one of the competing hypotheses may suit some specific subgroup. Moreover we have been looking at a single specific phenomenon: as we will see, it only suits some of the proposed hypotheses, however it is an open question how far the excluded hypotheses can account for other deficits M. shows in the course of his development.

Turning now to the interpretative hypotheses, they can be roughly split into those that assume a more or less deep deficit at the competence level and those that assume grammatical competence to be intact, the deficit being due to performance limitations of various sort.

5.4.1 Feature Blindness Hypothesis (Gopnik, 1990; Gopnik &Crago, 1991)

The most radical interpretation of dysphasia has been put forward by Gopnik (1990) and Gopnik and Crago (1991): dysphasics, at least those belonging to family aggregations, have a genetically determined core linguistic deficit in processing syntactic-semantic features. Research on a large family of English speaking dysphasics has revealed special difficulties in marking morphological features such as Tense or Number. Detailed analyses suggest that the occurrences of these morphemes are due either to rote-learning of inflected words or to a 'semantic' use, i.e., the Number morpheme "-s" may be used to express the semantic notion NUMBER though not the syntactic feature Number involved in Agreement relations (Gopnik, 1994).

The fact that the cliticization rule is in some way present in M.'s competence indicates that, as far as clitics are concerned, the Feature Blindness Hypothesis is to be questioned. Indeed, what we have seen is that none of the fundamentals of the grammar of clitics is missing in M.'s productions, including the possibility of controlling clitic-chains, albeit in some specific contexts. The core idea of Gopnik's theory is the very absence of one or some grammatical component: absence of clitic-chains in contexts other than present tense cannot be considered a manifestation of the fact that some fundamental feature of cliticization is missing.[17] In this sense, the results of this study go on a par with the results of studies made by Rice and Oetting (1993) and Bishop (1993) on the use of bound morphology in English speaking dysphasic children.

5.4.2. Clahsen (1989)

A less radical hypothesis on missing competence has been put forth by Clahsen (1989). Dysphasic children have a defective grammatical competence: either the parameters of UG are not fixed or they are fixed at a value that is different from that required by the native language. Moreover, they rely on semantic cues to guide their use of morphological markers. According to Clahsen, the use of grammatical morphemes will vary systematically. Dysphasic children should be able to produce those morphemes that express a semantic aspect of a word to which they are attached (i.e., noun plurals; see Clahsen et al 1992) but should be impaired in producing those morphemes which encode a relationship between syntactic structures. This hypothesis, as we will argue later on, may perhaps explain the dissociation between clitics and articles (and some other phenomena in M.'s overall production; cf. Cipriani, Chilosi and Bottari (1994)), however, for obvious reasons, it lies outside the issue as far as the clitic internal dissociation is concerned. Indeed, no parameter setting or mis-setting seems to be involved here (see however note 13). Moreover, and most importantly, even though clitic production can be conceived as a semantically driven strategy (clitics realize arguments of predicates; see next section), it cannot be regarded as void of grammatical content, given that, by assumption, M masters clitic-chains, no matter how simple they are. Thus, looking at clitics in Clahsen terms simply means specifying whether omission in certain contexts should really be interpreted in terms of missing competence. We will turn to this below, when we discuss the performance limitation hypotheses.

5.4.3. Auditory Hypothesis (Leonard et al. 1987)

Dysphasic children have difficulties in processing phonetically non-salient elements, so they cannot use auditory information to construct the general morphological paradigms

We have already taken into consideration Leonard's hypothesis: this has to be discarded by the selective pattern of clitic omission, namely, by the fact that there are specific contexts in which clitics are regularly omitted. [18]

5.4.4. Performance Limitation Hypothesis (Fletcher, 1992)

Dysphasic children have underlying grammatical competence but performance limitations prevent them from applying this knowledge consistently. There are some variants of this hypothesis, according to which specific components of speech are taken into consideration. Levelt's (1989) model of the processes involved in speech production provides a framework for conceptualizing the types of performance limitation that might be involved in dysphasia. So various hypotheses can be entertained. There could be an interference between the conceptualizer and the formulator, so that the grammatical encoding would be hampered if the intended message were conceptually complex. A second possibility is that slow grammatical encoding might be the problem. The prediction, in this case, is that grammatical problems will become increasingly apparent the more material the formulator tries to process. A third possibility is that problems emerge at the construction of the phonetic plan. A final potential source of errors is in the articulator, which converts the phonetic plan into a series of neuromuscular instructions.

Testing the predictions each possibility opens up lies outside the scope of the present study for want of sufficient quantitative data. Rather, we would like to point out that even assuming a performance limitation perspective, an explanation has to be formulated reasonably in grammatical terms. Indeed, the peculiar pattern of omission suggests that the deficit does not lie in processing overload in terms of number of items at various levels of linguistic organization (i.e., number of constituents, number of words, number of syllable, number of phonemes). It rather suggests that the deficit -- from the point of view of processing -- has a 'grammatical specificity' of its own. In particular, that the processing difficulties go on a par with the particular type of clitic-chain that would have to be construed in the omission contexts. This means that the deficit, independently of issues concerning processing or grammatical knowledge, is one that involves the syntactic representations. Thus, it seems that, as far as clitics are concerned, M.'s deficit is consistent with the representation deficit for dependent relations recently advanced by Van der Lely and Stolwerk (1997) and Van der Lely (1998) according to which what is specially affected in dysphasia are the structural dependencies between elements in the clause. In the case of clitics, the structural dependencies are of a particular kind, in that they involve access to non-adjacent positions in the structure.

6. CONCLUSION

In this paper, we have observed that the reasons for the selective pattern of clitic omission by a dysphasic child are to be searched in the complexity of the syntactic representations specifically involved in cliticization. In particular the difficulties seem to reside in the complexity of the clitic-chain: this child seems to be able to control structures containing simple clitic-chains but not structures containing complex clitic-chains or multiple clitic and non-clitic-chains. These results have some implications for various domains of linguistic research. As for linguistic theory the data provide support for a movement account of cliticization against a base-generation account and may also prove useful for understanding the exact configuration of the clitic-chain in specific Italian structures, like *passato prossimo* or imperatives. As for theories on dysphasia, the results appear very interesting because here we have a case in which a grammatical rule is learned in its fundamentals, but its application is contingent upon certain structural conditions. This conclusion rules out the most radical theories, like Gopnik's, that assume a deep deficit in competence. However, it also rules out theories assuming a bare performance limitation in traditional terms, since the omissions of clitics have to be accounted for with reference to special structural conditions.

Of course, many open questions remain as to which specific property of cliticization is affected in M.'s deviant productions. Some could find an answer in more speculative analyses led by a deeper understanding of cliticization as a grammatical phenomenon, but some call for empirical data that, given the fundamental tendency to avoid clitics, are hard to gather in dysphasics' spontaneous speech. Furthermore, as for theories on dysphasia, it must be pointed out that the conclusions we have reached can only have a preliminary value, suggesting some guidelines for more extensive research and appropriate testing by experimental work. Indeed, given the rather heterogeneous character of dysphasia, a single case can only have a value *per se*. Analogous limitations come from sticking to a single specific phenomenon: in principle it might be the case that deficits in different grammatical domains suit different interpretative hypotheses, even though, if this were the case, interpretations would turn out more superficial than one would desire. It is indeed reasonable to think of just one general cause for a deficit having manifestations in several grammatical domains rather than vice versa. In any case, we believe that the results of this study may prove stimulating for a better definition of the interpretative hypotheses, introducing grammatical specificity as an important parameter to take into consideration.

ACKNOWLEDGEMENTS

The aims and the methodology of the research presented are the outcome of discussions held at the Interdisciplinary Laboratory of SISSA-Trieste, on the occasion of the workshop on "Comparative Acquisition Studies", 5-16 July 1993. We wish to thank Luigi Rizzi and Kenneth Wexler who organized those meetings, and all the participants of the session on the acquisition of clitics. We also thank the audiences of the "Workshop on the L1- and L2-Acquisition of Clause-Internal Rules: Scrambling and Cliticization", Berne, 21-23 January 1994, and of the "First Lisbon Meeting on Child Language", Lisbon, 14-17 June 1994, where versions of this paper have been presented.

NOTES

[1] These data come from previous research on this single case study (see Cipriani et al. 1995).
[2] Language samples were transcribed independently by one of the authors (Chilosi) and by a trained research assistant; a reliability check was then performed on 80% of the utterances obtaining an inter-observer agreement of 91%. Particular attention has been paid to the vowels in positions that are relevant to carry morphological information, that is, vowels in word final position and in free morphemes. All revised data were transferred to an IBM computer and coded according to the set of conventions of the Child Language Data Exchange System (CHILDES) (Mac Whinney & Snow, 1985). Correct usage as well as errors were noted; pauses were coded in order to determine sentence boundaries.
[3] The normal child, R., has been followed from 1;7 to 3 years for a total of 16 sessions, each consisting of about 200-250 utterances. R. is the son of a middle-class family living in a region where a northern variety of Italian is spoken. Criteria for transcription and coding of R.'s productions were identical to those adopted for M.'s
[4] By 'substitutions' we mean phonetic reductions of the proper forms (i.e., *o* for *lo*); by 'errors' we mean misselection of the proper form of the functor.
[5] However, as reported in Cipriani, Chilosi, and Bottari (1995), he does not seem to treat all free morphemes alike: determinative articles, that according to recent theories share much with clitics, are by far less frequently produced notwithstanding the high number of contexts requiring them.
[6] This seems true for normal development in general, as reported in Cipriani, Chilosi, Bottari and Pfanner (1993).
[7] According to this hypothesis, which is reminiscent of the positions taken by Bowerman (1973), Brown (1973), Braine (1976), and others in the psycholinguistic tradition, and more recently advocated by Lebeaux (1988), Radford (1990), Platzack (1992), and others, early combinations are pure instantiations of lexical categories such as Noun, Verb, Adjective, etc. and (part of) their projections. See also Powers, this volume.
[8] It might be argued that right-dislocation is always associated with null object *pro*. This hypothesis may perhaps account for the agreement cases, but cannot support the hypothesis of the presence of a silent clitic in *passato prossimo* contexts.
[9] See also Leonard, Bortolini, Caselli, McGregor, and Sabbadini (1992) for an update. According to Leonard and his colleagues, the primary problem is not with the first stages of the auditory processing of the incoming acoustic signal, but at higher levels of auditory processing where the differences in sound are perceived but are not salient, therefore the dysphasic cannot use this auditory information to construct morphological paradigms.

[10] An analysis along the lines adopted in Guasti (1993) and Pizzuto and Caselli (1992) has been performed on M.'s production of verbs: subject agreement mistakes presented no significant values, like in normal children (see Bottari, Cipriani, and Chilosi, 1996). This suggest that in M.'s grammar the INFL component is operative.

[11] Of course one may wonder why certain forms and not others are missing. A plausible answer to this, to be worked out in the spirit of the conclusions we will reach in the present work, could be that the missing forms are not accessed and then not learned because they present special syntactic difficulties.

[12] Monosyllabic placehoders are [-tense] vocalic segments, mainly schwa, produced in front of lexical elements of various types. Some typical examples found in English speaking children are ∂ doll, ∂ more, ∂ hot. In recent years, monosyllabic placehoders have been ascribed a more overtly grammatical role as embryonic forms of free morphemes (cf. Peters and Menn, 1990; Cipriani, Chilosi, Bottari and Poli, 1990; Bottari, Cipriani, Chilosi, 1993/94). Monosyllabic placeholder insertion is a widespread phenomenon in normal language acquisition and is attested not only in Italian and English but also in many other languages possessing free morphology. It is worth noting that the absence of Monosyllabic placeholders in M.'s speech productions pleads against the hypothesis of a silent clitic in all the omission cases.

[13] See Sportiche (1992) for an overview and for the relevant literature.

[14] We are abstracting away from the formal and theoretical problems this hypothesis raises, among which specifying the relationship between the position occupied by a base-generated clitic and the position of full NPs, or accounting, in learnability theoretical terms, for how M. can learn clitic-chains in his late development.

[15] It could be argued that since M. is adopting an ad hoc rule, this rule could be reformulated so as to exclude post-verbal clitics and clitic clusters. This could be a logically possible move, but, actually, it contradicts the spirit of the base-generation hypothesis: this hypothesis assumes that M. is sensitive to the relationship between a clitic and a lexical predicate on condition of adjacency: this condition is present not only in the case of accusative and dative clitics occurring in present tense forms but also in contexts requiring clitic clusters and, more overtly, in contexts for post-verbal clitics.

[16] It could be argued that clitic-chains are bound to head-movement and that the ban on multiple links also applies. One interesting issue that emerges from this hypothesis concerns parameter setting. Supposing that in adult Italian cliticization always involves XP movement, as proposed by some authors, assuming bare head-movement for the dysphasic grammar would correspond to saying that a specific parameter has not been set to the correct values, a conclusion consistent with Clahsen interpretative hypothesis for dysphasia.

[17] Note that even in the case a base-generation explanation were assumed for clitic production by M., Gopnik's hypothesis could not be rescued: in his late development M. shows mastery of complex clitic-chains, thus it does not appear very plausible to associate a (presumed) absence of chain in the early period with a missing gene.

[18] There is one domain where an auditory hypothesis may retain some plausibility, namely in the *passato prossimo* contexts. The phonetic weakness of *l'* may induce misperception of input data, hence no learning of the rule in these specific contexts. There are, however, stringent reasons to discard this context bound hypothesis.
   i. The input also contains full clitics or non phonetically weak reduced clitics in *passato prossimo* contexts;
   ii. if cliticization is learned in simple contexts it still remains an open question why it is not applied in *passato prossimo* contexts;
   iii. since the auditory hypothesis may not account for omissions in other contexts, assuming it just for *passato prossimo* would mean assuming two coexisting and competing accounts for the general phenomenon of clitic omission, not a desirable move.

REFERENCES

Bishop, D.V.M.: 1992, 'The underlying nature of specific language disorder', *Journal of Child Psychology and Psychiatry* **33**, 3-66.
Bishop, D.V.M.:1993, 'Grammatical errors in specific language impairment: competence or performance limitations?', *Applied Psycholinguistics*.
Bloom, L.: 1970, *Language Development: Form and Function in Emerging Grammars*, MIT Press, Cambridge.
Bloom, L.:1973 *One word at a time*, Mouton, The Hague.
Borer, A. and Wexler, K.:1992, 'Bi-unique Relations and the Maturation of Grammatical Principles', *Natural Language and Linguistic Theory* **10**, 147-189.
Bottari, P., P.Cipriani, and A.M. Chilosi: 1996, ' Root infinitives in Italian SLI children' , in A. Stringfellow, D. Cahana-Amitay, E. Hughes and A. Zukowski (eds.) *Proceedings of the 20th annual Boston University Conference on Language Development* **1** Cascadilla Press, Somerville, 75-84.
Bottari, P., P. Cipriani and A.M. Chilosi: 1993/94, 'Proto-syntactic Devices in the Acquisition of Italian Free Morphology', *Language Acquisition*.
Bowerman, M.: 1973, *Early Syntactic Development: A Crosslinguistic Study with Special Reference to Finnish*. London: Cambridge University Press.
Braine, M.: 1976, 'Children's first word combinations'. *Monographs of the Society for Research in Child Development* **41**, 1-97.
Brown, R.: 1973, *A First Language: The Early Stages*, Harvard University Press, Cambridge.
Chomsky, N.: 1981, *Lectures on Government and Binding*, Foris, Dordrecht.
Chomsky, N.: 1986, *Knowledge of Language. Its nature, Origin, and Use*, Praeger, New York.
Cipriani P., A.M. Chilosi and P. Bottari: 1995, 'Language acquisition and language recovery in developmental dysphasia and acquired childhood aphasia', in K. Nelson (ed.) *Children's Language* **VIII**, Lawrence Erlbaum, Hillsdale.
Cipriani, P., A.M. Chilosi, P. Bottari and L. Pfanner: 1993, *L'acquisizione della morfosintassi in italiano: fasi e processi*, UNIPRESS, Padova.
Paola Cipriani, P., Bottari , P. Chilosi, A.M. & L. Pfanner: 1998, "A longitudinal perspective in the study of Specific Language Impairment: a case study from Italian", *International Journal of Language & Communication Disorders* **33**: 3, 245-280
Cipriani, P., A.M. Chilosi, P. Bottari and P. Poli: 1990, 'Some data on transitional phenomena in the acquisition of Italian', paper presented at the *5th International Congress for the Study of Child Language*, Budapest, Hungary, July.
Clahsen, H.: 1989, 'The grammatical characterization of developmental dysphasia', *Linguistics* **27**, 897-920.
Fletcher, P.: 1992, 'Sub-groups in school-age language impaired children', In P. Fletcher and D. Hall (eds.) *Specific Speech and Language Disorders in children*, Whurr, London, 152-163.
Gopnik, M.: 1990, 'Feature Blindness: A Case Study. *Language Acquisition* **1**, 139-164.
Gopnik, M.: 1994, 'Theoretical Implications of Inherited Dysphasia', in Y. Levy (ed.) *Other Children, Other Languages*, Lawrence Erlbaum, Hillsdale, 331-357.
Gopnik, M. and M. Crago:1991, 'Familial aggregation of developmental language disorders', *Cognition* **39**, 1-50.
Guasti, T.: 1993, 'Verb Syntax in Italian Child Grammar', *Language Acquisition*.
Lebeaux, D.: 1988, *Language Acquisition and the Form of Grammar*, Ph.D. Dissertation, University of Massachusetts Amherst.
Leonard L.B.: 1988, 'Is specific language impairment a useful construct?' In S. Rosemberg (ed.) *Advances in Applied Psycholinguistics*, Cambridge University Press, Cambridge, 1-39.
Leonard, L. B., L. Sabbadini and V.Volterra: 1987, 'Specific Language Impairment in Children: a Cross-linguistic Study', *Brain and Language* **32**, 233-252.
Leonard, L.B., U. Bortolini, M.C. Caselli, K.K. McGregor and L. Sabbadini: 1992, 'Morphological deficits in children with specific language impairment: the status of features in the underlying grammar', *Language Acquisition* **2**,151-179.
Levelt, W.J.: 1989, 'Speaking: from intention to articulation', . MIT Press, Cambridge.

Mac Whinney, B. and C. Snow: 1985, ' The Child Language Data Exchange System', *Journal of Child Language* **12**; 271-296.
McKee, C. and M. Emiliani: 1992, 'Il Clitico: c'è ma non si vede', *Natural Language and Linguistic Theory* **10**,
Peters, A. & L. Menn, L. 1990, 'The microstructure of morphological development: variation across children and across languages', ms.
Picallo, M. C.: 1990, 'Modal verbs in Catalan', *Natural Language and Linguistic Theory* **8**, 285-312.
Pinker, S.: 1984, *Language Learnability and Language Development*, Cambridge, Mass.
Pizzuto E. and M.C.Caselli: 1992, 'The acquisition of Italian morphology: implications for models of language development', *Journal of Child Language* **19**, 491-557.
Platzack, C.: 1992, 'Functional Categories in Early Swedish", in J. Meisel (ed.)*The Acquisition of Verb Placement*, Kluwer, Dordrecht.
Radford, A.: 1990, 'Syntactic Theory and the Acquisition of English Syntax', Blackwell, London.
Rapin, J. and D.A. Allen, 1983.'Developmental language disorders: nosologic considerations', in U. Kirk (ed.) *Neuropsichology of Language, Reading and Spelling*, Academic Press, New York, 155-184.
Rice, M. L and J. B. Oetting: 1993, 'Morphological Deficits of Children With SLI: Evaluation of Number Marking and Agreement', *Journal of Speech and Hearing Research* **36**, 1249-1257
Rizzi, L.: 1982, *Issues in Italian Syntax*, Foris, Dordrecht.
Rizzi. L.:1992, ' Early Null Subjects and Root Null Subjects', *Geneva Generative Papers* **1-2**.
Schaeffer, J.: 1992, 'Past participle agreement in Italian child language: a reply to Borer and Wexler (1992)' , ms., UCLA
Sportiche, D.: 1992, ' Clitic Constructions', ms., UCLA
Van der Lely, H. J. & Stollwerk, L.: 1997, 'Binding theory and specific language impairment in children', *Cognition*.
Van der Lely, H.: 1998, 'Grammatical SLI and the Representaion Deficit for Dependent Relationships', *Language Acquisition* **7**, 161-193.
Weissenborn, J.: 1990, 'Functional Categories and Verb Movement: The Acquisition of German Syntax Reconsidered", in M. Rothweiler, ed., *Spracherwerb und Grammatik. Linguistische Untersuchungen zum Erwerb von Syntax und Morphologie. Linguistische Berichte, Sonderheft* 3/1990.
Weissenborn, J.: 1994, 'Constraining the child's grammar: Local well-formedness in the development of verb movement in German and French', in B. Lust, J. Whitman and J. Kornfilt (eds.) *Syntactic Theory and Language Acquisition: Crosslinguistic Perspectives*, Vol. 1 , Lawrence Erlbaum, Hillsdale, 215-247

PIERO BOTTARI
University for Foreigners of Perugia & Scientific Institute 'Stella Maris'

PAOLA CIPRIANI
University of Pisa & Scientific Institute 'Stella Maris'

ANNA MARIA CHILOSI
University of Pisa & Scientific Institute 'Stella Maris'

VICENÇ TORRENS   KENNETH WEXLER

THE ACQUISITION OF CLITIC-DOUBLING IN SPANISH

1. INTRODUCTION

Clitic-doubling is an important morphosyntactic process in many languages (e.g., Spanish, Catalan, Romanian, and Hebrew) and functional categories are crucially involved. Clitic-doubling is a construction in which a full noun phrase is doubled by a clitic pronoun that receives the same theta-role and checks the same case:

(1)   Marta **te**   lo   dijo **a ti**
        Marta you-DAT it-ACC said to you-DAT
        'Marta told you it.'

The acquisition of clitic pronouns has been studied in many languages (Italian (Guasti, 1993); French (Friedemann, 1992; Hamann, Rizzi & Frauenfelder, 1996; Kaiser, 1994), German (Jakubowicz et al., 1995); Spanish (Varela, 1988); Catalan (Torrens, 1995)). The only study reported so far on the acquisition of clitic-doubling is the Ph.D. thesis by Varela (1988). In this study, however, the author only tested the comprehension of sentences with non-pronominal indirect objects. Therefore, that study does not provide any information about what children know about the obligatoriness of clitic-doubling or its optionality in different contexts.

Due to the lack of evidence on the acquisition of clitic-doubling it has been argued that clitic-doubling in languages like Spanish should not be found in the early stages (Fox & Grodzinsky, 1994; Fox, Grodzinsky & Crain, 1995). Fox, Grodzinsky & Crain propose that passives in English and clitic-doubling in Spanish are the same construction; these authors suggest that the delay on the acquisition of passives is based on the lack of clitic-doubling; therefore, they predict the delay of this clitic-doubling at the early stages.

S.M. Powers and C. Hamann (eds.), The Acquisition of Scrambling en Cliticization, 279–297.
© 2000 *Kluwer Academic Publishers. Printed in the Netherlands.*

The purpose of this paper is to provide evidence that shows that very young children know central aspects of clitic-doubling in Standard Spanish. The central goal of this study is the investigation of the productivity of this construction; another goal is to study the possible relation between the acquisition of clitic-doubling in Spanish and the acquisition of other constructions like floating quantifiers, dative experiencers, clitic left-dislocation, passives in English, and scrambling in Dutch.

2. THEORETICAL BACKGROUND

2.1 The structure of clitic-doubling

There are several accounts of the status and position of clitic pronouns. The base-generation hypothesis (Rivas, 1977; Jaeggli, 1982; 1986; Borer, 1984) proposes that the clitic is base-generated to the left of the verb, and the movement hypothesis (Kayne, 1975; 1991) proposes that clitics are base-generated in the canonical object position and move to the position of the verb by incorporation. Both accounts consider clitics to be arguments, and therefore clitics have to check case and must be assigned a theta-role.[1] The movement hypothesis has difficulties in accounting for the cases of clitic-doubling, where two arguments (the clitic and the co-referential NP) have to check the same case (accusative or dative) and must be assigned the same theta-role. Our acquisition evidence does not distinguish between syntactic theories of clitic-doubling. The base-generation theory at the moment seems to cover a great deal of syntactic ground; so, we will assume that theory for concreteness.

To account for clitic-doubling, we assume that clitics are heads, and that the object clitics are verbal agreement morphemes (Uriagereka, 1995; Franco, 1992). Following Sportiche (1992), we assume that clitics are heads of their own projection. In (2) below is the structural representation of the clause, including accusative and dative clitics (where Clio = Clitic Indirect Object, and Cldo = Clitic Direct Object):

(2)
```
                    IP
                 ..........
                   ClioP
                  /      \
               Spec      Clio'
                        /    \
                     Clio    CldoP
                            /     \
                         Spec     Cldo'
                                 /    \
                              Cldo    VP
                               |     /  \
                              XP2  Spec  V'
                                        / \
                                       V   DP
                                           |
                                          XP1
```

The specifier of the clitic phrase is a landing site for movement at LF of the co-referential DP, which is XP1 at the base-generated position; XP1 moves to the specifier of the clitic projection, XP2. The specifier position agrees on some features (person, number, gender, Case) with the co-indexed clitic. The following example illustrates the structure that we are assuming:

(3)   Carmen lo$_i$ prestó   XP1$_i$ a Javier
      Carmen it-ACC$_i$ lent   XP1$_i$ to Javier
      [CldoP XP2i [[Cldo lo$_i$] [... prestó XP1$_i$ [acc] ...]]]

Following Sportiche (1992), we assume that clitics license a feature [F]. This feature may be licensed at LF only in an appropriate agreement relationship. Sportiche states this relationship as follows:

(4)   Clitic Criterion (Sportiche, 1992:25):
      At LF
      i. A clitic must be in a spec/head relationship with a [+F] XP
      ii. A [+F] XP must be in a spec/head relationship with a clitic

where the argument XP1 has to move in order to satisfy the Clitic Criterion.

Following Sportiche (1992), we consider clitic-doubling as the concurrence of a clitic and of an overt XP1, and a covert movement of XP1 to XP2.

2.2. The contexts for clitic-doubling

Whether or not clitic-doubling is obligatory depends on the status and the case of the doubled object. The contexts described below correspond to Standard Spanish.

For direct objects, clitic-doubling with a pronominal direct object is obligatory; on the other hand, clitic-doubling with a non-pronominal direct object is impossible.

For indirect objects, clitic-doubling for non-pronominal indirect objects is optional with a goal theta-role and obligatory with a possessive theta-role; however, clitic-doubling for pronominal indirect objects is obligatory. For dative experiencers, which have a very different structure, clitic-doubling is obligatory. Examples for all the contexts described so far are listed in (5-10) below.

(5) *Pronominal Direct Object*
 *(**Los**) invité **a ellos**
 (them-ACC) invited-1s to them
 'I invited them.'

(6) *Non-Pronominal Direct Object*
 (***Lo**) comí **arroz con frijoles** anoche
 (it-ACC) ate-1s rice and beans last.night
 'I ate rice and beans last night.'

(7) *Non-Pronominal Indirect Objects with a goal θ-role*
 Dolores (**le**) llevó el libro **a Carlos**
 Dolores (him)-DAT brought-3s the book to Carlos
 'Dolores brought the book to Carlos.'

(8) *Non-Pronominal Indirect Objects with possessive θ-role*
 Javier *(**le**) rompió la cabeza **al boxeador**
 Javier (him-DAT) smashed-3s the head to the boxer
 'Javier smashed the boxer's head.'

(9) *Pronominal Indirect Objects*
 Carmen *(**le**) prestó el ordenador **a él**
 Carmen (him-DAT) lent-3s the computer to him
 'Carmen lent him the computer.'

(10)   *Dative experiencers*
        A ella   *(le)   gusta el té
        To her-DAT her-DAT likes tea
        'She likes tea.'

2.3. OTHER CONSTRUCTIONS

2.3.1 Clitic Left-dislocation

Clitic left-dislocation is a construction that contains a left-dislocated object and a co-indexed clitic. Some authors have suggested that the dislocated object is generated in its surface position (Cinque, 1990). On the other hand, Kayne (1994) and Cecchetto (1995) have proposed that the DP object moves from the argument position inside VP to the dislocated position (the two-steps movement hypothesis). In this view left-dislocation is a type of clitic-doubling, where the DP object moves to a dislocated position instead of staying in the argumental position. Evidence supporting this proposal comes from the island sensitivity effect found in clitic left-dislocation:

(11)   ??**Beppe**, temo la possibilità che **lo**   arrestino
              Beppe, fear-1s the possibility that him-ACC arrest-3p

The two-steps movement hypothesis (Ceccheto, 1995) proposes that the object DP moves to check a topic feature; first, the DP has to pass through Spec,CldoP (to check the agreement feature it shares with the clitic head); the second step is A' movement from Spec,CldoP to the topic position. The clitic incorporates into the verb, and checks case via incorporation into the verb (Belletti, 1993). Although Sportiche (1992) does not discuss clitic left-dislocation *per se*, under his base-generation theory clitic left-dislocation could arise by forcing the full DP to move to the topic position on the surface. This will force the clitic to also move to Spec,Cldo on the surface. If clitic-doubling and left-dislocation are syntactically similar, then one expects to find clitic-doubling and left-dislocation at the same stage in development.

2.3.2. Dative experiencers

Dative experiencers have a different structure than common clitic-doubling. Dative experiencers occur with psychological verbs like *gustar*, and in other non-psych unaccusative predicates like *se* constructions:

(12)   a Pedro le   gusta la bebida
         to Pedro him-DAT likes the drink
         'Pedro likes drinking.'

In these constructions the experiencer is the subject (but with a dative case), and the theme is in the object position (but triggers agreement on the verb) (Belletti & Rizzi, 1988). Montrul (in progress) has suggested that dative experiencer clitics are overt agreement in AgrS, manifesting case and agreement features and motivating movement of the dative NP into Spec, AgrS in the syntax. However, if the dative NP were in Spec, AgrS, we would expect it to agree with the verb, which it does not. Furthermore, an NP in Spec, AgrS should receive nominative case, but the NP receives dative case. Because the argument checks dative case, it seems more plausible to assume that dative experiencers are overt agreement in AgrIO, and that the doubled DP moves to position Spec, ClioP. Therefore, dative experiencers would be an instance of overt movement of XP1 to position XP2. On this analysis, we predict that the dative experiencer has dative case and that it does not agree with the verb. We predict that children produce dative experiencers as they produce clitic-doubling at the early ages.

2.4. Floating quantifiers

Sportiche (1988) suggests that floating quantifiers are adjacent to a silent DP (trace, *pro*, or *PRO*); this silent DP is bound by the quantified DP. Following are some examples of quantifiers in French, taken from Sportiche (1992):

(13)   a. **Les enfants** ont **tous**   mangé
            Les enfants$_i$ ont tous pro$_i$ mangé
         b. Je **les** ai vu **tous**
            Je les$_i$ ai vu tous pro$_i$
         c. Marie **les** a **tous** pris
            Marie les$_i$ a tous pris pro$_i$

where Sportiche suggests a XP/Cl analysis, under which *tous* has been floated under syntactic movement of an Accusative XP1 to its associated XP2. In Spanish, there are quantifiers of the kind showed in (13b).

If the structure of floating quantifiers and clitic-doubling is the same, we expect children to produce floating quantifiers and clitic-doubling at the same stage in development.

2.5. Scrambling

Sportiche (1992) suggests that clitic-doubling has the same underlying structure as other constructions like scrambling. Sportiche proposes that the differences between various clitic constructions can be captured by the following set of parameters:

i. Movement of XP1 to XP2 occurs overtly or covertly

ii. The clitic is overt or covert

iii. XP1 is overt or covert

For Sportiche, scrambling is the occurrence of an overt XP1 and a covert clitic, and the movement of XP1 to XP2 before LF, whereas clitic-doubling involves an overt XP1, an overt clitic, and the movement of XP1 to XP2 at LF. Table 1 shows the properties of clitic-doubling and scrambling:

Table 1.
Properties of clitic-doubling and scrambling

	XP	clitic	movement
scrambling	overt	covert	before LF
clitic-doubling	overt	overt	at LF

The distribution of the different objects is as follows: non-specific accusative objects raise to the Spec, AgrOP position, specific accusative objects raise to the Spec, CldoP position, and dative objects raise to the Spec, ClioP.

If clitic-doubling, left-dislocation and scrambling is syntactically similar, all else being equal, then perhaps clitic-doubling and left-dislocation will emerge at the same stage in development.

3. METHOD

3.1. Goals

This article investigates whether there is evidence of clitic-doubling in early language, or whether, on the contrary, this construction does not exist in the early stages – as suggested by Fox & Grodzinsky (1994) and Fox, Grodzinsky & Crain (1995).

The aim of this research is to find evidence for the productivity of clitic-doubling in a range of different possible contexts, and to study the relation between the acquisition of clitic-doubling and other constructions like dative experiencers, clitic left-dislocation, floating quantifiers, scrambling in Dutch, and passives in English. The right use of the contexts for clitic-doubling will be considered as evidence of knowledge of this construction.

Our proposal predicts that children will produce clitic-doubling in the correct contexts, that children will acquire floating quantifiers, dative experiencers, clitic left-dislocation and scrambling in Dutch at the same age because they have the same underlying structure; it also predicts that children will acquire passives at a different age than clitic-doubling because passives in English and clitic-doubling are different constructions.

If children discriminate the contexts where clitic-doubling can and must apply, correctly place the clitic and the co-referential XP1, and use correct agreement for number, person and gender, then there is evidence for the existence of this construction. If children's grammar does not have the construction of clitic-doubling (Fox & Grodzinsky, 1994; Fox, Grodzinsky & Crain, 1995), then children cannot discriminate the contexts of finite and nonfinite verbs.

If children use clitic-doubling productively while at the same age children have not acquired passives, then the proposal that these constructions are unrelated is borne out.

3.2. Design

The database employed was collected by López Ornat (1994). The child, María, speaks Standard Spanish. The design is longitudinal, and the frequency of recordings was once per month. This is a study of spontaneous speech in a natural and representative situation. All data have been transcribed into the CHILDES format (MacWhinney & Snow, 1990). The child's age ranges from 1;7 to 3;11, and there is a gap between 3;1 and 3;6.

The age range is relevant because Fox, Grodzinsky, & Crain postulate that at these ages children have not acquired clitic-doubling yet.

The utterances taken into account were sentences containing a verb and a complement, either a clitic pronoun or a full noun phrase. The complements taken into account in the study of clitic-doubling were non-pronominal direct objects, pronominal direct objects, non-pronominal indirect objects, pronominal indirect objects, dative experiencers, left-dislocated direct objects, right-dislocated direct objects, and indirect objects.

4. RESULTS

4.1. Clitic-doubling

If children know the structure of clitic-doubling and the rules governing movement of the NP1, the child will double the NP1 where they should double and will not double where they should not double, or will not produce a high number of errors on the different contexts. Following Fox, Grodzinsky & Crain, if children do not have the structure of clitic-doubling, then the child will not double the NP1 or they will commit many errors in the different contexts.

Instances of all possible contexts for clitic-doubling occur in María's transcripts. The data show that the child knows the obligatoriness, optionality and impossibility of use of the different contexts. We have found instances of clitic-doubling with pronominal direct objects, where it is obligatory in the adult language:

(14) a. **te**   he   regañado **a ti**   María 2;3
         you$_{DAT}$ have-1s scolded   to you
         'I have scolded you.'
      b. tú   no **me** mires **a mí**   María 2;9
         you$_{NOM}$ not me$_{ACC}$ look-2s at me
         'don't look at me.'
      c. **te**   veo **a ti**   María 3;11
         you$_{ACC}$ see-1s to you
         'I see you.'

We also found instances of clitic-doubling with non-pronominal indirect objects, where it is optional in the adult language:

(15) a. se   lo   digo **a mamá**   María 1;10
        her_DAT it_ACC tell-1s to mom
        'I tell her it.'
     b. **le** voy a dar arroz **a mi niño**   María 2;4
        him_DAT go-1s to give rice to my baby
        'I'm going to give rice to my baby.'
     c. Quíta/ **se** /las   tú   **a Irene**   María 2;5
        take her_DAT them_ACC you_OM to Irene
        'Take them from Irene.'
     d. **le**   quieren romper las alas **a Tobi** María 3;9
        him_DAT want-3p to.brake the wing to Tobi
        'they want to break Tobi's wings.'

Clitic-doubling with pronominal indirect objects also occurs in María's speech, where it is obligatory in the adult language:

(16) a. **te**   voy   a hacer una foto **a ti**   María 3;6
        you_DAT go-1s to take a picture to you
        'I'm going to take a picture of you.'
     b. no **te**   (lo) digo **a ti**   María 2;1
        not you_DAT (this) tell-1s to you
        'I do not tell you this.'
     c. **me** la   están   haciendo **a mí**   María 3;10
        me_DAT it_ACC are-3p doing   to me
        'they are doing it to me.'

Only one error was found in María's transcripts: in a single instance, the child does not double the clitic for a pronominal direct object, where it is obligatory in the adult language. The following is the only doubling error in María's transcripts. It shows a failure to double when the adult language requires doubling. There are no instances of doubling where the adult grammar disallows doubling.

(17)   *voy   a peinar a ti   María 2;5
          go-1s to comb to you
          'I'm going to comb you.'
          te   voy a peinar **a ti**   ADULT
          you_ACC go-1s to comb to you

The following table shows the number of utterances of doubled and non-doubled clitics for all the contexts and ages. The single error appears in boldface:

Table 2.
Productions of clitic-doubling for all contexts (where D Obl. = Doubling Obligatory, D Opt. = Doubling Optional, D Imp. = Doubling Impossible).

	1;7 - 2;3	2;4 - 3;1	3;6 - 3;11
A. INDIRECT OBJECTS			
Pronominal (D Obl.)			
Clitic-doubled	2	1	7
Omitted		**1**	
Non-pronominal (D Opt.)			
Clitic-doubled	6	9	14
Non clitic-doubled	1	1	3
Dative Experiencers (D Obl.)			
Clitic-doubled	5	8	
Non clitic-doubled			
B. DIRECT OBJECTS			
Pronominal (D Obl.)			
Clitic-doubled	2	1	2
Omitted			
Non-pronominal (D Imp.)			
Clitic-doubled			
Non Clitic-Doubled	182	255	198
Quantifier (D Opt.)			
Clitic-doubled		4	1
Non Clitic-Doubled	1	1	

The following table summarizes the frequency of clitic-doubling in impossible, optional and obligatory contexts:

Table 3.
Contexts for clitic-doubling

	impossible	optional	obligatory
doubled	0	34	28
non doubled	635	7	1

Based on these data we can conclude that the child knows that pronominal direct objects and indirect objects must double, direct object quantifiers can be doubled, non-pronominal indirect objects (with a goal or possessive theta-role) can be doubled, and that non-pronominal direct objects cannot double.

4.2. Other Constructions

María produces dative experiencers, and in all cases, she correctly doubles the clitic. Following are some examples:

(18)   a. **a mí** sí   **me** gusta   María 2;2
to me$_{DAT}$ me likes
'I like it.'
b. **a ti**   **te** gusta el limón?   María 2;8
to you you likes the lemon?
'do you like lemon?'
c. **a mí** no **me** gusta este café   María 2;8
to me not me likes this coffee
'I do not like this coffee.'

In addition, instances of clitic left-dislocation occur in María's speech at a very early age:

(19)   a. **ese cochecito**   **lo**   ha comp(r)ado   María 2;3
that car   it$_{ACC}$ has bought
'he has bought that car.'
b. **eso lo**   sabías?   María 2;6
that it$_{ACC}$ knew-2s?
'did you know that?'
c. yo **a ti**   **te**   voy   a hacer otra   María 3;9
I to you$_{DAT}$ you$_{DAT}$ going-1s to do another one
'I am going to do another one for you.'

Based on the data we can conclude that children have the structure of clitic left-dislocation and dative experiencers, and the rules of movement of the DP object to the position of Spec, FP and to the topic position. The theory we have been assuming claims that clitic left-dislocation, dative experiencers and clitic-doubling make use of the same grammatical resources; therefore, we expect that children who have clitic-doubling structures will also have the other structures. The data confirm this prediction. Future investigation will have to show whether other doubling theories make the same prediction. Of course, it is possible that the structures developed at different but very early times, before the age at which María started speaking.

María also produces some instances of floating quantifiers:

(20) a. me   **lo**   voy a comer   **todo**   María 2;5
         myself it$_{ACC}$ go-1s to eat all
         'I'm going to eat it all.'
      b. **lo**   llevo   yo   **todo**   María 2;5
         it$_{ACC}$ bring-1s I   all
         'I bring it all.'
      c. te   **lo**   tomas   **todo**   María 2;8
         yourself it$_{ACC}$ take-2s all
         'you take it all.'

In the adult language, this is an optional environment for clitic-doubling. This also seems to be the case for María; she also produces floating quantifier structures without clitic-doubling:

(21) a. ¿(los)   quieres todos?
         them-$_{ACC}$ want-2s all
         'do you want them all?'
      b. se   (las)   quería   comer a todas   María 2;9
         himself them$_{ACC}$ wanted-3s to eat to all
         'he wanted to eat them all.'

Based on the data we can conclude that the child knows that dative experiencers must double with a quantifier, and that floating quantifiers can optionally double. Therefore, the child produces these constructions at the same time as clitic-doubling.

Schaeffer (1995; this volume) has found that children scramble direct and indirect objects at a very early stage. However, this movement is optional in children's grammar, unlike in the adult grammar. These data show that the construction of scrambling in Dutch exists in the early stages, although it does not show the obligatoriness of the movement.

Sportiche's (1992) proposal about the structure of clitic-doubling and scrambling in Dutch is borne out by the occurrence of scrambling in the acquisition of Dutch, but it does not explain the initial optionality.

Note that in Schaeffer's data, the children tended to scramble pronouns much more often than they than other NPs. Schaeffer (this volume) suggests that the reason for the early observed optionally is underspecification of the feature specificity for DPs. As pronominals are inherently specific whereas other DPs are not and cases of clitic-doubling necessarily involve pronominals, the difference in the results may follow from this difference in feature specification.[2]

5. DISCUSSION

As we have already pointed out, Sportiche (1992) suggests that scrambling in Dutch and related languages shows a particular parametric variation on the structures of clitic-doubling. Scrambling involves the leftward movement of an object NP to a position in front of a class of adverbs, which start outside the VP. Thus, it seems to have in common with clitic-doubling, on Sportiche's account, the property that an NP moves leftward. In particular, Sportiche suggests that whereas clitic-doubling structures in Spanish involve a visible clitic head and LF movement of the doubled NP, scrambling in Dutch involves an invisible clitic head and surface movement of the doubled NP to the Spec, Clitic position. Thus, it might be worthwhile to compare what is known about the development of scrambling to what we have established about the development of clitic-doubling.

In a preliminary study, Schaeffer (1995), showed that very young children (Niek, 2;7-3;5; Laura, 1;9-3;4) have scrambling in Dutch, in that they, at least sometimes, scramble NPs which the adult language must scramble. However, Schaeffer's data seem to show that the scrambling is not obligatory in children even where it is obligatory in adults. This result, if it is substantiated, should be set beside our result which shows that a very young child obligatorily shows clitic-doubling when the adult grammar does. The question is: why should clitic-doubling be essentially obligatory from the beginning whereas scrambling is not? However, we should take into account the fact that children of Schaeffer's study may be in a previous stage of development, although ages are similar, because developmental stages and ages do not always correlate.

On Sportiche's account, if the relevant properties are types of movement, then both clitic-doubling and scrambling have the same types of movement, except that in clitic-doubling, the movement is LF movement (i.e., after spell-out) and in Dutch, it is surface movement (i.e., before spell-out). Is there any reason to believe that children treat adult surface movement as optional, i.e., that they sometimes do LF movement instead of surface movement? As far as we know, data are contradictory. If we look at a language like French, where there is both *in situ* and moved*wh*, Crisma (1992) has found that young children produce structures with moved *wh* rather than *in situ wh*; however, Hamann (1999) has found that a French-speaking child acquires moved *wh* much later than *in situ wh*.

The other parameter (on Sportiche's account) that distinguishes Dutch scrambling from Spanish clitic-doubling is whether or not the clitic head is visible or phonetically empty. Could it be that scrambling shows some delay because of a problem with an invisible clitic? Is there some problem with invisible elements in general?

This is possible, although it seems to us not very likely. Consider, for example, null subjects, which are standardly taken to involve an invisible *pro*. There is good evidence that in *pro-drop* languages like Italian, young children from the earliest ages know that the language is *pro-drop*, and have no problems with the invisible subject (for evidence which shows that Italian and English-speaking children know the relevant differences on *pro-drop*, see Bromberg & Wexler, 1995; Wexler, 1995). Thus, one can't say that there is a problem with invisible elements in general. Could there be a problem with invisible heads which are not full phrases, so that the problem is the invisible clitic head? Perhaps, but we know of no evidence.

Thus there seems to be some developmental difference (if Schaeffer's preliminary data is correct) between scrambling in Dutch and clitic-doubling in Spanish, such that the former is only sometimes done and the latter is done correctly, and it seems to be difficult to account for this difference in terms of the parameters proposed in Sportiche's theory. Of course we do not know why scrambling is only optional, if it is, in young Dutch children. The one point, however, that the two constructions do have in common is that they are both attested very early. If movement of the doubled NP is obligatory at LF in Spanish, it is surprising that this movement is obligatorily done by children acquiring Spanish, but that obligatory surface movement is not carried out in scrambling in young children in Dutch. We leave the question here.

With regard to the acquisition of passives in English Fox & Grodzinsky (1994) and Fox, Grodzinsky & Crain (1995) have suggested that the acquisition of passives is based also on the acquisition of clitic-doubling. These authors propose that passives in English and clitic-doubling in

Spanish are the same construction, and thus predict that the acquisition of clitic-doubling as well as the acquisition of passives will be delayed.

Following Baker, Johnson & Roberts (1989), Fox, Grodzinsky & Crain assume that the passive morphology is an argument and is theta-marked in INFL. The passive morphology -*en*, which is a clitic, forms a chain with the NP. After cliticizing on to the verb, the passive morphology transfers the thematic role to the NP.

Fox, Grodzinsky & Crain describe thematic role assignment in passives as following: for actional *be*-passives (i.e., those with agent or instrument *by*-phrases) the preposition assigns agenthood to the NP; also there is a syntactic mechanism that transfers the external compositional thematic role to *by*-phrases. For non-actional *be*-passives, the non-agentive *by*-phrase has to receive the external thematic role of the VP. For *get*-passives, the *by*-phrase does not receive the external compositional thematic role of the VP.

Fox & Grodzinsky (1994) studied the acquisition of passives in English and they found that children were good at non-truncated actional *be*-passives, bad at non-truncated non-actional *be*-passives and good at truncated non-actional *be*-passives.

Fox & Grodzinsky (1994) propose that the problem with non-actional *be*-passive *by*-phrases, occurs because the *by*-phrase has to receive the external thematic role of the VP; the passive morphology, which is an argument, receives the external thematic role from the verb, and transfers the thematic role to the *by*-phrase through a process of clitic-doubling.

Fox, Grodzinsky, & Crain conclude that in passive constructions children do not apply the process that transmits the subject theta-role to the subject: this is the reason for their failure in non-agentive passives. According to these authors, children have not yet acquired non-actional *be*-passives because they do not transfer the thematic role of the subject to the *by*-phrase (this transfer is considered the same structure as clitic-doubling), or because they do not transfer the thematic role in the particular passive construction.[3]

Based on the data on the acquisition of clitic-doubling that we have analyzed in this study, it seems that either clitic-doubling is a different structure than passives; or, assuming that both constructions have the same structure, that bad performance on non-actional *be*-passive results from some independent problem with this particular passive construction.

6. CONCLUDING REMARKS

The aim of this article was to study the early acquisition of clitic-doubling in Spanish. The contexts, status and productivity of this construction have been tested.

Instances of all contexts have been found: we have found instances of clitic-doubling with pronominal direct objects, pronominal indirect objects and dative experiencers, where it is obligatory in the adult language, and non-pronominal indirect objects, where it is optional in the adult language. However, we have not found instances of clitic-doubling with non-pronominal direct objects, which is impossible in the target. Therefore, any explanation on the acquisition of passives in English based on an early lack of the clitic-doubling construction does not apply.

The proposal made by Sportiche (1992) about the structure of clitic-doubling is consistent with the data on the acquisition of floating quantifiers because instances of this construction have been found in Spanish. Schaeffer (1995, this volume) finds that Dutch children scramble direct and indirect objects in a very early stage, although this movement is optional in children's grammar. These data show that the construction of scrambling in Dutch exists in the early stages, although children do not show knowledge of the obligatoriness of this construction. However, we should take into account that they may be in a different stage of development.

We have also found support for our hypothesis from the acquisition of clitic left-dislocation and dative experiencers: instances of both have been found in the speech of María.

We can conclude that data on the acquisition of clitic constructions, clitic left-dislocation, dative experiencers and floating quantifiers support the hypothesis that these constructions have the same underlying structure, and that the delay on the acquisition of passives is not due to the lack of the construction of clitic-doubling. Most important of all, we have shown that the very young child whom we have studied has excellent knowledge of the complex grammatical processes which are responsible for clitic-doubling. So far as we know, this is the first demonstration of this knowledge in young children.

ACKNOWLEDGEMENTS

We would like to thank Manuela Schönenberger, Carlo Ceccheto, Kevin Broihier, Esther Torrego, Cornelia Hamann, and Susan Powers for helpful comments on this research, the audiences of the Penn State conference on 'The Acquisition of Spanish as a First or Second Language' and the 'Boston Language Conference on Language Development', as well as the audiences of the meeting labs. at the Dept. of Brain and Cognitive Sciences. Another version of this paper has been presented at the Penn State Conference on 'The Acquisition of Spanish as a First or Second Language'. This research has received the support of the Generalitat de Catalunya.

NOTES

[1] Belletti (to appear) has recently suggested that the doubled NP is a complement of a clitic head (a D), and gets case from the preposition; however, we will not discuss this proposal here.
[2] The only exceptions in Spanish are dative experiencers, which must be doubled even if they are full NPs.
[3] In a newer version of their paper, revised in light of the clitic-doubling results of our paper, Fox & Grodzinsky changed their hypothesis so that they no longer assume that clitic-doubling in general is delayed in children, but only that something about the grammatical properties of the 'by-phrase' is delayed. Thus, our remarks in the text are relevant to their earlier views, but not to their later views. Note, of course, that even in the revised version, Fox & Grodzinsky have to assume that the child who cannot do non-actional verbal passives with 'by'-phrases' is lacking some grammatical capacity, though in light of our results, it can't be the ability to get clitic-doubling correct. At any rate, the sequence of scientific events is illuminating, Fox & Grodzinsky in their original paper were at liberty to assume that children as old as 4 or 5 couldn't do clitic-doubling because there had been no empirical study of the development of clitic-doubling constructions at an early age. Making the hypothesis that children lacked clitic-doubling was useful; it stimulated us to study the construction in a young child, for the first time in the literature, so far as we know.

REFERENCES

Baker, M., K. Johnson, I. Roberts, I.:1989, 'Passive arguments raised', *Linguistic Inquiry* **20**, 219-251.
Belletti, A.: 1993, 'Case Checking and Clitic Placement: Three Issues on (Italian/Romance) Clitics', *GenGenP* **1** (2), 101-118.
Belletti, A. : to appear, 'Italian/Romance clitics: structure and derivation', In H. Riemsdijk (ed.) *Clitics in the Languages of Europe*.
Belleti, A. and L. Rizzi: 1988, ' Psych verbs and theta theory', *Natural Language and Linguistic Theory* **6**, 291-352.
Borer, H. : 1984, *Parametric syntax*. Foris, Dordrecht.
Bromberg, H. S. and K. Wexler: 1995, 'Null subjects in Wh-questions', In C. Schütze, J. Ganger, K. Broihier (eds.) *Papers on Language Processing and Acquisition*: *MIT Working papers in Linguistics* **26**, 221-247.
Ceccheto, C. :1995, *Reconstruction in clitic left dislocation*, Unpublished document. DIPSCO, Instituto S. Raffaele, Milano.
Cinque, G. :1990, *Types of A'-Dependencies*. Cambridge, MA: MIT Press.

Crisma, P. 1992, 'On the acquisition of Wh-questions in French', *Geneva Generative Papers* **1**, 115-122.
Fox, D. and Y. Grodzinsky: 1994, 'Children's passive: A view from the by-Phrase', ms., MIT and Tel-Aviv University.
Fox, D., Y. Grodzinsky and S. Crain: 1995, 'An experimental study of children's passive'. In C. Schütze, J. Ganger, K. Broihier (eds.) *Papers on Language Processing and Acquisition. MIT Working papers in Linguistics* **26**, 249-264.
Franco, J. :1992, *On object agreement in Spanish*. Ph.D. Dissertation. University of Southern California, Los Angeles.
Friedemann, M.A.:1992, 'The underlying position of External Arguments in French', *Geneva Generative Papers* **1-2**, 123-145.
Guasti, T. :1993, 'Verb syntax in Italian child grammar', *Language Acquisition* **3**, 1-40.
Hamann, C., L. Rizzi and U. Frauenfelder:1995) 'On the acquisition of the pronominal system in French', *Recherches Linguistiques* **24**, 83-101.
Hamann, C.: 1999, 'The Acquisition of Constituent Questions and the Requirements of Interpretation', In M. A. Friedemann & L. Rizzi (eds.) The Acquisition of Syntax, Longman, London. 170-201.
Jaeggli, O. : 1982, *Topics in romance syntax*. Foris, Dordrecht.
Jaeggli, O.: 1986, 'Three issues in the theory of clitics', In H. Borer (ed.), *The syntax of pronominal clitics*. Academic Press, Orlando.
Jakubowicz, C., Müller, N., Kang, O.K., Rigaut, C., Riemer, B. :1995, 'On the acquisition of the pronominal system in French and German', Paper presented at the 20th Annual Boston University on Language Development, Boston, Massachusetts.
Kaiser, G.A.: 1994, 'More about INFL-ection and Agreement: The acquisition of Clitic Pronouns in French', In J. Meisel (ed.), *Bilingual First Language Acquisition*. Benjamins, Amsterdam.
Kayne, R. : 1975, *French Syntax*, MIT Press, Cambridge.
Kayne, R. : 1991, 'Romance clitics, verb movement, and PRO', *Linguistic Inquiry* **22**, 647-686.
Kayne, R. : 1994, *The Antisimmetry of Syntax*, MIT Press, Cambridge.
López Ornat, S.: 1994, 'La Adquisición de la Lengua Española', Siglo XII, Madrid.
MacWhinney, B. and C. Snow: 1990, 'The Child Language Data Exchange System: An Update', *Journal of Child Language* **17**, 457-472.
Montrul, S.: in progress, 'Thematic roles and functional projections in adult SLA: The issue of L1 Influence in Interlanguage', ms., McGill University, Montreal.
Rivas, A. :1977, 'A theory of clitics', Ph.D. Dissertation. MIT.
Schaeffer, J. :1995, 'On the acquisition of scrambling in Dutch', In D. MacLaughlin and S. McEwen (eds.) *Proceedings of the 19th Annual Boston University Conference on Language Development*, Cascadilla Press, Somerville, 521-532.
Sportiche, D.: 1988, 'A theory of floating quantifiers and its corollaries for constituent structure', *Linguistic Inquiry* **19**, 425-449.
Sportiche, D. :1992,*Clitic Constructions*. Manuscript. UCLA.
Torrens, V. :1995, 'The acquisition of Syntax in Catalan and Spanish: The Functional Category Inflection', Ph.D. Dissertation. University of Barcelona.
Uriagereka, J. : 1995, Aspects of the syntax of clitic placement in western romance. *Linguistic Inquiry*, 26, 79-123.
Varela, A.: 1988, 'Binding in Spanish: A theoretical and experimental study', Ph.D. Dissertation, University of Connecticut.
Wexler, K. : 1995, 'Feature interpretability and optionality in child grammar', Paper presented at the Workshop on Optionality, University of Utrecht, The Netherlands.

VICENÇ TORRENS
Universitat Ramon Llull

KENNETH WEXLER
Massachusetts Institute of Technology

SHYAM KAPUR   ROBIN CLARK

THE AUTOMATIC IDENTIFICATION AND CLASSIFICATION OF CLITIC PRONOUNS

1. INTRODUCTION

The dominant view of parameter setting is that setting a parameter is the same as setting a switch. On this view, the learner is seated at a control panel consisting of a fixed set of switches, where each switch corresponds to a point of cross-linguistic variation. The learner monitors the input stream waiting for evidence of a very particular type to appear; in response to this evidence, a 'trigger', the learner is allowed to set one of the switches. When the learner has encountered and responded to all the relevant 'triggers' in the input stream, the entire set of switches will be correctly set and the learner will have converged on the target sequence of parameter settings. We will refer to the above sequence of encountering and responding to a trigger as the problem of 'trigger detection'.

It might seem as though trigger detection is quite simple, almost pavlovian in nature, so that there is really very little of general scientific interest to explain. For example, the learner encounters a sentence like (1) in the appropriate context:

(1)   John saw Mary.

Assuming that the learner recognizes that *John* and *Mary* stand in the *see* relation with *John* as the EXPERIENCER and *Mary* as the THEME, and assuming that the learner has figured out that 'John saw Mary' is intended to encode this, then the learner will no doubt associate *John* with the external argument of *see*, *Mary* with the internal argument and set the parameters accordingly; specifiers preceded the head (*John* comes first) and complements after the head (*Mary* follows *see*). Of course, we must assume that the learner assumes that *Mary*, as a THEME, belongs in the complement position and so forth, so we'll need some extra bootstrapping principles.

And, naturally, the learner must have already figured out that (1) does not come from a verb second (V2) language with an underlying SOV order (like German).

Notice that, even in a simple case of trigger detection, we must appeal to a great deal of innate and empirical knowledge on the part of the learner.[1] Notice that extracting word order information from (1) seemed to presuppose that the learner already knows that the language, English, is not a V2 language. But how does the learner know that (1) doesn't come from a V2 language? German children seem, after all, to have little difficulty detecting that their target language is V2. What tricks do they use to do this? Alternatively, what tricks do English and French children use to detect that their target language is not V2?

Language acquisition is an automatic process that is apparently not subject to conscious control; a child does not will itself to learn the language of its caretakers and then proceed to do so in the manner of a miniature Sherlock Holmes. This suggests that there exists some set of algorithms that, when exposed to a sufficient body of evidence from the target language will automatically and relentlessly return the correct sequence of parameter settings. Therein lies the scientific interest in the problem of trigger detection; how is it that the learner is able to automatically and accurately detect triggers?

To fully appreciate the problem let us consider the learner in its initial state. It is given a linguistic parameter space and must locate the target language somewhere in the space on the basis of a text consisting of only grammatical sentences. It should be apparent that this problem is far from trivial. Since, given n two-valued parameters, there are 2 raised to n possible parsing devices, enumerative search through the space is clearly impossible. Because each datum may be successfully parsed by a number of different parsing devices within the space and because the surface properties of grammatical strings underdetermine the properties of the parsing device which must be fixed by the learning algorithm, standard deductive machine learning techniques are as complex as a brute enumerative search (Clark, 1992, 1994). In order to solve this problem, robust techniques which can rapidly eliminate inferior hypotheses must exist.

We have recently proposed a learning procedure which unites symbolic computation with statistical tools (Kapur, 1993; Kapur & Clark, 1994, 1996). Historically, symbolic techniques have proven to be a versatile tool in natural language processing. These techniques have the disadvantage of being both brittle (easily broken by new input or by user error) and costly (as grammars are extended to handle new constructions, development becomes more difficult due to the complexity of rule interactions within the grammar). Statistical techniques have the advantage of robustness, although the resulting grammars may lack the intuitive clarity found in symbolic systems. We propose to fuse the symbolic and the statistical techniques, a development which we view as inevitable; the resulting system will use statistical learning techniques to eventually output a symbolic parsing device. We also view this development to provide a nice middle ground between the problems of overtraining versus undertraining. Statistical approaches to learning often tend to overfit the training set of data. The resulting model lacks adequate generalizations and tends to pick up very specific characteristics of the input sample. Symbolic approaches, on the other hand, tend to behave as though they were undertrained (breaking down on novel input) since the grammar tends to be compact. Combining statistical techniques with symbolic parsing would give the advantage of obtaining relatively compact descriptions (symbolic processing) with robustness (statistical learning) that is not overtuned to the training set. In general, we would argue that learners must be sensitive to statistical (that is, distributional) properties of the input if they are to deal adequately with the full range of linguistic diversity that potentially confronts them. The child has no way of knowing which language it will be exposed to; given the ambiguity of the input evidence, the learner must be prepared to winnow out competing grammars quickly and efficiently.

In this paper, we will apply our new techniques to the problem of distinguishing clitic pronouns from free pronouns. The learner cannot distinguish these cases on the basis of semantic bootstrapping since clitic pronouns and free pronouns have the same denotation type. Instead, the learner must rely on phonological and syntactic properties. The decision to assign a pronoun to the free or clitic class is a crucial preliminary to converging on the target. We will show evidence that suggests that the learner can rely on robust evidence to correctly distinguish these cases and, furthermore, to partition the clitic pronouns into subclasses. While these case studies as yet do not provide a definitive solution to the problem of trigger detection, they do suggest a general research strategy that promises to explicate one of the fundamental problems of developmental psycholinguistics. In Kapur & Clark (1994, 1996), we have discussed the implications of such an approach for the very practical problem of parameterized parser construction for natural languages. We next investigate the source of complexity in parameter setting and conclude that there is only one realistic solution to the problem.

2. COMPLEXITIES OF PARAMETER SETTING

Theories based on the principles and parameters (P&P) paradigm hypothesize that languages share a central core of universal properties and that language variation can be accounted for by appeal to a finite number of points of variation, the so-called parameters. The parameters themselves may take on only a finite number of possible values, prespecified by Universal Grammar. A fully specified P&P theory would account for language acquisition by hypothesizing that the learner sets parameters to the appropriate values by monitoring the input stream for 'triggering' data; triggers being the sentences which cause the learner to set a particular parameter to a particular value. For example, the imperative in (2) is a trigger for the order "V(erb) O(bject)":

(2)   Kiss grandma.

under the hypothesis that the learner analyzes *grandma* as the patient of kissing and is predisposed to treat patients as structural objects.

Notice that trigger-based parameter setting presupposes that, for each parameter p and each value v, the learner can identify the appropriate trigger in the input stream. This is the problem of 'trigger detection'. That is, given a particular input item, the learner must be able to recognize whether or not it is a trigger and, if so, what parameter and value it is a trigger for. Similarly, the learner must be able to recognize that a particular input datum is **not** a trigger for a certain parameter even though it may share many properties with a trigger. In order to make the discussion more concrete, consider the following example:

(3)   a. John$_i$ thinks that Mary likes him$_i$.
        b. *John$_i$ thinks that Mary$_j$ likes her$_j$.

English allows pronouns to be coreferent with a c-commanding nominal just in case that nominal is not contained within the same local syntactic domain as the pronoun; this is a universal property of pronouns and would seem to present little problem to the learner.

Notice, however, that some languages, including Chinese, Icelandic, Japanese, and Korean, allow for long distance anaphors. These are elements which are obligatorily coreferent with another nominal in the sentence, but which may be separated from that nominal by several clause boundaries. Thus, the following example from Icelandic is grammatical even though the anaphor *sig* is separated from its antecedent *Jón* by a clause boundary (Anderson, 1986):

(4)   Jón_i segir ad Maria elski sig_i/hann_i.
        John says that Mary loves self/him
        'John says that Mary loves him.'

Thus, UG includes a parameter which allows some languages to have long distance anaphors and which, perhaps, fixes certain other properties of this class of anaphora.

Notice that the example in (4) is of the same structure as the pronominal example in (3a). A learner whose target is English must not take examples like (3a) as a trigger for the long distance anaphor parameter; what prevents the learner from being deceived? Why doesn't the learner conclude that English *him* is comparable to Icelandic *sig*? We would argue that the learner is sensitive to distributional evidence. For example, the learner is aware of examples like (5):

(5)   John_i likes him_j.

where the pronoun is not coreferential with anything else in the sentence. The existence of (5) implies that him cannot be a pure anaphor, long distance or otherwise. Once the learner is aware of this distributional property of him, he or she can correctly rule out (3a) as a potential trigger for the long distance anaphor parameter.

Under the classical view of parameter setting, it was sufficient to suppose that triggering evidence existed in the input text. This followed from the idea that a single exposure to a trigger could cause a parameter to be set. The view we are developing is more rigorous as to what can count as triggering evidence. Evidence in real input texts must be sufficiently frequent. If not, then the learner cannot be guaranteed to see the evidence at the relevant point. A putative trigger that occurs with vanishingly small frequency would not be an adequate trigger.

Distributional evidence, then, is crucial for parameter setting; no theory of parameter setting can avoid statistical properties of the input text. How far can we push the statistical component of parameter setting? We have shown elsewhere (Brill & Kapur, 1993, 1997; Kapur, 1993) that statistical algorithms can form the backbone of a successful parameter-setting system to acquire word order and, in particular, verb second constructions. In this paper, we suggest that statistically-based algorithms can be exploited to set parameters involving cliticization, i.e., the difference between free pronouns and proclitics. The work reported here can be viewed as providing further evidence for our theory of trigger detection; it seeks to establish a clear connection between the raw input text and the process of parameter setting.

3. TRIGGER DETECTION ALGORITHMS FOR THE PRONOMINAL SYSTEM

3.1. Entropy

Our analysis crucially relies on the concept of 'entropy' as this term is understood in Information Theory (see Cover & Thomas, 1991, for a detailed introduction). Entropy is a measure of the degree of uncertainty in a system. To make this definition more concrete, suppose that we are racing five horses and that each horse has a fixed probability of winning:

(6) Horse A $= \frac{1}{2}$
Horse B $= \frac{1}{4}$
Horse C $= \frac{1}{8}$
Horse D $= \frac{1}{16}$
Horse E $= \frac{1}{16}$

After any given race, we might play a guessing game where you try to find out which horse won the race by asking me a yes-no question. A rational strategy, one which minimizes the number of questions that need to be asked on any given round, would be to ask about the most likely winner first (Horse A) then move on to the next most likely winner (Horse B) and so on. Entropy gives an estimate of the expected number of yes-no questions which must be asked in order to discover the winner. Entropy of a random variable X ranging over some set S of possible outcomes, measured in bits, can be calculated according to the following formula:

(7) *Entropy*
$$H(X) = -\sum_{x_i \in S} p(x_i) \log p(x_i)$$

The function p is the probability distribution of the random variable X and log is the standard logarithmic function. The above equation sums up for all the events (e.g., each possible outcome of the horse race) the product of the probability of each event with the log of this probability. The result is multiplied by -1 for convenience (since the log of a probability value will always be negative). For the example in (6), the formula in (7) returns 1.875. Returning to the analogy with yes-no questions, we would expect, in general, to ask somewhat less than two questions in order to determine the outcome of the horse race. This is because Horse A wins half the time, so if we follow the strategy outlined above then half the time one question will suffice. Either Horse A or Horse B wins 70% of the time, so that generally we will only need about two questions. Intuitively, entropy can be considered to be the number of bits on average required to describe a random variable.

Of particular interest will be a calculation of the 'conditional entropy' of a random variable X given that we know the value of another random variable Y; this is denoted by H (X | Y) and can be thought of as a measure of how much about X can be predicted if we know Y. To take a linguistic example, we might take the X and Y to be various grammatical categories. We can try to use conditional entropy to predict the sequence of grammatical categories in a grammatical string of English as follows. Given that we know that Y = determiner, we have reasonable grounds to expect that the following word, the value of X, is a noun and not a verb. This is because the distribution of determiners and nouns are linked by the grammar of English. The presence of one is a fair predictor of the presence of the other in the neighborhood. In view of this, conditional entropy is a natural candidate measure for learning. Even though we have not investigated other similar measures, such as relative entropy and mutual information, systematically, we are convinced that we would obtain similar results with any reasonable measures. We next show that our techniques can lead to straightforward identification and classification of clitic pronouns in different languages.

3.2. Clitic Pronouns

Clitic pronouns are phonologically reduced elements which obligatorily attach to another element. Syntactic clitics have a number of syntactic consequences including special word order properties and an inability to participate in conjunctions and disjunctions. For example, in French declarative sentences, full direct objects occur after the lexical verb but accusative clitics appear before the inflected verb:

(8)   a. John a vu les filles.
              John has seen the girls
              'John saw the girls.'
        b. John les a vues.
              John clitic has seen
              'John saw them.'

Restricting our attention for the moment to French, we should note that clitic pronouns may occur in sequences, in which case there are a number of restrictions on their relative order. Thus, nominative clitics (e.g., *je, tu, il,* etc.) occur first, followed by the negative element *ne,* followed by accusative clitics (e.g., *la, me, te*) and dative clitics (e.g., *lui*) followed, at last, by the first element of the verbal sequence (an auxiliary or the main verb). There are further ordering constraints within the accusative and dative clitics based on the person of the clitic (see Perlmutter, 1971, for an exhaustive description of clitic pronouns in French).

In order to correctly set the parameters governing the syntax of pronominals, the learner must distinguish clitic pronouns from free and weak pronouns as well as sort all pronoun systems according to their proper case system (e.g., nominative pronouns, accusative pronouns). Furthermore, the learner must have some reliable method for identifying the presence of clitic pronouns in the input stream.

The above considerations suggest that free pronouns occur in a wider range of syntactic environments than clitic pronouns and, so, should carry less information about the syntactic nature of the positions that surround them. Clitic pronouns, on the other hand, occur in a limited number of environments and, hence, carry more information about the surrounding positions. Furthermore, since there are systematic constraints on the relative ordering of clitics, we would expect them to fall into distribution classes depending on the information they carry about the positions that surround them. The algorithm we report, which is based on the observation of entropies of positions in the neighborhood of pronouns, not only distinguishes accurately between clitic and free-standing pronouns, but also successfully sorts clitic pronouns into linguistically natural classes. In the test results reported next, the amount (only 3,000 utterances) and the quality of the input (unstructured unannotated input caretaker speech subcorpus from the CHILDES database, MacWhinney & Snow, 1990), and the computational resources needed for parameter setting to succeed are psychologically plausible.

It is assumed that the learner knows a set of first and second person pronouns. The learning algorithm computes the entropy profile for three positions to the left and right of the pronouns ($H(W \mid P = p)$ for the six different positions), where ps are the individual pronouns. Positions beyond three places on either side are considered too far to be influenced by the pronoun and are excluded from the entropy profiles. These profiles are then compared and those pronouns which have similar profiles are clustered together. Interestingly, it turns out that the clusters are syntactically appropriate categories. The entropy profiles for the ambiguous pronouns can be analyzed as a mathematical combination of the profiles for the conflated forms.

In French, as shown in Table 1, based on the Pearson correlation coefficients we could deduce that the object clitics *me* and *te*, the subject clitics *je* and *tu*, the non-clitics *moi* and *toi*, and the ambiguous pronouns *nous* and *vous* are most closely related only to the other element in their own class.

Table 1.
Correlation Matrix for the French Pronouns

```
VOUS 1
TOI  0.62 1
MOI  0.57 0.98 1
ME   0.86 0.24 0.17 1
JE   0.28 0.89 0.88 -0.02 1
TU   0.41 0.94 0.94 0.09  0.97 1
TE   0.88 0.39 0.30 0.95  0.16 0.24 1
NOUS 0.91 0.73 0.68 0.82  0.53 0.64 0.87 1

     VOUS TOI  MOI  ME    JE   TU   TE   NOUS
```

To distinguish clitics from non-clitics, we use the measure of stickiness (proportion of times they are sticking to the verbs compared to the times they are two or three positions away). These results are also quite good. The stickiness is as high as 54-55% for the subject clitics; non-clitics have stickiness no more than 17%.

The results we have obtained can be seen most dramatically if we chart the conditional entropy of positions around the pronoun in question. Let us begin with the free pronouns found in English as a control case. English pronouns do not cliticize syntactically in the way that Romance clitic pronouns do. Figure 1 shows the conditional entropy of the pronouns *I*, *you*, *me*, *us,* and *we*. The x-axis of the figure represents positions surrounding the pronoun. The positions marked 3L, 2L, and 1L are the three positions to the left of the pronoun, 1L being the closest, while the positions marked 1R, 2R, and 3R are to the right of the pronoun. Thus, the marker 1L represents the position immediately to the left of the pronoun and 1R the position immediately to the right. The y-axis corresponds to the conditional entropy of a position for a particular pronoun. Note that the category of the words in the various positions is not involved in the computation.

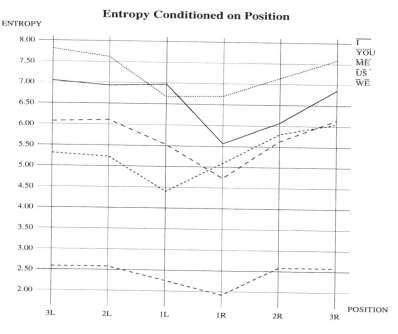

Figure 1 Some English pronouns.

For all the pronouns in Figure 1 excluding *us*, the entropy is greater than 4.50. Notice that the unambiguously nominative pronouns like *I* and *we* have a dip in entropy at the position immediately to their right. This is as we would expect given that this position tends to be a tensed verb, the source of nominative case. Similarly, *me*, the unambiguously non-nominative pronoun, has a dip in entropy for the position to its left; this is expected since this position will tend to be either a verb or a preposition, both assigners of accusative case in English. Notice that *you* occurs in both nominative and non-nominative positions; its curve shows a slight drop in entropy one position to the left and one position to the right. This is again expected since *you* occurs both as a specifier (where it receives nominative Case) and as a complement (where it receives accusative Case). Finally, we must mention *us*. This pronoun occurred with low frequency in our sample and, so, it is difficult to interpret its behavior. Given a larger sample, we would expect *us* to behave like *me*.

Clitic pronouns should distinguish themselves from free-standing pronouns in that the former merge syntactically with a head; this suggests that there should be a sharp drop in conditional entropy in the vicinity of a clitic pronoun since it must be adjacent to its host. The position to the right of a free-standing nominative pronoun in English tends to be a verb but it could be an adverb; an adverb can never intervene between a syntactic clitic and its host. In other words, a clitic pronoun should be associated with a steep curve at some position in its immediate neighborhood while free-standing pronouns should have a shallower curve, since they are slightly less informative about their surrounding environment. With this in mind, let us turn to the system of pronouns in French.

Figure 2 shows the entropy profiles for the unambiguous free-standing pronouns *moi* and *toi*. Notice that the conditional entropy is somewhat lower than the English free-standing pronouns shown in Figure 1. This may in part be due to the fact that their distribution is somewhat more restricted than their English equivalents.

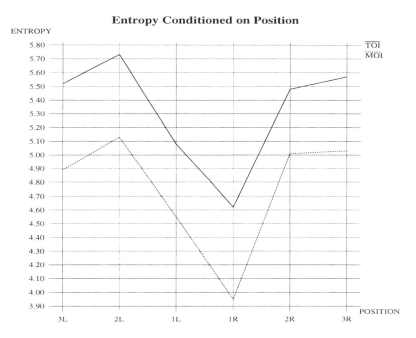

Figure 2 Unambiguous free-standing pronouns.

Compare *moi*, the free-standing pronoun, the other first person pronoun *je* (the nominative clitic) and *me* (the non-nominative clitic) as shown in Figure 3. The free-standing pronoun *moi* is systematically less informative about its surrounding environment, evidenced by a slightly flatter curve, than either *je* or *me*.

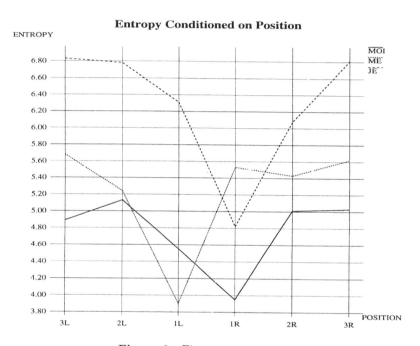

Figure 3 First person pronouns.

This distinction in the slopes of the curves is also apparent if we compare the curve associate with *toi* against the curves associated with *tu* (nominative) and *te* (non-nominative) in Figure 4; *toi* has the gentlest curve. This suggests that the learner could distinguish clitic pronouns from free-standing pronouns by checking for sharp drops in conditional entropy around the pronoun; clitics should stand out as having relatively sharp curves.

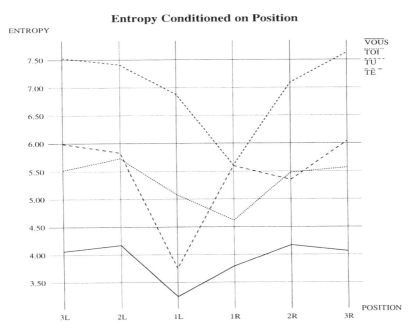

Figure 4 Second person pronouns.

Notice that we have three distinct curves in Figure 3. We have already discussed the difference between clitic and free-standing pronouns. Do nominative and non-nominative clitics sort out by our method? Figure 3 suggests they might since *je* has a sharp dip in conditional entropy to its right while *me* has a sharp dip to its left. Consider Figure 5 where the conditional entropy of positions around *je*, *tu* and *on* have been plotted. We have included *on* with the first and second person clitics since it is often used as a first person plural pronoun in colloquial French. All three are unambiguously nominative clitic pronouns. Notice that their curves are basically identical, showing a sharp dip in conditional entropy one position to the right of the clitic.

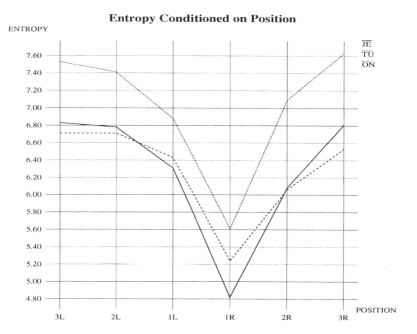

Figure 5 Nominative clitic pronouns.

Figure 6 shows the non-nominative clitic pronouns *me* and *te*. Once again, the curves are essentially identical, with a dip in entropy one position to the left of the clitic. The position to the left of the clitic will tend to be part of the subject (often a clitic pronoun in the sample we considered). Nevertheless, it is clear that the learner will have evidence to partition the clitic pronouns on the basis of where the dip in entropy occurs.

IDENTIFICATION AND CLASSIFICATION OF CLITIC PRONOUNS   313

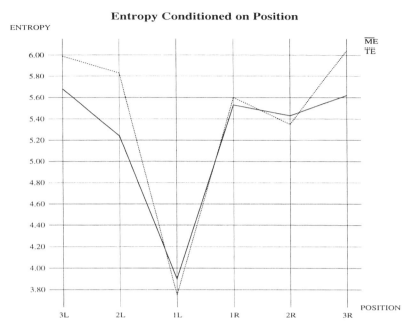

Figure 6   Non-nominative clitic pronouns.

Let us turn, finally, to the rather interesting cases of *nous* and *vous*. These pronouns are unusual in that they are ambiguous between free-standing and clitic pronouns and, furthermore, may occur as either nominative or non-nominative clitics. We would expect them, therefore, to distinguish themselves from the other pronouns, just as *you* did in English. If we consider the curve associated with *vous* in Figure 4, it is immediately apparent that it has a fairly gentle slope, as one would expect of a free-standing pronoun. Nevertheless, the conditional entropy of *vous* is rather low both to its right and to its left, a property we associate with clitics; in fact, its conditional entropy is systematically lower than the unambiguous clitics *tu* and *te*, although this fact may be peculiar to our sample. Figure 7 compares the conditional entropy of positions surrounding *vous* and *nous*. Once again, we see that *nous* and *vous* are associated with quite similar curves.

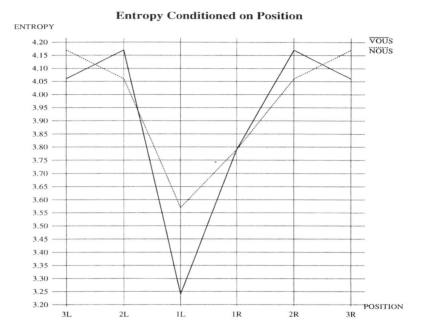

Figure 7 Ambiguous pronouns.

Summarizing, we have seen that conditional entropy can be used to distinguish free-standing and clitic pronouns. This solves at least part of the learner's problem of detecting the presence of clitics in the input stream. Furthermore, we have seen that conditional entropy can be used to break pronouns further into classes like nominative and non-nominative. The learner can use these calculations as a robust, noise-resistant means of setting parameters. Note the natural character of the properties of the input the learner needs to use to set parameter values. Close attention to differences in relative values of the entropy in the neighborhood of the items of importance (verbs, pronouns, etc.) appears to be a powerful and effective strategy for setting some of the core parameters. Not surprisingly, the absolute values, the means, the maximum and minimum values of entropies etc. are not meaningful because these quantities are of course highly sensitive to the choice of the input sample.

Thus, a part of the problem of trigger detection has been answered. We have shown that the input is such that the learner can detect certain systematic cues and exploit them in determining grammatical properties of the target. At the very least, the learner could use these cues to form a 'rough sketch' of the target grammar, allowing the learner to bootstrap its way to a full-fledged grammatical system.

3.3. The Dutch Clitic System

The Dutch clitic system is far more complicated than the French pronoun system (See for example, Zwart, 1993). Even so, our entropy calculations made some headway towards classifying the pronouns. We are able to distinguish the weak and strong subject pronouns. Since even the strong subject pronouns in Dutch tend to stick to their verbs very closely and two clitics can come next to each other, the raw stickiness measure seems to be inappropriate. Although the Dutch case is problematic due, in particular, to the effects of V2 and scrambling, we anticipate that the pronoun calculations in Dutch will sort out properly once the influence of these other word order processes are factored in appropriately.

4. CONCLUSIONS

It must be stressed that in our statistical procedure, the learning mechanism can determine when it has seen enough input to reliably determine the value of a certain parameter. Mechanisms such as these are non-existent in any standard trigger-based error-driven learning theory. In principle at least, the learning mechanism can determine the variance in the quantity of interest as a function of the input size and then know when enough input has been seen to be sure that a certain parameter has to be set in a particular way. In this way, facts such as late acquisition of object clitics could be explained.

Our work has assumed that the learner knows what the classification parameters are and merely needs to determine the specific parameter values for the target language. It is not hard to see that one could move one step further and argue that the classification parameters themselves are the result of the observation of simple statistical patterns in the input. We feel that at this stage in our research we lack adequate evidence to be able to make the stronger claim.

We are extending the results we have obtained to other parameters and other languages (as soon as suitable corpora become available). We are convinced that the word order parameters should be fairly easy to set and amenable to an information-theoretic analysis. Scrambling also provides a case where calculations of entropy should provide a straightforward solution to the parameter-setting problem. Notice however that both scrambling and V2 interact in an interesting way with the basic word order parameters; a learner may be potentially misled by both scrambling and V2 into missetting the basic word order parameters since both parameters can alter the relationship between heads, their complements and their specifiers.

Other parameters such as those involving adverb placement, extraposition and *wh*-movement should be relatively more challenging to the learning algorithm, given the relatively low frequency with which adverbs are found in adult speech to children. The interaction between adverb placement and head movement, in particular, will pose an interesting problem for the learner since the two parameters are interdependent; what the learner assumes about adverb placement is contingent on what it assumes about head movement and vice versa.

ACKNOWLEDGEMENTS

We are grateful to the anonymous referees for some valuable comments. We are also indebted to the audience at the Berne Workshop on the L1- and L2-acquisition of clause-internal rules: scrambling and cliticization held in 1994, where this work was first presented.

NOTES

[1] In fact, Clark (1990, 1992) showed that the complexity of this problem is potentially exponential because the relationship between the points of variation and the actual data can be quite indirect and tangled.

REFERENCES

Anderson, S.: 1986, 'The typology of anaphoric dependencies: Icelandic (and other) reflexives', in L. Hellan & K. Christensen (eds.) *Topics in Scandinavian Syntax*, Reidel, Dordrecht, 65-88.

Brill, E. and S. Kapur: 1993, 'An Information-theoretic Solution to Parameter Setting', *Technical Report IRCS-93-07*, Institute for Research in Cognitive Science, University of Pennsylvania, 200-216.

Brill, E. and S. Kapur: 1997, An Information-theoretic Solution to Parameter Setting. In S. Somashekar, K. Yamakoshi, M. Blume & C. Foley (eds.) *Cornell Working Papers in Linguistics: Papers on First Language Acquisition*, **15**.

Clark, R.: 1990, 'Papers on learnability and natural selection', *Technical Report 1*, Université de Genève.
Clark, R. :1992, 'The selection of syntactic knowledge. *Language Acquisition* **2(2)**, 83-149.
Clark, R.: 1994, 'Finitude, Boundedness and Complexity: Learnability and the Study of First Language Acquisition', in B. Lust, M. Suñer & Gabriella Hermon (eds.) *Syntactic Theory and First Language Acquisition: Crosslinguistic Perspectives.* Volume II. Lawrence Erlbaum, Hillsdale 473-489.
Cover, T. and J. A. Thomas: 1991, *Elements of Information Theory*, John Wiley & Sons,.
Kapur, S.: 1991, 'Computational Learning of Languages', Ph.D. Dissertation, Cornell University. Available as Computer Science Department Technical Report 91-1234.
Kapur, S.: 1993, 'How much of what? Is this what underlies parameter setting?' In *Proceedings of the 25th Stanford University Child Language Research Forum.*
Kapur, S. and R. Clark: 1994, 'The Automatic Construction of a Symbolic Parser via Statistical Techniques', In *Proceedings of the Association of Computational Linguists (ACL) Workshop on Combining Symbolic and Statistical Approaches to Language: The Balancing Act*, Las Cruces.
Kapur, S. and R. Clark: 1996, 'The Automatic Construction of a Symbolic Parser via Statistical Techniques', In J. Klavans & P. Resnik (eds.) *The Balancing Act: Combining Symbolic and Statistical Approaches to Language*, MIT Press, Cambridge, 95-117.
MacWhinney, B. and C. Snow: 1990, 'The Child Language Data Exchange System: An Update', *Journal of Child Language* **17**, 457-472.
Perlmutter, D.: 1971, 'Deep and Surface Constraints in Syntax', Holt, Reinhart and Winston, New York.
Zwart, C. J.: 1993, 'Notes on clitics in Dutch'. In L. Hellan (ed.) *Clitics in Germanic and Slavic*, Eurotyp working papers, Theme Group 8, **4**, University of Tilburg, 119-55.

SHYAM KAPUR
Infoseek Corporation

ROBIN CLARK
University of Pennsylvania

MARTHA YOUNG-SCHOLTEN

THE L2 ACQUISITION OF CLITICIZATION IN STANDARD GERMAN

1. INTRODUCTION

Whether adult second language (L2) learners are able to access the principles and parameters of Universal Grammar (UG) has been an intensely debated issue over the past decade (for an overview of the issues see White, 1989). Alongside an expanding body of evidence indicating that adult L2 learners do indeed have direct access to both the principles and parameters of UG, two observations regarding ultimate attainment remain relatively unchallenged. One, adult L2 learners frequently fail to attain native-like phonological competence in their L2. And two, even advanced adult second language learners may show signs of having failed to acquire various functional categories. Given that functional elements are often unstressed (in Germanic languages, for example), L2 learners' difficulties in acquiring functional categories could well be partly prosodic in nature.

The acquisition of pronominal cliticization in a Germanic language such as Standard German provides a means of examining whether the two observations above might derive from the same source. Prosodically speaking, the clitic forms in Standard German are as light as the unstressed syllables in words. In terms of the syntax, these clitics are involved in verb-related functional projections. Before a connection between phonological and syntactic development can be explored, whether adult L2 learners acquire the syntactic aspects of cliticization in standard German must be fully investigated. To this end, we will consider experimental data collected from a native German control group and from a group of advanced adult learners of German whose native languages were American English, Korean, Spanish and Turkish.

1.1. Cliticization in Standard German

Several recent works on Standard German have argued for the existence of a subset of personal pronouns which are (en)clitic allomorphs rather than the result of any productive phonological processes of reduction and deletion (see e.g., Wiese, 1988; Prinz, 1991; Abraham, 1991; Young-Scholten, 1991; 1993).[1] The forms included in this subset are not rate-dependent; rather they are found at normal rates of speech.[2] Moreover, while all personal pronouns in Standard German are more restricted syntactically than full NPs, clitics are even more restricted than full form pronouns. The surface forms of these full form and clitic pronouns are shown in (1).[3] The clitic allomorphs in the two rightmost columns distinguish themselves from their full form counterparts in the two leftmost columns not only in their reduced phonological forms, but also in terms of the positional requirement that they always appear as enclitics, following the finite verb in a matrix clause, a Wh-word or complementizer in an embedded clause or a subject NP in either. In addition, these forms display clitic-like phonological interaction with their hosts which free morphemes (including full form pronouns) following the same lexical items do not.

(1) Personal pronoun forms in Standard German

		full forms		clitic allomorphs	
		singular	*plural*	*singular*	*plural*
1p	nominative	[ɪç]	[viʌ]	[ç]	[vʌ]
	accusative	[mɪç]	[ʊns]	---	---
	dative	[mɪʌ]	[ʊns]	[mʌ]	---
2p	nominative	[du]	[iʌ]	[də]	[ʌ]
	accusative	[dɪç]	[ɔɪç]	---	---
	dative	[dɪʌ]	[ɔɪç]	[dʌ]	---
3p	*masculine*				
	nominative	[eʌ]	[zi]	[ʌ]	[zə]
	accusative	[in]	[zi]	[n]	[zə]
	dative	[im]	[inən]	[m]	---
	feminine				
	nominative	[zi]	[zi]	[zə]	[zə]
	accusative	[zi]	[zi]	[zə]	[zə]
	dative	[ɪʌ]	[inən]	[ʌ]	---
	neuter				
	nominative	[ɛs]	[zi:]	[s]	[zə]
	accusative	[ɛs]	[zi:]	[s]	[zə]
	dative	[i:m]	[i:nən]	[m]	---

1.1.1. The Phonological Behavior of Clitics

Despite the observation that the forms in the left and right columns in (1) would appear to be related, there are no productive phonological rules in German which can derive the forms in the columns on the right from those in the columns on the left (see Young-Scholten, 1991; 1993 for details). Such rules would have to result across the board in the reduction to schwa of vowels in unstressed syllables as well as in the deletion of such vowels and would have to operate at normal rates of speech. Yet schwa is neither the product of the reduction of unstressed vowels (as it is in English), nor is it a phoneme in German; the presence of schwa in German is limited to those instances in which schwa surfaces as the default vowel, either as the result of resyllabification after the application of morphophonological rules, or as the vowel in grammatical affixes and in non-derived words such as *Tasse* 'cup' (see Giegerich, 1985; Wiese, 1988; Hall, 1990). This, in combination with the absence of rules of vowel deletion in both unstressed syllables in monosyllabic function words and in the unstressed syllables of polysyllabic words at normal rates of speech, means that there is no way to derive from the full form pronouns the schwa clitic forms or the vowelless clitic forms. Moreover, the realization of pronouns as clitics is subject to a moraic constraint that a clitic be maximally comprised of a single, non-branching mora, ruling out monosyllabic clitics of the form CC and VC and all polysyllabic clitics, accounting for the gaps shown in (1).[4] The phonological interaction the clitics display with their hosts is also evidence for their clitichood.

(2)   a. hab   /hab/ → [hap]
         'have' 1SG (zero allomorph)
      b. habe   /hab + ə/ → [habə]
         'have' 1SG
      c. hab ich   /hab - ɪç/ → [hab ɪç]
         'have I'
      d. hab'n   /hab-n/ → [habm̩]
         'have'm'
      e. hab ihn   /hab#in/ → [hapin]/*[habin]
         'have him'
      f. Ich geb Angelika alles → [gepʔangelika]/*[gebangelika]
         'I'll give Angelika everything.'

Word-final underlyingly voiced obstruents in German are rendered voiceless, as in (2a). In (2b), the attachment of a vowel-initial suffix removes or bleeds the environment for final devoicing. The examples in (2c) and (2d), where the feature [labial] has spread from the final consonant of the host to the consonant of the clitic, illustrate that both subject clitics and object clitics can bleed final devoicing. That full form pronouns and full NPs cannot do so is shown in the second realizations in (2e) and (2f).

1.1.2. The Syntactic Behavior of Clitics

Standard German enclitics follow the finite verb, complementizers,*wh*-words and subject pronouns and NPs, as can full form pronouns, as shown in (3). (Henceforth orthographized forms will be used for the clitics).

(3)   a. Ich hab'n/ihn schon gestern gesehen
　　　　　　　I have him　already yesterday seen
　　　　　　　'I already saw him yesterday.'
　　　　　　b. Wollen'wr/wir 's/es/das morgen nicht diskutieren?
　　　　　　　want　we　　that　tomorrow not discuss
　　　　　　　'Don't we want to discuss that tomorrow?'
　　　　　　c. Ich freue mich, wenn'de/du kommst.
　　　　　　　I　please myself, if　you　come
　　　　　　　'I'll be happy if you come.'
　　　　　　d. Er weiβ nicht, ob's/es doch zu spät ist.
　　　　　　　he knows not whether it prt too late is
　　　　　　　'He doesn't know whether it's too late.'

As morphological entities, clitics can be and are subject to syntactic constraints. Thus while the examples in (3) do not reveal any differences in the distribution of full form pronouns and clitics,[5] the examples in (4) show that the positions in which clitics can appear are more restricted than for full form pronouns. A clitic or full form subject pronoun cannot follow an adverb (4a), a pronominal or NP object, as in (4b) versus (4c). The examples in (4d) and (4e) show that a NP subject behaves differently and can either be preceded or followed by a clitic or full form object pronoun. The syntactic behavior of postverbal pronominal subjects suggests that subject pronouns in their full form guise are actually clitics (cf. Tomaselli & Poletto, 1993). Phonological evidence (see (2c) above) further supports such an analysis for the full form of the first person singular pronoun *ich*.

(4) a. Natürlich hat gestern *'r/*er ihn gesehen.
naturally has yesterday he him seen
'Naturally he saw him yesterday.'
b. Gestern hat*'n er/*ihn er gesehen.
yesterday has him he seen
'He saw him yesterday.'
c. Gestern hat'r'n/ er ihn gesehen.
yesterday has he him seen
'He saw him yesterday.'
d. Gestern hat'n/ihn mein Vater gesehen.
yesterday has him my father-$_{NOM}$ seen
'My father saw him yesterday.'
e. Gestern hat mein Vater'n/ihn gesehen.[6]
yesterday has my father-$_{NOM}$ him seen
'My father saw him yesterday.'

Additional distributional differences between clitics and full forms are apparent when Kayne's (1975) criteria for clitics are applied, as shown in (5). Unlike the forms in the leftmost columns in (1), those in the rightmost columns in (1) can never be topicalized (5a), appear in isolation (5b), be conjoined (5c), be preceded by a parenthetical (5d) or otherwise be separated from their host (5e).

(5) a. Du/*de'kannst heute noch kommen.
you can today still come
'You can still come today.'
b. Wer soll das machen? *De/du.
who should that do? you
'Who should do that?' You.
c. Heute wollen*'r und'se/er und sie die Stadt besuchen.
today will he and she the city visit
'He and she want to visit the city today.'
d. Ich weiss was, um es nochmal zu sagen,*'de/du doch meinst.
I know what for it again to say you prt mean
'I know what - to repeat - you mean.'
e. Gestern war nur *'se/sie dabei.
yesterday was only she there
'She alone was there yesterday.'

The same set of criteria apply to the object forms in (6a-e), with the addition of the observation that clitic pronouns can never follow prepositions (6f).

(6)   a. Sie/*se'hat er in Dortmund kennengelernt.
           her   has he in Dortmund met
           'He met her in Dortmund.'
         b. Wen hast du gesehen? *Se/sie.
           whom have you seen? her
           'Whom did you see? Her.'
         c. Ich hab *'se und *'n/ sie und ihn nicht gesehen.
           I   have her and him   not seen
           'I haven't seen her or him.'
         d. Ich weiβ, daβ du, um es nochmal zu sagen,*'se/sie morgen siehst.
           I know that you for it again   to.say   her tomorrow see
           'I know that you - to repeat - will see her tomorrow.'
         e. Er hat heute *'n/ihn gesehen.
           he has today him   seen
           'He saw him today.'
         f. Ich hab was für *'se/sie mitgebracht.
           I have something for her with-brought
           'I've brought something with me for her.'

These examples suggest that clitics are heads, of the category X^o, since unlike full form pronouns they will be restricted from appearing in positions which must be occupied by an XP. Their adjunction is as in the tree in (7).[7]

(7)

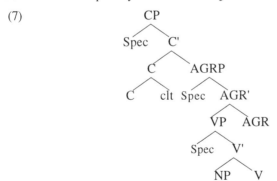

2. THE SECOND LANGUAGE ACQUISITION OF CLITICIZATION

Since clitic and full form pronouns (and NPs) are not in strict complementary distribution, their syntax will neither be readily apparent to the child nor the adult L2 learner of German. This is not to say that primary linguistic data is unable to accomplish the task of acquisition; subtle phonological cues do exist, informing the learner that those pronominal forms maximally consisting of a single non-branching mora only occur in a specific syntactic position.

Cardinaletti & Starke (1994, this volume) and Haegeman (1996) propose that in early Standard German and Dutch, respectively, children do not always activate the syntactic projection(s) associated with the "Pronoun Zone".[8] In addition, accounts of children's emerging phonologies in Germanic languages indicate that children initially lack the prosodic structure to allow analysis of clitics as distinct from full forms (see e.g., Demuth, 1996). While this suggests only a general picture of the acquisition of cliticization, the conclusion one can draw is that cliticization in Standard German is - predictably - not acquired during the early stages of first language acquisition. Proceeding from this conclusion, one would likewise not expect to see evidence of the acquisition of cliticization during the early stages of second language development. Yet, while we know that all normal German children attain adult competence in that language, the issue of whether adult second language learners reach complete native competence in German (or any L2) remains unresolved.

Do adult learners at advanced stages of L2 development demonstrate knowledge of the syntactic and morphophonological properties of Standard German clitics? Their attainment of such knowledge will depend on the extent to which both their syntactic and their phonological competence is native-like. If such learners fail to detect the phonological characteristics of the clitic and full form pronouns, analysis of these forms as distinct entities is blocked, and conclusions regarding their syntactic distribution can never be reached. Furthermore, if L2 learners have not acquired the correct syntactic projections for German, this will introduce an additional impediment in discerning those distributional differences. While recent studies have shown that L2 adults have access to X'-Theory such that they are able to arrive at non-L1 syntactic projections (see e.g., Vainikka & Young-Scholten, 1994), whether even advanced adult learners can be said to have completely acquired German syntax remains to be established (see e.g., Schwartz & Sprouse, 1994).

2.1. The Study

Second language learners of German who were deemed to be advanced were selected for an experimental study on the assumption that such learners represent (near) steady state L2 competence.[9] The aim of the investigation was to compare their competence with respect to cliticization with that of native-speaking Germans from the same population in order to examine the details of possibly incomplete L2 acquisition.

2.1.1. Test Subjects

The test subjects in the study were 21 non-native speakers (NNS) and 10 native speakers (NS) of German. The majority of the NNS had been living and either studying or working in Germany for at least a year at the time of testing and were considered to be advanced learners by dint of their full matriculation in various disciplines at the University of Bielefeld or their professional connection to the University. The NNS group consisted of nine American English speakers, five Korean speakers, four Turkish speakers, and three Spanish speakers. Although all had received at least some instruction in German prior to taking up residence in Germany, certainly their acquisition of cliticization could be considered to have taken place in a naturalistic setting, as this is not a topic included in a typical German course. The NS control group consisted of 10 speakers of German whose ages fell into the same range as those in the NNS group and who were also associated with the University of Bielefeld. All had grown up in central or eastern North-Rhine Westphalia, considered to be an area in which colloquial Standard German is the spoken dialect. None of the NS spoke a regional dialect.

2.1.2. Testing Procedure

The primary consideration in arriving at an appropriate means of eliciting clitics was the strong possibility that a formal testing situation would result only in the production of full form pronouns, since use of pronominal clitics is, strictly speaking, not obligatory (though use of full forms is marked in some idioms such as *Wie geht's?* 'How are you?'). This ruled out the reading of a passage as well as the elicitation of spontaneous speech. An elicited imitation task was therefore designed in an attempt to force the production of clitics. This task involved 80 'mini-dialogues' recorded by several Standard German-speaking linguistics students at the University of Bielefeld. Each dialogue contained two sentences, the first of which was a question or comment and the second of which was a response, as illustrated in (8); these test sentences also appear as some of the examples in (3) - (6) above. Except for several distractors, the second sentence in the pair contained at least one clitic. The 80 pairs yielded data consisting of 80 imitated sentences similar to (8b).

(8) a. Weiβt du, wo das Auto steht?
     know you, where the car stands
     'Do you know where the car is?'
  b. Ich hab's in der Goethestraβe stehenlassen.
     I have it in the Goethe street left
     'I've left it in Goethe street.'

Individual test subjects listened to each sentence pair, completed a short arithmatic calculation (designed to prevent automatic mimicking without processing), and then repeated the second sentence of the pair into a microphone. Test subjects were instructed to repeat sentences exactly, but to dispel possible instruction-based resistance to the use of these forms, the NNS test subjects were further reassured that this was the sort of natural speech they heard every day from fellow university students. An important feature of the task (about which test subjects were informed, but in a general sense) was that some sentences were ungrammatical in terms of the position of the clitic. The inclusion of such sentences was intended to see whether test subjects would automatically self-correct in line with their competence. The ability of the native as well as the non-native speakers to hold in their memory for the duration of the arithmetic calculation and repeat the correct clitic or corresponding full form pronoun in the majority of instances was an indication that speakers had indeed either accurately perceived these elements in the sentences when they heard them and/or were able to rapidly use the context of the preceding sentence to determine the pronoun in the test sentence.[10]

3. RESULTS

3.1. General Indications

The first indication that these L2 learners' cliticization is not native-like is suggested by the figures in Table 1 showing the mean frequency of clitic repetition. The table gives the verbatim repetition of clitics which were both grammatical and ungrammatical in the test sentences heard by the subjects. Figures include self-corrected repetitions of clitic forms.

Table 1.
Mean frequency of overall clitic repetition

GROUP	control n=10	American n=9	Korean n=5	Turkish n=4	Spanish n=3
% repetition	35%	13%	9%	6%	4%

There are a number of possible reasons for what is overall a low frequency of repetition of clitics by all groups (although the NNS repetitions are considerably lower). To begin with, recall that clitics are not obligatory. And in addition, even though the task was designed to force the production of clitics, the testing situation itself was likely to have had an inhibitory effect on their repetition. Moreover, increased processing demands may well have been involved in the perception of the ungrammatical cliticizations included in some of the test sentences. If both the NS and the NNS test subjects possessed similar competence, these effects should have had an equal impact on all test subjects' ability to repeat the clitics during the task. In that Table 1. shows that this was not the case, we have an initial indication of native - non-native differences in competence in these speakers' German. Table 1. illustrates further differences among the four non-native speaking groups. The Americans' frequency of repetition is the highest out of these four groups, for example. This is not surprising when one notes that English and German share more characteristics (particularly in terms of phonology, but also with respect to similar pronominal forms) than any of the other three languages do with German. This would be expected to have at least an initial facilitative effect in terms of the acquisition of the phonological properties of the clitics.[11] To address the question of whether learners show sensitivity to the different syntactic positions in which clitics and full form pronouns can occur in German, results from selected subsets of the 80 sentences must be examined (see also Young-Scholten, 1993).

3.2. Repetition of Clitics in Various Positions

Do second language learners repeat the pronominal forms in the test sentences in those positions in which they are allowed? Table 2 below addresses the question of whether the L2 learners repeated subject and object clitics when the word order involved was XVSY and SVO, respectively.

To begin with, this table shows that repetitions by the native speakers for subject and object clitics following the finite verb are nearly equally high for the clitic *s* and quite high for most other clitics, regardless of whether they are subjects or objects. When the non-native speakers repeated the clitics, the figures show a higher rate of repetition for post-verbal subject clitics than for object clitics following a finite verb. Taking into consideration what is an overall a lower rate of non-native speaker clitic repetition, we find relatively high rates of repetition for the subject clitics *s* for all four non-native speaking groups (although the Koreans score lower), and of *de* for two out of the four groups. This suggests that at least the clitic form *s* is present and allowed post-verbally in the L2 learners' competence and that *de* may be present for the Americans and Turkish speakers. It is not immediately apparent why post-verbal object clitics were not repeated with more frequency by the NNS groups. While this may have been due to an unfortunate choice of test sentence, with an increased processing load caused by the 'difficult' fricatives [x] and [ç] in the three words following a clitic: '... hab's doch noch nicht...' resulting in the clitic 'losing out', we again do not see this effect with the NS group.

Table 2.
Postverbal subject and object clitic repetitions
(Figures show frequency of clitic repetition w.r.t. the number of pronoun tokens produced by speakers.)

	SUBECT CLITICS				OBJECT CLITICS	
GROUP	s	de	wr	se	s	n/m
control	90% (9/10)	67% (12/18)	55%[1] (11/20)	100% (8/8)	100% (9/9)	85% (17/20)
American	56% (5/9)	41% (7/17)	6% (1/18)	0 (0/9)	11% (1/9)	5% (1/17)
Korean	20% (1/5)	20% (2/10)	0 (1/10)	0 (0/9)	0 (0/5)	0 (0/10)
Spanish	34%[2] (1/3)	20% (1/5)	0 (0/6)	0 (0/2)	0 (0/3)	20% (1/5)
Turkish	75% (3/4)	38% (3/8)	43% (3/7)	0 (0/4)	25% (1/4)	0 (0/6)

[1] The two forms on the task were the possible, yet ostensibly ill-formed assimilated forms [ˌvImʌ] 'swim we' and [lemʌ] 'live we'; figures represent repetitions of these forms and of non-assimilated forms with clitics, e.g. [ˌvImvʌ] and [lebmvʌ].
[2] One Spanish speaker produced the clitic -*s*, but with a case alteration (obvious from the rest of the sentence repeated).

Schwartz & Sprouse's (1994) study of an adult Turkish learner of German provides further evidence that second language learners are able to discern the post-verbal nature of subject clitics in German. At one stage of development, the learner they studied displayed an asymmetry - in favor of pronouns - between NPs and subject pronouns following the finite verb, revealing the learner's discovery that subject pronouns are enclitics in German.

It appears that both Schwartz and Sprouse's learner and the learners in the present study have some awareness of the 'Pronoun Zone' with respect to subjects in German. However, Table 2. also shows that object clitics were repeated by the non-native speakers to a much lesser extent, and in some cases not at all.

Is there a similar pattern of repetition when subject and object clitics follow a complementizer rather than a verb, when the syntax involves an embedded clause and hence a CP? Table 3. reveals that clitic repetition following a complementizer is lower for both the NS and NNS groups.

Table 3.
Post-complementizer subject and object clitic repetitions

	SUBJECTS			OBJECTS		
GRP	de	se	s	s	n/m	se
control	39%	70%	60%	56%	70%	70%
	(7/18)	(7/10)	(6/10)	(11/20)	(14/20)	(7/10)
American	6%	0	0	17%	11%	0
	(1/18)	(0/9)	(0/9)	(3/18)	(2/18)	(0/9)
Korean	11%	0	0	0	0	0
	(1/9)	(0/5)	(0/5)	(0/10)	(0/10)	(0/5)
Spanish	0	0	0	0	0	0
	(0/6)	(0/3)	(0/3)	(0/6)	(0/6)	(0/3)
Turkish	0	0	25%	0	0	0
	(0/7)	(0/4)	(1/4)	(0/8)	(0/8)	(0/4)

In fact in a good many instances there is no clitic repetition by the NNS groups. As was the case for clitics following finite verbs, NS repetition of clitics is comparable for both subjects and objects (particularly obvious for identical forms) in this position. The lower rate of repetition of clitics following complementizers may again be connected to the unfortunate complexity of some of the test sentences. Yet such an effect would have had an equal impact on the NS and NNS groups, given comparable competence; this is clearly not the case. These low rates of repetition and the non repetition of post-complementizer clitics - especially in comparison with their post-verbal repetition - are a further sign that these advanced non-native speakers do not possess native-like competence with respect to cliticization.

The three tables we have looked at so far indicate that these advanced learners' competence with respect to cliticization differs from that of native German speakers. However it is also apparent from the information in these tables that these L2 learners do manifest some awareness of clitics since the clitics in the test sentences are comprehended and then repeated at least some of the time. What further signs of acquisition of cliticization are manifested by these second language learners? Do they show sensitivity to ungrammatical cliticizations?

3.3. Clitics in Disallowed Positions

As mentioned earlier, clitics in some of the test sentences in the mini-dialogues were in ungrammatical positions. The test subjects were instructed to repeat every sentence as accurately as possible, but were also told that some of the sentences might be a bit wrong. While this introduced a bias to repeat verbatim even ungrammatical sequences, the expectation of hearing sentences that could be ungrammatical may have had the opposite effect, of priming test subjects for the subconscious correction of any such sentence prior to its reproduction. The latter is indeed, what the test subjects did when sentences were fully comprehended (which was not always the case). When successfully repeating sentences containing clitics in ungrammatical positions, test subjects typically either produced the full form of the pronoun or altered the order and then either repeated the full form or the clitic.

Table 4 shows that when confronted with clitics in ungrammatical topic position in German, native speakers repeated these as clitic forms less frequently than they did for clitics in grammatical positions (see Tables 2 and 3).[12]

Table 4.
Sentence-initial subject and object clitic repetitions

	SUBJECTS				OBJECTS		
GROUP	*de	*se	*s	*wr	*n/*m	*s	*se
control	10% (1/10)	0 (0/8)	0 (1/10)	0 (0/8)	25% (5/20)	37% (9/24)	20% (2/10)
American	25% (2/8)	0 (0/8)	0 (0/9)	0 (0/9)	0 (0/18)	0 (0/23)	0 (0/9)
Korean	0 (0/4)	0 (0/5)	0 (0/4)	0 (0/3)	0 (0/10)	0 (0/14)	0 (0/5)
Spanish	0 (0/3)	0 (0/3)	0 (0/3)	0 (0/3)	0 (0/6)	0 (0/9)	0 (0/3)
Turkish	0 (0/4)	0 (0/4)	0 (0/4)	0 (0/4)	20% (1/5)	0 (0/9)	0 (0/3)

The non-native speakers followed the trend of the native speakers and also repeated clitics in topic position less frequently (i.e., in most cases not at all). However, in addition to the one Turkish repetition of *m*, there were two American repetitions of *de* in this position, suggesting lexical transfer from American English of sentence initial subject clitic *ya* for 'you'.

The low frequency of repetition of topicalized clitics points to the conclusion that these second language learners generally do not allow clitics preverbally, except for those instances in which a subject clitic comparable to a form in the learner's native language is allowed in this position.

Do learners repeat clitics in other positions in which they are not allowed? Pronominal object (or subject) clitics are neither allowed following an adverb nor following a preposition. However, determiner clitics following prepositions are not only allowed, they are obligatory when the reading intended is generic, resulting in frozen forms such as *ins Theater* 'to the theater' and *zum Bahnhof* 'to the railway station'. Table 5 below illustrates how the test subjects dealt with these grammatical and ungrammatical cliticizations. We see in the two leftmost columns that the native speakers' rates of repetition are again relatively low, and nearly all of the non-native speakers do not repeat clitics in this position at all.[13] The Americans, however, demonstrate a rate of repetition of the clitic *s* following an adverb which is high compared to their rate of repetition for the object clitic *s* - 11% following a finite verb and 17% following a complementizer. In looking at whether non-native speakers allow pronominal clitics following a preposition, we can directly compare this to their repetition of the obligatory determiner clitics. The native speakers' frequency of repetition of these determiner clitics is very high (100% and 80%), comparable to their rate of repetition of postverbal object clitics *s* (100%) and *n/m* (85%). Of note is that the repetition rate of the clitic *s* exceeds that of *n/m*, indicating that phonological factors are involved in the attachability of individual clitic forms. The NS group's rate of repetition of the ungrammatical pronominal clitics following a preposition is much lower and is comparable to their rate of repetition of clitics following an adverb. A similar pattern prevails for the non-native speaker groups.

Table 5.
Post-adverb and post-preposition clitic repetitions

	ADVERBS		PREPOSITIONS			
			pronouns		determiners	
GROUP	*s	*n	*s	*m	s	m
control	40% (4/10)	30% (3/10)	30% (3/10)	50% (5/10)	100% (10/10)	80% (8/10)
American	38% (3/8)	0 (0/7)	22% (2/9)	22% (2/9)	44% (4/9)	67% (6/9)
Korean	0 (0/5)	0 (0/5)	40% (2/5)	0 (0/5)	20% (1/5)	20% (1/5)
Spanish	0 (0/3)	0 (0/3)	0 (0/3)	0 (0/3)	34% (1/3)	0 (0/3)
Turkish	0 (0/4)	0 (0/4)	0 (0/4)	0 (0/4)	50% (2/4)	25% (1/4)

Repetitions of determiner clitics represent - not surprisingly - some of the highest rates of repetition these speakers manifested in the entire test, especially by the non-American groups. This pattern appears to be reversed for two of the Korean speakers for *s*, although it is difficult to draw firm conclusions based on the difference of one response. The trend of increased repetition of determiner clitics turns out to be a bit weaker for the Americans, suggesting a possible influence of the reduction of pronouns following prepositions in English (as in *I've got something for'm in the car*).

3.4. Order alterations in reproduced sentences

The conclusion that can be drawn from Tables 1-5 is that second language learners have the strongest awareness of the obligatory determiner clitics along with some awareness that clitics, especially subject clitics, can appear post-verbally. However, the overall NNS reluctance to repeat clitics following complementizers coupled with the higher rate of repetition of clitics in some disallowed positions - particularly by the Americans - points to the L1 influence of low-level rules of reduction and deletion and also reveals a non-L1-based tendency to adopt such an analysis in the case of the Korean, Spanish and Turkish speakers.

Given the overall low rates of repetition by the NNS, the test results can be examined from a different angle in an attempt to paint a more detailed picture of these learners' competence. Let us therefore investigate what all groups did to (subconsciously) alter the test sentences when they did not repeat them verbatim. This information provides additional details regarding the positions in which the speakers prefer both clitic pronouns as well as full-form pronouns. In the repetitions of sentences with object clitics preceding a finite verb (i.e., ungrammatically topicalized clitics) shown in Table 6 (with repetitions which were full form pronouns) one of the strategies the non-native speakers employed was to alter the OVS order given in the test sentence to SVO, with repetition of the pronoun as a full form. However, the OVS order was only changed once to SVO by any of the speakers in the NS group. The table points to the conclusion that non-native speakers are reluctant to topicalize even full form non-subject pronouns, and show a preference for SVO order.

Table 6.
Preverbal object pronoun order alterations (Test sentence order is underlined; figures for altered orders show repetition of full forms rather than clitics).

	n & m repeated order		s repeated order		se repeated order	
GROUP	OVS	SVO	OVS	SVO	OVS	SVO
control	25% (5/20)	0 (0/20)	37% (9/24)	0 (0/24)	20% (2/10)	10% (1/10)
American	0 (0/18)	11% (2/18)	0 (0/23)	22% (5/23)	0 (0/9)	0 (0/9)
Korean	0 (0/10)	10% (1/10)	0 (0/14)	50% (7/14)	0 (0/5)	0 (0/5)
Spanish	0 (0/6)	17% (1/6)	0 (0/9)	56% (5/9)	0 (0/3)	0 (0/3)
Turkish	0 (1/5)	20% (1/5)	0 (0/9)	34% (3/9)	0 (0/3)	34% (1/3)

The non-native speakers' order alterations in Table 6 from OVS to SVO, always with repetition of full form pronouns, indicate that one cannot expect object clitics in this position if learners do not even allow any object pronouns in this position. The learners' rejection of clitics in this position - as shown in Table 4 - thus appears to be more complicated than at first glance, ostensibly involving incomplete acquisition of German syntax.

Table 7 further reveals the competence of the non-native speakers with respect to cliticization. This table shows the repetition of just the object clitic *s* - for which we've seen higher rates of repetition - preceding or following an NP subject in matrix clauses, both grammatical orders. The NS repetitions indicate a strong preference for OS order, with only a 5% order change to SO, and with repetition of the full form. Order changes from

SO to OS were more frequent (25%), with more frequent clitic retention under these circumstances.

Table 7.
Post and pre-NP subject repetition and order alterations for the object clitic s in matrix clauses (Test sentence orders are underlined)

TEST SENTENCE	NP subject - object clitic repeated order		object clitic - NP subject repeated order	
GROUP	<u>SO</u> clitics	OS full forms [clitics]	SO full forms [clitics]	<u>OS</u> clitics
control	40% (16/40)	25% [15%] (10/40)	5% (1/19)	95% (18/19)
American	17% (6/36)	0 (0/36)	17% [12%] (3/17)	41% (7/17)
Korean	0 (0/19)	16% [5%] (3/19)	30% (3/10)	30% (3/10)
Spanish	0 (0/9)	56% [11%] (5/9)	17% (1/6)	0 (0/6)
Turkish	7% (1/4)	21% [7%] (3/14)	14% (1/7)	14% (1/7)

The two leftmost columns in Table 7 provide some additional evidence of the NNS groups' awareness of the status of object clitics in German, as all NNS groups but the Americans altered the test sentence order from object clitic following an NP subject to object clitic preceding an NP subject, even retaining the clitic in a number of cases. The retention of clitic forms rather than replacement by full forms in such order alterations was a rare occurrence for other test sentences for the non-native speakers. Repetition of clitics in SO order was also lower, with the exception of the American group. This again suggests that the Americans are operating under low-level rules, which result in reduced pronouns following any stressed content word (see Young-Scholten 1993). On the other hand, the two rightmost columns show that object clitics preceding NP subjects were clearly preferred by most of the non-native speakers, including the Americans. Yet while there is only one instance of native speaker alteration to SO from OS order, the non-native speakers show either a tendency to or preference for SO. What is also interesting to note is that when the order is altered from OS to SO, only the American group exhibited any retention of the clitic, in further support of their having adopted low level rules. The figures in Table 7 strengthen the conclusion that our non-native speakers have some awareness that the 'Pronoun Zone' includes object as well as subject clitics, although they do not behave like native speakers and may fail to do so in various L1-related ways.

Let's now look at whether the same pattern of order alteration holds for object clitics following complementizers and preceding full NP subjects. Table 8 below involves the figures from Table 3, which showed minimal repetition for both subject and for all object clitics (not only *s*) following complementizers. This table presents the order alterations speakers made when repeating the sentences.

While the native speakers produced clitics following complementizers and preceding NP subjects between 56% and 70% of the time, what is most often produced by the non-native speaking test subjects when they repeat the sentences are full forms which reappear in an SO order. This is particularly striking for the clitics/full forms *n* and *m* (*ihn* and *ihm*), and *s* (*es*). Native speakers also altered the order from OS to SO, but they did so much less frequently, between 5% and 20% of the time.

Table 8.

Post-complementizer pre-NP subject repetitions and order alterations for all object clitics (Test sentence orders are underlined.)

GROUP	s repeated order		n & m repeated order		se repeated order	
	OS clitics	SO full forms	OS clitics	SO full forms	OS clitics	SO full forms
control	56% (11/20)	5% (1/20)	70% (14/20)	10% (2/20)	70% (7/10)	20% (2/10)
American	17% (3/18)	39% (7/18)	11% (2/18)	38% (7/18)	0 (0/9)	11% (1/9)
Korean	0 (0/10)	20% (2/10)[1]	0 (0/10)	30% (3/10)	0 (0/5)	20% (1/5)
Spanish	0 (0/6)	83% (5/6)	0 (0/6)	34% (2/6)	0 (0/3)	0 (0/3)
Turkish	0 (0/8)	50% (4/8)	0 (0/8)	50% (4/8)	0 (0/4)	25% (1/4)

[1]An additional five of the ten sentences repeated lacked any phonetic realization of the object.

Whether the object clitic *s* when it precedes an NP subject is treated differently depending on whether it follows a verb or complementizer can be determined from comparing Tables 7 and 8. All non-native speakers perform better with respect to post-verbal clitics, except for the Spanish speakers who repeat neither clitics nor full forms in OS orders after verbs or complementizers. The Americans exhibit the highest rate of repetition for the object clitic *s* after a verb: 41% in OS order and 12% when the order is changed to SO after a verb. After a complementizer, the rate of clitic repetition drops to 17% for OS order, with full forms, but no clitics repeated when the order has been changed to SO.

The figures for order alteration given in Table 8 for several of the non-native speaking groups may actually be too conservative. It is impossible to draw any conclusions from sentences which were not repeated accurately at all, but one can take the complete omission of object pronouns in otherwise accurate repetitions into account. Such omissions can be included as an additional indication of the rejection of an OS order after complementizers. The SO figures, representing preferred orders, can then be adjusted as follows: for the clitic *se*, the Spanish speakers' percentage of 'order altered' increases to 34%. For the clitic *s* for the Americans this increases to 56%, for the Turkish speakers it increases to 63%, for the Koreans speakers to 70% and for the Spanish speakers the order altered figure increases to 100%. With the addition of these figures, it becomes clear that OS order is dispreferred by non-native speakers with considerably more frequently following complementizers than following verbs. The non-native speakers' cliticization is not native-like, and we can offer the conclusion that the syntactic position in which reduced object pronouns are located in non-native German is not the same as the one in which object clitics are located in native German.

4. DISCUSSION

On the one hand, there is evidence from the above tables that non-native speakers exhibit some knowledge of the unique status of reduced pronouns in Standard German. However, as we have just asserted, there is also evidence pointing to lack of native competence with respect to the syntax implicated in cliticization. It would seem that with awareness of the 'Pronoun Zone', advanced learners would have come further in their acquisition of cliticization, even though cliticization seems to be something not acquired early on by children in their first language.

Now we can return to a consideration of the two observations noted in the introduction, that L2 adults rarely attain native-like competence in phonology and that difficulties with respect to functional elements may still exist at advanced levels of proficiency. Furthermore, the issue of whether adults attain native competence in an L2 syntax also remains unresolved. Thus one might want to connect our L2 learners' non-native cliticization to an across the board, age-related inaccessibility to the principles and/or the parameters of UG. If principled linguistic differences across languages with respect to cliticization involve parameterization, then this might simply be an illustration of these adult non-native speakers' inability to reset parameters. Yet while some researchers adopt the view that L2 adults no longer have direct access to UG (e.g., Clahsen & Muysken, 1989), findings on the acquisition of German for example from Vainikka & Young-Scholten (1994) and Schwartz & Sprouse (1994) provide convincing evidence that adult second language learners do indeed have access to principles of UG such as X'-Theory. In that learners have been shown to arrive at a syntax which is not only distinct from that of their native language but also at least resembles that of their L2, there is no a priori reason ruling out their ability to acquire cliticization. Moreover, under the Structure Building view held by Vainikka & Young-Scholten, learners would be predicted to be able to posit this projection based on the interaction of X'-Theory with the ambient input.

The Vainikka & Young-Scholten view holds that the L1 only exerts its syntactic influence at the initial, pre-functional stages of acquisition. So while there is an indication for the Americans that their native language may be exerting some influence, it is the case that they allow German clitics in positions which would not be possible in English.[14] There is less evidence of L1 influence with respect to cliticization for learners from other language backgrounds, even though one might expect to see such influence for learners whose native language has clitics, i.e., Spanish (see Young-Scholten, 1993 for further details on the L1 influence for the other NNS groups). For all four of these groups, it is not clear that L1 influence is more than phonological. It is also not clear that the speakers in these groups have completely acquired German syntax; there is evidence, albeit indirect, from the above tables that their CP is not that of native German.

4.1. Phonological Considerations

What might impede advanced learners in positing a clitic projection when they certainly show some awareness of the special status of reduced pronouns? What role might incomplete L2 phonology play in these learners' incomplete acquisition of cliticization? Do the learners show evidence that they are aware of the moraic constraint on clitics such that they have arrived at the native clitic paradigm in German? Table 9 points to the conclusion that the sole clitics which learners can be said to have begun to acquire is the clitic *s* (figures include determiner *s*), and perhaps *n* (figures include determiner *m*) and *de/se* for the Turkish speakers. That all groups demonstrate their highest rate of repetition with respect to the clitic *s* can be accounted for by the phonetic salience of [s] along with its status as obligatory determiner clitic and near-obligatory status as a pronominal clitic in certain common generic phrases and idioms, respectively. The American group's repetition of *s* is much higher, which is predictable in that only English approaches German in the complexity of a syllable structure which would allow incorporation of this single consonant clitic into a pre-existing syllable coda. Furthermore, syllabic nasals exist only in English, predicting the relatively higher rate of *n* and *m* clitic repetition shown in the table. Rather surprisingly, the Americans show a relatively lower rate of repetition for the clitics which involve reduced vowels (*r, wr, de* and *se*), even though one of these vowels, schwa, occurs in English. However, it is not surprising that the three other groups usually show low or no repetition of such clitics, given the lack of syllabic sonorant consonants or reduced vowels in unstressed syllables, particularly in syllable-timed Spanish (see Young-Scholten, 1993 for further details).

Table 9.
Total clitic repetition by phonological form

	s	*n* & *m*[1]	*r* & *wr*[2]	*de* & *se*
AMERICAN	27%	14%	9%	7%
TURKISH	18%	7%	5%	15%
KOREAN	13%	7%	1%	6%
SPANISH	11%	4%	0	0

[1] Figures include the sentential adverb clitic -*n* for 'denn'; repetition figures reduce to 7% for the Americans and slightly for other groups if these repetitions are excluded.
[2] Including the indirect object clitics *mr* and *dr*.

While we must keep in mind that any conclusions regarding clitic form are based on production data, an L2 learner's L1 phonology will also act as a filter on the input. Thus this low overall rate of repetition of the individual clitic forms leads us to propose that these second language learners have yet to acquire the phonological characteristics of cliticization. The figures in Table 9 reveal a patchy distribution of clitic forms such that it would be difficult for learners to arrive at a generalization pertaining to all clitics, i.e., that clitics observe the mono-moraic constraint.

Table 10 provides another glimpse at these speakers' L2 phonology. The table shows learners' pronunciation of various words in the test sentences and represents 14 consonant clusters and 14 of the reduced vowels schwa and [ʌ] in unstressed syllables in multisyllabic words. Non-target productions involved epenthesis or deletion in consonant clusters and full vowel realization for the reduced vowels.

Table 10.
Target-like forms for coda clusters and unstressed vowels (not in clitics)

	AMERICAN	TURKISH	KOREAN	SPANISH
coda C-clusters (n=14)	n/a	89%	84%	78%
reduced vowels (n=14)	64%	55%	36%	17%

The figures in the table echo the figures in Table 9 and provide additional support for the claim that these L2 learner's phonological competence is not completely native-like, (see also Young-Scholten 1993). Table 10 shows that the three non-native speaking groups (Americans would score 100%) whose L1 syllable structures are less complex than that of German have for the most part acquired the fact that German allows consonant clusters in the coda. Acquisition of German syllable structure would translate into acquisition of the clitic *s*, which, as we have seen, shows the highest rate of repetition for all groups. However, all four groups' acquisition of schwa (as default vowel) and the reduced vowel [ʌ] lags far behind, particularly for the Spanish speakers. Given these figures it is hardly surprising that the acquisition of cliticization in Standard German presents problems which can still be detected at advanced levels of proficiency.

5. CONCLUSION

What we have seen illustrated in the tables in the preceding sections reveals that advanced second language learners of German cannot be said to have absolutely no idea of the phonological and syntactic characteristics of cliticization. These non-native speakers display a budding awareness of the 'Pronoun Zone'. However, their second language competence with respect to cliticization clearly diverges from that of native speakers, and one of the culprits may well be their non-acquisition of either the status of vowels in unstressed syllables in German or the clitic forms which involve such vowels.

One important question which needs to be addressed is the extent to which the non-acquisition of what might be termed a clitic paradigm plays a decisive role in the overall acquisition of cliticization. Is it possible for learners to acquire cliticization only having acquired one or two of the clitics? If the learners' non-acquisition of this paradigm is connected to their non-acquisition of the moraic constraint on clitics, which is in turn due to general phonological difficulties in their second language, they will fail to process clitic forms as examples of the category clitic in German and will fail to detect their distributional differences from full form pronouns. Assuming this is not solely a matter of producing the right clitic form, the relevant input will be filtered through the learner's L1 phonological competence such that it ceases to represent what is presumably required for the learner to acquire cliticization.

Any further conclusions on the second language acquisition of clitics in Germanic languages must remain speculative at this point, since we lack sufficient data from the first and second language acquisition of cliticization in such languages.

ACKNOWLEDGEMENTS

Thanks go to the friends and colleagues at the universities of Bielefeld and Düsseldorf who offered support and advice several years back during the process of attempting to characterize the competence of native and non-native speakers of German with respect to cliticization. I am particularly grateful to the organizers of the Bern Workshop for providing a forum for the discussion of such a specialized area of linguistics. The comments of two anonymous reviewers have been particularly useful. Any omissions and inaccuracies remain my own.

NOTES

[1] Similar claims have been made for Dutch by Berendsen (1986). However, unlike in Dutch, conventional German orthography does not - with the exception of *s*, as in *Wie geht's*, allow the representation of clitics.

[2] See Kohler (1979) regarding those reduced forms of pronouns which are found at faster rates of speech, i.e., at Kaisse's (1985) P2 level.

[3] Meinhold (1973), Wiese (1988), and Prinz (1991) discuss dialectal and idiolectal variations which exist with respect to the register at which some of these clitics are found. See Young-Scholten (1991;1993) regarding the existence of [ç] as a clitic.

[4] The clitic [s] might be considered ideal in terms of its minimality; alone it does not even constitute a mora, but is simply incorporated into the final mora of the host to which it attaches. Note, too, that this moraic constraint allows the existence of the 1SG clitic [ç]. However, the form [ç] rarely surfaces in German, due to the infrequency with which this consonant can be successfully incorporated into the final syllable of its host. The unstressed 1SG pronoun typically retains its vowel, surfacing as [Iç]. It is this form which demonstrates clitic-like behavior such as the bleeding of final devoicing in sequences such as *hab-ich* (see below).

[5] In many of the examples in (3) when the discourse results in the assignment of stress to the full form pronoun, this pronoun can appear in those positions in which a full NP appears when not scrambled. Thus similar to a full NP, the pronoun in (3a) can follow the adverbs *schon gestern* when the discourse context results in stress on *ihn*: 'Ich habe schon gestern ihn/unsren neuen Mitarbeiter gesehen'

[6] Object clitics following full NP subjects do not appear to be grammatical for all speakers of Standard German.

[7] On the basis of several additional tests for clitic-hood, Haverkort (to appear) proposes that Germanic clitics are XPs, possessing the feature [+maximal] and, in addition [-projection]. This accounts for the XP-like behavior of the Standard German clitics while at the same time allowing these clitics to have head-like features and to be listed in the lexicon. The object clitics which precede NP subjects are adjoined to IP, while those which follow them are adjoined to VP.

[8] Cardinaletti & Starke (1994) in their discussion of the acquisition of personal pronouns in (L1) German, refer to the positions into which clitics move as the "Pronoun Zone. Under Haegeman's (1996) division of the Mittelfeld into three zones, this is "Zone 1" (simply a refinement of Wackernagel's position). See also Cardinaletti & Starke (this volume).

[9] Longitudinal or cross-sectional data from learners at various stages of acquisition would be required to investigate the actual acquisition of cliticization. Such data is, however, not yet available. Data from advanced learners suggest stage(s) which all learners might eventually reach.

[10] While overall the test was successful in forcing all test subjects to process sentences in terms of their competence, whereby deviant phrasing was typically corrected prior to repetition, it was occasionally clear that native speakers were able to override this 'competence filter' and repeat clitics in ungrammatical positions, exactly as they were given on the tape. This is obvious from the mocking tone, labored pauses and long syllabic sonorants or even fricatives which occur in those instances in which such ungrammatical sentences were repeated verbatim by the native speakers.

[11] However, it should be noted that the facilitative effects of these similarities may be short-lived, with the similarities between these two languages masking their important differences.

[12] Clitics are not allowed in this position, yet the 37% frequency with which the native speakers repeated sentence-initial object s suggests that fast speech forms with s (and n and m as well) might be permissible at normal rates of speech, particularly when the resultant forms involve the lengthening of consonants (they did in these instances).

[13] While a phonological explanation cannot be excluded for any of the examples presented here, the sequences of consonants which clitic attachment produced did not differ markedly across host-clitic constructions (see Young-Scholten, 1993 for details).

[14] Young-Scholten (1994) proposes that the less restricted behavior of pronouns in English involves a superset relative to the more constrained German cliticization. This creates a learnability problem for English learners of German in that they would have to engage in a futile search for the non-occurrence of pronouns in certain positions. On the other hand, allowing clitics in 'new' positions is something that can be acquired from the German input.

REFERENCES

Abraham, W.: 1991, 'Rektion und Abfolge pronominaler Glieder und ihrer klitischen Formen im Deutschen', in M. Kas, E. Reuland & C. Vet (eds.) *Language and Cognition 1: Yearbook of the research group for Linguistic Theory and Knowledge Representation of the University of Groningen*, Universiteitdrukkerij, Groningen.

Berendsen, E.: 1986, *The Phonology of Cliticization*, Dordrecht, Foris.

Cardinaletti, A. and M. Starke: 1994, 'The acquisition of pronoun placement', paper presented at the Workshop on the L1 and L2 acquisition of clause-internal rules: Scrambling and cliticization, Berne.

Clahsen, H. and P. Muysken.: 1989, 'The UG paradox in L2 acquisition', *Second Language Research* 5,1-29.

Demuth, K.: 1996, 'The prosodic structure of early words', in J.Morgan & K. Demuth (eds) *From Signal to Syntax: Bootstrapping from Speech to Grammar in Early Acquisition*, Lawrence Erlbaum, Hillsdale.

Giegerich, H.: 1985, *Metrical Phonology and Phonological Structure, German and English*, Cambridge University Press, Cambridge.

Haegeman, L.: 1996, 'Root infinitives, clitics and and truncated structures', in H. Clahsen (ed.) *Generative Perspectives on Language Acquisition*, Benjamins', Amsterdam, Philadelphia. 271-308.

Hall, T.: 1990, *Syllable Structure and Syllable Related Processes in German*, PhD dissertation, University of Washington.
Haverkort, M.: to appear, 'Romance and Germanic Clitics: A Comparison of their Syntactic Behavior', In T. Shannon & J. Snapper (eds.) *The Berkeley Conference on Dutch Linguistics 1993*, University Press of America, Lanham, 131-150.
Kaisse, E.: 1985, *Connected Speech*, Orlando, Academic Press.
Kayne, R.: 1975, *French Syntax: The Transformational Cycle*, MIT Press, Cambridge.
Kohler, K. J.: 1979, 'Kommunikative Aspekte satzphonetischer Prozesse im Deutschen', in H. Vater (ed.) *Phonologische Probleme des Deutschen*, Narr, Tübingen.
Meinhold, G.: 1973, Deutsche Standardsprache, Lautschwaechungen und Formstufen. Friederich-Schiller Universität, Jena.
Prinz, M.: 1991, *Klitisierung im Deutschen und Neugriechischen*, Niemeyer, Tübingen.
Schwartz, B. D. and R. Sprouse: 1994, 'Word order and nominative case in non-native language acquisition: A longitudinal study of (L1 Turkish) German interlanguage', in T. Hoekstra & B. D. Schwartz (eds.) *Language Acquisition Studies in Generative Grammar*, John Benjamins, Amsterdam, 317 - 368.
Tomaselli, A. and C. Poletto: 1993, 'Looking for clitics in Germanic languages: The case of standard German', *EUROTYP Working Papers*, ESF Publications.
Vainikka, A. and M.Young-Scholten: 1994, 'Direct access to X'-Theory: Evidence from Korean and Turkish adults learning German, in T. Hoekstra & B. D. Schwartz (eds.) *Language Acquisition Studies in Generative Grammar*, John Benjamins, Amsterdam, 265-316
White, L.: 1989, *Universal Grammar and L2 Acquisition*, John Benjamins, Amsterdam.
Wiese, R.: 1988, *Silbische und Lexicalische Phonologie. Studien zum Chinesischen und Deutschen*, Niemeyer, Tübingen.
Young-Scholten, M.: 1991, *Acquisition at the Interface*, Ph.D. Dissertation, University of Washington.
Young-Scholten, M.: 1993, *The Acquisition of Prosodic Structure in a Second Language*, Tübingen, Niemeyer.
Young-Scholten, M.: 1994, 'On positive evidence and ultimate attainment in L2 phonology', *Second Language Research* **10**, 193-214.

MARTHA YOUNG-SCHOLTEN
University of Durham

THOMAS ROEPER   BERNHARD ROHRBACHER

NULL SUBJECTS IN EARLY CHILD ENGLISH AND THE THEORY OF ECONOMY OF PROJECTION

1. INTRODUCTION AND OVERVIEW

It is well known that young children may omit referential subjects regardless of whether they are acquiring a *pro*-drop language such as Italian or a non-*pro*-drop language such as English. The classic proposal of Hyams (1986) according to which these early null subjects instantiate *pro* in both types of languages has recently come under attack from various sides. Bloom (1990, 1993) and Valian (1991) argue that missing subjects in early child English are a non-syntactic performance phenomenon that is due to a production bottleneck which severely limits the length of young children's utterances, a view which they support with an inverse correlation between subject-length (i.e., full NP, pronoun, null) and VP-length. Rizzi (1994a, b) and Hyams (1994) maintain that empty subjects in early child English are a syntactic phenomenon but relate them to adult English Diary Drop and German-style Topic Drop instead of Italian-style *pro*-drop. In particular, they argue that like adult Diary/Topic Drop and unlike adult *pro*-drop, these missing subjects in early child language are restricted to the first position of non-*wh* root clauses.

In this paper, we present new evidence from Adam (Brown, 1973; MacWhinney, 1995) that suggests that not all missing subjects in early child English can be reduced to performance limitations or Diary/Topic Drop. Between age 2;3 and 2;11 (Files 1-18), Adam produces numerous *wh*-questions without overt subjects (e.g., 'Where go?') and the VP-length of these examples is not greater than the VP-length in *wh*-questions with an overt subject pronoun. Adam's data moreover display a clear-cut distinction between finite (i.e., agreeing) and non-finite (i.e., non-agreeing) *wh*-questions. Whereas the number of empty subjects in finite *wh*-questions is negligible, there are almost as many non-finite *wh*-questions without an overt subject as non-finite *wh*-questions with an overt subject pronoun.[1] In the first eleven files, there are in fact five times as many empty subjects as overt subject pronouns in non-finite *wh*-questions. The same correlation between non-finiteness and lack of subject turns up in Adam's negative declaratives and has in fact been reported in the literature for many children acquiring languages other than English. Neither Bloom and Valian nor Rizzi and Hyams predict this correlation between non-finiteness and lack of subject.

We argue that the missing subjects in question are *pro*s and that their distribution follows from the theory of Economy of Projection developed in Speas (1994). Speas argues that in order to be syntactically licensed, each maximal projection must have independent semantic or phonetic content. Therefore, semantically empty AgrSP must have either its specifier filled by an overt subject at S-structure or its head filled by an agreement affix at D-structure. The former situation occurs in languages with weak agreement like English (where *pro*-drop is hence impossible) while the latter scenario occurs in languages with strong agreement like Italian (where *pro*-drop is hence possible). Unlike languages with weak or strong overt morphological agreement like English or Italian, languages without any overt morphological agreement like Japanese do not have AgrSP. Since projections such as T(P), V(P) etc. whose heads contain independent semantic content always allow their specifier to remain empty, languages without AgrSP also permit *pro*-drop.

Our central claim is that Adam's non-finite *wh*-questions without overt subjects have a Japanese-type structure, i.e., they lack AgrSP as long as agreement is overall rare (cf. the fact that in the first eleven files, only 4 out of 82 *wh*-questions containing either an empty subject or an overt subject pronoun are finite) and the highest specifier can be occupied by *pro*. Once weak English agreement is used more frequently, AgrSP is added to the tree even in non-finite *wh*-questions and since the head of this projection is underlyingly empty, its specifier must be occupied by an overt subject (cf. the fact that in Files 12-18, 108 out of 234 *wh*-Questions containing an empty subject or an overt subject pronoun are finite and there are now almost three times as many overt subject pronouns as empty subjects in non-finite *wh*-questions).

One advantage of this analysis is that it does not run into certain learnability problems that are often raised in connection with syntactic treatments of the missing subjects produced by children that are acquiring non-*pro*-drop languages. Although the child proceeds from a superset (containing both overt and empty subjects) to a subset (containing overt subjects only), this step is triggered by the acquisition of overt agreement morphology and no recourse to negative evidence is necessary. Neither do we have to appeal to the notion of parameter-resetting, since there is in fact no *pro*-drop parameter. Instead, the distribution of overt and empty subjects follows at any stage during the development from overt morphological properties of the particular grammar at that stage and from universal principles such as Economy of Projection.

The paper is organized as follows. Section 2 summarizes previous approaches to null subjects in early child English (*pro*-drop, Diary/Topic Drop and performance limitations). Section 3 introduces data from Adam, which are problematic for two of these approaches (Diary/Topic Drop and performance limitations). Section 4 discusses root infinitives, the environment in which Adam frequently omits the subject. Section 5 sketches the theory of Economy of Projection which in Section 6 is applied to Adam's data. The last section before the conclusion contains some speculations regarding the status of grammatical subject omissions in adult English subjunctive *wh*-questions (e.g., 'Why not keep a light on?').

2. EARLY NULL SUBJECTS: COMPETENCE OR PERFORMANCE, *PRO*-DROP OR DIARY/TOPIC DROP?

It is unsurprising that referential subjects are often absent in the earliest utterances of children acquiring *pro*-drop languages such as Spanish (cf. (1) from Pierce, 1992), where the adult grammar generally allows empty referential subjects. But such omissions are also widely attested in the earliest utterances of children acquiring non-*pro*-drop languages such as English, Dutch, German, Swedish or French[2] (cf. (2)), where the adult grammar generally does not allow empty referential subjects. The English example in (2a) and the French example in 2e come from Pierce (1992). The Dutch example in (2b) is from de Haan & Tuijnman (1988), the German example in (2c) from Verrips & Weissenborn (1992), and the Swedish example (2d) from Plazack (1993).

(1) puede   abrir   Rafael 1;6-2;0
    can-3S   open

(2) a. eating popcorn   Eve 1;9
    b. kann niet slapen op een schaap   David 2;2
       can not sleep on a sheep
    c. medizin drauftun mag nicht   Simone 2;0
       medication apply like not
    d. satt fel   Embla 2;0
       sat wrong
    e. avant veux chocolat   Nathalie 2;2
       before want chocolate

Examples like those in (2) have led Hyams (1986) to the conclusion that UG comes with the *pro*-drop parameter set to its positive value, i.e., that all children start out speaking a *pro*-drop language, and that this parameter is reset to its negative value only in the face of positive triggering evidence such as overt expletive subjects in the target non-*pro*-drop language.

Bloom (1990, 1993) and Valian (1991) argue against this view. In her comparison of the speech of 21 American children ranging in age from 1;10 to 2;8 and five Italian children ranging in age from 1;6 to 2;5, Valian (1991) observed that the American children with the lowest MLU (and the highest rate of subject omissions) included overt subjects in almost 70% of their utterances and that over 70% of these subjects were pronouns whereas Italian children included overt subjects in about 30% of their utterance and about 20-35% of these subjects were pronouns.[3] These findings suggest that empty subjects in the early speech of children acquiring *pro*-drop and non-*pro*-drop languages are not the same phenomenon. Both Bloom and Valian also point out that there is no abrupt decline in the rate of null subjects at any point during the development of children acquiring English, contrary to what might be expected if parameter (re)setting were involved (but see note 35). Instead, the rate of overt subjects gradually increases over time, apparently independently of possible triggers such as overt expletive subjects. Bloom and Valian conclude that the *pro*-drop parameter is initially set to its negative value which it retains throughout the development of children acquiring English and which is reset very early to the positive value by Italian children on the basis of positive evidence in the adult language. On this view, English children always have a non-*pro*-drop grammar but initially omit subjects because they simply cannot produce utterances beyond a certain length and subject omission is the least costly way to reduce utterance length given that the subject often represents old information. In other words, early English null subjects result not from a competence deficit, but from a performance deficit. This conclusion seems to be supported by a correlation between subject type and VP-length in the speech of Adam 2;3-2;7, Eve 1;6-1;10 and Sarah 2;3-2;7 reported in Bloom (1990).[4] On average, the VP is shortest with full NP subjects and longest when the subject is missing. Pronominal subjects co-occur with VPs of intermediate length (see Table 1). Valian (1991) partially reproduced these results for 6 of the 10 American children in her groups with the two lowest MLUs. These results are just what we would expect if a restriction on utterance length were responsible for the distribution of overt and empty subjects, but they are surprising if *pro* is a grammatical option for these children.

Table 1.
Average VP-Length and Subject Type in Child English (after Bloom, 1990)[5]

	VP-LENGTH (WORDS)		
	Full NP Subject	Pronoun Subject	Empty Subject
Adam	2.19	2.54	2.604
Eve	1.92	2.24	2.723
Sarah	1.47	1.88	2.462

It is however far from clear why phonetic length, number of words or (as is the case in Bloom's work) both of these factors should determine sentential complexity. Hyams & Wexler (1993) raise a number of other objections against Bloom (1990) and, less directly, Valian (1991). In their analysis of five transcripts from Italian-speaking adults, they found the same trend that was found for English-speaking children, i.e., VPs in sentences with full NP subject tend to be shorter than VPs in sentences with pronominal subjects which are themselves on average shorter than VPs in sentences with missing subjects. Yet Italian is standardly analyzed as a *pro*-drop language, and it would indeed be absurd to claim that adult Italians elide subjects because they suffer from a performance limitation on the length of their utterances. If this is correct, then the existence of a similar correlation between subject type and VP length in early stages of English does not bear on the question whether or not children at these stages have a *pro*-drop grammar. Another objection concerns the fact that according to the performance limitation theory, "lexical subjects will be omitted at lower processing loads (VP lengths) than pronouns" (Hyams & Wexler, 1993: 442), hence "the probability of omitting a lexical subject is greater than the probability of omitting a pronominal subject", while according to the *pro*-drop theory, pronouns but not full NP subjects are omitted. On the basis of File 30 in which overt subjects are more or less obligatory, Hyams & Wexler hypothesize that at any stage of his development, Adam intends to produce roughly one-third full NP subjects and two-thirds pronominal subjects. They find that in File 06, Adam uses full NP subjects in 33% of his utterances and pronominal subjects in 11% of his utterances. In other words, Adam's early (null subject) files contain the same proportion of lexical subjects as his later (obligatory subject) files, but these early files contain a dramatically lower proportion of pronominal subjects than the later files, thus supporting the *pro*-drop theory over the performance limitations theory.[6]

A look back at Table 1 reveals that for Adam, the child we will be concerned with below, the difference in VP-length between sentences with pronominal subjects and sentences without overt subject is very small (approximately 2.54 versus 2.604 words) and in all likelihood not statistically significant (Bloom (1990) tested his results for a linear trend but did not perform tests on the individual pairs of means). Moreover, we will see in Section 3 that Adam's *wh*-questions (which Bloom excluded from his corpus) exhibit a difference of the same magnitude, but in the opposite direction. Adam's empty subjects therefore do not support the performance limitation theory, and in as far as the latter cannot capture the non-finiteness effect to be discussed below, they contradict such a theory.

De Haan & Tuijnman (1988) observe that David, a Dutch child recorded at age 2;2, omits not only subjects, but also objects, and that he omits either of these elements only from utterance initial position, thus creating superficial V1 structures (cf. (2b)).[7] Poeppel & Wexler also report for Andreas, a German child recorded at age 2;1 that "subjects are never dropped when they are not in clause-initial position... If there is a non-subject in first position, then there is an overt post-verbal subject" (1993:14) but cf. (2c). On the basis of this generalization, de Haan & Tuijnman identify the null subjects in the speech of young children acquiring non-*pro*-drop languages with Topic Drop, a process familiar from adult Dutch and German which is subject to the same V1-restriction. Consider the (colloquial) adult German responses in (4-6) to the question in (3). A subject or object of a matrix clause can be elided if it precedes the finite verb, but not if it follows the latter (cf. (4)). In V2 languages, this pre-verbal position is usually taken to be Spec, CP, which among other things is a topic position (hence the name Topic Drop). Since Spec, CP also hosts fronted *wh*-elements, it follows directly that Topic Drop is excluded from *wh*-questions (see (5)). It is somewhat more mysterious why Topic Drop is impossible in all embedded clauses, even those which allow topicalization (cf. (6)).

(3) *Hans*:
Willst Du in den Zoo gehen, Nacktratten angucken?
want you in the zoo go naked mole rats at-look
'Do you want to go to the zoo and look at naked mole rats?'

(4) *Fritz:*
a. Nee, (ich) hab' *(die) schon gesehen.
   no I have them already seen
b. Nee, (die) hab' *(ich) schon gesehen.
   no them have I already seen
   'No, I have already seen them.'

(5) *Fritz:*
Warum sollte *(ich) *(sie) angucken gehen wollen?
why should I them at-look go want
'Why should I want to go look at them?'

(6) *Fritz:*
a. Nee, ich glaub' *(ich) hab' die schon gesehen.
   No, I believe I have them already seen
b. Nee, ich glaub' *(die) hab' ich schon gesehen.
   No, I believe they have I already seen
   'No, I think I've already seen them.'

De Haan & Tuijnman suggest that the Topic Drop analysis be extended to early child English although the latter does not allow object omissions (or allows them less frequently then Dutch and German). In fact, adult English has a process with apparently just the right properties. Like Topic Drop, Diary Drop (Haegeman, 1990) elides the clause-initial subject of a matrix declarative (cf. (7)) but not the clause-medial subject of a *wh*-question (cf. (8a)) or embedded sentence (cf. (8b)). Unlike Topic Drop, Diary Drop never elides objects (cf. (8c)), a difference that is probably due to the fact that English is not a V2 language.

(7) A very sensible day yesterday. Saw no-one.
(Virginia Woolf, *Diary* Vol. 5, from Rizzi, 1994a)

(8) a. Why should *(I) see anybody?
b. I'm glad that *(I) saw no-one.
c. No-one saw *(me).

The impossibility of Diary/Topic Drop in *wh*-questions (cf. (5) and (8a)) and embedded clauses (cf. (6) and (8b)) distinguishes these processes from Italian-style *pro*-drop, which is possible in both constructions (cf. (9)).

(9) a. Quante pietre hai preso?
how-many stones have-2SG taken
'How many stones did you take?'
b. Gianni mi ha chiesto se pensavo che tu avessi contattato nessuno.
Gianni me has asked whether thought-1SG that you had contacted anybody
'John asked me whether I thought that you had contacted anybody.'
(Italian, Rizzi, 1982:125,150)

Let us now briefly turn to the technical details of two Diary/Topic Drop analyses, i.e., those developed in Hyams (1994) and Rizzi (1994a).

According to Hyams (1994)[8], the null argument parameter determines language-specifically whether null arguments are licensed in A- or A'-positions, A-positions being theta-positions and specifiers construed with agreement. In languages like English or Dutch and German without rich agreement, null arguments must be identified via topic-identification which is possible only in Spec, CP (hence the V1 effect in Diary/Topic Drop). In English, the null argument parameter is set to "A-positions". Spec, CP is a non-thematic position and must therefore be construed with agreement in order to count as an A-position where null arguments are licensed. This is the case if the subject (bearing an agreement index) but not if the object (bearing no agreement index) has moved to Spec, CP.[9] The subject-object asymmetry in (7) and (8c) follows. In Dutch and German, the null argument parameter is set to "A'-positions". Null arguments are hence licensed (and identified) in Spec, CP regardless of whether they are subjects or objects, and both can be dropped (cf. (4a) and (4b)). Hyams assumes that the null argument parameter governing the licensing of null arguments is already correctly set during the early stages of the linguistic development and that it is merely the condition on the identification of null arguments which becomes more restrictive at a later point. She writes that "we do not expect to find a discrete shift in the development from null subject to non-null subject use since this is not the result of a parameter resetting. Rather, the change will be more gradual as the child determines the proper discourse conditions for topic identification in English" (1994:37). Below we will see that there are such discrete shifts in the development of Adam which suggests that the licensing of empty subjects is affected, although not via the resetting of a parameter.

Rizzi (1994a) proposes that the empty argument of Diary/Topic Drop is a null constant of category <-a,-p,-v> which must be a) located in an A-position and b) identified by a c-commanding discourse-linked null operator *if it can be* i.e., if the null constant is c-commanded by a specifier which could host such an operator. English does not have a discourse-linked null operator. Moreover, adult clauses are in general CPs in which all A-positions are c-commanded by Spec, CP, a specifier that could host a discourse-linked operator if one existed. Null constants of this type are therefore generally unavailable in adult English. Child clauses, on the other hand, may freely lack the CP-level. As a result, Spec, AgrSP, the S-structure (A-)position of the subject, is not c-commanded by a specifier and the subject can be a null constant in child English if and only if the CP is absent. All other A-positions are c-commanded by Spec, AgrSP, a potential host for an operator, and objects etc. cannot be null constants in child English irrespective of the presence or absence of CP. Rizzi (1994a:164) suggests that the requirement that adult clauses be CPs "may remain a weak principle, though, susceptible of being 'turned off' on abbreviated registers", thus accounting for adult English Diary Drop of the type illustrated in (7). As for Dutch/German, he assumes that these languages have a discourse-linked null operator which, if located in Spec, CP, can identify null constants in all argument positions.

Although strikingly different in their technical details, Hyams' and Rizzi's analyses both predict that early null subjects do not occur in *wh*-questions because Spec, CP, the landing site for *wh*-movement, is either occupied by an empty topic (Hyams) or altogether missing (Rizzi) in early null subject sentences. In fact, Valian's (1991) study of American children (see above for details) found only nine null subjects in 552 wh-questions (excluding subject questions). Crisma's (1992) analysis of the French child Philippe (age 2;1-

2;3) found only one null subject out of a total of 114 *wh*-questions (<1%, compare with 407 or 41% null subjects out of a total of 1002 declaratives). Clahsen, Kursawe, & Penke's (1995) study of nine German children (age 1;7-3;8) found null subjects in only 4% of their *wh*-questions with overt *wh*-elements. Radford on the other hand states that "null subject *wh*-questions are widely reported in the acquisition literature" (1994:4). In the next section, we will show that null subjects are indeed very frequent in Adam's *wh*-questions. In addition, we will show that null subjects are much more frequent in non-finite than in finite clauses, a conclusion that has been reached independently by many researchers. Like the performance limitation theory, the Diary/Topic Drop theory cannot capture this non-finiteness effect which is not attested in adult Diary/Topic Drop.

3. NULL SUBJECTS AND FINITENESS IN ADAM'S WH-QUESTIONS

Between File 1 recorded at age two years and three months and File 18 recorded at age two years and eleven months, Adam (Brown, 1973; MacWhinney, 1995) produced a total of 104 *wh*-questions without an overt subject. Some examples are given in (10) below.

(10) a. where go? ADAM01
 b. dining # where eat. ADAM02
 c. where find plier(s)? ADAM05
 d. what looking for? ADAM06
 e. what doing? ADAM07
 f. where zip it # uh? ADAM09
 g. why working? ADAM12
 h. what getting? ADAM12
 i. where going? ADAM13
 j. what call it? ADAM15
 k. why laughing at me? ADAM17
 l. where gone? ADAM18
 m. what think? ADAM18

Taking into consideration the fact that our corpus represents only a small fraction of Adam's utterances during this period (maybe 1%), we can project that Adam actually produced a large number of subjectless *wh*-questions (maybe 10,000). This immediately creates a serious problem for the

Diary/Topic Drop analysis, according to which such examples should be unattested.[10] The suggestion by Hyams (1994a, fn.13) that these cases are "derived via adjunction of the *wh*-phrase to CP" only evades the problem, especially since under this analysis the child seems to violate the *wh*-Criterion of Rizzi (1990:378) which goes back to May (1985:17) and states that "each wh-phrase must be in a Spec-Head relation with a +wh X^0". A further problem arises once we look in more detail at the distribution of null subjects in Adam's *wh*-questions, which we will do next.

For each of Adam's files, Table 2 lists the absolute number of overt personal subjects pronouns and missing subjects in *wh*-questions as well as the proportion of all *wh*-questions containing either an overt personal subject pronoun or no overt subject.[11]

Table 2.
Overt Personal Pronouns and Missing Subjects in Adam's Wh-Questions

	FINITE			NON-FINITE			ALL		
	overt	missing		overt	missing		overt	missing	
FILE	n	n	%	n	n	%	n	n	%
01	1	0	-	0	3	100	1	3	75
02	0	0	-	0	5	100	0	5	100
03	0	0	-	0	1	-	0	1	-
04	0	0	-	1	0	-	1	0	-
05	0	0	-	4	4	50	4	4	50
06	0	0	-	1	3	75	1	3	75
07	2	0	0	3	14	88	5	14	74
08	0	0	-	1	13	93	1	13	93
09	1	0	-	1	8	89	2	8	80
10	0	0	-	1	3	75	1	3	75
11	0	1	-	1	11	92	1	12	92
12	2	1	33	3	2	40	5	3	38
13	2	0	0	5	6	55	7	6	46
14	14	0	0	2	3	60	16	3	16
15	28	2	7	7	7	50	35	9	20
16	31	2	6	8	0	0	39	2	5
17	11	0	0	38	9	19	49	9	16
18	15	0	0	30	6	17	45	6	12
All	107	6	5	106	98	48	213	104	33

Overall, 104 *wh*-questions or 33% out of a total of 327 relevant examples lack an overt subject. A closer look reveals a clear non-finiteness effect: Whereas the subject is missing in 98 (or 48%) of all 204 non-finite *wh*-questions, it is missing in only six (or 5%) of all 113 finite *wh*-questions.[12] Subject drop is thus generally available only in non-finite sentences, but not in finite sentences. This becomes especially clear when we consider cases like (11) or (12) where the finite and non-finite versions of the same question appear side by side in adjoining or near-adjoining lines.[13] While the subject may be missing in the non-finite version, it is invariably overt in the finite version.

(11) a. where go?   ADAM11 line 913
      b. where dis goes.   ADAM11 line 914

(12) a. what d(o) you doing?   ADAM15 line 855
      b. what do [?] you doing? ADAM15 line 857
      c. what doing [?]?   ADAM15 line 876
      d. what d(o) you doing?   ADAM15 line 896

Before we proceed, let us take a look at the six counterexamples to the generalization that subject drop is restricted to non-finite clauses, i.e., clauses without subject-verb agreement. All of these counterexamples are listed below in (13).

(13) a. where can go?   ADAM11
      b. what said # Mommy?   ADAM12
      c. I simply where is?   ADAM15
      d. simply where is?   ADAM15
      e. where is.   ADAM16
      f. where is?   ADAM16

Note that none of these examples shows regular subject-verb agreement: Agreement is either altogether absent as with the modal in (13a) and the past tensed main verb in (13b) or realized in a suppletive verb stem as with the copula in (13c-f). Crucially missing are counterexamples of the form in (14), where a main verb bears regular subject-verb agreement, and the subject is null. In File 11, there are two (non-repetitive) examples with regular subject-verb agreement on the main verb and an overt demonstrative pronoun in subject position (cf. (11b)). Since in this file subject pronouns (including demonstrative pronouns, cf. (11a)) are dropped in 92% of all cases, then all other things being equal, we predict File 11 to contain 23 examples where the main verb bears regular subject-verb agreement and the subject is null (cf. (14)), whereas in fact, no examples of this type can be found. The systematic absence of examples like (14) shows that the presence versus absence of finiteness rather than the presence versus absence of auxiliaries governs the distribution of null subjects in child language. We will return to this point in Section 6.

(14)   *where goes?   unattested

Not only do null subjects practically never occur in finite clauses, but the proportion of null subjects in non-finite clauses also dramatically decreases with acquisition of finiteness and agreement. Judging from Table 2, finiteness is not yet productively used in *wh*-questions in Files 01-11[14] During this period, no two consecutive files contain finite clauses and the latter are overall rare (5 examples in 11 files). During the same period, null subjects are very frequent in non-finite *wh*-clauses, averaging 83%. Makowski (1993) reports that Adam's first agreeing and contrasting uses of *be*- and *do*-forms (which do not yet meet her criteria for 'productivity') occur in Files 10 and 11, respectively. Beginning with File 12, all files contain finite clauses and the latter became more numerous overall (108 examples in seven files). At the same time, the proportion of null subjects in non-finite *wh*-questions drops dramatically from 92% in File 11 to 40% in File 12 (or from 83% in Files 01-11 to 51% in Files 12-15). Makowski argues that agreement reaches the productive stage in File 15. The first productive use of agreement immediately precedes the second dramatic drop in the rate of null subjects in non-finite *wh*-questions from 50% in File 15 to 0% in File 16 (or from 51% 12-15 to 16% in Files 16-18). We will argue below in Section 6 that there is a causal relation between the acquisition of finiteness or, to be more precise, agreement and the loss of null subjects. Concretely, we will propose that as long as agreement is not acquired, clauses lack the AgrSP-level and *pro* is licensed in Spec, VP in accordance with the theory of Economy of Projection. Once agreement is acquired, AgrSP must be projected and the theory of Economy of Projection requires Spec, AgrSP to be filled by an overt subject, a situation that excludes *pro*.

The fact that empty subjects are much more frequent in non-finite *wh*-questions (which only contain main verbs) than in finite *wh*-questions (which contain an auxiliary and hence potentially an extra VP-element[15]) and especially the existence of n-tuples like the one in (12) intuitively suggest that there is no obvious link between missing subjects and long VPs in the sense of Bloom (1990, 1993). This intuition is confirmed by a formal comparison of the average VP-length in *wh*-questions without overt subject with the average VP-length in *wh*-questions with an overt personal pronoun as the subject:

Table 3.
VP-Length and Subject Type in Adam's Wh-Questions

	VP-LENGTH (WORDS)	
FILE	Empty Subject	Pronoun Subject
1-11	2.194	2.294
12-15	2.286	2.381
16-18	3.353	2.614
All	2.400	2.519

Overall, the difference in average VP-length is very small and, most importantly, in the wrong direction (*wh*-questions without overt subject tend to have slightly shorter VPs than *wh*-questions with an overt personal pronoun as the subject). Similar non-significant differences in the wrong direction appear if we limit the comparison to the files with the highest or second-highest rate of subject-drop (Files 01-11 and 12-15, respectively). It is only in the files with the lowest rate of subject-drop (Files 16-18) that VPs in *wh*-questions without overt subjects are longer than VPs in *wh*-questions with an overt personal pronoun as the subject, and this difference is almost significant according to a t-test ($t = 2.046$, $p = 0.056$).[16] What this means is that the performance limitations theory cannot explain those null subjects that occur in Files 01-15 where subject drop is a common phenomenon. Such a theory may be able to explain those null subjects that occur in Files 16-18 where subject drop has become rare. It is of course entirely conceivable that children employ more than one process to omit subjects, and this would account for the apparent gradualness in the loss of early null subjects that has been reported by Valian (1991), Bloom (1993) and others and that can -- to a limited degree -- also be observed in Table 2 above (But note the dramatic, non-gradual decline of the null subject rate after File 11 and after File 15 to be discussed in Section 6). The most important conclusion is that the bulk of null subjects in Adam's *wh*-questions is not amenable to a performance limitations analysis *à la* Bloom or Valian. Since these examples cannot be due to Diary/Topic Drop *à la* Hyams or Rizzi either, a different account is called for. In Section 6 we develop such an account based on the assumption that the missing subjects in question are in fact *pro*s which are licensed as long as AgrSP is not projected.

Other children produced fewer *wh*-questions than Adam and the evidence from these children is therefore often less compelling, but in all cases, a sizable portion of the *wh*-questions lacked an overt subject and these examples were in general non-finite. Claire (Hill 1982), a child acquiring English recorded nine times between ages 2;0 and 2;2, may be typical in this respect. Radford calculated that "39% (11/28) of [Claire]'s questions containing overt wh-words have null subjects" (1994:4). Again, we find a clear non-finiteness effect. An exhaustive list of Claire's types of *wh*-questions containing either an overt personal pronoun as the subject or no overt subject at all is given in (15) - (17). While non-finite *wh*-questions often lack an overt subject pronoun (compare (15) with (16)), the subject pronoun is never missing in finite *wh*-questions (cf. (17)).

(15)   a. where go?   CLAIRE01
         b. what doing?   CLAIRE01
         c. where tickle?   CLAIRE03
         d. what do?   CLAIRE06

(16)   where it?   CLAIRE02

(17)   a. Jane what is it?   CLAIRE06
         b. where is it?   CLAIRE08

It is instructive to compare the distribution of (the tokens of) overt and null subjects file by file throughout the corpus. To this end, consider Table 4 (Note that Files 4 and 5 were lost due to a malfunctioning tape recorder).

Table 4.
Overt Personal Pronouns and Missing Subjects in Claire's Wh-Questions

	FINITE		NON-FINITE	
	overt	missing	overt	missing
FILE	n	n	n	n
01	0	0	0	4
02	0	0	1	3
03	0	0	0	1
06	1	0	0	3
07	0	0	0	0
08	1	0	0	0
09	0	0	0	0
ALL	2	0	1	11

Null subjects occur only in Files 01 to 06, but not in Files 07 to 09, i.e., after the first finite *wh*-clauses have appeared in Files 06 and 08. Hill reports for File 01 that "when asked 'what's Kitty doing' Claire responded 'what doing'. When asked 'where's the doggie?' she responded 'where doggie?'". This behavior persisted until File 06 where 'what room is this' was echoed as 'what room this'. In Session 7 Claire used the question form 'who's this?' for the first time... Also in Session 7 she used the form 'where did the chair go?'" (1982:64ff). From what little we know about Claire, it thus appears that a major change concerning the finiteness of her *wh*-questions occurred around File 07, and it is at this very same point in her development that null subjects seem to disappear from her *wh*-questions. Although Claire's data perhaps do not constitute convincing evidence in their own right, these data are clearly compatible with the generalizations reached earlier in connection with Adam's data: Null subjects are restricted to non-finite (non-agreeing) clauses and vanish from the latter once finite (agreeing) clauses begin to take over.

Similar statements can be made with respect to the other children in the CHILDES database, although their material is again sparser and less easily quantifiable. A few of their subject-drop examples are given in (18) below. Radford supplies additional examples: "Klima & Bellugi (1966:200) report *What doing?* as a typical Stage I question; Plunkett (1992: 58) reports that one of the earliest *wh*-questions produced by her son was *Where go?*"" (1994:4).

(18) a. what doing?   EVE14
      b. where gone?   SAR15
      c. what got?   NAO31
      d. when eat eggs.   NIN01

It is interesting to note that children with language impairments appear to display the same pattern. For Penny, a child suffering from Down's Syndrome (Tager-Flusberg *et al.*, 1990; MacWhinney, 1995), overt subject pronouns are optional in non-finite *wh*-questions (like (19)) but obligatory in finite *wh*-questions (cf. (20)). 'B', a child diagnosed with Special Language Impairment from the Leonard-corpus on CHILDES (MacWhinney, 1995), produced numerous *wh*-questions without an overt subject. Like those shown in (21), none of them was finite.

(19) a. how you do this?   PENNY02 line 349
      b. how do this?   PENNY02 line 353

(20) a. where is it?   PENNY02
      b. *where is?   unattested

(21) a. what way go   SLIB
      b. how get it on?   SLIB
      c. how play that game?   SLIB
      d. where put it at?   SLIB
      e. where go to?   SLIB

There is another environment in English where finiteness is always visible even in the present tense. Like (non-subject) *wh*-questions, finite negative declaratives require an auxiliary, modal, or expletive. In the first ten files, Adam produced twenty non-finite and only one finite negative declarative without an overt subject (Note that the overall number of negative declaratives is much lower than the overall number of *wh*-questions). After File 10, subjectless negative declaratives become very rare. It is not always easy to distinguish non-finite negative declaratives from negative imperatives (which regularly omit the subject in adult English), but examples like those in (22) do not easily lend themselves to an imperative interpretation. As was the case with *wh*-questions there are cases where the finite and non-finite versions of the same negative declarative appear side by side in adjoining lines and the subject is absent in the non-finite version but present in the finite version (compare, (23) with (11) and (12)). In sum, the evidence from Adam's *wh*-questions and negative declaratives suggests that in both sentence types, null subjects are restricted to the same environment (non-finite clauses) and start disappearing at roughly the same point in the development (Files 12 and 11, respectively). In the remainder of this paper, we will say little on the issue of null subjects in Adam's negative declaratives, a topic to which we plan to return in future work. Suffice it to say that the analysis we propose in Section 6 covers null subjects in all non-finite clauses, including non-finite negative declaratives.

(22) a. no heavy.   ADAM03
      b no rocking.   ADAM05
      c. no singing song.   ADAM06
      d. no want dat op(en).   ADAM07
      e. no want stand head.   ADAM08

(23) a. no wan(t) (t)a sit dere.   ADAM07 line 1799
      b. no I don't want to sit seat.   ADAM07 line 1803

Sano & Hyams (1994) also observe a non-finiteness effect in early child English null subject sentences, although their corpus is more inclusive than ours and does not focus on *wh*-questions and negative declaratives.[17] Sano & Hyams report that the proportion of null subjects in sentences containing a copula (Table 5) or modal (Table 6), i.e., in necessarily finite utterances, is much lower than the overall proportion of null subjects in finite and non-finite utterances together (Table 7) and conclude that "it is the availability of root infinitives that makes null subjects possible in child English" (1994:545). We agree with this conclusion, but the perspective of the analysis we will propose in Section 6 is quite different from that of Sano & Hyams.

Table 5.
The Proportion of Sentences with Null Subjects out of Sentences Containing an Uncontracted Copula (from Sano & Hyams, 1994:548)

CHILD	FILE	AGE	am	are	is
Eve	01-20	1;6-2;3	0/4	0/36	0/109
Adam	01-20	2;3.4-3;0.11	0/1	0/71	13/114 (=11.4%)
Nina	01-07,09-21	1;11.16-2;4.12	0/0	0/19	2/50 (=4%)

Table 6.
The Proportion of Lexical Subjects in Sentences Containing the Modals (from Valian 1991) (from Sano & Hyams 1994:549)

	GROUP I	GROUP II	GROUP III	GROUP IV
Ave. Age	2;0	2;5	2;5	2;7
Ave. MLU	1.77	2.49	3.39	4.22
% Overt Subj.	94	95	98	99

Table 7.
The Overall Proportion of Sentences with Null Subjects (from Sano & Hyams, 1994:549)

CHILD	AGE		% Ø-SUBJECT
Eve	1;6-2;1		26%
Adam	2;5-3;0		41%
Nina	1;11.16	File Nina01	44%
	2;2.6	File Nina13	11%
(EVE & ADAM: out of sentences with lexical verbs, from Hyams & Wexler, 1993; NINA: out of all utterances, from Pierce, 1992)			

The non-finiteness effect discussed above also surfaces in the speech of children acquiring languages other than English. In their analysis of two German children, Katrin (age 1;5) and Nicole (age 1;8), Rohrbacher & Vainikka (1994) report that the subject was missing in 84% and 63% of all non-finite clauses and 36% of all finite clauses, respectively. Poeppel & Wexler (1993:15) found that Andreas, another child acquiring German recorded at age 2;1, left out the subject in 13 (or 35%) of his 37 non-finite utterances with the highest verb in V-final position as opposed to 17 (or 9%) of his 197 finite utterances with the highest verb in V2 position. Krämer gives even more divergent numbers for the same child: "Andreas uses overt subjects with infinitives 31.7% of the time [=32/101], and with finite verbs 87.[1]% of the time [=229/263]" (1993:199). Krämer also investigated Maarten, a Flemish child recorded at age 1;11 with overt subjects in 11 of his 100 infinitives and 69 (or 75%) of his 92 finite clauses, and Thomas, a Dutch child recorded between ages 2;3 and 2;8 with overt subjects in between 5.5% and 12.5% of his infinitives and between 66.1% and 78.1% of his finite clauses. The weighted average of overt subjects in root infinitives versus that in finite clauses in the speech of the Dutch children Peter (1;9-2;4) and Niek (2;7-3;6) is 66.4% versus 88.2% and 39.6% versus 82.9%, respectively (see Wijnen, 1994). Finally, Haegeman (1994) found that Hein (Dutch, 2;4-3;1) omitted subjects in 86% of his root infinitives but only 32% of his finite clauses. These results point in the same direction as our own results: Subjects are much more often missing from non-finite clauses than from finite clauses. The fact that the studies summarized in this paragraph consistently reported higher percentages of missing subjects in finite clauses than we did is probably due to their failure to exclude possible cases of Diary/Topic Drop (i.e., declaratives). The availability of Diary/Topic Drop in declaratives moreover explains why Adam continues to omit subjects in declaratives after he ceased to do so in *wh*-questions. In replicating our results, Bromberg & Wexler (1995:233) found that Adam omits the subject at an equal rate in declaratives and *wh*-questions (91% versus 94%) in File 11 (i.e., the last file in which we found subject omissions in *wh*-questions to be very frequent), he omits subjects much more often in declaratives than in *wh*-questions (16% versus 2%) in File 19 (i.e., after the last file we examined when subject omissions in *wh*-questions have become very infrequent). This again suggests that more than one process is responsible for subject drop in early child language; we will argue below that *pro*-drop is one of these processes and Diary/Topic Drop may be another one. The important point is that Diary/Topic Drop cannot account for all subject omissions in child language.

Let us sum up this section by saying that we found null subjects to be frequent in Adam's *wh*-questions. This finding is problematic for the Diary/Topic Drop theory which wrongly predicts that *wh*-Questions without overt subjects are rare or non-existent.[18] Equally problematic for the processing limitations theory is the fact that the VPs of *wh*-questions without overt subject are not longer than the VPs of *wh*-questions with overt pronominal subjects. Neither theory can explain why Adam freely omits subjects in non-finite (non-agreeing) *wh*-questions and negative declaratives but almost never does so in the finite (agreeing) counterparts of these constructions. Before we can develop an analysis that successfully addresses these questions, we have to briefly discuss the phenomenon of non-finite root clauses in early child language more generally.

4. ROOT INFINITIVES

The proper analysis of root infinitives[19] in child language is currently the subject of a vigorous debate, much of which does not concern itself directly with the issue of early null subjects. But since we have just seen in the previous section that early null subjects are largely restricted to non-finite contexts, we might expect a convincing account for root infinitives to significantly contribute to the explanation for early null subjects. We therefore now briefly turn our attention to the debate around root infinitives. Given the large and steadily growing volume of the literature on root infinitives on the one hand and the limitations of this paper on the other hand, the following comments must remain sketchy.

Non-finite root declaratives are often claimed to be universally ungrammatical in adult language, and the challenge is to explain why they are present in such large numbers in child language. According to one school of thought, the problem is only an apparent one and young children's 'root infinitives' are really finite utterances containing an empty finite auxiliary (Boser *et al.*, 1992).[20] Poeppel & Wexler (1993:16) point out that such an empty finite auxiliary should be able to license object- or adverb-topicalization in child German root infinitives and that Andreas, the German child they analyze, does in fact not produce any nonfinite object- or adverb-first sentences, contrary to the prediction of the empty auxiliary theory. Likewise, in their study of natural speech from 30 German children from 21 to 34 months and elicited imitations from 40 German two- to four-year-olds, Boser *et al.* found that "there is no instance in the data of a non-subject initial sentence with a null auxiliary" (1992:62). In other words, examples of the type *Kuchen Mama backen* 'cake mommy bake' are unattested. Boser *et al.* explain the absence of topicalization in root infinitives by assuming that empty finite auxiliaries, like empty pronouns, must be licensed (i.e., receive their φ-features) under S-structural Spec-head agreement. The S-structure position of finite verbs in German is Comp, where they Spec-head agree with a subject in Spec, CP, but not with a non-subject in Spec, CP. Hence an empty finite auxiliary will be possible only in utterances with the order subject-first. Boser *et al.* note that the empty auxiliary theory thus predicts "that a null pronominal specifier can be licensed by an overt X^0 head sharing the relevant set of feature specifications, and symmetrically, a null pronominal X^0 category can be licensed by an overt specifier sharing its relevant feature specifications... But instances where both head and specifier are null are not licensed..." (1992:61).[21] More concretely, an empty auxiliary can receive its φ-features from, and thus be licensed by, an overt subject and an empty subject can receive its φ-features from, and thus be licensed by, an overt verb, but an empty auxiliary and an empty subject cannot receive any φ-features from each other and both remain therefore unlicensed. This means that the empty auxiliary theory wrongly predicts subjectless root infinitives to be unattested. For example, (2a) could only have the ungrammatical S-structure in (24) below, where both [$_{Subj}$ *e*] and [$_{Aux}$ *e*] remain unlicensed.

(24)   [$_{AgrSP}$ [$_{Subj}$ *e*] [$_{AgrS'}$ [$_{Aux}$ *e*] [$_{VP}$ eating popcorn]]]

In Section 3, we have shown that subjectless root infinitives are in fact very common in child language. Since the empty auxiliary theory incorrectly rules them out, we must reject this theory.

Like Boser *et al.*, Wexler (1994) assumes that root infinitives are in fact finite clauses with the full array of functional projections, but unlike the former, he suggests that it is the seemingly non-finite overt verb itself which is the finite element of these clauses. Wexler proposes that at the stage where children produce root infinitives, they cannot distinguish different tense values and therefore take both agreeing finite verbs and non-agreeing infinitivals to be finite forms with strong (abstract) AgrS in the first case and weak (abstract) AgrS in the second case. In accordance with the theory developed in Chomsky (1992), the child overtly raises the agreeing 'finite' verbs to AgrS at S-structure but does so only covertly at LF with the non-agreeing 'infinitivals'.[22] This account is very successful in dealing with languages like French, German or Dutch where finite but not non-finite verbs overtly raise to AgrS in the adult language and where this distinction between finite verb raising and non-finite verb *in situ* is already in place in child language at the optional root infinitive stage (cf. Déprez & Pierce, 1993; Poeppel & Wexler, 1993; Rohrbacher & Vainikka, 1994 and many others). The overt/covert verb raising account is less successful in dealing with languages like English where neither agreeing finite nor non-agreeing non-finite main verbs overtly raise to AgrS in the adult language and where there is no reason to believe that either of them do so in child language at the optional infinitive stage. Following Pollock (1989), it is generally agreed that the obligatory position of the main verb after the sentential negation marker (cf. (25)) or an adverb (cf. (26)) indicates that adult English main verbs do not leave the VP in overt syntax. The overt/covert verb raising theory states that at the optional infinitive stage, English children raise agreeing finite forms to AgrS. This theory therefore predicts that children at the optional infinitive stage consistently produce sentences of the type illustrated in (25b) and (26b) instead of sentences of the type illustrated in (25a) and (26a), which does not seem to be the case. Thus Roeper notes that "Adam, like all others, shows *do*-insertion in the adult manner" (1993:82) and that "there are no instances of an adverb between the [main] verb and direct object" (19993:80). The examples in (25a) and (26a) were produced by Adam and are taken from Roeper (1993).[23]

(25)   a. [$_{AgrSP}$ I [$_{AgrS'}$ didn't [$_{NegP}$ e [$_{VP}$ see no tigers]]]]
         b. *[$_{AgrSP}$ I[$_{AgrS'}$ saw$_i$ [$_{NegP}$ not [$_{VP}$ t$_i$ no tigers]]]

(26)   a. [$_{AgrSP}$ He [$_{AgrS'}$ e [$_{VP}$ always [$_{VP}$ closes doors]]]
         b. *[$_{AgrSP}$ He [$_{AgrS'}$ closes$_i$ [$_{VP}$ always [$_{VP}$ t$_i$ doors]]]]

Another problem for the overt/covert verb raising analysis stems from the by now standard assumption that the (abstract) strength of AgrS depends on the (concrete) morphological richness of agreement (see Rohrbacher, 1993 and references cited there). Since agreeing finite main verbs in child English (with strong AgrS according to Wexler) show no more concrete morphological agreement than their counterparts in adult English (with weak AgrS), the overt/covert verb raising analysis has to conclude that the child determines the richness of agreement/strength of AgrS in ways that are fundamentally different from those in the adult grammar. If Rohrbacher

(1993, 1994) is correct in arguing that UG principles determine whether AgrS is strong or weak, this conclusion entails that children may violate core properties of UG, an undesirable consequence. Finally, note that it is unclear what moves English children to reset the AgrS value from strong to weak.

This is not to say that the main insights of Wexler's analysis could not be retained under a slightly different guise. Thus one might assume with Wexler that root infinitives are in fact finite and contain all functional projections, that children at this stage are unaware of the different values for Tns and that they hence freely produce agreeing 'finite' verbs and non-agreeing 'infinitivals', taking in fact both to be finite. Let us further assume that AgrS already has the adult value at this stage and that non-agreeing infinitivals (even if they are perceived as finite by the children) have weak AgrS and therefore stay *in situ* in all languages under consideration. In adult and child English, the agreeing finite forms of main verbs also have weak AgrS. As a result, they may not overtly raise to AgrS either. In adult and child French, German and Dutch, the agreeing finite forms have strong features in AgrS (French) and/or Comp (German and Dutch) to which they raise. It is not straightforward how this approach could account for the non-finiteness (or non-agreement) effect evident in early child English null subject sentences, since agreeing and non-agreeing child English utterances now share the same abstract features (finite Tns and weak AgrS). But this problem might not be insurmountable. What is more important in the context of this section is that there is evidence that at least some functional projections are missing in root infinitives and it is to this evidence that we now turn.

Note first that child English root infinitivals virtually never display the infinitival marker *to*. Under the reasonable assumption that *to* is base-generated in Tns, its absence from root infinitives suggests that this head and its projection, TP, are missing in this construction (see Radford, 1994). Next, it has been observed that root infinitivals typically do not contain auxiliaries. In adult English, modal auxiliaries are arguably base-generated in Tns and Guasti (1993) proposes that aspectual auxiliaries, too, are licensed by this head. If so, the absence of auxiliaries from root infinitives serves as a further indicator that TP is not projected here (see Haegeman, 1994; Radford, 1994; and Rizzi, 1994b). As for AgrS(P), Pierce (1992:87) reports that "from 88 to 99% of all subject clitics" produced by the four French children in her study "occur in overtly tensed clauses". Similarly, Haegeman

(1994) found that Hein (Dutch, 2;4-3;1) produced 472 (or 13%) subject clitics in 3768 finite clauses but none in 78 root infinitives. Assuming that subject clitics are either base-generated in or adjoined to AgrS, their absence from root infinitives can be interpreted as a sign that the latter lack AgrS and its projection, AgrSP (see Haegeman, 1994).[24] With arguments like this in mind, Rizzi (1994b) proposes the following account for root infinitives. Suppose Tns is a variable that needs to be bound. This can be done either selectively by finite features on the clause itself (in finite clauses) or a higher clause (in embedded infinitives) or unselectively by an operator (in non-finite, non-declarative matrix clauses, see Rizzi's Italian example *Che cosa dire in questi casi?* 'What to say in these cases?'). For matrix declaratives, only the first option is available which explains why these clauses must be finite in adult language. Young children on the other hand, may simply omit TP in which case there is no Tns variable to bind. In fact, Rizzi assumes that when this happens, none of the projections above TP can be present either. Given the order of projections in (27), this means that root infinitives lack not only TP and AgrSP, but also NegP and CP.

(27) $[_{CP}$ Comp $[_{AgrSP}$ AgrS $[_{NegP}$ Neg $[_{TP}$ Tns $[_{AgrOP}$ AgrO VP $]]]]]$

If NegP and CP must be absent in root infinitives, the latter cannot be negated or questioned. This conclusion seems to be supported by the following findings. Friedemann (1992) reports that only six out of 137 negative sentences in the data from Philippe and Grégoire (French) were root infinitives. Hamann (this volume) found 167 positive and no negative root infinitives in Katrin's file and 204 positive and only 14 negative root infinitives in Andreas's file (both children are acquiring German). According to Crisma (1992), none of the 35 *wh*-questions (but 117 of the 491 declaratives) in the first recordings from the French child Philippe (2;1 to 2;2) were root infinitives. For child Dutch, Haegeman reports that "in the entire Hein corpus there were 90 WH-questions, 88 of which were finite and only 2 were non-finite" (1994:17). Finally, Weissenborn (1992) claims that there are no *wh*-root infinitives in child German. But the data presented in Section 3 of this article and in particular the examples in (10) through (23) clearly show that child English root infinitives can be negative declaratives or *wh*-questions. Moreover, Haegeman (1994) found that while Hein negated root infinitives less often than finite clauses (5.2% versus 15.7%), negative root infinitives were a relatively robust phenomenon and the presence of adverbs that adjoin to NegP (or ΣP in non-negative sentences) in root infinitives further suggests that NegP can be present in child Dutch root infinitives. In keeping with Rizzi's theory, Haegeman proposes that NegP is projected above TP in the Romance languages and below TP in the Germanic languages. However, we see no theoretical reason for Rizzi's assumption that the omission of TP and AgrSP implies the omission of all functional projections above them and the empirical evidence for this assumption is equivocal at this point. We will therefore adopt a modified version of Rizzi's proposal according to which root infinitives are possible in early child language because unlike adults, young children can omit TP and other functional projections, the most notable among which is AgrSP. We will assume contra Rizzi that when they omit TP and AgrSP, young children can keep other, higher functional projections such as CP and NegP.[25] Here the underlying idea is that driven by considerations of Economy of Projection (see the next section), young children initially instantiate syntactic projections if and only if features of the head of that projection are overtly realized. In root infinitives, there is no overt material reflecting the presence of TP or AgrSP (i.e., no overt tense or agreement) and these levels are therefore initially not instantiated. Whenever an utterance contains negation or a fronted *wh*-element, there is overt material reflecting the presence of NegP or CP and these levels are therefore instantiated. For any given utterance, the instantiation of each functional projection is independent from that of all others and NegP and CP can therefore be projected in the absence of TP and AgrSP and vice versa.[26] In effect, young children are using two grammars, one with inflectional projections (in finite clauses) and one without inflectional projections (in non-finite clauses). The simultaneous use of multiple grammars by a single person is well documented in historical linguistics (see Kroch, 1990; Pintzuck, 1991; and Santorini, 1989) and bi-dialectalism and can therefore not be *a priori* excluded in language acquisition. Moreover, we will argue in the next section that central features of each grammar in question and in particular the absence or presence of AgrSP are also attested in adult languages such as English (with AgrSP) or Japanese (without AgrSP). Thus, the children presumably only make use of UG-options when they project or fail to project AgrSP (and TP). However, multiple grammars are in general unstable (see the sources cited above) and only the grammar with inflectional projections is compatible with all the input data and tensed/agreeing clauses in particular. When the child's productive use of contrasting agreement across different types of verbs signals that agreement has been recognized as a rule-based grammatical process, the grammar without inflectional projections is abandoned and TP and AgrSP become obligatory in all utterances, even non-finite ones. At this point, the option of root infinitives vanishes for the reason outlined in Rizzi (1994b): The tense variable introduced by TP must be bound and in matrix declaratives, this can be done only by finite features on these clauses themselves. In conclusion, when very young children are using inflectional projections (and they seem to do so at a very early stage if not the earliest observed stage, see e.g., Déprez & Pierce, 1993; Poeppel & Wexler, 1993; Rohrbacher & Vainikka, 1994), then they do it because they are also using the inflectional morphology which motivates these projections. When they do not use this inflectional morphology (as in root infinitives), then they chose a more economical structure without the corresponding inflectional projections.

5. ADULT PRO-DROP AND ECONOMY OF PROJECTION

Our analysis of young children's null subjects will be modeled on a theory of adult *pro*-drop that was recently developed by Speas (1994) and that is in turn based on work by Rohrbacher (1993) on the morpho-syntax of verbal paradigms. They have addressed an old question in linguistic theory: What is the status of paradigms? Paradigms continue to play an important role in theoretical morphology but no longer have any formal status in theoretical syntax. The core concept in Rohrbacher (1993) is that verbal paradigms in 'strongly' inflecting languages such as Spanish have independent lexical entries (and the affixes expressing subject-verb agreement are generated in AgrS) whereas verbal paradigms in 'weakly' inflecting languages such as English do not have such independent lexical entries (and the affixes expressing subject-verb agreement are generated in V). A more formal version of this generalization is given in (28).[27]

(28)   AgrS is a referential category with lexically listed affixes in exactly those languages where regular subject-verb agreement minimally distinctively marks all referential AgrS-features such that in at least one number of one tense, the person features [1st] and [2nd] are distinctively marked.

Behind this generalization lies the following reasoning.[28] The person features of AgrS are referential in that they determine whether the subject refers to the speaker(s), the hearer(s), or somebody else. If and only if both of these features are distinctively marked in an agreement paradigm, the latter becomes itself referential. Under the reasonable assumption that the lexicon lists all and only the referential elements of a language, agreement paradigms which distinctively mark both of the person features will have separate lexical entries and agreement paradigms which fail to distinctively mark at least one of the person features will not. If these ideas are on the right track, the agreement affixes in 'strongly' inflecting languages are inserted into AgrS at D-Structure and the verb raises to this position at S-Structure because affixes cannot stand on their own.[29] The result is overt V-to-AgrS raising. The agreement affixes in 'weakly' inflecting languages on the other hand are generated directly on the verb, either already in the lexicon as proposed in Chomsky (1992) or post-syntactically in a spell-out component as proposed in Anderson (1992). In either case, AgrS is empty at D-structure in this second type of language. Since Lasnik's Filter is inoperative in the absence of affixes under AgrS, there is no motivation for overt V-to-AgrS raising and this process is delayed until LF where the abstract agreement features of the verb must be checked (see Chomsky, 1992). The result is covert V-to-AgrS raising. We have arrived at the following two-way distinction:

(29)   a. Languages with strong overt agreement morphology have an AgrS-node that is filled at D- and S-structure.
           b. Languages with weak overt agreement morphology have an AgrS-node that is empty at D- and S-structure.

To these two types of languages, Speas (1994) adds a third type to which languages like Japanese belong:

(29)   c. Languages with no overt agreement morphology have no AgrS-node.

The idea behind (29c) is that languages without any overt agreement morphology also lack abstract agreement features and therefore AgrS(P) would have no role to play in these languages.

Based on the three-way distinction in (29), Speas develops a *pro*-drop theory that is arguably superior to its predecessors since it does not make use of a special licensing condition for *pro*. Instead, the 'licensing' of *pro* follows in Speas' theory from an independently motivated principle of UG, the Principle of Economy of Projection.

It is well-known that referential *pro* subjects[30] are licensed in languages like Japanese (see (30a)) without any overt agreement at all and in languages like Spanish (see (30b)) with strong overt agreement, but not in languages like English (see (30c)) with weak overt agreement.

(30) a. *pro* sasimi -o taberu-Ø.
        sashimi -ACC eat   [Japanese]
        'She eats sashimi.'

      b. *pro* habl $\left\{\begin{array}{l}\text{-o}\\\text{-as}\\\text{-a}\end{array}\right\}$ Espanol.   [Spanish]

      c. $\left\{\begin{array}{l}\text{I}\\\text{you}\\\text{she}\end{array}\right\}$ speak $\left\{\begin{array}{l}\text{-Ø}\\\text{-Ø}\\\text{-s}\end{array}\right\}$ Spanish.   [English]

Speas proposes that this state of affairs follows from the language typology in (29) in combination with a Principle of Economy of Projection of which we give a reformulated version in (31).

(31)   *Principle of Economy of Projection*
             Project XP only if its head X^0 or its specifier Spec, XP has independent semantic or phonetic content.

The intuition behind the Principle of Economy of Projection is that a phrase can be projected only if it contributes something to the utterance (i.e., if it is needed). In other words, a maximal projection is never vacuous and always contains more than its (independently motivated) complement. Economy of Projection thus allows a specifier position of a projection to remain radically empty only if the head of that projection contains phonetic or semantic material. Conversely, the head of a projection may remain radically empty only if the specifier of that projection contains phonetic or semantic material. Economy of Projection rules out any structure in which both the specifier and the head of a projection are radically empty since in such a structure the projection would be indistinguishable from its complement and considerations of economy dictate that it not be projected. We believe that this proposal is very much in the spirit of the Bare Phrase Structure Theory developed in Chomsky (1994).

As briefly mentioned, Speas assumes that AgrSP is projected in exactly those languages that have some overt morphological reflex of verb-argument agreement, i.e., for example Spanish and English but not Japanese. Being a purely relational projection, neither AgrS nor Spec, AgrSP ever has independent semantic content and one of them must be phonetically realized in order to satisfy Economy of Projection. AgrS can be phonetically realized only by an overt affix that has been base-generated there. Note in particular that "verb movement by itself is not sufficient to license null subjects... The projection of AGRP [has] to be licensed independently *as an AGRP*, before it [can] become the landing site of verb movement" (Speas, 1994 her emphasis). With perhaps the exception of expletive subjects, nothing is ever base-generated in Spec, AgrSP and this position can be phonetically realized only by an overt subject that has to move there for feature checking. Moreover, since phrases can be projected only during overt syntax, the phonetic realization of AgrS or Spec, AgrSP must take place at D- or S-structure. Recall from (29a) that in languages like Spanish with strong overt agreement morphology, AgrS is phonetically filled at D- and S-structure by an agreement affix. Therefore, Economy of Projection allows Spec, AgrSP to remain phonetically empty throughout syntax and subject *pro* is licensed in these languages (cf. (32a)). Recall further from (29b) that in languages like English with weak overt agreement morphology, AgrS is phonetically (and semantically) empty at D- and S-structure since the agreement affix is generated directly on the verb and the latter does not raise to AgrS in overt syntax. Therefore, Economy of Projection forces Spec, AgrSP to be phonetically filled with an overt subject at S-structure (cf. (32b)) and subject *pro* is not licensed in these languages (cf. (32c)).[31]

(32)

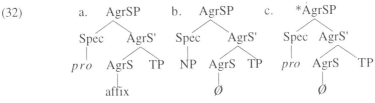

Recall from (29c) that in languages like Japanese with no overt agreement morphology, there is no AgrS node and hence no AgrSP that must conform to the Principle of Economy of Projection in (31). Let us assume that in these languages, TP constitutes the highest inflectional projection and Spec, TP constitutes the S-structural position of the subject.[32] Unlike AgrSP, TP is not a purely relational projection. Instead, its head always has independent semantic content in the form of a feature bundle which specifies the temporal reference of the clause. Spec, TP can therefore remain phonetically empty and subject *pro* is licensed in these languages. This is illustrated in (33).

(33)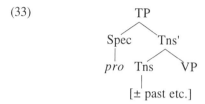

As for the identification of *pro*, we will assume that UG provides two different mechanisms. In languages with overt agreement morphology, *pro* will have to be identified via the agreement morphology.[33] In languages without overt agreement, *pro* will have to be identified by the discourse. At present, the formal properties of discourse identification remain to be worked out. Space limitations prevent us from addressing this less-than-well-understood topic; see Kawasaki (1993) for one approach to this problem.

Table 8 below summarizes the relation between agreement morphology and *pro*-drop in the system of Rohrbacher (1993, 1994) and Speas (1994). This table already anticipates the analysis we will propose in the next section for child English finite clauses (which like adult English show weak agreement and hence do not allow *pro*-drop) and child English non-finite clauses (which like adult Japanese do not show any agreement at all and hence allow *pro*-drop).

Table 8.
The Relation between Agreement Morphology and Pro-Drop

Agreement Morphology	AgrS	Spec, AgrSP filled	empty	*Pro*-drop
strong e.g., Spanish	filled	yes	yes	yes
weak e.g., English, child English finite clauses	empty	yes	no	no
none e.g., Japanese, child English root infinitives	–	–	–	yes

6. AN ECONOMY-DRIVEN APPROACH TO EARLY NULL SUBJECTS

In Section 3, we showed that early null subject sentences display a non-finiteness or non-agreement effect. This effect is most pronounced in *wh*-questions, where null subjects cannot be due to Diary/Topic Drop or to performance limitation induced deletion. We argue that these null subjects are instead instances of *pro*, and this conclusion naturally extends to all null subjects in root infinitives, at least during the early stage when the latter construction is common. In Section 4, we adopted a modified version of the proposal in Rizzi (1994b) according to which root infinitives lack both AgrS(P) and T(P). In Section 5, we outlined the *pro*-drop theory of Speas (1994): Economy of Projection allows *pro* if a) AgrS is underlyingly filled by a base-generated agreement affix or b) AgrS and its projection AgrSP are altogether absent from the derivation, but not if c) AgrS is underlyingly empty and the agreement affix is generated directly on the verb. Scenarios a - c obtain in languages with strong, no and weak overt agreement morphology, respectively. After these preliminaries, we can now directly turn to the analysis of null subjects in early child language.

If, as proposed by Rizzi, root infinitives instantiate the second of the three scenarios described above (i.e., AgrS(P) is missing), then the *pro*-drop theory developed by Speas predicts that referential *pro* subjects are possible in young children's root infinitives, in accordance with our earlier findings. We assign the examples in (34) and others like it the derivation in (35). Neither AgrSP nor TP are projected and the only projections that have to satisfy Economy of Projection are CP and VP. CP is licensed by independent semantic content in its head (i.e., the feature [+*wh*] in Comp) and independent phonetic content in its specifier (i.e., the *wh*-element *what* in Spec, CP). More importantly, VP is licensed by independent phonetic and semantic content in its head (i.e., the verb *doing* in V). As a consequence, Spec, VP does not need to have independent semantic or phonetic content and can hence be occupied by a discourse-identified *pro* (cf. (34a)). Non-finite negative declaratives (cf. 22 - 23) are analyzed in the same way, the only difference being that here CP is replaced by NegP, a projection that is licensed by independent phonetic and semantic content in its head (i.e., the negation marker *not* in Neg). The crucial part of the analysis goes through even if it turns out that non-finite *wh*-questions and non-finite negative declaratives lack the CP- and NegP-levels and that the *wh*-element and negative marker are directly adjoined to VP (cf. note 25). The child English structure in (35) should be compared with the adult Japanese structure in (33) with which it shares all relevant properties and in particular the ability to leave the subject phonetically empty because AgrSP is not projected. The analysis proposed here extends straightforwardly to subjectless root infinitives in the other child languages discussed in Section 3. One important feature of this analysis is that it is not the initial missetting of a (*pro*-drop) parameter which is responsible for the production of *pro* by children acquiring a non-*pro*-drop language, but rather the general availability of root infinitives (i.e., matrix clauses lacking AgrSP and TP) in early child language on the one hand and the independently motivated UG-Principle of Economy of Projection on the other hand. Arguably, this is precisely the form that explanations in language acquisition research should take.

(34) a. what doing?   ADAM07 line 15
      b. what you doing?   ADAM07 line 16

(35)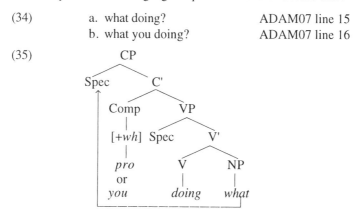

In child and adult English alike, finite clauses instantiate the third of the three scenarios described at the beginning of this section (i.e., AgrS is present but underlyingly empty). The *pro*-drop theory developed by Speas hence predicts that referential *pro* subjects in finite clauses are no more possible in child English than they are in adult English, and the absence of null subjects in Adam's finite *wh*-questions (where alternative means to omit the subject such as Diary/Topic Drop are unavailable) bears out this prediction. Examples like those in (36) have the derivation in (37) where AgrSP and TP are present in addition to CP and VP and all of these phrases must satisfy Economy of Projection. CP and VP are licensed in the fashion discussed above in connection with (35). TP is licensed by independent phonetic and semantic content in its head (i.e., the pleonastic *do* and the

NULL SUBJECTS AND THE THEORY OF ECONOMY OF PROJECTION 377

tense feature [-past] in Tns) and the specifier of this projection can therefore remain empty. AgrS on the other hand lacks such independent phonetic or semantic content. Recall from the last section that verb movement does not license projections and movement of the pleonastic *do* through AgrS to Comp does therefore not license AgrSP. As a consequence, Spec, AgrSP must have independent phonetic content and can hence not be occupied by *pro* (cf. 36a). The child English structure in (37) should be compared with the adult English structures in (32b, c) with which it shares all relevant properties and in particular the inability to leave the subject phonetically empty because AgrSP is projected with an empty head. As for German and Dutch, the other Germanic languages discussed in Section 3, we will simply assume for the moment that here, too, finite clauses have the same structure in early child and adult language and that referential *pro* in finite clauses is either not licensed (because the agreement paradigm is weak and AgrS is underlyingly empty) or not identifiable (because nominative is assigned from Comp, note 33). See Rohrbacher & Vainikka (1994) for a more complicated view.

(36)   a. *what do doing?   unattested
       b. what do you doing?   ADAM15

(37)

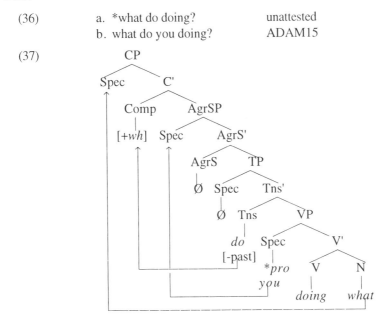

As mentioned in Section 3, none of the six (5%) counterexamples in Adam's speech against the generalization that finite Wh-questions do not allow subject drop exhibit regular subject-verb agreement. Instead, agreement is either altogether absent as with the modal in (38a) and the past tense verb in (38b) or realized in a suppletive verb stem as with the copula in (38c). Crucially missing are counterexamples of the form in (39), where a main verb bears regular subject-verb agreement and the subject is null. We are tempted to propose the following explanation. Sentences like the one in (39) are impossible because the presence of regular subject-verb agreement requires the presence of AgrSP and (39) could only have the structure in (40a) where AgrSP remains radically empty, contrary to the demands of the Principle of Economy of Projection. Sentences like those in (38) are possible because the absence of regular subject-verb agreement allows the absence of AgrSP and these sentences could have the structure in (40b) where TP is licensed by the modal, copula (see Section 4) or tense feature base-generated in its head (i.e., *can*, *is* and [+past] in Tns). As a consequence, Spec, TP does not need to have independent semantic or phonetic content and can hence be occupied by a discourse-identified *pro*. But this account does not explain why utterances of the type illustrated in (38) are so rare in Adam's speech, see for example the fact that in File 16, Adam said 31 times "Where is it?" but only twice "Where is?" (i.e., only 6% of all Wh-questions containing a form of the copula are missing the subject). The rarity of examples like (38a-c) might be taken to suggest that the presence of TP implies the presence of AgrSP, for reasons that are yet to be explored.[34] If this is correct, the explanation for Adam's few subjectless finite Wh-questions described in this paragraph does not go through. We will tentatively assume that the six examples listed exhaustively in (13) and partially again in (38) are real counterexamples to our theory. Since these counterexamples represent only 5% of all finite Wh-questions and are hence well within the range of adult production errors, they do not constitute a serious challenge to our theory.

(38)   a. where can go?   ADAM11
                 b. what said # Mommy?   ADAM12
                 c. where is?   ADAM16

(39)   *where goes?   unattested

(40)

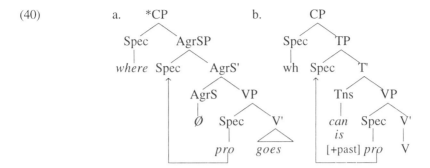

Recall from Section 2 that one of the arguments raised by Bloom (1990) and Valian (1991) against *pro*-drop approaches to null subjects in the early speech of children acquiring a non-*pro*-drop language was that the number of early null subjects declines gradually instead of suddenly, contrary to what might be expected if the (re)setting of a parameter such as the one traditionally assumed to govern the distribution of *pro* were involved.[35] Notice that this criticism does not directly carry over to the *pro*-theory defended here according to which there is in fact no *pro*-drop parameter and the licensing or non-licensing of empty referential subjects in any particular language instead falls out from the richness of the inflectional paradigm in that language on the one hand and independently motivated principles of Universal Grammar concerning the lexical representation of affixes (see 28) and Economy of Projection (see 31) on the other. If the child English option to omit the subject is lost as a function of the acquisition of the adult English agreement paradigm, then a gradual acquisition of the latter would go a long ways towards explaining an equally gradual loss of the former.

Let us see what the facts are for Adam, the child that is at the center of this study (see Table 2). In Files 01-11, 95% of Adam's *wh*-questions are non-finite and 83% of these non-finite *wh*-questions do not have an overt subject.[36] Only one of the four finite *wh*-questions produced in the first eleven files contains an empty subject. During this period, Adam's non-finite *wh*-questions have the structure in (35) without AgrSP (and TP) and hence with the possibility to leave the subject phonetically empty. Adam's finite *wh*-questions can have only the structure in (37) with AgrSP (and TP) and hence without the possibility to leave the subject phonetically empty. As noted in Section 3, Makowski (1993) reports that Adam's first agreeing and contrasting *be*- and *do*-forms occur in Files 10 and 11, respectively, i.e., towards the very end of this AgrSP-less root infinitive period. In Files 12-15, i.e., immediately after these first occurrences of contrasting agreement, the rate of non-finite *wh*-questions drops to 42% and the rate of empty subjects in non-finite *wh*-questions drops to 51%, with a sharp decrease in the null subject rate from 92% in File 11 to 40% in File 12. The rate of empty subjects in finite *wh*-questions is 6%. During this period, Adam's non-finite *wh*-questions may have either the AgrSP-less *pro*-drop structure in (35) or the AgrSP/obligatory subject structure in (37). Finite *wh*-question again only have the latter structure. Our claim is that AgrSP begins to emerge in nonfinite clauses precisely because agreement has started to occur. Again as noted before, Makowski (1993:28) argues that agreement reaches the productive stage in File 15, i.e., towards the very end of the period where AgrSP is optional in non-finite *wh*-questions. In Files 16-18, i.e., immediately after agreement has become productive, the rate of empty subjects in non-finite *wh*-questions again drops dramatically, this time to 16%, with a sharp decrease from 50% in File 15 to 0% in File 16. The rate of empty subjects in finite *wh*-questions is 3%. During this period, Adam's non-finite *wh*-questions may no longer have the AgrSP-less *pro*-drop structure in (35) and, like their finite counterparts, instead require the structure in (37) with AgrSP (and TP) and hence without the possibility to leave the subject phonetically empty. Our claim is that AgrSP becomes obligatory (and as a consequence, *pro* becomes impossible) in all clauses precisely because weak agreement has reached the productive stage.[37,38] It thus turns out that the loss of *pro*-drop is stretched out over a period of time only because the acquisition of agreement on which it depends is stretched out over that same period of time. Each milestone in the acquisition of agreement results in a dramatic drop in the rate of empty subjects, and there is nothing gradual about these drops in the empty subject rate.

We have just argued that whereas finite clauses are AgrSPs from the start, non-finite clauses initially lack this level (as well as the TP-level) and receive it only later as a function of the acquisition of the agreement morphology.[39] Let us assume that the acquisition of agreement morphology triggers the acquisition of (abstract) agreement features which require the presence of AgrSP for checking purposes[40] and which, once hypothesized, must be represented in finite clauses (where they may be strong or weak) and non-finite clauses (where they are perhaps universally weak) alike. One might argue that this view is more complicated than one that takes all projections for granted from the beginning, but within a framework that incorporates a theory of Economy of Projection, this is actually not the case. Children start out with the most economical representation for infinitives which, in the absence of overt agreement morphology or abstract agreement features from the grammar as a whole and the absence of TP from root infinitives in particular (see notes 35 and 38), does not include AgrSP. The latter projection is automatically added by universal principles once overt agreement morphology and abstract agreement features are acquired. As far as we can see, none of the learnability problems ensue that are often adduced against theories of incremental phrase structure acquisition (see also Radford, 1994).

To conclude this section, let us now briefly mention the analysis of early null subjects independently proposed by Sano & Hyams (1994) which in important aspects resembles our own analysis. Recall from Tables 5-7 that Sano & Hyams also found null subjects to be much more common in non-finite than in finite early child English utterances. They argue that "it is the availability of root infinitives that makes null subjects possible in child English... On this view, then, children's null subjects are not the result of a missetting of a null subject parameter *per se*, but rather derives from an independent aspect of child grammars which is found in many languages other than English, the property which is responsible for root infinitives" (1994:545). In particular, "the structure of null subject sentences in child English parallels the null subject sentences in adult Japanese and Chinese" (1994:544). So far, their interpretation of the facts is very close to ours. But Sano & Hyams go on to say that "we are not proposing that it is the absence of functional projections which creates a licit context for [the empty subject], but rather it is the lack of [AgrS] features, and hence of verb raising" (1994:548). Here the idea is that empty subjects in child English are big PRO rather than small *pro*, that big PRO must not be lexically governed at LF, that V-to-AgrS raising is triggered at S-structure by strong AgrS features and at LF by weak AgrS-features, and, crucially, that infinitives do not have AgrS-features. It follows from these assumptions that root infinitives in child English leave the verb *in situ* even at LF and thus allow PRO in the ungoverned Spec, AgrSP. Sano & Hyams suggest that L1 learners of English acquire AgrS features (and hence lose root infinitives and root null subjects) when they acquire the pleonastic *do* whose sole purpose it is to carry these AgrS features. "[This] hypothesis makes the prediction that we will not find pleonastic *do* during the null subject stage"

(1994: 554 fn. 14), a prediction that seems to be contradicted by the examples in (41).

(41)   a. what did you did? ADAM07
        b. no I don't want to sit seat. ADAM07
        c. yes # but where do you spit? ADAM14
        d. how do you know? ADAM15

Behind the change from child English (with root and embedded infinitives) to adult English (with embedded infinitives only) lurks another, more serious problem for Sano & Hyams' theory: The child must learn that AgrS features are obligatory in root clauses, but not in embedded clauses, or "Max promised *PRO* to do the dishes" would be excluded alongside "*PRO* to do the dishes". The proposed trigger, pleonastic *do*, appears in both root and embedded clauses and can therefore not yield the needed distinction between the two environments.[41] Rizzi's root infinitive analysis adopted in this article does not run into this problem. The generalization of TP to all clauses excludes non-finite declaratives from matrix contexts (where the Tns variable cannot be bound) while continuing to allow them in embedded contexts (where the Tns variable of the lower clause can be bound by the tense specification of the higher clause).

In Section 4, we mentioned independent arguments for Rizzi's truncation analysis of root infinitives such as the absence of the infinitival marker *to* from this construction. Insofar as these arguments go through, the analysis of early null subjects proposed in this article will be automatically superior to that proposed by Sano & Hyams. Clearly, the issue cannot be decided at this point, and we hope that it will be the subject of a lively debate.

7. WHY-QUESTIONS

In one corner of adult English, namely *why*-questions with a subtle non-declarative meaning (i.e., a lexically isolated domain), we find systematic evidence that AgrSP and TP are absent. In these questions, only unmarked verb-stems (see (42a)) but not verb forms marked for or agreement (see (42b)) or tense (see (42c)) are possible. These examples also show that in this type of question, the subject cannot be overtly expressed.

(42)   a. Why (*he) go downtown?
        b. *Why (he) goes downtown?
        c. *Why (he) goes downtown?

Each of the ungrammatical sentences is correctly excluded if we assume that no inflectional projections are allowed in this type of construction. Although the roughly subjunctive semantics and rarity of this form might lead us to expect that it will not be acquired until rather late, we find, remarkably, that Adam is able to isolate *why*-questions as the environment for structures without inflectional projections by age three.

In File 17, we suddenly find a fair number of subject-less *why*-questions, several of which seem to have this subjunctive character:

(43)
    a. why put string on it?   ADAM17
    b. why laughing at me?   ADAM17
    c. why not # see it dat one?   ADAM17
    d. why say oh oh?   ADAM17
    e. why say # right now?   ADAM17
    f. why not # take # take dose?   ADAM17

After File 19, all *wh*-questions without overt subject belong to this type (see (44)), therefore suggesting that the acquisition of AgrSP-less subjunctive *why*-questions is linked to the loss of AgrSP-less structures in all other constructions.

(44)
    a. why fall and hurt myself?   ADAM20
    b. why finish waiting for my water?   ADAM20
    c. why got paint?   ADAM22
    d. why going to open it?   ADAM22
    e. why always push this [= record button]   ADAM28
    f. why take it apart?   ADAM28
    g. why haven't finished?   ADAM28
    h. why broken?   ADAM28
    i. why have the yellow black thing [?]?   ADAM33
    j. d(o) you know why put de Bandaid on my finger?   ADAM33
    k. why go slowly?   ADAM34
    l. why have a nose?   ADAM46[42]

We are confronted with a classic subset problem: the child moves from a grammar in which both 'where go' and 'why go' are possible to one in which only 'why go' is possible. Our problem is that the AgrSP-less structure is general in the first grammar and lexically restricted in the second grammar. How does the child discover that the economic option is lexically restricted given that negative evidence is unavailable? We speculate now on how lexical 'narrowing' of a grammar may occur in acquisition.[43]

First we assume that Economy of Projection determines the initial state as lacking inflectional projections wherever this is possible within UG (i.e., in infinitivals but not in finite clauses). After inflectional projections have become productive, structures lacking them remain possible but only as a lexical exception:

(45)   If non-economical structures with inflectional projections are selected, then the economical structures without inflectional projections must be linked to lexical items.

This makes the following empirical prediction:

(46)   There are no non-economical exceptions.

That is, exceptions will be a) lexically linked, and b) choose an economical representation lacking inflectional projections. This means that a language such as Japanese which does not have a productive AgrS system will never have exceptional structures with AgrS and, depending whether this exceptional agreement is strong or weak, optional or obligatory overt subjects. A number of theories of underspecification in acquisition exist, but only this one leads to this cross-linguistic prediction. In its strongest form, this prediction reads as follows: all exceptions will be economical in both representation and derivation. A weaker version which is compatible with our evidence holds that exceptions will not add an inflectional projection, but only delete (or fail to project) an inflectional projection, in accordance with the theory of Economy of Projection.[44]

Let us now apply this proposal to *why*-questions. During the initial period when the child either does not project AgrSP in root infinitives at all or projects it only optionally, input data like "Why go outside when you can stay inside and watch TV?" are assimilated without problem to the AgrSP-less analysis. However, after the agreement affixes are recognized and AgrSP has become obligatory in all clauses, the same type of input data are now exceptional and by hypothesis, -AgrS must be lexically linked. This satisfies the constraint that lexical exceptions select economical projections. The child must choose a lexical entry for subjunctive *why* that requires a structure without AgrSP and TP.

How can we represent this choice structurally? First, let us note that the *why*-VP structure has some special features, in addition to genericity, which may follow directly from the absence of a subject. It disallows long-distance movement, as pointed out by Collins (1991):

(47)   a. *why say that Bill can swim t

We can therefore argue that *why* is not base-generated as an adjunct and moved to Spec, CP but that it is instead base-generated as the head of CP in Comp, which would make it ineligible for (long-distance) XP-movement (Chomsky, p.c.).[45]

How exactly can we prevent the child from generalizing the AgrSP-less structure from "Why put it down?" to "*where go to school" after inflections have been recognized? One distinction that might be expected to play a role is illocutionary force, which is naturally associated with CP.[46] Young children can distinguish declaratives, questions, and imperatives. Suppose that the set of illocutionary distinctions is larger and includes specific versus generic questions. This contrast is illustrated in (48).

(48)   a. Why did you go to school?
         b. Why go to school?

The former might be answered "Because it is Monday", while the latter is answered "To learn". Though many situations of overlap exist where an answer could be an answer to both, the crucial point is that some situations call for non-event generic answers. Children are known to make generic statements ("Lions are scary") early although no systematic study has been undertaken. The answer to (48b) would inform a child, in some context, that a generic and not a specific event is at the core of the question.

We must now project this distinction into the grammatical realm where a child represents different structures. We need a feature for generic questions which is distinct from that for specific questions such that it can be associated with a different structure, just as imperative force must be represented somewhere. One mode, which we add as a speculation, is that the higher nodes are marked with a feature that indicates their illocutionary force. This feature could in fact be carried on a lexical item, like *why*. Thus, the feature percolates to the higher CP node, marking it as a subjunctive question (as would be natural in Chomsky's (1994) theory of bare phrase structure). No other *wh*-word can assume this property unless the child receives specific input justifying the [+subjunctive] feature on this word.

(49)   CP [+subjunctive]
            /＼
         Comp   VP
          |
         why [+subjunctive]

It is the subjunctive Comp which then selects a VP as its complement, under the assumption that UG allows for the non-projection of AgrSP and TP.

This account relies once more on the assumption that higher projections (e.g., CP) can be present in the absence of lower projections (e.g., AgrSP and TP), contrary to what is assumed in Rizzi (1994b). In fact, whereas this assumption was not crucial for our *pro*-drop theory (see note 25 and Section 6), it is crucial for our treatment of subjectless, uninflected *why*-questions. The primary acquisition challenge now resides in the question of how the child chooses which subset of possible hierarchies of functional projections are permitted, and when, in her language.

8. CONCLUSION

In this paper, we have used the theory of Economy of Projection to provide a *pro*-drop account of early null subjects that does not refer to parameters and relies instead entirely on an interplay between the child's morphological knowledge on the one hand and universal principles on the other hand. A careful look at the data has revealed a series of sharp, non-gradual shifts in the change from *pro*-drop to non-*pro*-drop grammar which is closely linked to a series of similar shifts in the acquisition of contrastive agreement. This is expected if early null subjects are a grammatical phenomenon governed by universal principles but not if they reflect performance limitations which vanish as a pure function of time. Our account illustrates the acquisition consequences of the theories of paradigmatic knowledge developed by Rohrbacher (1993, 1994) and Speas (1994). On a more general level, it is compatible with Chomsky's influential suggestion that "parameters of UG do not relate to the computational system, but only to the lexicon" and that actually "only functional elements will be parameterized" (Chomsky 1989:44).[47] According to this view, crosslinguistic variation and diachronic change are governed solely by properties of functional elements. Taken at face value, it also predicts that only functional elements will play a role in language acquisition. A radical interpretation of this view would maintain that only overt (i.e., morphological) properties of the functional elements themselves are involved in crosslinguistic variation, diachronic change and language acquisition (see Clahsen *et al.*, 1994 for a similar view). We believe that this interpretation of Chomsky's proposal is in fact the only possible one if the following circular scenario is to be avoided. Assume that a certain property of a functional element (say a strong N-feature in AgrS) is responsible for a certain syntactic phenomenon (say obligatory movement of the subject to Spec, AgrSP). If the property in question is purely abstract and not reflected in the morphology of the functional element, then it is more likely than not that the syntactic phenomenon that depends on it will be the only evidence for it. In other words, a child acquires obligatory movement of the subject to Spec, AgrSP as a consequence of the acquisition of a strong N-feature in AgrS which in turn is motivated exclusively by obligatory subject-to-Spec, AgrSP movement. Such an account would have very little explanatory content beyond the statement that obligatory subject-to-Spec, AgrSP movement in the output is triggered by obligatory subject-to-Spec, AgrSP movement in the input, contrary to the spirit of Chomsky's suggestion.[48] If on the other hand the strength of the N-feature were determined by universal principles on the basis of overt morphological properties of the language-particular AgrS system, then the acquisition of the AgrS-morphology would automatically lead to obligatory subject-to-Spec, AgrSP movement or the lack thereof. Note that the acquisition of functional morphology, like the acquisition of lexical items but unlike the acquisition of abstract features, is motivated by the direct observability of this morphology in the input, independently of the syntactic phenomena that might depend on it, thus avoiding the circularity mentioned above. Our analysis of early null subjects and their disappearance is compatible with this program. We have proposed that the distribution of *pro* throughout the linguistic development of the child is determined by the (un)productivity of contrastive agreement and the (lack of) distinctive marking of the referential AgrS-features [1st] and [2nd] on the one hand and universal principles governing when AgrSP is projected and how it is licensed on the other hand. The program for crosslinguistic variation, diachronic change and language acquisition advanced in this final section of our article might well turn out to be too radical.[49] But as far as the concerns that motivated this program are real, it is worth exploring whether syntactic phenomena with major importance for the organization of grammar can be successfully treated within this program. Null subjects are such a phenomenon, and if our account is on the right track, then a successful treatment along the lines of the radical program is indeed possible. Needless to say, the correctness of our account does not depend on whether this program ultimately turns out to be right or wrong.

ACKNOWLEDGEMENTS

Portions of this paper where presented at the Workshop on the L1- and L2- Acquisition of Clause-Internal Rules at the University of Bern, the Conference on Generative Studies of the Acquisition of Case and Agreement at Essex University, at the Language Acquisition Group at the University of Massachusetts at Amherst and at the Computational Linguistics Feedback Forum at the University of Pennsylvania. We thank those audiences, Hagit Borer, Peggy Speas, Anne Vainikka, Ken Wexler, and two anonymous reviewers for helpful comments and criticism. Naturally, all errors are ours. One of us (Rohrbacher) was supported by NSF grant SBR-8920230.

NOTES

[1] Wh-questions in which the *wh*-word is the subject were excluded from the survey.

[2] The status of French as a non-*pro*-drop language is under dispute. See note 34 for a brief discussion.

[3] Valian reports that the American child with the lowest MLU used overt subjects in only 38% of their non-*wh*-utterances and admits that this child may be best analyzed as having a *pro*-drop grammar. In fact, the same child (and this child alone) also lacks modals and semi-auxiliaries (*gonna, wanna, hafta* and *gotta*), elements that are usually associated with higher functional projections. This suggests that this child's data is amenable to an analysis such as the one developed below according to which *pro* is possible when AgrSP is absent. The other American children in Valian's study may simply be too advanced in their development (as indicated by their higher MLU) to reflect this stage.

[4] Bloom excluded *wh*-questions and negative declaratives from his sample, i.e., exactly those environments where we will claim subject omissions are most telling.

[5] Bloom does not give separate raw numbers for the average VP-length of sentences containing full NP subjects and the average VP-length of sentences containing pronoun subjects. The relevant numbers in Table 1 have been estimated on the basis of Bloom's Figure 1. The combined raw numbers for the average VP-length of sentences containing either a full NP subject or a pronominal subject are 2.333, 2.024, and 1.800 for Adam, Eve and Sarah, respectively.

[6] Bloom (1993) discounts both of these counterarguments. With respect to the first argument, he notes that Hyams & Wexler's adult Italian corpus contains types of utterances not included in the child English corpus of Bloom (1990), a difference which allegedly renders Hyams & Wexler's results irrelevant. With respect to the second argument, he points out that the proportion of Adam's intended full NP and pronominal subjects is determined in an arbitrary fashion and that in Files 12-20, Adam uses much lower proportions of lexical subjects than in the reference File 30 (11-16% versus 30%), as predicted by the performance limitation theory. We will not attempt to resolve this matter, since the evidence presented in Section 3 stands on its own.

[7] De Haan & Tuijnman (1988:108) also report that "it is not the case that subjects/objects are more often absent in long sentences...or in sentences that are in some sense syntactically complex", contrary to the predictions of performance limitations theories of Bloom (1990, 1993) and Valian (1991).
[8] Hyams position has since evolved in a direction that has brought her views closer to ours. See Sano & Hyams (1994) and our discussion of this work at the end of Section 6.
[9] Hyams analysis contains at least two problematic assumptions. First, if Chomsky (1989) is correct that both subjects and objects have agreement projections (AgrSP and AgrOP), then it is unclear why subjects but not objects can pass on their agreement index to Spec, CP, thus turning the latter into an A-position by virtue of being construed with agreement. Second, there is no evidence that the subject in the second sentence in (7) has indeed been moved into Spec, CP.
[10] As mentioned by Hyams & Wexler (1993, fn. 25), these null subjects in *wh*-questions (as well as their counterparts in negative declaratives, see the discussion below) also create a problem for the theory developed in Gerken (1991) according to which subject drop is due to the omission of a weak syllable in iambic (weak-strong) but not trochaic (strong-weak) feet. The problem arises since fronted *wh*-elements and utterance-initial negation markers are often stressed, forming a trochaic foot with a following optional subject pronoun as in "whát (you) dóing?" (ADAM07).
[11] Only those *wh*-questions where the *wh*-word corresponds to an element other than the subject were considered. We disregarded *wh*-questions with full NP-subjects since here *pro*-drop is obviously not an option. We included self-repetitions in our counts but excluded all utterances with interruptions that could have possibly interfered with the production of an overt subject. Proportions were calculated only for files with more than one relevant example.
[12] Wh-questions were counted as finite if they contained a (finite) auxiliary (*have* or *be*), modal (*can*, *must*, etc.) or expletive (*do*) and as non-finite if they did not contain such an element. There were only two exceptions to this rule: In two utterances, no auxiliary etc. was present but the main verb carried regular 3rd person present tense agreement (see (11b)). Both utterances were counted as finite. The fact that examples of this type are very rare suggests that we were justified in counting *wh*-questions without an auxiliary, modal, or expletive as non-finite. Moreover, the highly significant correlation between finiteness (as defined above) and subjecthood also indicates that this assumption was correct.
[13] The examples in (11) and (12) already indicate that the phenomenon under observation is not lexically governed. In fact, *pro* occurs with all wh-words used in this stage except *how* (which shows up only in the probably formulaic *how are you?* and *how do you know?*) and with 18 different verbs, 10 of which are also among the 37 verbs that occur in wh-questions with overt pronominal subjects.
[14] The development of finiteness in *wh*-questions thus appears to lag behind that in other sentence types, possibly because it is linked to the acquisition of a discrete set of lexical items with special properties (see note 12). Based on the distribution of personal pronouns, Vainikka (1994) determines File 03 as the onset of Adam's IP stage, although it may in fact be the case that only the lower but not the higher inflectional projections (e.g., TP but not AgrSP) are available at this stage, a situation that would be compatible with the theory we develop below (but see the discussion around footnote 33).
[15] Strictly speaking, (finite) auxiliaries are probably not VP-elements (see Rohrbacher, 1993). But since Bloom (1990, 1993) uses VP-length as an indicator of processing load and since there is no reason not to believe that auxiliaries increase processing load, this detail is irrelevant. By the same token, it is reasonable to count all non-subject elements in this measure as was done in Table 3 below.
[16] We would like to thank Ken Matsuda and Sergey Avrutin for helping with the statistics.
[17] In addition, Valian (1991:65) found that her 21 American children never left out the subject in the 132 tensed subordinate clauses they produced. Rizzi (1994a:154) claims that this finding supports the Diary/Topic Drop analysis of early null subjects, since adult Diary/Topic Drop is ruled out in embedded clauses (see (6), (8b)). Valian's finding might however just as well be taken to support our *pro*-drop analysis, according to which early null subjects are excluded from finite clauses. The two theories would make different predictions for

embedded non-finite clauses that are not control-infinitives, but apparently (and not surprisingly), children do not produce such examples any more than adults do, presumably because finiteness is acquired before subordination.

[18] We have no detailed explanation for the scarcity of null subjects in *wh*-questions that has been reported for some languages (see the last paragraph of Section 2). Notice however that the languages in questions (e.g., French, German) are typically V-to-I raising languages with strong agreement, unlike English, which has weak agreement. It appears that strong agreement is acquired earlier than weak agreement (see Rohrbacher & Vainikka, 1994). In terms of the theory developed in Section 6, this means that AgrSP becomes obligatory in strong agreement languages like French or German before it becomes obligatory in weak agreement languages like English. Since the cases of *pro* discussed in this paper depend on the optionality of AgrSP, this might explain why null subjects in *wh*-questions have been observed only in child English but not in child French or child German. The details of this account remain to be worked out and go beyond the scope of the present paper.

[19] This term is widely used in the literature and we will continue to use it although it should be clear in the light of examples like (10d, e, g-i, k, l), (15 b), (18 a-c) and (22 b,c) that the term 'non-finite matrix clause' would be more appropriate.

[20] Similarly, Krämer (1993) argues that root infinitives with overt subjects contain an empty modal. However, she assumes that subjectless root infinitives (i.e., the kind we are interested in) do not as a rule contain an empty modal and that most of them are instead true root infinitives.

[21] The theory of Boser *et al.* is hence quite similar to the theory of Speas (1994) to be outlined in the next section, with the crucial difference that Boser *et al.* assume that all functional projections are always present.

[22] As an alternative, Wexler considers a verb raising/Infl lowering analysis along the lines of Pollock (1989) and Chomsky (1989). This proposal runs into the same problems (outlined below) as the overt/covert verb raising analysis. In addition, Wexler mentions that it might be the case that root infinitives simply lack Tns (and presumably its projection, TP) as independently proposed by Rizzi (1994b), Haegemann (1994), and others, but he does not discuss this possibility in great detail.

[23] Wexler acknowledges that the non-occurrence of (25b) in child English is a problem for his theory. In connection with the verb raising/Infl lowering analysis mentioned in the previous footnote, he writes that "English *not* has a property which prevents I from moving around it [hence *do*-support, R. & R.]. We can assume that the same property will prevent V from raising around *not* for the child" (1994:337). In fact, no such assumption can be easily integrated into the verb raising/Infl lowering analysis. Chomsky (1989) suggests that the trace of Infl lowering must be undone at LF via verb raising in order to avoid an ECP-violation. LF raising is substitution (since the landing sites are empty after Infl lowering), resulting in an intermediate verb trace in Tns. This trace, having semantic content, cannot be deleted at LF and the ECP demands that it be governed by its antecedent in AgrS which is impossible if a minimal governor such as *not* intervenes between AgrS and Tns (see (i)). Verb raising at S-structure as exhibited by English aspectual auxiliaries or French main verbs does not face this problem. Overt verb raising is adjunction (since the landing sites contain abstract or concrete affixes), resulting in an intermediate Tns trace. This trace, not having semantic content, can be deleted at LF and the ECP is trivially satisfied (see (ii)).

(i) *[$_{AgrSP}$ Baby [$_{AgrS'}$ [$_V$ like-Tns-AgrS]$_i$ [$_{Neg'}$ not [$_{TP}$ t$_{i'}$ [$_{VP}$ t$_i$ spinach]]]]]

(ii) [$_{AgrSP}$ Baby [$_{AgrS'}$ [$_{AgrS}$ [$_{Tns}$ have$_i$-Tns]$_j$-AgrS] [$_{Neg'}$ not [$_{TP}$ t$_j$[$_{VP}$ t$_i$ [$_{VP}$ eaten spinach]]]]]]

Notice that overt main verb raising in negative declaratives would result in a structure with all the relevant properties of (ii). Most importantly, this structure would satisfy the ECP. The ungrammaticality of overt main verb raising in negative declaratives can therefore not be linked to the presence of *not* and must instead be due to a general absence of overt main verb raising in adult English. Wexler's claim that agreeing finite main verbs overtly raise in child English assertive declaratives then wrongly predicts that they should do so in negative declaratives, too.

In connection with the overt/covert verb raising analysis discussed in the text, Wexler does not make a concrete proposal for the absence of (25b) from child English (see footnote 51, 1994:350). Whatever feasible explanation there might be in either theory, it is unlikely that this explanation will also cover the absence of pre-verbal, clause-medial adverbs in child English (see (26b)), a problem which Wexler does not bring up.

[24]Since subject clitics are also banned from adult French and adult Dutch infinitives, their absence from child French and child Dutch root infinitives might appear to be less than surprising. But recall that both Boser *et al.* (1992) and Wexler (1994) argue that child language root infinitives are, in fact, finite constructions and we therefore expect subject cliticization to be possible in the presence of AgrS(P). Haegeman (1994) shows that Dutch clitics can adjoin to empty heads, and Boser *et al.*'s assumption that the finite element in root infinitives is phonetically empty cannot play a role either.

[25]Not much hinges on this assumption. If it turns out that Rizzi is right and root infinitives necessarily lack CP and NegP, we might adopt an analysis according to which Adam's non-finite *wh*-questions and negative declaratives involve adjunction of the *wh*-element or negation marker to VP (see Radford, 1994 for a similar proposal). In either case, the account in Section 6 will go through: Since root infinitives do not show agreement, they lack the semantically empty projection AgrSP (whose specifier would have to be filled by an overt subject) and Spec, VP is available as a position for *pro*.

[26]See Section 6 for evidence suggesting that in child English (but not in child French, see footnote 34), the presence of TP implies the presence of AgrSP, a state of affairs which neither Rizzi's, nor our own theory predicts.

[27]Example (28) is taken from Rohrbacher (1994). The original formulation in Rohrbacher (1993) included the number feature [singular] in the list of referential AgrS-features. See Rohrbacher (1994) for the reason for this revision, which is immaterial in the context of this article. Speas (1994) advocates a different definition of agreement strength which is based on the notion of Morphological Uniformity. See Rohrbacher (1993,1994) for arguments for distinctive feature marking and against Morphological Uniformity as the decisive factor in the determination of agreement strength. Again, the theory we propose here is not directly affected by these details.

[28]See Rohrbacher (1993, 1994) for more details.

[29]This is formalized in Lasnik's Filter: "A morphologically realized affix must be realized as a syntactic dependent at Surface structure" (Lasnik, 1981).

[30]Space limitations prevent us from addressing the distribution of expletive and object *pro* in this paper. See Speas (1994) for discussion.

[31]Note that empty arguments such as *pro* "lack independent content, and hence cannot suffice to license the projection of an AGR phrase" (Speas, 1994).

[32]Neither of these two assumptions is crucial in order for the account to go through. Thus if Sano (1995) is right and Japanese lacks not only AgrS(P) but also Tns(P), then Asp(ect)P will play exactly the same role that TP plays in (33).

[33]We will adopt the idea by Jaeggli & Hyams (1988) that "AGR can identify an empty category as (thematic) *pro* iff the category containing AGR Case-governs the empty category." This explains why referential *pro* subjects are ungrammatical in V2 languages with strong overt agreement morphology such as Icelandic or German: Although *pro* is licensed in these languages, it cannot be identified because in V2 languages nominative Case is assigned by Comp instead of AgrS. See Rohrbacher (1993,1994) for details. Hamann (1992) offers an account along similar lines for late empty subjects in child German. She found that in the speech of the two 3-year-olds Elena and Christian, "10-20% of empty subjects are used even after the full acquisition of inflection and V2-structure" (1992:1). More surprisingly, at this point "11-17% of all -subject declarative constructions involve post-verbal 0-subjects and though there are no 0-subject *wh*-questions, there are 6-20% 0-subjects in Yes-No questions...Christian does not have one single embedded 0-subject,...but for Elena embedded 0-subjects are not negligible" (1992:20). In other words, many of these late empty subjects occur in constructions that exclude a Topic Drop analysis. Hamann identifies them as *pro*s in Spec, AgrSP that are licensed via government from Comp. Initially, V2-style movement of the finite verb to Comp results in syntactically visible agreement features in this position which can govern and identify *pro* in Spec, AgrSP. "Post-verbal thematic 0-subjects

would disappear when the child realizes that in Standard German...the AGR-features in C^0 in V2-structures do not count" (Hamann,1992:26; 1996). Our own account of these data differs from Hamann's only in the details, with *pro* in AgrSP licensed by strong agreement affixes in AgrS and identified by an agreeing Case-assigner in Comp. See Rohrbacher & Vainikka (1994) for a discussion of early 0-subjects in child German.

[34]This implication might hold only in English, but not in e.g., French. Pierce (1992) argues that adult French is a *pro*-drop language which base-generates subject-clitics in AgrS, leaving Spec, AgrSP phonetically empty in sentences like the following.

(i) $[_{AgrSP} pro_i [_{AgrS'} [_{AgrS} elle- [_{Tns} Tns\text{-}parle_k]_j] [_{TP} t_{i'} [_{Tns'} t_j [_{VP} t_i [_{V'} t_j]]]]]]$
                            she   speaks

In her study of the four French children Daniel (1;8-1;11), Grégoire (1;9-2;3), Nathalie (1;9-2;3) and Philippe (2;1-2;3) , Pierce (1992:114) found that while "the rate of null subjects over the course of development ... remains constant, and at a fairly high rate, for all four children", the nature of the null subject sentences changes substantially over time. In the beginning, many of the null subject sentences lack the subject clitic, regardless of whether they are finite or non-finite. Later the subject clitic and the structure in (i) becomes near-obligatory. In the terms of the theory we are proposing, this means that initially AgrSP does not have to be projected, resulting in the *pro*-drop structures in (ii) and (iii).

(ii) $[_{TP} pro_i [_{Tns'} [_{Tns} Tns\text{-}parle_j] [_{VP} t_i [_{V'} t_j]]]]$
                       speaks

(iii) $[_{VP} pro [_{V'} parler]]$
             speak

Note that the analog of (ii) was found to be very rare (if it exists at all) in Adam's speech, which lead us to conclude that AgrSP must be projected if TP is. In contrast, this structure is very common in the speech of Pierce's French children, accounting for 247 of Daniel's 782 utterances, 158 of Grégoire's 587 utterances, and so on. This suggests that the prohibition against bare TPs is language specific to (child) English. Verrips & Weissenborn (1992) independently propose a structure resembling the one in (ii) for two of their French speaking children, Fabienne (1;5-2;0) and Benjamin (1;9-2;3). Verrips & Weissenborn report that "there is an initial period ... in which finite main verbs only occur in the erroneous sequence *pas* + finite verb... Another intriguing aspect of the errors is the absence of pre-verbal subjects in [this] sequence" (1992:308). During this period, "the child has not yet figured out that the verb has agreement features" (1992:311) and therefore "there is no AGR projection" (1992:312). Given the hierarchical order of functional projections in (27), the absence of pre-verbal subjects in the sequence *pas* + finite verb now follows: The verb moves to Tns and Neg and since Spec, NegP is occupied by *pas* and Spec, AgrSP is absent, no pre-verbal position is available for the subject.

[35]Although it is commonly assumed that parameter (re)settings in the grammar are instantaneous and result in sudden changes in the linguistic output, we know of no *a priori* reasons to believe that this is in fact the case. Gradual change is possible not only because "the child's language is several steps removed from the parameters of core grammar, the level at which parameters are set" (Hyams, 1994b:36. Hyams' paper contains an insightful discussion of this matter). In our theory, gradual change is also possible because children may use more than one grammar (see the last paragraph of Section 4) and the gradual displacement of one grammar by another may be reflected in a gradual change in the data without necessitating recourse to the gradual resetting of parameters. Below, we refute Bloom's and Valian's factual claim (that the change of the rate of null subjects is gradual) without accepting their theoretical claim (that parametric change in language acquisition should be reflected in sudden data changes).

[36]Here and in the following, remember that we included only *wh*-questions with an empty or pronominal subject. In particular, we ignored all *wh*-questions where the subject was a *wh*-element.

[37] In Roeper & Weissenborn (1990) it is argued that non-clause-initial environments such as questions or subordinate clauses are the trigger domain for the loss of *pro*-drop, which would avoid the ambiguity between Diary/Topic Drop and *pro*-drop in clause-initial environments. Under the theory proposed here there is sufficient information in the agreement morphology of matrix clauses to determine the strong or weak nature of AgrS, and no recourse to embedded clauses is needed in order to establish the (non-)*pro*-drop nature of a language.

[38] If this analysis is on the right track, some if not most of Adam's root infinitives in Files 12-18 have both AgrSP and TP, in violation of the theory of root infinitives proposed in Rizzi (1994b) and discussed in Section 4. Root infinitives do of course disappear shortly after the AgrSP-structure becomes obligatory, but the question of why an ungrammatical structure is allowed for some time is interesting.

[39] That is, even before the acquisition of agreement, again suggesting that the presence of TP implies the presence of AgrSP (see note 34).

[40] Clahsen (1991) argues that in child German, the acquisition of the 2sg affix -*st* (the last singular agreement marker to be acquired) triggers the loss of *pro*-drop and the stabilization of verb movement. As far as *pro*-drop is concerned, Clahsen's position is very similar to our own, although we cannot delve into the details of child German null subjects (see note 33 and Rohrbacher & Vainikka, 1994). As far as verb movement is concerned, Clahsen's findings support the theory of V-to-AgrS raising developed in Rohrbacher (1993, 1994) alluded to in the previous section. See also Hamann (1996) for a detailed argument in favor of Rohrbacher's analysis.

[41] One could of course stipulate that the existence of embedded infinitives in the input data serves as an indication for the child that AgrS features are optional in embedded clauses, but we believe that such a solution would be incompatible with the program for language acquisition theory sketched in Section 7 according to which only overt morphological of the functional elements themselves are involved in language acquisition. Insofar as this program is attractive, a different solution should be sought.

[42] The examples in (44) have a number of non-adult properties. The use of gerunds (see (44d)) and participles (see (44c,h)) is widespread and may reflect the presence of an Aspect node. That Adam embeds subjunctive *why*-questions (see (44j)) is not surprising if root clauses can be 'merged' before they are subcategorized, as follows from the work of Roeper & de Villiers (1994) and Chomsky (1994).

[43] A historical note: There has always been an interaction between transformational operations and lexical items. Operations like tough-movement applied to some adjectives but not others (see "it is tough to eat" versus "*it is tasty to eat"). This was accounted for by putting a feature [±X-rule] on adjectives, much in the way in which we will propose the feature [+subj] on *why* selects a bare VP.

[44] This discussion is a more formal representation of the notion of "subparameter" discussed in Roeper & Weissenborn (1990).

[45] Alternatively, it could be maintained that *why* is moved to Spec, CP and that Spec-head agreement ensures that the lexical feature on *why* that specifies AgrSP and TP as absent (i.e., requires a bare VP complement) is copied onto Comp and percolates up to CP.

[46] See Roeper (1992).

[47] This idea goes back at least to Borer (1984).

[48] The problem would become less compelling (although it would by no means vanish completely) if each abstract functional feature was paired with clusters of syntactic phenomena instead of a single phenomenon. Whether this is possible in all or even most cases is far from clear.

[49] Thus it is hard to see how overt morphological properties of the English and German complementizer system (i.e., *that* versus *daß*) could account for the fact that V2, a phenomenon standardly associated with the CP-level, is severely restricted in the former but general in the latter language.

REFERENCES

Anderson, S.: 1992, *A-Morphous Morphology*, Cambridge University Press, Cambridge.
Bloom, P.: 1990, 'Subjectless Sentences in Child Language', *Linguistic Inquiry* 21, 491-504.
Bloom, P.: 1993, 'Grammatical Continuity in Language Development: The Case of Subjectless Sentences', *Linguistic Inquiry* 24, 721-734. .
Boser, K., B. Lust, L. Santelmann and J. Whitman: 1992, 'The Syntax of CP and V-2 in Early Child German (ECG). The Strong Continuity Hypothesis', *NELS* 22, 51-65.
Borer, H.: 1984, *Parametric Syntax*, Foris, Dordrecht.
Bromberg, S. and K. Wexler: 1995, 'Null Subjects in Child *Wh*-Questions', *MIT Working Papers in Linguistics* 26, 221-247.
Brown, R.: 1973, *A First Language. The Early Stages*, Harvard University Press, Cambridge.
Chomsky, N.: 1989, 'Some Notes on the Economy of Derivation and Representation', *MIT Working Papers in Linguistics* 10, 43-74.
Chomsky, N.: 1992, 'A Minimalist Program for Linguistic Theory', *MIT Occasional Papers in Linguistics* 1.
Chomsky, N.: 1994, 'Bare Phrase Structure', *MIT Occasional Papers in Linguistics* 5.
Clahsen, H.: 1991, 'Constraints on Parameter Setting: A Grammatical Analysis of Some Acquisition Stages in German Child Language', *Language Acquisition* 1, 361-391.
Clahsen, H., S. Eisenbeiss and A. Vainikka: 1994, 'The Seeds of Structure. A Syntactic Analysis of the Acquisition of Case marking', T. Hoekstra & B. Schwartz (eds.) *Language Acquisition Studies in Generative Grammar*, John Benjamins, Amsterdam.
Clahsen, H., C. Kursawe and M. Penke: 1995, 'Introducing CP: Wh-Questions and Subordinate Clauses in German Child Language', *Essex Research Reports in Linguistics* 7, 1-28.
Collins, C.: 1991, 'Why and How Come', ms., MIT.
Crisma, P.: 1992, 'On the Acquisition of Wh-Questions in French', *Geneva Generative Papers*, 112-122.
Déprez, V. and A. Pierce: 1993, 'Negation and Functional Projections in Early Grammar', *Linguistic Inquiry* 24, 25-68.
Friedemann, M.-A.: 1992, 'The Underlying Position of External Arguments in French: A Study in Adult and Child Grammar', *Geneva Generative Papers*, 123-144.
Gerken, L.: 1991, 'The Metrical Basis for Children's Subjectless Sentences', *Journal of Memory and Language* 30, 431-451.
Guasti, Maria T. 1993, *Causative and Perception Verbs. A Comparative Study*. Rosenberg & Sellier, Turin.
de Haan, G. and K. Tuijnman: 1988, 'Missing Subjects and Objects in Child Grammar', P. Jordens & J. Lalleman (eds.) *Language Development*, Foris, Dordrecht.
Haegeman, L.: 1990, 'Understood Subjects in English Diaries', *Multilingua* 9, 157-199.
Haegeman, L.: 1994, 'Root Infinitives, Tense and Truncated Structures', ms., Université de Genève.
Hamann, C.: 1992, 'Late Empty Subjects in German Child Language', *Université de Genève Technical Reports in Formal and Computational Linguistics* 4.
Hamann, C.: 1996, 'Null arguments in German child language', *Language Acquisition* 5, 155-208.
Hill, J.: 1982, 'A Computational Model of Language Acquisition in the Two-Year-Old', Ph.D. dissertation, University of Massachusetts at Amherst.
Hyams, N.: 1986, *Language Acquisition and the Theory of Parameters*, Reidel, Dordrecht.
Hyams, N.: 1994a, 'V2, Null Arguments and COMP Projections', T. Hoekstra & B. Schwartz (eds.) *Language Acquisition Studies in Generative Grammar*, Benjamins, Amsterdam.
Hyams, N.: 1994b, 'Nondiscreteness and Variation in Child Language: Implications for Principles and parameters Models of Language Development', Y. Levy (ed.) *Other Children, Other Languages. Issues in the Theory of Language Acquisition*, Erlbaum, Hillsdale.
Hyams, N. and K. Wexler: 1993, 'On the Grammatical Basis of Null Subjects in Child Language', *Linguistic Inquiry* 24, 421-459.

Jaeggli, O. and N. Hyams: 1988, 'Morphological Uniformity and the Setting of the Null Subject Parameter', *NELS* 18, 238-253.
Kawasaki, N.: 1993, 'Control and Arbitrary Interpretation in English', Ph.D. dissertation. University of Massachusetts at Amherst.
Klima, E. and U. Bellugi: 1966, 'Syntactic Regularities in the Speech of Children', J. Lyons & R. Wales (eds.) *Psycholinguistic Papers*, Edinburgh University Press, Edinburgh.
Krämer, I.: 1993, 'The Licensing of Subjects in Early Child Language', *MIT Working Papers in Linguistics* 19, 197-212.
Kroch, A.: 1990, 'Reflexes of Grammar in Patterns of Language Change', *Language Variation and Change* 1, 199-244.
Lasnik, H.: 1981, 'Restricting the Theory of Transformations: a Case Study', N. Hornstein & D. Lightfoot (eds.) *Explanation in Linguistics: The Logical Problem of language Acquisition*, Longman, London.
MacWhinney, B.: 1995, *The CHILDES Project: Tools for Analyzing Talk*, Erlbaum, Hillsdale.
Makowski, M.: 1993, 'The Structure of IP: Evidence from Acquisition Data', ms., Boston University.
May, R.: 1985, *Logical Form*, MIT Press, Cambridge.
Pierce, A.: 1992, *Language Acquisition and Syntactic Theory. A Comparative Analysis of French and English Child Grammars*, Kluwer, Dordrecht.
Pintzuk, S.: 1991, 'Phrase Structure in Competition: Variation and Change in Old English Word Order', Ph.D. dissertation, University of Pennsylvania.
Platzack, C.: 1993, 'Parameter Setting and Brain Structure: A Minimalist Perspective on Language Acquisition and Attrition from the Point of View of Swedish', ms., Lund University.
Plunkett, B.: 1992, 'Continuity and the Landing Site for Wh Movement', *Bangor Research Papers in Linguistics* 4, 53-77.
Poeppel, D. and K. Wexler: 1993, 'The Full Competence Hypothesis of Clause Structure in Early German', *Language* 69, 1-33.
Pollock, J.-Y.: 1989, 'Verb Movement, Universal Grammar and the Structure of IP', *Linguistics Inquiry* 20, 365-424.
Radford, A.: 1994, 'The nature of Children's Initial Clauses', ms., Essex University.
Rizzi, L.: 1982, *Issues in Italian Syntax*, Foris, Dordrecht.
Rizzi, L.: 1990, 'Speculations on Verb Second', J. Mascaró & M. Nespor (eds.) *Grammar in Progress. GLOW Essays for Henk van Riemsdijk*, Foris, Dordrecht.
Rizzi, L.: 1994a, 'Early Null Subjects and Root Null Subjects', T. Hoekstra & B. Schwartz (eds.) *Language Acquisition Studies in Generative Grammar*, Benjamins, Amsterdam.
Rizzi, L.: 1994b, 'Some Notes on Linguistic Theory and Language Development: The Case of Root Infinitives', ms., Université de Genève.
Roeper, T.: 1992, 'From the Initial State to V-2', J. Meisel (ed.) *The Acquisition of Verb Placement. Functional Categories and V2 Phenomena in Language Acquisition*, Kluwer, Dordrecht.
Roeper, T.: 1993, 'The 'Least Effort' Principle in Child Grammar: Choosing a Marked Parameter', E. Reuland & W. Abraham (eds.) *Knowledge and Language. Volume I: From Orwell's Problem to Plato's Problem*, Kluwer, Dordrecht.
Roeper, T. and J. de Villiers: 1994, 'Lexical Links in the Wh-Chain', B. Lust *et al.* (eds.) *Heads, Projections and Learnability*, Erlbaum, Hillsdale.
Roeper, T. and J. Weissenborn: 1990, 'How to make Parameters Work', L. Frazier & J. de Villiers (eds.) *Language Processing and Acquisition*, Kluwer, Dordrecht.
Rohrbacher, B.: 1993, *The Germanic VO Languages and the Full Paradigm: A Theory of V to I raising*, Ph.D. dissertation, University of Massachusetts at Amherst.
Rohrbacher, B.: 1994, 'Explaining the Syntactic Consequences of 'Rich' Agreement Morphology: On the Licensing of V-to-AgrS Raising and pro', to appear in *The Proceedings of the 13th West Coast Conference on Formal Linguistics*.
Rohrbacher, B. and A. Vainikka: 1994, 'On German Verb Syntax under Age 2', to appear in *The Proceedings of the 19th Annual Boston University Conference on Language Development*.

Speas, M.: 1994, 'Null Arguments in A Theory of Economy of Projection', *University of Massachusetts Occasional Papers in Linguistics* 17, 179-208.

Sano, T.: 1995, 'Roots in Language Acquisition: A Comparitive Study of Japanese and European Languages', Ph.D. dissertation, University of California at Los Angeles.

Sano, T. and N. Hyams: 1994, 'Agreement, Finiteness, and the Development of Null Arguments', *NELS* 24, 543-558.

Santorini, B.: 1989, 'The Generalization of the Verb-Second Constraint in the History of Yiddish', Ph.D. dissertation, University of Pennsylvania.

Tager-Flusberg, H., S. Calkins, T. Nolin, T. Bamberger, M. Anderson and A. Chandwick-Dias: 1990, 'A Longitudinal Study of Language Acquisition in Autistic and Down Syndrome Children', *Journal of Autism and Developmental Disorders* 20, 1-21.

Valian, V.: 1991, 'Syntactic Subjects in the Early Speech of American and Italian Children', *Cognition* 40, 21-81.

Vainikka, A.: 1994, 'Case in the Development of English Syntax', to appear in *Language Acquisition*.

Verrips, M. and J. Weissenborn: 1992, 'Routes to Verb Placement in Early German and French: The Independence of Finiteness and Agreement', J. Meisel (ed.) *The Acquisition of Verb Placement. Functional Categories and V2 Phenomena in Language Acquisition*, Kluwer, Dordrecht.

Weissenborn, J.: 1992, 'Null Subjects in Early Grammars: Implications for Parameter Setting Theory', J. Weissenborn, H. Goodluck & T. Roeper (eds.) *Theoretical Issues in Language Acquisition: Continuity and Change*, Erlbaum, Hillsdale.

Wexler, K.: 1994, 'Optional Infinitives, Head Movement and the Economy of Derivations', D. Lightfoot & N. Hornstein (eds.) *Verb Movement*, Cambridge University Press, Cambridge.

Wijnen, F.: 1994, 'Incremental Acquisition of Phrase Structure: A Longitudinal analysis of verb placement in Dutch Child Language', ms., University of Groningen.

THOMAS ROEPER
University of Massachusetts at Amherst

BERNHARD ROHRBACHER
Northwestern University

GUNLØG JOSEFSSON   GISELA HÅKANSSON

THE PP–CP PARALLELISM HYPOTHESIS AND LANGUAGE ACQUISITION: EVIDENCE FROM SWEDISH

1. INTRODUCTION

The main topic of this book is the acquisition of scrambling and cliticization. In this article we will, however, not explore reordering processes. Instead, we will focus on the other side of the same coin, namely the acquisition of the basic structure of the clause and the PP. It is, we believe, important to explore these basic structures, especially the setup and hierarchical order of functional categories, in order to understand the nature of reordering processes of different kinds. (For Swedish the object shift operation is the reordering process most closely related to scrambling and cliticization).[1]

In our paper we will elaborate on the idea of a structural parallelism between the functional categories of the PP and the CP.[2,3] Arguments in favor of our hypothesis will be taken mainly from Swedish. If the analysis proposed is correct it has important implications for language acquisition. A strong version of a PP-CP parallelism implies that children do not have to acquire the verbal and the nominal extended projections[4] separately, but that they need to acquire only one kind of extended projection, the two versions differing minimally in whether the lexical head has a [+N] or [+V] feature. Such a conclusion is desirable since it contributes to the understanding of how children can acquire a language so fast. The PP-CP parallelism hypothesis predicts that there will be a close correlation between the acquisition of the PP and the CP in child language, the two projections being identical in many respects. This prediction seems to be borne out by an investigation of the acquisition of the PP and subordinate clauses by nine Swedish children.

The outline of the paper is as follows: In Section 1, we first discuss the split CP hypothesis, modeled on Swedish. We propose that the CP consists of four functional projections, each one associated with a specific semantic domain. We also propose a PP-CP parallelism hypothesis, arguing that the nominal extended projection, the PP, has the same functional projections as the verb. In Section 2, we present an investigation on the acquisition of the subordinate clause and the PP by nine Swedish children.[5] The result is, in short, that there seems to be a clear connection in time between the acquisition of the subordinate clause and the PP in Swedish child language such that children first acquire the PP and then, directly after that the subordinate clause. In Section 3, we proceed to a more qualitative analysis of the parallelism, discussing correlations other than the purely temporal ones, as well as possible "bridges" between the PP and the CP.

2. THE CP-PP PARALLELISM HYPOTHESIS

2.1. The Split CP Hypothesis

The CP-PP parallelism hypothesis proposed in this paper exploits the so-called "Split CP Hypothesis". The idea that the CP consists of more than one functional projection has been argued for in several recent works (Shlonsky, 1992; Müller & Sternefeld, 1993; Hoekstra, 1993; and Platzack, 1994 among others. See Rizzi, 1997 and Platzack, 1998 for more recent treatments). The version of the split CP analysis proposed in this paper will draw from the ideas presented in Hoekstra (1993). Hoekstra proposes that the CP contains three kinds of functional projections, each of them with a specific semantic character. This is illustrated in the diagram in (1) below. (In (1) and throughout the paper intermediate specifiers are omitted.)

(1)
```
          ClP
         /   \
       Cl⁰    WhP
             /   \
           Wh⁰   TopP
                /   \
              Top⁰   IP
```

The topmost projection, (ClP), is, according to Hoekstra, associated with comparative contexts, the second projection contains wh-question words, and the third projection, what Hoekstra (1993) calls a Topic Projection, contains the complementizer dat 'that'. All three heads may be filled at the same time, as shown in (2) below, even though this, of course, is not necessary:

(2)   Dat is niet zo gek <u>als of dat</u> hij gedacht had.
       that is not as crazy C1 C2 C3 he thought had
       'That isn't so stupid as he had thought it was.'
                                              (Hoekstra, 1993:1)

What we intend to show is that Hoekstra's analysis, which is based primarily on Dutch data, could be applied to Swedish as well. We will however, argue, using data from Swedish, that there is an additional projection containing prepositions as well. We will thus propose the following structure of the CP in Swedish:

(3)
```
            CmP
           /    \
         Cm⁰    PP
               /  \
              P⁰   WhP
                   /  \
                 Wh⁰  AgrCP
                      /   \
                    AgrC⁰  IP
```

As the structure in (3) shows we have relabeled Hoekstra's TopP, calling it AgrCP (following Shlonsky, 1992). The reasons for this will be discussed below. We will use the term CP as a cover term for the whole projection and CmP for the Comparative Projection.

The default complementizer in Swedish is *att* 'that'. *Att* is used mainly in affirmative contexts (4a). It is sometimes used also after non-factive matrix verbs (4b):

(4)   a. Jag vet <u>att</u> han kommer.
         I know that he comes
      b. Jag misstänker <u>att</u> han kommer.
         I suspect that he comes

Att is diachronically derived from a nominal element, (the 3 person pronoun *thät* 'it'), thus corresponding to English *that* and German *daß*. This suggests that the complementizer is marked [+N]. Kayne (1982) argues from another angle that this complementizer is nominal. Arguments are, he concludes, prototypically nominal, whereas predicates are typically verbal. (This is also the standpoint in Holmberg, 1986:135ff. See also Vikner, 1991:63ff for a discussion.) A nominal complementizer provides the clause with a nominal head, which enables it to function as an argument. Diachronic evidence and Kayne's principle gives us good reasons to assume that the projection headed by *att* is nominal, thus motivating the name AgrCP.

As mentioned above, *att* is the default complementizer in Swedish. However, it could be exchanged with *om* 'if', making the embedded clause non-assertive, as shown in (5b), which should be compared to (5a).

(5)   a. Det är roligt <u>att</u> du kommer!
                it is fun that you come
         b. Det vore roligt <u>om</u> du kom!
                it is-subj fun if you come-subj/pret[6]

The two complementizers cannot however cooccur:

(6)   a. *Jag tror <u>att</u> <u>om</u> hon kommer.
                I think that if she comes
         b. *Jag tror <u>om</u> <u>att</u> hon kommer.

The fact that *att* and *if* are interchangeable in many contexts but are unable to cooccur gives us reasons to believe that they are generated in the same position, namely the head of AgrCP.

Many complementizers in Swedish are complex, consisting of two words. Very often the first part is a preposition, the second part either *att* 'that' or *om* 'if'.[7]

(7)   a. Jag är inte säker <u>på</u> <u>att</u> hon kommer.
                I am not sure on that she comes
                'I am not sure that she will come.'
         b. Jag är inte säker <u>på</u> <u>om</u> hon kommer.
                I am not sure on if she comes
                'I am not sure if she will come.'

(8)   Hon var glad <u>över</u> <u>att</u> hon hade klarat provet.
         she was happy over that she had succeeded-in the test
         'She was happy that she had passed the test.'

(9)   Hon lade barnen <u>efter</u> <u>att</u> de hade badat.
         she put-to-bed children-the after that they hade bathed
         'She put the children to bed after they had taken a bath.'

Examples of other complex complementizers of this kind are *för att* 'for that', *efter att* (after that) *över att* 'over that'.[8] These facts provide evidence of a functional projection above the AgrCP, yielding the structure in (10):

(10)
```
              PP
            /    \
          P⁰      AgrCP
          |      /    \
          på   AgrC⁰    IP
         över    |
         efter  att/om
                 att
                 att
```

Prepositions do not only govern *att*-clauses however; they may take *wh*-clauses as complements equally well:

(11) Fru Al var glad <u>över vad</u> man hade gjort.
   Mrs. Al was happy over what people had done
   'Mrs. Al was happy about the things that people had done.'

Kayne (1991) has proposed that *wh*-phrases are located in the specifier of CP. We will adopt this idea, but modify it to conform to the split CP analysis. We thus propose that there is a functional projection hosting the *wh*-words, located below the PP. Following Hoekstra (1993), we will call this phrase WhP. The next question is of course whether the WhP is located below or above the AgrCP. To answer this question we need to find a subordinate clause containing both a *wh*-word and *att*. Before giving such an example we do, however, need to demonstrate that a functional projection with a *wh*-word in its specifier at the same time may host the element *som* in its head. Consider (12):

(12) a. Jag vill veta <u>vem</u> (<u>som</u>) ni rånade.
    I wish know who (that) you robbed.
    'I want to know who you robbed.'
   b. Jag vill veta <u>vem</u> *(<u>som</u>) rånade mannen.
    I wish know who that robbed man-the
    'I want to know who robbed the man.'

In the example in (12a), the *wh*-word binds the object, in (12b) the subject. In the latter case *som* is obligatory. The reason is probably the need for some overt subordinator in an embedded clause if the *wh*-word binds the subject. If *som* is omitted in (12b) the subordinate clause introduced by the *wh*-word is interpreted as a main clause. In (12a) the position of the subject disambiguates the clause as being embedded; we clearly see that the verb has not raised to the CP domain since it remains to the right of the subject. The conclusion is that *som* occupies the head of the WhP, thus blocking verb raising, and that it is not always required to be spelled out. Let us now go back to the question of whether it is possible to determine the relative order between the AgrCP and the WhP in the clausal domain. In order to do this we need to find constructions where both the WhP and the AgrCP are phonetically realized. This kind of construction is found in colloquial expressions of the type illustrated in (13):

(13) När (som (att)) vi har målat färdigt skall vi tapetsera.
when that that we have painted ready will we redecorate-
walls
'When we have finished painting we will paper the walls.'

Example (13) shows that the WhP is located above the AgrCP. We thus arrive at the structure in (14):

(14)
```
            PP
           /  \
         P⁰   WhP
             /   \
          spec   Wh'
           |    /   \
          när Wh⁰  AgrCP
               |   /   \
              som AgrC⁰  IP
                    |
                   att
```

We have concluded so far that the CP consists of at least three projections, as illustrated in (14) above. The next question is whether there are additional types of complementizers not yet accounted for. Do we, for instance, have complex complementizers consisting of an X^0 followed by a preposition, a *wh*-clause, or an *att*-clause? The answer seems to be yes. Consider first (15), where the comparative particles *som* 'as' and *än* 'than' take preposition+*att*-clause as their complements.[9]

(15) a. Läraren gläds lika mycket över att barnen sjunger bra som över att barnen ritar vackert.
teacher-the is-happy as much over that children-the sing well as over that children-the draw beautifully.
'The teacher is as pleased about the children singing well, as about them drawing beautifully.'

b. Läraren gläds mer över att barnen sjunger bra än över att barnen ritar vackert.
teacher-the is-happy more over that children-the sing well than over that children-the draw beautifully
'The teacher is more pleased by the children singing well, than by them drawing beautifully.'

The comparative particles *som* 'as' and *än* 'than' may procede *wh*-clauses too:

(16) a. Läraren gläds lika mycket åt vad barnen är <u>som</u> <u>åt</u> <u>vad</u> de kan.
teacher-the is-happy as much for what children-the are, as for what they can.
'The teacher is just as pleased by what the children are, as by what they are able to do.'
 b. Läraren gläds mer åt vad barnen är <u>än</u> <u>åt</u> <u>vad</u> de kan.
teacher-the is-happy more for what children-the are than for what they can.
'The teacher is more pleased about what the children are, than about what they are able to do.'

Finally, *som* and *än* can precede "bare" *att* and *om*:

(17) a. Det är lika säkert <u>som</u> <u>att</u> du är Winston Churchill.
it is as sure as that you are Winston Churchill
'It is as sure as you being Winston Churchill.'
 b. Det vore lika dumt <u>som</u> <u>om</u> du hoppade från Eiffeltornet.
it would-be as silly as if you jumped from the Eiffel Tower
'It would be as stupid as jumping from the Eiffel Tower.'

It seems like comparative particles like *än* and *som* are generated in the highest projection within the CP domain, just like Hoekstra proposes. This means that we will have to add another functional projection on top of the PP in our system. This results in the structure anticipated in (3) above. (For the sake of convenience, the tree is repeated below.)

(3)
```
            CmP
           /   \
        Cm⁰    PP
              /  \
            P⁰   WhP
                /   \
              Wh⁰   AgrCP
                    /   \
                 AgrC⁰   IP
```

We have shown that the CP contains four different kinds of functional projections, each one associated with a specific semantic domain. We will not explore the question whether all these projections are present in all subordinate clauses, or whether we should apply some kind of economy considerations, assuming only the presence of the projections actually needed. Hoekstra (1993) concludes that the head of the lowest projection in his system is not obligatorily filled if the head of the intermediate projection, in his system the WhP, is filled. One possibility is that a C(omparative)P implicates the presence of a PP, WhP, and an AgrCP, and that the presence of a PP implicates the presence of a WhP and an AgrCP etc. For this system to work, we need to assume that the functional phrases located below an overtly realized phrase are inert or blocked by some mechanism. According to this proposal all the three heads below the Cm^0 would be blocked in subordinate CPs introduced only by a comparative particle, like in the example in (18):

(18)   Pelle sjunger lika bra som Lisa spelar.
              Pelle sings as good as Lisa plays.

We will not pursue this discussion here but just assume that the head(s) of the functional projection(s) of the CP are unavailable for the verb in subordinate clauses.[10]

In this subsection, we have proposed that the CP consists of four functional projections. The standard assumption is that the CP is but one projection. Platzack (1994) proposes that the CP be split into two functional projections while Hoekstra (1993) claims there are three. We propose four different projections. It is possible that we have not identified the complete set of functional projections either. We are however convinced that the ones proposed in this paper are the major ones. In the next subsection, we will propose that the structure of the nominal extended projection, the PP, has the same structure as the verbal extended projection, and that the same kind of functional projections as proposed above, and shown in (3), are present there too.

2.2. The Functional Projections of the NP

In this section, we will show that the nominal extended projection contains the same kind of functional projections as the verbal extended projection, the CP. The purpose is to show that there is a fundamental parallelism between the extended projection of the verb and the extended projection of the noun.

Let us start with a verb taking a complement consisting of a preposition governing an *att*-clause:

(19)   Läraren gladdes <u>över</u> <u>att</u> eleverna sjöng vackert.
              teacher-the was-happy over that students-the sang beautifully
              'The teacher was pleased that the children sang beautifully.'

According to the proposal in Section 2.1 both *över* and *att* are heads of projections contained within the CP. The preposition *över* can equally well govern a DP complement:

(20)   Läraren gladdes <u>över den</u> vackra sången.
         teacher-the was-happy over the beautiful song-the
         'The teacher was pleased about the beautiful song.'

The same principle applies to most prepositions; they can govern both a DP and a clause. A probable hypothesis is therefore that *över* in (19) stands in the same relationship to *att* (which was assumed to be in the head of AgrCP) as *över* to the determiner *den* in (20). Both *att* and the determiner are nominal in nature and both head their respective projections.[11] If we disregard the WhP for a while we get the common structure of (21) for subordinate clauses containing a complex complementizer (preposition + *att/om*) and preposition+determiner:

(21)

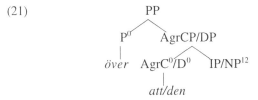

We have argued that there is a WhP between the PP and the AgrCP in the clausal domain. If the parallelism between the nominal and the verbal extended projection holds, it should be possible to have a preposition+*wh*-word+determiner. It is not so easy to test this since a *wh*-word in this position seems to preclude a [+def] noun, and, for some reason, the sequence preposition+*wh*-word+indefinite determiner, like in (22) is ruled out. We can see however that the *wh*-word in the construction type in question is preceded by a preposition and is followed by an adjectival modifier (see (23)).

(22)   *<u>med vilken en</u> vacker prinsessa
         with what a beautiful princess

(23)   <u>Med vilken</u> vacker prinsessa gifter han sig?
         with what beautiful princess marries he REFL
         'Which beautiful princess will he marry?'

The example in (23) indicates that the parallelism between the verbal and the nominal extended projection holds in that a preposition can take a WhP as its complement equally well as a DP (as in (20)).

The topmost of the four functional projections of the verbal domain is a Comparative Projection. The head of this projection hosts comparative particles, like *än* and *om*. If the parallelism between the CP and the extended projection of the noun holds, we predict that the comparative particles also may take preposition+DP complements, DPs introduced by *wh*-phrases or bare DP complements. The predictions are borne out, as examples (24 - 26) show. The a-sentences have clausal complements, and the b-sentences have DP complements.

(24) a. Läraren gläds lika mycket över att barnen sjunger bra <u>som</u> <u>över</u> <u>att</u> barnen ritar bra.
teacher-the is-happy as much over that children-the sings well as over that children draw well.
'The teacher is as happy about the children singing beautifully as about the children drawing well.'
b. Läraren gläds lika mycket över barnens sång <u>som</u> <u>över</u> <u>de</u> vackra teckningarna.
teacher-the is-happy more over children-the's song as over the beautiful drawings
'The teacher is as happy about the children's song, as about the beautiful drawings.'

(25) a. Carl är lika snabb <u>som</u> <u>när</u> han var 20 år.
Carl is as fast as when he was 20 years
'Carl is just fast as when he was 20 years old.'
b. <u>Vem</u>$_i$ var du lika snabb <u>som</u> t$_i$?[13]
who were you as fast as
'Who are you just as fast as?'

(26) a. Det är lika roligt att barnen sjunger <u>som</u> <u>att</u> de spelar.
it is as happy that children-the sing as that they play
'It is just as fun to hear the children sing as to hear them play.'
b. Den första pojken var lika duktig <u>som</u> <u>den</u> sista flickan.
the first boy-the was as good as the last girl
'The first boy was as good as the last girl'

The comparative particles *som* and *än* share one important property with ordinary prepositions; they can assign accusative case. This is not apparent in examples like (26b), since nouns do not bear morphological case in Swedish. It could therefore be claimed that the phrase *som den sista flickan* is elliptical with deletion under identity with the predicate part of the (presumed) matrix clause. Evidence that *än/som* do take DP/NP complements, and thus assign case, comes from the appearance of accusative pronouns in this position (in 27) and reflexive pronouns as modifiers (in 28).

(27)   Jag är längre än dej.
       I am taller than you$_{ACC}$
       'I am taller than you.'

(28)   Han$_i$ är längre än sin$_i$ bror.
       He is older than REFL brother
       'He is taller than his brother.'

Normative grammarians sometimes rule out sentences like (27), even though this is quite the normal way of expression for many speakers. To use a reflexive pronoun in (28), however, is the only way to express co-reference between the two participants of the comparative event. The use of a reflexive to modify the head noun of a subject is ungrammatical, which indicates that *sin bror* in (28) is not the subject of an elliptical sentence. Constructions like the one in (28) clearly indicate that comparative particles do take DP complements, thus assigning accusative case. Since comparative particles and prepositions share this important property, we will assume that comparative *som* and *än* are, in fact, a kind of preposition. We will call them **comparative prepositions**. As will be evident in the next subsection this kind of preposition seems to play a crucial role in the acquisition of subordinate clauses in child language. In the following, we will refer to projections where DPs are governed by either ordinary prepositions or comparative prepositions as PPs.

2.3. Summary

The purpose of Section 2 was to point out the close parallelism between the verbal and the nominal extended projection, or between the CP and the PP. If there is a fundamental parallelism between the CP and the PP in terms of positions, functions, and what kind of functional elements can occupy different positions, we expect this parallelism to be important for language acquisition. Economy considerations suggest that children apply properties of one of the constructions in acquiring the other. In Sections 3 and 4, we will show that this is borne out. It seems to be the case that children first acquire the PP. At the end of a period of variation in the use of prepositions, the first subordinate clauses emerge. Importantly, the first complementizer used is *som*, which, as was shown above, can govern both a clause and a DP.

3. THE ACQUISITION OF THE PP AND THE CP IN SWEDISH

3.1. Earlier Studies

The relation between the acquisition of the PP and the CP has not been discussed in earlier research of the acquisition of Swedish.[14] There are, however, separate studies focussing on one of these phenomena in Swedish child language. The acquisition of prepositions has been investigated in a study of one child by Lange (1976) and the acquisition of subordinate clauses in the speech of five children has been studied by Lundin (1987).

In the Lange (1976) study, different periods in the child's acquisition of prepositions are distinguished. Thus, there are very few prepositions in the first period, which is followed by a period of variation where prepositions are sometimes supplied and sometimes omitted. In the next period, the child uses prepositions correctly in more than 90% of obligatory contexts. The last period in Lange's study is characterized by new uses of old prepositions as well as new prepositions.

According to the analysis in Lundin (1987), subordinate clauses develop as follows. Before the age of 2;3, relatively few subordinate clauses are produced, and they often lack a complementizer. At the age of about 2;6 subordinate clauses occur quite frequently, and around the age of 2;9 all types of subordinate clauses that occur in adult speech are also found in the child's speech.

3.2. The Present Study

The aim of the present study is to investigate the acquisition of the PP and the acquisition of the CP within the same theoretical framework. In order to test the predictions, the data from the Stockholm project "Child language syntax" (Söderbergh, 1973; Lange, 1974; Lange & Larsson, 1973; Larsson, 1977), used in the aforementioned studies have been reanalyzed. In addition to this corpus, material from the Lund project "Variation and deviation in language acquisition" (Håkansson, Nettelbladt, & Hansson, 1991) is used. Transcriptions from nine children in total are used. Before we proceed to the analyses, a few words about data collection methods in the two different projects will be mentioned.

The children in both projects were recorded in interactions with an adult. The children from the Stockholm project, Ask, Embla, Nanna and Tor were followed from the age of 20 months to the age of 3;6 with fortnightly audio-recordings. The data from the Lund project consists of four to seven video-recordings of each of the six children included. These children, Erik,

Joakim, Karin, Martin, and Niklas were followed for a period of about one year. This implies that the time span between the recordings is greater in the Lund project. Because of the differences between the two corpora, we have decided not to conflate the results of the analyses, but to give detailed information about each child.

From the transcripts, clauses containing a PP and/or a CP were extracted, totaling approximately 1, 500 examples from these nine children. In the present study, recording number one for each child refers to the first recording where prepositions or a context for prepositions were found. This implies that we have not used the earliest transcripts where no contexts for prepositions occurred. Direct imitations of adult utterances have not been used. In sequences where the same utterance is repeated, only the first occurrence is used in our calculations.

On the basis of the quantitative analysis we propose a stage model for the acquisition of PP and CP in Swedish (For further details and total frequencies of occurrence for each child, see Tables 1- 9 in the Appendices).

Stage 1

At this stage, the children do not use prepositions. When there is a context for a preposition, the preposition is omitted. No CPs are used. This stage is represented by Karin 1, Nanna 1, and Niklas 1. Example (29) illustrates this stage.

(29)   Åka dagis   Karin 1;11
        go preschool

Stage 2

Prepositions in PPs are emerging and used to a varying extent. Sometimes a preposition is supplied, sometimes it is omitted. This pattern is shown in (30) from a recording of Joakim 2;5. Stage 2 is represented by Ask 1-5, Embla 1-9, Erik 1-3, Joakim 1-2, Karin 2-4, Nanna[15] 2, Niklas 2-3, Martin 1-4, and Tor 1-5.

(30)   a. Sitta ditt knä   Joakim 2;5
           sit your lap
        b. Jag bada i det   Joakim 2;5
           I swim in that

We find a few subordinate clauses at this stage, sometimes without complementizers. Example (31) illustrates these early subordinate clauses.

(31)   Här är dom äter   Tor 2;5.10
        here are they eat   (relative *som* omitted)

Stage 3

At Stage 3, PPs and CPs are acquired. This means that 90% of the prepositions and complementizers are supplied in obligatory contexts (For the 90% criterion, see Lange, 1976). The acquisition of CP comes slightly after the acquisition of PP, and most often, the children do not start using complementizers at all until they have reached a 90% use of prepositions in obligatory contaxtx. Stage 3 is represented by Ask 6-18, Embla 10-17, Erik 4-5, Joakim 3-5, Karin 5-6, Martin 5-7, Nanna 3-9, Niklas 4-6, and Tor 6-12.

(32)   a. Lägger - djuren i laggårn.   Embla 2;3.4
         put - animals-the in barn-the
         b. Precis som en kan/ som en kanin.   Embla 2;3.4
         just like a rab/ like a rabbit
         c. Och det är baby-grisen, den som   Embla 2;3.4
         heter Ola.
         and it is baby-pig, it that is-called Ola

In our material, we have found only seven exceptions to the generalization that all CPs have overt complementizers in obligatory contexts at Stage 3. Consider the examples in (33):

(33)   a. Handfat att tvätta sig man sk /kissat.   Ask 2;4.29
         basin to wash REFL one peed
         b. Du blir glad jag rita så /---/   Ask 2;4.29
         you become happy I draw so
         c. Där är bilar kör på gatan.   Ask 2;4.29
         there are cars drive on street-the
         d. Det är inte den blåser.   Nanna 1;10.2
         it is not that blow
         e. /e:/ den blåser.   Nanna 1;10.2
         is that blow
         f. Pang sa det, gick sönder.   Tor 2;7.11
         pang said it, went broken
         g. Sånt har man fiskar.   Erik 3;0
         such has one fishes
         'Such (things) does one have when one fishes.'

Some of the sentences in (33) are true counterexamples to our theory, some more doubtful. For instance, (33f) describes a sequence of events that are related temporally, as well as causally, and it is therefore natural to assume that the *wh*-word *när* 'when' is omitted. It could, however, also be the conjunction *och* 'and', since simple coordination of two events also implies that the two events are ordered temporally such that the first event precedes the second one.[16] Except for the sentences in (33), it seems to be a generalization to say that the children use CPs that accord to adult grammar when they have fully acquired the PP.

3.3. Embla: A Case Study

For a deeper analysis, we will follow the development of one child, Embla, between the age of 1;9.10 and 2;5.20. Her use of prepositions and complementizers in percentages over time can be seen in Figure 1 below.

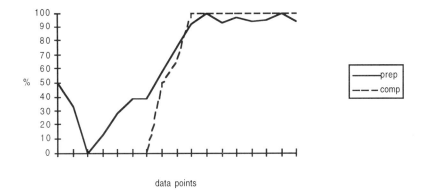

Figure 1 The use of prepositions and complementizers in the recordings of Embla 1;9.10 - 2;5.20, given in percentages of obligatory contexts at different data points.

There are 17 data points in Figure 1, with intervals of approximately two weeks. The first data point is taken from the recording when the first preposition appeared, at the age of 1;9.10. There is a great deal of variation in the use of prepositions in obligatory contexts in the first seven recordings. There are very few contexts for prepositions in the first two recordings, numbers 2 and 3, respectively. In recording 3, there are nine PP contexts, none of which is realized. There is a gradual increase in the use of prepositions during the next six recordings. In recording 10, Embla (2;1.28) has reached the 90% criterion of preposition acquisition. Interestingly enough, this is also the recording where Embla reaches the 90% criterion of acquisition of CPs. The rest of the children display basically the same pattern (see the appendices for details).

The proposed stages give the general view of the acquisition process. So much happens however, in children's development between the ages of 2 and 3, so the observed temporal coincidence between the acquisition of the PP and the CP is not sufficient to prove the proposed parallelism. If this were due to a more general developmental pattern, we would expect a similar sudden increase for example in the determiner phrase. This is not found, however. In a study of the acquisition of Swedish determiner phrases, Bohnacker (1997) shows that Embla already supplies overt determiners to a high degree at the age of 1;8, in other words before data point 1 in Figure 1 above.[17]

In Section 4, we will procede to a qualitative analysis of the acquisition of the PP and the CP. It will be shown that the first complementizer, *som*, is precisely the one that also may be used, and is in fact used by the children, as a preposition. This supports the idea that the acquisition of the PP should be viewed as an application of salient properties of the PP onto a new domain, the CP. If the proposed hypothesis were incorrect we would expect that other types of complementizers, like *wh*-words or the general subordinating *att* 'that', would be the first ones to be used by a child. A more thorough discussion of the syntactic properties of *som* as a complementizer and preposition which was introduced in Section 3, and will be continued in Section 4.

4. DISCUSSION

In Section 3, we showed that there is a correlation in quantitative terms between the acquisition of the PP and the CP. In this section, we will discuss the correlation in qualitative terms. First we will discuss a specific subtype of subordinate clauses, namely "quotation sentences", which emerges at the end of Stage 2. After that we will discuss *som,* the first complementizer used by the children, and discuss their reasons for this choice.

4.1. "Quotation Sentences"

One particularly interesting type of subordinate clause is the quotation sentence, shown in (34) below (Quotation sentences are marked Quot in the Appendices).[18]

(34)   "Jag vill ha mat" sa han   Embla 2;1.14
       "I want food" said he

Quotation sentences of the type in (34) have special properties which probably makes them easier to produce than other subordinate clauses. They lack complementizers, and deictic elements like pronouns or adverbs can remain unchanged. Of all the children in the investigation, Embla seems to use quotation sentences the most. We claim that this is a strategy that serves as an intermediate step in the development of full subordinate clauses that conform to adult language.

Interestingly enough, Håkansson (1987) found that teachers addressing second language learners tend to use more quotation sentences with beginners than with more advanced students. When the learners advance, the teacher's use of quotation sentences decreases significantly, and these are replaced by "true" subordinate clauses. A reasonable assumption is that the quotation sentences are easier to process and comprehend by learners.

4.2. *som*: A Lexical Bridge between the PP and the CP

The next question to address is the following: In what way do the children use the structure of the PP to acquire the CP? In other words, can we see any connection apart from the temporal one, discussed above, between the acquisition of the PP and the acquisition of the CP? As an answer, we will point out the importance of lexical items serving both as prepositions and complementizers. One particularly important preposition/complementizer seems to be the comparative or relative *som*. As shown in Section 2, *som* governs both DP and clausal complements. In comparative contexts, the semantic difference between the use of a DP or a clausal complement is very small. Consider the example in (35) below:

(35)   Den är inte så l/lång som hans.   Embla 2;5.6
                it is not as l/long as his

Here *som* governs a DP complement. The addition of a predicate would not add any new information since this predicate would be identical to the one of the matrix clause. If a predicate was to be inserted it would be something like (36) below:

(36)   Den är inte så lång som hans är lång.
                it is not as long as his is long

Comparative clauses with *som* therefore seem to be an "easy" type of subordinate clause. As Lundin (1987:78) notes, they express a comparison between events and things. The child is free to expand the DP to a syntactically more complex phrase, even though the semantics remain the same. This is exactly what Tor does in the examples shown in (37) below:

(37) a. Precis som Tor. Snurrar runt.   Tor 2;5.10
Just as Tor. Whirls around
b. Precis som Tor sn/ snurrar runt.   Tor 2;5.10

Observe that Tor first uses *som* as a preposition (37a). In (37b), he uses *som* as a complementizer. The semantics of (37a) is however equivalent to that of (37b). Comparative sentences are in a way simpler than many other subordinate clauses; the preposition *som* becomes a complementizer just by the addition of a predicate that in a way is pleonastic.[19] In this analysis, the term preposition or complementizer refers to the function of the element in question, not to lexical or context-independent properties. The type of extended projection in which the element in question appears determines whether it is a preposition or a complementizer. The structure of the PP can, as was shown above, very easily be carried over to the CP without a great increase in semantic complexity. We claim that *som* serves as a sort of bridge between the two construction types, this lexical item being able to govern both DPs and clausal complements. The step from using *som* as a preposition to using it as a complementizer is very small. It does, however, establish a principle, and once this principle is acquired the child will apply it to other prepositions, and will very soon be able to increase the complexity of the CP, using more complex complementizers as well. These complex complementizers consist of preposition+*att* or *om* (see 7 - 9). Given that it is easier to produce sentences with simple complementizers than with more complex ones, we understand quite easily why children start using *som* as complementizer, not any of the other prepositions.[20]

4.4. Concluding Remarks

We have argued that there is a parallelism between the PP and the CP in terms of the setup and hierarchical order of functional categories. This parallelism is crucial for language acquisition. In the present study, we have given empirical evidence for a correlation in time between the acquisition of the PP and the CP in child Swedish child; when children have acquired the PP structure (90% or more supplied in obligatory contexts) they also have acquired the CP structure. Determiner phrases are acquired at a different period of time and, it seems, in a different manner (Bohnacker, 1997), This shows that the observed parallel between prepositions and complementizers is not just an artifact of general developmental patterns. Moreover, there seems to be a lexical correlation between the CP and the PP. The first complementizer used by Swedish children is *som*, which the child already has acquired and used as a preposition. We argue that *som* serves as a "lexical bridge" between the PP and the CP.

ACKNOWLEDGEMENTS

A preliminary version of this paper was presented at "The Workshop on the L1- and L2-Acquisition of Clause-Internal Rules: Scrambling and Cliticization" in Berne, January 21 - 23, 1994. We thank the participants of the workshop for valuable comments. Special thanks to Christer Platzack for reading earlier versions of the manuscript and for giving good advice, useful suggestions and extensive comments, as well as to an anonymous reviewer for useful criticism. We are also in debt to Ragnhild Söderbergh for giving us access to her material. All errors and inadequacies are, of course, our own.

NOTES

[1] Object shift is, in short, the raising of a weak object pronoun to a position to the left of a sentence adverbial. Object shift is grammatical only in main clauses. An example of an object shift construction is given in (ii), which should be compared to (i) where the object is in its base position.

(i) *Jag ser inte den.*
     I see not it
(ii) *Jag ser den inte.*

An investigation by means of elicited imitation presented in Josefsson (in press) shows that the object shift construction is mastered rather late in the language acquisition process. The youngest child in the investigation, around 2 years of age, did not succeed in repeating any of the object-shifted sentences. Not until the age of 4 - 5 did the children seem to master the construction. For more details about the investigation, see Josefsson (in press).

[2] The term CP will throughout the paper refer only to subordinate CPs (unless otherwise specified). The possible structure of the main clause CP will not be discussed in this paper.

[3] Similar ideas concerning a parallelism between the DP and the CP, have been proposed in several works lately (Siloni, 1990; Åfarli, 1993; Penner, 1993). We do not take any stand as to the compatibility of these analyses and the one proposed in this paper.

[4] The term extended projection is used in the sense of Grimshaw (1991).

[5] The purpose of this paper is to explore the idea that there is a parallelism between the subordinate CP and the PP. Whether a child has access to all functional projections, including the CP from the very beginning, as proposed in Hyams (1992) or if they have only the lexical projection, the VP (e.g., Radford, 1990), is not discussed in this paper.

[6] *Vore* is morphologically a subjunctive form. For most other verbs in Swedish, the preterite forms have taken over the function carried out by subjunctives.

[7] Preposition+*att* seems to be far more common than preposition+*om*.

[8] In traditional grammar, some of the combinations preposition+*att* are classified as complex complementizers, some are classified as preposition+complementizer *att*. Jörgensen & Svensson (1987), for example, consider *trots att* 'despite that' and *för att* 'for that' complex complementizers but not *med att* 'with that' or *över att* 'over that'.

[9] Note that the relative particle *that* and the comparative particle *as* both are spelled out as *som* in Swedish.

[10] There is one important exception. Consider (i):

(i) *Han domderar som om han vore general.*
     he goes-on as if he was (a) general.
(ii) *Han domderar som vore han general.*

In the example in (ii), the verb of the subordinate clause has raised to the CP domain. This is made transparent by the fact that the verb *vore* precedes the subject. We have no good explanation of why this is possible. It is however restricted to conditional clauses where the verb seemingly raises to the position occupied by *om* in the example in (i). The construction in (ii) is stylistically marked.

[11] To circumvent the problem with the relation between the prenominal and the enclitic determiner we have chosen only examples containing an adjectival modifier, which requires the presence of a prenominal determiner, presumably located in D^0. The same function as determiner could be carried out by a possessive pronoun or a genitive.

[12] The possible presence of an AgrNP located between the DP and the NP is not of direct relevance for our thesis, and we therefore refrain from discussing that possibility.

[13] The comparative particle is preferably stranded in constructions of the type shown in (25a). To us *??Som vem var du lika snabb* sounds rather odd.

[14] The idea that the PP is important for the acquisition of subordinate clauses is, however, not new. Müller (1993:167ff) describes how bilingual children use the (French) preposition *pour* to govern infinitive clauses and German *für* 'for' as complementizer governing finite clauses. She also mentions that monolingual children use German *für* as a complementizer too. She concludes that there is a three-step development from the function as preposition to the function as complementizer: The complement of a preposition is in Stage 1 an NP. In Stage 2, the complement could be either NP or an IP. In third stage, the whole PP is reanalyzed as a (subordinate) CP, and the preposition is analyzed as a complementizer.

[15] Nanna imitates a lot, and it is difficult to interpret to which extent prepositions are really productive in her speech at this stage.

[16] Another possibility is that *gick sönder* is simply a verb first main clause. V1 sentences are quite frequent in narrative contexts also in adult language.

[17] For an earlier discussion about children's acquisition of definiteness in Swedish, see Svartholm (1978).

[18] We also have included other subordinate clauses, which lack overt complementizers but yet are grammatical in adult speech in this category.

[19] Interestingly, some children with specific language impairment (SLI) seem to be able to produce constructions with a comparative *som* taking a DP complement, but are unable to use *som* as a complementizer, taking a clausal complement. This may indicate that they have reached the stage in (36a), but are unable to proceed to the stage represented by (36b) (Kristina Hansson p.c.).

[20] Another kind of simple subordinate clause with *som* as complementizer, common in early child language, is the cleft construction. From a formal point of view, the matrix clause of the cleft construction contains a subject and a verb, *det är* 'it is', but neither the subject nor the verb refers to anything; *det* is an expletive and *är* the copula. The sole function of the matrix clause *det är* is to point out a focused element. *Det är* could thus be considered a sort of "dummy focus phrase". This taken into consideration, the steps from (i) to (ii) to (iii) in the following examples of Tor are therefore rather small:

(i) /a: e / det? (=Vad är det?) Tor 2;3.29
what is it
(ii) /e: san/ kryper ut. Tor 2;5.10
(it) is sand creeps out
(iii) Det är många bilar som jag öppn/ Tor 2;8.9
it is many cars that I ope/

For a discussion about the cleft construction in the acquisition of Swedish, see Plunkett & Strömqvist (1990).

APPENDICES

The tables in Appendix 1 and 2 show the frequency of prepositional phrases (PPs) and complementizer phrases (CPs) in the recordings of 9 Swedish children. The following abbreviations are used:

zero prep = preposition is omitted in an obligatory context
overt prep = preposition is supplied in an obligatory context
zero comp = complementizer is omitted in an obligatory context
overt comp = complementizer is supplied in an obligatory context
% corr = percentage of preposition supplied in obligatory contexts
Quot = Quotation -- The child quotes what someone has said, e.g.,

>"jag vill ha mat" sa han
>"I want food" said he   Embla 2;1.14

APPENDIX I

The Stockholm corpus (Söderbergh, 1973)

Table 1.
Ask 1;11.28-2;8.21

Rec nb	Age	zero prep	overt prep	PPs: % corr	zero comp	Quot	CPs: overt comp
Stage 2							
1	1;11.28	24	25	51	-	-	-
2	2;0.12	15	11	42	-	-	-
3	2;0.26	4	4	50	-	-	-
4	2;1.9	10	8	44	-	-	-
5	2;1.23	1	1	27	71	2	-
Stage 3							
6	2;2.6	1	17	94	-	-	-
7	2;2.22	1	12	92	-	1	-
8	2;3.4	1	15	94	-	1	1
9	2;4.1	1	23	96	-	-	-
10	2;4.15	1	27	96	-	-	-
11	2;4.29	1	24	96	3	-	-
12	2;5.12	1	15	94	-	4	-
13	2;6.5	-	18	100	-	1	2
14	2;6.19	-	20	100	-	1	10
15	2;7.9	-	17	100	-	2	2
16	2;7.24	-	38	100	-	2	9
17	2;8.7	-	36	100	-	-	7
18	2;8.21	-	24	100	-	-	5

Table 2.
Embla 1;9.10-2;5.20

Rec nb	Age	PPs: zero prep	PPs: overt prep	% corr	CPs: zero comp	CPs: Quot	CPs: overt comp
Stage 2							
1	1;9.10	1	1	50	-	-	-
2	1;9.25	2	1	33	-	-	-
3	1;10.8	9	-	-	-	-	-
4	1;10.22	13	2	13	-	-	-
5	1;11.5	5	2	28	-	-	-
6	1;11.21	5	3	38	1	-	-
7	2;0.3	13	8	38	-	2	-
8	2;1.1	5	7	58	1	-	1
9	2;1.14	4	13	76	1	6	2
Stage 3							
10	2;1.28	1	11	92	-	2	1
11	2;2.11	-	21	100	-	2	5
12	2;3.4	1	13	93	-	4	4
13	2;3.18	1	23	96	-	-	3
14	2;4.1	2	30	94	-	-	12
15	2;4.22	1	21	95	-	-	12
16	2;5.6	-	18	100	-	-	5
17	2;5.20	1	18	94	-	1	17

Table 3.
Nanna 1;8.12-2;1.17

Rec nb	Age	PPs: zero prep	PPs: overt prep	% corr	CPs: zero comp	CPs: Quot	CPs: overt comp
Stage 1							
1	1;8.12	4	-	-	-	-	-
Stage 2							
2	1;9.5	3	2	40	-	-	-
Stage 3							
3	1;9.19	-	6	100	-	-	-
4	1;10.2	-	10	100	2	-	-
5	1;10.25	1	9	90	-	-	-
6	1:11.12	2	4	67	-	-	-
7	1;11.21	-	23	100	-	-	4
8	2;0.4	5	19	79	-	1	-
9	2;1.17	1	7	88	-	-	-

Table 4.
Tor 2;2.17-2;8.30

Rec nb	Age	PPs: zero prep	overt prep	% corr	CPs: zero comp	Quot	overt comp
Stage 2							
1	2;2.17	7	5	42	-	-	-
2	2;3.15	2	10	83	-	-	-
3	2;3.29	4	5	56	-	-	-
4	2;4.13	6	2	45	3	-	-
5	2;5.10	4	22	85	2	-	2
Stage 3							
6	2;5.24	1	18	95	-	-	-
7	2;6.8	4	37	90	-	-	-
8	2;6.22	-	25	100	-	-	-
9	2;7.11	-	13	100	1	1	6
10	2;7.26	1	28	96	-	2	1
11	2;8.9	-	31	100	-	-	1
12	2;8.30	2	45	96	-	1	4

APPENDIX II

The Lund corpus (Håkansson, Nettelbladt & Hansson 1991)

Table 5.
Erik 2;5-3;0

Rec nb	Age	PPs: zero prep	overt prep	% corr	CPs: zero comp	Quot	overt comp
Stage 2							
1	2;5	4	2	33	-	-	-
2	2;7	2	2	50	-	-	-
3	2;9	4	-	-	-	-	-
Stage 3							
4	2;11	-	5	100	-	2	-
5	3;0	1	2	67	1	-	-

Table 6.
Joakim 2;3-3;4

Rec nb	Age	zero prep	overt prep	PPs: % corr	zero comp	Quot	CPs: overt comp
Stage 2							
1	2;3	2	1	33	1	-	-
2	2;5	4	3	43	-	-	-
Stage 3							
3	2;8	-	2	100	-	-	3
4	3;1	1	12	92	-	-	15
5	3;4	-	7	100	-	-	8

Table 7.
Karin 1;11-3;1

Rec nb	Age	zero prep	overt prep	PPs: % corr	zero comp	Quot	CPs: overt comp
Stage 1							
1	1;11	7	-	-	-	-	-
Stage 2							
2	2;0	2	1	33	-	-	-
3	2;3	2	-	-	8	-	-
4	2;7	1	5	83	3	-	-
Stage 3							
5	2;11	-	9	100	-	3	18
6	3;1	-	2	100	-	1	14

Table 8.
Martin 2;2-3;1

Rec nb	Age	zero prep	overt prep	PPs: % corr	zero comp	Quot	CPs: overt comp
Stage 2							
1	2;2	1	1	50	-	-	-
2	2;4	1	7	88	-	-	-
3	2;6	5	-	-	-	-	-
4	2;8	1	4	80	-	-	-
Stage 3							
5	2;10	-	17	100	-	3	2
6	3;0	-	5	100	-	-	1
7	3;1	-	20	100	-	-	6

Table 9.
Niklas 2;4-3;0

Rec nb	Age	zero prep	overt prep	PPs: % corr	zero comp	Quot	CPs: overt comp
Stage 1							
1	2;4	4	-	-	-	-	-
Stage 2							
2	2;6	4	1	20	-	-	-
3	2;7	7	1	12	-	-	-
Stage 3							
4	2;10	-	12	100	-	-	-
5	2;11	-	4	100	-	-	-
6	3;0	-	4	100	-	-	5

REFERENCES

Åfarli, T. A.: 1993, A Promotion Analysis of Restrictive Relative Clauses. Ms. University of Trondheim.

Bohnacker, U.: 1997, The Determiner Phrases and the Debate on Functional Categories in Early Child Language. *Language Acquisition* 7:1, 49–90.

Grimshaw J.: 1991, Extended Projections. Ms. Brandeis University.

Håkansson, G.: 1987, *Teacher Talk: How teachers modify their speech when addressing learners of Swedish as a second language.* Lund University Press: Lund.

Håkansson G, U. Nettelbladt, and K. Hansson: 1991, Variation and Deviation in Language Acquisition: Some Hypotheses and Preliminary Observations. *Working Papers* 3, Department of Linguistics, Lund University, 83–95.

Hoekstra, E.: 1993, On the Parameterization of Functional Projections in CP. *Proceedings of NELS 22.*

Holmberg, A.: 1986, *Word Order and Syntactic Features in the Scandinavian Languages and English.* Ph.D. Dissertation, Department of General Linguistics, University of Stockholm.

Hyams, N.: 1992, The Genesis of Clausal Structure. In Meisel J. (ed.) *The Acquisition of Verb Placement.* Kluwer Academic Publishers: Dordrecht, 371–400.

Jörgensen, N. & J. Svensson: 1987, Nusvensk *grammatik*. Liber, Lund.

Josefsson, G.: 1996, The acquisition of object shift in Swedish child language. In C. Johnson & J.H.V. Gilbert (eds.) *Children's Language* 9, Lawrence Erlbaum Associates, Hillsdale. 153–165.

Kayne, R: 1982, Predicates and Arguments, Verbs and Nouns. Talk presented at the GLOW Colloquium, Paris.

Kayne, R.: 1991, Romance Clitics, Verb Movement, and PRO. *Linguistic Inquiry* 22, 647–686.

Lange, S.: 1974, *En preliminär grammatisk analys av språket hos Freja från 20 till 41 månaders ålder*, del 1–3. Department of Scandinavian Languages. Stockholm University.

Lange, S.: 1976, *Prepositionerna i ett barns spontana tal. En längdsnittsstudie.* (P)reprint no 11. Department of Scandinavian Languages. Stockholm University.

Larsson, K.: 1977, *En preliminär grammatisk analys av språket hos Tor från 20 till 43 månaders ålder*, Department of Scandinavian Languages. Stockholm University.

Lange S. & K. Larsson: 1973, *Syntactic Development of a Swedish Girl Embla, Between 20 and 42 Months of Age*, Department of Scandinavian Languages. Stockholm University.

Lundin, B.: 1987, *Bisatser i små barns språk*. Lund University Press: Lund.

Müller G. & W. Sternefeld: 1993, Improper Movement and Unambiguous Binding, *Linguistic Inquiry* **24**, 461–507.
Müller, N.: 1993, *Komplexe Sätze*. Gunter Narr Verlag, Tübingen.
Penner Z.: 1993, The Earliest Stage in the Acquisition of the Nominal Phrase in Bernese Swiss German: Syntactic Bootstrapping and the Architecture of Language Learning. *Arbeitspapier* **30**, Universität Bern, Institut für Sprachwissenschaft.
Platzack, C.: 1998, A Visibility condition for the C-Domain', Working Papers in Scandinavian Syntax **61**, 53-99.
Platzack, C.: 1994, Mainland Scandinavian Evidence for a Split COMP. Talk presented at the GLOW Colloquium in Vienna.
Plunkett, K. & S. Strömqvist: 1990, The acquisition of Scandinavian languages. *Gothenburg Papers in Theoretical Linguistics* **59**. Department of Linguistics, University of Gothenburg.
Radford, A.: 1990, *Syntactic Theory and the Acquisition of English Syntax: The Nature of Early Child Grammars of English*. Basil Blackwell. Oxford.
Rizzi, L.: 1997, 'The Fine Structure of the Left Periphery', in L. Haegeman (ed.) *Elements of Grammar. A Handbook of Generative Syntax*, Kluwer, Dordrecht, 281-337.
Shlonsky, U.: 1992, Representation of Agr in Comp and subject clitics in West Flemish. *GenGen* **0**:0.
Siloni, T.: 1990, On the Parallelism between CP and DP: The Case of Hebrew Semi-Relatives. In *Proceedings of the LCJL,* Leiden.
Söderbergh, R.: 1973, Project Child Language Syntax and Project Early Reading. *Rapport från Barnspråksavdelningen*. Stockholm University.
Svartholm, K.: 1978, Svenskans artikelsystem. En genomgång av artikelbruket i vuxenspråket och en modell för analys av bruket i barnspråk. *Meddelanden från Institutionen för nordiska språk vid Stockholms universitet* **3**. Stockholm University.
Vikner, S.: 1991, *Verb Movement and the Licensing of NP-positions in the Germanic Languages*. Ph. D. Dissertation, University of Geneva.

GUNLØG JOSEFSSON
Lund University

GISELA HÅKANSSON
Lund University

CORNELIA HAMANN

NEGATION, INFINITIVES, AND HEADS

1. INTRODUCTION

In recent acquisition research, the position of the verb relative to the negation particle has been used to argue for the early existence of verb movement in children's grammars of French, German, and other languages. The argument is based on the well-established distribution of finite and non-finite verbs with respect to the negative particle in child French and child German. Pierce (1989, 1992) demonstrated that French children place the non-finite verb after the negative particle *pas*, but place finite verbs before this particle at a surprisingly early age and almost without errors:

(1) a. pas tomber bébé   Nathalie 2;0,1
 not fall baby
 'the baby doesn't fall'
 b. veux pas lolo   Nathalie 2;0,1
 want not pacifier.
 '(I) don't want the pacifier'

Pierce (1989:40) documents the following distribution over three French children covering an age span from 1;8 - 2;6:[1]

Table 1.
Verb movement in French (Pierce, 1989)

	+finite	-finite
pas verb	11	77
verb *pas*	185	2

Similar results were obtained by Verrips & Weissenborn (1989) (hereafter V & W) for French and German and have recently been corroborated for other French and German children as can be seen in Hamann (1993a) and the appendix.

The conclusion therefore is that in French and German finite verbs raise across negation and infinitives remain below, or in other words, finite verbs raise to IP, while infinitives stay in VP. The implication of these findings is that children at the age of around two years have the finiteness distinction and a functional projection for the finite verb to raise to, i.e., they have already acquired IP at least.

Leaving aside the implications for a Strong or Weak Continuity Hypothesis, there are two questions to be asked in the context of recent linguistic theory. These concern the status of the negative particle and the integration of the above findings into recent accounts of the optional infinitive phase. Both questions touch on the problem of the early availability of clause internal positions, projections, and movement where the early data on negation play a decisive role.

Given the introduction of the NegP as a functional category by Pollock (1989), and given the acquisition of (some) functional categories at about age 2, it seems to follow from the above that negative particles across which the verb can raise must be specifiers, as is clear for French *pas*. For German *nicht* and English *not* there is a lively debate, however, with regard to their status as negative heads or specifiers. If the acquisition literature assumes for reasons to be discussed below that these particles are heads at least in child language, then it has to answer the question how the verb can raise across another head unless there is cliticization, and how a reclassification comes about if the particle in question is a specifier in the adult language. If a reclassification takes place, there is the problem of discontinuity to be overcome. Therefore, the first question to be answered is whether the negative particle is a head or a specifier in the child grammar of a given language. Of course, these considerations hold only at a stage where the concept of finiteness is acquired and there is evidence for the existence of functional categories like IP or NegP. If that is not the case, then negation might simply function as an adjunct with no blocking effect at all. It is clear, however, that a decision as to the status of the negative particle in a specific child language will greatly influence the interpretation of the data concerning movement and available positions. I will argue that, in German, the negative particle is a specifier from the beginning.

The second problem concerns the child's truncation option as proposed by Rizzi (1992, 1994). Originally conceived to explain the optionality of infinitives and null subjects at a certain stage in acquisition, Rizzi's theory proposes that the child has the full array of functional projections from early on, but can truncate structure at any point in the tree, thus complying with the Minimize Structure Constraint proposed by Grimshaw (1993). The child projects only as much structure as is necessary to accommodate the material present in the phrase. Thus the child does not project further than VP or AgrOP for an infinitival clause, but can, in the next instant, use an inflected verb which has visibly been raised to IP.

Taken in isolation, this proposal seems to be just an ingenious way of compromising a Small Clause Analysis with the Full Competence Hypothesis, in so far as now the child has the full range of functional projections at its disposal, but uses them only if required - perhaps not at all in a first phase (Radford, 1996). But taken together with the assumption of a universally given order of projections, the hypothesis makes very precise co-occurrence predictions.

Most important of all is the following. If the NegP is located above TP, the use of negation will certainly activate tense or finiteness and thus exclude the sequence Neg+Infinitive in principle. So the second question is, whether the occurrence of negation with infinitives is really as robust as the data from Table 1 suggest. If it turns out that it is rare across languages, then Rizzi's proposal is proved correct. If it is robust in some languages, but rare in others then it follows that the order of projections is probably not universal (Haegeman, 1996), or negation in the particular language is an adverb or functions as an adjunct. If the phenomenon is rather robust across languages in which it is well established for adult language that NegP is above TP, then Rizzi's proposal seems to need revision.

Thus, the question about the occurrence of negation with infinitives will lead to insights about the universality of projection order or decide about the correctness of the truncation approach and so - together with the decision as to the status of the negative particle in child language - decide about the availability of projections and movement.

In order to deal with these questions, the structure of the article is the following. Section 2 outlines the theoretical background. In Section 2.1, the arguments for a NegP and the Neg-Criterion are called to mind, in Section 2.2. the Neg-Criterion is discussed in its manifestation in West Flemish and

German. Section 3 introduces the head/specifier problem in detail (3.1.) and argues that *nicht* is not a head in adult Standard German (3.2). Section 4 studies the acquisition of the negative particle in German with a view to the status of *nicht* in child language and the consequences for verb movement and scrambling (4.1). I then discuss the assumptions proposed in the literature that a) the negative particle *nicht* is a head in early child language (4.2), and b) that it remains unclassified for a time (4.3). 4.4. finally argues that a specifier analysis of *nicht* for child German explains all the data and so is preferable also for continuity reasons. Section 5 addresses the truncation theory and the problem of negative infinitives. 5.1. sketches the phenomenon of optional infinitives and the truncation hypothesis. Section 5.2. discusses French data on negation, 5.3. does the same for German and Dutch. It is argued that though the truncation hypothesis seems to be vindicated by the rarity of negation with infinitives, the German data show that the order of projections must be parameterized. This is the case even if, as is discussed in Section 6, *nicht* in child language is an adverb. Finally, Section 7 gives the conclusions.

2. THE NEGP AND THE NEG-CRITERION

2.1. The NegP and the Neg-Criterion in French

Based on Pollock (1989) and other work, it has generally been accepted that the clause structure of English and of French contains a functional projection NegP. In French this functional projection is headed by *ne* where *ne* has to co-occur with another negative constituent:

(2)   a. Jean ne viendra *(pas)
                  Jean ne come(fut) not
                  'Jean will not come'
          b. Jean ne viendra *(jamais)
                  Jean ne come (fut) (n)ever
                  'Jean will never come'
          c. Jean ne parlera *(a personne).
                  Jean ne speak(fut) to anybody
                  'Jean will not speak to anybody.'

For French it has been observed that there is a dependency relation between the negative head and negative constituents, because:

a. the head requires the presence of another negative XP (2a,b,c), and
b. there are ECP effects as in (3a,b).

(3) a. Je n'exige que tu voies personne.
    I ne insist that you see nobody
    'I insist that you see nobody.'
  b. Je n'exige que personne vienne.
    [*personne* only has narrow scope]
    I ne insist that nobody come
    'I insist that nobody come.'

In (3b), the negative element *ne* has moved to the higher clause, but its trace in the lower clause must be licensed by the presence of *personne* so that only a narrow scope reading is possible.

In parallel to work on *wh*-questions (Rizzi 1991, 1996), the dependency has been explained by postulating a well-formedness condition at LF, see Haegeman & Zanuttini (1991) and Haegeman (1991, 1995). This well-formedness condition, which determines the distribution of negative elements, is formulated as the Neg-Criterion.

(4) *The Neg-Criterion*
  a. A NEG-Operator must be in a specifier-head configuration with an X^0 [NEG].
  b. An X^0 [NEG] must be in a specifier-head configuration with a NEG-operator.

In order to account for cases where a *wh*-element or a negative constituent can stay *in situ* as in (5a,b), it is necessary to assume a functional definition of operator which exempts such elements in argument position from the relevant criteria at S-Structure.

(5) a. Niemand ist mit nichts zufrieden
    nobody is with nothing content
    'nobody is content with nothing'
  b. Who saw what

(6) *Operator*
  a. A negative phrase in a scope position is a Neg-operator
  b. A left-peripheral A'-position ([Spec, XP] or [YP, XP]) is a scope position.

2.2. Negation in West Flemish and German

The Neg-Criterion applies as late as LF in French (and in Italian), which will immediately account for the ECP effects in (3a,b). In these examples LF movement of *personne* 'nobody' is due to the Neg-Criterion. In other languages, we see that the Neg-Criterion applies at S-Structure. West Flemish (WF) is a case in point. WF has the negative head *en*, which cannot stand alone, but must be accompanied by the negative specifier *nie* 'not' or a negative constituent like *niemand* 'nobody', *niets* 'nothing'. Concerning word order, we see the following patterns in WF:

(7)   a. da Velere ketent me dienen boek was
             that Valere content with that book was
             'that Valere was content with that book'
        b. da Valere me dienen boek ketent was
             that Valere with that book content was
             'that Valere was content with that book'
        c. da Valere ketent was me dienen boek
             that Valere content was with that book.
             'that Valere was content with that book'

We conclude that in positive contexts the complement of *ketent* 'content', the PP *me dienen boek* 'with that book', may occupy a number of positions. It can be to the right of the adjective, to its left, in extraposition. When *ketent* takes a negative complement, however, the pattern changes. The negative complement can only be to the left of the adjective:

(8)   a. *da Valere ketent me niets en was
             that Valere content with nothing was
             'that Valere was content with nothing'
        b. da Valere me niets ketent en was
             'that Valere was content with nothing'
        c. *da Valere ketent en was me niets
             'that Valere was content with nothing'

Now observe that the word order is much freer when the negative head is absent as in (9a,b,c).

(9) a. da Valere ketent me niets was
        that Valere content with nothing was
        'that Valere was content with nothing'
     b. da Valere me niets ketent was
        that Valere with nothing content was
        'that Valere was content with nothing'
     c. da Valere ketent was me niets
        that Valere content was with nothing
        'that Valere was content with nothing'

In the examples (8a,b,c) the presence of *en* signals that there must be a NegP and hence the Neg-Criterion applies: *en* must have a negative XP as its specifier - at S-structure as the examples show. As *en* is optionally realized, (8b) has a grammatical counterpart in (9b), and both sentences get the reading where the negative constituent has sentential scope. For the sentences (6a) and (6b) to be grammatical, the negative head has to be absent and they have a reading where the negation has only constituent scope, and the interpretation is 'Valere is content with hardly anything'.

Haegeman (1991) also discusses instances of Negative Concord in WF, i.e., instances where the occurrence of two negative expressions leads to a simple negation reading. She shows that not just one, but all negative constituents must be in a specifier-head relation with *en* at S-structure. The idea is that the negative constituent moves to establish a specifier-head relation with *en* at S-structure and that this is achieved by either moving to Spec, NegP, or by moving to the specifier of a higher functional projection which thus becomes an extended projection of the NegP so that an extended specifier-head relation with *en* satisfies the Neg-Criterion.

The possibility to form an extended projection may be relevant for the acquisition sequence in German in so far as German shows many parallels to WF even if it does not have a two-partite negation. We find the same possible positions for adjectival complements as in (7a,b,c) and exactly the same pattern as in (9a,b,c) with negative complements.

(10) a. weil Peter auf seinen Freund stolz ist
because Peter of his friend proud is
'because Peter is proud of his friend'
b. weil Peter stolz auf seinen Freund ist
because Peter proud of his friend is
'because Peter is proud of his friend'
c. weil Peter stolz ist auf seinen Freund
because Peter proud is of his friend
'because Peter is proud of his friend'

(11) a. weil Peter stolz auf niemanden ist
because Peter proud of nobody is
'because Peter is proud of nobody'
b. weil Peter auf niemanden stolz ist
because Peter of nobody proud is
'because Peter is proud of nobody'
c. weil Peter stolz ist auf niemanden
because P proud is of nobody
'because Peter is proud of nobody'

As in WF, the negative constituent has sentential scope only when it has scrambled to the left of the adjective in (11b). In (11a) and (11c), we get an echoic or denial reading. If one substitutes *nichts* 'nothing' for *niemand* 'nobody', then one also gets either of the readings: 'because Peter is proud already of nothing' or 'because Peter is proud hardly of anything' as can be shown in the appropriate conversational contexts (see Hamann, 1993b). Thus, we are led to conclude that German patterns with WF in that the Neg-Criterion has to be satisfied already at S-Structure - something which might tie in with the properties of scrambling in these languages.

Such a parallel to WF certainly presupposes the existence of a NegP or a PolP in German. If we have a PolP, which is likely as it will emerge, then the negative particle will color it negatively and so to speak make it into a NegP. Let us now turn to a discussion of the German NegP and the properties of *nicht*.

3. GERMAN NEGATION AND THE HEAD/SPECIFIER PROBLEM

3.1. The Problem

In parallel to Pollock's assumptions about English, we can assume that *nicht* marks the position of the German NegP. This still leaves two choices: *nicht* could be a specifier like French *pas* as has been tacitly assumed in the above discussion, or it could be a head like French *ne* or West Flemish *en*.

Since Bayer (1990), it has often been assumed (especially in the acquisition literature, see Clahsen, 1988; V & W, 1989), that *nicht* is a head. This is surprising as pointed out in the introduction, because in such an account the verb must move across another head. This is excluded by the head-movement-constraint and more generally by the ECP. Thus, the alternative for the categorization of *nicht* is its being a specifier. This would allow a coherent analysis of the verb movement examples for children - and of the target sentences (12a,b), thus allowing for continuity.[2]

(12)   a. daß Maria nicht in die Schule geht
            that Maria not in the school goes
            'that Maria doesn't go to school'
      b. daß Maria diesen Brief nicht mit einem Bleistift schreibt
            that Maria this letter not with a pencil writes
            'that Maria doesn't write this letter with a pencil'

A decision as to the head or specifier status of *nicht* in child language is not made easier, however, by the considerable discussion in German linguistic theory about the proper categorization of adult *nicht*. Bayer (1990) gives an analysis of Bavarian cases of Negative Concord, i.e., cases where the occurrence of two negative expressions leads to a reading of simple negation, in which *nicht* is indeed a head. On the other side, we have Grewendorf (1990), Haegeman (1991) and others who assume that *nicht* is a specifier - mostly for the reason that it does not block verb movement and also, in the case of the latter, because of the striking parallels to WF. Let us therefore clear up the status of *nicht* in the target language before returning to its categorization in child language.

3.2. *Nicht* is Not a Head in Adult German

The following discussion will show that even if there is a way to account for verb-movement across *nicht*, there are other arguments for its specifier status.

A possible way across *nicht* is suggested by Roberts' (1992) work on long head movement, where the argument goes as follows. For V2-languages C is probably V-related, but negation is not, unless it is like a *wh*-feature in I as suggested in Rizzi (1991) for Wh, and unless we are dealing with a language which marks negation morphologically on the verb like Turkish. As we have one V-related chain of V-to-I and another V-related chain of V+I-to-C, the non-V-related head *nicht*, would not block this movement. Thus, verb movement across *nicht* would pattern with other cases of Long-Head-Movement.

Though there are reasons to assume that C is V-related in V2-languages, there are other arguments to assume it is not (Zwart, 1993). Also, the assumption about negation though descriptively adequate seems rather *ad hoc*. What makes French *ne* V related and cliticize to the verb, while German *nicht* is not V-related in the same sense? In fact, Haegeman (1995) assumes that West Flemish Neg is V-related, so that verb movement across Neg is certainly blocked. Let us therefore leave aside this possibility of escaping the HMC, and consider some other arguments against the head status of *nicht*.

The first two concern the fact that it is certainly not a clitic. As a clitic, it could move along with the verb and thus avoid violating the HMC. As it turns out, *nicht* is a free morpheme. *Nicht* does not cliticize to the finite verb or move along with it as the negative particle does in French and Italian AUX-to-C constructions:

(13) a. Pourquoi n' as   tu pas fait tes devoirs?
         why   ne have you not done your homework
         'Why haven't you done your homework?'
      b. *Pourquoi as   tu ne pas fait tes devoirs
         why   have you ne not done your homework
         'Why haven't you done your homework?'

(14) a. *Warum nicht hast du deine Hausaufgaben gemacht?
     why   not have you your homework   done
     'why haven't you done your homework?'
  b. *Warum hast nicht du deine Hausaufgaben gemacht?
     why have not you your homework   done
     'why haven't you done your homework?'
  c. Warum hast du deine Hausaufgaben nicht gemacht?
     why have you your homework   not done
     'why haven't you done your homework?'

While (14a) is completely unacceptable, (14b) is only unacceptable in the sentence scope reading. If the implication is that someone else has done a person's homework and there is heavy focus on *du* 'you', the sentence becomes interpretable. In that case, however, there would be no affinity to the verb, the constituent would be *nicht du* 'not you'.

The second argument is that material can intervene between the verb and the negative particle. This is excluded given a Bayer-type analysis where negation cliticizes to the verb.

we will assume that *nicht* is a syncategorematic expression....which in the unmarked case adjoins to V^0. The elements NEG and V together form a new V. It appears that a negative quantifier must be c-commanded by this negative verb (Bayer, 1990:17).

This sort of analysis, even if correct for Bavarian, certainly does not hold for WF (Haegeman, 1995) and cannot be right for Standard German. If we assume a *nicht*+V complex, this would have to dominate phrasal material of different types:

(15) a. daß Peter wahrscheinlich nicht sehr betrunken war
     that Peter probably not very drunk was
     'that Peter probably wasn't very drunk'
  b. daß Peter wahrscheinlich nicht nach Hause geht
     that Peter probably not to home goes
     'that Peter probably doesn't go home'
  c. daß Peter wahrscheinlich nicht darüber sprechen will
     that Peter probably not thereof talk wants
     'that Peter probably doesn't want to talk about this'

d. daß Peter da wahrscheinlich nich über sprechen will
   that Peter there probably not of   talk   wants
   'that Peter probably doesn't want to talk about this'
e. daß Peter wahrscheinlich nicht sehr glücklich mit dem Haus ist
   that Peter probably not very happy with the house is
   'that Peter probably is not very happy with the house'
f. daß Peter da wahrscheinlich nich sehr glücklich mit ist
   that Peter there probably not very happy with is
   'that Peter probably is not very happy with this'

In (15a), an AP intervenes between *nicht* and V; in (15b), it is a PP. In (15c), we see that the intervening constituent is a so-called R-PP. In (15d) the R-pronoun *da* has been extracted from the PP, which is possible in some varieties of Northern German as spoken in Hamburg or Niedersachsen. In this example, a trace intervenes between NEG and V. In (15e) it is again an AP that intervenes, this time with a PP complement. In the corresponding (15f) of the Northern variety, the R-pronoun *da* has been extracted from the AP. Again, a trace intervenes between *nicht* and V.

If we follow Bayer's analysis and assume that we have a NEG-V complex, then we would have to say that the complex head can dominate phrasal material of different categories, including traces of phrasal material. However, while the extraction of the head of a complex head is admitted in the literature as a type of excorporation, extraction of non-head material out of complex heads is not standardly assumed.

We propose therefore that exactly as WF *nie* in exactly the same kind of examples (Haegeman, 1991), German *nicht* does not incorporate and does not adjoin to other heads. Together with the fact, that it does not block verb movement, it is improbable that it is a head at all. Thus, it is a maximal projection.

The third fact, which argues for *nicht* being a specifier, is its historical development. If we adopt Jespersen's cycle (see Jepsersen, 1909-1949), German is just one step ahead of (written) French, in that the enforcement *niht* 'not' of the Middle High German head *en/ne/ni* can stand alone these days, i.e., the NegP has lost its head in Modern German as it seems to have done in spoken French as well. The problem is, of course, that *nicht* could be one step further in the cycle and be a head, as seems to be the case of Haitian *pa* (see Degraff, 1992).

The fourth argument for *nicht* as specifier is the fact that contrary to Bavarian, Negative Concord does not exist in Standard High German. Heads do not have to be present for Negative Concord to occur as WF infinitives prove (they do not allow *en* but show Negative Concord). But languages with strong negative heads usually have Negative Concord. As it has been argued that only languages with strong negative heads have Negative Concord (Haegemann, 1991, 1995), the lack of Negative Concord would point to either a weak or a null head though this is by no means a logical conclusion. It would be surprising if *nicht/nich* - which is after all a full form, can bear stress, and does not cliticize - were a weak head. As it seems to be a strong form, we would expect the usual pattern - which is Negative Concord. As German does not have Negative Concord, not even in child language, we have a strong indication, though not a proof, that *nicht* is not a head at all.

Though the verb-movement argument could be circumvented by some version of the Long Head Movement story, the remaining arguments seem strong enough, especially in view of parallels to closely related Germanic languages like WF, to conclude that *nicht* is not a head.

4. THE ACQUISITION OF *NICHT*

4.1. Negation, Verb-movement and Acquisition - a Dilemma?

In the recent acquisition literature on German negation (Clahsen, 1988; Verrips & Weissenborn, 1989) with the exception of Deprez & Pierce (1990, 1994), it is assumed that *nicht* is the head of a NegP, where *nicht* has VP as its complement, or where the NegP is adjoined to VP. This idea is very tenacious (Penner, Tracy, & Weissenborn, this volume), because it seemingly explains some well-attested child uses very straightforwardly. Many uses of early negation express non-existence or rejection, i.e. seem to involve a negative verb or modal auxiliary:

(16)   a. nein Ohr   Kathryn (Park, 1974)
             no   ear
        b. will nich, mag nich, kann nich etc.   (in all corpora)
           want not like not   can not
           '(I) don't want, (I) don't like, (I) cannot'

Given the position of the NegP "above" VP and the contrast in verb placement emerging from data like (17a) and (17b) from Verrips & Weissenborn, 1989, it is then argued that the finite verb has moved, thus giving an argument for the early existence of functional projections. Thus, we arrive at the dilemma outlined above.

(17)   a. macht nich aua   Simone 1;8.3
     makes not ouch
     'doesn't hurt'
     b. baby nich nuckel habe   Simone 2;0.0
     baby not pacifier have
     'the baby doesn't have (the/a) pacifier'

On the other hand, the fact that the object has stayed behind in the examples (17a) and (18), where adult language requires that the object be scrambled to the front of negation (at least in (18)), has served as an argument that the verb and negation do indeed form a complex, move together and leave the object behind.

(18)   brauche nich lala   Simone 2;0
     need   not pacifier
     '(I) don't need (the/a) pacifier'

If verb and negation are a complex, however, the position of negation with respect to the verb cannot be considered to provide evidence for verb movement.

4.2. Is *Nicht* (Mis)classified as a Head in Child German?

Nevertheless, it could be the case that there is a miscategorization at first which is put right later. Such an assumption is not ideal in view of the resulting discontinuity and the need for parameter resetting, which may be impossible as Penner (1992) or Müller (1994) have argued. But let us assume for the time being that the overwhelming production of utterances like (16b) and the affinity to the verb in examples like (18) warrants an analysis of early German child-negation as involving a head.

If that is so, and here lies the particular attractiveness of this assumption, then the creation of a NegP could well be "the beginning of syntax" (Penner, Tracy, & Weissenborn, this volume). The idea is that the specifier position of negation could provide a landing site for the first scrambled subjects or objects. Penner's early negation data for Bernese German (i.e., in the pre-V2 phase) show that it is either the subject or the object which moves, but not both. This leads to the formulation of a generalization in

In early *nicht* and *auch* constructions (which are infinitives) only one element can be scrambled at a time (Penner, Tracy & Weissenborn, 1994:8).

So it is natural to conclude that there is one and only one landing site available and that it is provided by the specifier of the new projection. This idea is well worth pursuing, because it is broad in conception, taking in not only the NegP, but also a FocusP in early *auch* phrases. So the argument would be that at this very early stage of about 18-20 months, the child has neither the Neg-Criterion nor the Wh-Criterion, but just a very general Affect Criterion which is purely configurational and requires only an A-position and a specifier-head relation of the relevant material. The creation of such an A'-position is assumed to be forced by the presence of the heads *nicht* or *auch,* which are scope bearing elements, and the existence of the "Ur"-form of the criteria: the requirement of a specifier-head relation. Later, i.e., after the acquisition of the Wh-Criterion and the Neg-Criterion, it will become the position for operators.

There are two problems here. One is that in this view the Neg-Criterion and the Wh-Criterion are not taken to be instantiations of the Affect Criterion.[3] The question then is how the child can know the general form of the criteria but not its specific instantiations. Couched in the terms of feature checking, the problem seems even more acute.[4] In a feature checking approach, the Wh- and the Neg-Criterion are two special formulations of the general process of feature checking. Then the assumption of a sort of Ur-criterion without assuming its specific form implies that the child does not know that negative or interrogative features have to be checked. So the child either does not know one of the most basic principles of grammar, or has to acquire checking for each feature separately - a very unlikely scenario. If the child treats the negative particle as a lexical item without recognizing the functional features it carries, then there is no reason to assume that the feature-checking configuration in the form of the Ur-criterion is needed at all. Thus it is very doubtful that the Affect Criterion can provide a position without also providing the knowledge of what sort of lexical item can occur in this position. In any case, this is a point that can be proved empirically. Thus it has to be established from data that the Neg-Criterion presumably together with the Wh-Criterion is acquired later. If this is not the case, and the Neg-Criterion is a direct spell-out of the Affect Criterion the said specifier position in a negative utterance would be available only for negative material and not for positive subjects or objects.

The second problem is that we expect the occurrence of Negative Concord, if only during the phase of the head classification of *nicht*. As soon as the Neg-Criterion is acquired and *nicht* is analyzed as a strong head, we should observe a phase of Negative Concord. While there is a very well documented stage in English where Negative Concord is the rule as Radford (1990) has shown with repetition tasks, such a phase cannot be said to exist in German.[5] Such a phase would not occur, of course, if the child has already concluded that *nicht* is a specifier.

Concerning the Neg-Criterion we must consider the possibility that it is in effect before it can manifest itself. One manifestation would be the occurrence of Negative Concord in languages that have Negative Concord. This can be observed only after the acquisition of negative operators. Another manifestation could be cases of doubling the negative particle as observed for Julia and Andreas. These seem to be rare, however, so that we cannot speak of a significant phase. A check of the CHILDES files of Julia (Clahsen Corpus) and Andreas (Wagner Corpus) reveals (19a-c). Note that Barbier's objection (this volume) concerning the intervention of material between the specifer and the head does not apply because the head may cliticize to the verb and can subsequyently move together with it (see Haegemann for a detailed discussuion of the phenomenon of Negative Concord).

(19)   a. mein platoffel is nich aber nich richtig   Julia 2;5
              my   slipper   is not   but   not   right
              'my slipper is not right'
        b. das nich alle Tiere nich   Andreas 2;1
              that not all animals not
              'that are not all animals'
        c. e ne Thorsten gibt nicht den Frosch   Andreas 2;1,
              nicht nicht gar
              e ne Thorsten   gives not   the   frog
              not   not   at all
              'Thorsten doesn't give the frog at all'

4.3. *Nicht* in Limbo

If we do not want to go along with a head-analysis of *nicht*, then another possibility short of a specifier classification remains. This grows out of another point made by Penner, Tracy, & Weissenborn (this volume), namely that their Standard German and Bernese data show a curious effect of what they call freezing: though the children under consideration use inflected verbs to a high rate (80-90%), they use *auch* and *nicht* almost exclusively with infinitives up to an age of two years.

Freezing at this particular moment, if firmly established, is significant in the framework of the NegP analysis and the head-specifier problem. We can reasonably assume that the child knows about head-movement as instantiated in the cases of verb movement in positive utterances, and also knows about the ECP as part of UG. So what the child does here is pick a form of the verb which does not have to be moved, i.e., the infinitive. With infinitives nothing can go wrong, and the child can wait for significant data in order to determine whether *nicht* is a head or a specifier. The evidence the child needs is a) intervening material between the verb and *nicht* to show that *nicht* is not a clitic but a free morpheme and b) verb raising to C in adult language. Once that is clear, the child will know what to do with the inflected verb in negative utterances. We have to assume some kind of maturation here or at least different phases of sensitivity to different phenomena. Otherwise we are confronted with the problem that the evidence in adult speech has been available all along.

This freezing phase is short in the acquisition of Bernese (Penner, p.c.), but establishing the existence or non-existence of such a phase and the facts about Negative Concord in or shortly after this phase for Standard German becomes important also for theoretical reasons as it might provide evidence for the location of NegP in German, which we will discuss in 5.3.

As it turns out, in Appendix C to Penner, Tracy, & Weissenborn (1994), the evidence for freezing in Standard German is rather flimsy, at least for negation. Only the very first example of Julia's (Tracy corpus) use of *nicht* involves an infinitive, and this use could well be an adult admonition use. To strengthen the argument, this infinitive remains the only one in the ten examples which are quoted for negative verbal utterances. It also is a separable verb, and separable verbs show a tendency to occur in the infinitive in this early phase of acquisition. The same holds for Stephanie

(Tracy corpus). Though she has two negative infinitives and only one negative finite construction in the first file where negation can be found, these two infinitives seem to be adult use as in *nicht anfassen, nicht hinauslehnen, nicht springen*. Her next files show no negative infinitives at all, but only finite uses. After such a finite phase of negation the last two infinitives, which are again separable verbs, cannot well considered as proof of freezing. The Katrin (1;5) corpus from CHILDES, Wagner does not show any use of infinitives with *nicht*. The children analyzed by Verrips & Weissenborn (1989) do not show freezing either: For Lukas we find one finite negation at 1;10, but no negative infinitives. At 1;11 Lukas has two finite negations and one infinitival negation. Simone uses 57 finite negations with *nicht* in the week before she uses her first negative infinitive at 1;10.28. Bo used nine finite negations before his first negative infinitive, and Benjamin has only finite negations (n=6) before his first negative infinitive at 2;6.27. Thus the existence of such a freezing phase is rather doubtful for Standard German (see Penner, Tracy, & Weissenborn, this volume who now propose freezing only in contructions with *auch*).

In any case, such a regression would be proof of knowledge of head movement and the ECP, so that we can deduce that once we get (XP) V_{+fin} XP-Neg structures, i.e., structures with intervening material and verb movement as in (20 a, b, c) the child has decided that *nicht* is in a specifier position and does not block verb movement.

(20)   a. kann das nich &a   Andreas 2;1
           can that not &a
           '(I) cannot do that'
       b. Caesar kriegt er nich   Andreas 2;1
           Caesar gets he not
           'he won't get Caesar'
       c. ich mach das nich   Andreas 2;1
           I do that not
           'I don't/won't do that'

The attractiveness of the early head analysis of *nicht,* was not motibvated only by the freezing facts but also by the distribution of unscrambled objects, which can be explained if verb and negation form a complex. Thus, the occurence of such unscrambled objects well into a regular use of finite negative structures is another problem for freezing and the head analysis. Consider the (S)-V-Neg-Obj pattern of unscrambled objects in (21a,b):

(21) a. brauche nich lala   Simone 2;0.0
         need   not pacifier
         '(I) don't need (the/a) pacifier'
      b. kann nich das zumachen   Julia 2;2.21
         can   not that close
         '(I) can't close that'

One way to deal with this problem were to assume that *nicht* is still a head, so that the explanation for the phenomenon again involves cliticization to the verb (Clahsen, 1988). This assumption has to deal with two problems. First, examples of negation with material intervening between the negative particle and the verb are easy to find, as Weissenborn (1990) has shown. Second, the triggering problem raises its head again: now it cannot be intervening material and verb movement which leads to a recategorization, it must be something else. It has been suggested that it is the acquisition of *kein*, clearly a negative constituent with quantificational force and so a maximal projection and a specifier, which teaches the child that *nicht* basically is the same thing.[6] Apart from theoretical considerations, there are two simple acquisition facts which argue against this assumption. Forms of *kein* are used quite early, even though its quantificational properties may be acquired only later.[7] The phenomenon of leaving the object "behind" does not cease to exist after we find fully correct use of *kein*. Examples (Simone & Benjamin are from Weissenborn (1990) and see note 15) with intervening material show the orders XP-V-XP-Neg, V-Adv-Neg, V-XP-XP-Neg:

(22) a. das macht der Maxe nich   Simone 2;1
         that does the Maxe not
         'Max doesn't do that'
      b. schmeckt auch nich   Simone 2;1
         tastes   also not
         doesn't taste good either
      c. brauch ich den nich   Benjamin 2;4
         need I that not
         (I) don't need that one

(23) Krisjan, ers brauchen wir die nich   Elisa 3;1
      Christoph first need we these not
      'Christoph, at first we don't/won't need these'

(24)	a. da kann Kleid auch nich there can dress also not 'the dress can't be put there neither'	Julia 2;4
	b. hier kann da nich wieder ziehen here can there not again pull '(I) can't pull here again'	Mathias 2;9
	c. kann noch nich fahrn can yet not drive '(I) can't drive yet'	Daniel 2;11
	d. das kann doch nich that can doch not 'Of course (I) can't do that'	Daniel 3;1
(25)	a. is se widder nich is she again not 'it's is not her either'	Katrin 1;5
	b. wijs du nich want you not 'you don't want (that)'	Katrin 1;5

Very early evidence for the use of *kein* and other negative constituents can be found in Tracy's Julia corpus as shown by Penner, Tracy, & Weissenborn (1994). The first correct occurrences of *kein* (n=2) (interestingly enough in finite phrases) come at the same time as the first occurrence of *nicht* (n=1), between the age of 23 and 25 months. In the even earlier Katrin data (Wagner Corpus on CHILDES), it is evident that the child has a form for *nicht*, which is phonetically distinct from her use of *kein* or *nichts*:

(26)	a. teiner [= keiner] da? nobody there 'is anybody there?'	Katrin 1;5
	b. nin din [= nichts drin] nothing in it 'there's nothing in there'	Katrin 1;5
	c. nis mehr din [=nichts mehr drin], nein nothing anymore in it, no 'there's nothing in there anymore'	Katrin 1;5

(27) a. is nich da   Katrin 1;5
       is not there
       '(it) is not there'
    b. Kakao nich   Katrin 1;5
       cacao not
       '(I) don't (want) cacao'

The later files of Mathias and Daniel (Clahsen Corpus) and the corpus of Elisa (Hamann), who is over three years at the time of these almost consecutive utterances, show clearly that the acquisition of *kein* does not exclude the possibility of leaving the object unscrambled.

(28) a. will nich ham nappa   Mathias 2;10
       want not have nappa
       '(I) don't want nappa'
    b. hab er kein Schuh mehr   Mathias 2;10
       has he no shoe any.longer
       'he doesn't have a shoe any longer'
    c. kanne nich Haus machen   Mathias 3;0
       can(I) not house make
       '(I) can't build a house'
    d. die hat keine trocken   Mathias 3;0
       this has no dry(er)
       'this one doesn't have dry ones/ a dryer'
    e. die hat keine waschschin   Mathias 3;0
       this has no washing.maschine
       'this one doesn't have washing-machine'
    f. Krisoff mag nich gouter   Elisa 3;1
       Christoph likes not gouter (French word)
       'Christoph doesn't like his biscuit'
    e. Jetz kriegs kein Kuchen, Krisoff   Elisa 3;1
       now get no cake, Christoph
       'Now you won't get a piece of cake, Christoph'

The explanation for the phenomenon of unscrambled objects can thus not be sought in the assumption that *nicht* is a head. There are some suggestions which seem to point the way. If accusative case is not yet acquired, then there is no reason for the object to raise in order to check case features in

AgrOP as Eisenbeiß (1994) assumes. For the late Elisa corpus, however, even this explanation does not seem to cover the facts, unless the French verb *gouter* 'to taste' in the German context is exempt from the case requirement. Another explanation relies on the fact that most of these unscrambled objects are perfectly acceptable as constituent negation, i.e., with a focussed object, and also if the negative particle itself is focussed. Penner, Tracy, & Weissenborn (this volume) also argue that unscrambled objects have nothing to do with case. It is in favor of this view that the same phenomenon can be found in adult speech, where the use of *ein* clearly depends on presupposition and pragmatic context. It means *irgendein* in (29), and the negative polarity *kein* is not required because the context is clearly positive (see Reinhart, 1976). The sentence is also acceptable with focus on *nicht*.

(29)   Wir brauchen nicht ein Buch, wir brauchen den Computer.
         we need   not   a book   we need   the computer
         'We don't need a (some) book, we need the computer."

Before a decision can be made about whether the object left behind in child language is actually a non-adult use, the analysis of natural speech data of adults is required, or, at least, a notation of intonation contour in the child data. Another way of checking the assumption about a gradual replacement of wrong *nicht +indefinite object* use would be to check if the same sort of replacement by *kein* is found with indefinite subjects. See Penner, Tracy, & Weissenborn (this volume) for an alternative explanation involving light nouns.

4.4. *Nicht* as a Specifier

Though we have sketched a scenario which assumes the categorization of *nicht* as a head and another one which includes a short early phase of holding off the categorization, it turns out that the phenomenon of unscrambled objects cannot be correctly explained with assuming that *nicht* is a head and that the existence of a freezing phase is rather dubious for Standard German negation. Thus we conclude that as soon as negative sentences with finite verbs occur - and this happens sometimes even before a negative infinitive is used as the data from Verrips & Weissenborn (1989) show - *nicht* cannot be a head any longer.

Let us therefore sketch a story where *nicht* is a specifier from the very beginning. Such an assumption would also avoid discontinuity problems and therefore certainly be preferable.

This does not mean, that the negative expression occupies a NegP and is a specifier also in the phase where external negation with *nein* is predominantly found.[8] In this phase, adjunction may be the right analysis. It can be applied, however, as soon as *nicht* is used. Thus we would assume a structure as in (30) for sentences with inflected verbs and also for infinitival phrases with IP not projected or inactive in that case. This is very much in the spirit of Deprez & Pierce (1990, 1994).

(30)
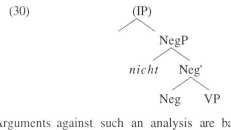

Arguments against such an analysis are based on the problem of case assignment in such structures (Radford, 1996). If, as Deprez and Pierce assume, nominative is assigned under government and strict adjacency, then the negative specifier would be a barrier to case assignment to Spec, VP in infinitives. If, on the other hand, Radford is correct in his proposal of an inherent case assignment inside VP in an early phase, then the existence of a NegP above VP does not play any blocking role for case assignment to infinitival subjects in Spec, VP. Therefore the assumption of a NegP in the phase following the external negation phase does not necessarily lead to problems with case (see Schütze & Wexler (1996), however, for a different view on case assignment).

If we thus assume a NegP with *nicht* as its specifier, then we would not expect any Negative Concord. This is borne out by the data. But there would neither be a phase where the NegP could provide an A' position for arguments to be scrambled to. Such a position could be provided, however, with the early acquisition of *kein*.

In parallel to WF, we can reasonably assume that *kein* is not in the specifier position of NegP. This follows for WF because there the specifier of Neg is occupied by *nie* 'not', so *niemand, niets* 'nobody, nothing' in

Negative Concord cases have to go higher up. Therefore *kein* would be the specifier of a higher projection, presumably AgrO, which thus becomes an extended projection of NegP, so that the Neg-Criterion can still be satisfied. We deduce that this projection becomes available with the acquisition of *kein*. To solve the problem of its accessibility for objects, subjects and negation which may cause conflicts with case assignment, we have three choices. Either we assume that case is not relevant yet, i.e., the case module or DP are not acquired (see Radford, 1990 and Friedemann, 1992); or we assume that the position is underspecified in the sense of Clahsen (1991) and Hyams (1996) so that case checking does not yet take place there; or following Chomsky (1993), we assume that we are dealing simply with an agreement projection, a collection of *phi*-features, where AgrS and AgrO are only different selections.

We could now apply Penner's idea and say that with the building of this projection, we have the beginning of syntax. In the absence of *kein* it provides an A' position where either objects or subjects could be scrambled to. This presumes that we take the first occurrences of *kein* - and not a consistently correct use as evidence for such a projection. These first occurrences are very early, as we have seen in the Katrin corpus (Wagner) and also from Tracy's data, so such a story could work.

The restriction that only either a subject or an object can be moved follows, because the one available position in infinitival sentences with *nicht* is not Spec, NegP, where *nicht* is itself sitting, but the one in the extended projection which would be occupied by *kein* if that item were present. It would also predict that the phenomenon of either subject- or object-scrambling occurs only in infinitives, because in inflected sentences there is always Spec, IP for the subject to move to. Thus the generalization about scramble-one-only in infinitives of Penner, Tracy, and Weissenborn (1994) still holds. What is not predicted is freezing and this is as it should be as was shown in Section 4.3. This scenario would assume the Neg-Criterion from early on for the construction of the extended projection and could be checked with data on *wh*-acquisition.

The analysis of infinitive examples like (31) where the subject has moved across Neg, indeed requires an intermediate projection if *nicht* is not simply adjoined to VP as suggested in Radford (1990).[9]

(31)   baby nich nuckel habe   Simone 2;0.0
        baby not pacifier have
        'the baby doesn't have a/the pacifier'

In example (31) from V & W (1989), the subject must be somewhere higher than NegP. This is problematic, if we do not assume an intermediate projection, because subjects of non-finite verbs do not necessarily go to Spec, IP. Now it could be the case that even in nonfinite contexts, the subject has to move to Spec, IP presumably for being licensed or getting case. This is a conclusion we are forced to buy, if we adhere to a NegP analysis, assume *nicht* as its specifier, and do not admit an intermediate projection. So an analysis with such a projection is more plausible.

(32)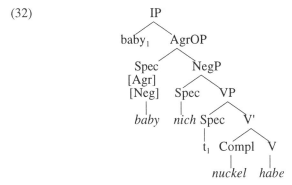

Let us briefly speculate on the structure of negative utterances with inflected verbs in German. As finite verbs are consistently moved across Neg, we would have to deduce that they are in a position higher than I^0 because IP is head final.[10] This could be C^0 itself, which is likely once we have instances of true topicalization, or it could be the head of an intermediate AGR-projection in the domain of IP which would also provide positions for clitics (cf. Cardinaletti & Roberts, 1991 and Haegeman, 1993 for the postulation of such projections). The child may well assume that because s/he hears sentences with clitics these positions are available and as heads can be landing-sites for the verb.

(33a)   brauch ich den nich   Benjamin 2;4
        need   I   that not
        'I don't need that one'

(33b)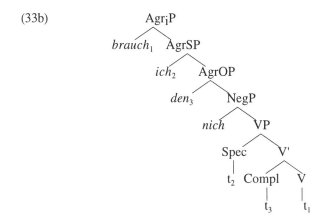

Such a scenario would predict the occurrence of a V1-phase: the subject is in Spec, IP (Spec, AgrS) for a finite sentence, the object has been scrambled only as far as the extended projection of NegP (the position where *nichts* or *kein* would be found), but the verb has gone higher to the head of another AGR-projection. Such a non-adult use of V1-sentences is indeed observable till after the age of three and it is not always clear that only a narrative chaining element like *dann* 'then', *da* 'there', or *jetzt* 'now' has been dropped. Some of these sentences seem to represent an independent option.[11]

There are data, however, which require a different analysis. These involve a very few examples where the subject of an inflected verb stays to the left of negation. We will have to assume that it stays in Spec, VP. Thus it could not receive case from I in (34a), so the only solution is that either case is not yet relevant or inherent case assignment is still available. Example (34b) seems to be an instance of the verb raising no further than I^0, so that the verb appears clause final. Again, case assignment, if required, must be inherent.

(34) a. darf nich Julia haben   Mathias 2;9
         must not Julia have
         'Julia must not have (this)'
      b. nich Julia soll   Mathias 2;10
         not Julia shall
         'Julia shall not (do that)'

5. NEGATION AND INFINITIVES

5.1. Truncated Structures

The three scenarios outlined above take one thing for granted - and the data and examples seem justification enough - in German child language negation does occur with infinitives, especially in an early phase. This is not surprising at all, because German has an imperative or admonition use of infinitives which is predominantly used negatively. The child will hear *nicht weinen, nicht anfassen, nicht hinauslehnen, nicht loslassen, nicht springen* ' don't cry, don't touch, do not lean out, don't let go, don't jump' etc. a hundred times a day. So some of the negative infinitives produced by the child will be such adult uses. Some of the child uses are clearly not like this construction, however, and this brings us to our second issue. The truncated structure approach as proposed in Rizzi (1992, 1994) coupled with the idea that NegP selects TP predicts that negation should not occur with infinitives at all.

The approach is designed to take care of the observation (cf. Wexler, 1994) that there is a cross-linguistic phase where the child can use infinitives as declaratives in a non-adult way, at a time where the child also inflects the verb and raises it. Such non-adult use of infinitives is called "root infinitive" by Rizzi (1994), a term we will adopt henceforth. The solutions proposed in Wexler (1994), in Rizzi (1994) and also in Haegeman (1996) and Hyams (1996) are all inspired by an observation made by Valian (1991) for English, Weissenborn (1990) for German, and Crisma (1992) for French: null-subjects and root infinitives do not occur in *wh*-questions. For different data see Rohrbacher and Roeper (1994, this volume) and Radford (1996), which will be discussed later.

This led Wexler (1994) to assume that children do not have tense or have underspecified tense features at an early age. Pursuing this seminal work of Wexler, Rizzi (1994) proposes, that adults necessarily have to analyze each sentence with a CP root, while children can localize the root of the phrase at any given projection. In Rizzi's formulation (35) is an axiom in adult language which is not yet operative for children and matures in the course in development.

(35)   CP = root

Therefore children can truncate at any place in the tree, and thus project only as much structure as is required to accommodate the material in a given phrase. So Rizzi assumes that children have the entire range of functional projections at their disposal. They can make use of them if they need them as would be the case when they form *wh*-questions, but they use only the projections which are absolutely necessary.[12] This leads to the proposal that root infinitives are structures which have been truncated above VP or at AgrOP as emerges from Haegeman (1996). Therefore a root infinitive comes out very much as one of Radford's Small Clauses.

The proposal goes further, however. Because one functional projection selects another one, it predicts that the activation of a projection by lexical material tacitly implies the activation of all lower projections. With a tree as in (36), assumed to be universal by Belletti (1990) it then follows that as soon as a projection higher than TP is involved, the tense morpheme necessarily has to be bound, so infinitives cannot occur.

(36)
```
         CP
        /  \
           AgrSP
          /    \
              NegP
             /    \
                  TP
                 /  \
                   AgrOP
                  /    \
                       VP
```

Hence as a corollary from the universality of (36) and Rizzi's truncation hypothesis we get (37).

(37)   Corollary:
        No Negation with Infinitives

This holds only, if all the assumptions are correct. In particular, it does not hold, if the order of projections is not universal and NegP is lower than TP as has been assumed for Germanic languages in particular for West Flemish and Dutch by Haegeman (1991) and for German by Grewendorf (1990) and in the account given of German in 3.4 of this paper.

The corollary would not hold either, if the negation used in infinitives turns out to be a special use as is suggested by the work of Hoekstra & Jordens (1994) where we consistently find V_{fin} *niet* 'not' but *nee* 'no' V_{-fin}.

Thus it can be argued that for the children studied by Hoekstra and Jordens there is an adverbial negation going together with infinitives. It might therefore turn out that the negative particle is an adverb in that phase - or in that language.

It does not hold, of course, if Rizzi's proposal is wrong. To establish this however, it does not suffice to show that in some language there are negative infinitives in child language. The reason for their occurrence may lie in one of the above possibilities. Only if acquisition data show that negation occurs with infinitives even in languages where the projection order (36) must hold in the adult language, Rizzi's proposal will need revision. What is needed therefore is a detailed data check on the occurrence of negation with infinitives across languages.

5.2. Negation and Non-finite Utterances in French

Let us begin with the data from French as discussed in the introduction. On the face of these data, we seem to need a new theory. This is not the case, however.

Table 2a.
Distribution of non-finite structures in verbal utterances in French

all verbal utterances			negative verbal utterances		
total	-Fin	+Fin	total	-Fin	+Fin
2035	694 (33.8%)	1359	275	79 (28.7%)	196

Table 2b.
Distribution of non-finite structures in verbal utterances in French (excluding 50 cases of negative infinitives in Nathalie's first file)

2035	694 (34.1%)	1359	225	29 (12.9%)	196

(Nathalie 21-27, Philippe 25-30, Daniel 20-23 months)

Table 3.
Distribution of non-finite structures in verbal utterances in French

all verbal utterances			negative verbal utterances		
total	-Fin	+Fin	total	-Fin	+Fin
-	-	-	984	158 (16.1%)	826 (83.9%)

(Five children with ages ranging from 1;8 to 2;10. For a detailed analysis see Appendix 2.)

The data of Table 2 are taken from Pierce (1989) so that I cannot describe the counting procedure in detail, they include infinitives and participles, however, and the same holds for the data in Table 3 from Verrips & Weissenborn, 1989.

At first glance, the percentages of non-finite structures in negative utterances and in positive utterances in the Pierce count seem to be of equal importance and is too high to be compatible with Rizzi's theory and the TP above NegP order as normally assumed for French. As Rizzi (1994) points out, however, 50 cases of the 79 negative non-finite forms all come from the first file of Nathalie, where she does not use any finite verbs at all. From this total lack of inflection, Radford (1996) argues, that here we have evidence for an early small clause phase in French. If that is the case, then the 50 cases of non-finite forms with negation are adjuncts and so are not relevant for arguments about the position of a functional NegP. Still, one might have scruples about discounting such an important number of occurrences. There is another problem with Nathalie's first verb forms, however. The great majority of these are baby-talk like *nja-nja* -'eat' or 'food' (46 *nja-nja* out of 68 utterances classified as verbal in the first file), do not carry either a finiteness marker nor an infinitive marker and should not enter into the count for these reasons. Therefore I feel justified in excluding Nathalie's first file from this numerical evaluation, (see also Levow, 1995 who includes only four cases of negation for Nathalie's first file). Without counting this first file, we are left with 29 cases, or 12.9% of non-finite structures in negative verbal utterances. The same magnitude of percentage for non-finite negative structures, namely 16.1%, was found across six French children ranging in age from 1;8-3;3 by V & W (1989), see Appendix 2 for the data of each single child. Unfortunately, no figures for the use of positive infinitives are included, so that there is no way of telling how many optional infinitives are used in all. Still, this figure seems to argue against Rizzi's truncation theory, as there is little doubt about the high position of NegP in French.

There is one big problem, however, which makes these figures, though indicative for verb movement and the use of non-finite structures, not at all conclusive for Rizzi's theory and the placement of the NegP in French: Both, Pierce (1989) and V & W (1989), include participles in their count which makes perfect sense for their purpose, but is not useful for ours in so far as participles and infinitives occupy different positions in the tree and are differently specified with respect to aspect which may also have consequences for their interplay with the tense projection. In fact, there are analyses of compound tenses where participles are tense heads, cf. Zeller (1994). So it makes sense to distinguish participles from infinitives, at least in the languages we are examining. Assuming that participles are situated at least as high as the aspect phrase and probably even in the TP, it is not surprising that participles do occur with negation: if the child activates the projections up to NegP, the material in the TP is available, though everything above the NegP may be missing, especially subject agreement. Infinitives, however, do not involve tense or aspect and are situated in VP. If child infinitives are due to truncation of all the material above AgrOP, negation is not expected to occur. Moreover, as Levow (1995) discusses, bare participles are highly ambiguous as to their interpretation. In many cases, they are simple adjectives, in other cases the auxiliary may have been dropped, and so the form may be tensed. Because participles pattern with infinitives in acquisition, Levow (1995) decides to follow Pierce and count participles as untensed forms. She finds that Grégoire has no negative non-finite forms, that Philippe uses these up to 8% in his negative utterances, but that Daniel and Nathalie use negative non-finite forms to a quite high percentage (44% and 32% respectively) which exactly corresponds to their overall use of non-finite forms. The individual differences lead her to conclude that not only a simple choice of the possible root can be involved. The same evidence is considered by Schönenberger, Pierce, Wexler & Wijnen (1996) who point to the inconclusiveness of the evidence with regard to the truncation option and decide for another account of optional infinitives involving underspecified tense.

Regarding the individual variation, much seems to depend on the counting procedure. With respect to the counting of participles, the many problems and ambiguities from the point of view of linguistic theory and the fact that the co-occurrence of negation with participles cannot serve as decisive evidence against truncation, lead Friedemann (1992) to decide in the opposite way from Levow (1995): he does not include participles and considers only infinitives. Because of the possible activation of a tense node by a participle, this decision was adhered to in the counts on Augustin, a corpus available in Geneva.[13] The count Friedemann (1992) made, indicates that participles are indeed different from infinitives. Without counting bare participles, the cases of negation with 'untensed' forms practically vanish: Friedemann's figures point to the correctness of Rizzi's assumptions.[14]

Table 4a.
Distribution of non-finite structures in verbal utterances

all verbal utterances			negative verbal utterances		
total	-Fin	+Fin	total	-Fin	+Fin
?	?	?	137	16 (11.7%)	121

Table 4b.
Distribution of infinitives in verbal utterances (excludinmg bare participles)

	negative verbal utterances		
	total	Inf	+Fin
	127	6 (4.7%)	121

(Philippe 2;1-2;3, Grégoire 1;11-2;3)

This very low number of infinitives in negative structures is indeed corroboration of Rizzi's theory. There also is a new French corpus available (see Hamann, Rizzi & Frauenfelder, 1996) which gives corroboration. A count of Augustin's first seven files was not conclusive because of the low number of sentential negation occurring in this period (see Hamann, 1996a). In this period and in the first 30 minutes of each of these recordings, Augustin used overall 17.5% infinitives in verbal contexts, and about 12.5% negative infinitives in negative verbal utterances. This analysis which takes into account only root infinitives and discounts any adult-like elliptical answer or any verbal form like (37) where it is not clear whether we are dealing with a modal verb and an infinitive (like in 37b) or an auxiliary and participle (as in 37a), was extended to the whole corpus in two steps.

(37)   [e] pas [deA~Ze] ça   =   [e] pas derang[e] ça

    a. [e] pas derangé ça
       is not disturbed that
       '(that) has not been disturbed'
    b. vais pas deranger ça
       will not disturb that
       '(I) will not disturb that'

First, 30 minutes of every recording (10 files) were transcribed and triple checked to show the development. The picture for negation has now changed dramatically: only 2% of all negative utterances occurred in the infinitive compared to an overall use of 10.8% root infinitives. In a second step, the last 15 minutes of each recording were transcribed and added to the data analysis. This last step, though giving better statistics, does not alter the result from the first step: It quite clearly indicates that Augustin does not use infinitives with negation as Table 5 shows (See Appendix 2 for tables giving the numbers for each recording).

Table 5.
Distribution of infinitives in verbal utterances in French
Augustin 2.0-2.4 and Augustin 2.6-2.10

File	all verbal utterances			negative verbal utterances		
	Total	Fin	Inf	Total	Fin	Inf
01-07	373	295 79.1%	78 20.9%	17	16 94.1%	1 5.9%
08-10	391	367 93.9%	24 6.1%	47	47 100%	0
Total	764	662 86.6%	102 13.4%	64	63 98.4%	1 1.6%

Given these results, there is reason to believe that for French, Rizzi's theory and the corollary are borne out, though some individual variation is to be expected.

5.3. Negation and Non-finite Structures in V2-languages

It has emerged from the theoretical discussion and the discussion of the examples so far, that German presumably has a low NegP. So the expectation is that we find a substantial percentage of negative infinitives. Let us start with a check on the data as known from the literature shown in Table 6 (from Tracy, 1991) and Table 7 (from Verrips & Weissenborn, 1989).

Table 6.
Distribution of infinitives in negated verbal utterances(German)

	total	Inf	+Fin
Julia 2;1 - 2;6	10	1	9
Stephanie 1;8 - 2;2,2	27	7 (25%)	20 (75%)

Table 7.
Distribution of non-finite structures in negated verbal utterances (German)

	total	-Fin	+Fin	
Lukas (1;10-2;1)	34	5 (14.7%)	29 (85.3%)	(8 files, 5 from 2;1)
Simone (1;10-2;2)	185	15 (8.1%)	170 (91.9%)	(19 files)
Bo (2;1.-2;6)	123	7 (5.7%)	116 (94.3%)	(10 files, 3 at 2;2., 3 at 2;3)
Benjamin (1;9-3;0)	16	3 (18.7%)	13 (81.3%)	(9 files spaced a month, 2;5 missing)

As in some of the children the phenomenon manifests itself at more than 10%, it certainly has to be dealt with. However, the data as drawn from the literature are not conclusive, as they do not allow a comparison to the use of infinitives in positive utterances at the same time. Thus it might well be the case that the low figure for Simone and Bo is simply the result of the fact that the children have passed out of the optional infinitive stage at some point of data taking. Moreover, just as for French, the count of Verrips & Weissenborn (1989) includes participles, so that the percentages are not conclusive for the problem at hand.

Three German corpora from the CHILDES Database[15] have been checked for the use of negative infinitives in correlation to the use of positive infinitives. One subject is Katrin (1;5), whose data were collected by Wagner. The second is Julia (1;11-2;5), collected by Clahsen. The third is Andreas (again collected by Wagner, see Wagner, 1985) for whom it has been established by Poeppel & Wexler (1993) that he is definitely in the optional infinitive stage.

The analysis of Table 8 shows the following. Katrin uses 42% infinitives in her positive verbal utterances, but not one single negative infinitive; Julia (1;11-2;3) uses infinitives to 52% in her positive verbal utterances, and to 20% in her negative verbal utterances. So far we would have to say that infinitives are much rarer in negation than in positive utterances, and that the moral to be drawn from only 12 cases of verbal negation for Katrin and only 25 cases for Julia are not statistically convincing. Andreas (2;1), however, provides us with 56 cases of verbal negation, and shows an equal distribution of infinitives in positive and negative utterances (about 25% in both). On the face of the data, we seem to get some individual variation as was observed for French by Levow (1995), but also an indication that negative infinitives are quite common. Let us keep in mind that the analyses made on the same basis, only considering infinitives not participles, already show a marked difference for French and German.

Though the data from Katrin and Julia are not conclusive, the cases of negative root infinitives in Andreas lead to the assumption, that here is a phenomenon to be accounted for. The same seems to emerge for Julia at the ages of 2;4 and 2;5 (see Appendix 3). Thus, either the German NegP is lower than TP[16], or German children treat *nicht* as an adverb, or both.

Data from Schaner-Wolles (1994) of two children speaking Austrian German corroborate the conclusion as shown in Table 9. Her data on negation are fully compatible with mine, because participles were not counted. In her data, however, infinitives in negation occur to a much higher percentage than in the overall distribution of verbal utterances. This might be due to the fact that the figures for the occurrence of infinitives in all utterances are drawn from her tables on verb-placement and thus do not include two-word verb-final utterances which are ambiguous as to a V2 or V-final position.

Table 8.
Distribution of infinitives in verbal utterances (German)

Katrin 1;5   Andreas, 2;1

	total	Inf	+Fin	total	Inf	+Fin
all verbal utterances	415	167 40%	248 60%	785	218 28%	567 72%
positive verbal utterances	403	167 42%	236 58%	729	204 28%	525 72%
negative verbal utterances	12	0	12	56	14 25%	42 75%
Julia 1;11- 2;5						
all utterances	193	93 48.2%	100 51.8%			
positive utterances	170	88 51.8%	82 48.2%			
negative utterances	25	5 20%	20 80%			

Table 9.
Distribution of infinitives in verbal utterances (Austrian)

Nico 2;2-2;9   Hannes 2;4-2;6

	total	Inf	+Fin	total	Inf	+Fin
all utterances	849	96 11.3%	753 88.7%	151	37 24.5%	114 75.5%
negative utterances	146	34 23.3%	112 76.7%	23	10 43.5%	13 56.5%

Therefore, on the evidence of these German data, we seem to be safe in concluding that the German NegP, or even the Germanic NegP, is low or *nicht* is an adverb. Confirmation of this conclusion comes from Dutch data as analyzed by Haegeman (1996). In the Hein corpus, Haegeman counts 635 cases of negative verbal utterances in all, of which 38 are in the infinitive.

Under modification of her calculation in order to adapt her figures to the format of the above tables we get from Haegeman's Table (13) that a total of 6% of verbal negative utterances in the Hein corpus occur in the infinitive, see Table 10. This, though admittedly a lower number than the one for German, is nonetheless taken by Haegeman to strengthen her other convincing arguments for a low NegP. This is corroborated by the fact that in the first phase, where infinitives are used in about 20% of all utterances, the percentage of negative infinitives is 9.3%. For a more detailed data analysis see Haegeman (1996).

Table 10.
Distribution of infinitives in verbal utterances (Dutch)

Hein 2;4-2;8	total	Inf	+Fin
all utterances	2326	484	1842
positive utterances	2008	455 22.6%	1553 77.4%
negative utterances	318	29 9.3%	289 90.7%

It seems to follow therefore that, given Rizzi's hypothesis, the order of projections is not universal. The data for German, however, can also be interpreted in another light. Poeppel & Wexler (1993) observe that separable verbs have a strong tendency to occur in their non-finite form during the optional infinitive stage. They find that "although 90% of the simple verb tokens occur in finite form, only 19% of separable verb tokens occur in finite form", (Poeppel & Wexler, 1993:8 footnote 12). If the German child thus has no choice in this phase but to leave a verb like *ausziehen* 'undress' or *Auto fahren* 'drive a car' in the infinitive, then there is reason not to include separable verbs in the counts for root infinitives at all. The reason would be the same which deducts subject questions from null-subject counts.

In this light, the data present a completely different view as the German data in Table 11 indicates. For Katrin, there is no change as none of her negative utterances contains a separable verb, and she did not use negative infinitives in any case. For Julia, a 20% use of infinitives in negation comes down to a mere 9% use of infinitives with negation. For Andreas, only four cases of negated infinitives remain, of which two seem to be normal adult use in any case.[17]

Table 11.

Distribution of infinitives in verbal utterances not counting separable verbs

Katrin, 1;5   Andreas, 2;1

	total	Inf	+Fin	total	Inf	+Fin
all verbal utterances	362	131 36%	231 64%	646	101 16%	545 84%
positive verbal utterances	350	131 37%	219 63%	603	97 16%	506 84%
negative verbal utterances	12	0	12	43	4 9%	39 91%

Julia, 1;11-2;5

	total	Inf	+Fin	total	Inf	+Fin
all utterances	193	93 48.2%	100 51.8%	143	44 30.8%	99 69.2%
positive utterances	170	88 51.8%	82 48.2%	121	42 34.7%	79 65.3%
negative utterances	25	5 20%	20 80%	22	2 9.1%	20 90.9%

Let us compare the German figures from Tracy (1990) shown in Table 12.

Table 12.

Distribution of infinitives in verbal utterances not counting separable verbs

verbal utterances   verbal utterances without separable verbs

	total	Inf	+Fin	total	Inf	+Fin
Julia 2;1-2;6. negative utterances	10	1	9	9	0	9
Stephanie 1;8-2;2 negative utterances	27	7 25%	20 75%	22	2 9.1%	20

Though 9% of infinitives in negative utterances looks still respectable as a figure, we see that for Julia (Clahsen) only two relevant cases remain, and for Andreas (Wagner) or Stephanie (Tracy) the same is the case.

Are we thus forced to conclude, that Rizzi's analysis is right on all counts, not only a) with regard to the truncation hypothesis, but also b) with regard to the universally high position of NegP? Concerning a), it is clear that the hypothesis has many merits, the least of which is its elegance. Remember, however, that one of the pillars of this hypothesis is the non-occurrence of infinitives or null-subjects in *wh*-questions as found by Valian (1991), Crisma (1992) and Weissenborn (1990). This has been challenged recently by Rohrbacher & Roeper (this volume), Bromberg & Wexler (1995), Phillips (1995), and Radford (1996). While Valian (1991) found 9 null-subjects in 552 *wh*-questions across 21 English children and Rizzi (1992) found only 12 null-subjects in 191 *wh*-questions for Eve (1;6-2;4), Radford (1996) quotes Klima & Bellugi (1966), Plunkett (1992) and Vainikka (1994) for examples of null-subjects in questions with overt *wh*-words and provides the following figures from Hill (1983): 39% (11/28) of the *wh*-questions of a child called Jane were null-subject phrases. From Rohrbacher and Roeper (this volume) who give a table of pronoun use and null-subjects in finite and non-finite *wh*-questions, we can deduce the following: of 327 *wh*-questions in the Adam corpus 115 had a null-subject and 204 were non-finite, i.e. 35% of all *wh*-questions contained a null-subject, 62.4% of all *wh*-questions of all *wh*-questions contained a null-subject, 62.4% of all *wh*-questions were non-finite. This count includes present and perfect participles, however, so that it does not provide us with the figure we need: the percentage of infinitives. Thus this conflicting evidence, though enough to leave some doubt about the correctness of truncation as a universal child option, is certainly not enough to discard the theory. This holds especially, as the evidence about negative infinitives across languages if inspected in all detail seems to corroborate the hypothesis.[18]

Concerning b) it has emerged from work on adult West Flemish, Dutch and German, especially from work on scrambling, that the position of NegP in these languages is in all probability lower than in Romance languages. This is corroborated in the data of Table 8 and Table 9. So we have to make a decision as to what to do with the separable verbs. There does not seem to be a good theoretical reason to exclude them, apart form the acquisition internal observation for which we have no explanation so far. On the other hand, these verbs occur quite frequently and even if the child should have no choice but to leave these verbs in the infinitive in a particular phase, the resulting structures must still be possible in the child's grammar. Thus we need an account for them along the lines of 4.4 which may, of course, lose a bit in generality but must be available for separable verbs. Thus we should count them in for our statistics.

Before we can establish the argument for the position of the NegP in German, there is one other possibility to consider. *Nicht* might be treated as an adverb in this phase, or there may be a lingering of the adjunction strategy suggested for English by Radford (1990) and for Dutch in Hoekstra and Jordens (1994) for the first phase of negation. This has been assumed for early phases of German negation in any case (Wode, 1977; Clahsen, 1988; Penner, Tracy, & Weissenborn, this volume).

6. *NICHT* AS AN ADVERB

The adverb possibility fits together not only with the use of infinitives but also takes care of the fact that, as suggested in treating the unscrambled objects, many cases of early negation seem to have properties of constituent negation.

That many cases of early child negation are constituent negation is indeed an impression one gets when checking through corpora manually and listening to the tapes. The problem is that we would require two negation strategies for the child, sentential negation with a base-generated NegP and with *nicht* base-generated in Spec, Neg, plus constituent negation, where *nicht* can move to the specifier position of any projection we would wish. It would be more plausible if there is one strategy with different versions coming out either as sentential or constituent negation. This would be available if *nicht* were an adverb in child language. As an adverb, it could become the specifier of the PolP thus coloring it as a NegP, it could occur higher up, in a FocusP or the position of topicalization and it could occur as the specifier of DPs thus admitting constituent negation for any NP to be negated. It could also simply adjoin to VP in the first phase. It would also fit in with the parallels we find in the acquisition of *auch* and *nicht*: These adverbs would only color the PolP differently, one creating a FocusP, the other a NegP. It also fits in very well with the fact that German children do not show Negative Concord.

This brings us to a set of data that to my knowledge have not been discussed in the acquisition literature so far, the order Neg-V-S-O, where *nicht* has topicalized.

(39) Nicht will ich das Schwarze   Elisa 3;5
      not   want I the black
      'I don't want the black one'

Topicalization of *nicht,* though rare, seems to mark a phase in the acquisition of negation for some children at least. We find the same phenomenon also for Daniel and Mathias from the Clahsen corpus, but more data and counts on this phenomenon would be necessary (see the Appendix for some more detail).

(40) fels noch nich is er putt   Daniel 2;9
      rock yet not is he broken
      'the rock is not yet broken'

(41) a. ni kommt zurück   Mathias 2;10
         not comes back
         '(it) doesn't come back'
      b. nich geht er putt   Mathias 2;10
         not goes he broken
         'it/he will not break'
      c. nich fährt   Mathias 2;10
         not drives
         '(it) does not drive'

Clearly, such data are incompatible with the idea that *nicht* is a head. Topicalization would be compatible with *nicht* being the specifier of NegP. However, such use most likely involves the adverb *nicht* as will emerge presently.

Topicalization was possible in Middle High German and could still be found in Luther's German, but is impossible in Standard Modern German. As Swedish and Norwegian *inte* and *ikke* can be topicalized this poses a problem. The existence of a NegP guarantees that *nicht* will be generated in its base position and the Neg-Criterion can be verified right there. This would prevent any further movement for economy reasons in adult German. It follows that child German (and for that matter Swedish and Norwegian) doesn't base-generate *nicht* in NegP - but treats it as a simple adverb in parallel to adult *gar nicht* which can be topicalized. The important idea here is that adverbs are not simply adjoined, but are the specifiers of their own projections, so the specifier status of *nicht* would be untouched by this new analysis.

If we assume that German (and English) children have adverbial negation initially, we could also explain the existence of the external negation phase which has been discussed above. The child could here simply treat *nein* like its counterpart from formal logic - i.e., as a sentential modifier. Interestingly, in the file of Katrin (CHILDES, Wagner) we find a negative or a positive marking at the end of her phrases:

(42) a. Hat diese Aua nein   Katrin 1;5
    has this ouch no
    'This one doesn't have a wound/ this one is not hurt'
   b. Aua macht am Bein ja   Katrin 1;5
    ouch makes on leg yes
    '(it) hurts on my leg'

As *nicht* is never used in this external sense, it might be the case that the child from early on distinguishes sentence modifiers and constituent modifiers - which in the case of IP/VP-modification acquire sentential scope. If we pursue this line of thought, it is not surprising that many of the problem cases about placement of negation turn out to be a form of constituent negation.

Let us remark that the assumption of an adverb analysis from the beginning does not change the scenario outlined in Section 4.4. As an adverb, *nicht* might either be adjoined to VP in which case no structure building takes place, or it would be sitting in the specifier of Neg, so that this position could not provide a landing site for scrambled subjects/objects. Therefore pre-*nicht* subjects must have arrived in a higher projection as was proposed in Section 4.4.

7. CONCLUSION

In the first part of this article it has been argued that in the phase where German children use negation in finite verbal constructions, they also have classified the negative particle as a specifier. This is preferable to an account where children start out with a head analysis of the negative particle because it assumes continuity. The arguments for such an analysis are drawn from the fact that finite negation occurs concomitantly or even before negation with infinitives, and children show clear knowledge of verb-movement across negation. It is shown that such an account together with the assumption of a NegP and the Neg-Criterion can account for the data on scrambling: in an early phase only one position is available in infinitive structures for either the subject or the object to go to. Later unscrambled objects are left in their base position not because the negative particle has incorporated to the verb, but for case reasons or the simple reason that such examples are examples of constituent negation or of the focussing of the object or of the negation.

From the phenomenon of negation with infinitives, it was then argued with the help of the truncation hypothesis[19] that the order of projections has to be parameterized, or negation must be an adverb in some languages. This conclusion was reached because a careful data analysis of French negative constructions shows that infinitives are indeed rare, while in German a good percentage of negative infinitives was found. Thus there is evidence that in French NegP is above TP also in child language, whereas in German NegP must be below TP. The evidence for the German child is a) the final distribution of the negative element in main clauses, which makes a low NegP likely, and b) the evidence of objects occurring before the negative particle. Thus AgrOP, the scrambling position of German objects, must be higher than NegP in German. An adverb-analysis of the German negative particle fits together with this order of projections because the adverb can occupy the specifier position of a PolP and thus color it negatively thereby fulfilling the Neg-Criterion, it fits together with the set of data about Neg topicalization found in child language and it takes care of the phenomenon of unscrambled objects which then can be read as constituent negation. The only problem would be the subset problem. But given a genetic learning algorithm or other statistic measures as outlined in Clark (1992) or in Kapur & Clark (this volume), this problem is not insurmountable.

ACKNOWLEDGEMENTS

This work was made possible by the Swiss National Fund Grant No. 11-33542.92 A version of the first part of this paper was presented during *The Cross-linguistic Acquisition Workshop* at the International School for Advanced Studies, Trieste, July 1993. The part on truncated structures grew out of discussions held in Trieste, especially with Amy Pierce, Ken Wexler, and other participants of the negation group. The paper took shape in discussions at the Seminar für Allgemeine Sprachwissenschaft in Tübingen in December 1993 and came close to its present form at the "The Workshop on the L1- and L2-Acquisition of Clause-Internal Rules: Scrambling and Cliticization" held in Berne, January 21 - 23, 1994. My thanks go to Arnim von Stechow, Gereon Müller, Rosemary Tracy, Ira Gawlitzek-Maiwald, Zvi Penner, Jürgen Weissenborn, and the participants of the Berne Workshop. I am indebted to Liliane Haegeman, Luigi Rizzi, and the two anonymous reviewers for many valuable suggestions.

NOTES

[1] The notation of age is "year;month,day."
In the following, apart from examples quoted from other sources like Pierce (1989) and Verrips & Weissenborn (1989), Schaner-Wolles (1994), Friedemann (1992), Haegeman (1996) etc., I have worked with corpora from the CHILDES Database (see footnote 15), with data from Elisa whose utterances I taped and transcribed myself in 1991 (see Hamann, 1992 and 1996c), with some diary notes of Elisa, which are marked as diary notes, and with the Augustin corpus taped and transcribed in Geneva (see footnote 13). The data quoted from Tracy are taken from the Penner, Tracy, & Weissenborn (1994) handout, but correspond to the data in Tracy (1991). The analysis of the CHILDES data and the Geneva corpora was performed with standard UNIX tools. The Elisa-corpus, though in Mac format, was analyzed by hand.

[2] For German, we always have to keep in mind that IP is head final in standard analyses so that movement to I does not show on the surface, hence (12ab).

[3] See Haegeman and Zanuttini (1991: 234) for the idea that the Neg-Criterion and the Wh-Criterion are instantiations of a general condition on scope bearing elements, called the Affect Criterion. Such a view implies that the Neg-Criterion is in effect as soon as the general condition is in effect, and thus there could not be a sequence of acquisition.

[4] See Rizzi (1995a) for an argument that feature checking and the satisfaction of the Wh or the Neg-Criterion are not equivalent.

[5] This has been discussed in Hamann (1993a). Also, all occurrences of two negative expressions in one phrase are listed and analyzed in Appendix 1.

[6] It can be argued that kein differs from nicht in a very important aspect: kein might be a negative polarity item.

[7] It is undeniable that something very impressive is going on in the acquisition of genuine operators. Consider the sequence in (i):

i. Christoph kommt heute nicht, Charlotte kommt heute nich, Sabine kommt heute nich. Alle kommen heute nich. - Keiner kommt heute.
'Christoph isn't coming today. Charlotte isn't coming today. Sabine isn't coming today. Everybody isn't coming today. - Nobody is coming today.' (Elisa 3;6, Hamann diary notes)

So it would not be surprising if a slow substitution is taking place as far as genuine quantifier use is concerned.

[8] It has been claimed that in German as in English we find a phase of external negation with nein (Wode, 1977, Clahsen, 1988). This has been challenged, however, because in many corpora *nein* does not occur earlier than *nicht*. Cf. Park (1974), Verrips & Weissenborn (1989), and Hamann (1993a).

[9] Radford's analysis is:

[$_{VP}$ [Kathryn] $_{V'}$[no $_{V'}$[fix this]]].

See Hamann (1993a) for a fuller discussion.

[10] As it is generally assumed that the head-complement parameter is set very early, the German child should be aware of the properties of IP. If the finite verb has moved only to I^0, then we would expect a word order as illustrated in i., which is found only rarely.

i. nich aua macht
    not ouch makes

If the finite verb has moved, and so much is uncontroversial, then it must have gone higher than IP, probably to CP- or to some intermediate AGR projection. More about this problem can be found in Hamann (1993a).

[11] The object is scrambled, i.e. A'-moved across nicht because AgrO is an extended projection of NegP, the subject is A-moved across Spec, AgrO and Spec, Neg. In a minimalist account, he subject will be able to cross the object because the verb has moved.

[12] Crisma (1992), following the original spirit of Rizzi's proposal, assumed that only morphological material can activate a projection, so that yes-no questions need not project higher than AgrSP. Recently, considerations about Full Interpretation and the Logical From of such questions have led to the assumption that interpretative necessities can also activate a projection. See Hamann (1996b,c).

[13] The Augustin corpus has been taped and transcribed in Geneva in a joint project of the Department of Linguistics and the Department of Psycholinguistics as described in Hamann, Rizzi, & Frauenfelder (1996).

For Augustin, we find that he does not use bare participles to any important percentage. From a total of 637 verbal utterances obtained from the transcription of the first 30 minutes of each of the 10 recordings, only 13 are bare participles. Of these, 4 are *cassé* 'broken', 1 is *assis* 'sitting' which are adjectives, 2 are *gagné* 'won' which is a fixed expression and perhaps also an adjective, 4 are clearly tensed because they are answers to questions where the auxiliary is provided, or are follow-ups in a narrative:

i. '[e] demandé à la dame et ....pis encore pas acheté'
    [e] asked of the lady and   then yet   not bought
ii. [e] pas derang[e]
    [e] not disturbed/ disturb

Two forms remain which appear to be untensed and could be counted with the infinitives. These examples and the obvious problem of deciding what is an infinitive and what is a participle for the verbs of the -er pattern makes more of an argument not to include participles in the count. The conventions for transcription also play an important role. As can be seen from i., so-called placeholders were transcribed as such not left out and not given an interpretation. This practice shows up the problems much more acutely, but also shows that many unclear uses of the participle are really tensed forms, see ii.

[14] Note that Levow (1995), counting bare participles, gives figures for these two children which correspond exactly to the non-finite part of Table 4.

[15] See MacWhinney & Snow (1990) and MacWhinney (1991). Katrin and Andreas are from the Wagner files, Julia is from the Clahsen file. Nicole (Wagner) and Julia's brothers, Daniel and Mathias (Clahsen) are also available on CHILDES for German.

[16] Note that a story as outlined in 3.4. will work only with a low NegP. As it is, TP can be built on top of the suggested structure, if TP were lower than NegP in adult structure, then a projection would have to be inserted, which is very improbable.

[17] For Andreas, 4 cases of negation with infinitive remain:

i. *normal elliptical answer to investigator's question*
    Annette: Was kann der nicht? (der=Ballon)
              what can he not
    Andreas: e nich fliegen
              e not fly

ii. *non adult use*
    Opa: Was bist du? Reporter?
              what are you reporter
    Andreas: e nich Reporter sein
              e not reporter be

iii. *non-adult use or elliptical*
    Mutter: Andreas, hier ist Tante Anni
              here is aunt Anni (holds out receiver to Andreas)
    Andreas: nich pechn
              not speak

iv. *unclear*
    Looking at a picture book where a child is crying
    Andreas: ne, nich weinen
              no, not weep
    Annette: doch, der weint
              but yes, he is crying

[18] A completely different account for negation and root infinitives is given in Harris & Wexler (1996). These authors find a percentage of only 9.6% of inflection in negated English child sentences whereas about 43% of all affirmative sentences where inflected in their sample. So, the use of non-finite forms in negation is very high indeed This count considers negation with no and not, however, so that again, it is not compatible with the above counts, which consider only the use of the particle for sentential negation. It is likely that their result can be interpreted in the light of Hoekstra & Jordens (1994).

As one reviewer pointed out, there also are counts on the occurrence of non-finite verb forms in *wh*-questions and declaratives for English which show that both occur to the same percentage. This casts doubts on the applicability of the truncation analysis for English (see Phillips, 1995). It has to be said that Phillips' count, which was delimited to subject questions in order to eliminate the notorious ambiguity of English forms like come as finite or infinitival, also disregarded utterances with missing auxiliaries. This implies that the very frequent examples of the type where going, who coming, who gone were not included in the count. Utterances like who played, however, still remain ambiguous between a finite and a non-finite reading. Moreover, the existence of adult utterances in English of the type why go there?, why leave now? suggests that English child questions may be modeled on these lines. It may indeed be the case that truncation cannot analyze every child utterance - precisely because language specific properties play a decisive role in the developmental sequence.

[19] It has been pointed out that the mere misclassification of a lexical item involves only parameter resetting and thus does not violate the continuity assumption, while truncation assumes that an axiom of UG is not consistently applied by the child, which is much worse. This may be so under a certain understanding of continuity. On the other hand, I believe that this particular sort of misclassification is rather undesirable in the course of development (see Penner, 1992 and Müller, 1994) because of the triggering problem and the lack of (new) evidence for resetting. I hope to have shown that the assumption of an early misclassification only creates problems and that we are better off if we dispense with it - as a bonus we are even satisfying continuity. At no point of the argument, continuity was put forward as the reason why the negative particle in German child language must be a specifier.

Truncation, on the other side, is either overcome by maturation, or it can be seen as the product of a process of reevaluating the strength of UG principles, not of their absence, as Rizzi (1995b) has pointed out. It can even be interpreted as the outcome of an incomplete matching of syntax and discourse, i.e. as an interface problem. This is so because the CP is the point of anchoring a phrase in the discourse, see Rizzi (1997) and Hamann (1996b, c). Seen in this light, truncation is not violating UG at all, but is a natural outcome of specific (formal) pragmatic anchoring problems, especially concerning tense and pronouns (see also Haegeman, 1996 and Hyams, 1996 on a pragmatic solution).

As Atkinson (1996) states very clearly, whatever one does within a continuity and full competence framework, there is likely to be a cost - appeal to maturation or pragmatics - because the changes in language development still remain to be explained. But the appeal to a global principle like maturation I find much less disturbing than the assumption of innumerable little breaks, which will always appear a bit ad hoc and will always invite the question of how the target item, classification or principle, could be acquired after the non-target start. This is why I find the little splinter very irksome while the beam will have to be dealt with in a concerted effort anyway.

APPENDIX

1. German Verb Placement and Other Negation Phenomena

Table A1.

Negation and verb placement (CHILDES, Wagner and Clahsen)

Katrin: 1;5, Julia: 1;11-2;5, Daniel: 2;9-3;6, Mathias: 2;9-3;6

Katrin	+fin	-fin	Julia	+fin	-fin
V Neg	6	0	V Neg	18	0
Neg V	0	1	Neg V	0	2
Mathias	+fin	-fin	Daniel	+fin	-fin
V Neg	100	0	V Neg	69	0
Neg V	4	1	Neg V	1	3

All cases of Neg V-fin involve null-subjects.

Elisa: 3;1-3;4

Elisa	+fin	-fin
V Neg	70	0
Neg V	0	1

The one case of Neg V-fin is an adult imperative structure with infinitive.

Table A2.
Negation, negative concord, external negation, topicalization

	Negation > 1 word	Neg Con	Ext. Neg	Top Neg
Katrin 1;5	17 (4 are strengthened with external negation)	0	12	0
Julia 1;11-2;5	30	1?	0	2
	(1 is strengthened by external negation)			
Mathias 2;9-3;6	136	0	1	4
Daniel 2;9-3;6	83	1	0	1
Elisa 3;1	79	0	0	0

(topicalization is not visible in the corpus, but occurred in the diary data)

The cases that involve two negative expressions (candidates for NC) are:

		CHILDES
nich da nein	Katrin 1;5	Wagner Corpus
nis mehr din nein	Katrin 1;5	Wagner Corpus
oda nich nein	Katrin 1;5	Wagner Corpus
braucht ju nich Angt, nein	Katrin 1;5	Wagner Corpus
will nich angel nein	Julia 2;1	Clahsen Corpus
mein platoffel is nich aber nich richtig	Julia 2;5	Clahsen Corpus
noch nich keine sik	Daniel 2;11	Clahsen Corpus

Only Daniel's utterance looks like true NC. As it turns out, it is not NC at all, because *keine sik* is in its base position as argument and thus does not enter into any relation with the negative head.

2. Negation and Infinitives/ Non-finite Utterances in French

Table A3.
Distribution of non-finite negative verbal utterances(from V &W, 1989)

	total	-Fin	+Fin
Fabienne 1;8.-3;3.	92	1 1.1%	91 98.9%
Loic 2;5.-2;11	238	77 32.4%	161 67.6%
Benjamin 2;0-2;9.	227	29 12.8%	198 87.2%
Philippe 2;1-2;8.	282	25 8.9%	257 91.1%
Florence 2;2.-2;10	98	13 13.3%	85 86.7%
Romain 2;4-3;0	47	13 27.7%	34 72.3%
Total	984	158 16.1%	826 83.9%

For Fabienne, Loic, Philippe there is equal spacing of files whereas there is a concentration at 2;3-2;6-2;7 for Benjamin, concentration at 2;6 and 2;7 for Florence, and concentration at 2;10 for Romain.

Table A4.
Distribution of infinitives in negative utterances in the Augustin corpus
Step 1: 30 minutes of each recording transcribed

	all verbal utterances			negative verbal utterances		
File	Total	Fin	Inf	Total	Fin	Inf
01 2;0.2	49	42 82.7%	7 14.3%	1	1 100%	0
02 2;0.23	23	14 60.8%	9 39.1%	0	0	0
03 2;1.15	15	8 53.3%	7 46.7%	0	0	0
04 2;2.13	44	38 86.4%	6 13.6%	0	0	0
05 2;3.10	33	29 87.9%	4 12.1%	1	0	1 100%
06 2;4.1	53	48 90.6%	5 9.4%	5	5 100%	0
07 2;4.22	46	38 82.5%	8 17.4%	1	1 100%	0
01-07	263	217 82.5%	46 17.5%	8	7 87.5%	1 12.5%
08 2;6.9	100	93 93%	7 7%	2	2 100%	0
09 2;9.2	141	133 94.3%	8 5.7%	20	20 100%	0
10 2;9.30	133	125 94%	8 6%	21	21 100%	0
08-10	374	351 93.9%	23 6.1%	43	43 100%	0
Total	637	568 89.2%	69 10.8%	51	50 98%	1 2%

Table A5.
Distribution of infinitives in negative utterances in the Augustin corpus
Step 2: Full transcription

File	all verbal utterances			negative verbal utterances		
	Total	Fin	Inf	Total	Fin	Inf
01 2;0.2	68	51 75%	17 25%	4	4 100%	0
02 2;0.23	33	20 60.6%	13 39.4%	0	0	0
03 2;1.15	21	11 52.4%	10 47.6%	0	0	0
04 2;2.13	60	54 90%	6 10%	3	3 100%	0
05 2;3.10	56	43 87.9%	13 12.1%	2	1 50%	1 50%
06 2;4.1	65	58 89.2%	7 10.8%	5	5 100%	0
07 2;4.22	70	58 82.9%	12 17.1%	3	3 100%	0
01-07	373	295 79.1%	78 20.9%	17	16 94.1%	1 5.9%
08 2;6.9	100	93 93%	7 7%	2	2 100%	0
09 2;9.2	141	133 94.3%	8 5.7%	20	20 100%	0
10 2;9.30	150	141 94%	9 6%	25	25 100%	0
08-10	391	367 93.9%	24 6.1%	47	47 100%	0
Total	764	662 86.6%	102 13.4%	64	63 99.5%	1 1.5%

3. Negation and Infinitives/ Non-finite utterances in German

Table A6.

Distribution of infinitives in verbal utterances for Julia

1;11-2;0	verbal utterances			verbal utterances not counting separable verbs		
	total	-Fin	+Fin	total	-Fin	+Fin
all utterances	2	3	0	2	2	0
positive utterances	2	2	0	1	1	0
negative verbal	1	1	0	1	1	0
2;1						
all utterances	4	4	0	3	3	0
positive utterances	4	4	0	3	3	0
negative utterances	0	0	0	0	0	0
2;2						
all utterances	22	18 81.9%	4 18.1%	13	9 69.2%	4 30.8%
positive utterances	21	18 85.8%	3 14.2%	12	9 75%	3 25%
negative utterances	1	0	1	1	0	1
2;3						
all utterances	43	30 69.7%	13 30.3%	26	15 57.7%	11 42.3%
positive utterances	39	30 76.9%	9 23.1%	22	15 68.2%	7 31.8%
negative utterances	4	0	4	4	0	4
2;4						
all utterances	66	28 42.4%	38 57.6%	49	10 20.4%	39 79.6%
positive utterances	56	25 44.6%	31 55.4%	39	9 23.1%	30 76.9%
negative utterances	12	3 25%	9 75%	10	1 10%	9 90%
2;5						
all utterances	55	10 18.2%	45 81.8%	50	5 10%	45 90%
positive utterances	48	9 18.8%	39 81.2%	44	5 11.4%	39 88.6%
negative utterances	7	1 14.3%	6 85.7%	6	0	6

REFERENCES

Atkinson, M.: 1996, 'Now, hang on a minute: Some reflections on emerging orthodoxies', in H. Clahsen (ed.) *Generative Perspectives on Language Acquisition*, Benjamins, Amsterdam, Philadelphia, 451-485.
Bayer, J.: 1990, 'What Bavarian Negative Concord reveals about the syntactic structure of German', in J. Mascaro & M. Nespor (eds.) *Grammar in Progress*, Foris, Dordrecht, 13-23.
Bromberg, H.S. and K. Wexler: 1995, 'Null subjects in Wh-questions in child French: Evidence for and against truncated structures', in C. Schütze, J. Ganger, & K. Broihier (eds.) *Papers on Language Processing and Acquisition, MITWPL* **26**, 221-248.
Cardinaletti, A. and I. Roberts: 1991, 'Clause structure and X-Second', ms., University of Geneva, University of Venice.
Chomsky, N.: 1993, 'A minimalist program for linguistic theory', in K. Hale and S. Keyser (eds.) *The View From Building 20: Essays in Linguistics in Honor of Sylvain Bromberger*, MIT Press, Cambridge, Mass. 1-52.
Clahsen, H.: 1988, 'Kritische Phasen der Grammatikentwicklung', *Zeitschrift für Sprachwissenschaft* **7**, 3-31.
Clahsen, H.: 1990/1991, 'Constraints on parameter setting. A grammatical analysis of some acquisition stages in German child language', *Language Acquisition* **1**, 361-391.
Clark, R.:, 1992, 'The selection of syntactic knowledge', *Language Acquisition* **2**, 83-149.
Crisma, P.: 1992, 'On the acquisition of Wh in French', *GenGenP* **0(1-2)**, 115-112.
Degraff, M.A.F.: 1992, 'A riddle on negation in Haitian', ms., City University of New York.
Deprez, V. and A. Pierce: 1990, 'A cross-linguistic study of negation in early syntactic development', paper presented at the 15th *Boston University Conference on Language Development*.
Deprez, V. and A. Pierce: 1994, 'Cross-linguistic evidence for functional projections in early grammar', in Hoekstra and Schwartz (eds.) *Language Acquisition Studies in Generative Grammar*, Benjamins, Amsterdam, 57-84.
Friedemann, M.-A.: 1992, 'The underlying position of external arguments in French' *GenGenP* **0(1-2)**, 123-144.
Eisenbeiß, S.: 1994, 'Kasus und Wortstellung im deutschen Mittelfeld', ms., *Lexlern-Projekt* , University of Düsseldorf.
Grewendorf, G.: 1990, 'Verb-Bewegung und Negation im Deutschen', *Groninger Arbeiten zur germanistischen Linguistik*, 57-125.
Grimshaw, J.: 1993, 'Minimal projection, heads and optimality', ms., Rutgers University.
Haegeman, L.: 1991, 'Negative Concord, Negative Heads', in D. Delfitto *et al.* (eds.) *Going Romance and Beyond, OTS Working Papers*, OTS-WP-TL-91-002, University of Utrecht.
Haegeman, L.: 1993, 'Object Clitics in West Flemish and the identification of A/A-bar', *GenGenP* **2(1)**, 1-30.
Haegeman, L.: 1995, *The Syntax of Negation*, Cambridge University Press, Cambridge.
Haegeman, L.: 1996, 'Root infinitives, clitics and truncated structures', in H. Clahsen (ed.) *Generative Perspectives on Language Acquisition,* Benjamins', Amsterdam. 271-307.
Haegeman, L and R. Zanuttini: 1991, 'Negative Heads and the Neg-Criterion', *The Linguistic Review* **8**, 233-251.
Hamann, C.: 1992, 'Late empty subjects in German child language', *Technical Reports in Formal and Computational Linguistics*, No. 4., University of Geneva.
Hamann, C.: 1993a, 'On the acquisition of negation in German', paper presented at *The Cross-linguistic Acquisition Workshop*, ISAS Trieste, July 1993, also ms., University of Geneva.
Hamann, C.: 1993b, 'Some scope phenomena in German negation', ms. University of Geneva.
Hamann, C.: 1996a, 'Negation and truncated structures', in M. Aldridge (ed.) *Child Language*, Multilingual Matters, Clevedon, 72-83.
Hamann, C.: 1996b, 'Wh-in situ, to move or not to move', *GenGenP* **4(1)**, 34-47.
Hamann, C.: 1996c, 'Null arguments in German child language', *Language Acquisition* **5**, 155-208.

Hamann, C., L. Rizzi and U. Frauenfelder: 1996, 'On the acquisition of subject and object pronouns in French', in H. Clahsen (ed.) *Generative Perspectives on Language Acquisition*, Benjamins', Amsterdam, Philadelphia, 309-334.

Harris, T. and K. Wexler: 1996, 'The Optional Infinitive Stage in Child English. Evidence from Negation', in H. Clahsen (ed.) *Generative Perspectives on Language Acquisition*. Benjamins, Amsterdam, 1-42.

Hoekstra, T. and P. Jordens: 1994, 'From Adjunct to Head', in T. Hoekstra & B. Schwartz (eds.) *Language Acquisition Studies in Generative Grammar*, Benjamins, Amsterdam, 119-149.

Hyams, N.: 1996, 'The underspecification of functional categories in early grammar', in. H. Clahsen (ed.) *Generative Perspectives on Language Acquisition,* Benjamins, Amsterdam, 91-128.

Jepsersen, O.: 1909-1949, *Modern English Grammar on Historical Principles I-VIII,* Munksgaard, Copenhagen (reprinted in 1954 by Allen and Unwin, London).

Klima, E.S. and U. Bellugi: 1966, 'Syntactic regularities in the speech of children', in J. Lyons and R. Wales (eds.) Psycholinguistic Papers, Edinburgh University Press, Edinburgh, 183-207.

Levow, G.-A.: 1995, 'Tense and subject position in interrogatives and negatives in child French: Evidence for and against truncated structures', in C. Schütze, J. Ganger, & K. Broihier (eds.) *Papers on Language Processing and Acquisition, MITWPL* **26**, 281-304.

MacWhinney, B. and C. Snow: 1990, 'The Child Language Data Exchange System: an update', *Journal of Child Language* **17**, 457-472.

MacWhinney, B.: 1991, *The CHILDES Project: Tools for Analyzing Talk*, Lawrence Erlbaum, Hillsdale, New Jersey.

Müller, N.: 1994, 'Parameters cannot be reset, evidence from the development of Comp', in J. Meisel (ed.) *Bilingual First Language Acquisition. French and German Grammatical Development*, Amsterdam, Benjamins, 235-269.

Park, T.-Z.: 1974, *A Study of German Language Development*, Ph.D. Dissertation, University of Berne.

Penner, Z.: 1992, 'The ban on parameter resetting, default mechanisms, and the acquisition of V2 in Bernese Swiss German', in. J. Meisel (ed.) *The Acquisition of Verb Placement. Functional Categories and V2 Phenomena in Language Acquisition*, Kluwer, Dordrecht, 245-282.

Penner, Z., R. Tracy, and J. Weissenborn: 1994, 'Scrambling in early developmental stages in standard and Swiss German', paper presented at the Workshop on the L1- and L2-Acquisition of Clause-Internal Rules: Scrambling and Cliticization, January 1994.

Pesetsky, D.: 1989, *Language Particular Processes and the Earliness Principle*, ms., MIT.

Pierce, A.: 1989, *On the Emergence of Syntax: A Cross-linguistic Study*, Ph.D. Dissertation, MIT.

Pierce, A.: 1992, *Language Acquisition and Syntactic Theory*, Kluwer, Dordrecht.

Phillips, C.: 1995, 'Syntax at age two: cross-linguistic differences', in C. Schütze, J. Ganger, & K. Broihier (eds.) *Papers on Language Processing and Acquisition, MITWPL* **26**, 325-382.

Plunkett, B.: 1992, 'Continuity and the landing site for Wh-movement', *Bangor Research Papers in Linguistics* **4**, 53-77.

Poeppel, D. and K. Wexler: 1993, 'The Full Competence Hypothesis of clause structure in early German, *Language* **69**, 1-33.

Pollock, J.Y.: 1989, 'Verb movement, Universal Grammar and the structure of IP. *Linguistic Inquiry* **20**, 365-424.

Radford, A.: 1990, *Syntactic Theory and the Acquisition of English Syntax: the Nature of Early Child Grammars of English*, Oxford, Blackwell.

Radford, A.: 1996, 'The nature of children's initial clauses', in M. Aldridge (ed.) *Child Language*, Multilingual Matters, Clevedon, 112-148.

Reinhart, T.: 1976, 'Polarity reversal: Logic or Pragmatics?', *Linguistic Inquiry* **7**, 697-705.

Rizzi, L.: 1990, *Relativized Minimality,* MIT Press, Cambridge.

Rizzi, L.: 1991, 'Residual Verb-Second and the Wh-Criterion', *Technical Reports on Formal and Computational Linguistics*, No. 2, University of Geneva.

Rizzi, L.: 1992, 'Early null subjects and root null subjects', *GenGenP* **0(1-2)**, 151-177.

Rizzi, L.: 1994, 'Some notes on linguistic theory and language development', *Language Acquisition 3*, 371-393.
Rizzi, L.: 1995a, ' A note on *do*-support', ms., University of Geneva.
Rizzi, L.: 1995b, 'Early null subjects and economy of representation', paper presented at the *Groningen Assembly on Language Acquisition, GALA*.
Rizzi, L.: 1997, 'The fine structure of the left periphery', in L. Haegeman (ed.) *Elements of Grammar. A Handbook of Generative Syntax*, Kluwer, Dordrecht, 281-338.
Roberts, I.: 1992, 'Two Types of Head-Movement in Romance', ms., University of Wales, Bangor.
Rohrbacher, B. and T. Roeper: 1994, 'True pro-drop in child language and the principle of economy of projection', paper presented at the Workshop on the L1- and L2-Acquisition of Clause-Internal Rules: Scrambling and Cliticization, Berne, January.
Schaner-Wolles, C.: 1994, 'The Acquisition of Negation', paper presented at GLOW, Vienna, April 1994.
Schönenberger, M., A. Pierce, K. Wexler and F. Wijnen: 1996, 'Accounts of root infinitives and the interpretation of root infinitives', *GenGenP* **3(2)**, 47-71.
Schütze, C. and K. Wexler: 1996, 'Subject case licensing and English root infinitives', in A. Stringfellow *et al.* (eds.) *BUCLD* **20**, 670-681.
Tracy, R.: 1991, *Sprachliche Strukturentwicklung*, Narr, Tübingen.
Vainikka, A.: 1994, 'Case in the development of English syntax', *Language Acquisition 3*, 257-325.
Valian, V.: 1991, 'Syntactic subjects in the Early Speech of American and Italian children', *Cognition* **40**, 21-81.
Weissenborn, J., M. Verripps and R. Berman: 1989, 'Negation as a Window to the Structure of Early Child Language', ms. Max-Planck Institute.
Wagner, K: 1985, 'How much do children say in a day?', *Journal of Child Language* **12**, 475-487.
Weissenborn, J.: 1990, 'Functional categories and verb movement: the acquisition of German syntax reconsidered', in M. Rothweiler (ed.) *Spracherwerb und Grammatik. Linguistische Untersuchungen zum Erwerb von Syntax und Morphologie, Linguistische Berichte, Sonderheft* **3**, 166-189.
Wexler, K.: 1994, 'Optional infinitives, head movement and the economy of derivations in child grammar', in D. Lightfoot and N. Hornstein (eds.) *Verb Movement*, Cambridge University Press, Cambridge, 305-350.
Wode, H.: 1977, 'Four early stages in the development of LI negation', *Journal of Child Language* **4**, 87-102.
Zeller, J.: 1994, *Die Syntax des Tempus*, Westdeutscher Verlag, Opladen.
Zwart, J.W.: 1993, *Dutch Syntax*, Doctoral dissertation, University of Groningen.

CORNELIA HAMANN
University of Geneva & University of Tuebingen

JACQUELINE VAN KAMPEN

LEFT-BRANCH EXTRACTION AS OPERATOR MOVEMENT: EVIDENCE FROM CHILD DUTCH

1. INTRODUCTION

The present paper deals with left-branch extractions in child language not supported by the adult input. These left-branch extractions appear in *wh*-questions (example 1a), topicalizations (example 1b), and scrambling environments (example 1c).

(1)   a. *welke* wil jij [*e* liedje] zingen?   S. 3;7.12
which want you [e song] sing?
'which song do you want to sing?'
b. *Cynthia* is dat niet [*e* pyama]   Jasmijn 2;5
Cynthia is that not [e pyama]
'That is not Cynthia's pyama.'
c. dat heb ik *zo* niet meer [*e* lang] gedaan! Loura 6;6
that have I so not more [e long] done
'I have not done that for a long time!'

This paper is organized as follows. Section 2 exemplifies the left-branch extractions in Dutch child language and raises the learnability question. Section 3 gives some additional facts that are relevant for the analysis of left-branch extractions in child language. Section 4 settles some questions about the categorial status of the subextracted elements. Section 5 takes a look into the present day analyses of left-branch extractions. Section 6 discusses the problem of a learning scenario for obligatory pied-piping. Section 7 considers whether universal LF representations might explain the child's long-standing preferences for the set of non-adult PF realizations. Section 8 serves as a conclusion.

2. FACTS AND THE LEARNABILITY QUESTION

2.1. Left-branch wh-extractions in child Dutch

Wh-movement in child Dutch may shift the left-branch element, leaving behind a nominal or adjectival projection (Hoekstra & Jordens, 1994), as in the examples in (2). This construction is not found in the adult input.

(2) *Stranding the nominal projection*
    a. *welk* wil jij [*e* boekje]?   S. 2;9.15
       which want you [e booklet]
       'which booklet do you want to read?'
    b. *welke* wil jij [*e* liedje] zingen?   S. 3;7.12
       which want you [e song] sing
       'which song do you want to sing?'
    c. {kom kijken} *hoe* R. [*e* veel plezier] heeft! Loura 6;6
       {come and see} how Rianne [e much fun] has
       'come and see how much fun Rianne is having!'
    d. *welke* wil je [*e* chocolaatjes]?   Nina 2;7.5
       which want you [e chocolates]
       'which chocolates do you want?'

(3) *Stranding the adjectival projection*
    a. {mag ik proeven} *hoe* het [*e* heet] is?   L. 4;3.0
       {may I taste} how it [e hot] is
       'may I taste how hot it is?'
    b. *hoe* is het [*e* laat]?   Tim C. 3;6
       how is [e late]   Loura 6;5
       'how late is it?'
    c. ik weet niet *hoe* het [*e* lang] is   Emma 3;1
       I know not how it [e long] is   Loura 3;6
       'I do not know how long it is'

The *wh*-extractions in (2)-(3) violate the Left-Branch Condition of Ross (1967) which generalizes over the ungrammaticality of examples like (2) and (3) in adult Dutch. Movement of an element - determiner, degree word, possessor - in the left-branch position is possible only by pied-piping the entire phrase.

The figures in (4) represent the distribution of complex *wh*-phrases in Laura and Sarah recordings and diary notes.

(4) a. No pied-piping (stranding)   recordings   diary notes
        Laura (2;9 - 5;6)   7   11
        Sarah (2;9 - 5;2)   17   4
     b. Pied-piping (no stranding)   recordings   diary notes
        Laura (2;9 - 5;6)   4   4
        Sarah (2;9 - 5;2)   11   2

The number of complex *wh*-phrases is not very high if one compares it to the total number of utterances with a *wh*-element (see note 1). This is due to the fact that children prefer simple *wh*-pronouns (Lebeaux, 1988; Radford, 1986). Since complex phrases do not occur frequently in early child language, statistics of the left-branch violations are not significant. The distribution in the files, though, shows that left-branch extractions (4a) occurred more often than pied-piping (4b) at the age indicated.

2.2. Left-branch [–wh] extractions in child Dutch: topicalization and scrambling

The sentence-initial position may be occupied by a subextracted [–wh] pronoun as well, as in the examples in (5) from Hoekstra & Jordens (1994).

(5)   *Topicalization of the left-branch element*
      Stranding the nominal projection
      a. *die* heb ik niet [*e* sok] aan   Jasmijn 2;3
         that have I not [e sock] on
         'I am not wearing that sock.'
      b. *Cynthia* is dat niet [*e* pyama]   Jasmijn 2;5
         Cynthia is that not [e pyama]
         'that is not Cynthia's pajama.'

Another kind of [–wh] subextraction is found in sentences where a pronoun is in a scrambling position at the left of a negative or positive adverb, as in the examples in (6) and (7).

(6)   *Scrambling of the left-branch element*
      Stranding the nominal projection
      a. ik wil *die* niet [*e* boek] lezen!   L. 2;9.2
         I want that not [e book] read
         'I do not want to read that book'
      b. doe jij *Laura's* ook [*e* haar]?   S. 6;3.16
         do you Laura's too [e hair]
         'are you fixing Laura's hair too?'

       c. e is *andere* nou [*e* puzzel]?   L. 2;6.24
         e is other then [e puzzle]
         '(where) is the other puzzle?'
       d. Cynthia mag *mij* niet [*e* navel] zien   Jasmijn 2;7
         Cynthia may my not [e belly button] see
         'Cynthia is not allowed to see my navel'

(7)   *Scrambling of the left-branch element*
       Stranding the adjectival projection
       a. is *heel* wel [*e* lekker]!   L. 3;3.4
         is very indeed [e nice]
         '(that) is very nice indeed!'
       b. dat heb ik *zo* niet meer [*e* lang] gedaan!   Loura 6;6
         that have I so not more [e long] done
         'I have not done that for a long time!'
       c. waarom moet dat *zo* nog [*e* heet]?   Tim B. 3;5
         why must that so yet [e hot]?
         'why does it have to be that hot yet?'

In the following sections I will use the distinction [+wh]/[−wh] element. Later on, in Section 7, I will define left-branch extractions in topicalizations and scrambling environments as A'-movement triggered by [+focus].

2.3. The Learnability Question: The Acquisition of the Left-Branch Condition

The subextractions of the previous section all violate Ross' Left-Branch Condition. The Left-Branch Condition is not a universal constraint. It does not apply in certain adult languages such as Polish, Russian, and Latin. Moreover, the D-elements in these languages are:

    i. highly inflected (Ross, 1967:131) and
    ii. optional (Uriagereka, 1988:113; Corver, 1990:332).

An example is the *wh*-subextraction in Polish is in (8) from Corver (1990:330).

(8)   jaki$_i$ wykreciles   [t$_i$ numer]?
         which$_i$ (you) dialed   [t$_i$ number]
         'which number did you dial?'

Rizzi (1990b:36) gives the Italian example of subextraction from an AP in (9a), although Italian lacks nominal inflection. Identical subextractions from APs are allowed in South American Spanish (Butt & Benjamin, 1988; S. Baauw, p.c.), compare the example in (9b).

(9)   a. quanto$_i$ è   [alto t$_i$]?
                   how   is (he)   tall
                   'How tall is he?'
         b. cómo·   somos   desgraciadas las mujeres!
                   how are(we)   unhappy   the women
                   'How unhappy we women are!'

The observations of Ross lead to the central problem of this paper, formulated in (10).

(10)   How is the Left-Branch Condition acquired?
                   a. Which parameter setting yields the Left-Branch Condition, that is which parameter setting forces pied-piping?
                   b. Why does the learner of Dutch start out with a grammar that tends to disregard the Left-Branch Condition?

Question (10a) will be discussed in Section 6. I will argue there that the Left-Branch Condition is a PF adjacency condition on Case assignment. Question (10b) will be discussed in Section 7. The result of subextraction is reminiscent of reconstruction at LF. I propose, as an answer to (10b), that the child may start off with the LF representation as a computationally more economic setting.

Before turning to these main questions, I will mention a few additional facts (Section 3) and define the categorial status of the subextracted element (Section 4). Section 5 presents a sketch of current standard solutions.

3. ADDITIONAL FACTS

Several phenomena can be related to both the [+wh] and the [–wh] subextraction facts. They are enumerated in (11) and elaborated below.

(11) a. Pied-piping, i.e., movement of the entire phrase, is a simultaneous option from the beginning.
b. Stranding data are still found, and are not uncommon, after the age of six, when the obligatory presence of D-elements has already been acquired for more than two years.
c. In the recordings there are no examples of violations of the Condition on Extraction Domains (Huang, 1982).
d. The subextracted elements seem to bear contrastive stress.

I will illustrate these facts below, beginning with observation (11a). Pied-piping of the *wh*-phrase follows subextraction quite soon, but at first only as a less frequent option. See the examples in (12).

(12) *Wh-movement of the entire projection*
a. [welk boek] ga jij t_{DP} lezen?   L. 3;6.30
   [which book] go you t_{DP} read
   'which book are you going to read?'
b. [welke lepel] wil jij t_{DP} hebben?   S. 3;5.30
   [which spoon] want you t_{DP} have
   'which spoon do you want to have?'
c. [hoe laat] is het t_{DegP}?   S. 3;1.23
   [how late] is it t_{DegP}
   'how late is it?'

Pied-piping in early Dutch also occurs for topicalized and scrambled elements.

(13) *Topicalization of the entire projection*
a. [deze man] gaat t_{DP} eruit   S. 2;5.25
   [this man] goes t_{DP} out of it
   'this man goes out of it'
b. [jouw lamp] is t_{DP} niet op de fiets S. 2;6.27
   [your lamp] is t_{DP} not on the bike
   'your lamp is not on the bike'
c. [mijn roosie] heb je t_{DP} vergeten   S. 2;8.3
   [my little rose] have you t_{DP} forgotten
   'you have forgotten to bring my little rose'
d. [heel moeilijk] ga ik een huis t_{DegP} bouwen S. 2;8.3
   [very complicated] go I a house t_{DegP} built
   'I am going to built a house in a very complicated way'

(14) *Scrambling of the entire projection*
   a. ik heb [zo een] nog niet t$_{DP}$ L. 3;3.7
      I have [such one] not yet t$_{DP}$
      'I have not such a thing yet'
   b. ik kan [mijn eigen] niet t$_{DP}$ dragen L. 3;4.8
      I can [my own] not t$_{DP}$ carry
      'I cannot carry myself'

Let me turn to the second fact (11b). Left-branch extraction gradually diminishes. Nevertheless, it remains a persistent phenomenon, as shown by the examples in (15).

(15) a. *hoeveel* denk je dat ik [*e* geld] heb? L. 8;3.30
      how much do you think that I [e money] have?
      'how much pocket money do you think I have?'
   b. *hoeveel* krijg ik dan [*e* zakgeld]? L. 8;3.30
      how much get I then [e pocket money]?
      'how much pocket money will I get then?'

The observation in (11b) is supported by the fact that [+/−*wh*] subextractions in Dutch child language extend far into the period in which the obligatory use of articles, demonstratives, interrogatives, and genitive marking is well-established in the child grammar (see the ages of L. in (15)). This is a clear difference with Latin and Polish in which D-elements remain an option. Significantly, these languages do not have articles, whereas Dutch does have articles and Dutch child language shows the systematic use of articles long before the left-branch extractions disappear. Consider the examples in (16).

(16) a. *waarom* wil jij dat in *de* auto zetten? L. 3;5
      why want you that in the car put?
      'why do you want to put that in the car?'
   b. *mijn* jurk is nat van *dit* water S. 3;1
      my$_{GEN}$ dress is wet from this water
      'my dress is wet from this water'
   c. de volgende keer ga ik *mijn* brood opeten S. 3;5
      the next time go I my$_{GEN}$ bread eat
      'next time I will be eating my bread'

At the age of three and a half, the children are already using articles, demonstratives, and genitive marking. I assume that they recognize these elements as functional heads, because they use them in adult-like fashion. Nevertheless, left-branch violations still occur.

The observation in (11c) is exemplified in (17) and (18). The [+wh] and [−wh] subextractions in Dutch child grammar involve only direct object DPs and predicative DegPs. Utterances like those in (17) and (18) probably do not occur in child language.

(17)   *Extraction out of a subject*
         a. **welk* leest [$_{DP}$ e kind] een boekje?
            which reads [$_{DP}$ e child] a booklet
         b. **dat* leest [$_{DP}$ e kind] een boekje
            which reads [$_{DP}$ e child] a booklet

(18)   *Extraction out of an adjunct*
         a. **hoe* heeft de kat [$_{DegP}$ e hoog] gesprongen?
            how has the cat [$_{DegP}$ e high] jumped
         b. **zo* heeft de kat [$_{DegP}$ e hoog] gesprongen
            that has the cat [$_{DegP}$ e high] jumped

There were eight examples of subject/adjunct [+wh] movement in the Laura and Sarah files. All show pied-piping of the full constituent, cf. (19).

(19)   a. welk meisje is t$_{wh}$ dan jarig?   L. 4;0.9
            which girl is t$_{wh}$ then celebrating her birthday
            'which girl celebrates her birthday then?'
         b. welke dieren komen t$_{wh}$ dr allemaal?   S. 4;4.28
            which animals come t$_{wh}$ there all
            'which animals will all come?'
         c. weet je hoeveel nachtjes ze t$_{wh}$ jarig is?   L. 5;6.12
            do you know how many nights she t$_{wh}$ is
            celebrating her birthday
            'do you know in how many nights she
            celebrates her birthday?'

This is reminiscent of the CED effects (Condition on Extraction Domains, Huang, 1982) of adult grammars. Adverbial phrases and subject DPs constitute islands for extraction, since they are not L-marked (Chomsky 1986, 1995:79)

The last point (11d) is illustrated by the stress pattern in (20). In the cases of subextraction, the stress falls on the subextracted element rather than on the complement.

(20)   waarom moet dat *zó* nog [e heet]?   Tim B. 3;5
         why must that so yet [hot]
         'why does it have to be that hot yet?'

Neutral stress falls to the right, i.e., on the most governed head (Cinque, 1993a). Other patterns in which the main stress falls on one of the other heads, are marked as special. The special stress on the subextracted head may be a crucial factor for the left-branch extractions in child language, as I will argue in Section 7.2.

4. THE CATEGORIAL STATUS OF THE SUBEXTRACTED ELEMENTS

The longstanding option between left-branch extractions and pied-piping supports the view that subextracted elements are based on a functional [+/−wh] feature from the very beginning (Van Kampen, 1994). Let us assume that the functional category D^0 or Deg^0, as well as its specific form, which is {[+d]/[+wh]}, belong to a universal set of functional categories accessible to the language learner *a priori*. It stands to reason that a learning procedure will be necessary to identify the universal [+d]/[+wh]-categories in their language-specific disguise. The phonological form, at least, is not given as a universal.

The [+/−wh] element must have been identified as a functional head quite early. Single *wh*-pronoun questions appear long before the left-branch extractions or pied-pipings. The identification of the [+wh] pronoun (*hoe* 'how', *welke* 'which', *wie* 'who', *wat* 'what') as a functional category D^0 or Deg^0 has to be fairly straightforward. The language learner first produces simple question words only (*wat* 'what', *waar* 'where', *wie* 'who'). The *wh*-element is in sentence-initial scope position, i.e., it is a [+wh]-marked marked operator. Moreover, it contains no further information than the typical *phi*-features allow (Lebeaux, 1988:444). In the same vein, the D-elements *die/dat* 'that', *mij* 'my' and the Deg-elements *zo* 'so' *heel* 'very' (see the examples in Section 2.2) have all the properties of functional, closed class elements and may be identified by the learner as such in a straightforward way.

I follow here Emonds' (1985:191) characterization, of grammaticalized (functional) categories which have the properties paraphrased in (21).

(21)   a. They are closed class elements and belong to a class that contains a small set of words which can't be added on to (no conscious coining).
             b. They differ only by syntactic features and cannot be differentiated from each other solely by purely semantic features.

Wh-elements, articles, and demonstratives are in general mutually exclusive. They compete for a single D^0 position and this restriction is respected in child language. The language acquisition device (LAD) must have recognized these elements as functional categories.

The Polish *wh*-elements, exemplified in (8), are equally straightforwardly captured as functional elements by Emonds' characterization. The same may be said of Rizzi's (1990b:36) degree element in the example *Quanto è alto?* in (9a). They trigger *wh*-movement, allow optional pied-piping, and have no more content than the [+wh] feature plus perhaps additional *phi*-features. I conclude that subextractions leave a gap t_D/t_{Deg} that is recognizable for the LAD.

5. LEFT-BRANCH VIOLATIONS AS ANALYZED IN PRESENT DAY SYNTAX

Ross' Left-Branch Condition has been reconsidered in Uriagereka (1988:113) and Corver (1990). They propose more or less the same type of analysis. Corver (1990) presents the most elaborate one. Roughly speaking and not entering into a set of subtleties (for these see Corver 1990:329ff), one might reinterpret Corver as follows. The [+/–wh] left-branch element is subject to a parameter [+/–projecting], in the spirit of Fukui & Speas (1986) (cf. Uriagereka, 1988). If the [+/–wh] element is [+projecting], we get a Dutch/German type of language. If the [+/–wh] element is [–projecting] we get a Polish type of language. The left-branch element in Polish is analyzed as an adjunction to the N-projection. Moreover, the left-branch element is a maximal projection as in (22).

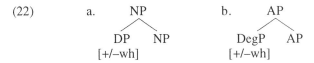

Hoekstra & Jordens (1994) assume this kind of adjunction structure for child language. As long as this structure holds the [+d]/[+wh] element may be subextracted if its containing NP is L-marked. It now follows that in Polish as well as in child language, subextraction is possible out of an object constituent, and not possible out of a subject or an adjunct. After all subjects and adjuncts are not L-marked.

As soon as the language learner recognizes articles, he/she will identify the left-branch element as a variant of the functional [+projecting] category D^0/Deg^0. The adjunction structure will be reanalyzed as in (23).

(23)   a.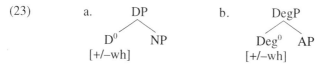

The D^0/Deg^0 head cannot be extracted due to (relativized) Minimality (Rizzi, 1990b; Chomsky, 1995:81). It cannot cross its L-governor. The Left-Branch Condition becomes relevant now and pied-piping of the full constituent is the only way to move the left-branch element into the sentence initial operator position.

All of this is according to the facts. A nice point of these analyses is that they fit well with Chomsky's (1995) analysis of X-bar structure. Chomsky (1995:chapter 4) states that a chain should obey the three requirements in (24) by definition.

(24)   a. Uniformity (either heads or maximal constituents)
        b. C-command
        c. A feature checking trigger

The left-branch element, which does not project, must be [–projecting/+maximal]. Hence, it can occupy [Spec, C]. If a subextracted element lands into this position, it allows a chain that satisfies Chomsky's conditions. Firstly, the chain is uniform as [–projecting/+maximal] (requirement 24a). Secondly, the chain is build on c-command since its head Spec, C c-commands its point of the tail in the object position (requirement 24b). Thirdly, the chain is created in order to obtain checking in [Spec, C] of the [+/–wh] operator feature against a feature [+Q]/[+topic] in C^0 (requirement 24c).

The contention that the subextracted elements are maximal projections is therefore supported by the structure-preserving uniformity condition (24a) combined with the checking condition (24c). Corver (1990) applies a somewhat different terminology but the fundamental difficulties of left-branch subextraction are clearly pointed out in his analysis.

It seems then that the *wh*-subextraction in Dutch child language fits into the present day ideas about generative syntax. For some of my readers, this may suffice as a reassurement.

6. THE LEARNING SCENARIO

6.1. The Current Analysis

There is a tension between the current analysis sketched in Section 5 and a plausible learning scenario. A closer look at the learning scenario for the category D questions the plausibility of Hoekstra & Jorden's (1994) account of [+/–wh] extraction in child Dutch. The crucial step in their analysis of left-branch extraction is a switch made by the language acquisition device (the LAD). At first, the LAD analyzes the left-branch element as a non-projecting functional category. The [+/–wh] element is adjoined to an N-projection during that period and it can be considered as an adjunct that is a maximal projection in its own right, see (22). Then reanalysis occurs and thereafter, the [+/–wh] element is analyzed as an item that projects and takes its NP companion as a kind of complement rather than being adjoined to it. This is a remarkable change in analyzing the input performed by the LAD. Initially, the LAD assumes that functional categories may or may not project. Then, for some reason, it decides that the category D does not project. This decision turns out to be correct for the Polish type of languages but incorrect for the German type. The early decision of a non-projecting D-element causes the correct left-branch extractions in Polish and the incorrect left-branch extractions in child Dutch/German. Subsequently, there is new evidence in the Dutch/German type of languages. This evidence comes in late, but is so strong that the LAD can retreat from its early but mistaken assumption that the functional category D in the Dutch/German type of language does not project. This is a general outline of the learning scenario for the Left-Branch Condition in Dutch/German.

The assumption of a plus/minus parameter for the projection of functional categories fits explanations by Rizzi (1990b) and Chomsky (1995:chapter 1.4.1). It follows from Minimality that an adjunct DP as in Polish may be subextracted out of an L-marked constituent, whereas a projecting head D in Dutch/German may not be subextracted and will bring about pied-piping. Be this as it may, the current analysis may rely on Minimality, but requires a retreat from [–projecting] into [+projecting].

Let me try to get a different view on the matter. Extraction of heads out of governed constituents is not unheard of. Baker's (1988) incorporation cases come to mind. Suppose then that functional heads may be extracted from L-marked constituents. Then we do not need the plus/minus parameter for the projection of functional categories, which might be a good thing anyway. It frees us from an almost impossible switching learning scenario and it allows a more uniform analysis of functional categories. Diagram (23) is relevant for all languages. The D-element always projects a DP and it is a [+N] element, sharing categorial features with its lexical complement. Pied-piping is now a far more limited question. Why will the D-element in the German type of language never strand its N-complement and have obligatory pied-piping? This is a learning issue since the D-element in the Polish type of languages may strand its N-complement and not apply pied-piping. Uriagereka (1988) and Corver (1990) notice, but do not derive, the fact that languages with obligatory pied-piping will have articles. This is a remarkable coincidence. Without further explanation one might as well expect no correlation at all, or even the reverse. That would be the (de facto) completely incorrect claim that only languages without articles have obligatory pied-piping.

The following derivation seems plausible. Languages with articles may be languages that have an obligatory D-element in all N-projections. Why should some languages, e.g., Dutch/German, require a D-element in (almost) all N-projections, whereas other languages have these D-elements as free additions only? A plausible answer might be that all N-projections require Case. Some languages use the D-elements as the Case carriers, whereas others allow autonomous Case on the N-element. The type with real Case on the D-element will need a D-element in each N-projection that should satisfy the Case Filter. Hence, such a language needs a kind of dummy D-element and this naturally is the article. The languages with autonomous Case on the N-element will have no use for an obligatory D-element and hence they will lack articles. The evidence for the obligatory presence of D-elements is overwhelming and hence learnable. The same must hold for optional presence and autonomous Case marking on the N-element. The articles in child Dutch appear long before the acquisition of pied-piping. More precise data is still required, but to get an impression of the enormity of the gap, articles may be in place around the age of 3 and pied-piping becomes a more or less reasonably adhered to principle around the age of 5.

This leads to the following three difficult questions.

(25)   a. How is it possible to (sub)extract the head D [+/–wh] in adult Polish and in child Dutch?
b. What is the landing site of the subextracted head D [+/–wh]?
c. If child Dutch allows subextraction of the head D [+/–wh] and yet satisfies the Case Filter with the unexceptional presence of D-elements, why is Ross' Left-Branch Condition acquired later on?

These questions will be dealt with in the next section.

6.2. An alternative proposal

None of the questions in (25) were relevant for the analysis of Hoekstra & Jordens (1994). Their answer to (25a) would be that the subextracted constituents are adjuncts not heads. If one were to insist that the [+/–wh] element is a functional category by force of Universal Grammar, they might grant that the subextracted constituent is a non-projecting D. Since it is non-projecting, it is at the same time maximal, hence a DP, see (22). Their answer to (25b) would be that subextraction of a head is impossible. Languages in which the [+/–wh] element is reinterpreted as a projecting D do not allow the subextraction of the head D. They move the DP which now includes the N-projection, see (23). The constituent affected by moving [+/–wh] is DP. Its landing site is Spec, C. All of this is available under a learning scenario that starts with non-projecting functional categories but may retreat from that position due to new language specific evidence.

Let me now assume a learning scenario that recognizes functional categories and projects them automatically over their associated lexical complements. The advantages of this approach will be clear.

(26)   a. There is no ambiguity of [+/–] projecting in functional categories.
              b. There is no retreat from [–projecting] D/Deg to [+projecting] D/Deg.

These advantages for the learning scenario are available only if the UG theory of syntax is weakened.

Let's start with the first question in (25a). The theory should allow the subextraction of functional heads. I tentatively propose that Minimality is to be further relativized in such a way that a head D[+/–wh]/[+N] may cross a c-commanding head [+V] (cf. Roberts, 1994). Only heads of the same A/A' type will cause a Minimality constraint. This should answer the question raised by (25a). See van Kampen (1997:126f) for an elaboration.

Question (25b) concerns the structure-preserving requirement (24a). The chain caused by the long movement of the D [+/–wh] could uphold the uniformity condition on chains if the D [+/–wh] is adjoined to the head C, where it could check the [+Q] element. The subextracted element that adjoins to C creates a chain satisfying the requirements of uniformity, c-command, and feature checking in (24). A potential objection may be that the single pronoun in (27a) ends up in a landing site different from the subextracted operator.

(27) a. [wat]$_{Spec,C}$ [ga]$_{+QC0}$ jij t$_{wh}$ doen?
       DP-chain

    b. [-]$_{Spec,C}$ [welk [ga]$_{C0}$]$_{C0}$ jij [t$_{wh}$ boekje] lezen?
       D^0-chain

The overwhelming majority of *wh*-questions in the files is of type (27a) (single pronouns; see note 1). It seems plausible that the emergence of (27b) (subextraction) is caused by the clear presence of (27a). However, it is possible to change position (27a) into position (27b) by an additional step as follows.

Let's assume the Head Cluster Principle in (28).

(28)   *Head Cluster Principle*
        Two adjacent heads that entertain a checking relation may adjoin to each other into a head cluster. The checked one adjoins to the one that checks.

This principle is string vacuous. It restructures the string, as in (29b), and escapes from a violation of the uniformity condition (24a).

(29) a.   [wat]$_{Spec,C}$ [ga]$_{+QC0}$ jij t$_{wh}$ doen?
                            ↓
      b.   [t$_{wh}$]$_{Spec,C}$ [wat [ga]$_{C0}$]$_{C0}$ jij t$_{wh}$ doen?

There is some independent motivation for the Head Cluster Principle in clitic movement (Chomsky, 1995: 249). The long moved clitic binds an argument position, i.e., a maximal projection. The uniformity of the chain must be one of a maximal projection. As soon as the top of the argument chain cliticizes into the V^0, it turns it into a [–projecting] head "at the last moment". Again, this seems to be restructuring between two adjacent heads with a checking relation. Looking at the restructuring in (29b) again, one may notice also that the relation between the incorporating head C^0 and the empty Spec, C is reminiscent of the relation between the finite verb and the empty Spec, I in a *pro*-drop language. In sum, the Head Cluster Principle might answer the question in (25b). The relation operator-argument is comparable to the relation clitic-argument.

The Left-Branch Condition, difficulty (25c), does not follow from any of these arrangements. I speculate that the Case function of the D-element in pied-piping languages is in addition subject to a PF adjacency constraint between the D-element and its N-complement. It is a nice point that this PF adjacency condition on Case-bearing elements derives independent support from a reanalysis of the Head-Final Filter in attributive APs (van Kampen, 1997:129f). van Kampen (1997:130f) proposed that the N-complement needs a string adjacent head [+D] in languages that obey the Left-Branch Condition. Latin and Polish N-projections by contrast do not need the D-element. They may violate the adjacency requirement when a D-element is present. The plus or minus PF adjacency requirement may be due to a Case-related parameter by the following speculation. Plausibly, N-elements in some languages are Case-marked due to the string adjacency of the D-element. In such languages, a D^0 is obligatorily present and string adjacent to each N if that constituent is to pass the Case Filter. In fact, the determiner is the spell-out of the Case feature (see Lebeaux (1988:242f) for a theory of Case assignment to D^0). The parameter is formulated in (30).

(30)   *Left-Branch Parameter*
        [+/−] D^0 dependent Case assignment to N

It is reasonable to assume that the Polish/Latin type of grammar has N-projections with a self-sufficient Case paradigm. The parameter value of (30) is negative in this system. In these languages nouns need no formal D-elements. German, Dutch and English nouns, by contrast, do need D-elements to satisfy the Case Filter. In these languages nouns themselves have only a Case paradigm dependent on a context [+D]. The parameter value of (30) is positive for these languages. They cannot subextract and they do apply pied-piping obligatorily. The stipulations above imply that the Case Filter is a matter of PF after all.

To summarize, [+/−wh] operators may be extracted from extended [+N] projections only if the latter are L-marked or marked under predication. The LAD obeys the CED (Condition on Extraction Domains, cf. Huang, 1982). It does not subextract out of subjects and adjuncts, cf. (17) and (18). This is consistent with recent locality theories. The fact that children do not comply with the language-specific Left-Branch Condition for a fairly long period is an issue of parameter setting. The parameter has been interpreted as involving a PF condition on Case marking. In Polish and similar languages, the checking of Case is not subject to PF adjacency with a D-element, whereas it requires D^0 adjacency in Dutch and German. In child language, the situation must be different. Rather, the Case-checking rules are not yet present as strict PF conditions and the adjacency of D^0 [+Case] and N [–Case] in child Dutch is not yet imposed by Case adjacency. Maybe this can be compared with the full acquisition of the Case endings in child Polish. The slow acquisition of Case conditions in Dutch (D^0 adjacency) and in Polish (N-suffixing) need not be unusual for a set of PF conditions.

7. LF AND SUBEXTRACTION

7.1. The [+wh] subextraction

In the last two sections, I have suggested an answer to question (10a). The learner of Dutch starts with a grammar not bounded by the Left-Branch Condition, because the initial grammar is not yet constrained by the PF adjacency requirement. A PF without pied-piping effects is closer to LF as it needs no reconstruction as I consider below. This may explain why the acquisition of obligatory pied-piping is remarkably slow. The subextractions find no support at all from the adult input and the learner progresses slowly towards the target language, since s/he is not informed by negative evidence. The same slow fade-out is found in overgeneralizations of *do*-insertion in child language (Evers & van Kampen, 1995; Hollebrandse & Roeper, 1996; van Kampen, 1997).

The idea that the subextractions are closer to the LF representation is in line with several recent proposals (Penner, 1993; Thornton & Crain, 1994; Penner & Weissenborn, 1996; van Kampen 1996, and others). Just like some other phenomena in child language, the *wh*-subextractions in child grammar may find support from the universal representation at LF. The LAD is enlightened by LF *a priori* and corrected by PF input.

Let me make the familiar distinctions between an operator *wh*, a restriction (N, A) and a variable t_{wh}. The interpretation of the restriction has to take place in the position prior to *wh*-movement, in an A-position. For architectural reasons, Chomsky (1977:84) proposed that syntactic *wh*-movement must precede all semantic co-indexing rules.

(31)   [wh (restriction)]$_{X''}$ [........ t_{wh} (restriction)]

The *wh*-constituent moved into an A'-position marks the scope of the question, but the restriction on the *wh*-operator *which picture of himself* in (32) cannot be fully interpreted in that position.

(32)   [which picture of himself] does John$_i$ like [t_{wh} picture of himself$_i$]

The interpretation of the restriction in the trace position is crucial in (33) when *Bill* functions as the antecedent for *himself*.

(33)   [which picture of himself] John thinks that Bill$_i$ made [t$_{wh}$ picture of himself$_i$]

Chomsky proposed that the *wh*-constituent gets reconstructed at LF. The restriction part had to be moved back into the argument position occupied prior to *wh*-movement. Alternatively, but also by stipulation, the structure of the restriction part is preserved in the pre-*wh* position, and deleted later on. In view of this fairly complex arrangement, it is remarkable that the effect derived by LF reconstruction is directly present in the child's *wh*-subextractions.

For languages with overt movement, the *wh*-phrase requires reconstruction at LF. The sentences in (2)-(3) seem a direct reflection of LF, with the lexical argument in θ-position and the functional element in scope-assigning position. For that reason, I suggest that the LF representation is immediately available to the learner and supports the *wh*-subextraction cases.

This accounts for the [+wh] subextractions. The same kind of explanations holds for the [–wh] subextractions (illustrated in 5 - 7). The [–wh] subextractions in child language also show an LF effect, as will be shown now.

7.2. The [–wh] subextraction

All subextractions of the D- and Deg-element in (5), (6), and (7) have a contrastive focus-marking function. There are two arguments for this claim.

(34)   a. The appearance of negative and positive focusing operators.
         b. The contrastive stress on the D-/Deg-element.

The first argument (34a) is illustrated in (35) and (36). All examples involve a [+/–neg] or [+Q] focusing operator that marks illocution (*wel* 'indeed', *niet* 'not', *nog* 'yet', *ook* 'too', *nou* 'then').

(35) *Contrastively focusing the Deg^0*
    a. is *heel* **wel** [*e* lekker]!   L. 3;3.4
        is very indeed [e nice]
        '(this) is very nice indeed'
    b. dat heb ik *zo* **niet meer** [*e* lang] gedaan!   L. 6;6
        that have I so not more [e long] done
        'I have not done that for a long time'
    c. waarom moet dat *zo* **nog** [*e* heet]?   Tim B. 3;5
        why must that so yet [e hot]?
        'why does it have to be that hot yet?'

(36) *Contrastively focusing the D^0*
    a. doe jij *Laura's* **ook** [*e* haar]?   S. 6;3.16
        do you Laura's too [e hair]?
        'are you fixing Laura's hair too?'
    b. is *andere* **nou** [*e* puzzel]?   L. 2;6.24
        is other then [e puzzle]?
        '(where) is the other puzzle?'
    c. K. gaat *die* **niet** [*e* twee bananen] opeten   Sacha 3;7
        K. goes that/those not [e two bananas] eat
    d. jij kan *mij* **niet** [*e* muts] opdoen   Jasmijn 3;0
        you can my not [e cap] on put
        'you cannot put my cap on'

A second argument (34b) that the [–wh] movements are instances of marked focus is provided by the contrastive value of the D-element in (37) in child language. The focus marking of the D-element has a contrastive effect and attracts non-neutral stress (for contrastive (disanaphoric) stress see Williams, 1994).

(37)   ik wil [díe]$_i$ niet [t$_i$ boek] lezen!   L. 2;9.2
        I want [thát]$_i$ not [t$_i$ book] read
        I do not want to read *that* book
        'If there is a book I want to read, it is not that one'

The special stress on the element D^0/Deg^0 in (35) and (36) (*heel* 'very', *zo* 'so', *dat/die* 'that', *Laura's* 'Laura's', *mij* 'me'), as well as the presence of focusing operators indicate that the D^0/Deg^0 is interpreted as a contrastive element by the child. This fits into the analysis of Association with Focus as given by von Stechow, 1991.

The rule Association with Focus moves the focus to the immediate domain of the operator at LF. The examples in child language show a similar rule in the syntax, be it that only the D^0/Deg^0 element is in the domain of the focusing operator. A grammatical analysis in terms of LF and X-bar representation of these items is as yet uncertain. I would like to suggest that the target of the subscrambled head is as follows (cf. 27b).

(38)   {is}   [-]$_{Spec,FP}$ [[andere [nou]$_F$]$_F$ [.. [$_{DP}$ D^0 N]]......]VP
                            [+focus]   [+focus] t_{focus}

The focusing operator marks the constituent as [+focus]. The contrastive element is adjoined to the head F, where it checks on the [+focus] element. The contrastive element is now in an operator position with respect to the predicate. This [+focus] analysis also accounts for the fact that articles in child Dutch, which are [–focus], will not subextract, whereas demonstratives [+/– focus] may subextract. This is according to fact.

The LAD may receive input evidence from adult Dutch. In adult Dutch objects with a contrastive reading on the D-element may move out of the VP to the left of adverbial material. The sentence in (39) has a contrastive value, meaning something like 'I don't want to read that one'.

(39)   ik wil dát boek niet lezen
                    I want thát book niet read

The contrastively focused DP ends up in an A'-position, as argued by Mahajan (1990) and Neeleman (1994). The LF representation separates the focus D-operator and the reconstructed N-complement.

To summarize, I have analyzed the [–wh] left-branch extractions as A'-movement triggered by [+focus]. Languages differ as to whether they have the means of making the A'-raising operation visible in the syntax. From the present point of view it is significant that the effect obtained by LF, reconstruction is directly present in child language as in the [+wh] subextractions.

8. CONCLUSION

The initial questions in (10), repeated in (40), have been answered as in (41).

(40) How is the Left-Branch Condition acquired?
a. Which parameter setting yields the Left-Branch Condition, that is which parameter setting forces pied-piping?
b. Why does the learner of Dutch start out with a grammar that lacks the Left-Branch Condition?

(41) a. A PF adjacency requirement.
b. A preference for a direct LF representation in PF.

Child grammar avoids reconstruction by applying subextraction. However, the subextractions seem to respect Huang's (1982) Condition on Extraction Domains. The CED as a universal constraint need not be learned. The Left-Branch Condition by contrast is not universal. I have proposed to derive it from a PF adjacency parameter.

The full acquisition of the pied-piping parameter is as slow as the setting of a parameter can be. This longstanding alternative between subextracted and full movements implies an early optionality and its disappearance in a development from a superset language to a subset language. Moreover, the optionality does not disappear in Polish adult language. This clearly contradicts the Subset Principle which demands that acquisition is always accretional. Other parameter settings that contradict the Subset Principle are not rare at all as observed earlier by Lebeaux (1988:173ff). See van Kampen (1997:169ff) for a discussion of optionality in acquisition along the lines of Lebeaux, in terms of computational economy. Constructions in child language that are not supported by adult input, may find support from the universal representation at LF. A more elaborated view of the influence of LF on child language acquisition would not fit in the present paper.

ACKNOWLEDGEMENTS

I am grateful to Judy Bernstein, Peter Coopmans, Martin Everaert, Arnold Evers, Aafke Hulk, Fred Weerman, Ken Wexler, Frank Wijnen, two anonymous reviewers, and the editors of this volume for valuable comments and disagreement. The research reported here was supported by a grant (300-171-027) from the Netherlands Organization for Scientific Research (NWO).

NOTES

[1] The examples are from 130 audio-recordings of my two daughters, Sarah (50 recordings; ages 1;7-5;5) and Laura (80 recordings; ages 1;9-6;0) and from diary notes. The transcripts of the recordings contain 24,127 analyzable utterances of Laura and 16,546 analyzable utterances of Sarah. The total number of finite sentences with realized *wh*-elements is 263 in Laura's files and 370 in Sarah's files. The diary notes contain 1,659 utterances of two words and more of Laura and 873 utterances of Sarah. The total number of finite sentences with realized *wh*-elements is 92 in the diary notes of Laura and 47 in the diary notes of Sarah. The material will be, and has already partially been, incorporated into CHILDES. The audio-recordings have been transcribed in CHAT format. The left-branch extractions that have been found in the corpora were uttered at the following ages: Sarah (S.): 2;9 - 6;4/Laura (L.): 2;6 - 8;4 (age in [years;months.days]). Jacomine Nortier has provided me with some additional data of her daughters Emma and Loura, Nienke Bijholt of her sons Joep and Tim, Peter Coopmans of his son Tim and Wim Zonneveld of his daughter Nina. Jeannette Schaeffer's experiments on the acquisition of scrambling in Dutch, yielded several left-branch extractions by Dutch children aged 3;7-3;9. See Hoekstra & Jordens (1994) for more Dutch examples, and Penner (1993) for Swiss German ones.

[2] The first subextraction in *wh*-phrases wasrecorded for Sarah at 2;9.12, and for Laura at 3;5.5. The first pied-piping of the *wh*-phrase was recorded for Sarah at 3;1.23, and for Laura at 3;6.30.

[3] As I said in Section 2.1, statistics of the left-branch violations are not significant. But there is a little decrease in left-branch violations if one compares the first year (roughly 3;0-4;0) with the second year (roughly 4;0-5;0) for both children. Sarah: First year: 31.25% pied-pipings/68.75% left-branch extractions. Second year: 65% pied-pipings/35% left-branch extractions. After the age of 5;0 left-branch extractions become less frequent. Laura: First year: 34% pied-pipings/67% left-branch extractions. Second year: 75% pied-pipings/25% left-branch extractions. After the age of 5;4 left-branch extractions become less frequent. It would be highly relevant if more data were available to get reliable percentages. Nevertheless, it is a fact that child Dutch shows long-lasting left-branch violations that disappear completely in adult Dutch.

Clearly, the overall number of utterances with subject and adjunct movement is not very high. The present analysis would gain in plausibility if more data were available. The only counterexample I found is the one in (i), extraction out of a temporal adjunct.

(i) dat heb ik zó niet meer [e lang] gedaan!   Loura 6;6
that have I só not more [e long] done!
'I have not done that for a long time'

For the moment, I tentatively adhere to the analysis since I have found no counterexamples in the recordings and since it fits the theoretical picture. Adult languages that may violate the Left-Branch Condition obey the CED as well (Corver, 1990:334).

[5] There is a difference between subextraction out of DegP in predication structures, as in (3) and (7), and subextractions out of DegP in adjunct positions, as in (18). Only in the latter case do we have a DegP barrier. I derive the subextractions in (3) and (7) by assuming that copular verbs L-mark their complement. This assumption is contrary to the one made in Chomsky (1986:78). See van Kampen (1997) for an additional argument.

[6] In English child language *wh*-elements also appear first as *wh*-pronouns rather than as *wh*-phrases, see Radford (1986:67) and Lebeaux (1988:443).

[7] The classification of *wh*-elements, demonstratives, possessives, and quantifiers in (2), (5) and (6) as D^0 is quite common (see Corver, 1990:34; Demske, 1995 and Chomsky 1995:263,282 for recent examples). The same may be said of the classification of the *wh*-elements and modifiers in (3) and (7) as Deg^0 (Corver, 1990:41). I extend D^0 to proper names. They have clear parallels with demonstratives as non-characterizing identifiers and they fit the present subextraction pattern, see examples (5b) and (6b,d) (see van Kampen, 1997:33 for the idea that proper names serve as an identifier for D^0 in acquisition). I also

assume that the child interprets *andere* in (6)c as a quantifying D^0 (comparable to *many* in adult languages, see Abney 1987:290f).
[8]For expository reasons I will abstract away from split DP and split DegP. See Szabolsci (1983), Abney (1987), Cinque (1993b), Giusti (1995), Longobardi (1996) and De Wit (1997) for some complications and some proposals for a split DP/DegP. A split analysis is not relevant to the main points of the analysis proposed here. My basic claim is that all subextracted single elements are functional heads within an extended N- or A-projection and that they appear as operators.
[9]DP in (22) stands for [– projecting]/[+maximal].
[10]In fact, the adjoined projection is lexical in Corver (1990) and Hoekstra and Jordens (1994) but this is irrelevant for the point I make here.
[11]See also Rizzi (1990a).
[12]For clitic movement as long head movement see De Rivero (1991), Roberts (1994).
[13]The Head Cluster Principle was suggested to me by Arnold Evers.
[14]I follow Neeleman (1994) in interpreting the Head-Final Filter as a string adjacency condition. For an autonomous view on adjacency see Lattewitz (1997). She argues that adjacency is a secondary effect of general syntactic principles.
[15]It is true that (30) does not account for the restrictions on the Deg^0 extractions in (i).

(i) * hoe is hij groot?
How is he big?
'how big is he?'

D^0 extractions arise from both the Left-Branch Parameter and LF primacy. Deg^0 extractions only arise from LF primacy. I will elaborate on the LF primacy idea in Section 7. It might be relevant that Deg^0 extraction is allowed in some adult languages that do in general obey the Left-Branch Condition and are subjected to the Head-Final Filter (Cinque, 1993b), for instance Italian and South American Spanish (cf. the examples in 9). Moreover, Deg^0 extractions seem to be more persistent in child language than D^0 extractions (Peter Coopmans, p.c.).
[16]See for variants and alternatives: Ruys, (1993 and references therein); Chomsky (1995:206ff).
[17]See Hornstein & Weinberg (1990) for the idea that at LF quantifier raising and *wh*-raising move only the head. The same point is made in Lasnik (1993:29), for reasons of minimalist grammar. I adhere to the idea that operators are heads that may optionally pied-pipe their lexical complement towards PF. Reconstruction (lowering) of the pied-piped complement is a countermovement towards LF. See for an elaboration van Kampen (1997).
[18]The topicalizations in (5) show also the properties in (34). They are to be analyzed as contrastively focused elements as well.
[19]Evidence of focus movement in the syntax and in violation of the Left-Branch Condition, has been registered in adult Bengali (Bayer, 1994):

(i) kalke ama-r baba -r -o EkTa notun baRi bikri hoe gEche
yesterday I-poss father –poss –too one new house sell
become went
'yesterday a new house of my father too was sold'

In the example in (i), -*o* 'too' is the focusing operator and *amar baba* 'my father' is the focused element that has been subextracted.
[20]I may add that the proposal by von Stechow was not developed in terms of X-bar theory. However, see Haegeman (1992) for A'-phrases above VP in which operators may appear. See Penner, Tracy, & Weissenborn (this volume) for a comparable Focus Phrase in child German.
[21]Focus scrambling with contrastive focus is different from scrambling in neutral contexts. Only the former is movement to an operator, i.e. an A'-position. Scrambling in neutral contexts may be analyzed as movement to an A-position (Spec, AgrO in Mahajan, 1990) or it may concern base-generation in an A-position (Neeleman, 1994). It lacks reconstruction effects. For neutral focus of non-scrambled definite objects see Reinhart (to appear).

REFERENCES

Abney, S. P.: 1987, The English Noun Phrase in its Sentential Aspect, Ph.D. Dissertation, MIT.
Baker, M. C.: 1988, *Incorporation. A Theory of Grammatical Function Changing*, University of Chicago Press, Chicago.
Bayer, J.: 1994, 'Focusing particles: Aspects of their syntax and logical form', Paper presented at the 'Workshop on L1 and L2 Acquisition of Clause Internal Rules: Scrambling and Cliticization', January 21-23, Berne.
Butt, J. and C. Benjamin: 1988, *A New Reference Grammar of Modern Spanish*, Edward Arnold, London/New York.
Chomsky, N.: 1977, 'On wh-movement', in P. Culicover, T. Wasow, & A. Akmajian (eds.) *Formal Syntax*, Academic Press, New York, 71-133.
Chomsky, N.: 1986, *Barriers*, MIT Press, Cambridge Mass.
Chomsky, N.: 1995, *The Minimalist Program*, MIT Press, Cambridge Mass.
Cinque, G.: 1993a, 'A null theory of phrase and compound stress', *Linguistic Inquiry* **8.3**, 425-504.
Cinque, G.: 1993b, 'On the evidence of partial N movement in the Romance DP', ms. University of Venice.
Corver, N. F. M.: 1990, The Syntax of Left-branch Extractions, Ph.D. Dissertation, Tilburg University.
Demske, U.: 1995, 'Prenominal genitive phrases as definite determiners', ms. University of Tübingen/Stuttgart.
Emonds, J.: 1985, *A Unified Theory of Syntactic Categories*, Foris, Dordrecht.
Evers, A. and N. J. van Kampen: 1995, 'Do-insertion and LF in child language', in J. Don, B. Schouten, W. Zonneveld (eds.) *OTS Yearbook 1994*, Utrecht University, 24-41.
Fukui, N. and M. Speas: 1986, 'Specifiers and projections', MIT Working Papers in Linguistics **8**, 128-171.
Giusti, G.: 1995, 'A unified structural representation of (abstract) case and article', in H. Haider *et al.* (eds.) *Studies in Comparative Germanic Syntax*, Kluwer, Dordrecht, 77-93.
Haegeman, L.: 1992, 'Sentential negation in Italian and the Neg Criterion', ms. University of Geneva.
Hoekstra, T. and P. Jordens: 1994, 'From adjunct to head', in T. Hoekstra & B. D. Schwartz (eds.) *Language Acquisition Studies in Generative Grammar*, John Benjamins, Amsterdam, 119-149.
Hollebrandse, B. and T. Roeper: 1996, 'The concept of do-insertion and the theory of INFL in acquisition', in C. Koster & F. Wijnen (eds.) *Proceedings of the Groningen Assembly on Language Acquisition*, 261-272.
Hornstein, N. and A. Weinberg: 1990, 'The necessity of LF', *The Linguistic Review* **7**, 129-167.
Huang, J. C.-T.: 1982, Logical Relations in Chinese and the Theory of Grammar. Ph.D. Dissertation, MIT.
Kampen, N. J. van: 1994, 'The learnability of the left-branch condition', in R. Bok-Bennema & C. Cremers (eds.) *Linguistics in the Netherlands 1994*, John Benjamins, Amsterdam, 83-94.
Kampen, N. J. van: 1996, 'PF/LF convergence in acquisition', in: K. Kusomoto (ed.) *Proceedings of the North Atlantic Linguistic Society 1995* (NELS 26), October 23-27, 149-163.
Kampen, N.J. van: 1997, First Steps in Wh-movement, Ph.D. Dissertation, Utrecht University.
Lasnik, H.: 1993, 'Lectures on minimalist syntax', ms. University of Connecticut.
Lattewitz, K. T.: 1997, Adjacency in Dutch and German, Ph.D. Dissertation, Groningen University.
Lebeaux, D.: 1988, Language Acquisition and the Form of Grammar, Ph.D. Dissertation, University of Massachusetts Amherst.
Longobardi, G.: 1996, 'The syntax of N-raising: A minimalist theory', ms. Utrecht University.
Mahajan, A.: 1990, The A/A'-Distinction and Movement Theory, Ph.D. Dissertation, MIT, Cambridge Mass.

Neeleman, A.: 1994, Complex Predicates. A Comparative Analysis of Dutch and English Verb-Predicate Constructions. Ph.D. Dissertation, Utrecht University.
Penner, Z.: 1993, 'The earliest stage in the acquisition of the nominal phrase in Bernese Swiss German: Syntactic bootstrapping and the architecture of language learning', Arbeitspapiere **30**, Universität Bern, Institut für Sprachwissenschaft.
Penner, Z. and J. Weissenborn: 1996, 'Strong continuity, parameter setting and the trigger hierarchy: On the acquisition of the DP in Bernese Swiss German and High German', in H. Clahsen (ed.) *Generative Perspectives on Language Acquisition*, John Benjamins, Amsterdam, 161-200.
Radford, A.: 1986, 'The acquisition of the complementizer system', *Bangor Research Papers in Linguistics* **2**, 55-76.
Reinhart, T.: 1995, 'Interface strategies', OTS Working Papers, Utrecht University.
Rivero, M.-L. de: 1991, 'Long head movement and negation: Serbo-Croatian vs. Slovak and Czech', *The Linguistic Review* **8**, 319-351.
Rizzi, L.: 1990a, 'Speculations on verb second' in J. Mascaró & M. Nespor (eds.) *Grammar in Progress*, Foris, Dordrecht, 375-386.
Rizzi, L.: 1990b, *Relativized Minimality*, MIT Press, Cambridge, Mass.
Roberts, I.: 1994, 'Two types of head movement in Romance' in N. Hornstein & D. Lightfoot (eds.) *Verb Movement*, 207-242.
Ross, J. R.: 1967, Constraints on Variables in Syntax, Ph.D. Dissertation, MIT.
Ruys, E. G.: 1993, The Scope of Indefinites, Ph.D. dissertation, Utrecht University.
Stechow, A. von: 1991, 'Focusing and backgrounding operators', in W. Abraham (ed.) *Discourse Particles, Proceedings of the Workshop at the Groningen University 1986*, May 24-26, John Benjamins, Amsterdam.
Szabolsci, A.: 1983, 'The possessor that ran away from home', *The Linguistic Review* **3**, 89-102.
Thornton, R. and S. Crain: 1994, 'Successful cyclic movement', in T. Hoekstra & B. D. Schwartz *Language Acquisition Studies in Generative Grammar*, John Benjamins, Amsterdam, 215-252.
Uriagereka, J.: 1988, On Government, Ph.D. Dissertation, University of Connecticut, Storrs.
Williams, E.: 1994, Thematic Structure in Syntax, *Linguistic Monographs* **23**, MIT Press, Cambridge, Mass.
Wit, P. de: 1997, Genitive Case and Genitive Constructions, Ph.D. dissertation, Utrecht University.

JACQUELINE VAN KAMPEN
OTS Utrecht University

INDEX

A'-adjunction, 34
A-bar position, 122, 123
A'-bound, 218
A'-chains, 5, 19, 32, 33, 46
A-chains, 4, 5, 19, 32, 33, 46
A'-dependencies, 218
A'-movement, 49, 138, 191, 201, 283
A-movement, 49, 104, 107, 138
A-movement to VP adjunct, 108
A'-position, 32
A-positions, 32, 353, 437
A'-traces, 24
A-structure projection, 32
accusative case, 443
accusative clitics, 280
acquisition, 381
acquisition of agreement, 380
acquisition of CP, 410
acquisition of PP, 410
acquisition of scrambling, 1
adequate trigger, 303
adjunct, 491
adjunction, 19, 31
adult input, 479
adverbial infinitival, 25
adverbials, 22, 23
adverbs, 83
affect configurations, 127, 139, 155, 160
affect criterion, 140, 437, 438
affective operator, 140
agreement, 13, 251, 284, 357, 369, 379
agreement index, 352
agreement markers, 10
agreement morphology, 209, 373
agreement paradigm, 379
agreement requirements, 248
agreement system, 8
allomorphs, 320
American English, 319
anaphor, 303
anaphoric, 132, 178, 267
argument absorption, 12, 207, 208, 231
argument clitics, 240
argument drop, 62
argument slots, 243
argument structure, 238, 260
argument structure manipulation, 208

arguments, 23, 280
articles, 492
association with focus, 499
auch, 130, 132, 144
auxiliaries, 207, 213, 223, 226, 232
auxiliary selection, 228–230, 232

bare phrase structure, 372
base generation, 264
base order, 29, 30
base-generated, 4, 100, 107, 108, 122
base-generated word orders, 3
base-generation, 5, 15, 95, 96, 105, 195, 273, 283
base-order, 106, 111
basic structure of the clause, 397
Bernese Swiss German, 5, 46, 140, 193, 195
bilingual, 230
bilingualism, 228
binary branching, 105
bootstrapping, 299
bottom-up application of move, 196

C-system, 216, 219, 220
case, 11, 42, 49, 280, 492
case features, 11, 495
case filter, 492, 495, 496
case marking, 157
case system, 306
case-parameter, 23
caseless, 112, 120
Catalan, 279
categories, 488
causatives, 214
chain complexity, 267
chain formation, 12, 238, 263
chains, 262, 267
character of data, 96
checking difficulties, 261
checking domain, 33, 34
checking positions, 34
child language, 2
CHILDES, 77, 286, 456, 464
clause bound, 118
clause-internal, 15

clause-internal processes, 1
clitic, 166, 432
clitic climbing, 241
clitic climbing in Romance, 193
clitic clustering, 251
clitic clusters, 246, 247, 260, 268
clitic criterion, 281
clitic doubling, 11, 251
clitic left-dislocation, 280, 283, 290, 295
clitic movement, 191, 266, 495
clitic omission, 260, 273
clitic omission/realization, 259
clitic paradigm, 340
clitic placement, 204
clitic pronouns, 15, 171–173, 248, 279, 301, 305
clitic pronouns from free and weak pronouns, 306
clitic voice, 12
clitic-argument, 495
clitic-chain, 262, 273
clitic-climbing, 186, 266
clitic-doubling, 14, 257, 279, 280, 282–284, 286–290, 292, 294, 295
clitic-like, 113
clitichood, 174
cliticization, 2, 7, 10, 15, 201, 238, 244, 248, 249, 252, 273, 303, 325, 330, 340, 441
clitics, 8, 223, 238, 239, 322
closed class, 488
cognitive development, 239
coindexation, 211
comparative prepositions, 407
competence, 327, 330, 349
competence deficit, 237
competence level, 238
complementizers, 410
complex complementizers, 400
complex *wh*-phrases, 481
complexity, 273
computational economy, 501
computational overload, 267
computationally, 484
condition on extraction domains, 484
Condition on Extraction Domains (CED), 487, 496
conditional entropy, 305, 309, 314
conditions on movement, 12
configurational readiness hypothesis, 147, 156
constituent, 41
constituent negations, 46, 58, 462
constituent order, 50

continuity, 128
continuity hypothesis, 424
contituent negation, 49
contrastive focus-marking function, 498
control relations, 238
coordination, 174, 184
corefer, 165
covariation, 174, 176
covert (LF), 123
CP-PP parallelism hypothesis, 398
cross-over effects, 24
crosslinguistic variation, 387
crossover, 27

D(et), 90
D-elements, 492
dative case, 284
dative clitics, 280
dative experiencers, 280, 283, 284, 286, 290, 295
default choices, 128
deficiency, 165–167, 173, 178, 182
deficient pronouns, 183–185
deficit, 238
definite DPs, 46
definite noun, 137
definiteness, 30, 151, 157
deictic particle, 129
dependencies, 19
descriptive adequacy, 19
determiner clitics, 332, 333
detransitivizer, 209
developmental changes, 55, 128
developmental dysphasia, 237
diachronic change, 387
diary data, 6, 96, 147
diary drop, 351, 353
diary/topic drop, 354, 355, 358, 363, 374, 376
direct objects, 52, 53, 282
discourse, 88
discourse linking, 152
discourse referent, 178
discourse topic, 217, 244
dislocated, 102
disorder, 237
double negation, 64
Down's syndrome, 360
DP type, 52
Dutch, 3, 5, 6, 195, 280, 286, 292, 377, 461, 480
dysphasia, 238, 259, 273
dysphasic, 237

economic, 484
economical structure, 370
economy, 88
economy considerations, 403, 407
economy of projection, 346, 347, 357, 369, 372, 373, 375, 376, 379, 383, 386
ECP, 431, 440
ECP effects, 427
elicited imitation, 50
elicited imitation task, 48, 326
elicited production, 225
ellipsis, 25
Emonds, 488
empty subjects, 350, 357
English, 5, 96, 280, 346, 374, 375
entropy, 304, 307
entropy profiles, 306
ergative *se*, 232
ergativizer, 209
errors, 51, 54, 55, 103, 225, 227, 288
expressive language, 239
extended projection, 182, 190, 195, 397, 429, 446
external argument, 211

faire-causatives, 214, 290
familiar, 88, 90
feature, 49
feature checking, 437
finite *wh*-questions, 359, 378, 380
finiteness, 357, 361
floating quantifiers, 280, 284, 286, 295
focus, 28, 42, 49, 155, 482, 499
focus agreement, 140
focus particle phrase, 139
focus particles, 128, 129, 145
focus projection, 28–30
focus scrambling, 503
focus spreading, 20
focusing operator, 498
free, 260
free pronouns, 15, 301
free-standing and clitic pronouns, 314
freezing, 439, 440
French, 9, 15, 191, 218, 279, 305, 457
frequency counts, 97
fronted *wh*-element, 369
full competence hypothesis, 425
full continuity, 12
full form, 320
full noun phrase, 279
full NPs, 240, 243

functional case, 32
functional categories, 4, 7, 13, 238, 279, 319, 397, 414, 488, 491
functional head, 85, 486
functional projections, 2, 4, 12, 31, 104, 398, 403

gar nicht, 464
genetic deficit, 237
German, 3, 5, 19, 187, 279, 457, 461
German clitics, 197
Germanic, 19
Germanic clitics, 15
Germanic pronominal clitics, 9
Germanic pronouns, 170
governed case, 32
grammatical SLI, 239
grammatical specificity, 272

head cluster principle, 494, 495
head movement, 8, 189–191, 440
head-final filter, 495
head-movement, 11, 195
headedness-parameter, 23
heads, 187
heavy and light nouns, 147
heavy NP-shift, 3, 20
hierarchical order, 414
Hindi, 19
human constraint, 180

identification, 353, 374
impoverished elements, 11
incremental, 381
indefinite, 75
indefinite DPs, 36, 46
indefinite objects, 75, 137
indexicality, 165
indirect object, 52, 53
infinitives, 453
inflected for case, 112
information theory, 304
inherently definite objects, 137
input stream, 302
interim solutions, 128
internal argument, 211
islands, 487
Italian, 9, 12, 13, 15, 191, 346

Japanese, 2, 5, 6, 19, 346, 374, 375

kein, 47, 441, 443, 446
Korean, 319

L-marked, 487
L2 acquisition, 326
L2 learners, 319
landing, 160
landing sites, 11, 116, 128, 437, 493
language acquisition, 387
Language Acquisition Device (LAD), 488, 491, 496, 497, 499
language development, 1
language impairments, 360
language variation, 302
learnability, 479
learnability problems, 342, 347, 380
learning algorithms, 14
learning mechanism, 315
learning scenario, 491, 493
left-branch condition, 480, 483, 489, 490
left-branch extractions, 479
left-dislocation, 286
lexical bridge, 413, 414
lexical NPs, 240
lexical transfer, 332
lexicalized chunks, 249
LF, 500
LF reconstruction, 497
LF representation, 497
liaison, 175, 178
licensing, 7, 352
licensing conditions, 128
licensing of case, 47
light nouns, 141
like verbal prefixes, 142
linking position, 32
local scrambling, 20, 139, 160
local syntactic domain, 302
Local Wellformedness Condition, 203
locality, 7, 33, 496
locally-scrambled, 141
long distance anaphors, 302
long head movement, 435
long scrambling, 20
long-distance clitic movement, 193
long-distance scrambling, 20, 192
long-movement, 266

marked, 49, 54, 55
marked focus, 499
marked scrambling, 56
maximal projections, 187
medial, 232
middle field, 138
middle *se*, 208, 211, 212
minimal projection domain, 35

minimalist, 41
minimize structure, 425
moraic constraint, 321, 338, 340
morphological deficiency, 183
morphological paradigms, 238
morphological richness, 208
movement, 3, 7, 11, 15, 19, 31, 96, 107, 184, 273, 285, 290
movement type, 52
multiple focus, 43
multiple grammars, 369

natural classes, 306
naturalistic setting, 326
neg-criterion, 427, 437, 438, 446, 463
negation, 7, 52, 58, 59, 65, 83, 132, 369
negation doubling, 58, 59
negation markers, 145
negation particle, 132, 137, 423
negative concord, 140, 143, 429, 431, 435, 438, 445, 446, 462
negative constituent, 429, 430, 441
negative declaratives, 361, 364, 368, 375
negative infinitives, 449, 457, 459
negative particles, 423, 424, 433
nicht, 47, 142, 426, 431, 432, 434–436, 438, 440, 441, 444, 445, 447, 463, 464
niet, 47
No Functional Problem hypothesis (NFP), 105
No Functional projections Hypothesis, 4, 111
nominal extended projection, 404
nominal extended projection PP, 398
nominal specificity, 72, 86
nominative and non-nominative clitics, 311
nominative case, 116, 284
non-agreement effect, 374
non-finite *wh*-questions, 345, 359, 379, 380
non-finiteness, 346, 374
non-finiteness effect, 354, 362
non-*pro*-drop, 348
non-reflexive object clitics, 207
non-reflexives, 220
normal pronouns, 168–171
novel, 88
nuclear scope, 76
null arguments, 352
null constants, 353
null subjects, 355, 357, 360

INDEX

object agreement, 208
object clitics, 9, 11, 12, 14, 329, 330, 335
object drop, 62, 63, 219
object forms, 323
object scrambling, 49, 139, 200
object shift, 3, 6, 20, 21, 41–43, 47–50, 52–56, 61, 64–67, 397
obligatorily scramble, 74
obligatory, 49, 54, 56, 64, 83, 282, 287, 288, 350
obligatory contexts, 408, 410
obligatory D-element, 492
obligatory pied-piping, 479, 492
occurrences, 240
occurrences and omissions of clitics, 239
omissions, 63, 239–242, 252, 253, 261, 267, 347
operational overload, 261
operator, 353, 427, 488
operator *wh*, 497
operator-argument, 495
optional, 42, 49, 54, 282, 287
optional infinitive phase, 424
optional infinitive stage, 71, 366, 456
optional infinitives, 89
optional scrambling, 56, 64
optionality, 72, 501
optionality in acquisition, 501
order of projections, 459
overt (S-structure), 123
overt coplementizers, 410
overt subject pronouns, 346
overt subjects, 103, 346, 348, 355, 357, 359

paradigms, 370
parallelism, 414
parallelism hypothesis, 397
parameter setting, 2, 128, 271, 299, 301, 303
parameter-resetting, 347, 348
parameters, 2, 13, 23, 285, 302, 319, 338
parametric variation, 14
parasitic gaps, 19, 24, 25, 191
parser construction, 301
parsing, 263
parsing device, 300
participles, 452, 453
partitive, 268
passato prossimo, 241, 245, 247, 251, 253–255, 258, 260, 261, 266–268, 273
passives, 293–295

past participle agreement, 255–258
pattern of emergence, 111
performance, 238, 349
performance factors, 252
performance limitations, 272, 358
personal pronouns, 168, 320
phi-features, 202, 365, 488
phonetic drop hypothesis, 253
phonologic-syntactic subtype, 239
phonological cliticization, 11
phonological properties, 301
pied-piping, 481, 484, 492
pied-piping parameter, 501
pitch accent, 28
placeholder, 128
placement errors, 207, 223, 224, 230
post-complementizer clitics, 330
post-verbal clitics, 329
post-verbal subject, 328
PP-CP parallelism hypothesis, 397
pre-functional, 252
pre-functional stages, 338
prepositions, 410
principle of economy of projection, 14
principle of structure preservation, 187
principles, 13, 319
PRO, 381
pro, 14, 106, 172, 209, 293, 345, 346, 357, 371, 373, 374, 381
pro object, 219
pro-drop, 10, 345, 349, 363, 386, 495
pro-drop language, 293
processing limitations, 364
proclitics, 303
procrastinate, 88
projection position, 32
pronominal, 7
pronominal cliticization, 319
pronominal clitics, 1, 13, 14
pronominal subject, 118
pronominal system, 174
pronoun fronting, 37
pronoun zone, 335, 337, 340
pronouns, 36, 86, 301
prosodic, 319
pseudo-topics, 120
putative trigger, 303

quantifier, 27
quotation sentences, 412

raising and copula, 213
raising verb, 212, 213

reconstitution, 57, 60, 64, 65
reconstruction, 22, 27, 484, 496, 500
reduced, 178
reduced pronouns, 335, 337
referential, 165
referential *pro*, 375
referential subjects, 345, 347
reflexive clitics, 12, 207, 223, 224, 230
reflexives, 12, 211, 220
reflexivization, 208
relativized minimality, 194
restriction, 497
restrictive clause, 76
restructuring, 495
retrieval, 262
retrieval difficulties, 261
richness, 379
right-dislocation, 247, 251, 257
robust, 314
robustness, 301
Romance, 9
Romance clitics, 15
Romance subject clitics, 10
root infinitives, 89, 364, 365, 367–369, 375, 382, 449
rote learning, 249

scope, 22, 42, 49, 488
scope domain, 144
scrambled, 48, 484
scrambling, 2, 3, 6, 7, 15, 19, 23, 27, 29, 34, 36, 37, 42, 52, 54, 55, 60, 66, 67, 73, 74, 76, 88, 95, 118, 122, 158, 280, 285, 286, 292, 316, 479, 481, 485
scrambling in Dutch, 22
scrambling of definites, 88
scrambling of pronouns, 82
scrambling proper, 20, 21
se, 229
se and R-clitics, 208
second language (L2), 13
semantic bootstrapping, 301
semantic effects, 20
sentence accent, 28
sentential negation, 64, 140
sentential scope, 144
separable verb, 439
silent clitic, 257, 258
silent clitic hypothesis, 252, 253, 255, 257
situation linking, 152
small clause, 12

small clause analysis, 425
Spanish, 9, 12, 15, 319
special, 179
special language impairment, 360
special pronouns, 168–170
specific, 75
specific language impairment, 237
specific semantic domain, 403
specificity, 72, 85, 88, 292
specifier, 7, 31, 434
specifier-head configuration, 140
specifier-head relation, 437
split CP, 397
split CP hypothesis, 398
spontaneous, 6
spontaneous data, 6
spontaneous speech productions, 239
stage model, 409
Standard German, 140, 319
Standard Spanish, 280, 282, 286
statistical tools, 300
statistically-based algorithms, 303
steady state L2 competence, 326
stimulus sentences, 49, 51
stressed, 248
stressed pronouns, 240, 248
string complexity, 262
strong, 166
strong overt agreement morphology, 371
strong pronouns, 11, 171–173, 175, 180
structural parallelism, 397
structure building, 129, 338
structure complexity, 262
stylistic inversion, 209
subextraction, 484
subject agreement, 261, 275
subject and object clitics, 328
subject clitics, 9, 10, 13, 391
subject drop, 253
subject omission, 348
subject pronouns, 322, 345
subject-verb agreement, 377
subjunctive, 347
subordinate clauses, 397
subscrambled, 499
subset, 347
subset language, 501
subset principle, 203, 501
substitution, 19, 31
superset, 342, 347
superset language, 501
Swedish, 3
Swiss German, 187
symbolic algorithm, 14

symbolic computation, 300
syntactic chains, 263
syntactic head, 177
syntactic movement, 3
syntactic phrase, 177
syntactic precedence principle, 123
syntactic properties, 301
systematic use, 486

T-model, 176
temporal auxiliaries, 214
temporal specificity, 71
tense features, 13
thematic role, 207, 294
theta-role, 11, 279, 280, 282
three-word combinations, 107
topic drop, 350, 351
topic position, 121
topicalization, 26, 122, 463, 479, 481, 485
topicalized, 484
topicalized clitics, 332
topics, 101, 103, 120, 290
trace, 497
trigger detection, 14, 299–301, 303, 315
triggering data, 302
triggering mechanisms, 14
triggers, 128, 173, 176, 177, 180, 299
tripartition, 167, 169, 174, 181, 182
truncated structures, 449
truncation, 382, 425
truncation hypothesis, 461
Turkish, 4–6, 319
two-word combinations, 107

UG-options, 369
ultimate attainment, 319
unaccusatives, 106, 109
underspecification, 72, 89
underspecified, 71, 72, 88
universal base hypothesis, 4, 124
universal base-order, 108
Universal Grammar (UG), 1, 2, 6, 12, 13, 303, 319, 348, 367, 372, 374, 379
unmarked, 49, 54, 56
unscrambled objects, 440, 443

V2, 316
V2 and scrambling, 315
V2 language, 300
V2 pattern, 133
V2 position, 135
V2 rule, 133

verb movement, 191, 268, 423, 435
verb placement, 134
verb projection raising constructions, 197
verb raising, 71
verb second, 303
verbal and the nominal extended projections, 397
verbal clitic, 114
verbal extended projection, 404
verbal particles, 129
very special pronouns, 170, 171
VP Internal Subject Hypothesis, 116
VP-adjuncts, 108
VP-length, 345, 358

weak, 166
weak overt agreement morphology, 371
weak pronouns, 11, 171–173, 175, 180
West Flemish, 461
wh-criterion, 139, 355, 437, 438
wh-extractions, 480
wh-movement, 23, 27, 480
wh-questions, 14, 345, 346, 355, 357, 358, 359, 360, 364, 368, 375, 427, 461, 479, 494
why-questions, 382, 384
word combinations, 97
word order errors, 3, 4, 95, 96, 105, 116
word-order variation, 3, 5
word orders, 4, 6, 8, 29, 48, 303, 316

STUDIES IN THEORETICAL PSYCHOLINGUISTICS

1. L. Solan: *Pronominal Reference.* Child Language and the Theory of Grammar. 1983 ISBN 90-277-1495-9
2. B. Lust (ed.): *Studies in the Acquisition of Anaphora.* Volume I: Defining the Constraints. 1986 ISBN 90-277-2121-1; Pb 90-277-2122-X
3. N. M. Hyams: *Language Acquisition and the Theory of Parameters.* 1986 ISBN 90-277-2218-8; Pb 90-277-2219-6
4. T. Roeper and E. Williams (eds.): *Parameter Setting.* 1987 ISBN 90-277-2315-X; Pb 90-277-2316-8
5. S. Flynn: *A Parameter-Setting Model of L2 Acquisition.* Experimental Studies in Anaphora. 1987 ISBN 90-277-2374-5; Pb 90-277-2375-3
6. B. Lust (ed.): *Studies in the Acquisition of Anaphora.* Volume II: Applying the Constraints. 1987 ISBN 1-55608-022-0; Pb 1-55608-023-9
7. G. N. Carlson and M. K. Tanenhaus (eds.): *Linguistic Structure in Language Processing.* 1989 ISBN 1-55608-074-3; Pb 1-55608-075-1
8. S. Flynn and W. O'Neil (eds.): *Linguistic Theory in Second Language Acquisition.* 1988 ISBN 1-55608-084-0; Pb 1-55608-085-9
9. R. J. Matthews and W. Demopoulos (eds.): *Learnability and Linguistic Theory.* 1989 ISBN 0-7923-0247-8; Pb 0-7923-0558-2
10. L. Frazier and J. de Villiers (eds.): *Language Processing and Language Acquisition.* 1990 ISBN 0-7923-0659-7; Pb 0-7923-0660-0
11. J.A. Padilla: *On the Definition of Binding Domains in Spanish.* Evidence from Child Language. 1990 ISBN 0-7923-0744-5
12. M. de Vincenzi: *Syntactic Parsing Strategies in Italian.* The Minimal Chain Principle. 1991 ISBN 0-7923-1274-0; Pb 0-7923-1275-9
13. D.C. Lillo-Martin: *Universal Grammar and American Sign Language.* Setting the Null Argument Parameters. 1991 ISBN 0-7923-1419-0
14. A.E. Pierce: *Language Acquisition and Syntactic Theory.* A Comparative Analysis of French and English Child Grammars. 1992 ISBN 0-7923-1553-7
15. H. Goodluck and M. Rochemont (eds.): *Island Constraints.* Theory, Acquisition and Processing. 1992 ISBN 0-7923-1689-4
16. J.M. Meisel (ed.): *The Acquisition of Verb Placement.* Functional Categories and V2 Phenomena in Language Acquisition. 1992 ISBN 0-7923-1906-0
17. E.C. Klein: *Toward Second Language Acquisition.* A Study of Null-Prep. 1993 ISBN 0-7923-2463-3

STUDIES IN THEORETICAL PSYCHOLINGUISTICS

18. J.L. Packard: *A Linguistic Investigation of Aphasic Chinese Speech.* 1993
    ISBN 0-7923-2466-8
19. J. Archibald: *Language Learnability and L2 Phonology:* The Acquisition of Metrical Parameters. 1993 ISBN 0-7923-2486-2
20. M.W. Crocker: *Computational Psycholinguistics.* An Interdisciplinary Approach to the Study of Language. 1996 ISBN 0-7923-3802-2; Pb 0-7923-3806-5
21. J.D. Fodor and F. Ferreira (eds.): *Reanalysis in Sentence Processing.* 1998
    ISBN 0-7923-5099-5
22. L. Frazier: *On Sentence Interpretation.* 1999 ISBN 0-7923-5508-3
23. S. Avrutin: *Development of the Syntax Discourse Interface.* 1999
    ISBN 0-7923-5936-4
24. B. Hemforth and L. Konieczny (eds.): *German Sentence Processing.* 2000
    ISBN 0-7923-6104-0
25. M. De Vincenzi and V. Lombardo (eds.): *Cross-linguistic Perspectives on Language Processing.* 2000 ISBN 0-7923-6146-6
26. S.M. Powers and C. Hamann (eds.): *The Acquisition of Scrambling and Cliticization.* 2000 ISBN 0-7923-6249-7

KLUWER ACADEMIC PUBLISHERS – DORDRECHT / BOSTON / LONDON